South Vietnam

Volume 7

U.S.-Communist
Confrontation in
Southeast Asia

1972–1973

South Vietnam

Volume 7

U.S.-Communist Confrontation in Southeast Asia

1972–1973

Edited by Edward W. Knappman
Contributing Editor: Hal Kosut

FACTS ON FILE, INC.   NEW YORK, N.Y.

South Vietnam Volume 7

U.S.-Communist Confrontation in Southeast Asia

1972–1973

© Copyright, 1973, by Facts on File, Inc.

Published by Facts on File, Inc.,
119 West 57th Street, New York, N.Y. 10019.
Library of Congress Card Catalog No. 66-23943
ISBN 0-87196-239-X
9 8 7 6 5 4 3 2 1
PRINTED IN
THE UNITED STATES OF AMERICA

Contents

Preface

THE 7TH VOLUME OF FACTS ON FILE'S week-by-week chronicle of the war in Indochina records the final stages of direct American involvement in that conflict.

During the period covered by this volume—January 1972 through March 1973—peace negotiations finally began to overshadow events on the battlefields. The war, however, still raged on the ground in South Vietnam, Laos and Cambodia and in the air over North Vietnam. Early in 1972 the Communists launched a major offensive in the northern provinces of South Vietnam. Although President Nixon refused to let the stepped-up fighting delay withdrawals of American troops, he responded to the offensive by ordering an all-out effort to interrupt the flow of supplies to the Communists in South Vietnam. American planes pounded the roads, airfields, harbors and railroads of North Vietnam. For the first time during the war, American mines were dropped in the harbors, rivers and coastal waters of North Vietnam.

In the fall of 1972 reports began to filter out of the negotiations in Paris that real progress was being made in private talks between Presidential advisor Henry A. Kissinger and Le Duc Tho, Hanoi's chief negotiator. The rumors seemed to be entirely confirmed in late October when Kissinger made a dramatic statement that he believed "peace is at hand" in all of Indochina. But it was soon apparent that several crucial differences of interpretation remained to be resolved. When talks on these differences were broken off in mid-December, President Nixon again ordered increased bombing raids against the North. Kissinger and Tho, however, resumed their secret Paris talks in January after a halt in the bombing and initialed an agreement on a ceasefire accord Jan. 23, 1974. Despite problems and delays in implementing the agreement, all U.S. troops were withdrawn from Vietnam and all U.S. prisoners of war held by North Vietnam were released by the end of March. Completion of these two provisions of the ceasefire accord seemed to conclude the U.S. role in the war, but repeated violations of the ceasefire in South Vietnam and continued fighting in Cambodia demonstrated that for the people of Indochina peace remained only a hope.

This book consists almost exclusively of the printed record from the weekly issues of FACTS ON FILE. Any editorial changes, generally minor, were usually made to eliminate repetition, correct errors or add facts that might not have been available when the original record was being compiled. As in all FACTS ON FILE books, great pains were taken to make this volume a balanced and accurate reference work and to keep it free of bias.

U.S. & Communist Peace Plans

Discussions in Paris cited. President Richard M. Nixon said during a televised interview Jan. 2 that U.S. troop withdrawals from Vietnam would continue but that a force of 25,000–35,000 troops would be retained in Vietnam until all U.S. prisoners of war were released. He said the issue of release of the POWs in return for a pullout deadline had been discussed in Paris with the peace negotiators but the North Vietnamese had "totally rejected it."

That statement was attacked as untrue by several antiwar sources, including Sen. George McGovern (S.D.), a candidate for the Democratic presidential nomination. Administration officials later clarified that U.S. negotiators in Paris had never proposed a firm withdrawal date in exchange for a POW release because of Communist insistence on linking the issue to an end to U.S. aid for the current Saigon government.

Discussion of Vietnam policy formed much of the hour-long interview, which was conducted by Dan Rather of the Columbia Broadcasting System. Nixon made several important comments during the interview relating to the war and related problems:

Amnesty to draft evaders—There would be no amnesty "for those who have deserted their country" as long as GIs were serving in Vietnam or held prisoner by the North Vietnamese.

Vietnam discussion—The President said the Vietnam pullout would continue at its current rate or faster and this would bring the U.S. troop level in South Vietnam "to a very low level well before the [November presidential] election." Another withdrawal announcement would be made "well before" February.

But, he said, in order to have any bargaining leverage with the North Vietnamese, "we will have to continue to retain a residual force in Vietnam and we will have to continue the possibility of air strikes on the North Vietnamese."

"Why should having 25,000 or 35,000 as a residual force have any effect?" Nixon asked. "And the answer is, does the enemy want the United States to withdraw from Vietnam or doesn't it?" As President, he said he could not withdraw all U.S. forces as long as the enemy held one U.S. prisoner. And, when the enemy viewed the alternatives, with the American involvement ending, Nixon said, "it would be well for them not to retain our POWs and run the risk that it would be necessary" for the U.S. to stay in Vietnam.

The President said the recent heavy bombing of North Vietnam had been undertaken to counteract increased Communist troop infiltration, firing at U.S. aircraft and the shelling of Saigon. The enemy, he said, "violated the under-

3

standing of 1968 when the bombing halt was agreed to with regard to firing on our unarmed reconnaissance planes." All in all, he had "no other choice but to bomb, in this case, selected military targets and supply buildup areas. Those were the only areas that were hit. The results have been very, very effective."

Nixon was asked by Rather: "If you have to maintain a residual force and keep open at least the threat of additional air strikes, then how can you campaign saying you've ended the American involvement?"

Nixon replied that "the important thing is not how I can campaign with regard to the American involvement, but . . . whether the American people are convinced that the President . . . has done everything that he can to bring this desperately difficult war to an end and . . ., in view of dealing with international outlaws, to protect American men and to get back" American POWs.

Rather asked the President whether the enemy had ever been asked if they would release the POWs and guarantee the safety of the withdrawing U.S. troops if the U.S. set a date for total with-

drawal. Nixon replied [see box] that the matter "has been under discussion at various times in the Paris peace talks" but the "North Vietnamese totally rejected it."

When the issue had been broached to Communist negotiators by a U.S. senator (McGovern), Nixon said, the North Vietnamese "said deadline for prisoners was no deal." Nixon called this "a very cruel action on their part to reject out of hand even the possibility of that kind of discussion."

Furthermore, Nixon said, the question of the POW return for a total U.S. pullout was one the enemy would "have a chance to answer" when "we come down to the end" of U.S. involvement in Vietnam.

The issue also had been discussed with Soviet Foreign Minister Andrei A. Gromyko, he said, and Presidential aide Henry A. Kissinger had discussed it with Chinese Premier Chou En-lai on his two visits to China.

POW remark termed 'deceitful'—McGovern charged Jan. 3 that Nixon had "deceived the American public" by as-

---

'Under discussion at various times

Text of the exchange on the prisoner of war issue between President Nixon and CBS correspondent Dan Rather:

Rather's question—Mr. President, speaking of POW families, a lady from Florida called in this afternoon and asked that I ask you this question. She is Mrs. Gerald Garley from Florida, who is the mother of a 27-year old Navy lieutenant who is a prisoner. Her question, which I take this opportunity to ask on her behalf is, have we ever asked the North Vietnamese and the provisional Revolutionary Government if they will release the POWs and guarantee the safety of our withdrawing troops if we set a date for the withdrawal of all U.S. forces from South Vietnam?

Nixon's answer—Mr. Rather, that particular matter has been one that has been under discussion at various times in the Paris peace talks, but you yourself recall, because you reported it on CBS, and I think even NBC and ABC had this as well, that when that was floated out this fall, the North Vietnamese totally rejected it.

In other words, that is the deal of saying if we set a deadline, then they will give us back our POWs . . . That was publicly done . . . You remember the United States Senator [George McGovern (D, S.D.)] had met, he said, with some of the people from North Vietnam. He was convinced that in the event that we set a deadline, that that would mean that they would release the prisoners. The North Vietnamese said

deadline for prisoners was no deal. That was publicly stated.

Under those circumstances, this, of course, is a very cruel action on their part, to reject out of hand even the possibility of that kind of discussion.

I would say this, looking to the future, that as I have just pointed out, that when we come down to the end, as far as our own involvement in Vietnam is concerned, the question of whether or not they will return our prisoners in exchange for a total American withdrawal is one they will have a chance to answer, and I could also point out that we have participated in a great number of discussions other than those public discussions in Paris.

Sitting right here in this room—as a matter of fact, you are sitting in my chair, Mr. [Andrei] Gromyko was sitting in this chair—I raised the subject of POWs with him. Dr. [Henry] Kissinger raised the subject with Chou En-lai on both of his visits to the People's Republic of China . . .

In the event that at the time of the meetings that I will have in China and later on in the Soviet Union, we have not made progress in this area, the subjects will again be raised . . .

I am going to tell you we have pursued every negotiating channel, that we have made a number of offers in various channels and when the total record is published and it will be published in due time and at an appropriate time, our lady from Florida and the others will realize that we have gone the extra mile as far as POWs are concerned. I do not want to disclose any further details because negotiations are under way. . . .

serting the Communist negotiators had rejected attempts to obtain release of the POWs in return for a pullout date. (A statement issued Jan. 2 by a spokesman for the National Peace Action Coalition, an antiwar group, called Nixon's answer on the matter "a blatant and shocking lie.")

"It is simply not true, and the President knows it is not true," McGovern continued, "that our negotiators in Paris ever discussed with the North Vietnamese the question of total American withdrawal from Indochina in conjunction with the release of our prisoners."

What he had told the Communist negotiators in Paris and "what I maintain today," he said, "is that if we set a date for the complete withdrawal of our forces and the cessation of the bombing of Indochina, it would signal the end of support for the Saigon regime, and our troops would be allowed to withdraw safely and our prisoners freed. The North Vietnamese did not reject this approach." McGovern accused the Nixon Administration of refusing "to admit that we are propping up the corrupt Thieu regime" and said that was why the American involvement in Indochina continued.

Administration   clarification—White House Deputy Press Secretary Gerald L. Warren Jan. 3 provided some clarification of the President's remarks. After McGovern's meeting with the Communist negotiators, Warren said, the Administration in September 1971 had pressed for clarification on the issue— whether a pullout deadline would lead to release of the POWs—and had found the North Vietnamese intransigent.

Warren also clarified another point— the Administration was not conditioning a pullout solely on release of the POWs. Despite the President's preoccupation during the interview with the point, Warren said, a pullout also still depended on South Vietnam's ability to defend itself.

The clarification continued Jan. 4 from "administration officials," who said U.S. negotiators in Paris had never proposed a firm date for total pullout in exchange for the release of the POWs.

They were convinced that the North Vietnamese would reject this because of their insistence that the issue could not be separated from the Communist demand that the U.S. end all its support for the South Vietnamese government of President Thieu.

In Paris Jan. 3, a statement from the North Vietnamese delegation said the POWs could have been freed "by application of the seven-point peace plan" presented by the Communists in July 1971 and that the first two points, covering a pullout date and support for Thieu, were "closely related to each other."

Paris peace talks resume. The Paris peace talks resumed Jan. 6 after a month's suspension with the Communist delegations restating the conditions for the release of American prisoners of war.

Nguyen Van Tien, the Viet Cong delegate, said freeing the captives was contingent on the pullout of American forces and the withdrawal of American support of the South Vietnamese government of President Nguyen Van Thieu. These two conditions, part of the Viet Cong's seven-point peace plan, were "closely linked," Tien said.

The Communist position was also stated by North Vietnam's chief delegate, Xuan Thuy: "If the Nixon Administration really wants to disengage from the Vietnam war and to rapidly repatriate all American servicemen, in combat or in captivity," then it should "give up aggression, stop the 'Vietnamization' of the war, pull out from South Vietnam all troops . . . stop backing the Nguyen Van Thieu bellicose puppet group."

Thuy's demand for an end to Vietnamization appeared to be a toughening of Hanoi's stand. Previously North Vietnam had linked only troop withdrawal and the resignation of Theiu with release of American prisoners.

The American press spokesman at the Paris talks, Stephen J. Ledogar, agreed that the question of prisoner release and troop withdrawal had never been put to the Communist side by the U.S. delegation. This statement appeared to contradict President Nixon, who had said Jan. 2 that the matter had been "under discussion at various times" at the Paris talks but that the North Vietnamese had "totally rejected" the approach.

Ledogar made clear that any settlement that called for American troop withdrawal must also provide for the pullout of North Vietnamese troops from South Vietnam, Laos and Cambodia and not merely the recovery of captives.

North Vietnam's new position on the prisoners had first been expressed by Hanoi radio Jan. 5. A broadcast said the abandonment of Vietnamization as well as U.S. troop withdrawal was "the only way for President Nixon to get the United States prisoners of war back to their families."

India, North Vietnam widen ties. India and North Vietnam Jan. 7 expanded diplomatic relations by upgrading their respective consulates in New Delhi and Hanoi to embassies. The U.S. and South Vietnam rebuked New Delhi's action and challenged its membership on the three-nation International Control Commission (ICC) in Vietnam.

The New Delhi announcement on the agreement with Hanoi explained that its purpose was "to strengthen further friendly relations" between India and North Vietnam.

In criticizing India's move, the U.S. State Department Jan. 7 questioned India's neutral role on the ICC, which had been established by the 1954 Geneva conference on Indochina to supervise the cease-fire and partition agreements. The commission had been largely dormant since the fighting began in 1959. Its two other members were Poland and Canada.

State Department spokesman Charles W. Bray 3rd said India "would in effect be abandoning a neutral attitude" on the ICC "by taking steps to accord a relatively favorable diplomatic status to North Vietnam."

Bray added: "Considering the very tough line the North Vietnamese are currently taking" in the Paris peace talks, "this would be a particularly poor time to raise a consulate general to an embassy and at the same time leave their mission in Saigon at the level of a consulate-general."

Saigon retaliated against India Jan. 8 by barring its newly-appointed chairman of the ICC, L. N. Ray, from entering South Vietnam. Ray had been due to arrive in Saigon Jan. 8. Foreign Minister Tran Van Lam, assailing India's action as an "unfriendly and unnecessarily provocative gesture," said unless India "simultaneously upgrades the status of her representatives in Saigon, India shows a political partiality toward Communist North Vietnam which would destroy the very foundations of the International Control Commission under its present composition."

Nixon sets further withdrawal. President Nixon announced Jan. 13 that 70,000 more U.S. troops would be withdrawn from South Vietnam over the next three months, reducing the authorized troop ceiling to 69,000 by May 1. The withdrawal rate would be increased slightly from the current 22,500 men a month to 23,000.

It was the seventh withdrawal announcement since the President assumed office in January 1969. The authorized troop level at that time was 549,500.

Nixon said he would make another withdrawal announcement before May.

In expanding upon the President's brief announcement, Defense Secretary Melvin R. Laird said "the Vietnamization program has moved forward with sufficient vigor and progress so the South Vietnamese are in a position where they can provide for the security responsibilities in-country which are theirs." The South Vietnamese, he said, had assumed complete responsibility for ground combat in South Vietnam and were assuming an increasing share of "air and logistics responsibilities."

After completion of the latest withdrawal, Laird said, there would no longer be any U.S. combat divisions in South Vietnam. Troop ceilings will have been cut to about 48,000 for the Army, 16,000 for the Air Force and 4,500 for the Navy. (The Marine withdrawal had been completed. The totals did not include air-strike forces based in Thailand or on Navy vessels off the coast of Vietnam.)

Laird made clear, however, that an American "presence" in Vietnam would be maintained until the issue of prisoners of war "has been resolved."

Asked about reports of an impending enemy offensive in South Vietnam, Laird said several "spectaculars" might be mounted but that the South Vietnamese could survive and win "75% or more" of the battles.

Laird said the Cambodian units were doing better than expected and there was "no question" the North Vietnamese had "pushed a little further [in Laos] this year than they did in the last three years, but this swings back and forth."

The defense secretary also commented on the domestic political side of the withdrawal issue. "Some of those individuals who are going around the country criticizing the program to withdraw Americans from Vietnam," he said, "were silent in 1968 and before, when we were on the escalator going up and up and up. Now that we are going down, down, down, it seems they have changed their position, and are critical of the President and the program which he has approved to withdraw Americans from Southeast Asia."

Nixon reveals new peace plan. President Nixon, in a nationwide address Jan. 25, announced that he had submitted to the Communists through secret channels an eight-point program to end the war in Vietnam.

The President also disclosed that Henry A. Kissinger, his national security adviser, had privately discussed peace prospects with two North Vietnamese diplomats in Paris on 12 occasions between Aug. 4, 1969 and Aug. 16, 1971. Those talks ended before Kissinger was able to submit Nixon's new plan in its entirety, but the eight-point formula had been sent to the North Vietnamese peace conference delegates in Paris in a private communication from the President Oct. 11, 1971.

The North Vietnamese and Viet Cong delegations at the Paris peace talks denounced Nixon's peace program Jan. 26 and 27.

Among the major elements in the Nixon plan [See text on p. 9].

All U.S. and foreign allied troops would be withdrawn from South Viet-nam within six months of a peace agreement with the Communists and the Communists would remove their forces from South Vietnam, Cambodia and Laos; all military and civilian prisoners of both sides would be released "in parallel with the troop withdrawals"; a cease-fire was to go into effect when the agreement was signed; military aspects of the agreement would be subject to "international supervision"; and new presidential elections were to be held in South Vietnam, organized and operated by an "independent body" comprised of all political forces, including the Viet Cong, with President Nguyen Van Thieu and Vice President Tran Van Huong resigning one month before the balloting.

Nixon's formula did not mention withdrawal of American planes stationed aboard aircraft carriers off the coast of Vietnam or in bases in Thailand.

The President explained in his radio and television broadcast that he had decided after 10 months in office to attempt to end the impasse at the Paris conference by entering into the secret talks with the Communists. But the disappointing results of those private contacts, Nixon said, prompted him to make them public to the American people now in a further "try to break the deadlock at the negotiations."

The President gave this account of the events leading up to his decision to publicize the private discussions in Paris:

During the course of his meetings with the two North Vietnamese diplomats (seven times with Le Duc Tho and five times with chief delegate Xuan Thuy), Kissinger had advanced several proposals, which the President's Democratic critics had accused him of not making. One of them, submitted May 31, 1971, called for total American withdrawal in exchange for release of all prisoners and a cease-fire. The North Vietnamese rejected the proposal June 26 and presented their own nine-point plan "which insisted that we overthrow the government of South Vietnam."

Following three fruitless 1971 meetings, July 12, Aug. 16 and Sept. 13, the President Oct. 11 "sent a private communication to the North Vietnamese that contained new elements that could move negotiations forward" and requested that they be discussed with Kissinger Nov. 1. The North Vietnamese agreed to such a meeting, to be held Nov. 20, but canceled it Nov. 17, claiming Le Duc Tho was ill. After that, the Communists expressed no further interest in meeting to discuss the Nixon plan.

The Nixon proposal for new elections in South Vietnam, preceded by the resignation of that country's president and vice president, was reaffirmed by President Thieu in a radio address Jan. 26. After reiterating the main political points outlined by Nixon, Thieu declared that "the unification of Vietnam will be decided by the North and South alone and neither side should impose its position on the other."

Nixon said if the Communists rejected his proposal, he would continue the policy of American withdrawal and Vietnamization. He warned "if the enemy's answer to our peace offer is to step up their military attacks, I shall fully meet my responsibility as commander in chief to protect our remaining troops."

The President said, in a conciliatory gesture to Hanoi, his plan included an American offer to help all the states of Indochina, including North Vietnam, to carry out a major reconstruction program to recover from the ravages of the war.

(Although Nixon did not mention a specific figure for Indochina war relief, a White House official said Jan. 27 that Kissinger, in his private talks with Hanoi officials in Paris, had raised the possibility of an American offer of $7.5 billion, with $2.5 billion earmarked for North Vietnam.)

Kissinger gives more details—Henry A. Kissinger told a news conference in Washington Jan. 26 that North Vietnam's demand that the U.S. end all its support to the South Vietnamese government was one of two points in Hanoi's nine-point plan that prevented an agreement in the private U.S.-Communist talks in Paris. The other point, Kissinger disclosed, was the Communists' conception of the term "withdrawal," which they interpreted to mean the removal of all American equipment, economic aid and all American arms held by the South Vietnamese army. Compliance with this request, Kissinger said, would

mean the collapse of the Saigon government.

Kissinger said he would not release all of Hanoi's nine points because it would not be "consistent with our attempt to protect the confidentiality of these negotiations."

Kissinger said that in his May 31, 1971 meeting in Paris he had offered to set a deadline for the removal of American troops in return for a cease-fire throughout Indochina and the exchange of prisoners, a proposal turned down by Hanoi. Kissinger noted that "this was the first time that the United States had indicated a willingness to set a date, . . . unilaterally; that is, without an equivalent assurance of withdrawal on the other side."

"So our attempt to negotiate the military issue separately was simply rejected," Kissinger said, because of Hanoi's insistence "that the only possible proposal is one that included the political elements."

Domestic political reaction—Republican senators appeared to preempt strong criticism of President Nixon's proposals by declaring Jan. 26 that the plan ought to satisfy all but those who favored a U.S. capitulation in Indochina.

Sen. Hugh Scott (Penn.) said, "There was general agreement that last night's speech is an answer to reasonable people with reasonable doubts. Of course, it would never be an answer to people who demand total surrender." Scott's remarks were amplified by Sen. Barry Goldwater (R, Ariz.), who said, "Any Democrat who fails to support the current initiative to end the war is either committed to the total surrender of all America's strategic interests in Indochina or is more interested in gaining political advantage than in ending the tragic hostilities."

Democratic senators generally welcomed the Nixon plan, although many of them expressed reservations.

Sen. Mike Mansfield (Mont.), the majority leader, called the proposals a "long step forward" and an "advance over previous positions," containing "concessions that could lay the groundwork for the start of negotiations for the first time." Mansfield said, however, that he would keep his amendment to secure a precise date for the withdrawal of U.S. troops from Indochina "on the front burner because it faces up to the most important element in the situation . . ."

Sen. Hubert Humphrey (D, Minn.) criticized the lack of a definite withdrawal date. Sen. Edmund Muskie (D, Maine) felt the proposal for new elections in South Vietnam might make the Viet Cong feel their political rights were not being protected.

The severest criticism was voiced by Sen. Edward Kennedy (D, Mass.), who declared, "We do not need an eight-point plan to end the war. All we need is a one-point plan—a complete withdrawal of American ground, sea and air forces by a date certain, in exchange for a return of our prisoners. . . . So long as we try to

Text of Joint U.S.-South Vietnamese Proposal

The White House Jan. 25 released this text of a proposal by the governments of the U.S. and South Vietnam for a negotiated settlement of the Indochina conflict:

1. There will be a total withdrawal from South Vietnam of all U.S. forces and other foreign forces allied with the government of South Vietnam within six months of an agreement.

2. The release of all military men and innocent civilians captured throughout Indochina will be carried out in parallel with the troop withdrawals mentioned in Point 1. Both sides will present a complete list of military men and innocent civilians held throughout Indochina on the day the agreement is signed. The release will begin on the same day as the troop withdrawals and will be completed when they are completed.

3. The following principles will govern the political future of South Vietnam:

The political future of South Vietnam will be left for the South Vietnamese people to decide for themselves, free from outside interference.

There will be a free and democratic presidential election in South Vietnam within six months of an agreement. This election will be organized and run by an independent body representing all political forces in South Vietnam which will assume its responsibilities on the date of the agreement. This body will, among other responsibilities, determine the qualification of candidates. All political forces in South Vietnam can participate in the election and present candidates. There will be international supervision of this election.

One month before the presidential election takes place, the incumbent president and vice president of South Vietnam will resign. The chairman of the Senate, as caretaker head of the government, will assume administrative responsibilities except for those pertaining to the election, which will remain with the independent election body.

The United States, for its part, declares that it:

■ Will support no candidate and will remain completely neutral in the election.

■ Will abide by the outcome of this election and any other political processes shaped by the South Vietnamese people themselves.

■ Is prepared to define its military and economic assistance relationship with any government that exists in South Vietnam.

Both sides agree that:

■ South Vietnam, together with the other countries of Indochina, should adopt a foreign policy consistent with the military provisions of the 1954 Geneva accords.

■ Reunification of Vietnam should be decided on the basis of discussion and agreements between North and South Vietnam without constraint and annexation from either party, and without foreign interference.

4. Both sides will respect the 1954 Geneva agreements on Indochina and those of 1962 on Laos. There will be no foreign intervention in the Indochinese countries, and the Indochinese people will be left to settle their own affairs by themselves.

5. The problems existing among the Indochinese countries will be settled by the Indochinese parties on the basis of mutual respect for independence, sovereignty, territorial integrity and noninterference in each other's affairs. Among the problems that will be settled is the implementation of the principle that all armed forces of the countries of Indochina must remain within their national frontiers.

6. There will be a general cease-fire throughout Indochina, to begin when the agreement is signed. As part of the cease-fire, there will be no further infiltration of outside forces into any of the countries of Indochina.

7. There will be international supervision of the military aspects of this agreement, including the cease-fire in its provisions, the release of prisoners of war and innocent civilians, the withdrawal of outside forces from Indochina and the implementation of the principle that all armed forces of the countries of Indochina must remain within their national frontiers.

8. There will be an international guarantee for the fundamental national rights of the Indochinese peoples, the status of all the countries of Indochina and lasting peace in this region.

Both sides express their willingness to participate in an international conference for this and other appropriate purposes.

condition our withdrawal on things like free elections, a cease-fire, or any of the other trappings disclosed last night, reasonable as they may seem, we shall be pursuing the same blind alley in public negotiations that we have followed with such futility in private."

U.S. plan debated in Paris—The Communist delegations at the Paris peace talks Jan. 26 and 27 assailed but did not reject outright President Nixon's eight-point formula to end the war.

In a statement issued Jan. 26, one day before the regular weekly session, the North Vietnamese representatives said that in both the public and private meetings "the Nixon administration did not respond to the two questions fundamental for the just and logical peaceful settlement of the Vietnam problem." The U.S. had refused, they said, to agree to halt Vietnamization of the war and withdraw its forces, arms and dismantle its bases and had "persisted in maintaining" support of the South Vietnamese government.

The statement called Nixon's Jan. 25 speech "a brazen challenge to the Vietnamese people, the American people and peace-loving people around the world."

The Viet Cong delegation charged that Nixon "spoke of sham peace but made real war." The statement called the President's proposal for a cease-fire "only a maneuver aimed at forcing" the Indochinese people "to renounce" their struggle against the U.S.

Nixon's plan for election in South Vietnam, the Viet Cong said, was "only a maneuver aimed at forcing the South Vietnamese people to allow the present Saigon administration" to influence the selection of its successor.

At the regular weekly session Jan. 27, the Communists formally responded to the Nixon peace program by denouncing all eight points and by reiterating their own position, stating that a peace settlement must provide for total American withdrawal and the ouster of the present Saigon regime. Xuan Thuy, North Vietnam's chief delegate, assailed Nixon for breaking his pledge not to reveal the secret U.S.-Communist talks.

"If Mr. Nixon cannot keep such a promise, then what credibility will his other statements have?" Thuy said. Thuy, however, did not flatly reject the Nixon plan and another delegation spokesman did not rule out further secret talks with the U.S. Thuy said "We shall have other comments to make on President Nixon's Jan. 25 speech and on the U.S. government's eight-point proposal."

William J. Porter, chief American delegate, urged the Communists to accept the American plan "in complete form as an overall agreement in principle." Once this principle had been accepted, he said, it would be possible "to begin implementing certain military aspects," such as troop withdrawal and prisoner exchange. On the matter of troop withdrawal, Porter warned that "although they could start on the date of the agreement in principle, they wouldn't be totally completed until final agreement on all aspects of the problem is signed."

After speaking by telephone with Porter, Secretary of State William P. Rogers told a news conference in Washington Jan. 27 that he was encouraged by the outcome of the latest Paris session. He expressed optimism over the fact that the Communist delegations had not "rejected our proposal. There has been a good deal of invective about it, but it hasn't been rejected. Rogers also said "it was a good sign" that the Communists "have been asking a few questions about what we mean" by the proposal.

Previous Paris sessions—In the Jan. 20 peace session in Paris, the U.S. delegation asked the North Vietnamese why 14 American pilots shot down over North Vietnam were not on Hanoi's list of U.S. war prisoners. A roster released by the North Vietnamese Dec. 22, 1970, described by them as "complete and final," listed 339 captured Americans. Heyward Isham, deputy American delegate, said all the 14 airmen were "known to have been alive on the ground in North Vietnam or were at one time actually identified by you as having been captured." (Sweden had announced March 7, 1970 that North Vietnam had provided it with a list of the 14 captured pilots.

The Viet Cong had charged at the Jan. 13 meeting that the U.S. and Saigon governments were planning to increase in February the movement of civilians from the northern provinces of South Vietnam to the south in order to create a free-fire zone for the deployment of nuclear weapons. Viet Cong delegation spokesman Ly Van Sau said one million persons were involved in the repatriation shift to "concentration camps" in the southern part of the country.

The U.S. and South Vietnamese representatives denied the Communist charges. South Vietnamese spokesman Nguyen Trieu Dan said about 50,000 persons figured in the transfer, about 5% of the population of the five northern provinces. He said they had requested resettlement in the south.

China assails Nixon plan. President Nixon's plan for a Vietnam settlement was denounced by China Jan. 28 and 31.

A Peking government statement Jan. 28 described it as a "plan for persisting in and prolonging the war of aggression against Vietnam and Indochina" and for "perpetuating the forcible occupation of South Vietnam." Peking scorned the American proposal that made an agreement to end the war a condition for removal of U.S. troops. The way to terminate the conflict, the statement said, was for the U.S. to "immediately, unconditionally and totally" withdraw its forces, and end the bombing, Vietnamization and support of the South Vietnamese government.

Premier Chou En-lai declared Jan. 31 that if the U.S. "goes along with its eight-point program, I think it will not be possible for the war to be ended in Indochina, especially in Vietnam."

Rift called 'fundamental.' North Vietnam made public Jan. 31 a nine-point plan to end the war in Vietnam. It said the plan had been submitted to U.S. representatives in secret talks in Paris June 26, 1971. The plan [text p. 12] was published along with a communique released by the North Vietnamese delegation to the Paris peace talks in response to President Nixon's disclosure Jan. 25 of the secret peace negotiations.

The Viet Cong delegation to the Paris peace talks presented a revised version of their seven-point plan at the Feb. 3 session. South Vietnam rejected it but the U.S. took a less definitive stand.

In addition to making known their own plan, the North Vietnamese presented their version of the eight-point U.S. proposal received by them Oct. 11, 1971, the seven-point plan submitted by the Viet Cong July 1, 1971, and the texts of an exchange of messages between the U.S. and North Vietnam on a private meeting set for Nov. 20 but canceled by the U.S.

Nguyen Thanh Le, press spokesman for the North Vietnamese delegation, released all the documents. He told a news conference that the proposals of Hanoi and Washington reflected a "fundamental" difference in their approach to ending the conflict. North Vietnam's plan was essentially a reiteration of its oft-stated demands for resolving the Indochina struggle, and, according to Le, was "fully conforming" to the Viet Cong's seven-point plan.

There were two principal differences between the U.S. and North Vietnamese positions as outlined in their respective programs:

(1) President Nixon's call for a military withdrawal from Vietnam was conditioned on agreement in principle on a final settlement. The Communists insisted that the U.S. set a date for withdrawal without conditions. The U.S. plan called for withdrawal of all foreign forces from the territory of South Vietnam; the Communist plan demanded the withdrawal of U.S. and allied troops from all Indochinese countries.

(2) The American plan provided for a presidential election in South Vietnam, to be run by a commission with Communist participation. President Nguyen Van Thieu and Vice President Tran Van Huong would resign one month before the balloting. North Vietnam proposed that the U.S. withdraw its support from the current Saigon government immediately and replace it with a tripartite coalition government, including the Communists, that would hold the elections.

Some differences were noted between the American eight-point plan as disclosed by President Nixon and its text as released by the North Vietnamese. According to Hanoi's version of the proposal, a small American residual force would remain in Vietnam to help enforce the cease-fire that would go into effect with the final peace agreement. The text stated that once a "statement of principles" were signed by Dec. 1, 1971, the remaining American forces would leave by July 1, 1972. This constituted a seven-month period in which American forces would be pulled out, compared with a six-month interval cited by Nixon Jan. 25.

On another point, North Vietnam's version of the American plan said the U.S. residual force would be pulled out of Vietnam by the date of the proposed presidential elections in South Vietnam and the balloting would be held "within six months of the signature of the final agreement based on the principles of this statement." In his Jan. 25 address, Nixon proposed that both total withdrawal and a presidential election take place "within six months of an agreement."

The Hanoi communique asserted that President Nixon in his Jan. 25 address and national security adviser Henry A. Kissinger in his Jan. 26 news conference had "unilaterally divulged the substance" of the secret U.S. and North Vietnamese talks and had "even distorted the facts." In disclosing these private meetings, the statement said, the U.S. government wanted to give the impression "that it has goodwill" and to hold Hanoi responsible "for the deadlock in the negotiations." Actually, it was the U.S. that had created the impasse, Hanoi said.

The communique also held the U.S. to blame for cancellation of the Nov. 20, 1971 meeting at which the two sides were to have continued the secret negotiations. According to the statement: The North Vietnamese had accepted Kissinger's Oct. 17 proposal for the Nov. 20 meeting. The North Vietnamese in-

---

Text of 9-Point North Vietnamese Peace Proposal

The North Vietnamese delegation to the Paris peace talks issued the text Jan. 31 of the nine-point peace plan said to have been presented at a private meeting of North Vietnamese and American envoys in the Paris area June 26, 1971. Appended to the document was the text of the seven-point Viet Cong peace plan submitted to the Paris talks July 1, 1971.

1. The withdrawal of the totality of U.S. forces and those of foreign countries in the U.S. camp from South Vietnam and other Indochinese countires should be completed within 1971.

2. The release of all military men and civilians captured in the war should be carried out [in] parallel and completed at the same time with the troop withdrawal mentioned in Point 1.

3. In South Vietnam, the United States should stop supporting Thieu-Ky-Khiem so that there may be set up in Saigon a new administration standing for peace, independence, neutrality and democracy. The Provisional Revolutionary Government of the Republic of South Vietnam will enter into talks with that administration to settle the internal affairs of South Vietnam and to achieve national concord.

4. The U.S. government must bear full responsibility for the damages caused by the United States to the people of the whole Vietnam. The

government of the Democratic Republic of Vietnam and the Provisional Revolutionary Government of the Republic of South Vietnam demand from the U.S. government reparations for the damages caused by the United States in the two zones of Vietnam.

5. The United States should respect the 1954 Geneva agreements on Indochina and those of 1962 on Laos. It should stop its aggression and intervention in the Indochinese countries and let their peoples settle by themselves their own affairs.

6. The problems existing among the Indochinese countries should be settled by the Indochinese parties on the basis of mutual respect for independence, sovereignty and territorial integrity, and noninterference in each other's internal affairs. As far as it is concerned, the Democratic Republic of Vietnam is prepared to join in resolving such problems.

7. All the parties should achieve a cease-fire after the signing of the agreements on the above-mentioned problems.

8. There should be an international supervision.

9. There should be an international guarantee for the fundamental national rights of the Indochinese peoples, the neutrality of South Vietnam, Laos and Cambodia, and lasting peace in this region.

The above points form an integrated whole.

formed the U.S. Nov. 17 that Politburo member Le Duc Tho, who was to have conferred with Kissinger, was ill and could not come to Paris. The North Vietnamese chief negotiator to the Paris peace talks, Xuan Thuy, was suggested as the alternate negotiator, but on Nov. 19 the U.S. called off the meeting.

U.S. releases text of Hanoi plan—The U.S. Feb. 1 released its own version of North Vietnam's nine-point plan and reiterated its willingness to negotiate an agreement on the basis of the Hanoi plan. Both texts were virtually identical with the exception of minor grammatical differences.

White House Press Secretary Ronald L. Ziegler, who released the text, discussed the controversy over the cancellation of the Nov. 20 meeting. He acknowledged that Kissinger had turned down a proposal to meet alone with Thuy. Ziegler held these private talks could not produce results unless a representative of North Vietnam's political leadership, such as Le Duc Tho, was present.

Kissinger had said in his Jan. 26 news conference "Now everyone who has been engaged in these negotiations knows that in his [Tho's] absence no major change can occur." The U.S. had replied Nov. 17 that since illness prevented Tho from attending, "No point would be served by the meeting."

Viet Cong's revised peace plan—The Viet Cong's new version of their seven-point plan presented at the Paris peace talks Feb. 3 called for the immediate resignation of President Thieu before negotiations on a coalition government in South Vietnam could start. Unlike its previous proposal, the Viet Cong did not ask the U.S. to oust Thieu and did not restate earlier demands for a new administration in Saigon prior to coalition talks.

The Viet Cong's delegation spokesman, Ly Van Sau, said another new aspect of the proposal was the call for "a precise date for the complete withdrawal from South Vietnam of all troops, military advisers and personnel, arms, war equipment of the United States and of other foreign countries in the American camp without putting any condition

whatever." Sau recalled that the Viet Cong had previously suggested a withdrawal date for the U.S. to accept. This proposal had generally been accompanied with the suggestion that if the deadline was not acceptable to the U.S. it could select a "reasonable" date of its own.

The new Viet Cong plan did not mention a cease-fire, in contrast to the first point in its July 1 1971 proposal and in the seventh point of North Vietnam's nine-point plan. Unlike the old formula, it also failed to mention parallel release of war prisoners as troops were withdrawn.

The Viet Cong's new plan on a political settlement differed widely from its previous one. According to the original version, there would be a "new administration favoring peace, independence, neutrality and democracy," which the Viet Cong would negotiate to form a coalition. The revised program, in addition to calling for Thieu's resignation, said Saigon must abandon "its bellicose policy, abolish its apparatus of repression and coercion against the population, put an end to the policy of pacification, liberate persons arrested for political reasons and guarantee the democratic freedoms stipulated by the 1954 Geneva accords on Vietnam."

In rejecting the revised Viet Cong plan, the South Vietnamese delegation said, "What the Communists want is the destruction of the legality and the legitimacy of the regime in the person of President Thieu."

The Communist representatives declined to give direct replies to questions about the new plan asked by William J. Porter, chief U.S. delegate. They merely said it should be considered. Stephen J. Ledogar, spokesman for the American delegation, later said the military proposals appeared to be a hardening of the Viet Cong position. But he said the American side would study the political aspects of the new program.

Also at the Feb. 3 Paris session, Xuan Thuy, chief North Vietnamese delegate, called President Nixon's eight-point plan "unacceptable" because its purpose was "to pursue a policy of Vietnamization of the war" and to prolong the conflict itself.

Hanoi rejects U.S. peace plan. North Vietnam Feb. 5 formally rejected President Nixon's eight-point peace plan to end the war in Vietnam. A government statement said the proposal was "deceptive" and that Hanoi expressed "unreserved support" for the Viet Cong's seven-point formula to terminate the conflict.

Communist rejection of the Nixon plan had been voiced Feb. 4 by the North Vietnamese and Viet Cong envoys to Moscow. The Soviet news agency Tass reported that in their·meeting with Soviet Premier Alexei Kosygin, the "Vietnamese envoys stressed that the U.S. proposal meant nothing but an attempt to impose a solution of the Vietnamese problem according to the American pattern."

Hanoi clarifies peace stand—The major gulf between the U.S. and North Vietnamese positions on peace was further stressed in clarification of Hanoi's stand expressed Feb. 4 and 5 by Xuan Thuy, North Vietnam's chief delegate to the Paris peace talks.

Thuy declared Feb. 4 that North Vietnam would not release American war prisoners until the U.S. ended its support of South Vietnamese President Nguyen Van Thieu and until the war was over. He further stated that setting a specific date for U.S. withdrawal would no longer be enough to bring about the release of the American captives.

Thuy's views were announced on the CBS television program "Face the Nation," recorded in Paris Feb. 4 and broadcast Feb. 6. Secretary of State William P. Rogers appeared on the second segment of the program.

Thuy said that in July 1971 North Vietnam had proposed freeing American prisoners in exchange for a U.S. withdrawal date. But he implied that North Vietnam had been forced to harden its position by linking the military and political issues after the re-election of President Thieu Oct. 3.

Thuy was asked what his government's reply would be to the proposals of some aspirants in the American Presidential campaign, that "if the United States proposed a date for total withdrawal, the North Vietnamese would re-release all American prisoners." Thuy answered: "You should realize the difference of the conditions in 1971 and the present conditions in 1972. As you realize, after the Oct. 3 elections in South Vietnam, the Vietnamese people understand still more clearly that Mr. Nixon's words and deeds do not match."

Secretary Rogers denied that North Vietnam had ever offered to free the prisoners in return for a troop withdrawal date. According to Rogers' version of the U.S.-North Vietnamese exchanges in 1971: "There was never any discussion of that kind. In every session we had with the North Vietnamese, they made it clear that they would not talk about a military solution, except in the context of an overall political solution."

Thuy reiterated Feb. 5 that Hanoi's military and political conditions for ending the war had been separable in the summer of 1971, but were now inseparable. His views were expressed in an interview in Paris with Richard J. Barnet and Peter Weiss, co-director and chairman of the Washington-based Institute for Policy Studies. Thuy said that in his 1971 secret talks with Henry A. Kissinger, President Nixon's adviser on national security, he had told Kissinger that if the U.S. encouraged Thieu not to run for re-election, this would be a "favorable opportunity" for settling the war without getting the U.S. further involved in South Vietnamese politics. Thuy told his interviewers that Thieu would not have been returned to office if the U.S. had set a specific date for withdrawal. American refusal to denounce Thieu's one-man election race left no doubt that the U.S. had no intention of leaving Vietnam, Thuy said.

Thuy denied that in the 1971 secret talks the U.S. had offered to draw up a date for total withdrawal in return for the release of American prisoners. All offers, Thuy said, were based on the "unacceptable conditions" of Nixon's eight-point formula.

Thuy explained that the election of a new government in South Vietnam, one of Nixon's eight points, was unacceptable to his side. He asked: "How could we accept an election when Thieu's forces, including a million-man army, pacification forces, civil guard and police, are operating down to the hamlet level?" The "electoral commission," as proposed by Nixon, would have only nominal control of the election and the balloting would result in favor of the U.S., Thuy said.

Nixon comments on talks. In his third annual report on foreign affairs, delivered to Congress Feb. 9, President Nixon declared that the differences between the two sides in the Paris peace talks could be boiled down to one issue: "Will we collude with our enemies to overthrow our friends? Will we impose a future on the Vietnamese people that the other side has been unable to gain militarily or politically?" His answer: "This we shall never do."

But, he said, if the North Vietnamese were "willing to compete fairly in the political arena" in South Vietnam, "they will find our side forthcoming to meet their concerns."

The President again stated his willingness to provide a five-year, $7.5 billion postwar reconstruction program for Indochina, $2.5 billion of which would go to North Vietnam.

As for the prisoners of war, Nixon pledged to retrieve the American POWs held by North Vietnam "either as part of an overall settlement or through other means."

Nixon assures Thieu on peace plan. President Nixon assured President Nguyen Van Thieu Feb. 10 that "under no circumstances" would the U.S. "undercut" South Vietnam in negotiations with the North Vietnamese and Viet Cong to end the Indochina war. Nixon made the statement at a news conference to ease Thieu's anxiety about possible American concessions to the Communists on Saigon's future.

Thieu said in a broadcast interview Feb. 10 that he would refuse to go any further than Nixon's eight-point peace plan in efforts to reach a political settlement. His remarks were largely in response to a statement Feb. 3 by Secretary of State William P. Rogers that the U.S. was taking a "flexible" position on the matter of holding new elections in South Vietnam.

At his news conference, Nixon said he sought to clear up the "misunderstanding" resulting from Rogers' state-

ment. The President reaffirmed that every proposal submitted by the U.S. in the Paris peace talks had been made jointly and in consultation with the Saigon government and that this practice would continue. The latest eight-point formula, Nixon said, was a joint U.S.-South Vietnamese proposal and "is going to stand until we get a reply" from the Communists.

Rogers' remarks on flexibility, Nixon pointed out, referred to "what we have always said that we have put a proposal on the [negotiating] table" and that "we are ready to negotiate on it." This meant that the U.S. would not "go a step further than we have in that proposal." The President added: "The enemy has not responded to it. Until the enemy does respond to it, there will be no further proposals and no further concessions on our part."

In his Feb. 3 news conference, Rogers had been questioned as to whether the U.S. was "flexible" on the makeup of the group that would organize the election in South Vietnam and "the length of time that President Thieu would resign prior" to the balloting, one of Nixon's eight points and agreed to by Thieu. Rogers replied. "Yes we are. And I think those are considerations that if the other side was interested in negotiating in good faith, they could raise. I think they are perfectly logical, sensible considerations that we would have to think about. We are flexible on those."

Thieu said in his Feb. 10 interview, "I think Mr. Rogers does not understand thoroughly the relationship between Mr. Nixon and myself as it has already been agreed that the American government would not deal with questions involving Vietnam's internal affairs at the Paris peace talks, in particular those involving political problems in South Vietnam, without prior consultations" with the Saigon government.

Thieu said if Nixon planned to give the Chinese proposals on Vietnam during his forthcoming visit to Peking "he should first meet with me to discuss and get my agreement."

Thieu said if Rogers had "actually" made a statement "interfering with our rights." . . . "I will bring the matter to the attention of President Nixon."

South Vietnamese Foreign Minister Tran Van Lam said Feb. 10 that his government had read the transcript of Rogers' statement and was satisfied that the secretary had not deliberately suggested that the U.S. negotiate directly with the Communists on the matter of Thieu's resignation.

U.S. cancels peace session. The U.S. delegation to the Paris peace talks refused at the Feb. 10 session to agree to a date for the next meeting that would normally be held seven days later.

Chief delegate William J. Porter announced the decision to protest a three-day anti-war rally scheduled to open in nearby Versailles Feb. 11. He described the rally as "a horde of Communist-controlled agitators" who placed "intolerable" pressure on the peace talks. Porter said he would inform the Communist representatives "when we have determined how soon another meeting will be desirable."

The North Vietnamese and Viet Cong delegates denounced Porter's refusal to agree to the date of the next meeting as an "act of sabotage."

Stephen J. Ledogar, spokesman for the American delegation, charged after the Feb. 10 session that North Vietnam had organized the Versailles rally.

The U.S., with the support of South Vietnam, Feb. 10 protested to the French government against the mass meeting. The government reportedly replied it had no legal way of blocking it.

The three-day conference, known as the "World Assembly in Paris for Peace and Independence of the Indochinese People," was in support of the Vietnamese Communist peace proposals. Its official organizers were listed as 48 French leftist organizations and the Conference of Stockholm on Vietnam. About 1,000 persons representing mostly left-wing groups in 80 countries were to attend. They included the North Vietnamese and Viet Cong and a group of 70 from the U.S.

Japanese mission to Hanoi. Two Japanese Foreign Ministry officials visited North Vietnam on a diplomatic mission Feb. 8-11. The U.S. was reported Feb. 24 to have objected to the visit, originally scheduled for the week of Feb. 20, on the ground that it might embarrass President Nixon during his visit to China. Japan was said to have rejected the American protest but agreed on a compromise by sending its representatives to Hanoi more than a week before Nixon left for China.

The U.S.-Japanese negotiations on the mission to Hanoi were said to have been conducted in Washington between U. Alexis Johnson, deputy undersecretary of state for political affairs, and Ambassador Nobuhiko Ushiba.

Tokyo had declined to comment on the objectives of the mission. One of the visiting diplomats, Wasuke Miyake, said Feb. 12 that he had gone to Hanoi on the invitation of the North Vietnamese Chamber of Commerce. He said no concrete talks were held. Accompanying Miyake was Yushisaburo Inouye.

Paris peace talks resume, halt. The Paris peace talks, suspended for a week, resumed Feb. 24 but came to an abrupt halt when the North Vietnamese and Viet Cong delegations walked out only a few minutes after the meeting had convened.

The Communist walkout was in protest against recent American air raids on North Vietnam. Xuan Thuy, North Vietnam's chief delegate, declared "as a sign of energetic protest" his delegation had decided to suspend the current meeting and that the next session would be held March 2. All delegations, however, were required to agree on a date, and both the U.S. and South Vietnam refused to grant immediate consent.

William J. Porter, chief American delegate, stated after the Communists left the meeting room, "We have just seen a remarkable example of the intentions of the other side to conduct the 'serious negotiations' for which they asked us to come back to the table."

At the Feb. 10 session the U.S. and South Vietnam had canceled the following week's meeting in protest against a left-wing anti-war rally in nearby Versailles. The allied side formally advised the Communists of the decision Feb. 15. The North Vietnamese and Viet Cong protested the delay Feb. 16 and insisted that the next meeting be held Feb. 24. The U.S. and South Vietnam later agreed.

North-South Vietnam contacts—Xuan Thuy had held private talks in Paris with a South Vietnamese representative Dec. 19, 1971, it was confirmed by both sides Feb. 23. The North Vietnamese delegation said in the two-hour meeting Thuy had merely received former Foreign Minister Tran Van Do as a private person since he was not a member of the Saigon government.

Do said in Saigon that his meeting with Thuy had accomplished nothing. He said Thuy had expressed the hope they would meet again. Do, who conducted the secret contacts with the approval of President Nguyen Van Thieu, reported to the South Vietnamese leader on his return to Saigon.

Vietnam discussed during China visit. President Nixon discussed the Indochina peace negotiations with Chinese leaders during his Feb. 21–28 visit to Communist China. A communique released Feb. 27 reiterated the previously-stated positions of the two countries on the war. The U.S. emphasized its support for the eight-point proposal advocated in January by itself and South Vietnam for an end to the Indochina war. It added that "in the absence of a negotiated settlement the U.S. envisages the ultimate withdrawal of all U.S. forces from the region consistent with the aim of self-determination for each country of Indochina." In its statement, China announced its support for the revised 7-point Viet Cong proposal elaborated in February and the Joint Declaration of the Summit Conference of the Indochinese Peoples.

North Vietnam's first comment on the visit appeared Feb. 24 in the Communist party newspaper Nhan Dan. It said Nixon was responsible for "dark plotting to carry out continued U.S. neocolonialist war in South Vietnam and throughout the Indochina peninsula." The paper added: "And never before has a president gone to an international meeting in an area which before was a very strange place for a great majority of all American people. The situation stated above clearly shows how more and more the

U.S. aggressors are deadlocked in a position from which they strive to extricate themselves."

A Viet Cong radio broadcast Feb. 24 accused Nixon of trying to "capitalize on the internal disagreements of the Socialist camp in order to further his interests."

Indian Prime Minister Indira Gandhi told an election rally Feb. 21 in New Delhi: "If the meetings between the American and Chinese leaders are meant to forge friendship, it is welcome to us. But apprehensions are being expressed that the talks are meant to form some sort of a new power group. If so, India—though a small nation—will not be bound by any such decision which seeks to dictate terms to Asian countries."

The Soviet government newspaper Izvestia Feb. 21 said China was keeping silent about the U.S. bombing of North Vietnam during Nixon's visit. The paper declared: "At present it is no secret for anyone that Nixon's trip to Peking, advertised in every way by Washington propaganda as 'a visit in the name of peace,' is taking place against a background of severe enlargement of the U.S. military clique's piratical actions in Indochina."

Other reaction. South Vietnam's first official comment on President Nixon's visit to China came March 1 in remarks by Foreign Minister Tran Van Lam, who said he was not upset by the Sino-U.S. communique's reference to the ultimate withdrawal of U.S. forces from Indochina.

Lam declared: "It has already been agreed between our two governments that when Vietnamese troops are fully trained and equipped the American troops will go home." He also said: "We fully approve of Mr. Nixon's trip. No one can deny that it helped create an atmosphere of eased tensions. . . . The U.S. has been very correct and faithful in its commitments to Vietnam, and we especially appreciate the mention of our eight-point peace proposal."

Green reassures allies on U.S. policy. Marshall Green, assistant U.S. secretary of state, visited the capitals of Asian countries allied to the U.S. during early March to discuss aspects of President Nixon's visit to China.

After arriving March 5 from Manila, Green met South Vietnamese President Nguyen Van Thieu March 6 in Saigon. A March 7 dispatch from the Vietnamese Foreign Ministry said Green had "strongly affirmed that there had been no secret arrangements between the U.S. and Communist China concerning the Vietnam issue" and that "there had been no secret contacts between the U.S. and North Vietnam under any form and by any persons during the China visit."

Green left that morning for Thailand and made stops on the way in Laos and Cambodia. He had a meeting with Laotian Premier Souvanna Phouma in Vientiane and later saw Cambodian Deputy Premier Sisowath Sirik Matak and Foreign Minister Koun Wick. He reportedly told them that the U.S. was looking for a settlement in which "the armed forces of all Indochinese states will remain within their national frontiers." Sirik Matak remarked March 8 that he had been assured by Green that the Nixon trip to China had not affected the Cambodian situation. "We will continue to receive U.S. aid and all guarantees that we would desire to have," he said. In Bangkok March 8, Green met with Thai Premier Thanom Kittikachorn.

Chinese premier visited Hanoi. Former Cambodian Chief of State Prince Norodom Sihanouk disclosed March 9 that Chinese Premier Chou En-lai had briefed North Vietnamese leaders on his talks with President Nixon and assured them of Peking's support in the Indochina struggle. The U.S. government was said to have received authoritative reports confirming that the discussions had been held in Hanoi March 3–4 and that Chou had returned to China March 5.

It was disclosed that Sihanouk also had been in Hanoi, meeting with North Vietnamese leaders Feb. 12–March 5 to discuss mutual problems. Sihanouk's representatives in Paris published a joint communique March 5, the day the prince returned to China; his government-in-exile was based in Peking.

Speaking in Shanghai, Sihanouk said March 9 that Chou had informed him in a three-hour conversation that Nixon had been told in the Peking summit talks that China would not mediate the Indochina war by acting as an intermediary between Washington and the "Indochinese resistance." Chou "told me it was China's duty to support these resistance movements until total victory," Sihanouk said.

According to the exiled Cambodian leader, Peking had informed Nixon that "if the U.S. desires sincerely to improve and normalize relations with China it should end the aggressive war against Indochina." Chou had told Nixon that if the U.S. continued to stay in Indochina, "tensions will be lasting and perhaps will increase if you continue your air escalation," Sihanouk said. The prince said Chou had told the President that the U.S. must solve the Indochina problem before the Taiwan dispute.

White House Press Secretary Ronald L. Ziegler refused March 9 to make a direct comment on Sihanouk's statement that Nixon had sought to have China serve as intermediary in Indochina. Ziegler only referred to that section of the Feb. 27 joint U.S.-Chinese communique that stated neither country was "prepared to negotiate on behalf of any third party or to enter into agreements or understandings with the other directed at other states."

The joint communique released by Sihanouk's representatives in Paris also bore the signature of North Vietnamese President Ton Duc Thang. It pledged that "the problems existing between the two countries will be settled by the two peoples through negotiations in fraternal friendship." The problems referred to were believed to pertain to a reported dispute between Hanoi and Sihanouk over the insurgency against Cambodian Premier Lon Nol. North Vietnam reportedly had been undermining Sihanouk's influence by supporting Communist cadres loyal to Hanoi rather than the prince's supposedly non-Communist followers.

The joint communique also said that Sihanouk's government-in-exile, the Royal Government of National Union of Cambodia, was "the only and authentic legal and legitimate government of Cambodia."

China assails U.S. air raids. China March 10 denounced the U.S. for its recent air strikes on North Vietnam and reiterated support for Communist forces in Indochina. The statement was Peking's first attack on Washington since President Nixon's visit to China.

The statement by the Foreign Affairs Ministry endorsed North Vietnam's Foreign Ministry declaration of March 6 condemning the U.S. for the raids and other "acts of aggression." China called "the wanton bombings a vain attempt to hold back the victorious advance of the Vietnamese and other Indochinese people in their war against United States aggression." The statement demanded that the U.S. halt the bombings and other attacks, withdraw unconditionally "before a set terminal date" and "cease to support the puppet cliques in the Indochinese countries."

Paris peace talks resume. The first full session of the Paris peace talks in three weeks was held March 16 with the prisoner of war issue the principal topic.

The U.S. proposed that prisoner of war camps be opened to international inspection "in return for an undertaking by both sides to refrain from efforts to liberate prisoners from locations visited."

The Communist delegation called the proposal an evasion of the fundamental issue. North Vietnamese press spokesman Nguyen Thanh Le said after the meeting that "all American troops, prisoners or not, can certainly be back in the United States before Easter" if the U.S. accepted the two main points of the Communist peace plan—withdrawal of all American troops from Vietnam and replacement of the Thieu government in Saigon and negotiations toward a coalition government.

Quoting the North Vietnamese delegation as saying that the U.S. proposal was "a hypocritical maneuver that fizzled," Le referred to the prisoner issue raised in private U.S.-North Vietnamese talks the previous year by Henry A. Kissinger, President Nixon's national security adviser. Le said "In the course of a private meeting we had with Mr. Kissinger in July 1971, Mr. Kissinger declared this: 'Don't think we are negotiating with you

to settle the war only because of the prisoners'—which shows that the Nixon Administration doesn't care about the prisoners."

The previous peace session, held Feb. 24, had been cut short abruptly after the Communist delegations walked out to protest U.S. bombing attacks on North Vietnam. The U.S. and South Vietnam retaliated the following day by announcing they would not attend the next meeting scheduled March 2. The allies said March 7 they also would absent themselves from the March 9 meeting but proposed instead that talks reconvene March 16. The Communists accepted the new date March 15. The allies attributed their boycott of the two previous meetings to the Communists' Feb. 24 walkout and the "tone and contents of recent official announcements from Hanoi," which were critical of President Nixon.

U.S. suspends peace talks. The U.S. delegation to the Paris peace talks announced an indefinite suspension of the conference at the March 23 session.

In announcing the decision in an opening statement, chief U.S. delegate William J. Porter said there would be no further meetings until the North Vietnamese and Viet Cong representatives entered into "serious discussions" on concrete issues determined beforehand. The Communists rejected Porter's contention, asserting that he was posing unacceptable conditions.

Porter noted that President Nixon "has declared next week as a week of national concern for our men held prisoner by you and your associates. It would be a mockery of our concern for them were we to ... listen to more of your blackmail and distortions to the effect that the prisoner of war issue is an 'imaginary problem.' Therefore our side does not agree to a meeting next week."

Porter told the Communists they could use "any convenient channel, including our liaison officers" to convey their intentions to resume "serious discussions." He did not provide any further clarification of the criteria for resuming the talks.

Xuan Thuy, North Vietnam's chief delegate, asserted later at a news conference that the following week's session would be the sixth canceled by the U.S. "without a valid reason."

Viet Cong spokesman Ly Van Sau said the U.S. cancellation of the talks constituted "a new escalation in the sabotage of the conference. Mr. Porter has posed a whole series of conditions we can never accept." Sau then demanded: "Who has given Mr. Porter the right to decide what is significant or not."

The U.S. State Department March 23 declined to describe the Paris talks as "finished." The U.S., the department said, would be making a "continuous assessment" "to determine whether future meetings would be useful in any given week."

Hanoi accuses U.S. on POWs. North Vietnamese officials contended that the prisoner of war issue was a secondary one which the U.S. was exploiting to divert American public attention from the principal problem—settling the Indochina war through negotiations. The North Vietnamese views were contained in a dispatch filed from Hanoi March 16 by New York Times correspondent Seymour Hersh and published March 24.

Hersh quoted Hoang Tung, editor of the Communist party newspaper Nhan Dan, as saying: "We have to find the areas of importance. The prisoners are only a small part of the war as a whole. They are not the cause of the policy but the consequence of it."

Another North Vietnamese official, Col. Ha Van Lau, roving ambassador to the Paris peace talks, told Hersh: "This question of prisoners is a matter President Nixon will stick to because it is a point of great concern to the American people. He will continue to make distortions and frauds about it."

One of two American prisoners Hersh was permitted to interview said his captors were improving conditions of his imprisonment. Marine pilot Lt. Col. Edison W. Miller, captured Oct. 13, 1967, said: "I have never been tortured and I have never been beaten. In my opinion the treatment has always been satisfactory, and today I would say that in recent few years the treatment is good."

Nixon defends peace talk halt. President Nixon said March 24 that North

Vietnam's "propaganda" and "filibuster" tactics at the Paris peace talks for the past three and a half years had prompted the U.S. decision the previous day to call an indefinite suspension of the meetings.

Speaking at a news conference, Nixon said he personally had ordered the halt in the talks. Accusing the North Vietnamese of refusing "to negotiate seriously," Nixon repeated the American position, stated at the latest Paris session, that "whenever the enemy is ready to negotiate seriously, we are ready to negotiate and I would emphasize we are ready to negotiate in public channels or in private channels."

Nixon emphasized that the current trend of the talks offered "no hope whatever" of a negotiated settlement. The President acknowledged that his decision to cancel the meetings was not going "to bring a negotiation," but he said "it was necessary to get the talks off dead center."

Mrs. Nguyen Thi Binh, head of the Viet Cong delegation, declared March 24 that the American decision to call off the negotiations represented "a new act of sabotage." Mrs. Vinh made the statement on arriving in Paris after a six-month absence.

Nguyen Thanh Le, spokesman for the North Vietnamese delegation, said March 29 that the U.S. must take the initiative in bringing about a resumption of the peace talks. "It is up to the American side to remedy its error" in suspending the meetings, he said. Le said that although "the Nixon Administration has torpedoed all negotiating paths," both public and private, Hanoi was still not ruling out secret meetings.

Le's remarks followed a North Vietnamese Foreign Ministry statement March 28 calling for a resumption of the talks and appealing to "brother Socialist and peace-loving countries" to put pressure on the U.S. to that end.

William J. Porter, the chief American delegate at the Paris talks, returned to Washington March 30 for consultations. Deputy Press Secretary Gerald L. Warren said it had not yet been decided how long Porter would remain, but that he would "most assuredly" be returning to Paris.

The Fighting Continues

North Vietnam raid aftermath. Hanoi Jan. 1 revised upward to 24 the number of American planes it claimed to have downed in the Dec. 26–30, 1971 raids on North Vietnam. The report said seven U.S. airmen had been captured. The U.S. command Jan. 1 acknowledged that four American aircraft, not three as originally announced, had been downed in the attacks and that five crewmen were missing.

The U.S. Defense Department Jan. 3 said that 35–40 military strongpoints in North Vietnam had been pounded in the five-day raids but conceded that not all planned targets had been hit. As a result, the department said it would not rule out future raids on the North.

Saigon military sources Jan. 2 had expressed disappointment with the results of the air strikes, blaming them on a sudden "freak weather change" that had caused fog and rain over the North Vietnamese coast. The sources said if the weather had held the raids could have continued for another three days.

(The U.S. command reported Jan. 2 that 10 American planes had been downed over North Vietnam and Laos in the last three weeks of December 1971 with 13 crewmen missing and six rescued. Two U.S. helicopters had been shot down by ground fire on the South Vietnamese side of the Laos border Dec. 31, the command said. Two crewmen were killed and two wounded.)

Meanwhile, the U.S. continued its air pressure against the North Vietnamese. A force of more than 200 planes struck Communist supply lines in Cambodia and Laos Jan. 1. American B-52s pounded North Vietnamese supply routes, depots, troop concentrations and bunkers in the South Vietnamese, Laos and Cambodian border regions Jan. 5–7. About one-fifth of the raids were concentrated in the southwestern section of the demilitarized zone. The planes reportedly made 100 strikes in the 72-hour period, dropping nearly 3,000 tons of bombs.

U.S. jets Jan. 5 carried out two "protective reaction" strikes against antiaircraft radar installations in North Vietnam. The two targets were located 10 miles north of the Bankarai Pass and 64 miles southwest of Hanoi. The American planes attacked after they were reportedly menaced by the installations during bombing missions over the Ho Chi Minh Trail in Laos.

The number of "protective reaction" strikes on North Vietnam in 1971 had totaled 108, the U.S. command said.

New Year's truce ends. The Saigon command announced Jan. 1 that Viet Cong forces had violated the allied 24-hour New Year's truce Dec. 31 with 20 attacks that had killed nine South Vietnamese and wounded 20. The Viet

21

Cong had unilaterally declared the truce would run until Jan. 3.

The U.S. command reported Jan. 2 that 19 enemy soldiers had been killed during the 24-hour cease-fire. The command said U.S. combat deaths in 1971 through Dec. 25 had totaled 1,386, the lowest number since the similar period in 1965 when 1,369 were listed as slain in action.

Long Tieng evacuated. Most of the Meo tribal forces of Maj. Gen. Vang Pao evacuated Long Tieng in northern Laos as a result of North Vietnamese pressure on the base, the Laotian government reported Jan. 3.

The troops pulled out were said to have been deployed in nearby villages and on high ground around the strongpoint. Long Tieng itself was downgraded to a forward operations base. Its airstrip was still in use and contact was being maintained with Vientiane, the capital of Laos. U.S. officials said Jan. 5 that there was a "better than 50-50 chance" that the Communists would overrun Long Tieng in the next few weeks.

Long Tieng had been under heavy North Vietnamese artillery attack since Dec. 31, 1971 and several North Vietnamese regiments were reported to have surrounded the base. The shelling destroyed an ammunition dump, a radio transmission center and the headquarters of Military Region II. Communist pressure had momentarily eased Jan. 1, enabling American planes to fly in ammunition to the beleagured garrison that day.

In other action in Laos, North Vietnamese troops were advancing on Pakse near the Boloven Plateau in southern Laos. Government troops were reported Jan. 1 to have been driven back 11 miles and set up a main defense line 21 miles from Pakse.

North Vietnamese forces, supported by two MiG aircraft, destroyed a bridge on the only road between Vientiane and the royal capital of Luang Prabang and overran a government outpost in the area, the Laotian Defense Ministry reported Jan. 4. The attack, occurring 20 miles from Long Tieng, was said to be the deepest MiG penetration of Laos in the Indochina war.

North Vietnamese missiles in Laos. American sources Jan. 10 reported that North Vietnam had strengthened its air defenses by placing surface-to-air missile installations inside Laos for the first time and attacking U.S. planes bombing the Ho Chi Minh Trail in Laos. Until now, U.S. aircraft on such missions had been fired at by missile sites from inside North Vietnam.

The U.S. command reported Jan. 11 that one such enemy installation, located near Tchepone, in southern Laos, about 30 miles southwest of the North Vietnamese border, had fired two missiles at an American fighter-bomber Jan. 10. A command report Jan. 12 said the missile site was apparently destroyed when attacked later by another U.S. jet.

In other air action, U.S. planes carried out two protective reaction strikes on antiaircraft positions in North Vietnam Jan. 10–11. The first target was 90 miles northwest of the coastal city of Vinh, the second was 35 miles north of the demilitarized zone near the Bankarai Pass on the Laotian border.

Communist guerrillas Jan. 10 attacked an air base used by American B-52 bombers in Utapao, Thailand, wrecking the engine of one plane and slightly damaging another. Thai authorities said one of the three attacking guerrillas was killed and another captured.

During early January the Indochina conflict intensified as Communist forces mounted heavy attacks and made advances on three war fronts—in South Vietnam, Cambodia and Laos.

South Vietnam—North Vietnamese and Viet Cong troops carried out 34 attacks against South Vietnamese military and civilian targets in the 24-hour period ending at 6 a.m. Jan. 12. The raids, including 12 rocket and mortar assaults, were the highest number for any 24-hour period since October 1971. The most serious attack occurred when a Viet Cong unit ambushed a 30-man government militia platoon in the Mekong Delta, killing three.

In another action Jan. 12 Communist infiltrators entered the U.S. air base at Bienhoa, 15 miles northeast of Saigon, and blew up a stockpile of small-arms ammunition. One of the infiltrators was killed.

In previous action in South Vietnam, 18 Americans were wounded Jan. 7 when Communists fired 20 mortar rounds at a U.S. fire support base 20 miles northeast of Saigon.

A terrorist Jan. 8 hurled a grenade into a government-sponsored rally of 1,200 students at Quinhon in the north, killing at least nine and wounding 111 persons, including Col. Nguyen Van Chuc, newly appointed chief of Binhdinh Province.

A Viet Cong squad Jan. 10 struck within six miles of downtown Saigon, wounding seven militiamen in the local administrative office of Binhthuan hamlet.

The government started an airlift Jan. 5 of refugees in northern Quangtri Province to Phuoctuy Province in the south. The relocation move was expected to involve more than 10,000 persons.

Saigon troops quit Cambodian area—
A force of 10,000 Vietnamese troops began pulling out of the Krek area of eastern Cambodia Jan. 2 in a move to bolster the defenses around Saigon, 90 miles south, for a possible Communist Tet offensive in mid-February. The pullback, followed by a similar Cambodian withdrawal in the area, was confirmed by a South Vietnamese military spokesman Jan. 11.

The Saigon spokesman said fewer than 5,000 South Vietnamese troops would remain in the area. They were to be deployed along the border and in one base inside Cambodia three miles south of Krek. A communique said the troops that had been removed would be operating northeast of Saigon in two border provinces, Tayninh and Binhlong, and in neighboring Binhduong Province.

A 2,400-man Cambodian brigade was reported Jan. 12 to have deserted en masse and quit the Krek area. The men had fled their posts and many had abandoned their weapons when the South Vietnamese began to leave the area.

The Cambodian deserters changed to civilian clothes and fled to South Vietnam. About 3,000 Cambodian families also had fled the Krek region, it was reported Jan. 12. Elements of three North Vietnamese divisions occupied the Krek area, 10 miles from South Vietnam's border.

While South Vietnamese troops were leaving southeastern Cambodia, an 1,800-man Saigon force carried out a limited operation in the northeastern part of the country Jan. 7. The commander of the Central Highlands, Gen. Ngo Dzu, said the men were flown in by helicopters and established six fire bases six miles inside Cambodia, about 200 miles northeast of Saigon. The major objective of the mission, Dzu said, was to destroy Communist bases and capture supplies being massed for an expected Tet offensive. The incursion was preceded by U.S. B-52 bomber attacks.

Reds threaten Long Tieng, Pakse—
North Vietnamese forces in Laos continued to make progress in their drives against a government base at Long Tieng in the north and against Pakse in the south.

A 1,000-man Laotian force Jan. 11 was driven from the village of Ban Nhik and pulled back several miles to the west toward Pakse. The abandonment of Ban Nhik, on the edge of the Boloven Plateau and 18 miles from Pakse, came after heavy North Vietnamese assaults launched Jan. 7. Government forces were said to have suffered 200 casualties in the retreat.

In their drive to capture Long Tieng, North Vietnamese forces Jan. 11 captured two government positons on high ground overlooking the base.

Farther north, Laotian troops were said to have lost their position at Phou Khoun, 20 miles northwest of the Plaine des Jarres, Jan. 10.

Laotian Defense Minister Sissouk na Champassak said Jan. 9 that the North Vietnamese had committed 32,-000 men to their drive in northern Laos. He said the offensive was supposed to reach its climax before President Nixon's visit to China Feb. 21. Sissouk said the North Vietnamese were "planning to break through and threaten Vientiane in the north, and Pakse in the south, possibly bringing Thailand into the war because the Mekong border will be menaced. They are intentionally bringing about a big escalation in the war, and little Laos is again the victim of outside forces and events."

Saigon opens Cambodian drive. South Vietnamese and Cambodian forces opened a joint drive in southern Cambodia Jan. 12. The operation was launched outside Antgassom, 42 miles south of Pnompenh, but there were no reports of contact with the enemy.

Among other military developments:

Cambodian sources reported Jan. 16 that more than half of the 2,000 North Vietnamese troops based in the temple city of Angkor in the northwest had been withdrawn to fight on other fronts in Cambodia.

The Cambodian high command reported Jan. 19 that an additional 5,000–10,000 North Vietnamese troops had moved into Cambodia via the Ho Chi Minh Trail in Laos. This raised Hanoi's troop strength in the country to 65,000–70,000.

Heavy fighting erupted Jan. 24 in marshlands 12 miles east of Pnompenh. The clash followed reports of 600 North Vietnamese troops moving in the direction of the capital. The battle occurred at the village of Peak Sbai, with U.S. planes providing government forces with air support.

Long Tieng siege eased. Laotian and Thai reinforcements flown into beleaguered Long Tieng in northern Laos the previous week were reported Jan. 15 to have partially eased the North Vietnamese siege of the base. The Communist encirclement was penetrated in one area as the government and Thai troops moved out of the base and recaptured Skyline Ridge, high ground two miles to the north. Casualties in the day's battle were placed at 47 Laotian troops and 13 enemy soldiers. Heavy fighting, however, continued around the base through Jan. 18.

Involved in the Long Tieng operation were about 6,000 North Vietnamese, an equal number of Meo tribal irregulars and Laotian regular forces and about 2,000 Thais.

U.S. officials said Jan. 19 that since the outbreak of fighting for Long Tieng in late December 1971, at least 600 Laotian troops were killed, wounded or missing. North Vietnamese deaths were estimated at 600–700.

A group of foreign newsmen were given a guided tour of Long Tieng Jan.

19. An American official said the U.S. and Laotian governments had decided to permit a public inspection of the hitherto secret base for the first time in 10 years.

"This is a North Vietnamese invasion of Laos, and there's no point in keeping you people from seeing it for yourselves," he said. One of the visitors to the base, an American correspondent, confirmed that Long Tieng was badly damaged and had been effectively put out of action by the Communists. The base had consisted of a mile-long paved runway, a complex of communication buildings and a large cluster of villages that housed 30,000 civilians, who had been evacuated before the Communist attacks.

Warning to Thailand—Thailand's involvement in the Indochina war had prompted a warning from North Vietnam Jan. 16. The Communist party newspaper Nhan Dan, alluding to the Jan. 10 Communist guerrilla attack on the American air base at Utapao, Thailand, said the "thunder blows dealt them in the recent past are severe warnings to the Thai reactionaries who are perpetrating towering crimes against the Thai and Indochinese people in serving the U.S. imperialist objectives."

The newspaper warned of further "punishment" if Thailand kept "following the U.S. on the road of military adventure in Indochina."

Enemy raids pressed in South Vietnam. The increased North Vietnamese and Viet Cong attacks mounted against South Vietnam Jan. 10 continued through Jan. 19 with government troops and civilians suffering heavy losses. Nearly 250 incidents were reported in the nine-day period.

Saigon headquarters reported 33 enemy soldiers were killed in attacks on government outposts Jan. 13. Government losses were put at 15 killed and 25 wounded.

Twelve Communists were reported slain Jan. 14 in a series of coordinated attacks on three major towns in northern Quangngai Province.

Widespread Communist assaults Jan. 15 resulted in the killing of 15 government soldiers, 15 civilians and 89 enemy troops, according to Saigon reports.

The American air base at Camranh Bay was the target of one of 30 Communist rocket, mortar and ground assaults across South Vietnam Jan. 16. Several vehicles and buildings were hit.

The U.S. command had reported Jan. 13 that five Americans were killed and 47 wounded Jan. 2–8. South Vietnamese losses in the same period were 221 killed and 497 wounded. The allied commands reported 803 North Vietnamese and Viet Cong killed Jan. 2–8.

South Vietnamese combat fatalities in 1971 were said to have totaled about 21,500 while Communist deaths that year were said to have been approximately 97,000.

U.S. jet downs North Vietnamese MiG. An American jet Jan. 19 downed a MiG-21 over North Vietnam for the first time since March 29, 1970.

The action came amid an intensification of the air war over Indochina that was marked by two previous encounters between U.S. jets and North Vietnamese MiGs, an increase in Communist surface-to-air missile (SAM) attacks on American planes, a step-up of American bombing of Communist supply lines in Laos and South Vietnam and continued U.S. protective reaction strikes on North Vietnam.

The reported objective of the mounting U.S. bombing campaign was to neutralize Communist preparation for a possible offensive during Tet, the lunar new year, in mid-February.

The MiG-21 was shot down by a U.S. Navy plane near Quanglang, 170 miles north of the demilitarized zone. The Communist jet appeared on the scene after eight surface-to-air missiles and antiaircraft guns fired at five American planes. One of the aircraft was slightly damaged, but all returned safely to their carrier in the Gulf of Tonkin, the U.S. command said. According to American records, the downed North Vietnamese plane brought to 112 the number of MiGs lost to U.S. fighters in the war. This compared with 50 American planes lost to MiGs.

Hanoi's Foreign Ministry announced Jan. 19 that two U.S. planes had been shot down that day during raids on populated regions in North Vietnam.

The other American encounters with North Vietnamese MiGs had occurred in northern Laos Jan. 15 and 17. The MiGs fired missiles at the U.S. aircraft in both engagements but missed.

Other air developments—The North Vietnamese were reported Jan. 15 to have moved their mobile missile launchers closer to South Vietnam's northern border, precipitating new encounters with U.S. fighter-bombers within three miles of the frontier. In one such engagement, a U.S. jet Jan. 14 struck and apparently destroyed a mobile missile unit three miles north of the DMZ. An American air strike in the same area Jan. 15 was said to have destroyed another missile position.

U.S. planes Jan. 15 carried out the eighth protective reaction strike on North Vietnam since Jan. 1. The target was a radar-controlled missile site 40 miles north of the demilitarized zone.

The Ho Chi Minh Trail in Laos came in for heavy pounding by American planes Jan. 16–19. About 30 B-52s dropped nearly 1,000 tons of bombs Jan. 16 while an additional 200 strike missions were flown by smaller fighter-bombers. More than 200 strikes were flown against the trail network Jan. 17 and another 250 planes were out Jan. 18 to hit supply routes and depots. The four days of aerial attacks also were directed at North Vietnamese troop concentrations and supply buildups in South Vietnam's Central Highlands. Enemy supply lines, including those in Cambodia, were attacked Jan. 19 by another 250-plane force.

Long Tieng battle continues. North Vietnamese and pro-Communist Pathet Lao troops seized a ridge overlooking the base of Long Tieng in northern Laos in heavy fighting Jan. 20–21. Government forces, however, recaptured the high ground Jan. 25, reoccupying two positions that served as helicopter landing zones on the eastern rim of the ridge. As a result of the Laotian success, an American source said Jan. 25 that Long Tieng "is clearly out of danger but the enemy is still there."

Two weeks of fighting around Long Tieng was said to have resulted in the killing of more than 500 men on each side.

In fighting northwest of Long Tieng, North Vietnamese and Pathet Lao forces drove government defenders from Phou Khoun Jan. 21. In another action 28 miles to the southeast, Communist forces Jan. 22 seized the airfield and Laotian military post of Mouong Phou.

Laotian Defense Minister Sissouk na Champassak said Jan. 23 that North Vietnam's current offensive had subjected his country to the heaviest fighting and casualties it had ever experienced. Without citing exact figures, Sissouk claimed the losses inflicted on government forces by Hanoi troops in the Plaine des Jarres amounted to "real genocide."

Laotian Premier Souvanna Phouma had said Jan. 22 that despite heavy government setbacks in northern Laos, he would not appeal for American aid "unless the situation gets worse."

U.S. presses air attacks. U.S. jets intensified the air war over Indochina Jan. 21–26 with attacks on North Vietnamese troop concentrations in the Central Highlands of South Vietnam and continued strikes on missile sites in North Vietnam. The "protective reaction" raids brought to 19 the number of such strikes on the North since Jan. 1. The U.S. attributed the increase in these raids to a concentration of enemy antiaircraft defenses along the Laotian border, aimed at counteracting the American bombing of the Ho Chi Minh Trail in Laos.

B-52 bombers Jan. 21–24 pounded suspected Communist troop masses and supply dumps in the Central Highlands near the Laotian border. North Vietnamese tanks, numbering six, were said to have been spotted in the area for the first time Jan. 25.

U.S. fighter-bombers Jan. 22 attacked the demilitarized zone between North and South Vietnam, knocking out two enemy antiaircraft guns and damaging another, the U.S. command reported the following day. The raid came after the North Vietnamese guns had fired on four Phantom jets flying missions over Laos. The enemy installations were in the

northern half of the DMZ, 21 miles northwest of Khesanh. A missile site in North Vietnam, three miles east of the Bankarai Pass, 45 miles north of the DMZ, came under American air attacks the same day.

The U.S. command disclosed Jan. 23 that enemy ground fire in South Vietnam had shot down the fifth and sixth helicopter in the past seven days. Two Americans were killed and at least two were wounded.

Missile and antiaircraft sites in North Vietnam were the targets of American air strikes Jan. 23, 24 and 26. The installations were located near the Bankarai Pass and Donghoi, about 50 miles north of the buffer zone.

U.S. assesses 1971 raids—U.S. Defense Department officials were reported Jan. 24 to have expressed the belief that White House orders restricting targets had made the Dec. 26–30, 1971 American raids on North Vietnam ineffective. The Washington Post quoted one official as saying: "The targets themselves were terribly nonlucrative. Even if we destroyed them all, we would not have done much good."

U.S. jets hit North Vietnam. U.S. planes attacked North Vietnam Jan. 28–Feb. 1, striking at missile sites, antiaircraft batteries and radar installations.

The U.S. command announced Feb. 2 that the 11 strikes carried out Jan. 31–Feb. 1 were the heaviest of the year.

The Saigon command confirmed Feb. 1 that its subsonic A-37 jet bombers had been operating since Dec. 1, 1971 in the bombing campaign against the Ho Chi Minh Trail in Laos. U.S. and South Vietnamese officials had unofficially reported earlier the appearance of the A-37 in combat.

Reds prepare major drive. U.S. intelligence sources reported Jan. 30 that the North Vietnamese and Viet Cong were preparing to launch a major offensive in South Vietnam during President Nixon's visit to China in February. An impending Communist drive also was predicted by Defense Secretary Melvin R. Laird Jan. 30 and by Gen. William C. Westmoreland, Army chief of staff, Jan. 31.

According to the American intelligence report: North Vietnamese and Viet Cong units were being exhorted by their political officers to deliver "decisive blows" against U.S. and South Vietnamese forces in February. Since the start of the current dry season in October 1971, about 120,000 of the enemy had moved down the Ho Chi Minh Trail, 30,000 more than a year ago. The Communist infiltrators were fanning out from the supply routes into South Vietnam, Laos and Cambodia.

(The American airbase at Bienhoa, 15 miles northeast of Saigon, had been placed on heightened alert Jan. 27. The action was ordered following intelligence reports indicating possible enemy assaults in the Central Highlands, on the central coast and along the northern approaches to Saigon.)

John Paul Vann, the senior U.S. civilian adviser in South Vietnam's Military Region II, which included the Central Highlands, was quoted as saying Jan. 30, "It is absolutely certain that an offensive will take place."

Defense Secretary Laird said Jan. 30 that he anticipated the Communists "will try to have several spectaculars this year, probably some time in February and undoubtedly again this summer and some time before the Presidential elections in the United States."

Gen. Westmoreland, concluding a six-day visit to Indochina, said in Saigon Jan. 31 that he expected the Communists to mount a major drive in South Vietnam soon, with the fighting centered largely in the northernmost provinces and in the Central Highlands. But Westmoreland expressed confidence that the attacks could be contained because, he said, the South Vietnamese were stronger and the Communists were weaker than at the time of the 1968 Tet offensive.

In ground action in South Vietnam, the Saigon command claimed the killing of 107 Communist troops in scattered clashes throughout the country Jan. 27. The biggest fight occurred in the Central Highlands where government troops stumbled on a North Vietnamese base near Benhet. In the battle that followed, 25 enemy soldiers were killed, 20 by air strikes, the command reported.

Another 116 enemy soldiers were slain in scattered clashes Jan. 28, the Saigon command announced. In one incident, the Viet Cong fired more than 100 mortar shells at a government command post and artillery position in the Mekong Delta.

South Vietnamese planes Jan. 30 destroyed three North Vietnamese tanks in the Central Highlands. This brought to five the number of tanks knocked out by government aircraft in the region. Five enemy trucks also were destroyed in the same period.

North and South Vietnamese troops fought sharp clashes along the demilitarized zone Jan. 29–30. Government bases just south of the buffer strip were struck by more than 200 rocket and mortar shells Jan. 29. The Saigon command reported that 54 enemy troops had been killed in the two days of fighting. South Vietnamese losses were put at nine killed and 22 wounded.

The U.S. command had reported Jan. 28 that two Americans had been killed in action Jan. 16–22, three less than the previous week. The Saigon command said its losses in that period were 326 killed, compared with 390 slain Jan. 9–15. Total officially listed war losses: U.S.—45,639 killed and 302,549 wounded; South Vietnam—138,803 killed and 300,552 wounded; North Vietnamese and Viet Cong—792,487 killed.

Thais leave South Vietnam. The last members of Thailand's 12,000-man force in South Vietnam left the country Feb. 4. The Thai contingent, 824 soldiers, withdrew without any ceremonies. Their departure was first disclosed by the U.S. command Feb. 5.

U.S. strengthens B-52 force. The U.S. was reinforcing its arsenal of B-52s in the Western Pacific to protect the remaining American troops in South Vietnam in the event of a Communist offensive, Administration sources reported Feb. 9.

The additional planes, totaling at least a squadron of 15, were believed to have been ordered to Guam to await a possible transflight to Thailand to reinforce more than 40 other B-52s stationed there for the bombing of the Ho Chi Minh Trail in Laos.

In another precautionary move, the aircraft carrier Constellation was reported Feb. 9 to have cut short a stop in Hong Kong and apparently sailed to join two other carriers in the Gulf of Tonkin off the Vietnamese coast. The warships were deployed there for possible retaliatory air strikes on North Vietnam.

In the air war, two more "protective reaction" strikes on North Vietnam were reported Feb. 1. This brought to seven the number of such raids on the North that day. Since Jan. 1 U.S. jets had made nearly one-third as many protective reaction strikes on the North as in all of 1971.

American planes Feb. 4 destroyed a North Vietnamese missile site and the vehicle transporting it in southern Laos, three antiaircraft guns in North Vietnam's section of the demilitarized zone and struck another gun site in North Vietnam, 45 miles north of the DMZ. A U.S. command report Feb. 5 said the target in Laos was southeast of Tchepone, about 25 miles west of the South Vietnam border.

U.S. planes had bombed a hospital near Thanhhoa, North Vietnam Dec. 26, 1971, killing nine people, including four patients, and wounding 11, an American correspondent reported Feb. 9. The reporter was Banning Garret, who had visited the hospital Jan. 20. Two buildings were said to have been destroyed and three damaged in the raid, by four American jets. The raid was one of those carried out against the North Dec. 26–30. A Hanoi communique had reported Dec. 26 that a civilian hospital had been bombed in Thanhhoa that day and two U.S. pilots had died when their plane crashed near the city.

Communist shellings increase. Communist forces carried out about a dozen rocket and mortar attacks in and near the coastal cities of Danang and Quinhon in South Vietnam Feb. 9–10, but no major ground assaults were reported. Twenty-nine attacks occurred throughout the country Feb. 9.

The American air base at Danang was struck in the Feb. 9 attack. Three South Vietnamese civilians were killed and 17 persons, including 10 American servicemen, were wounded. At least one aircraft and some installations were reported damaged.

In other action in South Vietnam, heavy fighting continued in the Central Highlands, where a major North Vietnamese and Viet Cong offensive was expected. The Saigon command reported Feb. 5 the killing of 54 North Vietnamese in encounters with government troops in the highlands. A brief North Vietnamese rocket attack was directed Feb. 7 at a regional militia camp in Kontum.

Sharp fighting broke out suddenly Feb. 3 in the Mekong Delta's U Minh Forest, which had been quiet for some time. Saigon said South Vietnamese troops killed 14 Viet Cong in four separate clashes. Government casulties were nine killed and 16 wounded.

American helicopters Feb. 6 dropped napalm on what appeared to be newly-built North Vietnamese bunkers 25 miles northeast of Saigon.

On other Indochina battle fronts:

Laos—Vientiane government sources reported Feb. 3 that North Vietnamese and Pathet Lao troops the previous day had captured Muong Kassy, on the main road between Vientiane and the royal capital of Luang Prabang. Another Laotian strongpoint, Dong Hene, fell to North Vietnamese troops Feb. 7. The enemy action in southern Laos was part of a drive to protect the western flank of the Ho Chi Minh Trail.

Cambodia—North Vietnamese and Viet Cong troops continued attacks on government positions less than two miles from the ancient temple ruins at Angkor Wat Feb. 7. The Cambodian command reported Feb. 6 that 20 civilian workers taken prisoner by Communist forces in January near Angkor had been killed by their captors Feb. 3.

The Saigon command reported Feb. 3 that South Vietnamese jets had destroyed four North Vietnamese tanks inside Cambodia, near the South Vietnamese-Laotian frontier.

(The U.S. General Accounting Office reported Feb. 5 that Cambodia's Public Health Ministry estimated that more than 2 million Cambodians had been left homeless by the fighting in that country since 1970. The GAO report quoted refugees as saying that Viet Cong and South Vietnamese forces had "looted property, destroyed what they could not carry, burned villages, and raped, beat and murdered the villagers.")

Angkor offensive starts. Cambodian forces totaling about 6,000 men were reported Feb. 12 to have launched a major drive against North Vietnamese troops around the ancient Buddhist temples at Angkor. The government had announced Feb. 10 that such an offensive might be necessary to retake the temples seized by the North Vietnamese in June 1970.

The Angkor clashes mounted in intensity through Feb. 15. A military spokesman said that the government offensive was closing in from two sides of the temple city, 150 miles northwest of Pnompenh. A force of 4,000 enemy troops were dug into heavily wooded areas west and south of the perimeter walls surrounding the temples, holding off government units based in the nearby town of Siemreap.

It had been disclosed Feb. 11 that an internal clash over the temple area had erupted at Angkor in November-December 1971 between the North Vietnamese and the Khmer Rouge, the Cambodian Communist guerrilla group. Refugees from the area reported that 15 North Vietnamese had been slain in one such engagement. According to the refugees, the fighting had broken out after the Khmer Rouge had accused the North Vietnamese of looting the temples of their treasures.

Cambodian Information Minister Long Boret had charged Feb. 3 that the temples were being threatened with destruction because the North Vietnamese had forced a halt to the restoration work. The government had confirmed Jan. 20 that the North Vietnamese expelled French archeologist Bernard-Philippe Groslier and his 300 Cambodian workmen from Angkor; 20 of the workmen had been killed by the North Vietnamese in apparent retaliation for the soldiers killed in the fighting with the Khmer Rouge.

U.S. jets hit North & South Vietnam. American jets launched a "limited-dura-

tion" bombing offensive Feb. 16 against North Vietnamese artillery positions in the southern province of North Vietnam and in the northern section of the demilitarized zone. The raids ended Feb. 17. They followed sustained U.S. air strikes launched Feb. 9 on suspected North Vietnamese troop buildups and infiltration trails in the Central Highlands in South Vietnam. The attacks on the South had halted for most of Feb. 15, for an allied-proclaimed 24-hour cease-fire for Tet, the lunar new year, and resumed at 6 p.m. that day.

The U.S. command, reporting Feb. 17 on the new raids on the North, said five artillery pieces had been destroyed in Quangbinh Province and in the northern sector of the DMZ since the strikes began.

The U.S. command Feb. 18 acknowledged the loss of three planes in the 29-hour attack—one Feb. 16 and two the following day. Six crewmen were missing. Hanoi claimed Feb. 18 that seven U.S. jets had been downed in the two days and that "many pilots" had been killed or captured.

The command said "these strikes were necessary to counter a threat to the security of the remaining United States forces posed by the introduction of these new offensive weapons [artillery] into the area."

The raids in the South were aimed at averting a possible Communist offensive during the Tet holiday. They were concentrated in two enemy base areas west of the Central Highlands city of Kontum and northwest of the Ashau Valley in Thuathien and Quangtri Provinces. U.S. authorities believed more than 20,000 North Vietnamese troops were there.

An official explanation of the raids was given by the U.S. command Feb. 14. It said: "These strikes come under the heading of interdiction rather than direct air support. Their purpose is to disrupt enemy troop movements and to destroy their supplies. They are directed against known Communist base areas, infiltration routes and new locations obtained by reconnaissance."

More than 100 strikes were carried out each day against enemy targets in the Central Highlands. The largest number of attacks, 172, occurred in the 24-hour period that ended at 6 a.m. Feb. 12. This was the highest number since Sept. 24, 1970, the U.S. command said.

Hanoi radio claimed the downing of two American planes Feb. 10–11. The aircraft were shot down while over Vinhlinh, just north of the DMZ, and over Nghean Province, in central North Vietnam bordering Laos, the broadcast said. The U.S. command said it had no reports of American planes being downed.

During the raids on the South, other U.S. planes continued protective reaction strikes on missile sites in North Vietnam.

Tet truce violated—In ground action in the South, a 24-hour cease-fire proclaimed by South Vietnam and the U.S. for the Tet holiday ended at 6 p.m. Feb. 15. The allies refused to recognize the Communists' unilateral 96-hour truce, which had started at 1 a.m. Feb. 14 and was to end at 1 a.m. Feb. 18, on the ground that the enemy would use the period to move in men and supplies for attacks on the South. The allies claimed that during their 24-hour cease-fire the Communists had committed 33 violations, killing eight South Vietnamese and wounding 21.

The U.S. command had reported Feb. 2 that two Americans had been killed in combat Jan. 30–Feb. 5, three fewer than the previous week. This brought to 45,-646 the number of Americans killed since 1961. Wounded totaled 302,602.

U.S. loses 7 planes. The U.S. high command Feb. 18 conceded the loss of seven American planes in the continuing air war over Indochina. In a delayed report, the command said three aircraft had been shot down during the raids on North Vietnam Feb. 16–17, a spotter plane had been downed in Cambodia Feb. 17 and three others had been lost between Feb. 4 and Feb. 13. All six fliers aboard the planes lost in North Vietnam were missing and three crewmen were known killed and one was injured in other crashes.

North Vietnam publicly displayed in Hanoi Feb. 19 five American airmen it claimed had been captured in the Feb. 16–17 raids. The captives were brought into a room at the International Club one at a time and were presented before a group of newsmen and diplomats. The men spoke brief messages to

their relatives in front of television cameras.

Before the men were brought in, Hanoi's press director, Ngo Dien, said 12 U.S. airmen had been captured and 33 planes had been shot down over the North since Dec. 26, 1971. U.S. raids on the North during January had increased 300% from January 1971, he said.

In the latest air action, U.S. planes continued their heavy raids on Communist troop and supply concentrations in the Central Highlands of South Vietnam, carrying out 148 strikes Feb. 17–18. The attacks smashed two Communist convoys near Kontum, destroying 10 trucks, 30 supply-carrying bicycles and other equipment, according to military spokesmen.

U.S. planes Feb. 19 destroyed six North Vietnamese trucks in the Central Highlands and destroyed six or seven antiaircraft guns in North Vietnam, the command reported.

The U.S. command reported Feb. 22 that U.S. fighter-bombers had shot down a North Vietnamese MiG-21 interceptor over northern Laos the previous day and carried out four strikes on North Vietnam. At least four antiaircraft guns were said to have been destroyed.

South Vietnam ground action. Communist forces carried out sharp attacks throughout South Vietnam Feb. 19–22, with heavy action concentrated in the Central Highlands.

In one of the worst government defeats in several months, Communist forces Feb. 19 overran a South Vietnamese outpost in Baxuyen Province in the Mekong Delta, killing 27 militiamen and four civilians. An additional seven persons were killed in other battles in the Mekong Delta, the Saigon command reported. South Vietnamese rangers battled 150 North Vietnamese troops in the Central Highlands that day. Two rangers were killed.

The U.S. command reported Feb. 21 that Communist troops shelled three American air bases, shot down two helicopters and damaged four others Feb. 20–21. Two Americans were killed in the downing of one of the 'copters 25 miles northwest of Saigon. The airbases struck were at Danang, Bienhoa and Phuloi.

The Saigon command claimed 88 North Vietnamese and Viet Cong troops had been killed in two operations in the northern part of South Vietnam Feb 21–22. The action occurred in the Queson Valley, 20–25 miles south of Danang. Government forces and U.S. installations within 12 miles of Saigon came under Communist attacks during those two days. The U.S. Army support command compound in Quinhon in the Central Highlands was shelled by Communist forces Feb. 22.

Plaine des Jarres battle. About 4,000 Laotian troops, aided by American air strikes, launched a drive Feb. 7 against North Vietnamese forces occupying the Plaine des Jarres in northern Laos. The Communist soldiers counterattacked Feb. 22, driving government troops from a hillside overlooking the southeast corner of the plain. The withdrawal followed heavy Communist rocket and mortar attacks on the nearby base at Phou Ke. The Plaine des Jarres had been captured by the North Vietnamese Dec. 20, 1971.

In first disclosing the government offensive, Defense Minister Sissouk na Champassak had said Feb. 18 that its purpose was to ease enemy pressure on the bases of Sam Thong and Long Tieng, 18 miles southwest. Although government forces had eased the Communist threat to those two bases, the strongholds continued under enemy fire.

In military developments elsewhere in Laos, government troops recaptured two strategic towns previously lost to the North Vietnamese. Muong Kassy, 92 miles north of Vientiane, was reoccupied by the Laotians Feb. 13. Dong Hene, 70 miles west of Tchepone in southern Laos, was retaken Feb. 22. Government troops had recaptured Ban Nhik near Pakse Feb. 12 but were forced by the Communists to retreat a few hours later. Ban Nhik had first been seized by the North Vietnamese Jan. 11.

Thieu says Soviets urged Hanoi drive. President Nguyen Van Thieu charged Feb. 23 that the Soviet Union had urged North Vietnam to launch an offensive in South Vietnam to prevent the U.S. and China from ending the Indochina war during President Nixon's visit to China. In a New York Times interview published Feb. 25, Thieu said U.S. air attacks and South Vietnamese ground assaults had prevented the Communists from mounting such a drive.

Thieu said he believed that Moscow was determined that it and not China must provide a solution to the Indochina conflict.

Saigon forces drive into Cambodia. The Saigon command disclosed that South Vietnamese forces had carried out three separate drives into southeastern Cambodia Feb. 1, 23 and 27. The offensives were aimed at blocking Communist infiltration routes into South Vietnam and at smashing suspected Communist preparations for attacks on South Vietnam's Mekong Delta.

The Feb. 27 operation, described as a "reconnaissance in force," ended the following day after penetrating three miles into Cambodia, about 130 miles northeast of Saigon. The Saigon command said eight enemy soldiers had been killed and there were no casualties among the government's 1,500 troops.

The two other operations, further south in Cambodia, were continuing and involved 5,000 men. In one action, South Vietnamese troops were reported to have killed 52 North Vietnamese and Viet Cong 12 miles from the Vietnam border while losing 16 men killed and nine wounded.

In fighting in South Vietnam:

An American army unit was ambushed by Communist troops 42 miles east of Saigon Feb. 25. The attack set off a five-hour battle in which 21 Americans were wounded. Fourteen more Americans were wounded in two other Communist ambushes further north that day. One involved an attack on a 35-truck convoy between Quinhon and Pleiku and the other occurred 13 miles southwest of Danang. Five of those wounded in the Danang area clash were hit during an accidental strafing attack by American helicopters.

A U.S. Army helicopter crashed in Danang harbor Feb. 25, killing seven persons, including four Americans. Among those killed were Brig. Gen. Phan Dinh Soan, deputy commander of

South Vietnam's Military Region I, and his deputy commander. A U.S. spokesman said the crash was not the result of enemy fire.

Saigon reported that government troops Feb. 27 killed 33 enemy soldiers, 28 of them by artillery and air strikes, in the Queson Valley, 25 miles south of Danang. Another 10 enemy soldiers were said to have been killed by South Vietnamese troops that day in a clash on the coast, 45 miles southeast of Saigon.

The U.S. command reported Feb. 27 that American forces had suffered their highest weekly casualties since Jan. 1 during Feb. 20–26. Four soldiers were killed and 47 were wounded in that period.

In the air war, the U.S. Air Force Feb. 29 carried out its 67th "protective reaction" strike on North Vietnam since Jan. 1. A fighter-bomber struck a missile site 40 miles north of the demilitarized zone, but the results were not known. A Communist surface-to-air missile site in Laos had been destroyed by a U.S. jet Feb. 26, according to the American command. The target was located southwest of Tchepone, a main junction on the Ho Chi Minh Trail.

U.S. casualties up. American forces Feb. 20–26 suffered their highest weekly casualties since Jan. 1, the U.S. command reported March 2. Six Americans were killed, an increase of four over the previous week, and 56 were wounded, 35 more than the week before. South Vietnamese and Communist losses also increased. A total of 360 Saigon soldiers were killed and 729 were wounded Feb. 20–26, compared with 208 killed and 531 wounded the week before. The allied commands said 1,026 North Vietnamese and Viet Cong soldiers were killed, up from 637 the previous week.

South Korean troops withdraw. South Korea completed the first phase of the withdrawal of part of its 48,000-man force from South Vietnam when the last contingent of a marine brigade landed at the port of Pusan Feb. 29. The ROK force in South Vietnam was thus reduced to 38,000.

U.S. ends troop alert. A three-week alert that had confined American troops to their barracks in South Vietnam was lifted by the U.S. command March 2. The alert had been imposed Feb. 13 in anticipation of a Communist Tet offensive, which never materialized. U.S. intelligence officers, however, said they still expected a Communist drive in 1972.

Fighting in South Vietnam March 3–8 ranged from the area around the demilitarized zone to the Central Highlands, where a Communist offensive had been expected. A force of about 10-000 South Vietnamese troops opened a drive March 2 in the western part of the highlands. The thrust was assisted by U.S. B-52 bombers, which carried out the fifth day of saturation raids in the area. Government soldiers made little contact with the enemy through March 8.

Government troops opened two more drives against suspected enemy concentrations in the northern sector. One sweep of 1,500 men was centered March 3 south and west of Quangtri City, just below the DMZ. The other, involving the same number of troops, was launched March 5 west of Hue.

Another Communist buildup in the north prompted the B-52s March 4 to shift their attacks to an area stretching from Khesanh in the northwest corner to the Ashau Valley about 60 miles to the south. The targets were bunker complexes, storage areas and infiltration routes. The B-52s flew more than 20 missions in the same area March 8.

A South Vietnamese ship convoy on the Dongnai River exploded 10 miles east of Saigon March 5, resulting in a loss of 300 tons of ammunition, including bombs and artillery shells. Three ammunition barges sank and several escort vessels either sank or were damaged. Allied officers said the blast was caused either by a Communist mine or by a rocket fired from the riverbank.

South Vietnamese positions guarding the DMZ were struck by 10 Communist mortar and rocket attacks March 8. No casualties were reported.

Laotians end drive on plain. Increasing North Vietnamese attacks were reported March 6 to have forced Laotian troops to call off their offensive around the Plaine des Jarres in northern Laos. The government drive was first launched Feb. 7. Several thousand Laotian and Meo tribal guerrillas were said to be in full retreat toward the U.S.-supported base at Long Tieng, 20 miles southwest.

Vietnamese sources said despite the government setback, the attacks around the plain had succeeded in relieving enemy pressure around the immediate vicinity of Long Tieng. Hanoi's forces, however, continued to press their attacks not far from the base, overrunning Phou Thung, a government mountain position 30 miles from Long Tieng March 3. Thirty-three government troops were said to have been killed in the action.

Government forces also suffered a defeat in southern Laos March 7 as Communist attacks forced them to retreat about a mile toward Pakse. Supported by tanks and rockets, North Vietnamese troops overran government positions east and northeast of the strategic commercial center and reportedly shelled other posts overlooking the Pakse airfield.

Hanoi charges U.S. air offensive. Hanoi radio reported March 7 that the U.S. had launched a major, widespread bombing offensive against North Vietnam, striking "many populated areas."

The North Vietnamese report was followed by a U.S. command announcement March 8 that it would no longer disclose the number of planes involved in American raids. "To continue to reveal the number of aircraft would be useful to the enemy and endanger the lives of U.S. pilots," a command spokesman said.

In the air war, the U.S. claimed the probable downing of one of two North Vietnamese MiG-21 interceptors March 1 in a dogfight with two U.S. fighter-bombers along the North Vietnam-Laos border, 125 miles southwest of Hanoi.

Hanoi reported that U.S. jets attacked the southernmost provinces of Quangbinh and Hatinh March 3–4, killing "many civilians." The broadcast claimed a Phantom jet and an unmanned reconnaissance aircraft were shot down in the raids.

Hanoi radio also said that villages in Quangbinh had come under heavy U.S.

air attacks March 1 and 2. The U.S. command had acknowledged protective reaction strikes those two days against North Vietnamese air defense systems and radar sites.

A force of more than 20 American jets March 6 carried out the heaviest assault in months against antiaircraft defenses in North Vietnam. One of several MiGs attempting to intercept the raiders was reported shot down. The news agency Reuters said the MiG was destroyed near Quanglang airfield, between the demilitarized zone and Hanoi.

Air activity over the North was particularly intense March 7 as U.S. jets carried out six protective reaction raids while other U.S. planes engaged five MiGs 170 miles north of the DMZ. One MiG was claimed by U.S. pilots to have been shot down. Hanoi contended that two of the jets were lost. The protective reaction raids brought to 86 the number carried out since Jan. 1, equal to the total for all 1971. Twenty of the raids had occurred in the past six days.

Communists move on Long Tieng. A North Vietnamese force of 4,500–6,000 men threatened to capture the north Laos base of Long Tieng after seizing Sam Thong, a village seven miles to the northwest, March 11. Sam Thong, defended mainly by 4,000 Thai troops, was first attacked March 10 and fell 36 hours later.

A heavy North Vietnamese artillery barrage forced the closing of the Long Tieng airstrip March 12. Poor weather limited U.S. and Laotian air support, but government sources March 13 said that a Laotian T-28 plane had killed or wounded 50–100 North Vietnamese around Sam Thong.

The Hanoi forces followed up their capture of Sam Thong by taking control of a ridge overlooking Long Tieng March 14. The Laotians were driven from the high ground by enemy artillery and abandoned three helicopter pads. One key position overlooking Long Tieng was reported March 21 to have been recaptured by Thai and Laotian troops, but the base itself was said to have come under heavy North Vietnamese mortar attack from two other positions.

A force of 1,000 troops stationed at Long Tieng was said to have rebelled March 18 and forced 15 truck drivers to take it to a supply base 20 miles southwest. The men, trained by the U.S. Central Intelligence Agency, charged that their commander had reneged on a promise to ship them out of the base at the end of their three-month assignment there. Long Tieng was largely defended by CIA-trained Meo tribesmen.

In other Laotian military developments, the rebel pro-Communist Pathet Lao claimed March 12 to have shot down two U.S. planes and one helicopter, killing six CIA spies. The report said one plane was brought down over the Ban Nhik region March 4 and that the other plane and helicopter were downed over Sayabury Province Feb. 28 and 29.

Government troops were reported March 17 to have opened a new drive to reopen the highway between Vientiane and the royal capital of Luang Prabang, 150 miles north of Vientiane. One column of troops, flown by helicopter from Luang Prabang, advanced toward the Communist-held crossroads town of Sala Phoukhoum, 12 miles farther south. Another government unit was 10 miles south of the town and heading north.

China backs Sihanouk. A statement by former Cambodian Chief of State Norodom Sihanouk's government in exile in Peking condemning South Vietnam's latest drive into Cambodia was upheld March 17 by the Chinese Foreign Ministry.

The exiled regime March 15 had assailed Saigon's drive launched March 10 as a "criminal operation perpetrated by the U.S. imperialists and their Saigon lackeys." The assault "laid bare the deceitful utterances of [U.S. President] Nixon, who loudly professes his desire to seek peace in Asia and reduce tension while obdurately carrying on his war of aggression in Cambodia and Indochina," the statement said.

A further Chinese endorsement of the Sihanouk regime was expressed March 19 by Premier Chou En-lai, who charged that attempts were being made to split Sihanouk's National United Front of Cambodia. Speaking at a banquet hon-

oring the second anniversary of the front, Chou said "what calls for special attention is that at the present certain powers are creating a so-called 'Khmer third force' to carry out activities for a compromise in a vain attempt to split the National United Front of Cambodia and undermine the militant unity of the Cambodian and Indochinese people."

Chou reiterated continued backing of forces fighting the U.S., saying it was the "duty of the Chinese people to render all-out support and assistance to the Cambodian and other Indochinese people in their struggle against U.S. aggression." He said "we have been doing so in the past and we will continue to do so in the future."

In an address to the banquet, Sihanouk denounced Lon Nol's seizure of total power in Cambodia March 10. Sihanouk called Lon Nol's assumption of "the title of 'President of the Republic' at a time where there is no possibility to consult the people or hold a plebiscite" a "trumped up" action.

Thailand fights insurgents. Thai government forces, heavily armed with American equipment, were reported March 22 to have made little headway in an operation launched Jan. 20 against Communist insurgents in northeast Thailand, 300 miles from Bangkok.

Government units totaling 12,000 men were said to be fighting a guerrilla force of 150–200 defending a mountain base at Lom Sak. Thai commanders acknowledged government deaths in the operation had totaled at least 30. Other sources placed the number of fatalities at 60 with at least 200 wounded.

Praphas Charusathien, deputy chairman of the ruling National Executive Council, had said March 17 that government troops had reached a suspected enemy base area, which he described as "a big central headquarters that issued orders coordinating activities of terrorists in the north with those of terrorists in the northeast."

Thai military officials and Western diplomats in Bangkok were reported March 22 to have said that the insurgents' activity in Thailand had increased 15%–20% over the past year and a half and that they were receiving better arms through Laos. The Thai director of the command for the Suppression of Communists, Lt. Gen. Saiyud Kerdphol, said the guerrillas were "still in phase one, building their organization, infrastructure and secure areas, . . . But they are moving close to phase two—launching guerrilla offensive operations against us."

The guerrilla forces were deployed in three areas of Thailand: in the northeast around the Phu Phan Mountains, about 1,500 men; in the northwest, with an estimated 3,000 Meo tribesmen, led by Thais and ethnic Chinese born in Thailand; and near the Malaysian border to the south, about 500 rebels.

Government casualties in three years of fighting as reported by Western diplomatic sources: 1969—300 killed and 500 wounded; 1970—450 killed and 500 wounded; and 1971—500 killed and 500 wounded.

Communist attacks in Pnompenh. Communist demolition squads carried out three attacks in Pnompenh March 23, 24 and 28.

Enemy frogmen March 23 blew up a 5,000-ton cargo vessel and two barges carrying fuel in the Bassac River on the southern end of the city.

Communist saboteurs March 24 knocked out a bridge over the Tonle Sap River, which lead to a naval base and a large army garrison. At least three persons were killed when an explosive device in a parked truck blew a 50-foot hole in the center span.

Six persons were killed by a saboteur explosion in Pnompenh March 28.

A government directive issued March 28 urged residents of Pnompenh and nearby villages to "prepare defensive positions and shelters and prepare knives, swords or guns" in case of another enemy attack on the city, such as the one March 21 in which 112 persons were killed and 280 wounded by a Communist rocket barrage.

The government directive followed a Cambodian command report March 27 which had said that 800 Communist soldiers had been sighted 10 miles southwest of Pnompenh. The enemy force was observed by fighter-bomber pilots who dropped bombs on the suspected Communist positions. The report was coupled with a communique that claimed the killing of 70 Communists near Paing Kasey, 20 miles southwest of the capital. Government losses were put at two dead.

South Vietnamese forces stepped up their operations in eastern Cambodia by sending in another 2,000 men March 22 but then temporarily ended the drive five days later. The Saigon reinforcements had brought to more than 10,000 the number of government troops taking part in the latest offensive to destroy enemy base camps near the South Vietnamese border. The new task force headed toward Krek, along Highway 7.

According to Saigon, the first phase of the drive into eastern Cambodia launched March 10 had ended and left 743 Communists killed, 583 by artillery and air strikes. South Vietnamese losses were placed at eight killed and 65 wounded. Thousands of South Vietnamese withdrew from the Parrot's Beak area of eastern Cambodia March 27 to regroup for a new assault on Communist bases.

South Vietnam military action. The military situation in South Vietnam March 9–21 was relatively quiet with the exception of a few sporadic attacks by Communist forces.

Enemy forces carried out widespread assaults across the country March 13 with most of the action centered in the Central Highlands provinces of Kontum and Pleiku. A field report said that in one raid 13 North Vietnamese were killed and one was captured. The clash occurred southeast of Fire Base 5.

Another large outbreak of Communist attacks occurred March 15–16. The Saigon command said the North Vietnamese and Viet Cong had initiated 41 attacks during the 24-hour period ended at dawn, compared with 23 in the previous 24-hour period. The forays were launched mainly in the coastal lowlands province of Quangngai, 75 miles south of Danang. Local militia took the brunt of the assaults. Four enemy attacks in the province killed 31 persons, 18 of them civilians.

Thirteen South Vietnamese troops were killed in a Communist demolition assault March 13 on the Tayninh West base camp, 60 miles northwest of Saigon.

Sixteen of the infiltrators were killed. The camp was the headquarters of South Vietnam's drive into eastern Cambodia.

A U.S. helicopter carrying an American combat team into action crashed 20 miles north of Saigon March 17. All 11 aboard were killed.

U.S. presses air war. The air war in Indochina continued without letup as U.S. aircraft March 19 carried out the 100th protective reaction strike on North Vietnam. The U.S. command reported March 20 that a Navy A-6 fighter-bomber had attacked a radar site 35 miles north of the demilitarized zone. Two other U.S. jets had destroyed an antiaircraft battery and a radar site in the North March 19 and another antiaircraft artillery battery, about 15 miles north of the DMZ, had been destroyed by F-4 fighters March 17.

American sources reported March 12 that U.S. planes had destroyed several North Vietnamese tanks in raids on southern Laos the previous week. The tanks, believed to be Soviet-made T-54s or later-model T-55s, had been destroyed near the South Vietnamese border, east of the Laotian town of Tchepone and just south of the DMZ.

Three American airmen downed on the Ho Chi Minh Trail in southern Laos were rescued March 19. More than 50 U.S. aircraft attacked enemy troops for 24 hours to cover the rescue operations.

Lon Nol forms new government. Cambodian President Lon Nol named a new premier March 18 and announced the formation of a new 17-member Cabinet March 21 in the wake of his assumption of total power the previous week.

The new premier was Son Ngoc Thanh, who also held the post of foreign minister. Thanh was a long-time nationalist leader, first serving as premier during the Japanese occupation of Cambodia in World War II. He was born in South Vietnam.

At least five political leaders were said to have rejected offers to become premier before Thanh accepted Lon Nol's bid.

The new Cabinet announced by Lon Nol March 21 had been made public by the Cambodian radio the previous day. The broadcast said the Cabinet was provisional and was subject to further change.

Eight ministers had been in the previous Cabinet and most of the others were well-known government officials. Two of Lon Nol's supporters held key posts: Maj. Gen. Sak Suthsakham was defense minister and Maj. Gen. Thapana Nginn was interior minister. The only member of the new government who had been associated with the opposition was Yem Sambaur, who was appointed chief justice.

Former Premier Sisowath Sirik Matak, whose ouster from government had been demanded by protesting students for two weeks, was not appointed to the new regime. Despite his exclusion and announced retirement from political life, students of Pnompenh University and of the city's high schools continued their protests against him and boycotted all classes. The youths accused Sirik Matak of corruption and of being undemocratic for denying them free speech during his term in office.

Communists shell Pnompenh. Communist artillery and rockets pounded the Cambodian capital of Pnompenh and its outskirts March 21, killing more than 100 civilians and wounding more than 100 others. It was the heaviest attack on the city since the war in Cambodia had started in 1970.

The enemy launching sites were believed located about five miles southwest of the city limits. They had fired an estimated 75 shells, many directed at the international airport on the western edge of the city.

The shelling was followed by a Communist ground attack with the largest assault centered on Takhmau, six miles southeast of Pnompenh. A force of 500 Communists entered the town and killed at least 25 civilians, the Cambodian command reported. A government radio station six miles from the center of the city also was attacked. The main transmitter was damaged, briefly disrupting communications.

The Communists also were reported to have surrounded the district capital of Preyveng, 30 miles east of Pnompenh. The government garrison there was attempting to break out southward on Route 15 to link up with other Cambodian troops moving north. The Cambodian command said Preyveng was "isolated" and the situation was "serious."

South Vietnamese troops with American air support had launched a new drive into eastern Cambodia March 10 in an attempt to prevent enemy attacks on the approaches to Saigon. The operation was started by a force of 5,000 men. An additional 2,000 men carried out another drive in the same region March 11. The offensives, located 6–10 miles inside Cambodia north of the Pnompenh-to-Saigon highway, made no major contact with the Communists through March 18.

The Saigon command reported March 11 that U.S. B-52s assisting the operation had struck a North Vietnamese base camp 12 miles inside Cambodia north of Tayninh, South Vietnam, destroying reinforced concrete bunkers and supplies, and killing a number of enemy troops.

Two large caches of enemy supplies were found in the area of the operation by South Vietnamese troops, the Saigon command reported March 18. They included 90 tons of rice, five tons of ammunition and more than 50,000 gallons of gasoline. In one of the few engagements of the drive, 10 enemy soldiers were killed in scattered fighting 12 miles northwest of Kompang Trach, the Saigon command reported. Government losses were one killed and six wounded.

A smaller South Vietnamese offensive launched 25 miles to the southwest Feb. 1 was still in progress and Saigon reported 35 enemy troops were killed there March 10. South Vietnam lost two men.

Cambodian forces were engaged in fierce fighting with North Vietnamese soldiers around the Angkor temples Feb. 18–March 1. A temple in the western sector was reported Feb. 18 captured by Cambodian troops. Heavy clashes broke out within three miles of Angkor Feb. 21 with 11 government soldiers killed and 39 wounded. Enemy losses were not known. North Vietnamese troops March 1 struck out from fixed positions at Angkor and attacked the surrounding Cambodian forces.

The Cambodian command reported March 7 that its forces that day had successfully concluded a 10-day operation by capturing an island in the Mekong River, 50 miles northeast of Pnompenh. Government losses were 15 killed and 63 wounded.

Air war intensifies. The air war intensified over Indochina with the U.S. suffering heavy losses in planes.

Eight American aircraft were reported downed March 24–26.

A U.S. and a South Vietnamese helicopter were lost in the Central Highlands of South Vietnam March 26. The South Vietnamese aircraft was brought down first and the American 'copter coming to its assistance was fired on and crashed. The North Vietnamese then attacked the allied crewmen on the ground, killing one American and wounding four others and 11 South Vietnamese.

All five crewmen were killed when a U.S. Air Force HH-53 rescue helicopter was shot down by Communist ground fire in Laos March 27.

Two U.S. AC-130 gunships were shot down by Communist antiaircraft in Laos March 29 and 30. All 14 aboard the first plane were missing and feared dead. Fifteen crewmen of the second gunship were rescued.

A U.S. fighter-bomber March 30 shot down a North Vietnamese MiG-21 with a missile near the Laotian border as it was flying near the Bankarai Pass. It was the fifth MiG downed since Jan. 1.

U.S. Policy Debated

War an election year issue. From the very beginning of the year, it was apparent that the Nixon Administration's conduct of the war in Indochina would be an important issue during the 1972 presidential campaign.

Humphrey enters race. Sen. Hubert H. Humphrey of. Minnesota announced in Philadelphia Jan. 10 that he would seek the 1972 Democratic presidential nomination. Humphrey, 60, was the 1968 Democratic standard-bearer.

Humphrey launched his campaign with a stinging broadside at President Nixon's Vietnam war policy. Humphrey declared that "our most urgent immediate need is to end the war" in Southeast Asia "and to do it now."

"It has taken Mr. .Nixon longer to withdraw our troops than it took us to defeat Hitler. Had I been elected [in 1968] we would now be out of that war."

Muskie announces candidacy. Sen. Edmund S. Muskie (Me.) Jan. 4 announced his candidacy for the Presidential nomination of the Democratic party with a pledge to give the nation "a new beginning."

Without once mentioning the Democratic party in his address, Muskie lashed out at President Nixon's failure to fulfill his 1968 campaign pledges to end the war in Vietnam, establish price stability and prosperity and bring about domestic peace. He said more could have been accomplished if the Administration had been "candid with the country."

Muskie said "we were promised an end to the war. We have been given a continuing war—with more American deaths, more American prisoners taken and a resumption of the massive bombing which was stopped in 1968."

Muskie urges total Vietnam pullout. Sen. Muskie opened his campaign in the New Hampshire Presidential primary Jan. 6 with a call for a total U.S. withdrawal from South Vietnam regardless of consequences. In a televised statement in Manchester, Muskie said the U.S. should end the war "not by dropping more bombs, but by withdrawing every soldier, sailor and airman from Vietnam." He said the Vietnamese would then "find their own way to settle their problems" and implied acceptance of whatever resolution was reached.

At a news conference earlier the same day in Concord, New Hampshire, Muskie said President Nixon's decision to build a $5.5 billion spaceship shuttle had "merit", but he doubted whether it had "priority given the other pressures on our resources."

Senate Democrats urge deadline. The Senate Democratic Policy Committee adopted a resolution Jan. 19 calling upon the President to set a final date for withdrawal of all American forces from Indochina within the next six months, negotiation of an immediate cease-fire and a phased withdrawal of U.S. forces in return for a phased release of American prisoners of war.

Senate Democratic Leader Mike Mansfield (Mont.) Jan. 29 declared his intention to persist in his effort to attain enactment of his end-the-war amendment for a total pullout within six months. Although he had previously praised the President's peace plan, he expressed concern that the President had not "separated the political and military aspects." The military aspect, he said, was "the most important" and the political aspect "secondary in significance."

Muskie's Vietnam peace plan. Sen. Edmund S. Muskie (D, Me.) presented his own Vietnam peace plan Feb. 2 and criticized President Nixon's as deceptive to the public and unproductive diplomatically.

Muskie proposed a two-point plan: "First, we must set a date when we will withdraw every soldier, sailor and airman and stop all bombing and other American military activity, dependent only on an agreement for the return of our prisoners and the safety of our troops as they leave.

"Second, we must urge the government in Saigon to move toward a political accommodation with all the elements of their society. Without such an accommodation, the war cannot be ended, and it is clear that the American people will not support an indefinite war either by our presence or by proxy."

While he welcomed "Administration proposals to move American troops out of Indochina," Muskie said, he questioned "the wisdom of a course which attaches so many conditions to our leaving that it can only leave us where we are now, watching our sons fight and die, not for a cause but for a mistake, looking to a future where more human beings will suffer at our hands in a senseless and immoral conflict." The President's proposals, he said, were no more than an attempt "to win at the conference table what we have

not won and cannot win on the battlefield."

Muskie cited what he called three deficiencies in the Nixon peace proposals. "Most Americans thought they heard the President agree to set a date certain for our withdrawal," he said, but the President actually offered to withdraw troops within six months of a general settlement.

Also, the President's proposal to hold free elections in South Vietnam 30 days after President Nguyen Van Thieu would step down, Muskie said, would still leave Thieu's "handpicked agents" in control of the government process. "What opponent then would risk his liberty or even his life in open opposition?" he asked, and, "How could anyone call such elections free?"

In the third deficiency, Muskie called the President's cease-fire proposal a diplomatic "stumbling block" by requiring the North Vietnamese, in effect, to "concede Saigon's control over most of the countryside, abandoning their supporters to the police power of an enemy regime."

Ziegler rebuttal—White House Press Secretary Ronald L. Ziegler stressed later Feb. 2 the Administration view that a cease-fire was not a serious barrier in the peace negotiations. He cautioned that "unfounded criticism" would complicate the talks.

Rogers denounces Muskie—Secretary of State William P. Rogers Feb. 3 said Muskie jeopardized prospects for a negotiated peace by rejecting the President's peace plan before the enemy had done so.

He said Muskie's remarks were "most inappropriate and harmful to our national interest" and that every man running for public office, particularly a presidential candidate, "should ask himself every time he makes a statement whether it serves the national interest or not."

Rogers remained optimistic about the President's peace proposals. The Communists had indicated "some interest" in the plan, he said, and added, "we have diplomatic conversations with others that indicate they think the President's proposal might be a way out."

In reply, Muskie said later Feb. 3 he believed the other side "would respond seriously to the terms I have suggested" and he did not think it was "against the national interest to try to promote" the goal of stopping the killing of American boys in Vietnam sooner.

Aid bill's defeat tied to Paris talks. The New York Times reported Feb. 3 that Henry A. Kissinger, President Nixon's adviser for national security, had remarked at an unpublicized White House meering Jan. 28 that the Senate defeat of a foreign aid program Oct. 29, 1971 had been a factor in the suspension of secret negotiations between the U.S. and North Vietnam in November 1971. Kissinger said the defeat might have led the North Vietnamese to believe that U.S. economic support for the Saigon regime could be ended without concession by Hanoi in the Paris peace talks. Kissinger reportedly expressed this view during a meeting with relatives of U.S. prisoners of war.

Sen. J. W. Fulbright (D, Ark.), chairman of the Senate Foreign Relations Committee, cited the newspaper report in the Senate Feb. 3 and called Kissinger's remark "an outrageous abuse" of his White House position. Fulbright urged the Senate to find a way to force Kissinger to testify before Congress on foreign policy. "If we ask him to explain his statement to the Foreign Relations Committee," Fulbright said, "he would say as he has in the past that he is not responsible to the Senate but only to the President," or, in effect, invoke executive privilege and decline to testify.

Sen. Stuart Symington (D, Mo.) joined in the criticism Feb. 3. Citing subsequent Senate approval of foreign aid bills, Symington called Kissinger's view "ridiculous."

Nixon cautions war critics. President Nixon called on his Democratic rivals for the presidency Feb. 9 to dampen their criticism of his Vietnam peace initiatives or risk that their words "might give the enemy an incentive to prolong the war until after the [November] election."

Nixon's remarks were made in a morning radio broadcast in which he set forth the main themes of his foreign policy report to Congress.

In his speech, Nixon emphasized that he was not questioning the sincerity or patriotism of his war critics.

But while he said "there should always be free debate and criticism," Nixon asserted that such criticism should contribute to, not deter, the search for an "honorable peace."

Without mentioning his Democratic presidential rivals by name, Nixon reminded them that "we have only one President at a time, [and] only the President can negotiate an end to the war."

(Nixon's broadcast came two days after H. R. Haldeman, a top White House aide, charged that the criticisms leveled by leading Democrats at the new peace plan seriously undermined the chances for ending the war. [See below])

The sharpest criticism of Nixon's comments came from New York Mayor John Lindsay, who charged that the President's statement was close to what Lindsay called "character assassination." Lindsay said "the Nixon technique is all too familiar. He disclaims any attack on the patriotism of his opponents and then accuses them of consciously aiding the enemy."

Sen. George S. McGovern (D, S.D.) said Nixon's speech, while milder in tone than the comments by Haldeman, did not entirely dispel his suspicion that Haldeman's remarks had White House approval.

Sen. Edmund S. Muskie (D, Me.) indicated that he was in accord with Nixon in some of his remarks and that he had no intention of pre-empting the President's role as the chief negotiator. But Muskie said dissent in the U.S. over the war was "not about to be put down by his [Nixon's] dislike of criticism."

Sen. Hubert H. Humphrey (D, Minn.) said if Nixon wanted responsible criticism, he had to keep his presidential rivals fully informed of developments. Humphrey said Nixon "has failed to do so, either in regard to candidates or the American people."

Haldeman assails peace plan critics— H. R. Haldeman, one of President Nixon's chief White House counselors, charged in a television interview broadcast Feb. 7 that those who criticized the

President's latest Vietnam peace plan were "consciously aiding and abetting the enemy of the U.S."

Haldeman's remark touched off a series of rejoinders from several leading Democratic politicians, some of whom had criticized several aspects of Nixon's Jan. 25 peace initiatives.

But the Republican Congressional leadership, while avoiding direct comment on Haldeman's charge, asserted that potential presidential candidates who offered alternative peace plans might undermine Nixon's new peace efforts.

Shortly after Haldeman's remarks were broadcast, White House Press Secretary Ronald L. Ziegler said that the comments were "his own personal point of view" and not necessarily those of the President.

Haldeman made his charge during an interview with Barbara Walters of the National Broadcasting Company (NBC) on the "Today" show. The interview was taped Jan. 28—three days after Nixon announced the peace plan—but held for airing until Feb. 7. It was Haldeman's first television appearance.

Haldeman has been described as the President's chief of staff and a man with considerable influence in the White House. During the interview, Miss Walters asked Haldeman what kind of criticism upset the President. He replied that Nixon was "naturally concerned by the kind of criticism that can get in the way of what he's trying to do and that would be unfair criticism."

Haldeman said that before Nixon made his new peace plan known, "you could say that his critics—people who were opposing what he was doing—were unconsciously echoing the line that the enemy wanted echoed."

He said the new plan made all the points that the President's war critics had sought—"except one, which is turning South Vietnam over to the Communists, putting a Communist government in South Vietnam."

Haldeman continued that "the only conclusion that you can draw now is that the President's critics are in favor of putting a Communist government in South Vietnam and insisting that that be done, too. That's something we aren't going to do."

When Miss Walters reminded Haldeman that some of the President's Vietnam critics were U.S. senators, he replied, "In this particular posture, I think they are consciously aiding and abetting the enemy."

Miss Walters sought to have Haldeman identify those senators he spoke of, but he said, "I don't want to characterize any individual in this respect. I am expressing a personal feeling that I think applies where it applies."

Nixon comments on his critics. The President, at his Feb. 10 news conference, elaborated on his ' views of criticism by Democratic candidates of his Vietnam peace proposals.

Nixon said that while his opponents had a right to suggest proposals "that would overthrow the government of South Vietnam, or some other proposal that would satisfy the enemy," as a consequence "the responsibility for the enemy's failing to negotiate may have to be borne by those who encourage the enemy to wait until after the election."

Responding to a question about the Feb. 7 interview of his staff chief H. R. Haldeman, [See above] Nixon said he considered his opponents' statements "a matter of judgment," not of "patriotism."

However, he recalled his own stand in the 1968 election. Although he had earlier been a critic of the partition of Laos and of actions which "contributed to the assassination of Diem," and while he had been "a strong critic of the conduct of the war," he said that once he became a candidate, and once President Johnson had begun peace talks, he announced that he "would say nothing that would, in any way, jeopardize those peace talks." He asked 1972 presidential candidates to "consult their own consciences" and follow his example.

Candidates to get policy briefings. The Nixon Administration offered Feb. 11 to make foreign policy briefings available to presidential candidates and members of Congress.

State Department spokesman Charles Bray 3rd said Secretary of State William P. Rogers was "entirely prepared to make himself available" to brief the candidates on Vietnam and other foreign policy problems. Deputy White House Press Secretary Gerald L. Warren said Vietnam briefings would be available to members of Congress and candidates and "if any figure in public life" wanted to call the National Security Council, he said, "I'm sure that call would be welcomed."

The matter had arisen in the recent flare-up of Democratic criticism of President Nixon's peace proposals and Administration rebuttal that the criticism could undermine the peace talks in Paris. Sen. Hubert H. Humphrey (D, Minn.) had suggested Feb. 9 that opposition candidates might be more sympathetic to the Administration viewpoint if they were provided detailed information about its strategy.

The controversy over the criticism continued. The Senate Democratic Policy Committee unanimously approved a resolution Feb. 15 condemning a recent remark by a Presidential assistant (H. R. Haldeman, who was not named in the resolution) that the Democratic critics were "consciously aiding and abetting the enemy." The statement, it said, reflected "an extraordinarily undeveloped sense of the basic right of every American citizen under the Constitution."

In Manchester, N.H. Feb. 11, Sen. Edmund S. Muskie (D, Me.) said dissent had been useful in the past "in turning our policy around" and that if he had hurt the national interest by offering ideas about the peace negotiations, President Nixon had hurt the national interest in offering "ideas on how to speed up the war" in criticism of Johnson Administration policy in 1965, 1966 and 1968.

Defense Secretary Melvin R. Laird said in San Diego Feb. 11 that "responsible men will not encourage the enemy to hold out in anticipation of a more generous settlement, thus risking delay in the return of American fighting forces and the release of the prisoners."

In Jacksonville, Fla. Feb. 11, Sen. Henry M. Jackson (D, Wash.) continued to call for "a little moratorium" on Vietnam policy criticism.

Jackson and Humphrey, along with Senate Democratic Leader Mike Mans-field (Mont.), had been singled out by Attorney General John Mitchell Feb. 10 as having acted with "high responsibility" for having "refrained from doing or saying anything which could undercut the President's negotiating position or encourage Hanoi to prolong the war in the hope of getting a better deal after election day."

More Viet medical aid urged. Sen. Edward M. Kennedy (D, Mass.) charged March 4 that the Nixon Administration was "establishing a national policy of walking away from our humanitarian responsibilities to the people of Vietnam" by "sabotaging" and reducing health programs in South Vietnam as U.S. troops were withdrawn.

The statement accompanied a General Accounting Office report showing hospital admissions for civilian war casualties in South Vietnam averaged 3,508 a month for the first eight months of 1971. Kennedy was chairman of a Senate Judiciary subcommittee on refugees.

Laos aid diversion reported. Sen. Edward M. Kennedy (D, Mass.) made public March 18 a General Accounting Office (GAO) report that the diversion of funds intended for relief of civilian victims of war in Laos was continuing despite Nixon Administration assurances in 1971 the practice would be ended. The report said almost half the relief funds were being diverted to the clandestine guerrilla force in Laos.

Kennedy, chairman of a Senate Refugees and Escapees Subcommittee, released another GAO report April 22 that aid funds were being diverted to feed and otherwise assist paramilitary forces and their dependents in Laos, including Meo tribesmen serving in the clandestine army operated by the Central Intelligence Agency.

Sen. Stuart Symington (D, Mo.), chairman of a Senate subcommittee on U.S. overseas commitments, issued a subcommittee report May 7 that the U.S. had pledged to provide up to $100 million a year to support a Thai irregular army of 10,000 men in Laos.

The report, prepared by staff members James G. Lowenstein and Richard M. Moose, also reported that U.S. helicopter gunships, under U.S. Army command but apparently flown by Thai pilots, were being used in Northern Laos to support medical evacuation missions. The report also said the Thai Air Force was flying combat support missions in Laos with equipment and ammunition supplied by the U.S.

Agnew assails Vietnam critics. At a meeting of the American Society of Newspaper Editors in Washington April 21, Vice President Spiro Agnew assailed Democratic Senators J. W. Fulbright (Ark.), Hubert H. Humphrey (Minn.), Edward M. Kennedy (Mass.), George McGovern (S.D.), and Edmund S. Muskie (Me.) for having "staked their credibility and some of their political future" on the failure of the President's Vietnam policy. Agnew said such men, "who played a central role in pushing America into an everdeepening involvement in Vietnam, are now charging that the President desires a military victory more than he desires peace." "This is a transparent lie," he charged. Agnew added that "the New York Times, an early and ardent advocate of getting America into Vietnam [was] doing public penance regularly by scourging the President who is getting us out." (Addressing the same meeting later April 21, Times Vice President James Reston asserted that "never since before the last world war, not even in Lyndon Johnson's time, have I seen a trickier Administration than this one.")

In a speech to the Maine GOP Convention in Augusta April 28, Agnew berated Muskie for exhibiting "a singular lack of enthusiasm for his native land." In response to a Muskie campaign theme: "Wouldn't it be nice if we had a country we can love, believe in, work for and die for?" Agnew replied: "Well, I have news for the Senator. We have such a country. It is called the United States of America."

Communists Launch Spring Offensive

Biggest enemy attack since 1968.
Thousands of North Vietnamese troops
launched a major offensive March 30
across the demilitarized zone (DMZ)
that divided North and South Vietnam.

By April 1 the Communist ground
and artillery attacks had forced defending South Vietnamese troops to abandon a number of base camps near the
DMZ and the enemy was pushing the
government forces in disarray toward
their rear bases. It was the biggest
Communist offensive since the siege
of the allied bases at Conthien and
Khesanh in the same area in 1968.

U.S. advisers believed the objective
of the enemy drive was to seize Quangtri, capital of Quangtri Province. Its
fall would pose a serious threat to Hue
and Danang further south. The scope
of the Communist operation was confirmed by South Vietnam April 1. Lt.
Gen. Hoang Xuan Lam, commander of
Military Region I in the northern provinces, issued a statement saying "the
Communist North Vietnamese are
crossing the demilitarized zone to in-
vade Quangtri Province." He said the
enemy was employing three artillery
regiments and antiaircraft units
equipped with surface-to-air missiles.
About two North Vietnamese divisions
with an estimated 20,000 men were believed involved in the operation.

The North Vietnamese launched the
offensive March 30 by firing more than
5,000 rockets, long-range artillery
shells and mortar shells on 12 South
Vietnamese positions just south of the
demilitarized zone. The government
announced March 31 that 285 enemy
soldiers and 31 government troops had
been killed in the first two days of fighting.

Six South Vietnamese outposts were
abandoned near the DMZ March 31.
They included fire support bases
Fuller, Mailoc, Holcomb and Pioneer
and two other small camps.

Heavy cloud cover restricted U.S.
air support for the retreating government troops. B-52 bombers carried
out attack missions April 1 just south
of the buffer zone, striking suspected
Communist troop concentrations northeast of Khesanh. The planes also
dropped bombs on Kontum in the Central Highlands. A Communist attack
on a government outpost 20 miles
northwest of Kontum March 31 was repulsed by Saigon troops, the South
Vietnamese command reported April 1.
It said 87 North Vietnamese were slain
while government casualties totaled
one killed and 14 wounded.

The Communist thrust across the
DMZ had been preceded by heavy
clashes in the northern sector, around
Hue, between March 16 and 29, with
Hanoi's forces reported suffering heavy
losses. Fighting 18 miles southwest of
the city March 16 resulted in the death

45

of 72 North Vietnamese, according to Saigon. South Vietnamese troops attempting to prevent 400 enemy troops from moving down the coastal plain suffered three killed and 15 wounded. A clash in the same area March 18 raised the North Vietnamese death toll by another 180, many of them being killed by air and artillery strikes. Three clashes erupted within 15 miles of Hue March 26 and 180 North Vietnamese were killed. The Saigon command said the heaviest battle occurred when government patrols encountered a 130-man enemy force and killed 85 of them Government losses in the three clashes were put at four dead and 25 wounded. A South Vietnamese sweep 18 miles southwest of Hue March 29 killed 52 of the enemy.

Elsewhere in South Vietnam, Communist forces March 22 attacked the Mekong Delta district town of Trucesgiang, 50 miles southwest of Saigon, killing 19 local militiamen and policemen and nine civilians. Twenty-nine other defenders were wounded, and nine of the attackers were killed, Saigon reported.

Two American soldiers were killed and four wounded by a booby-trap explosion March 29, 31 miles east of Saigon.

Communists press Quangtri drive— South Vietnamese troops abandoned the northern half of Quangtri Province April 2 as North Vietnamese soldiers pressed their drive southward. Only three major bases in the northern part of the province remained in government hands— Quangtri city, the Quangtri combat base and Dongha city, all reported under heavy enemy attack. The last two government bases just south of the demilitarized zone fell April 2. They were Mailoc and Camp Carroll, 12 miles west of Dongha.

The South Vietnamese commander moved his division staff out of the Quangtri combat base to Quangtri city, three miles south, after the base was struck by more than 1,000 rocket and artillery shells.

The Saigon command claimed 19 North Vietnamese tanks had been destroyed by low-flying South Vietnamese planes north of Dongha April 2. Ground

fighting in the area also was heavy. After the battle, government forces blew up the highway bridge from Dongha north across a branch of the Cua Viet River to prevent Hanoi's troops from moving their artillery and tanks further south. The Cua Viet marked the South Vietnamese northern line of defense in Quangtri Province.

In the air war April 2, U.S. B-52s flew six missions west of Quangtri city, dropping bombs on suspected enemy troop concentrations. Some of the few American fighter planes that were able to fly despite the thick clouds were fired on by ground missile sites in and just north of the DMZ and in southern Laos, but none of the aircraft were hit, the U.S. command said. Three U.S. helicopters and an observation plane were shot down by enemy ground fire in Quangtri Province. The 'copter crewmen were missing, but the observation pilot was rescued. North Vietnam claimed that its forces had shot down a B-52 in the northern part of the DMZ April 2, but the U.S. command said it doubted the report. Hanoi also claimed the shooting down of three American planes April 1 during a raid over residential areas in Vinhlinh district, just north of the DMZ.

Heavy fighting continued April 3 north of Dongha with the city reported in flames after being hit by thousands of shells fired from North Vietnamese tanks and artillery. South Vietnam claimed its forces had destroyed 25 of the 30 enemy tanks that had pushed out from the DMZ since March 30.

Although allied communiques made mention of only North Vietnamese involved in the fighting, a statement issued by the Viet Cong April 3 suggested that its forces were also engaged in the offensive. The Viet Cong said its men had "wiped out" nearly 5,500 South Vietnamese and took more than 1,000 prisoners between the start of the drive March 30 and April 2. In addition, a large number of Saigon troops had been "disbanded," the Viet Cong statement said.

The Communist menace to Quangtri city was further heightened as South Vietnamese troops abandoned one of their remaining defense points on the northern bank of the Cua Viet River

April 4. Government troops were forced to pull out of Fire Base Anne, a small artillery position eight miles southwest of the city. Saigon claimed the killing of 23 North Vietnamese troops in a battle nine miles to the southeast. Enemy troops also were advancing on the city from the southwest. Saigon claimed 65 North Vietnamese troops were killed in fighting three miles northeast and two miles southwest of Dongha.

A Communist broadcast April 4 said "the liberation forces are fiercely attacking, razing to the ground a series of bases north and south of Route 9 and along Route 1" in Quangtri Province. The broadcast claimed "the United States aggressors are losing and are being forced to withdraw" and appealed to South Vietnamese troops to surrender to the "liberation command."

North Vietnam's forces in the area below the DMZ were estimated at 15,000–20,000 men, while South Vietnamese troops in Quangtri were said to number about 26,000.

The U.S. command said American planes made nine retaliatory strikes on Communist radar sites and artillery positions in the northern section of the DMZ April 4 and above the zone inside North Vietnam April 3 and 4. The protective reaction strikes against the North now totaled 120 since Jan. 1. Other U.S. planes April 4 flew 145 strike missions against North Vietnamese positions in a 10-mile strip below the DMZ. Meanwhile, five U.S. Navy destroyers offshore in the Gulf of Tonkin fired at North Vietnamese troop positions and along Route 1 in the same area.

Communist pressure spread to Thuathien Province, the province south of Quangtri, as two government fire bases southwest of Hue, the capital, came under enemy fire April 5. U.S. planes April 5 conducted three retaliatory raids on North Vietnamese missile and antiaircraft artillery sites north of the DMZ while other aircraft carried out 217 tactical air strikes below the buffer strip. North Vietnam claimed the downing of another B-52, over Vinhlinh, but the U.S. State Department denied the claim.

A state of alert was declared in Quangbinh, North Vietnam's province border-ing on the DMZ, it was reported by the North Vietnamese press agency April 4. The agency said regional army militia and self-defense groups in the province were mobilized, training exercises in antiaircraft and antitank warfare had started and preparations were being taken for possible air or amphibious commando assaults.

Communists open Binhlong front— The Communist drive into Binhlong Province was launched from eastern Cambodia April 5. Initial reports said several hundred North Vietnamese of a 1,000-man attacking force cut Highway 13 between Anloc and Saigon only 37 miles north of the capital. The Communists, equipped with tanks, increasingly expanded their operations and were reported April 7 to be in control of the northern section of the province.

Two strategic province towns were under heavy enemy assault. The district headquarters town of Locninh and Anloc, a few miles to the south of Route 13, were the targets of the enemy thrust. A few American advisers were among the South Vietnamese defenders in the district compound of Locninh, the focal point of the enemy attack. Government troops were reported to have abandoned the airfield at Quanloi, four miles northwest of Anloc.

The Saigon command reported its forces had killed 37 enemy soldiers April 5 in Tayninh Province, south of Binhlong.

Government troops engaged North Vietnamese soldiers inside Cambodia across the Tayninh border April 6. The Saigon command said 73 North Vietnamese and 10 government soldiers were killed in the clash near Kompong Trach.

South Vietnamese forces had suffered heavy casualties in Tayninh the previous weekend, American authorities reported April 7. Fifty South Vietnamese were killed and 200 were missing or wounded when the Communists attacked a government artillery position, Fire Base Pace, three miles south of the Cambodian border.

*Thieu sees 'decisive battle'—*South Vietnamese President Nguyen Van Thieu declared in a television address April 6 that "the decisive battle" of the war was under way. "This is the decisive moment where the survival or loss of our country is at stake," he said.

Thieu said the objective of the Communist drive was to capture Quangtri and Thuathien Provinces and to establish a capital for the Viet Cong's National Liberation Front. He warned that if the enemy leaders succeeded "they would go on to demand a policical solution which would either consist of a coalition government or territorial concession to the Communists toward ultimately taking over all our country."

The president said Hanoi's further aim was "to cause the failure of the Vietnamization program so as to create political dissension within the United States that would make the government and people of America cease all aid, military as well as economic, to the republic of Vietnam."

Hanoi urges 'complete victory'—North Vietnamese Defense Minister Gen. Vo Nguyen Giap called on "the Vietnamese people's armed forces" April 2 to press their offensive "to complete victory." In a statement made to North Vietnamese troops, Giap asserted that "the United States imperialists who have sustained heavy defeats are facing innumerable difficulties and are in a fix."

Giap's avoidance of reference to North Vietnamese forces was in line with Hanoi's policy of not openly admitting that its troops were fighting in the South. The Viet Cong's role in the offensive in the DMZ area was specifically cited in a report from Hanoi April 5, which said that the fighting was being waged by the "people's liberation armed forces of South Vietnam."

In a further apparent refutation of the claim that North Vietnamese troops had invaded the South, Hanoi's Foreign Ministry accused Washington April 5 of "cynically distorting the South Vietnamese people's struggle against the U.S. aggression." Anticipating U.S. retaliatory strikes on North Vietnam, the ministry also said that American threats of "heavier bombing raids" would not undermine the Communists' "determination to fight and win" the war.

U.S. troop exit continues. Despite the latest North Vietnamese offensive, the U.S. continued to withdraw its troops from South Vietnam. The American command announced April 3 that 6,200 men had been pulled out the previous week, bringing the total to 95,000, almost a seven-year low. A total of 26,500 remained to be withdrawn in the next four weeks to meet President Nixon's goal of leaving no more than 69,000 Americans in Vietnam by May 1.

U.S. sources said the North Vietnamese drive would have no affect on the American withdrawal rate.

U.S. losses at 6-month high. The U.S. high command reported April 6 that 10 Americans had been killed in combat March 26–April 1. It was the highest weekly American loss in six months. The command also reported that 15 Americans were listed as missing as a result of air crashes the previous week.

The number of Americans wounded in the March 26–April 1 period were put at 33, an increase of 20 over the previous week. U.S. fatalities since Jan. 1, 1961 were now 45,679.

Other losses the previous week as reported by Saigon: South Vietnam—466 killed, 1,073 wounded and 74 missing; Communists—2,150 killed and 80 captured.

Hanoi urges secret talks with U.S. North Vietnam was reported April 6 to have urged the resumption of secret peace talks with the U.S. The request was submitted to President Nixon by Le Duc Tho, a member of the North Vietnamese Politburo, through three American labor leaders who had recently visited Hanoi.

The labor officials told of Tho's offer following their testimony at a closed hearing April 6 before the Senate Foreign Relations Committee. The men, who had returned from Hanoi March 28, were David Livingston, president of District 65, Distributive Workers of America; Harold Gibbons, vice president of the Teamsters Union; and Clifton Caldwell, vice president of the Amalgamated Meat Cutters and Butchers Union. They had met March 31 with Henry A. Kissinger, President Nixon's national security adviser, to tell him of

Tho's suggestion that he and Kissinger resume their secret talks that had broken off in 1971.

The continued refusal of the U.S. to resume the public Paris peace talks it had canceled March 23 was denounced again April 6 by Mrs. Nguyen Thi Binh, head of the Viet Cong delegation as "sabotage." "She said the "Popular Liberation forces" were fighting to "free all of South Vietnam" and set up a "government of national concord" in Saigon. Mrs. Binh denied that North Vietnamese forces were involved in the battle. "All the units that are participating in the fight for Quangtri are part of the popular armed forces of liberation of South Vietnam," she said. The Viet Cong leader denied that her movements' forces would use Quangtri city, if captured, as its seat of government. Without specifying its location, Mrs. Binh said "we have a liberated zone where the services of the National Liberation Front and of the provisional revolutionary government are established."

The U.S. and South Vietnam April 4 had turned down a renewed Communist request that the Paris talks be reopened. The Viet Cong and North Vietnamese representatives suggested that the next meeting be held April 6 "as usual." In rejecting the bid, Saigon spokesman Nguyen Trieu Dan said "it is ridiculous to talk about wanting to negotiate while carrying out an invasion." Dan's American counterpart, Stephen J. Ledogar, declared the Communists "are interested in military victory, not a compromise. There will be no more meetings 'as usual.'"

Laird warns Hanoi on drive. U.S. Secretary of Defense Melvin R. Laird warned Hanoi April 7 that the American air strikes on North Vietnam would continue until it ended its offensive in the South, withdrew its forces across the DMZ and displayed "a willingness to seriously negotiate" in Paris.

Laird complained that North Vietnam remained obdurate at the peace discussions, had "shown no movement back across the DMZ, and until these conditions are met . . . we will continue to use the necessary power in order to protect our forces as we withdraw them from Southeast Asia." Despite the enemy at-

tacks, the U.S. would "meet or beat" the goal of reducing its force in South Vietnam to 69,000 men by May 1, Laird said.

The secretary was critical of Soviet military aid to North Vietnam, saying it was a "major contributor to the continuing conflict" and that Moscow was providing Hanoi's troops with 80% of the equipment being used in the current offensive. Moscow, he asserted, had "placed no restraints upon the use of this equipment outside of North Vietnam."

An extension of American raids on the North had been threatened April 6 by Adm. Thomas H. Moorer, chairman of the Joint Chiefs of Staff. Moorer did not indicate how much farther north the American jets would range, but said the American air strikes that day had hit targets "40–50 miles" above the demilitarized zone.

"As long as there are valid military targets supporting this [North Vietnamese] operation, the air strikes will continue," Moorer said.

U.S. may halt further troop exit— The North Vietnamese offensive might affect President Nixon's decision to pull more American troops out of South Vietnam after the May 1 deadline of reducing the U.S. force there to 69,000 men, U.S. officials said April 12.

Nixon was scheduled to make an announcement before May 1 on additional withdrawals, but White House Press Secretary Ronald L. Ziegler cautioned against drawing "conclusions one way or another." Although it was the President's "intent, hope and policy to continue with troop withdrawals," he was now confronted with a "somewhat different set of circumstances," Ziegler said.

Similar views were expressed April 12 by Rep. Gerald Ford (Mich.), House Republican leader, and Sen. Hugh Scott (Pa.), Senate Republican leader, after being briefed on the war by Nixon Administration officials. Ford said "there has never been a commitment" implied in previous withdrawal announcements that a future pullout "would automatically follow."

U.S.. air & naval raids. The U.S. air and naval strikes around the DMZ continued through April 7. American jets had been striking Communist targets in that region sporadically since the start of the North Vietnam drive March 30, but bad weather had limited the raids. The emergence of clear weather April 6 permitted systematic strikes for the first time since the opening of the Communist offensive.

The launching of the attacks was announced by the U.S. command in Saigon, which said that "in response to the invasion of the Republic of South Vietnam by North Vietnamese forces across the demilitarized zone, U.S. Air Force tactical aircraft and Navy components are attacking military targets in the area north of the demilitarized zone in order to help protect the lives of the diminishing U.S. forces in South Vietnam." The statement said the raids would be of "limited duration," but did not elaborate.

The U.S. reported three aircraft were downed in the first day's operations. According to the American command, two Navy A-7 jets were destroyed by ground missiles over the North. One pilot was rescued and the other was missing. The third plane, a rescue helicopter, was shot down by antiaircraft fire while conducting a search and rescue mission northwest of Quangtri city. North Vietnam April 6 claimed 10 American planes were downed over its territory.

One of the five Navy warships, a destroyer, firing on Communist targets from the Gulf of Tonkin, was struck by enemy artillery and automatic weapons from the Camlo district, just below the DMZ. It sustained light damage and three U.S. sailors were slightly wounded.

The American air strikes thus far were limited to the area south of the 18th Parallel. American pilots interviewed in Danang said their immediate targets were about 20 surface-to-air missile positions just north of the DMZ.

The American air strikes had followed an order by President Nixon April 4 to dispatch an additional 10–20 B-52 bombers to Indochina to reinforce U.S. airpower to counter the enemy offensive. The Defense Department said Nixon had made clear that he was prepared "to take whatever steps are necessary to protect the remaining United States forces in South Vietnam."

The air armada the U.S. was building up in the DMZ area totaled about 500 tactical fighter-bombers and 60 B-52s. In addition to the five Navy warships stationed in the Gulf of Tonkin, three aircraft carriers were deployed in the area and a fourth was on the way.

U.S. decision on air strikes—The U.S. decision to carry out reprisal air and naval strikes on North Vietnam was authorized by President Nixon following meetings in Washington of the Special Action Group April 3–5. The panel, under the chairmanship of Henry A. Kissinger, Nixon's national security adviser, met during periods of emergency. It included representatives of the State and Defense Departments, the Central Intelligence Agency and other interested departments.

After the Special Action Group meeting April 3, State Department spokesman Robert J. McCloskey, who had attended the conference, called the latest Communist offensive an invasion of South Vietnam. He said it was "a flagrant violation" of the 1954 Geneva agreement on Indochina and the 1968 understanding between the U.S. and North Vietnam on the halt in the American bombing of the North. "And by any definition, what has occurred is an invasion of South Vietnam," McCloskey said.

According to the U.S. interpretation of the 1968 understanding, North Vietnam was obligated not to violate the demilitarized zone and was to refrain from shelling South Vietnamese cities.

McCloskey asserted April 4 that North Vietnam had added "a new factor to the battlefield situation in South Vietnam" with the use of major supplies of Soviet tanks and heavy artillery. The Soviet equipment, McCloskey contended, permitted Hanoi's forces to conduct "conventional warfare rather than their traditional guerrilla attacks."

North Vietnamese Foreign Minister Nguyen Duy Trinh denounced the American raids April 7 as "an extremely grave military adventure." He said the Nixon Administration must "bear full responsibility for all the serious consequences of their acts."

The American air strikes prompted the North Vietnamese high command to issue orders to its forces April 7 to "deal thunderblows at the enemy" by "shooting down many aircraft, capturing many pilots, and sinking many U.S. warships."

Hanoi asks French intervention. North Vietnam appealed to France April 7 to persuade the U.S. to halt the bombing of its territory. The request was submitted by North Vietnamese Charge d'Affaires Nguyen Tuan Lieu in a meeting with Herve Alphand, secretary general of the Foreign Ministry.

France called for a resumption of the Paris peace talks April 12 after the Viet Cong and North Vietnamese delegates reiterated their demand that day for renewal of the canceled negotiations. A government statement issued after a Cabinet meeting did not mention the American bombing of the North, but said the Paris talks "should resume without delay" because the "conflict must receive a political solution and such a solution remains possible."

The Communist representatives charged in their statement that American refusal to re-enter the Paris talks was based on "unreasonable and entirely erroneous pretexts." It said if the U.S. continued to stay away from the negotiations, "it will only further expose before public opinion its opposition to a peaceful settlement of the conflict and its aim of seeking military victory."

The U.S. State Department April 12 criticized France's call for an immediate resumption of negotiations. Undersecretary of State U. Alexis Johnson told French Charge d'Affaires Emmanuel de Margerie in Washington that the U.S. regarded the Cabinet statement as one-sided and ill-timed. Department spokesman Robert J. McCloskey later told a news briefing that the Cabinet declaration was biased since "it picks up the demands" of North Vietnam and the Viet Cong which the U.S. held to be unacceptable because it was opposed to negotiating under the threat of military pressure.

Battle for Anloc. The battle for Anloc began to emerge following the North

Vietnamese capture April 7 of Locninh, a district capital of Binhlong Province at the northern end of Route 13, 75 miles north of Saigon. The South Vietnamese troops, 15,000 men of the 5th Infantry Division, retreated to Anloc, several miles south, and were immediately surrounded by enemy soldiers. Meanwhile, other North Vietnamese troops moved parallel with Route 13 from the south, attacking the towns of Laikhe and Chontanh, below Anloc.

Heavy fighting broke out around Anloc April 8. Some engagements were fought inside the city as advance enemy elements made their way into the town. In a move aimed at rescuing the beleaguered Anloc garrison, the Saigon command April 9 ordered the 21st Division shifted from the Mekong Delta. The relief column moving up Route 13, however, reached only as far as 15 miles from Anloc because of heavy enemy resistance.

The major enemy assault on Anloc was launched April 13 as a force of 3,000 men spearheaded by 40 tanks stormed into the city. After more than 24 hours of close combat, the Communists captured half the provincial capital, with government troops holding the other half. Heavy U.S. B-52 raids on North Vietnamese troops one mile west of the city April 12–13 and fighter-bomber strikes in the general area the previous days failed to slow the Communist advance. The Saigon command claimed that 30 Communist tracked vehicles, including seven Soviet-made T-54 tanks, had been destroyed or damaged in the Anloc fighting.

The North Vietnamese troops in Anloc distributed leaflets, saying the Viet Cong planned to establish a government in "liberated Anloc" April 20.

Quangtri & other battle fronts. Enemy activity in Quangtri Province just below the demilitarized zone eased as more than 500 U.S. fighter-bombers and B-52s pounded Communist troop concentrations and antiaircraft positions above and below the demilitarized zone April 7. The American fleet pounding enemy targets from offshore was reinforced April 7. Three aircraft carriers were joined by a fourth and two cruisers reinforced five destroyers.

Although Communist activity in Quangtri was not as heavy as in the previous week, the Saigon command claimed a heavy toll of North Vietnamese soldiers in a series of engagements in the area. Saigon reported that government rangers killed 217 North Vietnamese in two battles four miles south of Quangtri city April 7. In a delayed report, the government command said more than 100 North Vietnamese had been killed April 6 in tank battles and air strikes around Dongha northwest of Quangtri city.

The North Vietnamese launched a massive assault against South Vietnamese positions west of Quangtri city April 9 but were thrown back with a heavy loss of life. Allied commanders reported that 1,000 of the enemy had been slain and 30 tanks destroyed. The exact number of government troop casualties was not given, but their losses were believed heavy. In the wake of the battle, several clashes were fought in the same area April 10. Saigon claimed 243 more enemy soldiers were killed. More clashes around Quangtri city and Dongha April 11 resulted in 111 enemy soldiers killed, while government losses totaled four wounded, according to Saigon.

Enemy activity erupted for the first time in three areas since the start of the North Vietnamese drive March 30 —in the Hue area, in the Central Highlands between Kontum and Pleiku and in the Mekong Delta. U.S. officers reported April 8 the Communist troops had cut the main highway between Kontum and Pleiku in several places. Most of the 33 B-52 missions flown in South Vietnam April 6–8 concentrated in the mountains west of Kontum. Government troops sweeping the area April 8 reported finding the bodies of 154 Communist soldiers. Ten government positions near Kontum were shelled by the enemy April 11, but continued B-52 strikes in the area apparently thwarted any bolder Communist move against the city.

The fighting near Hue was centered around Fire Base Bastogne, the government strongpoint 20 miles west, which came under North Vietnamese siege. The heaviest fighting occurred there

April 11, with government forces repelling a strong North Vietnamese attack. The enemy was reported to have lost 102 men killed.

Several hundred U.S. infantry troops were airlifted April 12 north from Danang to bolster American defenses at Phubai, 42 miles south of the DMZ, and at a Navy radar station at Tamky, near Hue. About 50 of a 142-man company at Phubai at first refused an order to go out on patrol, but later agreed to go. Many of the men complained about the danger of the assignment.

A score of government soldiers were killed in a series of scattered but coordinated small enemy attacks on militia and army outposts in the Mekong Delta April 7. The South Vietnamese claimed 40 of the enemy were killed. Viet Cong troops staged 19 more assaults on government positions in the delta April 8, killing an estimated 50 government soldiers and wounding more than 200. Another 15 Viet Cong assaults were carried out in the delta April 9.

Communist drive assessed. U.S. officials, including Ambassador to South Vietnam Ellsworth Bunker and Gen. Creighton W. Abrams, head of U.S. forces in South Vietnam, were reported April 8 to have informed the White House and Defense Department that the North Vietnamese offensive was an all-out drive that would last for months. Both officials said they believed the Communist objective was to capture Quangtri and Thuathien Provinces in the north, perhaps Kontum in the Central Highlands, and Tayninh and Binhlong Provinces near Saigon.

Interviewed April 8 by the Washington Post, Abrams said that the Communist push would "turn out to be a big mistake . . . an even bigger miscalculation" than the 1968 Tet offensive.

The U.S. repeated its pledge April 8 to do "what is necessary" to help South Vietnam stop the Communist drive, but said that it was not "contemplating the use of ground forces." The statement, made by White House Press Secretary Ziegler, said the U.S. would not limit its support to air and fire power and logistical assistance, but he declined to say what form the other aid would take.

B-52s strike North Vietnam. U.S.
B-52s began bombing deep inside North
Vietnam April 10 for the first time since
November 1967. The U.S. command said
the raids were "in response to the Communist invasion across the demilitarized
zone." The command refused to disclose the targets, but the Associated
Press said the B-52s struck the Vinh
area, 145 miles north of the DMZ. If
true, the Vinh area raid marked the
deepest penetration into North Vietnam
by B-52s.

The command also reported that
U.S. fighter-bombers had carried out
225 strike missions against North Vietnam April 6-9 and that two planes were
lost. One pilot was rescued and the other
was missing.

In a change of policy, the Defense
Department announced April 11 that the
U.S. command would no longer make
daily announcements about American
air strikes over North Vietnam. Department spokesman Jerry W. Friedheim said the object of the new policy
was to protect U.S. pilots who were
"flying against the most sophisticated
air defense in the history of air warfare." Reports on the air strikes would
be issued periodically at the discretion
of Gen. Creighton W. Abrams, U.S.
commander, Friedheim said.

The U.S. was reported April 10 to
have sent another 20 B-52s to Indochina,
raising the force to 70. Other American
plane totals in the area: 530 fighter
bombers, including 220 Air Force jets
in South Vietnam and 280 Navy fighters
on four aircraft carriers in the South
China Sea; and 30 Marine fighters that
had arrived earlier in the week from
Thailand.

China assails U.S. raids. China assailed American air strikes on North
Vietnam April 10 and described the raids
April 12 as representing a "serious incident of expanding the war."

A Foreign Ministry statement April
10 said the U.S. was "committing new
crimes against the Vietnamese people"
by employing more planes in its bombing operations and by increasing naval
shelling of North Vietnam. The ministry
said the Peking government endorsed
the North Vietnamese Foreign Ministry statement April 6 expressing the de-

termination of "the Vietnamese people
to smash all military adventures of the
U.S. aggressors."

The charge that the U.S. was widen-
ing the conflict was expressed by Premier
Chou En-lai April 12 at a meeting in
Peking with Nguyen Tien, North Vietnam's acting charge d'affaires. Tien formally handed Chou a copy of his government's communique of April 11 denouncing American "escalation" of the
war. Chou said China backed the declaration and pledged to give "all-out support and assistance to the Vietnamese
people" in their struggle against the
U.S.

North Vietnam's April 11 communique came close to acknowledging that
Hanoi's forces were fighting in South
Vietnam. The statement first accused
Washington of attempting to perpetuate
"the partition of Vietnam" and of constantly repeating "shopworn contentions" that the North was invading the
South. The communique then added:
"Wherever there are U.S. aggressors
on Vietnamese territory, all Vietnamese
have the right and duty to fight against
them to defend the independence and
freedom of their fatherland."

Denouncing the the the U.S.' "new extremely serious move of war escalation,"
the communique said that since April 6
hundreds of U.S. planes and American
warships "have launched unceasing attacks against North Vietnamese territory, including the city of Vinh."

The North Vietnamese government
issued another appeal to its people April
11 to press the fight against the U.S.
and South Vietnamese government. The
exhortation was contained in a report
on resolutions adopted at a recent meeting of the Central Committee of the
ruling Communist party. The report,
titled "patriotic fight and economic tasks
for 1972," stressed plans to expand the
economy, with greater emphasis on increasing agricultural yield.

Kissinger delays visit. A scheduled visit
to Japan by Henry A. Kissinger, President Nixon's national security adviser,
was postponed until "early May," the
White House announced April 11. The
trip was called off because of the intensified fighting in Vietnam. The White

House had announced March 29 that Kissinger would go to Tokyo April 15–18.

U.S. urged peace talk renewal. The U.S. disclosed April 13 that President Nixon had proposed to the Communists the resumption of the Paris peace talks it had canceled March 23. The disclosure was made in Paris by William J. Porter, head of the American delegation, as he was about to return to Washington.

Porter said Nixon's offer had been made in a message sent through a private channel April 1 and received "by the other side" the following day. The proposal called for resumption of the talks April 13, but the Communists' "only response to this overture came in the form of a mushrooming invasion of South Vietnam by North Vietnamese troops, and a classic prevarication in the Viet Cong statement that North Vietnamese ground troops were not involved in the military operation," Porter said.

The State Department April 13 indirectly confirmed that Nixon's message to the Communists contained the stipulation that the conference could resume only if the Communists halted their current offensive in South Vietnam. The department said the President's note contained a warning that "continued enlargement" of the Communist drive "would not be conducive to serious negotiations" in Paris.

Losses on all sides increase. The heavy fighting in South Vietnam resulted in a sharp increase in U.S., South Vietnamese and Communist casualties.

The Saigon command reported April 13 that 641 government troops had died April 2–8, compared with 466 the previous week. North Vietnamese and Viet Cong were said to have suffered 2,987 dead, compared with 2,150 in the March 26–April 1 period.

The U.S. command said its forces had lost 12 killed April 2–8. This was two more than in the previous week. Total American casualties since 1961 stood at 45,691 killed, 302,852 wounded and 1,536 missing or captured.

Battle losses soared even higher April 9–15, with government and Communist troops suffering a record weekly toll. South Vietnamese casualties were 1,002 killed, 2,656 wounded, and 408 missing. The South Vietnamese claimed 7,117 Communists were killed and 71 captured. U.S. casualties in the April 9–15 period were 12 killed, 63 wounded and 10 missing.

Senate approves war-power curbs. The Senate approved by a 68–16 April 13 a bill to limit the President's power to wage war without Congressional authorization. Despite the Administration's opposition to the measure, the large majority for passage included all four Senate Republican leaders. The bill explicitly exempted the Vietnam conflict from its provisions.

The bill specified that there were emergency situations in which the President could commit the armed forces to combat without prior Congressional approval, but it provided that any such action must cease within 30 days unless Congress sanctioned it. The emergency situations specified were an attack on the U.S. or its armed forces, imminent threat of such an attack or a threat to the lives of U.S. nationals in other countries or on the high seas.

Under an amendment adopted unanimously April 5, the President would be allowed to take military action beyond the 30-day limit to protect the lives of U.S. troops and U.S. nationals and citizens in danger on the high seas. The amendment also provided that the legislation would not be a barrier to U.S. officers' continued participation in the NATO joint command structure.

The bill specified that the President had no "specific statutory authority" to commit the armed forces to combat under any current treaties.

During debate, which opened March 29, the Senate overwhelmingly rejected Republican attempts to delay the bill for a determination on its constitutionality or for a study of the warmaking roles of Congress and the president. It also rejected, by 56–26 April 12, a GOP move to dilute the bill to conform with a version previously adopted by the House, which merely required a presidential report to Congress whenever armed forces were committed to combat without congressional sanction.

A proposal by Sen. Mike Gravel (D, Alaska) to require the U.S. to end its participation in the Vietnam war within 45 days unless Congress voted a declaration of war, was defeated April 11 by a 74–11 vote. Gravel also proposed that a test vote be taken on declaring war on North Vietnam, but this was tabled 78–7.

U.S. scored for peace talk lapse. The North Vietnamese delegation to the Paris peace talks asserted April 15 that it had accepted President Nixon's April 1 proposal to resume the meetings but that Washington had canceled the offer four days later.

The Hanoi representatives, who called for a resumption of the talks April 27, said there had been an exchange of at least six messages with the U.S., all "through a private channel," since the American cancelation of the talks March 23. The statement said one of the American messages, received April 11, rejected a North Vietnamese proposal for a meeting April 20 "under the pretext that the Vietnamese people had intensified their military activities in South Vietnam." The North Vietnamese statement rejected this argument as "absolutely untenable," charging that it was the U.S. that had invaded Vietnam, extended the war in Cambodia and Laos and intensified the bombing of North Vietnam.

The North Vietnamese statement differed from chief U.S. delegate William J. Porter's assertion April 13 that the Communists had responded to Nixon's bid April 1 by launching an invasion of South Vietnam. Porter April 15 refused to comment on the contradiction, referring the matter to the White House, which also refused comment.

Xuan Thuy, Hanoi's chief delegate, suggested April 17 that new secret talks could be held if the U.S. halted its air attacks on North Vietnam and resumed the regular meetings in Paris. Thuy said North Vietnamese Politburo member Le Duc Tho, who had held private meetings in 1971 with Henry A. Kissinger, Nixon's national security adviser, would return to Paris if the two conditions were met. If they were not, Thuy said, "then there is no basis for private meetings."

The U.S. delegation April 19 rejected Thuy's proposal as nothing new. Delegation spokesman Stephen J. Ledogar said "the mere presence in Paris of Le Duc Tho has not amounted to anything in the past, so his mere presence is not something to be bargained for." "We are interested in negotiation, not just an opportunity to talk" to Tho, Ledogar said.

Hanoi-Haiphong area bombed. The U.S. command in Saigon announced April 16 that waves of U.S. Air Force and Navy fighter-bombers and B-52 heavy bombers had struck the vicinity of the North Vietnamese port of Haiphong, 60 miles east of Hanoi. The attack on Hanoi was carried out a few hours later, but the command said B-52s were not involved in this raid. The command reported the strike on Hanoi April 17. It said the attacks on the two cities occurred within a 16-hour period.

The initial communique on the Haiphong attack said: "Targets included logistical facilities such as fuel dumps, warehouses, truck parks and other activities which are supporting the invasion of South Vietnam by North Vietnamese forces. In response to the massive invasion across the DMZ, previous B-52 strikes were conducted against military targets in the vicinity of Vinh and Binthuong. All B-52s returned safely."

A more detailed account by the U.S. command April 18 said 18 B-52s and about 100 Navy and Air Force jet fighter-bombers had carried out the raids on the supply dumps near Haiphong harbor. A second wave of 60 fighter-bombers hit petroleum storage areas on the outskirts of Hanoi seven hours later. A third wave hit the storage areas again later in the afternoon. (The previous deepest penetration of B-52s into North Vietnam had occurred April 10, when the bombers struck at Vinh, 145 miles north of the DMZ.)

The command acknowledged the loss of two planes in the operations. It said a Navy A-7 and an Air Force F-105 were shot down by ground fire.

The command also said other Air Force planes, F-4 Phantoms, flying north of the 20th Parallel between the second and third bombing waves, intercepted four North Vietnamese MiG-21s and shot down three of them just southwest of Hanoi. A fourth MiG was believed to have crashed after running out of fuel.

North Vietnam claimed 15 American planes, including a B-52, were shot down over Hanoi and Haiphong by ground gunners. A Hanoi broadcast April 16 said "the U.S. imperialists have sent many groups of planes to come and bomb and attack many populous areas in Haiphong city" and that other "waves of many fighters and bombers struck at areas both inside and just outside Hanoi."

A North Vietnamese report April 18 said 60 civilians had been killed in the attacks—13 in Hanoi and 47 in Haiphong. The wounded totaled 27 in Hanoi and 101 in Haiphong, the report said. Authorities claimed U.S. planes had flown more than 1,000 sorties over North Vietnam since April 6, killing or wounding several hundred civilians.

Attacks on Soviet ships protested—A Soviet note handed to American Ambassador Jacob D. Beam in Moscow April 16 charged that four Soviet ships had been struck and damaged during the American air strikes on Haiphong harbor that day. A government statement issued April 16 by Tass denounced the bombings of Hanoi and Haiphong as "crimes of the American military against the peoples of Indochina." The statement said Haiphong and "the suburbs of Hanoi were bombed and strafed. There are victims among the civilian population and serious material damage has been inflicted."

Moscow's protest, published April 17, said "the Soviet merchant ships Simferopol, Boris Lavrenev, Samuil Marshak and Selemdzha, anchored in the port of Haiphong, sustained damages in the form of numerous shell holes." The note made no mention of Soviet casualties, but said there were "dead and wounded among the port workers" loading the Soviet ships. The note demanded that the U.S. "immediately adopt strict measures to prevent similar provocations in the future."

An American reply to the Soviet protest, handed to Deputy Foreign Minister Anatoly G. Kovalev by Ambassador Beam April 16, declined to accept blame for the alleged attacks on the Soviet ships

but pledged "to continue to make every effort to avoid damage to international shipping." The note said the damage to vessels in Haiphong harbor could have been caused by North Vietnamese anti-aircraft guns. But if the American planes had damaged foreign ships in the harbor, "it was inadvertent and regrettable," the statement said.

Hanoi had reported the Soviet ship Simferopol hit and an officer wounded. Two other foreign ships also were reported damaged in the Haiphong raid—a British and an East German vessel.

U.S. jets strike North again—After a two-day lull, U.S. planes struck deep inside North Vietnam April 18, attacking supply and transportation centers up to 150 miles north of the demilitarized zone. All of these raids were on targets south of the 19th Parallel and no B-52s were involved. The same area was pounded by 125 missions April 19.

U.S. officials had reported April 14 that President Nixon had ordered B-52 strikes throughout North Vietnam's southern panhandle. The report had said up to 150 of the heavy bombers would take part in the attacks.

Gulf of Tonkin clashes. U.S. warships bombarding the southern panhandle of North Vietnam from the Gulf of Tonkin were challenged by North Vietnamese shore guns, speed boats and jet planes.

An American destroyer April 17 fired on two enemy patrol boats in the gulf, between the demilitarized zone and the 20th Parallel of North Vietnam. In a delayed report on the engagement, the U.S. command said April 20 that the warship sank one of the boats and probably damaged the other.

Another American ship, the guided missile destroyer Buchanan, was struck by North Vietnamese shore guns April 17. One crewman was killed and seven were wounded. The ship put into Danang harbor for repairs.

Two American destroyers and a cruiser pounding North Vietnamese coastal defenses April 19 were attacked by two Communist MiGs 20 miles north of the DMZ. One plane struck and destroyed the gun turret of a destroyer and wounded three sailors. Guided missiles from another ship in the task force shot down one of the MiGs and sank two North Vietnamese patrol boats in the area, it was reported.

The guided missile frigate Worden was accidentally fired on by American planes during the U.S. air strikes on Haiphong April 16. One sailor was killed and nine were wounded. North Vietnamese torpedo boats were in the vicinity at the time and it was first believed that the Worden had been fired on by the enemy vessels.

U.S. increases naval strength. While the U.S. was continuing to reduce the number of its Army ground troops in South Vietnam, it was increasing the size of its naval force in the area, the U.S. command reported April 17.

According to the command, the number of offshore naval personnel had nearly doubled the previous week to 34,-000 men. One thousand more Marines were sent into the country, raising the corps' force to 1,400. An additional 5,000 soldiers were removed from South Vietnam, reducing the total force to 85,000.

Chou scores U.S. 'escalation.' Chinese Premier Chou En-lai assailed the American raids on Hanoi and Haiphong, April 16, asserting that the U.S. had "embarked on the old track of war escalation." The attacks on the two cities as well as an "unprecedented amount" of U.S. air and naval assaults in South Vietnam were "in defiance of the opposition of the people of the world, including the American people," Chou said.

The reaction of other Asian countries to the bombings varied. The nations aligned with the U.S. responded with either strong approval or reserved comment. They included Japan, South Korea, the Philippines, Indonesia, Singapore, Malaysia and Nationalist China.

India and North Korea joined China in condemning the air strikes. A Pyongyang statement April 18 called the bombings "an atrocious crime against the Vietnamese people."

Soviets accuse China on Red support. The U.S.S.R. accused China April 19 of rejecting a Soviet proposal for joint support of the Vietnamese Communists.

A Moscow broadcast beamed to China said Peking had "refused to issue a joint statement denouncing U.S. crimes" in Vietnam and had turned down "any step for united action in support of the Vietnamese patriots." The broadcast noted that the Soviet Union had provided North Vietnam with material and political assistance, while China, it charged, merely issued statements on Hanoi's behalf. The broadcast added: "The authorities in Washington have long treated such statements casually, especially since Nixon's China visit, because the U.S. ruling clique is well aware that the Chinese ruling clique, to carry out its selfish political conspiracy, is prepared to sacrifice the interests of the people of various countries in Asia."

Chinese Premier Chou En-lai April 5 had vowed continued support to the Vietnamese Communists in their struggle against the U.S. "war of aggression." His statement was made in a filmed interview in Peking with British journalist Felix Greene and was broadcast over NBC television April 19. The premier pledged that if the U.S. "war of aggression against Indochina does not stop. . . . and the bombings are expanded, the free Indochinese peoples can only fight on to the end and the Chinese people will certainly support them to the end."

Chou characterized President Nixon's trip to China in February as "at least a start" toward the understanding of each other's views. "The most outstanding question in the Far East remains that of the United States war of aggression against Vietnam and Indochina," he said.

Communist aid to Hanoi drops. Arms aid given to North Vietnam by the Soviet Union and other Communist countries totaled about the same in 1971 as in the previous year but was well below the peak reported before the U.S. halted the bombing of the North in 1968, U.S. government sources reported April 11.

According to the figures cited by U.S. intelligence:

China, the Soviet Union and other East European Communist nations provided North Vietnam with $1.02 billion in economic and military help in 1967, $756 million worth in 1970 and $775 million in aid in 1971. North Vietnam had received $505 million in Soviet arms aid in 1967, $70 million in 1970 and $100 million in 1971. Soviet economic aid to Hanoi came to $200 million in 1967, $345 million in 1970 and $315 million in 1971. Chinese military assistance to North Vietnam totaled $145 million in 1967, $85 million in 1970 and $75 million in 1971. Peking's economic aid in those three years came to $80 million, $60 million and $100 million respectively.

Communist aid figures for 1972 were not available.

Rogers, Laird defend bombing. Secretary of State William P. Rogers told a televised hearing of the Senate Foreign Relations Committee April 17 the Nixon Administration would take "whatever military action is necessary" to repel North Vietnam's "massive invasion" of South Vietnam.

He justified the renewed bombing of North Vietnam, including the raids on Hanoi and Haiphong, as necessary (1) to protect the 85,000 U.S. troops remaining in South Vietnam, (2) to guarantee continuance of the troop withdrawal program and (3) to give the South Vietnamese a chance to defend themselves against the North Vietnamese invasion.

Rogers' testimony at the hearing, originally scheduled to consider the foreign aid bill, was the Administration's first explanation of the renewed bombings. The only immediate comment from President Nixon was contained in a report April 17 that he had remarked to a member of Congress at a Capitol Hill luncheon that "you have to let them have it when they jump on you."

Rogers' defense of the bombings was reinforced by Defense Secretary Melvin R. Laird, who appeared before the committee April 18 and, in a verbal joust with Chairman J. W. Fulbright (D, Ark.), defiantly asserted that protection of U.S. personnel was sufficient reason in itself to justify the bombing. Fulbright questioned whether there was any connection between the bombing and protecting the GIs. Laird countered that that was Fulbright's, not his, assumption.

Rogers said only "military targets" had been bombed in the Haiphong area and Laird and Adm. Thomas H. Moorer, chairman of the Joint Chiefs of Staff,

who accompanied Laird April 18, said the raids there and in the Hanoi area had been effective and precise. Some of the Hanoi targets were said to have been about six miles from the center of the city.

On other points, Rogers told the committee that the U.S. would not resume negotiations during "this major invasion," that the North Vietnamese were "lying through their teeth" in claiming their forces were not fighting in South Vietnam, that the Administration had ruled out use of nuclear weapons and reintroduction of U.S. ground forces in the situation but retained every other military option to repel the enemy's "naked aggression."

In reply to skeptical questions about the effectiveness of the Vietnamization program in light of the enemy action, Rogers said the South Vietnamese had been fighting "very well" and if the enemy offensives were turned back South Vietnam would be "able to defend itself successfully in the future." He said the bombing would slow the invasion and "result in a failure of these offensives."

The committee questioned Rogers about the status of President Nixon's planned Moscow trip, especially in view of Soviet complaints of bombing damage to Soviet ships in Haiphong harbor. Rogers said there was "no evidence" that the trip would be canceled.

Laird, however, was critical of the Soviet Union in his testimony April 18. He said there had been "no restraints" set by the Soviet Union on the military equipment it provided to North Vietnam and the current enemy invasion would not have been possible without the Soviet aid. On the other hand, he said, the U.S. had been "very careful" to provide South Vietnam only military equipment that could be used for an "in-country capability" of defending its security.

Laird indicated that the U.S. response to the enemy invasion could underscore for North Vietnam and the Soviet Union the need for military restraint. The U.S. had been "very restrained," he said, but was "answered by an invasion" across a demilitarized zone in "flagrant, massive violation" of the 1968 understanding that had ended the previous bombing of the North. The violation, he said, "must be treated as a very serious matter."

Laird, like Rogers, stressed that all North Vietnam was subject to bombing as long as the invasion lasted. He said the Administration had contingency plans to seal off Haiphong harbor to stop the entry of military shipments and he "would not rule out" that possibility.

Before testifying April 18, Laird denied reports from Saigon that the bombing of the Hanoi-Haiphong region had been suspended by President Nixon to see if there would be any political response from the North Vietnamese. "The bombing continues south of the demilitarized zone, in the demilitarized zone and north of the demilitarized zone," he said. A White House statement later April 18 called Laird's statement "the authorized position" of the U.S. government.

Panel votes war-funds cutoff—Meeting after Rogers' appearance April 17, the Senate Foreign Relations Committee voted to approve a cutoff of funds for all U.S. combat operations in Indochina after Dec. 31, subject to an agreement for release of American prisoners of war. In the form of an amendment attached to a State Department appropriation authorization, the fund cutoff was proposed by Sens. Frank Church (D, Idaho) and Clifford Case (R, N.J.) and supported by several Democrats and Republicans Jacob K. Javits (N.Y.) and Charles H. Percy (Ill.). Sen. George D. Aiken (Vt.), ranking Republican on the committee, cast the lone vote against the amendment, although Sens. John Sherman Cooper (R, Ky.) and William B. Spong Jr. (D, Va.), abstained.

Fulbright said in a television interview April 9 the issue of a war-funds cutoff could be a "very live" one in Congress. The recent enemy offensive in Vietnam proved Vietnamization was not "a valid way" to end the war, he said. "The negotiation process is all." He called the U.S. bombing "a major re-escalation of the war."

Democratic aspirants vs. raids. The resumption of the bombing of North Vietnam was denounced by several Democratic Presidential contenders and

appeared to have revived the war as a political issue. A Republican counter-attack was led by Sen. Barry Goldwater (Ariz.), the 1964 GOP presidential candidate.

The Democrats commenting viewed the enemy offensive in Vietnam as proof of the failure of Vietnamization. They warned that the bombing was a dangerous and reckless re-escalation of the war. They called for an immediate renewal of peace negotiations and accused President Nixon of failing to keep his 1968 campaign promise to end the war.

Sen. Edmund S. Muskie (D, Me.) pledged April 17 to withdraw all U.S. forces from Indochina within 60 days of his inauguration if he was elected president. He said he would "cut off military aid to the government in Saigon if it is not making substantial progress toward peace."

Sen. George McGovern (D, S.D.) said April 7 that the bombing would not end the war and the only way to end it was "to recognize we made a mistake and to set a date now to terminate operations."

Sen. Hubert H. Humphrey (D, Minn.) campaigned against the bombing as "dangerous retaliation" but encountered heckling April 18 from a student audience because of his identification with Vietnam policy during the Johnson Administration.

Gov. George Wallace (D, Ala.) and Sen. Henry M. Jackson (D, Wash.) did not join the anti-bombing chorus. In statements April 18, both supported whatever action was deemed necessary to insure the safe withdrawal of U.S. troops. Wallace said he accepted the Administration explanation that the bombing was necessary. Jackson said that the air strikes against Haiphong had come six years "too late" and that he was puzzled about why it was mounted now when most GIs had been withdrawn.

Other Democrats also attacked the bombing: Senate Majority Leader Mike Mansfield (Mont.) said April 3 that bombing North Vietnam "will not bring about a settlement." Sen. Edward M. Kennedy (Mass.) denounced the bombing April 17 as dangerous "brinkmanship." Sen. Harold Hughes (Iowa) called it a "reckless gamble" April 17 and

Sen. Alan Cranston (Calif.) said the same day it reflected a "false vision of military victory."

Goldwater defends bombings—Sen. Goldwater made a series of statements defending the renewal of bombing. He said April 3 that the raids against North Vietnam were preferable to "dilly-dally bombing" aimed at enemy supply shipments. He advocated April 7 the bombing of "every conceivable" supply target in the North, and he pointed out April 16 he had been advocating such action for nine or 10 years. He added, "With our accurate bombing, I feel there's no worry about hitting civilians."

In the Senate April 19, Goldwater assailed the Soviet Union as "the principal culprit" on the enemy raid and said, "If a Russian ship is hit, that's too damn bad. I hope we hit them all. They have no business being in Haiphong. I would rather blow the living daylights out of Haiphong than lose one more American life."

Republican senators also rebutted in Senate debate April 19 Democratic charges that the President was endangering chances for peace in order to preserve the Thieu regime in Saigon.

Goldwater introduced April 19 a resolution condemning the North Vietnamese as aggressors and endorsing Administration policy in Vietnam, but an objection by Senate Democratic Whip Robert C. Byrd (W. Va.) prevented immediate consideration of it.

Sen. Gordon P. Allott (Colo.), chairman of the Senate Republican Policy Committee, also denounced "the reckless rulers in the Kremlin" for fueling Hanoi's war machine. He told the Senate April 19 that Communist governments "cannot expect to be completely immune from all the risks of the war" and should "take the sensible precaution of staying out of the war zone" if they wanted safe shipping.

House Republican Leader Gerald R. Ford (Mich.) April 17 dismissed warnings about the risk of an international incident in the bombing of Haiphong as a "red herring."

Vice President Spiro T. Agnew defended the bombing and characterized the U.S. Vietnam effort as one "of the most moral acts that this world has ever seen" in a speech to California Republicans April 8 in Palo Alto.

Sen. Robert Dole (Kan.), Republican national chairman, advised the Democratic presidential challengers April 16 to review the nation's Vietnam war role under Democratic Administrations before attacking a President who was "getting us out of their war."

House Democrats vote pullout—The House Democratic caucus passed a resolution by a 144–58 vote April 20 ordering Democrats on the House Foreign Affairs Committee to report to the floor within 30 days a bill "promptly setting a date" to end "military involvement in and over Indochina," provided U.S. prisoners were released.

The speaker of the House, Carl Albert (Okla.), voted for the motion after language was inserted condemning the "military invasion of South Vietnam by the forces of North Vietnam." Albert said the vote was binding on committee members unless they felt constrained by pledges to constituents or by constitutional questions. The Foreign Affairs Committee chairman, Thomas Morgan (Pa.), who was not present at the vote, said he would allow the committee to act on a bill.

It was the first time that House Democrats took so strong a stand on ending the war.

Antiwar protests renewed. Hundreds of antiwar demonstrators were arrested April 15–20 in incidents across the country as the escalation of the bombing in Indochina provoked a new wave of protests centered on college campuses and near military or military-industrial installations.

Maryland Gov. Marvin Mandel ordered 800 National Guardsmen onto the campus of the University of Maryland at College Park April 20, and imposed a curfew. Demonstrations against the war and against the Reserve Officers Training Corp (ROTC) had begun on the campus April 17 and had culminated in two days of pitched fighting between state police and up to 2,000 students who blocked traffic on nearby U.S. Route 1. Several hundred were arrested.

At Columbia University in New York, President William J. McGill April 20 ordered suspension of all classes the following day. McGill's order came after 250 students had broken up a meeting of the University Senate that had been discussing a one-day strike. The students were protesting Columbia's summoning of police, who had been called to the campus April 20 to enforce a court injunction barring coercive picketing of the School of International Affairs and other buildings.

Other campus violence was reported at Harvard University (Cambridge, Mass.) April 18 and Boston University April 20; offices in both schools were ransacked by a few hundred protesters and arrests were made. Arrests or minor violence were also reported at the University of Wisconsin in Madison, and Stanford University in Palo Alto, Calif. April 17, at Rutgers University in Newark, the University of Oregon in Eugene and in Madison again on April 19, and at the University of Massachusetts at Amherst April 20.

National Student Association (NSA) president Margery Tabankin issued a call April 17 for a national one-day student strike, after a meeting of student leaders from 30 colleges. Letters were sent to NSA's 515 member colleges, and by April 20 a number of campuses had endorsed the strike call. Demonstrations were reported at scores of campuses, often directed at ROTC and military recruitment activities. (Recruitment was suspended at the University of Massachusetts April 20 by President Robert Wood.)

The presidents of the eight Ivy League colleges and the Massachusetts Institute of Technology (Cambridge, Mass.) issued a statement April 19 condemning the renewed bombing raids on North Vietnam, and supporting antiwar protests "if they are not at the expense of the rights of others" or the "educational and scholarly" activities of the schools.

A spokesman for the Student Mobilization Committee said in Cambridge, Mass. April 20 that 44 New England colleges had seen some form of antiwar protest in the past few days.

At the Alameda Naval Air Station in California, 41 demonstrators were arrested April 17, and in San Francisco the same day, 16 protesters, including 12 members of Vietnam Veterans Against the War, were arrested while occupying an Air Force recruiting station. In Dayton, Ohio April 20 160 persons, most of them Antioch College students, were arrested while trying to block the gates of Wright Patterson Air Force Base.

Police arrested 60 persons standing in the entrance of a United Aircraft plant in Stratford, Conn. April 17, protesting production of assault helicopters used in Vietnam.

In Washington more than 200 were arrested April 15 for demonstrating without a permit in Lafayette Park, across from the White House.

Hanoi version of 1968 'understanding'. At a news conference in Paris April 20, North Vietnam's chief negotiator, Xuan Thuy, released Hanoi's version of the private talks that led to the halting of the U.S. bombing of North Vietnam Oct. 31, 1968 and the agreement to hold four-sided peace talks in Paris beginning in January 1969.

The Hanoi version refuted U.S. contentions that in return for the bombing halt, North Vietnam had agreed tacitly not to violate the demilitarized zone between the two Vietnams, not to shell populated areas in South Vietnam, and not to interfere with U.S. reconaissance flights over North Vietnam.

According to the North Vietnamese document, the U.S. negotiator in 1968, Ambassador W. Averell Harriman, had first insisted on the following "circumstances" for a bombing halt:

■ Restoration of the demilitarized zone.

■ No military build-up by the two sides.

■ The start of substantive talks in which each side could be free to raise any question. The U.S. side would include Saigon representatives, and Hanoi could invite whatever representatives it chose.

■ No major attacks against Saigon, Hue and Danang.

North Vietnamese negotiator Le Duc Tho, the document continued, had rejected Harriman's conditions. In subsequent meetings, Harriman allegedly insisted only on the participation of the Saigon government in future negotiations in return for an unconditional bombing halt.

At a meeting Oct. 15, 1968, Harriman reportedly announced that the U.S. was prepared to stop bombing and all other acts of force if the other side agreed to begin "serious talks" the day after the bombing halt. Xuan Thuy replied that after an unconditional bombing halt North Vietnam would accept a foursided peace conference.

Hanoi said it had asked that the unconditional agreement to halt bombing be placed in the minutes of the meetings, and Harriman replied Oct. 24: "We recognize your statement about 'no condition,' Therefore we are quite ready to assure you that, in any statement on the cessation of the bombing, the United States government will not refer to any word such as the word 'conditional.' "

Hanoi added that the U.S. refused to put that agreement in the minutes, and after some argument, Hanoi consented to leave it out. At the last meeting Oct. 30–31, 1968, Thuy said, "We understand that this is an unconditional cessation of the bombing."

Thuy explained April 20 that although the agreement was kept out of the minutes, both sides had kept records of what had been said.

U.S. reply—The State Department charged April 21 that Hanoi was trying to rewrite history in denying there was an understanding that it would show military restraint in return for the 1968 bombing halt.

State Department spokesman Robert J. McCloskey said the document released by Thuy was heavily edited and "designed obviously to support arguments made from time to time by North Vietnam." However, McCloskey refused to make public a documented U.S. version of the exchanges that preceded the bombing halt.

Battle for Anloc. The fierce fighting that had broken out around Anloc April 8 raged through April 20, with the defenders of the capital of Binhlong Province coming under increasing attacks by North Vietnamese and Viet Cong forces. Government reinforcements that had

been trying since April 10 to move north on Route 13 to reach the isolated 9,000 defenders of Anloc remained unable to break through enemy defenses on the road.

U.S. B-52s and Navy fighter-bombers pounded enemy troops around Anloc April 15, reportedly killing 200 of them. North Vietnamese troops struck at Anloc from all sides that day, using tanks and artillery. The Viet Cong radio reported April 15 that its forces had "liberated" Anloc and that they had "completely destroyed" government troops in the city.

The Viet Cong claim was contradicted by a Saigon report April 16 that said all North Vietnamese troops and tanks had been driven out of Anloc. The Communists had been in control of half the city during heavy fighting April 13.

North Vietnamese tanks pushed into Anloc April 18, but were driven out by government defenders, the Saigon command said. The city came under further Communist artillery and tank assaults April 19–20. Six enemy tanks were destroyed in the April 20 fighting and 52 of the enemy attackers were slain, according to South Vietnamese military authorities.

Other military developments—North Vietnamese and Viet Cong troops April 19 overran Hoaian, district capital of Binhdinh Province in the Central Highlands. An American adviser reported April 20 that the government defenders had abandoned the town without being attacked by the Communist troops surrounding it. It was said the decision to yield Hoaian had been made April 18 when it became apparent that government reinforcements would not reach the town.

In other fighting in Binhdinh Province, the Communists had cut strategic Route 19 at the Ankhe Pass between the coastal city of Quinhon and Pleiku. A senior American adviser, John Paul Vann, said April 20 that about 200 South Koreans had been killed or wounded attempting to break through a North Vietnamese roadblock at the pass. Vann estimated that in scattered and gradually intensifying fighting in the Central Highlands since early April "the government forces had lost 1,100 killed or missing and had inflicted losses of 5,300 deaths on their enemies."

Government troops had suffered a previous setback in the Central Highlands April 15 when North Vietnamese soldiers drove them out of Fire Base Charlie, 20 miles northwest of Kontum city.

In fighting 60 miles north of Quinhon April 16, North Vietnamese forces were repelled in attacking the rear base of government infantry regiment. The enemy lost 220 killed while government casualties were placed at 26 killed and 23 wounded.

In the northern provinces, Hanoi forces fought two engagements with South Vietnamese troops near Dongha. Government troops assisted by tanks and artillery killed 109 of the enemy while suffering only one fatality.

Fire Base Bastogne, 19 miles west of Hue, remained under North Vietnamese siege, but was resupplied April 16 by parachute and some government troops who slipped through enemy forces that had been surrounding the strongpoint since April 11. The base's 500 defenders had been running low on food, water and ammunition the previous three days.

Communist rockets struck Danang April 15, killing 13 civilians and wounding 22.

The U.S. command reported April 21 that three American planes and eight crewmen had been lost in Quangtri Province just below the DMZ at the start of the North Vietnamese offensive March 29. The announcement was delayed while unsuccessful rescue operations were under way.

Although military activity in Quangtri Province remained relatively quiet, officials in Washington predicted April 20 that the North Vietnamese were preparing for a long campaign in that sector. The prediction was based on a report that advance elements of Hanoi's last combat division remaining in North Vietnam were entering the demilitarized zone toward the fighting in South Vietnam. The division, identified as No. 325C, totaled 10,000 men and was said to be accompanied by tanks, long-range artillery and antiaircraft weapons. No. 325C was said to be the

last of 13 North Vietnamese combat division committed to operations in South Vietnam, Cambodia and Laos.

Raids on North continue. U.S. bombers struck North Vietnam April 21 and 24 in the vicinity of Thanh Hoa, 80 miles south of Hanoi.

The April 21 raids were carried out by B-52s and by Air Force and Navy fighter-bombers. All the B-52s returned safely, but an Air Force F-4 Phantom was brought down 42 miles southeast of Thanhoa. Its two crew members were rescued at sea.

The U.S. military command in Saigon declared April 21 that the attacks had been directed at "military targets in North Vietnam that are helping to support the Communist invasion across the demilitarized zone into South Vietnam." According to the dispatch, none of the raids had been near Hanoi or Haiphong and they had all taken place "in areas where the enemy has been assembling and moving supplies and troops to support the invasion forces."

An F-4 Phantom was shot down April 23 east of Donghoi and the guided-missile destroyer Benjamin Stoddert was hit by enemy coastal fire. No injuries were reported.

In the April 24 attacks, American planes flew more than 100 missions against targets in the Thanh Hoa area. One B-52 had to return to Danang after suffering light damage.

(The U.S. command April 21 announced the end of a 20-day search-and-rescue operation in which four planes and a helicopter were lost in Quangtri Province. Sixteen U.S. airmen were presumed dead.)

Cambodia: Communist advance in southeast. Communist troops had taken effective control of all Cambodian territory east of the Mekong river along the border with South Vietnam, except for government strongholds such as the provincial capital of Svayrieng, the New York Times reported April 25.

Communist forces broke through government positions along Route 1 April 20, seizing a 50-mile stretch of the highway and posing a threat to Saigon, 40 miles to the southeast. The collapse of government positions began with the fall of the market town of Kompong Trabek, 50 miles southeast of Pnompenh, where 450 of the town's 500 defenders were either killed or captured.

Communist troops April 24 overran an important government outpost near Svayrieng, 68 miles southeast of Pnompenh, which had been under siege since April 15. Another southeastern provincial capital, Preyveng, 27 miles from Pnompenh, was also under siege.

Elsewhere in Cambodia:

Rebel forces cut off and surrounded 1,000 government troops near the temples of Angkor Wat, 145 miles north of Pnompenh, April 17. A government relief column trying to reach the troops April 18 was reported subjected to "fierce attacks."

Communist troops April 23 occupied the town of Kompong Trach, 75 miles southwest of Pnompenh near the border with South Vietnam. Joint Cambodian and South Vietnamese forces garrisoned in the town had been under heavy pressure for 17 days, and the town had briefly been occupied by 1,500 rebel troops April 9.

Communist troops were reportedly massing near Pnompenh April 26. Cambodian pilots reported sighting about 800 of the enemy 10 miles southwest of Pnompenh.

(Shooting broke out around the Pnompenh University law school April 26 after hundreds of students broke through a police cordon to give food to students barricaded inside the building. Military police had besieged the school, where 100 students demanding government reforms had shut themselves in six weeks before.)

(Two foreign journalists—Terry L. Reynolds of the U.S. and Alan Hirons of Australia—were reportedly captured by Communist troops on Route 1 south of Pnompenh April 26. Their capture raised to 19 the number of foreign newsmen missing in Cambodia.)

(The Cambodian command had barred foreign journalists from the southeastern front April 22 after accusing them of sensationalism and exaggerating government losses.)

Methodists ask pullout. A majority of 1,000 delegates attending the general

conference of the United Methodist Church in Atlanta April 25 approved a resolution asking President Nixon to withdraw all U.S. forces in Southeast Asia by Dec. 31, 1972 and asking Congress to stop funding these forces beyond that date. After defeating by a 534–405 vote another resolution praising U.S. efforts to end the war and condemning "the appetite of North Vietnam to wage cruel and inhuman war," the majority approved a statement calling U.S. involvement "a crime against humanity."

Nixon address on withdrawals. President Nixon announced April 26 that 20,000 more U.S. troops would be withdrawn from Vietnam over the next two months despite the intense North Vietnamese offensive launched in Indochina three weeks ago.

Addressing the nation by television and radio, the President also:

■ Expressed confidence about the Paris peace talks, scheduled to be resumed April 27;

■ Pledged to continue U.S. air and naval attacks against North Vietnam to stop its "massive invasion" of South Vietnam;

■ Reported that the South Vietnamese were defending themselves well and the invasion would fail if the U.S. continued to provide air support;

■ Appealed to the American public to be steadfast in support of the U.S. commitment in Vietnam.

The 20,000-man withdrawal, to be carried out by July 1, would reduce the authorized U.S. troop strength in Vietnam to 49,000 men. It was Nixon's eighth troop withdrawal announcement since he assumed office on Jan. 20, 1969, when the authorized U.S. troop strength in Vietnam was 549,500. It was the first announcement in which he did not promise another statement on completion of the latest phase of the pullout. U.S. troops had been leaving Vietnam at a rate of about 23,000 men a month under the last withdrawal announcement Jan. 13.

Hopeful on Paris peace talks—In his address, Nixon said the U.S. was returning to the Paris peace talks "with the firm expectation that productive talks leading to rapid progress will follow through all available channels." The U.S. negotiators would be at the table, he said, "with one very specific purpose in mind," "to get on with the constructive business of making peace." The first order of business in Paris, he declared, would be "to get the enemy to halt his invasion of South Vietnam and to return the American prisoners of war."

Hanoi assailed for invasion—The President assailed North Vietnam for its "massive invasion" of South Vietnam and its "unprovoked aggression across an international border," the demilitarized zone (DMZ). He declared that the North Vietnamese attack was in violation of the 1954 treaties on Indochina and Hanoi's 1968 understanding with the Johnson Administration that the bombing of North Vietnam would be halted in return for its pledge not to violate the DMZ nor shell civilian population centers.

"Whatever pretext there was for a civil war in South Vietnam has now been stripped away," the President asserted.

Saigon forces lauded—The President said that the U.S. commander in Vietnam, Gen. Creighton W. Abrams, had reported that the South Vietnamese were "fighting courageously and well" and were "inflicting very heavy casualties on the invading force."

Nixon said Gen. Abrams had reported: "there will be several more weeks of very hard fighting" and "if we continue to provide air and sea support, the enemy will fail;" The U.S. air strikes were essential to protect the U.S. troops remaining in South Vietnam and to assist the South Vietnamese in the current fighting; with the failure of the North Vietnamese offensive, "the South Vietnamese will then have demonstrated their ability to defend themselves on the ground against future enemy attacks."

Bombing to continue—Nixon said that he had rejected all suggestions that he halt the renewed bombing of North Vietnam. He asserted that U.S. air and naval attacks on military installations in North Vietnam "will not stop until the invasion stops." He said he had repeatedly

warned that the U.S. would retaliate against any Communist step-up in the war in order to protect U.S. troops, permit continuation of the withdrawal program and prevent "imposition of a Communist regime on the people of South Vietnam against their will, with the inevitable bloodbath that would follow for hundreds of thousands who have dared to oppose Communist aggression."

Americans asked to back policy—The President declared that the Communists "have failed in their efforts to win over the people of South Vietnam politically, and Gen. Abrams believes that they will fail in their efforts to conquer South Vietnam militarily." Their one remaining hope, he said, was to win in the U.S. Congress and among the American people "the victory they cannot win" among the people of South Vietnam or on the battlefield.

Bidding for the public's support of his Vietnam policy, Nixon said the stakes were "the cause of peace in the world." He warned that a Communist military victory in Vietnam would "enormously" increase the risk of similar wars in other parts of the world and stain America's record of world leadership.

Nixon vowed that "we will not be defeated and we will never surrender our friends to Communist aggression." He urged Americans to "be steadfast," if they faltered in Vietnam, he said, it would amount "to a renunciation of our morality" and "an invitation for the mighty to prey upon the weak, all around the world."

"Let us therefore unite as a nation in a firm and wise policy of real peace, not the peace of surrender, but peace with honor, not just peace in our time, but peace for generations to come," the President declared.

Kissinger briefs newsmen. The President's national security adviser, Henry A. Kissinger, briefed reporters April 26 prior to Nixon's address. Among his points: The Administration would ask Hanoi at the Paris peace talks to withdraw the troops that had crossed the DMZ; its position on the troops that had entered South Vietnam from Cambodia and Laos would be defined at the negotiating table; the purpose of the heavy U.S. bombing was to "defeat" the Communist offensive in South Vietnam by preventing seizure of provincial capitals or large sections of countryside, and to reduce the enemy's capacity to mount a major offensive later. The latter was the primary reason for the bombing of the Hanoi-Haiphong area, Kissinger said.

Peace talks resume. The Vietnam peace talks resumed in Paris April 27 after a month's break. President Nixon had suspended the talks indefinitely March 23.

Negotiators attending the meeting were William J. Porter, U.S.; Pham Dang Lam, South Vietnam; Mrs. Nguyen Thi Binh, Viet Cong; and Xuan Thuy, North Vietnam.

It was a fruitless session, each side accusing the other of aggression and of refusing to negotiate seriously. However, there were prospects of renewed secret talks between the U.S. and North Vietnam.

Hanoi spokesman Nguyen Minh Vy announced at the session that Le Duc Tho, a North Vietnamese Politburo member who had negotiated privately with U.S. presidential aide Henry A. Kissinger, would be in Paris by the end of the week. Vy said "it is probable there will be private meetings" after Tho's arrival.

The North Vietnamese and Viet Cong delegates had formally proposed resuming the talks April 20, indicating they would agree to meet whether or not the U.S. halted its current bombing campaign over North and South Vietnam. Hanoi previously had demanded an end to the bombing as a condition for resumption of the peace talks.

The White House replied in a statement April 25 that the U.S. and South Vietnam would resume negotiations provided the first order of business was discussion of measures to put an end "to the flagrant North Vietnamese invasion of South Vietnam." The U.S. had previously demanded North Vietnam stop its military offensive in the south.

In his televised address on Vietnam April 26, President Nixon expressed op-

timism about the negotiations, but warned that "we are not resuming the Paris talks simply in order to hear more empty propaganda and bombast from the North Vietnamese and Viet Cong delegates."

In his briefing for newsmen before the President's address, Kissinger, who recently had returned from a secret mission to Moscow, said "we have evidence" suggesting the time was right to resume the talks. According to the New York Times April 27, Kissinger gave the impression that he had received hints in Moscow that the talks might be productive.

(The Washington Post reported April 28 that Kissinger and Nixon statements April 26 implied the U.S. had indicated to the Soviet Union it would avoid bombing the Hanoi-Haiphong heartland of North Vietnam for a limited time to test that nation's willingess to bargain seriously for a peace settlement.)

Reaction in Congress. Nixon's address drew strong reactions April 27 from both sides of the aisle in Congress. Some Republicans held that critics of the President were abetting the enemy and some Democrats protested that the war should not be continued to preserve a dictatorial regime in South Vietnam.

In the House, Republican Leader Gerald R. Ford (Mich.) said that to continue the bombing until the enemy invasion stopped was "the right course" for the nation.

In the Senate, the President was defended by Sen. George D. Aiken (Vt.), ranking Republican on the Senate Foreign Relations Committee, who hinted that the Administration could not complete its troop withdrawal program by midsummer because of "encouragement given" North Vietnam "to escalate and prolong the war. "All I ask of the critics of President Nixon," Aiken said, "is please do not encourage this war to go on, please do not take the side of the enemy." Senate GOP Whip Robert P. Griffin (Mich.) made the same point and specifically directed it against Sen. George McGovern (S.D.), a leading war critic.

McGovern called the President's speech "a piece of political trickery and calculated deception to save the President's face and Gen. [Nguyen Van] Thieu's job" as South Vietnamese premier. He called Thieu "a dictator."

Another Democratic presidential candidate, Sen. Hubert Humphrey (Minn.), welcomed the resumption of peace talks but deplored the intensive bombing.

Sen. Edward M. Kennedy (D, Mass.) said Nixon's speech was replete with "obsolete cold war rhetoric" and assailed his "timetable for Vietnamization" as "a timetable for war" not peace. While backing the reopening of the Paris talks, Kennedy deplored the "total absence of any indication that ... [the President] is prepared to make a genuine compromise in the negotiations." Sen. J. W. Fulbright (D, Ark.), chairman of the Senate Foreign Relations Committee, said the President had "changed the character of the war" to "unlimited air and naval bombardment" and by so doing had "removed one of the normal human restraints upon the savage cruelty and inhumanity present in all wars." He protested that Americans would "continue to fight and die as long as it is necessary for them to do so in order to save the South Vietnamese government from military defeat."

U.S. protests continue. American protests against involvement in Indochina continued April 21–27, with rallies on the East and West Coasts, and demonstrations at several major universities and military installations.

In New York, a crowd estimated at 30,000–60,000 marched in the rain April 22, while a San Francisco rally attracted 30,000–40,000 protesters and another 10,000–12,000 took part in a Los Angeles march the same day. Smaller marches were held in Chicago and other cities April 22, and a few thousand marched in Salt Lake City April 24.

In Washington, 200 law school students protested at the Supreme Court building April 21 against the Court's refusal to review the constitutionality of the war. In Detroit the same day 15 protesters were arrested for blocking a federal building, and in Boston April 27 police arrested 44 demonstrators at a television studio when they demanded

time to reply to President Nixon's speech the night before.

About 95 protesters were arrested April 21 and another 35 April 24 trying to block the gates of the Westover Air Force base in Chicopee, Mass. An attempt to blockade the Groton, Conn. submarine base ended in 42 arrests April 26.

Seven crewmen of a Navy munitions ship jumped overboard April 24 near Middletown, New Jersey as the ship was leaving port escorted by canoes manned by antiwar protesters from Philadelphia. The day before, 21 civilian protesters had been arrested for attempting to interfere with loading operations. Several sailors on board had complained to the Navy Department April 20 about allegedly unsafe equipment and procedures. The crewmen were returned to the ship by Coast Guard vessels.

Campus developments—Although the national student strike called by some student leaders failed to materialize, protesters seized buildings or offices at several colleges and universities.

At Columbia, groups of counter-demonstrators ended the blockade April 27 of two of several buildings occupied by protesters. Police had been called to the campus April 25 to clear one of the buildings, and at least five students were arrested and several minor injuries incurred on both sides in the ensuing melee.

A group of black students at Harvard peacefully left an administration building April 26 they had occupied since April 20, demanding the University sell $18 million in Gulf Oil stock to protest the company's operations in Angola.

Sister Elizabeth McAlister, a defendant in the Harrisburg 7 case persuaded 350-Princeton students April 22 to end a 12-hour occupation of the Woodrow Wilson School of International Affairs, while at Cornell April 26 over 100 students occupied a library building, demanding an end to military research and the Reserve Officers Training Corp. (ROTC) at the University, and asking that University-owned stock in Gulf Oil be voted in favor of ending Angola operations. Similar demands were made by 400 University of Pennsylvania students and faculty members April 27 in a building they took over the night before. At Reed College, Portland, Ore., 200 students sat in April 25 at an administration building. Forty Boston University students conducted a sit-in April 21 in a dean's office, but 500 others were rebuffed April 24 when they tried to seize an administration building.

Violence was reported at the University of Michigan, where ROTC offices were ransacked and armed forces recruitment offices vandalized April 21. A subsequent march through Ann Arbor that day by 1,500 students was dispersed by police using clubs. Austin, Tex. police used tear gas and made at least five arrests to disperse a demonstration of University of Texas students. Arrests were also reported at Stanford and Syracuse Universities and at Boise State College April 21, while large peaceful rallies occurred at Yale and at Fordham University in New York April 21. That day about half the students at the University of California in Berkeley stayed away from classes in protest.

Army Chief of Staff Gen. William C. Westmoreland was hit by a tomato in El Paso, Tex. April 21 during a demonstration by civilians and some servicemen.

National Academy in antiwar vote. The National Academy of Sciences passed a resolution April 27 asking President Nixon and Congress to downgrade "reliance on military force" in American foreign policy, and to use American technology and resources to improve conditions in other countries. Nearly all the 125 members attending (out of 700 in all) backed the statement.

The conference also passed a proposal to send all members descriptions of any proposed classified military research for consideration before contracts were signed. Two members had resigned to protest classified research, which accounted for 2% of the Academy's yearly $35 million budget.

Heavy fighting in South Vietnam. North Vietnamese troops continued to exert strong pressure on three fronts April 28 after a week in which the ground war in South Vietnam was substantially expanded. In the Central Highlands and Binhdinh Province, the Communists appeared to be intensifying efforts to cut the country in two with a front stretching from Cambodia to the South China Sea. Kontum Province's capital city was surrounded, as was Anloc, capital of Binhlong Province between the Cambodian border and Saigon. In the north, invading forces penetrated to within several miles of Quangtri city.

Kontum & Highlands—An estimated 20,000 North Vietnamese soldiers were reported converging on Kontum by April 28 and enemy forces had cut Route 14 on both the north and south sides of the Central Highlands city. Their approach was speeded when Saigon forces abandoned more than half a dozen fire bases in the area. These included Fire Bases 5, 6, Yankee, Hotel, Dakto 2, Zulu, Victor, Metro and Bravo.

Tancanh, forward command post of the 22nd Division, was overrun April 25 and Col. Le Duc Dat, its commander, was listed as missing Fleeing government forces took refuge at Benhet, nine miles east of the Cambodian border, and others were reported April 26 to have regrouped in defensive positions 10–11 miles north of Kontum.

A government convoy was reported to have succeeded in fighting its way along Route 19 between the coastal town of Quinhon and Pleiku April 26.

John Paul Vann, senior U.S. adviser in the Central Highlands, said April 26 that South Korean troops had cleared the Ankhe Pass after more than two weeks of heavy fighting. Communist losses in the battle were put at 705, according to reports by the South Korean command, with the Koreans losing 51 killed and 15 wounded.

The defense of the area was hampered April 26 when Lt. Gen. Ngo Dzu, commander of Military Region II, embracing the Central Highlands, was taken to Saigon after suffering a heart attack. He was replaced by Maj. Gen. Duong Quoc Dong, commander of the Airborne Division. (The deputy senior U.S. adviser for the region, Brig. Gen. George E. Wear, had been flown out after collapsing from exhaustion.)

The Communist position in Binhdinh Province was enhanced April 25 by the capture of Fire Base Dunglieu, east of Kontum. Battalion-size North Vietnamese and Viet Cong units at Hoainhon, some 60 miles east of Kontum, were reported to have attacked remnants of the 22d Division's 42d Regiment, which had suffered heavy losses the previous week at Hoaian.

Anloc—The city's 8,000 defenders were subjected April 27 to 2,260 artillery shells, although little infantry or tank action was reported. A government spokesman said that in blunting an attack on the district town of Dautieng, 45 miles northwest of Saigon, South Vietnamese troops had killed 133 North Vietnamese and captured one. U.S. B-52s flew five missions of three planes each in the area immediately around Anloc, dropping bombs in rectangular patterns.

The Saigon command said April 23 that its planes had destroyed two North Vietnamese tanks one mile east of Anloc. Helicopters were able to land and evacuate some 200 300 wounded. A 10,000 man South Vietnamese relief force abandoned April 21 its drive up Route 13 to reach Anloc.

Quangtri—An unknown number of enemy troops broke through Quangtri's northern defenses April 27 and penetrated to within two and a half miles of the city. A Saigon spokesman listed the number of North Vietnamese killed at 317. He placed South Vietnamese casualties at 13 dead and 73 wounded.

U.S. intelligence officers reported April 27 that the North Vietnamese were moving artillery closer to the city. They said that the South Vietnamese defenders had destroyed 30–40 enemy tanks. Bad weather prevented B-52 raids in close support of government troops, but seven raids were reported as near as 10 miles to Quangtri.

South Vietnamese marines left Dongha and another base nine miles north of Quangtri April 28 after an attack by North Vietnamese troops. Three North Vietnamese tanks had been destroyed near Dongha April 23 when they forded the Cua Viet river west of the South Vietnamese defense lines. Government sources said 131 North Vietnamese troops were killed and two taken prisoner, while Saigon lost seven killed and 44 wounded.

Casualties heavy—The South Vietnamese command reported April 27 that in fighting during the week of April 16 22 it had lost more soldiers than in any other week of the war. The command said 1,149 of its troops had been killed and 3,376 wounded. It estimated that the number of North Vietnamese and Viet Cong killed was 4,890. No figure was given for enemy wounded. The U.S. command set its losses at 10 Americans killed, 78 wounded and 8 missing.

Military sources in Saigon April 23 said the South Vietnamese had suffered at least 10,000 casualties, with 3,000 men killed, since the beginning of the North Vietnamese offensive some three and a half weeks before. Enemy losses were estimated as 13,000 killed.

Nixon confident. During a visit to Treasury Secretary John Connally's ranch near Floresville, Tex. April 30, President Nixon told a group of guests that, according to the latest assessment by Gen. Creighton Abrams, the current enemy offensive there would continue in its intensity over the next four or five weeks, that the South Vietnamese would lose some battles and win some but would hold provided the U.S. continued its air and naval support.

The South Vietnamese were resisting "very bravely," according to Abrams, Nixon said. The President pointed out that the enemy had failed to rally to its cause the South Vietnamese people, more than 90% of whom, he said, were still under the government of South Vietnam.

Nixon stressed that the U.S. would use its military and naval strength against military tagets in North Vietnam and warned that "the North Vietnamese are taking a very great risk if they continue their offensive in the South." He said he believed the U.S. could limit its strikes to military targets "without going to targets that involve civilian casualties."

In upholding the air and naval strikes in North and South Vietnam "to prevent a Communist takeover" in the South, Nixon reiterated points set forth in his Vietnam speech April 26—that the strikes were necessary to protect American servicemen in Vietnam, to prevent a bloodbath in South Vietnam by the Communists if they took over, to avoid encouraging similar Communist war efforts elsewhere in the world and to prevent loss of respect for the office of president of the United States.

Nixon also told the group he would defend the oil depletion allowance against any Democratic push for tax reform. "The energy crisis of the 1980s requires more incentives for oil exploration," not less, he said.

Communists capture Quangtri city. North Vietnamese forces captured Quangtri city May 1. An estimated 8,000 South Vietnamese troops abandoned the city, capital of Quangtri Province, after putting up little resistance.

The loss of the city gave the North Vietnamese control of the entire province, the northernmost in South Vietnam. The Communist victory posed an immediate threat to Hue, capital of Thuathien Province to the south. Some North Vietnamese units were reported to have moved to within 15 miles of Hue, whose population was swelled to more than 300,000 by refugees fleeing Quangtri.

Hue itself was the scene of wild disorders. Government troops that fled to the city were reported May 3 to have gone on a rampage, looting, intimidating civilians and exchanging fire with other deserters. At least 500 deserters were rounded up in Hue and forced back into service.

The fall of Quangtri prompted President Nguyen Van Thieu to revamp his army command May 3. Lt. Gen. Hoang Xuan Lam, commander of the northern military region, was replaced by Maj. Gen. Ngo Quang Truong, who had been commander in the Mekong Delta. Brig. Gen. Vu Van Giai was relieved as commander of the Third Division, which was routed at Quangtri. Gen. Lam asserted later May 3 that he had not been dismissed, but had resigned because his troops had disobeyed his orders to defend Quangtri. Lam said: The defenders "withdrew without orders. Quangtri had not been hit yet. The order to hold Quangtri was not executed."

The Third Division commander and his staff, accompanied by 80 American advisers, had been flown out of Quangtri in four rescue helicopters. Third Division troops with 10 remaining American advisers had retreated toward Hue under cover of B-52 bomber attacks on the advancing enemy troops.

The North Vietnamese seizure of Quangtri was preceded by the capture April 28 of Dongha, seven miles to the north of the city and 12 miles south of the demilitarized zone. This led to a tightening of a Communist ring around Quangtri city and to heavy shelling which left many sections of the provincial capital in flames. An estimated 320 North Vietnamese were reported killed April 28 as they moved on Quangtri city.

North Vietnam claimed May 2 that its forces had killed, wounded or captured nearly 10,000 South Vietnamese and other allied troops in the five-day battle for Quangtri.

Communist pressure against Hue began to tighten with the capture April 28 of Fire Base Bastogne, a government strongpoint guarding the western approaches to the city. The base, under siege for a month, fell after enemy commandos penetrated the camp's barbed-wire defenses. The 500 defenders withdrew to Fire Base Birmingham four miles to the east, but continued to come under heavy ground and artillery fire. Another outpost 20 miles northwest of Hue, Fire Base Nancy, was pounded by enemy artillery May 2 and abandoned by the government defenders the following day. Fire Base Nancy was the northernmost position held by the South Vietnamese and their last base in Quangtri Province.

Viet Cong forms Quangtri regime—The establishment of a provisional revolutionary administration in captured Quangtri city was announced by the Viet Cong May 4. The governing apparatus was described by a Viet Cong broadcast as the Quangtri Provincial Capital Provisional People's Revolutionary Committee.

A four-point communique issued by the committee called on the South Vietnamese people to "eliminate the administration . . . set up by the United States-Thieu clique." It appealed to South Vietnamese soldiers, police and administrative personnel in the city to "turn in weapons, documents and radios" and warned they would be "severely punished" if they tried "to escape to continue to operate for the enemy." The communique said "everyone must strictly abide by security" and must refrain from stealing equipment "belonging to the army or left behind by the enemy." The statement said the revolutionary committee would welcome anyone cooperating with its rules.

U.S. intelligence specialists in Washington reported May 4 that the Communists had established similar provisional administrations in other villages and towns in captured Quangtri Province. The Communists also had formed a district-level administration in Locninh, the district capital northwest of Saigon captured April 6.

In a separate broadcast earlier May 4, the Viet Cong radio had appealed to the people of Hue and surrounding Thuathien Province to "take to the streets" to overthrow the Saigon government and to "fight until the Americans leave." It also urged South Vietnamese military forces to "'mutiny, drop their weapons, quit their ranks and return to the people." The broadcast said the recent Communist victories had created "the most favorable condition ever known for our people's anti-United States national salvation struggle."

Kontum surrounded—North Vietnamese troops surrounded the Central Highlands provincial capital of Kontum and threatened to cut South Vietnam in two, according to battlefield reports April 29. Enemy units were three to five miles from the city and were reported poised for a major assault. As the Communist forces moved closer, thousands of persons were evacuated from Kontum to Pleiku by plane and helicopter. An estimated 10,000 persons, including military men, were removed April 29-30.

Washington officials reported May 3 that a battle report received the previous day from Gen. Creighton W. Abrams, commander of American forces in South Vietnam, had pointed up the critical nature of the Communist offensive in the Central Highlands. Abrams was said to have expressed the belief that if Kontum could hold out for a "few days" the Communists might not be able to capture it.

Another serious situation appeared to be developing in the coastal province of Binhdinh, where the Communists had captured three districts in two weeks with little resistance. The North Vietnamese strengthened their hold on the northern section of the province by capturing Tamquan District May 1 and seizing Landing Zone English, six miles north of Bongson, May 3. Several hundred government troops abandoned Landing Zone English and made their way to the coast, where they were picked up by landing ships.

Col. Nguyen Van Chuc, the Binhdinh Province chief, warned May 2 that unless he received reinforcements immediately, the Communists would overrun all of Phumy District. Its capture, he said, would lead to the eventual loss of the entire province.

U.S. planes continued strikes in an attempt to blunt the North Vietnamese drive on all fronts in South Vietnam. Among the highlights of the raids, most of which occurred in the northern areas of the country: B-52s flew 28 missions April 30, the highest number ever carried out by the big bombers in a single day. Fourteen of the attacks were centered around Kontum.

U.S. fighter-bombers carried out 618 strikes on enemy targets May 3 and B-52s flew 24 missions. More than half the missions were flown against enemy targets in the Hue area.

B-52 raids on North assessed—The U.S. Air Force announced April 30 that B-52s had flown 720 sorties over North Vietnam April 20-29. The raids had destroyed or damaged 250 enemy trucks, logistics craft and port facilities, 19 bunkers and 16 warehouses and supply depots, the authorities said.

Cambodian military developments. Communist troops captured four Cambodian positions in Takeo Province, the Cambodian military command reported May 12. This brought to 11 the number of such positions that had fallen since the loss of the border town of Kompong Trach April 30. The command said 31 government troops and eight Communists had been killed in another clash in which Cambodian forces captured a bridge position on Route 5, linking Pnompenh with Battambang

Province, 40 miles northwest of the capital.

A force of 4,000 Cambodians launched a drive May 16 to recapture the temple ruins at Angkor Wat, occupied by the North Vietnamese for nearly two years. The attackers seized the Bakheng monument atop a hill in the area May 18. Two government probes directed at the east and west entrances of the temple May 19 brought Communist counterfire and resulted in the death of 21 Cambodian soldiers.

The provincial capital of Svayrieng in southeastern Cambodia came under heavy Communist attack May 25–28. About 20 of the enemy were killed May 27 with the help of allied planes. Four civilians were killed by enemy shelling of Svayrieng May 28.

Pnompenh came under daylight artillery shelling June 5 for the first time in nearly two years of war. Six persons were killed and 11 were wounded. The attacks were directed at the Defense Ministry building and in an area near President Lon Nol's villa. Pnompenh had previously come under enemy shelling May 14.

Gravel blocked on airing Vietnam study. The Senate, in an unusual secret session called by Sen. Mike Gravel (D, Alaska) May 2, rejected Gravel's efforts to publish excerpts from a classified Vietnam policy study in the Congressional Record. The 63 pages of excerpts questioned the effectiveness of the U.S. bombing of North Vietnam prior to 1969.

The study, called National Security Study Memorandum No. 1, was prepared for President Nixon immediately after his inauguration in 1969. It was compiled by the National Security Council staff under the direction of Henry A. Kissinger, the President's national security adviser, from responses to 28 questions submitted to military, intelligence and foreign affairs agencies.

An earlier effort by Gravel to place the excerpts in the Congressional record had been blocked April 25 by Minority Whip Sen. Robert P. Griffin (R, Mich.), who had said it would be "very unfortunate" if Gravel "takes it on himself to be the sole judge of the declassification of highly sensitive papers."

Gravel had said April 25 that the material demonstrated that President Nixon, in deciding recently to resume the bombing of North Vietnam, was "pursuing a reckless, futile, and immoral policy which he knows will not work, but which is intended to enable him to save face." Gravel handed out copies of the excerpt to senators then on the Senate floor and said he would supply copies to all other senators.

State Department spokesman Charles W. Bray III April 25 disputed Gravel's evaluation that the pre-1969 bombings were comparable to those currently underway in Indochina. He said the current situation "is something quite different from what was essentially a small-scale and guerrilla warfare" before 1969. The present use by North Vietnam, Bray said, of "greater conventional tactics, larger units, and tanks and heavy artillery, surface-to-air missiles, antiaircraft artillery" offered "individual targets which rarely or ever were available in the past and they are much more heavily dependent on logistics and resupply facilities, which are more accessible to retaliation from the air."

A summary of the Kissinger study was first published by the Washington Post April 25, prior to Gravel's move. The New York Times published excerpts April 26. Syndicated columnist Jack Anderson and Newsweek magazine also published early accounts of the study.

Some of the contents of the study:

The government's Vietnam policy makers often divided into two clear-cut groups: the Joint Chiefs of Staff, the U.S. military commander in Vietnam, the commander in chief of Pacific forces and the U.S. embassy in Vietnam generally took "a hopeful view of current and future prospects in Vietnam," while the Office of the Secretary of Defense, the State Department and the Central Intelligence Agency were "decidely more skeptical about the present and pessimistic about the future."

The two groups disagreed over the effectiveness of U.S. bombing in Laos and North Vietnam. The military and the U.S. embassy insisted it had succeeded, while the other groups said it failed. The Joint Chiefs of Staff had recommended resumption of bombing early in 1969.

They said it "would assure almost total interdiction of truck and water-borne movement of supplies into the demilitarized zone and Laos."

The two groups also disagreed over the effectiveness of "pacification" in South Vietnam's countryside. The military claimed the Saigon regime controlled three-fourths of the total population while the Defense and State Departments and the CIA offered "more cautious and pessimistic responses." Estimates by the two groups on the period required to bring the entire South Vietnamese population under Saigon's control ranged from 8.3 years to 13.4 years.

Both groups agreed that the South Vietnamese "could not, either now or even when fully modernized, handle both the Viet Cong and a sizable level of North Vietnamese forces without U.S. combat support in the form of air, helicopters, artillery, logistics and some ground forces." They felt the South Vietnamese alone could cope with just the Viet Cong forces.

Both generally agreed Hanoi had not entered the Paris peace negotiations out of "weakness." The State Department noted that the Soviet Union had played a major role in facilitating the Paris talks and it said "the Russians can use leverage upon Hanoi in measured, highly selective and carefully timed fashion."

The excerpts showed that the U.S. ambassador then in Saigon, Ellsworth Bunker, had predicted that North Vietnam's military prospects were "bleak" enough to force Hanoi to "make significant concessions" in the Paris negotiations.

U.S. cancels Paris peace talks. The U.S. and South Vietnam called an indefinite halt to the Paris peace talks following the 149th session May 4. The meetings had resumed on April 27 after a one-month break.

William J. Porter, chief American delegate, told newsmen after the May 4 meeting that the decision was made because of "a complete lack of progress in every available channel," an implication that secret talks had been held and were as deadlocked as the public meetings. Porter said the U.S. and South Vietnam had informed the Communists

that "we would not agree to set a date for the next meeting."

The Viet Cong representative in Paris, Mrs. Nguyen Thi Binh, delcared "if the Nixon Administration thinks it can use intimidation and force to subjugate the Vietnamese people, it is mistaken." Other Communist officials expressed the belief that the decision to cancel the negotiations might signal a new war escalation with the resumption of American air attacks on North Vietnam. Mrs. Binh and Xuan Thuy, the chief North Vietnamese delegate, denounced President Nixon's April 30 statement [See p. 324A2] on the need to prevent a Communist take-over and a "bloodbath" in in Vietnam. "The only bloodbath is the slaughter committed by the United States and the Saigon administration over the last 10 years," Mrs. Binh said.

At the 149th session, Porter had opened the meeting with questions he had posed at previous conferences. They ranged from "Will you discuss measures to end your invasion [of South Vietnam]?" to "Will you consider any solution that does not include the overthrow of the elected leadership in South Vietnam?"

The Communist reply to Porter reiterated queries submitted at the April 27 session: Would the U.S. "end its aggression" and would it "give a serious response" to the Communist peace plan?

Porter responded by asserting that the Communist statements "consisted of sterile denunciations, arrogant ultimatums and clumsy evasions. Let it be recorded that it is impossible to discuss with you particular subjects bearing on a peaceful settlement. That proof is as clear as your military aggression in South Vietnam."

The U.S. State Department indicated May 4 that Washington had been misled about North Vietnam's purported readiness to participate in "serious" negotiations. Department spokesman Charles W. Bray 3d noted that in his April 26 statement announcing that the U.S. was returning to the peace talks President Nixon had said it was doing so with the "firm expectation that productive talks leading to rapid progress will follow through all available channels."

(The resumption of the peace talks April 27 was said to have been worked out by Henry A. Kissinger, Nixon's national security adviser, in his meetings with Leonid I. Brezhnev, Soviet Communist party leader, in Moscow April 20–24. According to a Washington source quoted by the New York Times April 28, arrangements had been worked out with Hanoi and Moscow for the renewal of private talks as well.)

Tho reiterates Hanoi demands—Le Duc Tho arrived in Paris from Hanoi April 30 and said that he had come to negotiate with the U.S. "a just and equitable peaceful solution to the Vietnamese problem." In a statement that appeared to be intended as a rebuttal to President Nixon's April 26 address on the war, Tho repeated his government's main conditions for a settlement.

He said the U.S. would have to end the bombing of North Vietnam and "determine a deadline for the rapid withdrawal from South Vietnam of the totality of American troops and those of the other countries of the American camp." Those U.S. soldiers "that are against the war and aspire to be repatriated" would "not be the object of attacks on the part of liberation troops" as long as they did not participate in military operations.

Hanoi wanted the "immediate resignation of Nguyen Van Thieu" and a "change of policy of the Saigon administration," Tho declared. All "coercion and oppression of the people" would have to be abolished in order to insure implementation of "Article 14C of the 1954 Geneva agreements on Vietnam." (The article pledged the parties "not to engage in any reprisals or discrimination against persons or organizations by reason of their activities during hostilities, and to guarantee their democratic liberties.")

Tho also declared: "In South Vietnam, what we want is a government of national harmony with three components. We in no way want to impose a 'Communist regime' in South Vietnam, such as Mr. Nixon has fabricated."

State Department spokesman Charles W. Bray 3rd told reporters May 1 that Tho's statement had been "something of a disappointment." He added, however: "Quite frankly, we did not expect to find anything new in Le Duc Tho's public statement. In that respect, we were not surprised." A South Vietnamese spokesman said May 1 in Paris that there was nothing in Tho's remarks "which permits hope for a rapid end to the conflict. He only repeated the absurd and unreasonable demands formulated at the meeting table and repeated by the Communist side at the last session. . . . We are always ready to negotiate but we will never cede to armed pressure."

Kissinger-Tho talks rumored—A report that Henry A. Kissinger had met secretly with Le Duc Tho in Paris April 30 and agreed on a broad peace settlement was denied by the U.S. government May 3. The report, first circulated by the Paris newspaper France-Soir May 2, was reportedly confirmed by Vietnamese Communist sources in Paris.

According to the account, the U.S. had proposed a seven-day cease fire, and both sides had agreed in principle on a mutual troop withdrawal of U.S. and North Vietnamese forces, the exchange of prisoners and the resignation of President Nguyen Van Thieu. Kissinger and Tho also were reported to be in Paris negotiating the composition of the government that would take over in Saigon after Thieu's resignation.

Kissinger was said to have made another secret trip to Paris, presumably to meet again privately with North Vietnamese officials. He reportedly had left Washington May 1 and returned May 2. Kissinger was known to be in Washington May 3.

Charles W. Bray 3rd denied May 3 that the U.S. had proposed a seven-day cease fire. But he refused to confirm or deny that Kissinger had met with Tho. Bray said, however, that the Communists were misleading the public by "misrepresenting the substance cf discussions which have taken place."

U.S. builds up air, naval forces. The U.S. May 4 ordered 50 more fighter-bombers to Indochina and a sixth aircraft carrier with 75 planes to the waters off Vietnam. The additional planes would bring total American attack aircraft in the battle zone to nearly 1,000.

The decision to reinforce American air strength came amid reports that plans were underway to resume the heavy bombing of North Vietnam now that the Paris peace talks had been suspended. Renewed attacks on Hanoi and Haiphong were not ruled out.

The Defense Department May 4 released what it said were photographs of Communist-bloc supply ships in Haiphong harbor. The department also released pictures of Soviet-made tanks, heavy artillery, surface-to-air missiles and antiaircraft artillery it said were being used for the first time in the war. One of the weapons was a shoulder-fired SA-7 missile that homed on the heat generated by an aircraft engine. The weapon reportedly had recently downed one light plane and a helicopter in Quangtri Province. Department spokesman Jerry W. Friedheim said "sophisticated weapons had arrived through Haiphong and were providing "a new dimension to the battle."

Communists shell Cambodian capital. Viet Cong forces shelled Pnompenh May 6 and followed up the assault with an unsuccessful ground attack on a key bridge in the city only one mile from the American embassy.

About 25 rocket shells struck the downtown section of the city, killing two persons and wounding 44. Two American homes were hit but no casualties were reported. A ground attack involving about 100 Viet Cong was directed against Pnompenh's only bridge across the Bassac River leading to Route 1, the main road to Saigon. Government defenders, fighting the invaders from house-to-house, drove them back. The government reported that losses in the day's fighting totaled 28 dead, including 11 civilians, and 135 wounded. Communist casualties were not given.

In other ground action, Cambodian and South Vietnamese troops April 30 abandoned the village of Bavet and the border stronghold of Kompong Trach in the face of heavy Communist attacks. The withdrawal left the provincial capital of Svayrieng and its 40,000 refugee inhabitants isolated. The Cambodian command said 4,600 government troops and their 705 dependents had fled Bavet to South Vietnam. Svayrieng was on Route 1, 60 miles of which had been under Communist control for the past two weeks. Cambodian forces launched a counter-drive to reopen the highway but military authorities reported May 2 that heavy Communist resistance had stalled the action.

Cambodian troops, however, were able to reopen two major roads leading into Pnompenh in the previous 24 hours, military authorities announced May 3. They were Routes 5 and 7.

Cambodian troops May 8 abandoned Tani, a town near Kompong Trach, following heavy North Vietnamese assaults. Communist occupation of Tani, 58 miles sough-west of Pnompenh, gave them a 20-mile corridor leading from mountain sanctuaries to the Mekong Delta in South Vietnam.

Two more government positions, in Takeo Province 24 miles from the South Vietnamese border, fell to Communist forces May 9. This brought to six the number of Cambodian bases seized in three days of fighting.

U.S. senators return from China. Senators Mike Mansfield (D, Mont.) and Hugh Scott (R, Pa.), who returned from a visit to China May 7, filed separate reports with the Senate May 11 on conclusions reached as a result of their trip.

Mansfield said he thought it "illusory" to hope that, out of a desire to improve relations with the U.S., China would influence North Vietnam to end the war or release American prisoners. He also declared that "the new sorties into North Vietnam have tarnished the significance of the President's visit to China and, of course, the visit of the Senate's joint leadership. They have thrown into at least temporary eclipse the possibilities of Chinese-U.S. rapprochement."

Scott said the U.S. and China should "normalize relations to the greatest extent possible. At the same time we must remain alert to the fact that there are basic philosophical differences in our views of man and society."

Nixon Orders Ports Mined

Nixon orders ports mined. President Nixon announced to the nation May 8 that he had ordered the mining of North Vietnamese ports and interdiction of land and sea routes to North Vietnam in a move to prevent delivery of war supplies to that country. "Rail and all other communications will be cut off to the maximum extent possible," the President said, and "air and naval strikes against military targets in North Vietnam will continue."

The President stressed that the actions were not directed against other nations, such as allies of North Vietnam. "Their sole purpose," he said, "is to protect the lives of 60,000 Americans who would be gravely endangered in the event that the Communist offensive continues to roll forward and to prevent the imposition of a Communist government by brutal aggression upon 17 million people" of South Vietnam.

Pullout set if conditions met—Nixon said the interdiction and bombing would cease if the following conditions were met: the return of all U.S. prisoners of war, and an internationally supervised cease-fire throughout Indochina. Once these conditions were met, Nixon said, "we will stop all acts of force throughout Indochina" and "proceed with a complete withdrawal of all American forces from Vietnam within four months." This would permit, he said,

negotiations and a political settlement between the Vietnamese themselves.

The President, addressing the nation by television and radio, directed special remarks "to each of the major parties involved" in the Vietnam war—the leaders of Hanoi, the people of South Vietnam, the Soviet Union and the American people.

He asked Hanoi's leaders not to compound the agony of the North Vietnamese people "with continued arrogance" but to choose a peace that "guarantees true independence."

He told the South Vietnamese people they would continue to have the "firm support" of the U.S. and it was their spirit that would "determine the outcome of the battle."

Nixon told the Soviet Union that each nation must recognize the other's right to defend its interests and help its allies. But he said great powers should help allies "only for the purpose of their defense—not for the purpose of launching invasions against their neighbors." Doing otherwise would "seriously" jeopardize world peace, he cautioned, adding that significant progress had been made in negotiations on nuclear arms curbs, trade and other issues and that the Soviet Union should not "permit Hanoi's intransigence to blot out the prospects we together have so patiently prepared."

77

Nixon held out the prospect of "a new relationship" that could serve the interests of both countries and "the cause of world peace." "We are prepared to continue to build this relationship," he said. "The responsibility is yours if we fail to do so."

Nixon appealed to the American people for their support in his newly-stated policy, saying, "it is you, most of all, that the world will be watching."

"We Americans did not choose to resort to war," he said, "it has been forced upon us by an enemy that has shown utter contempt toward every overture we have made for peace."

In three years of negotiations, he said, the U.S. had "offered the maximum" any President could offer but Hanoi had responded with "insolence and insult" and "arrogantly refused to negotiate an end of the war."

There were "only two issues left for us in this war," Nixon said: the first involved the enemy's invasion, jeopardy to the GIs remaining in Vietnam and the "long night of terror" to the South Vietnamese if the Communists took over; the second involved the enemy's intransigence at the peace table and attempt to install a Communist government in Saigon.

In making his decision to interdict the enemy's supplies, Nixon said he rejected the alternatives of immediate withdrawal and continued reliance on negotiation to end the war. "By simply getting out," he said, "we should only worsen the bloodshed. By relying solely on negotiations, we would give an intransigent enemy the time he needs to press his aggression on the battlefield."

"There is only one way to stop the killing," the President said. "That is to keep the weapons of war out of the hands of the international outlaws of North Vietnam."

Rogers summoned from Europe—Further Presidential action on the latest Vietnam crisis had been foreshadowed when Secretary of State William P. Rogers was called back to the U.S. from a European tour to attend a National Security Council meeting May 8 preceding the televised presidential address.

Rogers was summoned from Bonn by the President May 7, the same day the White House announced postponement of a trip to Tokyo planned for May 11 by Henry A. Kissinger, the President's adviser for national security. Rogers was in Bonn during an eight-nation tour of Western Europe in preparation for President Nixon's scheduled visit to the Soviet Union May 22. (The State Department said May 9 Rogers would not resume his European trip, which would be continued by the Rogers' party.)

While in Brussels May 5 attending a meeting of the North Atlantic Treaty Organization, Rogers urged the members of the alliance to support Nixon's policy in Vietnam and warned that a precipitate U.S. pullout would undermine the trust put in the U.S. commitment to NATO. He also told the alliance the Soviet Union "bears a responsibility" for North Vietnam's invasion of South Vietnam and that the issue would be raised by Nixon in his Moscow visit.

While in London May 4, Rogers told reporters "strong military action" would have to be taken to counter the North Vietnam offensive in South Vietnam and that President Nixon would take "whatever military action" was necessary "to prevent a military takeover by force."

Connally, Kissinger advice sought—The National Security Council was composed, in addition to the President, who was chairman, and Rogers, of Vice President Spiro T. Agnew, Defense Secretary Melvin R. Laird and the director of the Office of Emergency Preparedness, George A. Lincoln. Kissinger also attended meetings as head of the council's staff. The meeting May 8 also was attended by Treasury Secretary John B. Connally Jr. The President reportedly had drafted his speech himself before the council meeting, which was considered a formality to confirm his policy. After the meeting, Nixon met privately with Connally and Kissinger to again review his decisions.

Prior to appearing on television that evening, Nixon briefed Congressional leaders at the White House, told them of his decisions and, reportedly, "gently" urged their support.

Kissinger discusses Soviet position. At a White House news conference May 9, Henry A. Kissinger, President Nixon's adviser for national security, described the latest Vietnam policy decisions as "very painful and difficult" but necessary because "no honorable alternative was available." While the closing of North Vietnam supply routes "involves some risks" and "short-term difficulties" for Soviet leaders, he said, the Administration concluded that it "did not involve an unacceptable risk" to the U.S.

Kissinger spoke of the "massive difficulties" for the U.S. arising from a situation the Soviet Union "permitted to evolve," the "real choices" facing both sides and of his opinion that "if one wants a genuine improvement in relations, as we do, one cannot also at the same time maximize the pressures all around the periphery."

The Administration still believed, he said, that "a new era in East-West relations" was possible and would "pursue it with the same intensity as before." The Administration was proceeding with preparations for Nixon's Moscow visit, he said, and saw no reason at the moment to postpone it.

Kissinger said the Vietnam situation had been discussed during his recent secret trip to Moscow and he did not believe "that there could be any doubt in the minds of the Soviet leaders of the gravity with which we would view an unchecked continuation of a major North Vietnamese offensive and of an attempt by the North Vietnamese to put everything on the military scales." He noted that the enemy had launched three "major onslaughts" after his return from Moscow and the renewal, at Soviet urging, of secret and public peace talks in Paris.

While he did not think the Soviet Union had "a deliberate plan to inflict a humiliation" on the U.S. in Vietnam, Kissinger stressed, "we are saying that any thoughtful national leader, looking at the masses of offensive equipment, might have considered the consequences and, prior to a meeting that had, and still has such high prospects, should ask himself whether it can be in the interest of either party to impose a major setback on the other."

U.S. still ready to negotiate—Kissinger also emphasized at the press conference May 9 that the U.S. had not renounced negotiation as a way to end the war but was willing to negotiate a military solution, as advanced by President Nixon in his address, or a comprehensive political-military solution.

Kissinger disclosed details of his May 2 secret meeting in Paris with Le Duc Tho, a member of North Vietnam's Politburo. The meeting (rumored at the time and confirmed by the White House May 5) had been six months in the making, Kissinger said, and the result of "innumerable exchanges." Then, he said, Tho had refused to negotiate and presented previously published demands. "What we heard could have been clipped from a newspaper and sent to us in the mail," Kissinger said. The unproductive meeting, and its nature, and the Soviet role in getting the U.S. to attend, were said to have been part of the planning background influencing Nixon's decision to cut off North Vietnam's war supply routes.

On stopping supply ships—On the specifics of cutting off the delivery of war supplies to North Vietnam, and whether a Soviet ship would be stopped from entering a port, Kissinger said May 9 "the instructions are to warn all foreign ships of the existence of these minefields, but not to interfere with them if they decide to proceed into the minefields at their own risk."

As for the U.S. reaction to supplies being landed outside the minefields, he said the U.S. "would interfere with it to the maximum degree possible."

Laird firm about stopping cargoes. Defense Secretary Melvin Laird said May 10 the U.S. would "take those actions that are necessary" to halt delivery of war supplies to North Vietnam. He made the statement repeatedly at a news conference in answer to questions about how the blockade-type action would work concerning airlifted supplies or ships landing cargo.

Laird said: "Our policy is to stop the delivery to the North Vietnamese of these supplies and we will take those ac-

Text of President Nixon's May 8 Address on Vietnam Policy

Good evening.

Five weeks ago, on Easter weekend, the Communist armies of North Vietnam launched a massive invasion of South Vietnam—an invasion that was made possible by tanks, artillery and other advanced offensive weapons supplied to Hanoi by the Soviet Union and other Communist nations.

The South Vietnamese have fought bravely to repel this brutal assault. Casualties on both sides have been very high.

Most tragically, there have been over 20,000 civilian casualties, including women and children, in the cities of which the North Vietnamese have shelled in wanton disregard of human life.

As I announced in my report to the nation 12 days ago, the role of the United States in resisting this invasion has been limited to the air and naval strikes on military targets in North and South Vietnam.

As I also pointed out in that report, we have responded to North Vietnam's massive military offensive by undertaking wide-ranging new peace efforts aimed at ending the war through negotiation.

On April 20, I sent Dr. Kissinger to Moscow for four days of meetings with General Secretary Brezhnev and other Soviet leaders.

I instructed him to emphasize our desire for a rapid solution to the war and our willingness to look at all possible approaches.

At that time, the Soviet leaders showed an interest in bringing the war to an end on a basis just to both sides.

They urged resumption of negotiations in Paris and they indicated they would use their constructive influence.

I authorized Dr. Kissinger to meet privately with the top North Vietnamese negotiator, Le Duc Tho, on Tuesday, May 2, in Paris. Ambassador Porter, as you know, resumed the public peace negotiations in Paris on April 27, and again on May 4.

At those meetings, both public and private, all we heard from the enemy was bombastic rhetoric and a replaying of their demands for surrender.

For example, at the May 2 secret meeting, I authorized Dr. Kissinger to talk about every conceivable avenue toward peace. The North Vietnamese flatly refused to consider any of these approaches. They refused to offer any new approach of their own. Instead, they simply read verbatim their previous public demands.

Here is what over three years of public and private negotiations with Hanoi has come down to: The United States, with the full concurrence of our South Vietnamese allies, has offered the maximum of what any President of the United States could offer.

We have offered a de-escalation of the fighting. We have offered a cease-fire with a deadline for withdrawal of all American forces.

We have offered new elections, which would be internationally supervised, with the Communists participating—both in the supervisory body and in the elections themselves. President Thieu has offered to resign one month before the elections.

We have offered an exchange of prisoners of war in a ratio of 10 North Vietnamese prisoners for every one American prisoner that they release.

And North Vietnam has met each of these offers with insolence and insult. They have flatly and arrogantly refused to negotiate an end of the war and bring peace. Their answer to every peace offer we have made has been to escalate the war.

In the two weeks alone since I offered to resume negotiations, Hanoi has launched three new military offensives in South Vietnam.

In those two weeks the risk that a Communist government may be imposed on the 17 million people of South Vietnam has increased, and the Communist offensive has now reached the point that it gravely threatens the lives of 60,000 American troops who are still in Vietnam.

There are only two issues left for us in this war.

First, in the face of a massive invasion, do we stand by, jeopardize the lives of 60,000 Americans, and leave the South Vietnamese to a long night of terror?

This will not happen. We shall do whatever is required to safeguard American lives and American honor.

Second, in the face of complete intransigence at the conference table, do we join with our enemy to install a Communist government in South Vietnam?

This, too, will not happen. We will not cross the line from generosity to treachery.

We now have a clear hard choice among three courses of action: Immediate withdrawal of all American forces, continued attempts at negotiation or decisive military action to end the war.

I know that many Americans favor the first course of action—immediate withdrawal.

They believe the way to end the war is for the United States to get out and to remove the threat to our remaining forces by simply withdrawing them.

From a political standpoint, this would be a very easy choice for me to accept. After all, I did not send over one-half million Americans to Vietnam. I have brought 500,000 men home from Vietnam since I took office.

But abandoning our commitment in Vietnam here and now would mean turning 17 million South Vietnamese over to Communist tyranny and terror. It would mean leaving hundreds of American prisoners in Communist hands with no bargaining leverage to get them released.

An American defeat in Vietnam would encourage this kind of aggression all over the world—aggression in which smaller nations, armed by their major allies, could be tempted to attack neighboring nations at will, in the Mideast, in Europe and other areas. World peace would be in grave jeopardy.

The second course of action is keep on trying to negotiate a settlement. Now this is the course we have preferred from the beginning and we shall continue to pursue it. We want to negotiate. But we have made every reasonable offer and tried every possible path for ending this war at the conference table.

The problem is, as you all know, it takes two to negotiate. And now, as throughout the past four years, the North Vietnamese arrogantly refuse to negotiate anything but an imposition, an ultimatum, that the United States impose a Communist regime on 17 million people in South Vietnam who do not want a Communist government.

It's plain then that what appears to be a choice among three courses of action for the United States is really no choice at all. The killing in this tragic war must stop.

By simply getting out, we should only worsen the bloodshed. By relying solely on negotiations, we would give an intransigent enemy the time he needs to press his aggression on the battlefield.

There's only one way to stop the killing. That is, to keep the weapons of war out of the hands of the international outlaws of North Vietnam.

Throughout the war in Vietnam, the United States has exercised a degree of restraint unprecedented in the annals of war. That was our responsibility as a great nation—a nation which is interested, and we can be proud of this as Americans, as America has always been, in peace not conquest.

However, when the enemy abandons all restraint, throws its whole army into battle on the territory of its neighbor, refuses to negotiate, we simply face a new situation.

In these circumstances, with 60,000 Americans threatened, any President who failed to act decisively would have betrayed the trust of his country and betrayed the cause of world peace.

I have therefore concluded that Hanoi must be denied the weapons and supplies it needs to continue the aggression.

In full coordination with the Republic of Vietnam I have ordered the following measures, which are being implemented as I am speaking to you:
■ All entrances to North Vietnamese ports will be mined to prevent access to these ports and North Vietnamese naval operations from these ports.
■ United States forces have been directed to take appropriate measures within the internal and claimed territorial waters of North Vietnam to interdict the delivery of any supplies.
■ Rail and all other communications will be cut off to the maximum extent possible. Air and naval strikes against military targets in North Vietnam will continue.

These actions are not directed against any other nation. Countries with ships presently in North Vietnamese ports have already been notified that their ships will have three daylight periods to leave in safety. After that time, the mines will become active and any ships attempting to leave or enter these ports will do so at their own risk.

These actions I have ordered will cease when the following conditions are met:

First, all American prisoners of war must be returned.

Second, there must be an internationally supervised cease-fire throughout Indochina.

Once prisoners of war are released, once the internationally supervised cease-fire has begun, we will stop all acts of force throughout Indochina.

And at that time we will proceed with a complete withdrawal of all American forces from Vietnam within four months.

Now these terms are generous terms. They are terms which would not require surrender and humiliation on the part of anybody. They would permit the United States to withdraw with honor. They would end the killing. They would bring our POWs home.

They would allow negotiations and a political settlement between the Vietnamese themselves. They would permit all the nations which have suffered in this long war—Cambodia, Laos, North Vietnam, South Vietnam—to turn at last to the urgent works of healing and of peace. They deserve immediate acceptance by North Vietnam.

It is appropriate to conclude my remarks tonight with some comments directed individually to each of the major parties involved in the continuing tragedy of the Vietnam war.

First, to the leaders of Hanoi: Your people have already suffered too much in your pursuit of conquest. Do not compound their agony with continued arrogance. Choose, instead, the path of a peace that redeems your sacrifices, guarantees true independence for your country and ushers in an era of reconciliation.

To the people of South Vietnam: You shall continue to have our firm support in your resistance against aggression. It is your spirit that will determine the outcome of the battle. It is your will that will shape the future of your country.

To other nations, especially those which are allied with North Vietnam: The actions I have announced tonight are not directed against you. Their sole purpose is to protect the lives of 60,000 Americans who would be gravely endangered in the event that the Communist offensive continues to roll forward and to prevent the imposition of a Communist government by brutal aggression upon 17 million people.

I particularly direct my comments tonight to the Soviet Union. We respect the Soviet Union as a great power. We recognize the right of the Soviet Union to defend its interests when they are threatened. The Soviet Union in turn must recognize our right to defend our interests. No Soviet soldiers are threatened in Vietnam. Sixty thousand Americans are threatened.

We expect you to help your allies and you cannot expect us to do other than to continue to help our allies. But let us, and let all great powers, help our allies only for the purpose of their defense—not for the purpose of launching invasions against their neighbors.

Otherwise, the cause of peace, the cause in which we both have so great a stake, will be seriously jeopardized.

Our two nations have made significant progress in our negotiations in recent months. We are near major agreements on nuclear arms limitation, on trade, on a host of other issues.

Let us not slide back toward the dark shadows of a previous age. We do not ask you to sacrifice your principles or your friends. But neither should you permit Hanoi's intransigence to blot out the prospects we together have so patiently prepared.

We, the United States, and the Soviet Union are on the threshold of a new relationship that can serve not only the interests of our two countries but the cause of world peace.

We are prepared to continue to build this relationship. The responsibility is yours if we fail to do so.

And finally, may I say to the American people: I ask you for the same support you've always given your President in difficult moments.

It is you, most of all, that the world will be watching. I know how much you want to end this war. I know how much you want to bring our men home.

And I think you know, from all that I have said and done these past three and half years, how much I too want to end the war—to bring our men home.

You want peace. I want peace. But you also want honor and not defeat. You want a genuine peace, not a peace that is merely a prelude to another war.

At this moment, we must stand together in purpose and resolve. As so often in the past, we Americans did not choose to resort to war—it has been forced upon us by an enemy that has shown utter contempt toward every overture we have made for peace.

And that is why, my fellow Americans, tonight I ask for your support of this decision—a decision which has only one purpose—not to expand the war, not to escalate the war but to end this war and to win the kind of peace that will last.

With God's help, with your support, we will accomplish that great goal.

Thank you and good night.

tions that are necessary to stop that delivery."

Laird disclosed that one Soviet freighter headed toward Haiphong harbor at the time the mining operation began had changed course. He said there were 36 ships in Haiphong harbor at the time the mining began: 16 Russian, 5 Chinese, 4 British (Hong Kong), 2 Cuban, one East German, three Polish and 5 Somalian.

U.S. mines North Vietnamese ports.
U.S. Navy planes May 9 dropped mines into the port of Haiphong and six other harbors of North Vietnam to block the arrival or departure of North Vietnamese and foreign ships. The mines became activated May 11. The other ports affected were Thanhhoa, Hongai, Campha, Vinh, Donghoi and Quangkhe.

The Defense Department reported May 11 that five ships—four Russian and one British—had left Haiphong before the mines had been armed. About 25 ships, half of them Soviet, had been heading for Haiphong when the first mines were dropped, but none had entered the port. Thirty-one ships remained in Haiphong, according to department spokesman Jerry W. Friedheim. They included 12 from the U.S.S.R., five from China, three each from Hong Kong and Poland, five from Somalia, two from Cuba and one from East Germany.

It was not known whether any foreign ships were trapped in the other six North Vietnamese ports.

(Defense Department sources estimated May 11 that the mining operation would increase U.S. financing of the war by as much as $1.5 billion over the next 13 months.)

Hanoi radio warned May 12 that North Vietnam would sweep the U.S. mines from the harbors and sink naval vessels blocking the ports. A Le Monde correspondent in Haiphong had reported May 10 that North Vietnamese minesweeping preparations were "actively under way," but had not yet begun.

U.S. launches new air phase. U.S. planes launched heavy attacks May 8 in the opening phase of the new interdiction effort ordered by President Nixon. Hanoi and Haiphong came under air attack during raids May 10. The U.S. command said before the new campaign started, the U.S. had made more than 1,000 strikes on the North between May 3 and May 8.

In the May 8 raids, an undisclosed number of Navy fighter-bombers struck storage facilities, barracks and training facilities in an area 15 miles west of Hanoi. A U.S. command announcement May 9 said the strikes were directed at "military targets" that "are helping to support the Communist invasion" of South Vietnam. Three North Vietnamese MiGs were shot down in the vicinity of Hanoi, the command said. Another MiG was brought down by Navy planes dropping mines on North Vietnamese harbors. The exact area was not specified.

Hanoi radio charged May 9 that American planes had "deliberately struck at the dike system in Namha Province," southeast of the capital. The U.S. command denied the dikes had been hit.

North Vietnam was struck May 9 by 200 U.S. fighter-bombers, with the attacks ranging from the demilitarized zone to Hanoi. One North Vietnamese MiG was reported shot down.

A Hanoi broadcast May 10 claimed that two U.S. destroyers were set ablaze by coastal artillery while the warships shelled the port of Haiphong. The U.S. command did not confirm the report.

A force of 150–175 fighter-bombers May 10 struck at "North Vietnamese military transportation and supply distribution activities," the U.S. command announced. The targets included rail and fuel storage sites in Hanoi and Haiphong and rail lines leading to China. The announcement also said the planes attacked bridges, repair shops and petroleum storage areas. The command said 10 North Vietnamese MiGs had been shot down by American jets during the raids. Hanoi reported 16 U.S. aircraft had been destroyed and several pilots captured. The U.S. conceded the loss of only three American aircraft.

A Hanoi broadcast said 32 civilians had been killed in the capital's suburban district of Gialam during the May 10 raids. The broadcast said the Chinese economic mission and a hospital in Hanoi were bombed.

Chinese ships hit by U.S. jets—Two Chinese freighters anchored off Hon Ngu island in North Vietnam were shelled by U.S. warships May 6 and bombed and strafed by U.S. planes May 7 and 8, the Peking Foreign Ministry charged May 9. The statement said the vessels were badly damaged and Chinese crew members and Vietnamese civilians were injured. The ministry called the attack "a grave provocation against the Chinese people" and said the government had "lodged a strong protest with the U.S."

(U.S. Administration officials disclosed May 2 that a Soviet freighter had been sunk during the American raids on Haiphong April 16. At the time the Soviet Union had protested the damaging of four of its ships in the harbor, but neither Moscow nor Hanoi mentioned any ship sinking.)

Earlier U.S. air activity—Other American air activity over North Vietnam prior to the new bombing phase:

Hanoi claimed May 5 that U.S. planes had killed many civilians, including 10 children, in an attack May 3 in three southernmost provinces of the country.

North Vietnam claimed that U.S. planes raided Namdinh city May 6 and killed "many civilians" and destroyed "many houses and other property." The targets were 50 miles south of Hanoi. The Communists said three American planes were shot down that day over the North—two over Namha Province and one over Thanhhoa Province. This brought to 3,537 the number of American planes lost over the North, according to Hanoi's count.

The downing of three North Vietnamese MiGs by U.S. Navy F-4 Phantom jets May 6 was reported by the U.S. command the following day. The announcement said the Communist aircraft were destroyed in two dogfights 50–75 miles southwest of Hanoi. The MiGs apparently were attempting to intercept an American strike against the Baithuong airfield, the command said.

U.S. authorities in Saigon May 8 conceded the loss of a Navy A-7 attack plane during a raid over North Vietnam

May 6. The command also reported that a U.S. destroyer had been hit by fire from shore batteries while bombarding the North Vietnamese coast from the Gulf of Tonkin.

Agence France-Press correspondent Joel Henri reported in a dispatch from North Vietnam May 8 that he and other foreign newsmen had witnessed air raid damage to non-military targets, including a hospital and a school, during a tour of Thanhhoa and Namha Provinces. Twenty persons had been killed and 25 wounded in an April 27 raid on a school in Dongyen in Thanhhoa, Henri reported. He said there were no signs of military targets in the area.

Hanoi scores Nixon 'ultimatum.' The North Vietnamese delegation to the Paris peace talks May 9 assailed the mining of North Vietnamese ports and the escalation of the air war as a violation of the 1954 Geneva agreements and of a 1968 U.S. pledge to end air attacks on the North.

The mining of the ports, the statement said, and the intensified bombing constituted "the gravest step in the escalation of the war to date" and posed "an insolent challenge to the Vietnamese people, to the Socialist countries, to all peace-loving nations, to the American people and to peoples the world over."

The "Vietnamese people will never accept Mr. Nixon's ultimatum," the North Vietnamese delegation asserted.

"As long as the Nixon Administration continues its aggression in Vietnam, continues its policy of Vietnamization of the war and escalation of the war," it said, "all the Vietnamese people, united as ever, will resolutely continue their resistance struggle until they reach their fundamental objectives, namely, independence, freedom and peace."

North Vietnamese Defense Minister Vo Nguyen Giap had declared in a broadcast May 7 that his country had defeated U.S. forces during the administrations of Presidents Eisenhower, Kennedy and Johnson and were about to win "the war of Nixon."

In an address marking the 18th anniversary of the victory over the French at Dienbienphu, Giap said U.S. "bombs and insolent threats cannot shake the solid determination of the heroic Vietnamese people."

Viet Cong reject Nixon peace offer. The Viet Cong May 10 rejected President Nixon's May 8 offer to halt the latest American military escalation against North Vietnam in return for release of U.S. prisoners of war and an internationally-supervised cease-fire.

Mrs. Nguyen Thi Binh, head of the Viet Cong delegation to the suspended Paris peace talks, said Nixon's proposal was more stringent than his eight-point peace plan of Jan. 25. She also denounced the President's order to mine North Vietnamese harbors and to increase the bombing of the North as "the gravest step in escalation of the war to date."

According to Mrs. Binh, Nixon's call for an immediate cease-fire prior to a political settlement "means we must drop our weapons before the problems are solved and we must release all the prisoners. And only after these things are carried out, will Mrs. Nixon decide on a troop withdrawal."

Mrs. Binh noted that by contrast Nixon, in his Jan. 25 proposal, had called for a troop withdrawal and a cease-fire after settlement of political and military issues.

Ly Van Sau, chief spokesman for the Viet Cong delegation, also denounced Nixon's new position on the pullout of American troops. According to Sau's interpretation, Nixon "did not set a date for withdrawal."

Sau added: "Four months, he said. Four months after when? After 1976? Or after 1979? When?" Sau said Nixon in effect sought "to impose a solution on our people while the military situation of the United States is not so brilliant."

Soviet denounces Nixon move. In a statement distributed May 11 by the official press agency Tass, the Soviet Union called on the U.S. to end its "blockade" of North Vietnam, declaring that the mining of ports in the area and the bombing of rail lines were "fraught with serious consequences for international peace and security." The statement did not mention the possible effect of the U.S. initiative on President Nixon's forthcoming visit to Moscow.

The dispatch characterized the mining of North Vietnam's harbors as an "inadmissable" threat to "the safety of Soviet and other ships" and urged that the "blockade" be "canceled without delay" and that the U.S. cease its "acts of aggression" against North Vietnam. (The New York Times May 12 reported the belief in journalistic circles that two Soviet freighters had been hit in the previous three days during raids on Haiphong.) "All responsibility for the possible consequences of these illegal actions will be borne by the government of the U.S.," the message said.

It described the U.S. measures as a "gross violation of the generally recognized principle of freedom of navigation —ignoring the fact that the Geneva conventions of 1958 on maritime law affirming that principle bear, alongside other signatures, the one of the U.S." The U.S. had thereby "demonstrated its contempt for one of the basic requirements of international law: the observance by states of commitments assumed under international treaties."

Moscow asserted that the "real purpose of these actions is clear. It is not to 'save the U.S. from humiliation,' but to save the notorious policy of 'Vietnamization,' which has obviously failed. It is not to enable the Vietnamese to settle their affairs through negotiation, but to extend American military support to the antipopular puppet regime in Saigon." The Soviet Union "has rendered and will continue to render the necessary support" to the "heroic Vietnamese people."

(Xuan Thuy, chief North Vietnamese negotiator at the Paris peace talks, stopped in Moscow May 11 on his way back to Hanoi for a meeting with Soviet Premier Aleksei N. Kosygin. Tass said only that the talks had been held "in a cordial, comradely atmosphere in the spirit of friendship and solidarity.")

A Tass dispatch from Washington May 9, viewed as a preliminary Kremlin reaction to the Nixon announcement, had called the bombing and mining "overt acts of aggression" which violated "norms of international law."

Soviet aides visit Nixon—At the time of the Russian announcement criticizing the latest U.S. moves against North

Vietnam, two Soviet officials were in Washington visiting President Nixon. One of them indicated after the meeting that the President's trip to the Soviet Union was likely to take place as scheduled.

The Soviet officials were Ambassador Anatoly F. Dobrynin and Foreign Trade Minister Nikolai S. Patolichev. They were received by Nixon; Henry A. Kissinger, the President's adviser on national security affairs; Secretary of Commerce Peter G. Peterson; and Peter Flanigan, assistant to the President for international economic affairs.

After the meeting, which lasted about an hour, Patolichev reportedly answered a newsman's question about Nixon's proposed Soviet visit by remarking: "We never had any doubts about it. I don't know why you asked this question. Have you any doubts?"

Ronald L. Ziegler, White House press secretary, declared that Patolichev had been paying a "courtesy call" in return for recent interviews given by Soviet leaders to U.S. officials visiting Moscow. Ziegler said that neither Vietnam nor Nixon's planned trip to Moscow had been discussed.

China assails U.S. action. The Chinese Foreign Ministry released an official government statement May 12 calling the U.S. actions against North Vietnam a "grave new step" that "grossly violates the freedom of international navigation and trade and wantonly tramples upon the charter of the United Nations and international public law."

In a related development, Huang Hua, the Chinese delegate to the U.N., had said in a May 11 letter to Secretary General Kurt Waldheim that "the Vietnam question has nothing to do with the U.N." Huang also referred to limits on the "freedom of international navigation."

Peking sees U.S. 'provocation'—An article appearing May 11 in the Chinese Communist party newspaper Jenmin Jih Pao and distributed by the official news agency Hsinhua had called President Nixon's action a "dangerous move" and a "flagrant provocation against the people of Vietnam and the world over."

The statement declared: "The Chinese people express the gravest indignation at and the strongest condemnation of this grave act of war escalation of U.S. imperialism."

As long as the war "against Vietnam and Indochina continues in any form," the article said, "we shall firmly support the Vietnamese and other Indochinese peoples . . . to the end and final victory." Jenmin Jih Pao added that "the people of North Vietnam are fully entitled to support their own flesh and blood compatriots in the South" as long as the U.S. maintained its "aggressor troops" and those of its "hirelings" in support of the "puppet clique in South Vietnam."

Other world reaction. Broadcasts from Eastern European countries were unanimous May 9 in reflecting official condemnation of President Nixon's new moves in Vietnam.

The Budapest radio compared the situation to the 1962 Cuban missile crisis and said the latest developments limited the prospects for Nixon's scheduled visit to Moscow. Yugoslavia took a similar view, indicating that chances for such a meeting had been reduced by half. The Bulgarian radio said Nixon was "not ready to realize that his policy of Vietnamization is a complete failure."

Among nations often considered sympathetic to the U.S., Nixon's decision to mine ports and bomb rail lines in North Vietnam drew a generally cool reaction. A major exception was a British Foreign Office statement, which said that "countermeasures by the U.S. were, in the circumstances, inevitable." Foreign Secretary Sir Alec Douglas-Home disclosed during House of Commons debate that British ships were being warned to stay out of Vietnamese waters. The London Times, however, declared editorially that "the question has to be asked, has President Nixon chosen the right way out. Surely it is much too late to keep the weapons of war out of North Vietnamese hands."

French Foreign Minister Maurice Schumann remarked that "far from burning itself out, the war is feeding upon itself." He said that France "for its part can only deplore once more that things have come to this stage." (After a Cabinet meeting May 10, Schumann expressed his government's "deep concern" over the "brutal aggravation" of the war represented by Nixon's mining of North Vietnamese ports. The statement warned against the "risk of confrontation between the great powers." It advised a political solution, saying that "chances have been present to conclude peace on a basis and under conditions which humiliate no one.")

The Japanese government said it was "regrettable that the Vietnam situation has become serious after North Vietnam launched offensives, trespassing over the DMZ."

The strongest criticism came from Sweden, whose premier, Olof Palme, asked in a television address, "How many people must die . . . how great must the destruction be before the U.S. realizes that negotiations aiming to guarantee the independence of the Vietnamese people is the only way to peace?"

Waldheim offers U.N. forum. Kurt Waldheim, United Nations secretary general, urged May 9 that the "full machinery of the U.N.," particularly the Security Council, be employed to help end the war in Vietnam. He said the U.N. could be used "first to achieve a cessation of hostilities and then to assist in the search for a peaceful and lasting settlement of the problem."

Waldheim appealed to "all the parties" in the war "to act with the utmost restraint" and said: "The most recent developments have confirmed my conviction that a solution to the problem of Vietnam can only be found through negotiations."

In meetings May 8–10, Waldheim consulted with all members of the Security Council on the Vietnam issue.

Legal justification invoked at U.N.— The State Department May 8 released a letter George Bush, U.S. representative to the United Nations, sent to the Security Council citing Article 51 of the U.N. Charter as justification for President Nixon's action to seal off North Vietnam's war supplies from abroad.

The U.S. acted in response to a "massive invasion across the demilitarized zone and international boundaries by the forces of North Vietnam," Bush stated, and Article 51 said that "nothing in the present charter shall impair the inherent right of individual or collective self-defense if an armed attack occurs against a member of the United Nations, until the Security Council has taken the measures necessary to maintain international peace and security."

Congressional polarization. Nixon's new Vietnam policies caused a further polarization in Congress, with most Republicans backing the President and most Democrats expressing varying degrees of opposition, ranging to the filing by some House Democrats of an impeachment resolution.

House Republican Leader Gerald Ford (Mich.) said May 8 that Nixon had been "generous in his bid for peace but firm in his determination that we will not surrender." Senate Minority Leader Hugh Scott (Pa.) said May 9 of the harbor mining operation, "I took the position this should be done as far back as 1965 to 1966. Within the rules of war, it is one of the limited options available to the President."

Scott said May 10 that Republican senators were considering censure or discipline measures against antiwar Sen. Mike Gravel (D, Alaska), who had read into the Congressional Record May 9 portions of a classified report on Vietnam prepared in 1969 by Presidential aide Henry Kissinger. Gravel had reported that Defense Department information cited in the report showed that interdiction of supplies transported over two roads from China to Laos had been extremely difficult, and noted that China and North Vietnam were connected by seven main arteries.

Nixon received further backing from conservative Republicans James Buckley (N.Y.), who said May 8 the new military moves would "preserve the credibility of American mutual security agreements around the world," and Barry Goldwater (Ariz.), who said the same day that Kissinger had assured Congressional leaders at the White House briefing that Nixon's Moscow trip would not be affected.

However, some Republicans expressed reservations, including Jacob Javits

(N.Y.), and George Aiken (Vt.), who called the harbor minings "brinkmanship" May 9. Sen. Lowell Weicker Jr. (Conn.), while backing the President's actions, said May 9 he would vote for a fund cutoff for the first time.

In the House, Speaker Carl Albert, noting May 9 that Nixon had moved without consulting Congress, said "now that the decision has been made, we can only hope that the strategy shortens the war." But four Democratic representatives filed a resolution May 10 to impeach Nixon for "high crimes and misdemeanors" in waging illegal war. They were John Conyers (Mich.), Bella Abzug (N.Y.), William F. Ryan (N.Y.) and Ronald Dellums (Calif.).

Seventeen House Republican moderates had written Nixon May 5 urging him to seek a cease-fire in Indochina and a political settlement with Soviet and United Nations cooperation. The representatives, 12 of whom had voted against the 1971 fund cutoff proposal, asked for limitations on bombing of North Vietnam, and said "in light of our apparent, indefinite commitment of American air support to South Vietnamese ground forces, we do not see how even a near-total 'de-Americanization' of the ground war in Indochina can bring the conflict and its current carnage to an early end."

Candidates react. Democratic presidential candidates Sens. Hubert Humphrey (Minn.), George McGovern (S.D.), Edmund Muskie (Me.) and Henry Jackson (Wash.) expressed criticism of Nixon's moves, although Jackson opposed attempts by war opponents to throw "roadblocks" in the President's way. Gov. George Wallace (Ala.) confined himself May 9 to a hope that Nixon made "the right decision."

Humphrey and McGovern both suspended their campaigning in the Nebraska primary after Nixon's speech May 8 to return to Washington. Humphrey, in Omaha, called the decision to mine Haiphong harbor "a serious escalation" which "requires an immediate response by the Congress." In Washington May 9 he said "I cannot and do not support the President's action."

McGovern said in Nebraska that "the only purpose of this dangerous new course is to keep Gen. Thieu in power a little longer." On the Senate floor the next day he called the move "the most dangerous act of the entire war," and a "flirtation with World War III."

Muskie said May 9 that Nixon, "trapped by his own failures and faced with a series of unpleasant options," had chosen "the worst option of all."

Jackson, who had condemned Democratic war critics before his withdrawal from active campaigning May 2, questioned the efficacy of mining North Vietnam ports in May 9 Senate debate, and said he was "also deeply concerned that through these latest developments our program for the withdrawal of U.S. troops will be adversely affected, and that the SALT [Strategic Arms Limitation Talks] talks will be jeopardized." He also criticized the Administration for having been unprepared by a "North Vietnamese classic heavy-fire operation."

Antiwar moves progress in Senate. The Senate Democratic caucus voted 29–14 May 9 for a resolution "disapproving the escalation of the war in Vietnam," and endorsed a newly revised Indochina fund cutoff by a 35–8 vote. Majority leader Mike Mansfield (Mont.) noted it was the first time the caucus had backed a fund cutoff for the war.

In the debate over the resolution criticizing President Nixon's latest military moves, Sens. Gale McGee (Wyo.), Henry Jackson (Wash.) and Alan Bible (Nev.) joined Southern and Border state senators in arguing that Nixon should be given more time to "luck out," in McGee's words. But the caucus voted 44–0 against a delay in Senate consideration of the fund cutoff, which had not been expected to come to a vote until after the President returned from his scheduled Moscow trip.

The cutoff proposal, sponsored by Sens. Clifford Case (R, N.J.) and Frank Church (D, Idaho) and attached by the Foreign Relations Committee to a State Department fund authorization bill, was approved by the caucus in a modified form suggested by Case and Church May 9 after Nixon's address the night before. The new version would conform to

Nixon's four-month withdrawal schedule after prisoner release, and was designed to attract additional Republican support.

Sen. Edward Brooke (R, Mass.) offered a substitute amendment May 9 to cut off funds after Aug. 31, claiming that his measure would in effect endorse and sanction Nixon's latest proposal.

House committee Democrats for pullout. A caucus of Democratic members of the House Foreign Affairs Committee voted May 10 to back a bill in the full committee setting Oct. 1 as a final date for withdrawal of all U.S. ground and air forces from Indochina, subject only to prior release of U.S. prisoners and safe withdrawal for U.S. troops. If the committee, which had a Democratic majority of 21–17, passed the measure it would be the first end-the-war legislation originating in the House to get floor consideration. The House had rejected Senate versions of such legislation in the past.

Committee Chairman Thomas E. Morgan (Pa.), who had previously backed the Administration in opposing pullout measures, said he had decided to vote in favor this time after President Nixon offered in his May 8 television address to withdraw all troops four months after release of U.S. prisoners. But the caucus rejected Nixon's additional prerequisite of a cease-fire throughout Indochina.

A full caucus of House Democrats had instructed Democrats on the committee April 20 to report out a pullout deadline bill, but some Democrats had challenged the authority of the caucus to bind party members. Democratic Whip Thomas P. O'Neill (Mass.) subsequently sent a letter to all House Democrats stating that the Foreign Affairs Committee's Democratic members were "absolutely bound as agents of the caucus" at least in committee, although not necessarily on the final floor vote.

Suits filed. Two U.S. senators and 21 representatives filed suit in federal court in Washington May 11 to enjoin President Nixon and Cabinet officers from continuing to wage war in Indochina, which the plaintiffs said violated the 1971 Mansfield amendment and the 1907 Hague Convention provisions about naval mines. Nixon had said he would not abide by the amendment.

In a similar case, U.S. District Court Judge John F. Dooling Jr. ordered Nixon and Defense Department officials May 11 to show cause why they should not be enjoined from their new offensive against North Vietnam, in response to a suit filed by the New York Civil Liberties Union in behalf of Spec 4 Ernest DaCosta, currently serving in Vietnam. Dooling had rejected two earlier suits brought by DaCosta challenging his orders to go to Vietnam, first ruling in a July 1971 suit that Congress had in effect supported the war, then ruling in a Feb. 16 suit that Nixon was in effect following the Mansfield amendment by withdrawing troops and decreasing hostilities.

Administration scores critics. Top Administration figures criticized Democratic opponents of Nixon's Vietnam policies in speeches and statements May 15.

Secretary of State William P. Rogers testified before the House Foreign Affairs Committee that the current North Vietnamese offensive had been timed to "blackmail" Nixon before his Moscow visit. He said Congress should close ranks behind Nixon at least "until the campaign begins."

In a prepared speech, Interior Secretary Rogers C. B. Morton said he was "saddened by the vicious partisan reaction of those who should know better," and said "most Democrats in the Congress" had failed to support Nixon "in contrast to the majority of Americans."

Agriculture Secretary Earl Butz called for a moratorium on domestic criticism for several weeks at an American Advertising Federation meeting in Washington.

Senate backs Nixon terms. The Senate voted 47–43 May 16 to add a clause to pending end-the-war legislation, linking American withdrawal from Vietnam with an internationally supervised cease-fire as proposed by President Nixon May 8.

The clause had been offered by Sen. Robert Byrd (D, W. Va.) with Administration support to modify the Case-

Church amendment to a routine fund bill. The amendment had called for a fund cutoff for American forces in Indochina four months after North Vietnam agreed to release U.S. prisoners. Sen. Frank Church, speaking against the Byrd provision, said it would emasculate the amendment since neither North or South Vietnam was likely to approve a cease-fire.

Fourteen Democrats and 33 Republicans backed the Byrd provision, including antiwar Republican John Sherman Cooper (Ky.), who explained his vote as protecting Nixon's bargaining power in his forthcoming Moscow visit. Ten Republicans and 33 Democrats opposed the change.

Majority Leader Mike Mansfield (Mont.) immediately suggested a substitute proposal that accepted the cease-fire provision, but without requiring South Vietnamese government approval, and mandating a complete withdrawal of all troops and complete cessation of air and naval hostilities after Aug. 31. It was expected that a vote on the new Mansfield proposal would be delayed until after Nixon's Moscow trip.

Poll finds Nixon support. A poll by the Harris Survey, reported May 14, found that 59% of a sample of 1,385 Americans supported the mining of Haiphong harbor, 24% opposed it and 17% were unsure. Those surveyed supported a status quo cease-fire by 51%–31%, and would agree to let North Vietnam retain the territory its troops occupied in the South in return for peace.

POW group meets Nixon. President Nixon met three women representing the National League of Families of American Prisoners and Missing in Southeast Asia May 15, and promised to maintain the naval blockade of North Vietnam until the prisoners were released, according to the group's spokeswoman. The three women said they were reassured of Nixon's concern.

Antiwar protests escalate. Nixon's speech touched off an intense wave of antiwar protest on college campuses and in major cities May 8–11, and widespread use of civil disobedience tactics led to violent clashes with police, scores of injuries and a reported total of 1,800 arrests in several cities. Protesters, largely college students, massed on streets, highways and railroad tracks, and attempted to block entrances at military and other federal installations, including the Capitol Building in Washington. Arson, bombings, rock throwing and looting were reported in a few areas.

Serious incidents were reported in Minneapolis, Albuquerque, N.M., Madison, Wis., Berkeley and San Jose, Calif., Gainesville, Fla., Boulder, Colo. and the Chicago area. Sporadic demonstrations, violence or arrests occurred in varying locations in New York, Boston, Washington and Philadelphia among other cities, while demonstrations or rallies were reported in dozens of areas.

Minnesota Gov. Wendell Anderson activated 715 National Guardsmen May 11 after an outbreak of violence at the University of Minnesota at Minneapolis the previous day. At least 25 students and three policemen had been injured and 30 arrests made as 2,000–5,000 students and city police battled for control of a street running through the campus with rocks, bottles and tear gas.

At least nine persons were injured, one seriously, by police fire during disorders in Albuquerque involving University of New Mexico students May 10 and 11. Three Madison, Wis. policemen were shot May 11 while pursuing bomb suspects after three nights of clashes in which over 50 demonstrators had been arrested. Police in Berkeley fired wooden and putty pellets and used tear gas to disperse as many as 1,000 rioters May 8–11; at least 52 injuries and 32 arrests were reported.

In San Jose, suspected arson at a Naval Reserve armory and an Army veterinary center caused over $200,000 damage May 9. About 1,000 students from the University of Florida at Gainesville were driven from a stretch of U.S. highway 441 by tear gas and clubs May 9, and pitched battles continued the next day, with a total of 395 arrests; hundreds of students took part in these marches and rallies in Tampa and Tallahassee.

At least 70 persons were arrested in Boulder, Colo. as 1,000 protesters blocked intersections with burning automobiles and logs May 9. Over 22 persons were arrested for blocking expressways in Chicago and Evanston May 9–11, while 2,000 University of Illinois students rioted in Champaign-Urbana May 9, breaking windows and looting. Incidents of violence were also reported from the University of Maryland, Ohio State College at Bowling Green, the University of California at Los Angeles and Stanford University.

Protests began in New York immediately after Nixon's May 8 television appearance and continued through the week, with the largest crowd demonstrating at the headquarters of the International Telephone and Telegraph Co., a military contractor, May 10. There were repeated demonstrations by antiwar veterans at the United Nations building. Demonstrations in Philadelphia culminated in a battle May 11 between protesters and workers at a naval shipyard.

The Capitol Building was the focus of much of the protest activity in Washington, with almost continuous demonstrations on the steps by antiwar groups and congressmen, and a counter-demonstration by some Republican senators and about 400 supporters May 11. House Speaker Carl Albert closed public galleries May 9 after 40 vocal protesters were ejected in three incidents, and again the next day as 500 D.C. high school students marched on the building. Police arrested 28 demonstrators in two groups who refused to leave the building after closing time May 11.

Arrests at the Westover Air Force Base near Chicopee, Mass. reached about 1,000 by May 11 in demonstrations that had begun April 21. Among those arrested was President John William Ward of Amherst College. Over 36 protesters were arrested May 10 at the Kirtland Air Force Base in Albuquerque, N.M., and over 100 arrests were made as protesters blocked federal buildings in Binghamton, N.Y. May 9 and Burlington, Vt. May 10.

Railroad tracks were blocked for periods of up to 12 hours in Davis, Calif. and New Brunswick, N.J. May 11.

Protests slacken—War protests continued May 12–18 on college campuses and at government facilities,

but the scale and extent seemed to decline from the previous week.

The week's major confrontation occurred in San Francisco May 12, where police used clubs to disperse a crowd of 3,000 protesting outside a hotel where Govs. Ronald Reagan (R, Calif.) and Nelson Rockefeller (R, N.Y.) were opening Nixon's California re-election campaign.

Protests and arrests continued at the Institute for Defense Analyses at Princeton University May 12–16, at the Capitol in Washington, where 120 were arrested at a rotunda sit-in May 16 by Clergy and Laymen Concerned, and at Westover Air Force Base in Chicopee, Mass. May 16–17.

Among other developments, the United Nations headquarters building in New York was closed to visitors May 12 after a group of construction workers battled demonstrators.

Earlier protests—Public opposition to U.S. involvement in Indochina and the renewed heavy bombing of North Vietnam had continued April 26–May 8, including such new developments as a protest by nuns in St. Patrick's Cathedral in New York, protests at stockholder meetings of defense contracter firms and a critical resolution by the major organization of wives and families of U.S. prisoners.

The National League of Families of American Prisoners and Missing in Southeast Asia passed a resolution at its national convention in Washington May 7 expressing "extreme distress" at Nixon's failure to obtain release of the prisoners, and asking the President to adopt policies to "insure an accounting of the missing men and the release of the prisoners of war, not just the withdrawal of combat troops."

Police arrested seven of 12 nuns who lay down in the aisles of St. Patrick's Cathedral April 30 to symbolize the Indochina war dead, but the archdiocese announced later it would not press charges. About 60 other nuns, mostly from the Order of Sisters of Charity, had simultaneously conducted an antiwar vigil outside the cathedral.

Stockholders defeated by 98% margins two antiwar proposals offered at the annual meeting of Honeywell, Inc. in

Minneapolis April 26. The proposals called for a written report of the firm's involvement in the war, and plans to convert from weapons production to consumer goods. About 150 demonstrators temporarily blocked the entrance to Honeywell headquarters in New York May 4. Demonstrators, including stockholders, protested General Electric Co. (GE) participation in the war at the company's annual meeting in Houston April 26.

At least 29 congressmen and 80 Congressional staff members supported an antiwar vigil on the steps of the Capitol in Washington May 3–4. During the vigil May 3, 13 protesters staged a sit-in at the office of Rep. Thomas Morgan (D, Pa.), chairman of the Foreign Affairs Committee.

Campus protests continued during the week. A survey by the American Council on Education reported May 5 found that war protests took place on 27% of a representative sample of college campuses in April, compared with 16% reported after the 1970 invasion of Cambodia.

About 100 protesters abandoned a sit-in at a Cornell University library building May 1, and campus security guards ousted 30 demonstrators from a building at Columbia University May 2, leaving only one building occupied on that campus. At the University of Pennsylvania, 200 students at a sit-in were handed an injunction April 28, while 60 students were suspended that day for a sit-in at William Paterson College in Wayne, N.J. The presidents of 60 private Midwest colleges issued a statement May 6 calling for a total immediate withdrawal of U.S. forces from Indochina.

In two separate actions, American Civil Liberties Union (ACLU) lawyers filed suit in Washington May 1 against the Justice Department and federal and local officials for conspiring to abuse police powers in planning and carrying out 7,000 arrests during Mayday protests in 1971, and filed damage suits totaling $12.1 million in Cleveland May 4 against Ohio and the Ohio National Guard in connection with the 1970 shootings at Kent State University.

Thieu declares martial law. President Nguyen Van Thieu declared martial law

throughout South Vietnam May 10. The action was seen aimed at arousing a sense of urgency among the people in the face of the Communists' continued offensive. It was the first time since the 1968 Communist Tet offensive that martial law had been imposed in South Vietnam.

The imposition of martial law followed Thieu's plea May 9 for emergency powers that would enable him to rule by decree to cope with the current crisis. He did not formally ask the National Assembly to grant him the powers, but implied that he was putting the deputies on notice that he was leaving it up to them to approve his request.

Thieu's plea for special powers was made in a television broadcast in which he said: "All the people must be one. Legislature, judiciary and executive must be one. It is time that we stop permitting ourselves normal politics and time only to save the country."

Thieu lauded President Nixon's order to mine the harbors of North Vietnam and increase the bombing of the North as "the strongest measures ever taken to punish" the Communists. He pledged that his country's forces would "destroy the enemy and will reoccupy our territory" captured by the Communists during their offensive. Thieu attributed South Vietnamese battlefield reverses to "mistakes" and "a defeatist spirit" by "some field commanders." He promised they would be "severely punished."

A Cabinet decree announced May 11 contained a series of measures affecting military mobilization and further restricted civil rights. Draft deferments were curbed, the draft age was lowered to 17 from 19, an estimated 45,000 draftees excused from military service were to be recalled and some militiamen and Home Guard members were ordered transferred to the regular army.

On civil matters, strikes and political demonstrations were banned, central and local authorities were to control the distribution of essential goods, travel to foreign countries was sharply restricted and a 10 p.m.–5 a.m. curfew was instituted.

Thieu's request for special emergency powers brought a counter-demand from opposition senators and deputies May 12 that he dissolve the National Assembly rather than permit it to serve as "decor for a false democracy."

Thieu relieved a field commander for the second time in a week May 10. He dismissed Lt. Gen. Ngo Dzu as commander of Military Region II, whose forces had suffered a series of setbacks at the hands of the Communists in Binhdinh and Kontum Provinces. Dzu was replaced by Maj. Gen. Nguyen Van Toan, deputy for operations to the commander of Military Region I in the northern provinces.

Sieges of Anloc, Kontum continue. Communist forces made no significant ground advances since their capture of Quangtri city May 1, but Kontum city in the Central Highlands and Anloc north of Saigon remained surrounded by North Vietnamese and Viet Cong forces. Government marines were holding a line about 20 miles northwest of Hue along a river marking the southern border of captured Quangtri Province.

Meanwhile, U.S. planes continued to provide heavy air support to hard-pressed Saigon troops on all fighting fronts in South Vietnam. Fighter-bombers as well as B-52s flew hundreds of missions May 5-10 against Communist troop positions and artillery and tanks.

South Vietnamese attempts to open the blocked highways to besieged Anloc and Kontum city were repulsed May 5 with heavy losses. A government relief column trying to move north on Route 13 about 10 miles from Anloc was beaten back by the North Vietnamese who overran a fire base supporting the South Vietnamese push.

Route 14 leading to Kontum city had been reopened briefly by South Vietnamese forces May 4 but was closed again by North Vietnamese troops the following day as they repelled a government paratrooper attack supported by American's air strikes. Following the government's aborted attempt to break through to Anloc, North Vietnamese forces continued to pound the already battered city with artillery, rocket and mortar fire through May 10.

(The Saigon government had announced May 6 that it would evacuate all 30,000 civilians from Kontum city May 10, but the removal plan did not materialize.)

(Mychanh, a South Vietnamese village 20 miles north of Hue, was accidentally attacked by a U.S. fighter-bomber May 5, killing nine government marines and wounding 21.)

Government bases and positions around Kontum city came under North Vietnamese ground and artillery attack May 7. A government base at Lekhanh, 14 miles west of Kontum city, was also hit by Communist fire, but air strikes killed 300 soldiers and knocked out four tanks, according to Saigon military authorities.

Two more bases west of Kontum city— Poleikleng and Benhet—were struck by Communist guns May 8. Part of the Benhet camp was occupied by the North Vietnamese attackers, who were later driven out. Poleikleng, 14 miles west of Kontum city, was overrun by the North Vietnamese May 9.

U.S. losses at 7-month high—The U.S. command reported May 11 that 19 Americans had been killed in combat April 30–May 6. This was 17 more than in the previous week and was the highest U.S. fatality toll in seven months. U.S. wounded totaled 28, four more than in the April 23–29 period.

The South Vietnamese command reported that 603 of its troops were killed April 30–May 6, 2,028 were wounded and 737 were missing. Saigon's losses in the previous week were 769 killed, 2,794 wounded and 319 missing.

Refugee flow increases—Thousands of civilians were reported to have fled south to Danang in the wake of the North Vietnamese capture of Quangtri Province and the subsequent threat to Hue. Refugees began leaving Hue for Danang May 4 and by May 6 city authorities reported that more than 300,000 persons had poured into Danang from the northern front. The influx swelled Danang's population to more than 700,000. A U.S. official who flew over Hue May 6 estimated that 80% of the city's 200,000 residents had fled.

South Vietnamese civilians also were streaming north into Danang from Quangtin and Quangngai Provinces to the south. There had been no significant fighting there, but U.S. officials believed those refugees had also been prompted by fear.

A U.S. Administration official said in Washington May 8 that 700,000 South Vietnamese civilians had fled their homes since the start of the Communist offensive March 30. The statement was made by Robert H. Nooter of the Agency for International Development in testimony before a hearing of the Senate subcommittee on refugees.

U.S. passes withdrawal goal—President Nixon's goal to reduce the American troop force in South Vietnam to 69,000 men by May 1 had been exceeded by 2,700. The U.S. command reported May 1 that as of midnight April 30 U.S. troop strength in the country had dropped to 66,300.

Meanwhile, U.S. naval strength off Vietnam continued to increase. Three thousand U.S. sailors had joined the 55 warships in the Gulf of Tonkin and the South China Sea, bringing the force to 41,000 men, according to the command.

Hanoi rejects Nixon plan. North Vietnam's chief negotiator Le Duc Tho May 12 rejected President Nixon's four-part peace plan, but offered to resume the suspended Paris negotiations. He insisted, however, private discussions could not be held without a renewal of the public meetings.

In an interview in a Paris suburb, Tho demanded that the military and political problems of the Indochina dispute be linked and not be treated separately, as Nixon suggested in his latest plan. "Everyone knows that the most arduous problem now existing between the two sides is the problem of power in South Vietnam," Tho said. He said North Vietnam and the Viet Cong had no intention of taking complete control of any future post-war government in Saigon. Tho then delineated the components that would make up the Communists' proposed "government of national harmony of three elements".

The current Saigon government, after removing President Nguyen Van Thieu and other members of the "repressive apparatus," would name its own segment

of the new regime. Another element would consist of the Viet Cong, and the third would represent other South Vietnamese, "including people who don't approve of government policy but don't approve of PRG [the Viet Cong's Provisional Revolutionary Government] policy either."

A May 10 British proposal that Britain and the Soviet Union as co-chairmen reconvene the Geneva Conference on Indochina was rejected by Tho. He said that because of London's support of the latest American escalation, Britain "no longer has any qualification to serve as co-chairman of the Geneva Conference."

Tho said that in his May 2 meeting with Henry A. Kissinger, President Nixon's national security adviser had "offered nothing other than [Nixon's] eight old points; instead he tried by every means to maintain the Nguyen Van Thieu administration, which the Vietnamese people will never accept."

A Vietnamese Communist proposal May 16 that the Paris talks be resumed May 18 was promptly rejected by the U.S. delegation. A North Vietnamese and Viet Cong note sent to the U.S. and South Vietnamese representatives also demanded that the U.S. halt "immediately" the mining and bombing of "the two zones of Vietnam," but did not state this as a condition for resuming the talks.

A joint allied note formally rejecting the Communist proposal said May 17 that the offer was unacceptable because it takes two to negotiate." North Vietnam's actions and words suggested that it had "no serious purpose in demanding another plenary session at this time," the U.S. and South Vietnamese statement said.

North Vietnamese Premier Pham Van Dong said in an interview published May 17 that the Communists were ready to negotiate the end of the war in 24 hours and would offer President Nixon "the honorable exit we are determined to give him." Dong accused Nixon of refusing "to negotiate seriously" and warned that his side was prepared to continue the struggle "for years, time is on our side."

Waldheim pushes efforts. U.N. Secretary General Kurt Waldheim May 12 pressed his efforts to get the Indochina issue before the U.N. He held separate talks with Soviet delegate Yakov A. Malik and Chinese delegate Huang Hua, but contents of the discussions were not disclosed.

In a follow-up development May 15, Waldheim made public a message he had written the previous week in reply to Huang's May 11 letter, which had stated that "the Vietnam question has nothing to do" with the U.N. Waldheim said in his reply that because other efforts to halt the war had failed, "I feel strongly that the United Nations can no longer remain a mute spectator of the horrors of the war and of the peril it increasingly poses to the international peace."

Chinese, Japanese comment. The American mining of North Vietnamese harbors was again denounced by China May 14. Premier Chou En-lai said that the sealing off of the Communist ports "far from intimidating the heroic people of Vietnam, could only inspire them to redouble their efforts to wage, . . . the war of resistance against American aggression, . . ."

Japanese Premier Eisaku Sato May 11 voiced doubts about the stepped-up American war moves. Sato said Nixon's "determination to bring the war to an end" was understandable, but he hoped the measures taken would not result in "an endless war."

Saigon forces counterattack. South Vietnamese forces launched a series of counterattacks in Quangtri Province and in the Central Highlands around Hue May 13 and 14, attaining limited gains. In the fighting around Anloc, government forces advanced to within two miles of the besieged city north of Saigon May 17.

The government thrust into Quangtri Province was the first counterattack since the start of the Communist offensive March 30. About 1,000 marines, accompanied by six American advisers, were landed by 17 U.S. helicopters behind Communist lines May 13 and re-

portedly killed more than 300 North Vietnamese before returning to friendly positions on foot the following day. The attack, which took place southeast of Quangtri city, captured May 1, was said to have taken the North Vietnamese by surprise. Another 500-man government unit that served as a blocking force for the assault troops were reported by a Saigon spokesman May 14 to have rescued "a number of civilians from enemy-held territory and brought them back behind friendly lines." No government losses were reported in the Quangtri fighting.

In their second counterthrust, government troops May 14 pushed out from two points southwest of Hue and reoccupied Fire Base Bastogne on the southern approaches to the city May 15. The assault force, ferried in by five helicopters, encountered no Communist fire as they landed at the base, the North Vietnamese having abandoned the strongpoint, which they had seized from Saigon troops April 28. A Saigon spokesman reported May 16 that the government troops had killed 120 North Vietnamese in six clashes while moving up the coastal plain toward Fire Base Bastogne. Government losses were put at "two or three." The operation was aimed at disrupting Communist preparations for an expected attack on Hue, but it was believed the base's capture had not completely eased the threat to the city.

In a series of operations after Bastogne's capture, government troops claimed the seizure and destruction of nearly eight tons of Communist ammunition at three separate caches in the area. Government forces were reported May 18 to have been airlifted to two former fire bases 10–15 miles southwest of Hue that had been abandoned by the North Vietnamese.

In the fighting around Anloc, South Vietnamese troops May 17 were transported by helicopter to within two miles of the city, which had been surrounded by Hanoi forces for more than a month. The advance was supported by five B-52 strikes that reportedly killed 300 Communist soldiers just south of Anloc, the Saigon command announced May 18. North Vietnamese gunners surrounding the city continued the heavy shelling of Anloc, pounding the defenders May 18 with 1,600 artillery rounds. Another government relief force moving north on Route 13 was reported to have reached within six miles of Anloc May 13.

Intensified North Vietnamese shelling of Anloc had begun May 11, with about 10,000 artillery shells striking the battered city that day.

In other action in the Central Highlands, North Vietnamese forces May 14 launched their first ground assault on Kontum city, but were driven back two and a half miles from the town. The Communists lost 173 men and 10 tanks in the five-hour clash, according to allied accounts. Twenty-three more Communists were slain in the same area May 15. The city came under heavy Communist shelling May 17. The airfield was hit, resulting in destruction of two South Vietnamese transport planes and the damaging of two U.S. helicopters. A U.S. cargo plane loading ammunition at Kontum city May 17 was struck by a Communist rocket. Seven Americans were killed.

U.S. bolsters fleet—The arrival of the Saratoga off the Vietnamese coast May 15 brought to six the number of aircraft carriers involved in the sea operations against the Communists. A total of 60 warships were now stationed off the coast. The flagship of the fleet, the cruiser Oklahoma City, sank 10 Communist supply boats and damaged 20 others off Quangtri Province May 17, the U.S. Navy announced.

Viet Cong claims victories—A Viet Cong representative May 16 claimed a series of victories for Communist forces in South Vietnam. Nguyen Phu Soai, acting head of the Provisional Revolutionary Government's "special representation" in Hanoi, claimed: "The Saigon army had been broken in many places. Of 13 divisions in the regular army, two have been put out of action— the 3rd Division in the north and the 22nd in the Central Highlands. Four others have been battered heavily." Communist forces had killed or wounded 80,000 men in April and captured 10,000.

U.S. jets cut vital lines in North. American air strikes on North Vietnam May 11-17 severed vital supply links in the country. At the same time, U.S. warships continued to bombard North Vietnamese coastal positions and other targets.

In the May 11 raids, the U.S. claimed that a bridge knocked out by fighter-bombers cut North Vietnam's northeastern rail link with China. One of the returning pilots said several of the span's concrete supports collapsed during the 15-minute attack. The railroad bridge was located at an unspecified distance northeast of Hanoi.

North Vietnam charged that U.S. planes had struck again at dikes along the Red River in a suburb of Hanoi May 10 and 11. Hanoi radio also said that the May 10 raids had heavily damaged a Soviet ship in one of North Vietnam's lesser ports. A sailor was killed and the captain was wounded, according to Hanoi.

U.S. air strikes May 12-13 were confined to the southern part of North Vietnam, with petroleum pipelines, pumping stations and bridges among the principal targets. U.S. authorities reported that the May 13 attacks had knocked out the entire petroleum-pumping network supplying North Vietnam's offensive in South Vietnam.

A U.S. command report May 17 confirmed that air strikes during the previous five days had cut North Vietnam's main fuel pipeline to the South by destroying all the pumping stations in the southern panhandle. Prior to these raids, the pipeline "could carry 1,130 metric tons of fuel per day to support enemy mechanized equipment and trucks operating in the demilitarized zone and the northern areas of Quangtri Province," the command said.

A major road and rail bridge 80 miles south of Hanoi was struck in raids May 14. According to an Air Force account, 80-100 feet of the bridge had been destroyed, effectively cutting an important supply link.

Summarizing the May 7-15 strikes on the North, the U.S. command said May 17 that 1,800 sorties had been flown, seven American planes were lost and 11 Communist jets were downed. The report added: North Vietnam's main air defense complex at Bachmai airfield, three miles south of Hanoi, had been attacked during the week by F-4 jets, which had destroyed "several structures," including the headquarters. The jets had destroyed 15,000 gallons of fuel oil in a raid on a supply funnel near the Mugia Pass. The route channeled supplies from North Vietnam into the Ho Chi Minh Trail.

Hanoi radio reported May 18 that two U.S. planes had been shot down May 16 and three more the following day. U.S. planes flew about 250 strikes against the North May 17.

(North Vietnam May 11 released an antiwar statement it claimed had been signed by eight captured U.S. pilots. The statement protested the renewed bombing of the Hanoi-Haiphong areas and urged the American people and Congress to "end the war now.")

Hanoi civilians evacuated—The intensified U.S. bombing campaign against North Vietnam led Communist authorities to evacuate much of Hanoi, it was reported May 12.

David Jackson, Canadian member of the International Control Commission, said in Saigon that "a major evacuation of residents has taken place. It has been going on since the outset of recent hostilities."

Foreign missions in the North Vietnamese capital had been advised to prepare to leave, Jackson said. Most of the missions' dependents already had left. Jackson said there were no indications that the central part of Hanoi had been struck by the American raids.

Another diplomatic source in Saigon said May 12 that the civilian exodus from Hanoi had begun with the April 16 air strikes and that whole city wards were being re-established in the countryside. Essential government officials, military personnel and industrial workers remained in the city.

(Haiphong officials reported May 18 that 244 persons had been killed in the U.S. raid on the port city April 16. The report also said that 513 persons were injured and nearly 2,000 homes were destroyed.)

U.S. says mining '100% effective.' A U.S. claim May 12 that the mining of North Vietnam's ports was "100% effective" was challenged by a report from Haiphong May 17 that the devices

were being cleared from the harbor and that ship traffic was unimpeded.

In two other related developments, the U.S. disclosed May 15 that North Vietnamese rivers and canals also had been mined and Soviet sources indicated May 18 that the sealing off of the ports had spurred cooperation between Moscow and Peking in the transport of Soviet supplies to North Vietnam via China.

The Defense Department's May 12 statement said that several North Vietnam-bound merchant ships, reportedly all Soviet, had apparently changed course to avoid running into the mines. The department disclosed that two or three additional vessels, one or two of them Soviet, had been able to leave Haiphong May 11 before the mines became activated. This reduced to 28 or 29 the number of ships trapped in Haiphong harbor. Those ships were "completing their unloading," apparently without U.S. air or naval interference, Administration officials said May 14.

A further Administration report on the movement of Soviet freighters said May 16 that "virtually all" 13 Russian ships heading for Haiphong seemed to have been diverted to other ports, possibly Chinese. Three of the ships were reported diverted May 17 and the Administration said May 18 that the last two of the Russian vessels had been ordered to other harbors.

The U.S. contention that Soviet ships were staying away from North Vietnamese ports was contradicted by a Moscow radio report May 13 that eight Soviet freighters were on their way from Black Sea ports to Haiphong. The broadcast said the ships would "deliver mineral fertilizers, agricultural machines, food, clothing and medicine to North Vietnam and are now crossing the Atlantic and Indian Oceans." The broadcast did not indicate when the ships would arrive.

In a parallel development, U.S. officials disclosed Soviet naval movements in the Paracel Islands, 200 miles east of the Vietnamese coast, May 16. It was said that two flotillas totaling eight warships had joined forces in the area. One unit was comprised of two destroyers, an oil tanker and a submarine. The other force was made up of a cruiser and three destroyers, which reportedly had sailed from Vladivostok.

The May 17 Haiphong report on the clearing of the American mines came from New York Times correspondent Anthony Lewis. He said independent sources supported the Communist claim that the mines were being cleared from the harbor as planes dropped them, and that ships were moving in and out. At least one vessel, an East German freighter, had entered the harbor earlier in the week, according to these sources.

The Defense Department May 17 denied Lewis' report, saying that no ships had entered or left Haiphong since it was mined, and that there had been no evidence of mine-sweeping activities there or in any other North Vietnamese port. The East German freighter referred to by Lewis remained in Haiphong, the department insisted.

The Times' Haiphong dispatch was further denied by the White House May 18. Kenneth W. Clawson, deputy director for communications, accused the Times "in at least two specific instances of being a conduit of enemy propaganda to the American people." The previous Times report challenged by Clawson was a May 13 dispatch from Washington which had said the mines were designed to deactivate themselves before President Nixon's trip to Moscow.

The Defense Department disclosed May 15 that the North Vietnamese rivers, including the Red River that ran through Hanoi, and canals had been mined during the same operation that had sealed off the country's ports May 9–11. In his May 8 address announcing the action, Nixon had mentioned that the operation would include inland waterways, but the Pentagon's announcement was the first public disclosure that the measure had been carried out. Hanoi radio reported May 16 that U.S. planes had sown more mines in North Vietnamese ports.

Sino-Soviet moves to aid Hanoi—A Reuters dispatch from Peking May 18 said the Soviet Union was moving military equipment across China by rail to help North Vietnam bypass its mined ports. Quoting Soviet sources in the Chinese capital, the dispatch said U.S. efforts to cut off North Vietnam's sea routes would not stop Moscow from sending military equipment to Hanoi. Chinese officials were quoted by Western diplomatic sources as saying that Peking would "put no obstacle in the way" of Soviet and other East European assistance to the North Vietnamese.

Soviet-Chinese cooperation on the aid effort was said to be the topic of discussion in Peking between Chinese officials and a North Vietnamese delegation headed by Communications Minister Brig. Phan Trong Tue and Deputy Minister of Foreign Trade Ly Ban. Soviet Ambassador Vasily Tolstikov had left Peking for Moscow May 17 following what were believed to be high-level talks with the Chinese.

Hanoi warns Soviet on 'weakness.' The North Vietnamese Communist newspaper Nhan Dhan warned May 20 that "a few signs of weakness will encourage the truculence" of the U.S in its battle against the Vietnamese Communists. Foreign observers in Hanoi were said by New York Times correspondent Anthony Lewis to regard the statement as a veiled warning to Soviet officials as they were about to engage in summit talks with President Nixon.

The Nhan Dhan article said the Vietnam dispute must be settled through direct talks in Paris and not through outside mediation by the U.S. or by the Soviet Union. This view was reiterated May 22 by Mrs. Nguyen Thi Binh, head of the Viet Cong delegation at the Paris peace talks. Warning against any "maneuver" in the U.S.-Soviet summit talks, Mrs. Binh insisted that "the war will not be solved in Moscow or elsewhere. It can only be solved here in Paris."

Another Communist request May 23 to resume the suspended Paris peace talks was turned down again by the U.S. and South Vietnam May 24. The allied note said: "In calling for a new meeting on Thursday May 25, your side limited itself to repeating the same lines of propaganda without however giving the slightest indication of what it is ready to discuss . . . In these conditions our side sees no use in meeting Thursday May 25."

Sino-Soviet meeting on war aid. Soviet and Chinese officials met with North Vietnamese and Mongolian representatives in Peking May 19 to map plans to speed up war assistance to North Vietnam in view of the American mining of its harbors. China and the Soviet Union were said to have known in advance of the North Vietnamese offensive that had begun March 30 and were prepared for possible U.S. response.

A North Vietnamese source in Peking was quoted as saying that Hanoi was "very, very satisfied" with China's assistance efforts. "We have received everything we have sought from the Chinese," the source said. The statement was in comment on the continuing visit of a North Vietnamese delegation headed by Deputy Foreign Trade Minister Ly Ban that had arrived in Peking May 3.

The presence of the Mongolian ambassador in the Peking talks was an indication of his country's role in the transshipment of Soviet goods through China to North Vietnam. He was said to have been discussing the speed up of traffic across Mongolia's Gobi Desert and the Soviet Union.

Diplomatic sources in Peking reported May 21 that the Chinese were diverting trains to carry increased war aid to North Vietnam from the Soviet Union and other Communist countries. Train engines and freight cars that normally operated between north and south China on the Peking-Canton line had been shifted to the Nanking-Hanoi link. Different gauges, however, required unloading and reloading trains at the Chinese-North Vietnamese border.

Another report by diplomatic sources in Peking May 23 said China had begun to prepare its railways for the new aid program to North Vietnam not long after the mining of its ports.

Prior to the mining of North Vietnam's ports, about 80% of Soviet supplies were reaching North Vietnam by sea, according to U.S. estimates.

Agnew sees offensive failing. Vice President Spiro T. Agnew returned to Washington May 18 after a visit to Japan, Thailand and South Vietnam. Meeting newsmen after he reported to President Nixon May 19, Agnew said that Thieu had told him that the recent U.S. mining and bombing operations against North Vietnam had wrecked the enemy's plans for a nine month offensive and that North Vietnam would be incapable of sustaining its campaign for more than four months. Agnew asserted he possessed information "which shows substantially that there has been a great deterioration in morale in Hanoi in recent weeks."

Bomb damages Pentagon. An explosive device was detonated in a section of the Pentagon building early May 19, causing damage estimated at $75,000 but no injuries.

The Washington Post received a telephone call from someone identifying himself as "a weatherman" and announcing the explosion just before it occurred. At the same time, the New York Post received a call saying the explosion was in honor of the birthday of the late North Vietnamese leader Ho Chi Minh, and directing the receiver to a phone booth where a six-page statement criticizing President Nixon's war policies was found. A similar statement was received later May 19 by the Washington Post, signed by "Weather Underground No. 12," and bearing insignia identical to markings on 1971 Weather Underground letters claiming credit for a Capitol Building bomb.

Spokesmen for the National Peace Action Coalition and the Peoples Coalition for Peace and Justice, in Washington May 19 to prepare for weekend antiwar marches, denied any connection with the explosion.

The bomb was the 63rd to be exploded in a federal building since Jan. 1, 1970, according to the General Services Administration. Total damage costs were set at $829,400. According to Federal Bureau of Investigation figures reported May 20 there were 607 bombings in the U.S. and its territories in the first four months of 1972, killing 10 persons and injuring 56 others. The National Bomb Data Center in Washington claimed that "53% of the bombings have some sort of political motivation—right wing or left."

Hundreds arrested in D.C. More than 400 protesters were arrested during battles May 21-22 between Washington police and war protesters, while up to 15,000 demonstrators attended a peaceful antiwar rally on the Capitol grounds May 22.

In the skirmishes near the Capitol May 21 and at the Pentagon the next day several minor injuries were reported, including District of Columbia Police Chief Jerry Wilson May 22, as rocks, bricks and bottles were traded with tear gas and police charges.

The Capitol Building continued as a scene of protest May 24, when 94 protesters, including prominent entertainers and educators were arrested for refusing to leave the building. Several protesters had been evicted from the House of Representatives gallery May 22 for an antiwar disturbance.

About 3,500 people attended a "victory in Vietnam" rally May 20 at the Washington Monument sponsored by evangelist Carl McIntire.

Cooke, Presbyterians ask war end. Terence Cardinal Cooke, head of the Roman Catholic archdiocese of New York and Catholic military vicar of the Armed Forces, issued a pastoral letter to 2,200 priests and members of religious orders in the New York area May 20 asking for a "speedy end" to the Indochina War through United Nations intervention.

While Cooke praised the motives behind U.S. intervention in Vietnam, he wrote that "all wars are to be deplored whether they are fought for just causes or ill." Cooke's predecessor, Frances Cardinal Spellman, had called the Vietnam conflict "a war for civilization."

In its strongest antiwar statement to date, the General Assembly of the United Presbyterian Church in the U.S.A. asked May 22 for a total, immediate U.S. withdrawal from Indochina, to be brought about by "an escalation of conscientious protest" including civil disobedience.

Fighting rages around Kontum, Anloc. The heaviest fighting in South Vietnam May 18–24 continued to rage around the two besieged government strongpoints of Kontum city and Anloc and in the vicinity of Hue on the northern front.

A North Vietnamese attack one and a half miles northwest of Kontum was beaten back May 18–19 by intense U.S. air strikes and government ground resistance. Forty-one Communists were reported killed in a series of five major attacks before the North Vietnamese withdrew. No government losses were reported.

North Vietnamese forces made another unsuccessful thrust toward Kontum May 20–21. They twice occupied South Vietnamese trenches just north of the city, but were driven out by U.S. jet strikes and artillery fire. An estimated 100–200 North Vietnamese were involved in the operation.

Despite Communist failure to gain ground around Kontum, South Vietnamese troops May 20 reportedly abandoned Fire Base November, about five miles north of the city. No reason for the withdrawal was given. Sporadic clashes continued in the Kontum city area through May 23, with the Communists making no gains.

South Vietnamese troops fighting their way up Route 13 to relieve the besieged garrison at Anloc battled closer to the city May 19. Elements of two divisions and airborne battalions clashed with the North Vietnamese along a 15-mile stretch of the road and some units were two miles from the city. But in fighting May 20 the government relief column was battered by a heavy North Vietnamese attack and was forced to halt. The Saigon command said 81 Communists were killed in the day's fighting and that 10 North Vietnamese tanks were knocked out. Government losses were put at 15 dead.

South Vietnamese forces aided by American air strikes repelled North Vietnamese attacks on their forward positions northwest of Hue May 21–23. A total of 200 Communist troops were killed and five tanks destroyed in the first attack May 21. Another 300 North Vietnamese were reported slain May 22 and 18 of their tanks were destroyed. The Communists' principal target appeared to be a South Vietnamese brigade on the south bank of the Mychanh River, about 18 miles northwest of Hue. The Mychanh was the northernmost line of defense for Hue.

South Vietnamese troops May 24 carried out another spoiling attack in Communist-occupied Quangtri Province.

Six hundred government troops were flown in by U.S. Army helicopters after 500 others were carried ashore in U.S. tank-landing ships 10 miles northeast of Quangtri city. Naval gunfire from seven destroyers covered the attack. The government force struck at three separate points near Quangtri city. The Saigon command said almost 300 Communists had been killed before the government attacking force withdrew.

Saigon, Communist losses rise—South Vietnamese and Communist battle losses increased while American casualties declined May 7–13. Saigon said 750 of its troops were killed, 2,319 were wounded and 344 were missing. This compared with 603 killed, 2,028 wounded and 737 missing the previous week.

The South Vietnamese command said Communist losses May 7–13 totaled 3,613 killed, up from 2,349 the previous week. It said 56 Communist soldiers were captured.

The U.S. command said 13 Americans were killed, six less than the week before. Twenty-six GIs were wounded, two less than the week earlier.

Communists push into Kontum. North Vietnamese commandos slipped into the besieged Central Highlands city of Kontum May 25 and remained in control of scattered pockets of the town despite fierce South Vietnamese attacks through May 31. Losses were reported heavy on both sides. U.S. planes providing support bombed Communist positions in the area.

The original North Vietnamese force, totaling about 100 men, seized houses near Kontum's airport May 25, isolating the city from its only means of supply. About half the Communist force was said to have been killed or driven out of the city the same day, but the rest clung to sniper positions, while more North Vietnamese apparently made their way into Kontum.

Fighting intensified in and around Kontum May 26, with Saigon claiming 316 of the enemy killed. Government losses were listed at 42 killed and 140 wounded.

Another 155 North Vietnamese were reported killed in fighting in and around the city May 28, while Saigon listed its casualties at only six dead. The infiltrators were reported by South Vietnam to have been driven out of a school and an orphanage. The South Vietnamese claimed killing 115 North Vietnamese March 29 and placed their losses at 18 killed. Saigon troops May 31 reoccupied more lost ground, taking an abandoned field hospital next to the former headquarters of the South Vietnamese 22nd Division, part of which remained in Communist hands. South Vietnam's official press agency reported May 31 that in the past six days of fighting at Kontum 1,155 North Vietnamese had been killed and 18 tanks destroyed.

In other fighting:

A South Vietnamese relief force attempting to evacuate wounded soldiers from around the besieged city of Anloc suffered a heavy blow May 26 when they were struck by a series of North Vietnamese ambushes on Route 13, seven miles south. The report said 42 government troops were killed, 159 were wounded and 23 of their armored personnel carries destroyed.

Heavy fighting erupted May 23 along the Mychanh River line 25 miles north of Hue. In subsequent developments, North Vietnamese forces May 25 managed to get some troops and tanks across the river near Route 1, but were repulsed with a loss of 246 men and four tanks. South Vietnamese losses were placed at 12 dead and 59 wounded. In another action on the Mychanh front, Saigon troops claimed to have killed 172 North Vietnamese May 27.

A report May 26 on the South Vietnamese thrust into Communist-occupied Quangtri Province May 24 said the operation apparently had failed in its objective of destroying a pocket of North Vietnamese troops on the beach.

U.S. intensifies air strikes. The U.S. command in Saigon reported May 23 that U.S. planes had flown more than 1,000 sorties against North Vietnam May 19–21 with apparent unusual effectiveness. A spokesman claimed that bridges, which had been difficult to hit in previous years, had in many instances been knocked out in single raids.

This led to speculation that some pilots were employing "smart bombs," bombs guided by laser beams.

The command said targets bombed May 20 included an electrical transformer station eight miles northwest of Hanoi. Six bridges on rail lines connecting Hanoi with China were destroyed by fighter-bombers May 22, the command said. At least 13 other North Vietnamese rail and highway bridges had been bombed since May 19, and four of them were destroyed, according to the command.

The command conceded May 24 that two U.S. planes had been downed in the previous two days, one by a MiG. Hanoi claimed eight U.S. planes had been downed May 23.

U.S. raids carried out in the Hanoi-Haiphong areas May 23-24 struck at power plants and oil storage tanks. The May 23 strikes included attacks on an electrical power plant at Hongai, 24 miles northeast of Haiphong, and the Namdinh power plant, 48 miles south of Hanoi. Four North Vietnamese planes were shot down during the May 23 raids, and one American aircraft was lost, the command said. Hanoi claimed 11 U.S. planes were downed May 23 and three more the following day.

In previous raids, Agence France-Presse reported from Hanoi May 11 that the Soviet-Vietnamese Friendship Hospital in the capital had been hit by six missiles and a 500-pound bomb dropped from U.S. planes. Heavy damage was caused and some patients were injured, the report said.

The North Vietnamese radio reported that "many populated areas" had been struck in Hanoi and Haiphong May 18. Another broadcast said five American planes had been shot down.

U.S. planes May 20 "savagely attacked a number of areas of heavy population in the periphery of Hanoi," the North Vietnamese Foreign Ministry said. Two U.S. planes were downed in the attacks, according to the ministry.

U.S. expands air war—A decision to further expand the U.S. air war against North Vietnam was announced May 23 by the Defense Department, which said that more industrial sites and other non-military targets would be subject to bombing. Department spokesman Jerry W. Friedheim said the jets "will be hitting some of the other targets, such as power plants and some of the industrial facilities which support the military effort of the North." Freidheim said the U.S. commanders "probably have more flexibility in their targeting than was exercised in the 1967-68 period."

Friedheim's statement confirmed a report from military sources in Saigon May 19 that U.S. planes were bombing targets throughout North Vietnam with even fewer restrictions than before the 1968 bombing halt. The new stepped-up air offensive, code named "Linebacker" by the Defense Department, encompassed targets in the Hanoi-Haiphong area that previously had been bypassed.

Soviet ships attacked—Hanoi disclosed May 20 that a Soviet seaman was killed and two others were injured May 10 when U.S. planes bombed the Russian freighter Grisha Akopyan in the North Vietnamese harbor of Campha, northeast of Haiphong.

A Los Angeles Times report May 18 said the Soviet Union had protested the incident to Washington. The State Department May 18 said it had "no confirmation on the death of a Soviet seaman."

Another American jet attack on a Soviet ship in Haiphong May 9 was disclosed in a report from Hanoi May 22, saying that a stewardess seriously injured aboard the vessel left for Moscow that day after being treated in a Hanoi hospital.

A Soviet ship damaged in the U.S. raid on Haiphong April 16 was granted permission by China to put in at Canton for repairs, diplomatic sources in Washington reported May 19. The vessel, the Pevek, was one of 16 in the harbor during the attack. It had departed before the mines were armed.

U.S. continues air raids on North. U.S. planes continued to pound North Vietnam May 25-30, averaging nearly 300 raids a day and concentrating on vital highways and railroad bridges, among other targets.

U.S. planes flew more than 290 raids May 25. The U.S. command said they knocked out two bridges six miles from Haiphong, a highway and railroad bridge one mile west of the city and two other rail spans between Hanoi and the Chinese border. Two U.S. Navy planes were reported to have been shot down. One pilot was rescued, the other was missing.

The U.S. command said 270 strikes were flown over the North in a 24-hour period ending at 5 p.m. May 26. The command claimed all highway bridges leading from Quangtri Province in South Vietnam to the North Vietnamese panhandle had been destroyed and that all major rail bridges in the North had been made unusable.

The command also disclosed May 28 that 27 American planes had been downed since the North Vietnamese offensive had started March 30. Twelve of the planes were lost to surface-to-air missiles.

Bridges, rail lines and other targets in North Vietnam were hit by more than 500 U.S. air strikes May 26–28.

It was reported June 1 that U.S. Navy planes from three carriers in the Gulf of Tonkin had launched a concerted campaign to isolate the mined North Vietnamese port of Vinh, a major transshipment point for supplies to support the Communist offensive in the South. Three bridges around Vinh had been bombed May 30, while five warships shelled targets around the city and near Donghoi, further south, the U.S. Navy reported.

Hanoi's Vietnam news agency reported May 28 that several Chinese had been killed in U.S. raids against North Vietnam. The agency did not list the number of fatalities nor did it clarify the status of the Chinese victims. The report quoted a statement by the General Association of Chinese Residents in North Vietnam as saying that despite the deaths of a "number of them," other "Chinese workers and co-op members in Hanoi, Haiphong and Namdinh did not budge an inch from their places of work" during the American air strikes.

U.S. bolsters B-52 fleet—The U.S. Defense Department reported May 24 that an undisclosed number of additional B-52 bombers would be sent to Southeast Asia for use in the Indochina

war. They would reinforce 140–150 other B-52s now based in Guam and Thailand. About 90 of them had been shifted to the war theater since Jan. 1.

U.S. mining controversy continues. The effectiveness of U.S. mining of North Vietnamese ports remained questionable amid continued contradictory reports of the offshore operations.

A New York Times report from Hanoi May 22, quoting foreign observers in the capital, said the mining had effectively blocked the movement of ships in and out of the harbors. Correspondent Anthony Lewis said some sources believed the Communists were sweeping Haiphong's inner harbor at night, but that the North Vietnamese themselves said the Americans were continuing to plant more mines there.

A North Vietnamese official, asked May 21 to clarify the situation in Haiphong harbor, said: "In Haiphong we Vietnamese cannot sit idle . . . , so the people there have done a number of things to insure that port activity continues. As to how, we cannot tell you . . . In any case, if the mines have been cleared the Americans will drop more. If more are dropped we will try our best to clear them."

North Vietnamese Politburo member Le Duc Tho said in Paris May 23 that the U.S. mines were being cleared from Haiphong harbor and added "our supplies will continue" to enter.

The U.S. Defense Department reiterated May 23 that there was no evidence the North Vietnamese were sweeping the minefields. The department said the 25 ships that had been heading for North Vietnamese ports when the mines were planted May 9 had "changed course" and some had gone to Hong Kong. The Pentagon also said a Soviet and Chinese ship had been warned to keep clear of North Vietnamese ports by a U.S. destroyer shortly after the mines had become activated May 11. Three cargo ships, two from East Germany and one from Bulgaria, were reported by the London Times May 19 to have entered Hong Kong after being diverted from Haiphong.

V. Belov, captain of the Soviet cargo ship Zeya, told Singapore newsmen

May 20 that he had sailed his vessel out of Haiphong harbor May 13, two days after activation of the mines, "without trouble. There were times we came close to American gunboats but nothing happened."

The Defense Department denied May 22 that the Zeya had crossed the Haiphong minefield. Spokesman Jerry W. Friedheim said the ship "was not within the minefield when the minefield was activated." The vessel "was outside of Haiphong harbor—near Haiphong but outside the harbor" when the mines became activated, he said.

Hanoi reported May 19 that a Bulgarian freighter, the Tzanko Tzerkovski, had been ordered May 17 to defy the U.S. mines and sail for North Vietnam with its cargo.

Military aid cut by Senate panel. The Senate Foreign Relations Committee approved May 23 a $1.7 billion fiscal 1973 foreign military aid program with an end-the-war amendment sponsored by Majority Leader Mike Mansfield (D, Mont.) and other policy curbs. The Mansfield amendment called for withdrawal of all U.S. forces from Vietnam by Aug. 31 and a fund cut-off for all U.S. combat operations in and over Indochina as soon as U.S. prisoners were released and a cease-fire set.

The military aid total was $550 million less than requested by the Nixon Administration. The committee also imposed a $275 million ceiling for spending on military and economic aid to Cambodia (Administration request $348 million); curbed U.S. payments for Thai forces fighting in Laos; and barred transfer of foreign aid funds to other agencies.

Refugee toll rises. The U.S. Senate Refugees and Escapees Subcommittee reported May 24 that the toll of civilian war casualties in South Vietnam from the current enemy offensive was more severe than the previous high point— North Vietnam's 1968 Tet offensive.

The panel estimated that the enemy offensive begun in March resulted in 40,000–50,000 civilian casualties, including about 15,000 dead, by the first week in May, with the same toll

expected by the end of the first week in June. The 1968 offensive had resulted in about 62,000 civilian casualties in two months, with about 20,000 deaths. The total number of refugees on the Saigon government rolls increased during the current drive by about one million to a total of 1.5 million homeless or displaced persons.

Subcommittee Chairman Edward M. Kennedy (D, Mass.) said the "people problems in Vietnam" were greater today than at any time during the war. He called the refugee total "an appalling commentary on the Administration's policy of continuing the war."

U.S. on Hanoi supply problem. As a result of the mining of North Vietnam's ports and the bombing of its rail and road networks, there was "very little evidence of any significant expansion in the movement of supplies through China to North Vietnam," U.S. intelligence officials in Saigon reported May 29.

The U.S. assessment of North Vietnam's supply problems came amidst contradictory reports on Sino-Soviet efforts to continue providing North Vietnam with war equipment.

Soviet diplomatic sources in Peking were quoted as saying May 18 that Hanoi-bound Soviet military equipment was moving across China by rail. However, following the American bombing of two principal China-North Vietnam rail links, the New York Times noted May 25 that up to 1,000 freight cars carrying war material were reported backed up in Chinese rail yards.

Washington diplomatic sources reported May 25 that China had rejected a Soviet request to permit 12 of its freighters to enter Chinese ports to unload arms for North Vietnam. The Chinese were said to have informed the Russians if they were determined to deliver military material to the North by ship, they should "clear the mines" planted by the U.S.

A report from Hong Kong June 6 said Peking was now permitting Soviet and other East European ships to unload war cargoes for North Vietnam in Chinese ports. Agence-France Presse had reported from Hong Kong May 30 that two East German freighters and three Polish cargo vessels were on their way to

Chinese ports to unload war equipment for North Vietnam. The Polish ships, presumed heading for Chanchiang, were said by the French news agency to have been authorized to unload their cargo as a result of a Chinese-Polish navigational accord that predated the mining of North Vietnam's ports.

North Vietnam reported that U.S. planes had dropped more mines in North Vietnamese harbors June 3. A Foreign Ministry statement June 5 also said that U.S. planes continued to "savagely bomb Haiphong port city."

U.S. troop level drops. The U.S. command announced June 5 that American troop strength in Vietnam had fallen to 63,700 the previous week, the lowest level in seven years. In the largest weekly troop withdrawal in four weeks, 1,100 men were removed, including 510 from eight units that were deactivated.

The command had reported May 8 that the U.S. force in Thailand, mostly airmen, had been increased to the record of 50,000 set in 1968.

Cost of war seen rising. Defense Secretary Melvin R. Laird told the House and Senate committees that held the Congressional purse strings June 5 that the expanded U.S. military activity in Vietnam could add $3 billion–$5 billion to the defense budget in fiscal 1973. Such an addition would nearly double the Administration-projected annual cost of the war.

Appearing before the Senate and House Appropriations Committees, Laird said the additional money would be needed to pay for the air and naval activities ordered to counter the current North Vietnamese offensive.

Rep. George Mahon (D, Tex.), chairman of the House Appropriations Committee and generally a supporter of Nixon Administration policies, expressed surprise that spending in Vietnam was going up in view of the Administration's statements about the success of Vietnamization. Mahon said he was "astonished" to hear Laird call Vietnamization "astonishingly successful."

Aides to Laird told Mahon's committee that much of the projected $3 billion–$5 billion cost increase would be used to

pay for munitions used in the bombing of North Vietnam as well as to replace equipment. One aide said that in two-and-a-half months the U.S. had used $400 million worth of munitions. According to other figures supplied by Laird and his aides, the cost of the war had increased by $1.5 billion since North Vietnam began its offensive in late March.

Laird told the Senate committee that the annual cost of the war had been reduced from about $22 billion in the Johnson years to about $7 billion in the current fiscal year.

Later, he told the House panel that the Administration planned a $400 million increase in military aid to South Vietnam to replace lost combat equipment. For fiscal 1973, the Administration had asked Congress to authorize a defense budget of $83.4 billion.

Hanoi admits difficulties. North Vietnam admitted June 5 that the intensified U.S. bombing was causing it "very difficult" economic problems. The official Communist party newspaper Nhan Dan insisted, however, that "even if the enemy succeeds in the bomb destruction of our cities and our large industrial installations, they can never paralyze our economy to the point of preventing our survival and our ability to supply the South."

U.S. jets raid near China. The U.S. command reported June 8 that American planes raiding North Vietnam June 5–6 had made possibly their closest attack to the Chinese border, bombing targets only 20 miles away. Among the strategic points struck during the 24-hour period were a highway bridge 10 miles southwest of Langson and a railyard 15 miles southwest of the city. The U.S. communique also reported that the planes struck the Bacgiang thermal power plant 25 miles northeast of Hanoi. More than 270 strikes were carried out.

In raids on the North May 31–June 6, U.S. pilots claimed the destruction of large numbers of bridges, oil tanks, trucks, boats, supply dumps and surface-to-air missile sites. Among highlights of the raids:

U.S. fighter-bombers May 31 downed two MiG-21s over North Vietnam. This brought to 34 the number of North Vietnamese Migs claimed destroyed since Jan. 1.

The North Vietnamese press agency claimed June 2 that three U.S. planes had been downed the previous day over Langson, Vinhphu and Yenbai Provinces. This brought to 3,625 the number of American aircraft downed over the North, according to the agency's estimates. The U.S. conceded the loss of one plane June 1. The American command said a fighter-bomber was struck by ground fire and managed to make its way to Thailand, where it crashed. The two crewmen reportedly parachuted to safety.

The Bacgiang thermal power plant was among the targets hit by U.S. planes flying more than 220 missions May 31–June 1.

U.S. planes June 4 were reported to have destroyed a 150-foot-long railroad bridge over the Namlam River, 85 miles northwest of Hanoi.

The U.S. command reported American raids June 6 knocked out eight bridges, including a highway bridge near Haiphong, and destroyed more than 100 supply boats. The command said the North Vietnamese were using more small craft and barges to move supplies now that their harbors were mined, their two railways to China were cut and their highway system damaged.

Hanoi claimed two U.S. planes were downed June 6 while attacking "a number of populated areas" in the provinces west and northwest of Hanoi.

Communists ousted from Kontum. The North Vietnamese force that had infiltrated into the city of Kontum May 25 was reported by the South Vietnamese command June 7 to have been virtually driven out of the Central Highlands provincial capital. Only a handful of Communist troops remained and they were being mopped up, the command said. In fighting in and around the city June 6, 200 North Vietnamese troops but only about 10 government soldiers

were killed, it reported. Another 303 North Vietnamese were reported killed in the area June 4. Although the enemy threat inside Kontum was eased, a large North Vietnamese force continued to surround the city. Only two Communist battalions had been committed to the fighting inside Kontum. U.S. sources estimated that since the start of the fighting in Kontum May 25 South Vietnamese forces had lost 1,000 killed and wounded, while 3,000–5,000 North Vietnamese were slain.

Anloc, other action—In the fighting for besieged Anloc, a South Vietnamese relief column pushing up Highway 13 for the past two months was reported to have made contact June 7 with a rear element of the garrison. A Saigon command spokesman June 8 said the linkup had taken place at a point on the defense line slightly less than a mile south of Anloc. The spokesman acknowledged, however, that "the main mission of the relief force is to clear Highway 13 and this mission has not been completed."

Heavy fighting raged around Phumy in coastal Bindinh Province June 3–4 as the North Vietnamese made an unsuccessful assult on the district capital. The Saigon command said the Communists lost more than 140 killed in the two days of fighting, 106 of them slain June 4. Government casualties were listed as seven killed and 24 wounded.

Casualty reports—The U.S. command reported June 2 that 10 Americans had been killed and 35 wounded in action May 21–27. Ten other Americans died of noncombat causes and 134 were listed as missing but not in action. A Defense Department aide told Facts On File June 8 that the latter figure was largely made up of men unaccounted for following R & R (rest and recreation) leaves or absent without leave.

Saigon listed its losses in the May 21–27 period as 754 killed, 2,781 wounded and 312 missing.

Eight Americans had been killed, 22 were wounded and seven missing in combat May 14–20, the U.S. command reported May 25. In that period South Vietnam lost 757 killed, 2,351 wounded and 214 missing, while Communist losses were claimed to be 4,028 killed and 106 captured.

Hanoi radio claimed June 7 that more than 90,000 South Vietnamese and Americans had been killed, wounded or captured between the start of the Communist offensive March 30 and May 1.

Troops relieve Anloc. Elements of the South Vietnamese 21st Division, which had been bogged down for weeks in its efforts to relieve Anloc, succeeded in reaching the town June 9.

A South Vietnamese spokesman said that in fighting around Anloc that day 81 enemy soldiers had been killed while Saigon's forces had suffered eight dead. As many as 10,000 civilian refugees were reported to have fled Anloc June 12.

A group of 1,500 South Vietnamese soldiers were flown to Anloc June 13 from Laikhe, 30 miles south, and were joined the following day by more troops brought in by helicopter. Route 13, the only road access to the town, remained blocked by North Vietnamese forces.

In other ground action, South Vietnamese marines fighting three miles within Communist-occupied Quangtri Province June 9 reported killing 94 North Vietnamese and Viet Cong soldiers in a two-day period ending that day.

North Vietnamese forces moved into the Plain of Reeds 63 miles west of Saigon June 10 and shelled Mochoa, the provincial capital. The shelling occurred again June 14 as large concentrations of enemy troops were reported building up in the area.

U.S. troop cuts—A U.S. command announcement June 12 said the total American troops in South Vietnam had dropped the previous week by 1,800 men to a level of 61,900. The reduction consisted of 1,100 army personnel and 700 air force men. (The New York Times said in reporting the move June 13 that some or all of the servicemen might be transferred to Thailand.)

Casualty reports—According to a U.S. command dispatch June 8, 11 Americans were killed and 20 were wounded in combat during the week of May 28–June 3. South Vietnamese casualty figures for the week were listed as 912 killed, 3,281

wounded and 274 missing. North Vietnamese and Viet Cong forces suffered 4,314 killed, an allied military spokesman said.

The New York Times reported June 11 that a Chinese Nationalist chartered transport plane carrying U.S. and South Vietnamese soldiers normally engaged in secret operations had crashed in the Central Highlands June 3. Fourteen Americans, 11 South Vietnamese and a six-man Chinese crew were reported missing.

Top U.S. adviser killed. John Paul Vann, considered one of the most experienced U.S. civilian advisers in South Vietnam, was killed June 9 when the helicopter in which he was traveling crashed near the end of a flight from Pleiku to Kontum in the Central Highlands.

Vann, 47, had been director of the U.S. 2nd Regional Assistance Group, a position which gave him a rank equivalent to that of major general. Two other Americans were also killed in the accident.

Ronald L. Ziegler, White House press secretary, read a tribute to Vann June 9 on behalf of President Nixon. The statement said Nixon "feels that Vann was one of the nation's finest citizens and a truly extraordinary public servant. For more than a decade he worked tirelessly to achieve an honorable peace in Southeast Asia and to bind up the wounds of its ravaged peoples."

The Viet Cong took responsibility for Vann's death June 10. A Radio Hanoi broadcast monitored in Saigon that day said the Viet Cong command had "sent a cable congratulating the anti-aircraft unit in Kontum Province for good shooting" in bringing down the helicopter carrying Vann, whom the broadcast described as "one of the most important and most cruel advisers" in South Vietnam.

U.S. blasts power plant in North. A U.S. military spokesman in Saigon announced June 11 that B-52 bombers the previous day had destroyed a major hydroelectric plant supplying electricity to the Hanoi-Haiphong area.

According to the spokesman, the U.S. aircraft had used 2,000-pound bombs guided by laser beams in attacking the Langchi plant, 63 miles northwest of Hanoi, without hitting a dam located some 300 feet from the target area.

B-52s struck targets June 7 in the lower panhandle of North Vietnam just above the DMZ, in what was believed to be the first use of the heavy bombers against the North since April 24. The B-52s again crossed into the North June 9–10 to bomb supply caches near Donghoi.

Some 60 rail cars stranded northeast of Hanoi and 25 miles below the Chinese border, believed to be carrying military equipment destined for use by the North Vietnamese, were reported demolished by U.S. B-52s June 12. The U.S. command also said that two navy Phantoms from the carrier Coral Sea had shot down two MiG-17 jets 26 miles south of Hanoi.

More laser-guided bombs were used June 12 to knock out two railroad bridges located 55 and 60 miles northeast of Hanoi. A total of 290 strikes were flown that day by U.S. planes. B-52s were used again against Donghoi June 13.

The main rail line connecting Hanoi and Haiphong was reported by U.S. military sources June 14 to have been cut the previous day when U.S. jets destroyed a bridge at Haiduong, midway between the two cities. Twenty-eight buildings of a factory producing pontoon bridges on the northwest edge of Hanoi were wrecked that day in another U.S. air strike.

China sees threat—A Chinese Foreign Ministry statement released June 12 denounced the "grave provocations against the Chinese people" it said had been brought about by U.S. bombing raids in the northern parts of North Vietnam.

The dispatch said the U.S. had "steadily expanded the sphere of bombing up to areas close to the Sino-Vietnamese borders, threatening the security of China."

In a statement June 13 apparently designed to reassure Peking that its borders were not in danger of violation, U.S. State Department spokesman Charles W. Bray 3rd said "the actions we are taking against military targets in North Vietnam are taken with considerable care and precision, and are not in any way intended to threaten the security of China." Bray expressed confidence in the "effectiveness of some of the newer techniques involving, for instance, laser beams and television control of the bombs."

Hanoi claims dikes hit—Nguyen Thanh Le, a North Vietnamese spokesman in Paris, charged June 8 that the U.S. had intentionally and repeatedly bombed dams, dikes and locks in his country in raids April 10–May 24.

Le said 42 raids had been conducted and 580 bombs dropped on waterworks of the Red River and other streams and that U.S. naval vessels had fired up to 500 shells on the coastal dikes of Haihau district, about 70 miles southeast of Hanoi.

The allegations were denied June 8 by U.S. Vice Adm. William P. Mack, former commander of the 7th Fleet and recently named superintendent of the U.S. Naval Academy, and by Lt. Gen. George J. Eade, Air Force deputy chief of staff for plans and operations.

(Also in Paris June 8, the Viet Cong press agency released what it said was a public appeal to the U.S. Congress signed by 15 American servicemen taken prisoner in South Vietnam during 1967–71. The appeal was said to have called the war "a mistake" and to have urged Congress to require the Nixon Administration to obtain peace. It was reportedly signed by Capt. Harold Kushner, M.D.; WO Frank G. Anton, Sgt. Jon Robert Caviani, Spec. 4 John A. Young, Pfc. King D. Rayford, Cpl. Frederick L. Elbert Jr., Pfc. John G. Sparks, Sgt. Jose Jesus Anzaldua Jr., 1st Lt. Richard C. Anshus, WO David W. Sooter, Cpl. Alfonso Ray Riate, Spec. 4 Robert P. Chenoweth, Pfc. James A. Daly, Pfc. Don A. MacPhail and Pfc. Abel L. Cavanagh.)

U.S. jets raid MiG bases. American planes directed attacks against North Vietnamese MiG bases considerably south of Hanoi June 15–18 during the period of Soviet President Podgorny's visit there.

In four days of concentrated strikes aimed at damaging MiG air fields, the U.S. jets attacked bases at Baithuong, 80 miles south of Hanoi, at Quanlang and at Khephat, near Donghoi. The U.S. command reported that runways at all three bases had been partially destroyed.

A U.S. spokesman said June 19 that American jets had destroyed more of North Vietnam's antiaircraft system during the previous 24-hour period than at any time since Hanoi's offensive against South Vietnam began. More than 300 tactical strikes were carried out in North Vietnam's southern panhandle from the DMZ to the vicinity of Quangkhe, 65 miles north. A total of 140 "pieces of air defense equipment," including 76 surface-to-air missiles, were reported destroyed or severely damaged. (In a related announcement, the U.S. command said June 19 that an F-4 Phantom had been shot down June 13 some 60 miles north of Hanoi by a MiG fighter and that two crewmen were listed as missing.)

The attacks continued June 20 with 46 North Vietnamese missiles reported knocked out. Navy fighter-bombers hit two storage depots 27 and 30 miles northwest of Haiphong. The official North Vietnamese press agency said two U.S. jets had been shot down north of Hanoi June 20.

House panel drops end-war bill. The House Foreign Affairs Committee narrowly defeated a bill June 13 calling for U.S. withdrawal from Indochina by Oct. 1, and substituted a resolution backing the withdrawal terms offered by President Nixon May 8. The vote was 19–18.

Democrats on the committee led by chairman Thomas E. Morgan (Pa.) had offered a bill ordering an end to all U.S. military action in or over Indochina by Oct. 1 if American prisoners were released and the safety of withdrawing troops were guaranteed. Republicans, responding to a White House lobbying effort, offered a substitute resolution, stating that it was the intent of Congress that U.S. forces be withdrawn four months after an internationally supervised cease-fire was implemented

throughout Indochina and after all prisoners were returned and missing troops accounted for.

Five Democrats joined 14 Republicans in support of the substitute measure, with two Republicans and 16 Democrats in opposition; two antiwar Democrats were absent for the vote. The committee had never approved a withdrawal measure in the past.

Civilian casualties running high. South Vietnamese civilians had suffered heavy casualties since the start of the North Vietnamese offensive March 30 with the losses running higher than those inflicted in the Communists' Tet offensive in 1968, according to two separate U.S. reports made public June 15.

Sen. Edward M. Kennedy (Mass.), chairman of the Senate Judiciary Subcommittee on Refugees, said his panel estimated that "as many as 25,000 deaths" had occurred and that another 55,000 civilians were wounded since March 30. The comparable figure for the Tet offensive was 62,000 civilian casualties, including 20,000 deaths. The subcommittee's estimate of civilian losses between 1965 and May 1972 totaled 1,250,000, including 380,000 killed.

Kennedy said the Agency for International Development had informed him that the number of new refugees created by the fighting in South Vietnam had risen by 100,000 since May 8 and that the subcommittee estimated "up to 1.2 million new refugees since April 1."

U.S. Ambassador Ellsworth Bunker estimated that the number of civilian casualties admitted to hospitals in the second part of 1972 would double the total in the first six months of the year.

Bunker's report, sent to Secretary of State William P. Rogers June 11 and made public June 15, noted that the Tet drive had produced an average 37.3% increase in monthly hospital admissions of civilians in the six-month period after the fighting in February–March 1968. Bunker said hospital admissions of civilians in April and May 1972 "appear proportionately greater than initial increases following the 1968 Tet offensive." "The next six-month period," he predicted, "will show a monthly average substantially in excess of the 37.3%."

Mayors meet, back Nixon on Vietnam. The 40th annual U.S. Conference of Mayors met in New Orleans June 17–21, and voted to endorse President Nixon's Vietnam policies. It was a reversal of a 1971 conference position.

The Vietnam resolution, passed June 21 by a 2–1 show of hands, stated that although the war "distorts national priorities" and had divided the country, Nixon had taken "encouraging steps" to end it. While the 1971 resolution had called for a U.S. troop withdrawal within six months, the 1972 version supported Nixon's offer to withdraw four months after a cease-fire and release of American prisoners.

A group of antiwar mayors, including John V. Lindsay of New York, Thomas A. Luken of Cincinnati, Norman Mineta of San Jose, Calif. and Richard G. Hatcher of Gary, Ind. had submitted a resolution calling for a complete cessation of U.S. military activity in Indochina by Oct. 1. Republican Mayor John Driggs of Phoenix sponsored the successful pro-Nixon proposal. Mayor Richard Daley of Chicago said his vote for the Driggs resolution was out of loyalty to the "old-fashioned way" of supporting the President on foreign policy.

Casualty reports. The South Vietnamese command reported June 22 that 724 government troops were killed and 2,529 wounded in fighting June 11–17. The U.S. command said eight Americans had been killed and 27 wounded in that weekly period.

Battle casualties in the June 4–10 period as reported by the U.S. command June 15: six Americans killed and 32 wounded, raising total losses since 1961 to 45,782 dead, 303,118 wounded and 1,598 missing or captured; 632 South Vietnamese killed, 2,302 wounded and 167 missing; and 3,719 North Vietnamese and Viet Cong killed.

Total losses since the start of the North Vietnamese offensive March 30 stood at 121 Americans killed, 85 dead from nonhostile causes and 450 wounded; 9,159 South Vietnamese killed and 30,656 wounded; and 48,515 Communists killed.

U.S. raid ruins North steel mill. U.S. air raids on North Vietnam June 21–27 were marked by the reported destruction of the country's only steel mill, the bombing of a power plant—resulting in the partial blackout of Hanoi—and the pounding of targets within the city limits of Hanoi and Haiphong.

The U.S. command reported that the steel plant was struck June 24 at Thainguyen, 35 miles north of Hanoi. Pilots, using 2,000-pound bombs guided by laser and television beams, reported destroying "numerous double-bay warehouses and the plant's open-hearth furnaces for making steel." The plant had been bombed four times before the 1968 bombing halt. It was North Vietnam's only producer of structural steel used for bridges, railroads and buildings.

North Vietnam claimed two U.S. Phantom jets were downed during the June 24 raids "over populous areas" in nine provinces.

A U.S. raid June 25 destroyed a power plant at Viettri 25 miles northwest of Hanoi and blacked out part of the North Vietnamese capital, the U.S. command reported the following day. The command said 20 fighter-bombers had "effectively destroyed the plant's capability to produce power."

Targets within the city limits of Hanoi and Haiphong were pounded by more than 320 air strikes June 26. The U.S. command said planes based at Udon, Thailand bombed the Bacmai airfield and adjacent storage areas two miles south of the center of Hanoi, while other pilots attacking Haiphong bombed within one mile of the city's center.

The North Vietnamese press agency claimed a hospital and a residential block were destroyed in the June 26 raid on Hanoi, and that two dispensaries were destroyed in the attack on Haiphong and many persons were killed or wounded. The agency report said a dike at the nearby hamlet of Dongtru was hit by an American rocket.

Hanoi radio claimed air and ground defenses shot down 10 U.S. planes over North Vietnam June 27. Five of the aircraft were destroyed over Hanoi, the report said. The North Vietnamese

press agency said U.S. planes the same
day bombed a hospital at Bacmai and
other civilian targets. "Numerous"
civilians were killed in the hospital attack, the agency said.

Hanoi claims U.S. bombs dikes—
Hanoi again charged June 22 that U.S.
planes and Navy vessels had embarked
on a deliberate campaign to destroy
North Vietnamese dikes and renewed
an international appeal "to force the
United States to stop."

Speaking at a news conference in
Paris, Vo Van Sung, the North Vietnamese delegate general in France, said
U.S. planes had attacked dikes 68 times
April 10–June 10, dropping 665 bombs
along the Red River and other waterways. Calling the campaign "premeditated," Sung said "possible bursting of
dikes in North Vietnam during the rainy
season—from the end of June until
October—threatens the lives of millions
of people and threatens hundreds of
thousands of square kilometers of cul-
tivated land with flooding."

The North Vietnamese government
had charged in a broadcast May 30 that
in Thanhhoa Province, about 100 miles
south of Hanoi, "for many times in a
day of April 19, 20, 24, 26 and 27, and
May 13, 17, and 18, U.S. aircraft attacked the irrigation works, dropping a
total of 158 big-sized bombs on the em-
bankments of the Ma and Len Rivers in
Hoanghoa, Dongson, Theiuhoa, Vinh-
loc, and Hatrung districts."

The U.S. Defense Department had
repeatedly denied any deliberate or inadvertent attacks against the dikes. One
Air Force official, Lt. Gen. George J.
Eade, deputy chief of operations, said:
"We haven't targeted any dikes and to
my knowledge we haven't accidentally
hit any dikes which have caused any
problem."

The Defense Department June 23
said it believed "Hanoi might be making these allegations so that they could
claim, if there were any floods caused
by natural phenomenon, that they resulted from erroneous charges that we
have been bombing dikes."

Agence France-Presse correspondent
Jean Thoraval June 24 confirmed
Hanoi's charges that dikes in North
Vietnam were being damaged. In a dis-

patch from Hanoi, Thoraval said he and
other foreign newsmen that day had
seen bombed dikes 14 miles from Namdinh, a textile center about 60 miles
south of Hanoi. According to Thoraval,
the commercial center of Namdinh
"was in total ruin" as a result of U.S.
air strikes.

Sweden's ambassador to North Vietnam, Jean-Christophe Oeberg, said in
Hanoi June 24 that the U.S. air campaign over North Vietnam was directed
at almost "anything," "not only
military targets but also economic targets." "The destruction, the devastation,
is more complete now than at any time
before," he said.

Lon Nol elected president. Marshal
Lon Nol was elected June 4 to a full five-
year term as president of Cambodia. He
had taken the title of president after assuming full power in March.

Running against candidates In Tam,
former chairman of the dissolved National Assembly, Keo An and Hou Mong,
Lon Nol received slightly less than 55%
of the vote. Keo An had called for
the return to Cambodia of exiled former
Chief of State Prince Norodom Sihanouk as a private citizen.

Lon Nol further consolidated his rule
June 21 by announcing the formation
of a new political organization—the
Nationalist Union Movement—with
himself as its head. Political circles in
Pnompenh were shocked at the news
because the movement appeared to be
similar to the Sangkum, the political
organization with which Sihanouk had
effectively controlled political life in
Cambodia from 1955 until his overthrow
in 1970.

U.S. airmen shifted to Thailand. The
shift of American pilots and planes
from the Danang air base in South
Vietnam to bases in Thailand 500 miles
west was disclosed June 19. The U.S.
command in Saigon announced that the
transfer of more than 2,000 pilots and up
to 150 planes was completed June 26.

Marine Corps Commandant Gen.
Robert E. Cushman Jr. said June 20
that the shift to Thailand was "part of

the move to get out of Vietnam, to get a base that's more secure."

The Defense Department further explained June 21 that the "driving factor" of the withdrawal was the decision June 17 to pull out the 196th Infantry Brigade, which provided security at Danang for the airmen. "We are not going to leave these Air Force people there without American security," a department statement said.

The July 3 issue of Newsweek magazine predicted that Thailand would soon replace South Vietnam as the major U.S. military base in Southeast Asia. The article said that in the past six weeks there had been a tremendous buildup of American airpower in Thailand: the number of B-52s at the Utapao air base had doubled to 80; the Takhli base, closed in 1970, had been reopened and at least two new squadrons of F-4 Phantoms were stationed there; and the first U.S. Marine air base was opened in Nam Phong.

Newsweek estimated that U.S. air strength in Thailand had increased from 450 to 750 planes and that the number of U.S. military personnel in the country had risen from 32,000 to 49,000 men.

According to a New York Times report June 29, the Defense Department had provided statistics showing that there were 45,000 Americans in Thailand, compared with 32,000 when the North Vietnamese launched their offensive at the end of March. The Pentagon also estimated that there now was a 42,000-man naval force offshore. In March, there were 18,000 offshore troops, in January 15,000.

The Times also reported that various support forces whose activities were related to the war had been increased at American bases in the Pacific. One report estimated that as many as 15,000 men may have been added to those forces since the enemy's March offensive.

Taken together, those increases were estimated to total 50,000–60,000 men.

New troop cut set—President Nixon announced June 28 that 10,000 more troops would be withdrawn from South Vietnam by Sept. 1, reducing the size of the U.S. force there to 39,000 men.

At the same time, Nixon said that henceforth no draftees would be sent to Vietnam unless they volunteer for duty there. The President's order, however, would not affect the 4,000 draftees now serving in Vietnam or draftees already under orders to go there.

Both of Nixon's decisions were announced by White House Press Secretary Ronald L. Ziegler. Ziegler said the President had made them "based on an assessment that the troops could be withdrawn without jeopardizing U.S. troops in Vietnam or the Vietnamization program." Vietnamization was the Administration's program for turning over the major combat burden to South Vietnamese forces.

Senate acts on military aid. In a series of votes June 13–28, the Senate moved toward adoption of the foreign military aid authorization bill, retaining most of the fund cuts and checks on the Executive branch proposed by the Foreign Relations Committee. The Senate planned to resume consideration of the bill, including the Mansfield Vietnam pullout provision, after the recess for the Democratic National Convention. In a defeat for antiwar forces Sen. Clifford P. Case (R, N.J.) agreed to an amendment June 23 killing a provision he had sponsored to cut off funds for Thai forces in Northern Laos. Current law barred aid to third-country mercenaries in Laos, and Sen. Stuart Symington (D, Mo.) charged June 24 that Thai troops designated by the Administration as volunteers had told Congressional investigators they had been ordered to Laos. The Senate retained a provision barring funds for third-country troops in Thailand.

House rejects pullout amendment. The House approved by a 334–59 vote June 27 a military procurement bill authorizing the $1.3 billion increase in strategic weapons spending requested by the Nixon Administration. The House also rejected, by a 224–152 vote, an end-the-war amendment requiring a U.S. pullout from Vietnam by Sept. 1 subject only to an agreement for release of American prisoners of war.

International Peace Efforts

Report on Vietnam discussions. President Nixon reported to Congress on his Moscow visit within a half-hour of his return to the U.S. June 1. He told Congress, assembled in joint session that evening in the House chamber, that the war in Incochina and the peace talks had been among the subjects he had discussed with Soviets leaders.

Nixon said the problem of ending the Vietnam war "was one of the most extensively discussed subjects on our agenda" of the Moscow talks. But "it would only jeopardize the search for peace if I were to review here all that was said on that subject," he declared. "I will simply say this: each side obviously has its own point of view and its own approach to this very difficult issue. But at the same time, both the United States and the Soviet Union share an overriding desire to achieve a more stable peace in the world."

His Administration "has no higher goal" than "bringing the Vietnam war to an early and honorable end," he said. "We are ending the war in Vietnam, but we shall end it in a way which will not betray our friends, risk the lives of the courageous Americans still serving in Vietnam, break faith with those held prisoners by the enemy or stain the honor of the United States of America."

Paris talks renewal bid. The U.S. and South Vietnam refused to take up the suspended Paris peace talks June 14, although North Vietnamese and Viet Cong spokesmen had earlier indicated apparent willingness to do so.

In a message sent to the North Vietnamese and Viet Cong delegations June 14, the allies declared that "continued North Vietnamese military activities in South Vietnam do not indicate an intention on your part to take the path of negotiations." Concerning the eventual resumption of talks, the dispatch said, "our side shall be guided by all relevant factors, including the result of procedures which provide that the time for each session will be specifically agreed in advance."

The message was believed to have been a response to a June 13 statement by North Vietnam and the Viet Cong which asked the U.S. to halt its acts of war and "participate in the work of the Paris conference each Thursday as usual." William J. Porter, chief U.S. negotiator at the talks, had remarked June 12 on his return to Paris after a month's absence that "President Nixon has been intensely interested in arriving at some kind of negotiated settlement of the Vietnam problem."

Porter had also said: "My return here at this time is an additional indication of his strong preference and hope that such a settlement can be achieved. . . . We understand, I think, some of the problems which beset the other side, at least we try to understand. We are going to keep trying. This is the essential message that I bring back."

State Department spokesman Charles W. Bray 3rd said June 12 that Porter's "relative optimism" had been inspired by reports that the chief North Vietnamese negotiator, Xuan Thuy, would soon be returning to Paris with new instructions.

Podgorny in Hanoi; U.S. raids suspended. Soviet President Nikolai V. Podgorny flew to Hanoi June 15 after a stopover in Calcutta June 14. A Moscow dispatch published in the pro-Moscow New Delhi newspaper, The Patriot, said June 14 that Podgorny was expected to discuss with North Vietnamese leaders a possible resumption of the Paris peace talks.

U.S. Air Force officers in Danang said June 15 that a suspension of U.S. bombing raids in the Hanoi area had begun the day before and would last as long as Podgorny was in Hanoi. However, they added, the suspension would not apply to the rest of North Vietnam.

A spokesman for the U.S. command in Saigon said June 15 that he did not know of any limitation of the bombing in the North. In Washington, the White House refused to comment on reports of a partial halt, but Administration officials privately confirmed them, according to the New York Times June 16.

Podgorny June 18 ended his visit to the North Vietnamese capital with no apparent sign that the trip had produced substantial agreement between the two countries on ways of ending the Vietnam war.

A joint communique released June 19 said the Soviet Union would "continue to render all the necessary assistance" to the North Vietnamese in their fight against "imperialist aggression" and that Moscow wished Hanoi "fresh successes." Both sides called upon the U.S. to "resume constructive talks in Paris" and end its bombing and mining of North Vietnam.

At a brief airport stopover in Calcutta on his way to the Soviet Union, Podgorny said June 18 he was "very happy with the outcome" of his trip and that everything had gone "as I wanted." Asked if he thought the Paris peace talks would be taken up again, Podgorny replied: "Yes, soon."

Kissinger arrives in Peking. President Nixon's adviser on national security, Henry A. Kissinger, arrived in Peking June 19 to begin a series of talks with Chinese officials.

Kissinger held four hours of talks June 19 with Premier Chou En-lai and afterwards attended a banquet given by Chou. Another four hours of discussions took place June 20 between Kissinger and Chou, with Foreign Minister Chi Peng-fei and other officials in attendance.

In a related development, Le Duc Tho, a member of the North Vietnamese Politburo and special adviser to the Paris peace talks, had arrived in Peking June 17. Tho had a meeting June 18 with Chou and left later in the day for Hanoi.

Kissinger returned to Washington June 23. After reporting to President Nixon June 23, Kissinger told a White House news conference the following day that he had discussed the Indochina war at length with Chinese leaders, but detected no break in the political impasse. He said he agreed with a statement made earlier in the day by Secretary of State William P. Rogers that there were no "clear signs" of progress toward ending the conflict. Kissinger noted that even if the major Communist powers pressured North Vietnam to reach a solution, the war could only be settled by "direct negotiations" between Washington and Hanoi.

Kissinger also said the Peking meetings had left him confident that the U.S. and China would make "steady progress" in bilateral talks on expanding trade and on arranging cultural, scientific and educational exchanges.

An official joint statement issued simultaneously in Washington and Peking June 24 said the Kissinger-Chou meetings "consisted of concrete consultations to promote the normalization between the two countries." The statement expressed the "desirability of continuing" these discussions in the future.

Paris peace talks to resume. President Nixon disclosed at a news conference June 29 that the Paris peace talks on the Vietnam war would resume July 13. The U.S. was returning to the talks, he said, "on the assumption that the North Vietnamese are prepared to negotiate in a constructive and serious way." If they were, he said, the war could be ended "well before" the end of his first term of office (Jan. 20, 1973); but if they did not engage in serious negotiations, then the U.S would continue its policy of increased bombing and the mining of North Vietnamese ports.

Nixon defended the bombing and mining as necessary to gain diplomatic concessions from the enemy—serious consideration of the U.S. peace plan and the return of American prisoners of war. "The only way we're going to get our POWs back," he said, "is to be doing something to them [the North Vietnamese], and that means hitting military targets in North Vietnam, retaining a residual force in South Vietnam and continuing the mining of the harbors of North Vietnam."

Nixon said the effects of the mining and bombing had "turned around" the battlefield situation and the South Vietnamese were "now on the offensive."

The President denied that the U.S. had bombed dikes and dams in North Vietnam. Reports of such bombing had been checked, he said, and found to be "inaccurate." Only military targets were permitted, he said.

Communists firm on peace stand. The North Vietnamese and Viet Cong delegations to the Paris peace talks asserted June 30 that President Nixon had been forced by domestic and world opinion to resume the conference, but they indicated no change in their conditions for reaching an agreement. The Communists' statements were in response to President Nixon's announcement June 29 that the Paris conference would resume July 13.

Hanoi's representatives again demanded that the U.S. end the naval blockade and bombing of North Vietnam, withdraw support of President Nguyen Van Thieu, abandon the Vietnamization policy and unconditionally remove its troops from Vietnam. The North Vietnamese reiterated the call for U.S. acceptance of the Viet Cong's seven-point peace plan. The Viet Cong statement called the plan the "correct and realistic basis for a settlement of the Vietnamese problem permitting the United States to withdraw honorably from its war of aggression."

The North Vietnamese Communist party newspaper Nhan Dan June 30 denounced as a "fraud" Nixon's announcement the previous day of plans to withdraw 10,000 more American troops from South Vietnam in July and August. Those troops would not be returned to the U.S., the newspaper said, but would be sent to Thailand "or some other places in Southeast Asia from where they will be rushed back to Vietnam if necessary."

A North Vietnamese embassy source in Vientiane, Laos was quoted as saying June 30 that Hanoi would demand the withdrawal of the U.S. force from Thailand as part of a peace settlement. North Vietnam regarded the American force there as a threat to its security and as an attempt to "maintain American influence in Indochina without an American presence," the source said. The embassy official also warned that Thailand "cannot permit the American bases in Thailand to remain and hope to normalize relations with North Vietnam or China."

American use of bases in Thailand had been denounced by China June 28. The Communist party newspaper Jenmin Jih Pao singled out the American air attacks on North Vietnam which orginated at Thai airfields.

Souvanna agrees to peace talks. Laotian Premier Souvanna Phouma July 7 accepted an offer from the Lao Patriotic Front leader, Prince Souphanouvong, for resumption of talks aimed at halting fighting between government and rebel Pathet Lao forces. Souphanouvong had proposed sending his personal envoy, Souk Vongsak, to reopen contacts broken off in 1971.

Souphanouvong followed up his peace offer with a statement July 14 saying that "the only way to obtain genuine peace and independence for the fatherland is to persist in our nationwide struggle till complete victory." He asserted that unless the "U.S imperialists and their henchmen" were "defeated on the battlefield, they will not renounce their aggressive schemes."

Laos cabinet change—A sweeping change in Laos' tripartite government was announced by Premier Souvanna Phouma July 12. Four ministers were dismissed, eight new members were appointed and three current ministers were promoted or shifted.

Souvanna said the Pathet Lao ministers absent from the government since 1963 would retain their posts even though their duties had been taken over by secretaries of state.

A new political group aimed at forcing the resignation of Souvanna's government and ending the ruling three-party coalition had been formed May 8. It was made up of National Assembly members and was headed by the assembly president, Phoui Sananikone, a former right-wing premier. The organization, called the Group for the Protection of the Constitution, had 32 members, a majority in the 60-seat assembly.

Schumann visits China. French Foreign Minister Maurice Schumann visited China July 5-11 and the Indochina war was the principal topic of discussion. Before leaving China, Schumann told newsmen July 11 that "the Chinese are preoccupied by Taiwan and Korea, but for them the No. 1 problem is Vietnam."

Schumann had conferred with Chairman Mao Tsetung, Premier Chou Enlai and Foreign Minister Chi Peng-fei.

Paris peace talks resume. The Paris peace talks resumed July 13 after a 10-week suspension. The allied and Communist delegations restated their opposing positions of previous meetings, but a spokesman for the North Vietnamese delegation said later that chief negotiator Xuan Thuy had raised "some new aspects" in his presentations. He did not specify what they were.

Thuy repeated Hanoi's demand that the U.S. abandon its support of South Vietnamese President Nguyen Van Thieu and end "its intervention in the internal affairs of Vietnam." He then said there was a second aspect to the political question, a matter of "power in Saigon—a question for the Vietnamese people to negotiate, excluding all outside influence." The State Department said the American delegation had expressed interest in the latter statement, and wondered whether Thuy was expressing a new position or rephrasing a previous one. Heretofore, the U.S. had called for discussion of all political problems among the Vietnamese, but Hanoi had insisted on a full political as well as military settlement with the U.S.

In the presentation of formal positions at the meeting, U.S. chief delegate William A. Porter summarized President Nixon's May 8 proposals on releasing prisoners of war, a cease-fire and withdrawal of American troops. Thuy and Mrs. Nguyen Thi Binh, chief of the Viet Cong delegation, rejected this proposal as "illogical and unreasonable." Mrs. Binh asserted that an immediate cease-fire "would not serve to end the war but simply to legalize the administration of Nguyen Van Thieu and the American military presence" in Vietnam.

Henry A. Kissinger, Nixon's national security adviser, had said July 8 that he had "some reason to believe" that North Vietnam would engage in "serious negotiations" when the peace talks resumed. Speaking at a Western White House briefing, Kissinger said there had been "very intense diplomatic activity" since the U.S. broke off the talks May 4 and was hopeful that progress could be made.

Pope Paul VI had appealed to both sides in the Paris negotiations July 9 to display "courage for peace" in their new discussions. He said both sides must "give proof of wisdom and magnanimity capable of putting human life and dignity above any other interest."

U.S.-North Vietnamese private talks. Henry A. Kissinger, President Nixon's national security adviser, held a 6½-hour private meeting in Paris July 19 with Le Duc Tho, North Vietnamese Politburo member and chief adviser to his country's delegation to the Vietnam peace talks. The secret talks were disclosed simultaneously by the White House and the North Vietnamese government. The session was the 14th Kissinger had held with Tho and was their first meeting since May 2.

Kissinger flew back to Washington later July 19 and reported to President Nixon. A White House statement on the talks said "further meetings will be announced as they are held. By mutual agreement neither side will reveal the substance of these meetings."

The Kissinger-Tho discussions were followed by another plenary meeting of the Paris talks July 20. William J. Porter, chief U.S. delegate, said after the conference that he had found "a slight improvement" in the tone, if not the substance, of the meeting. Porter said his instructions were to elicit a North Vietnamese statement that their conditions for a settlement were "negotiable." The meeting concluded, however, without his being able to "evoke any kind of statement that their proposals are negotiable," Porter said.

Private talks continue. U.S. Presidential adviser Henry A. Kissinger conferred privately in Paris Aug. 1 with Le Duc Tho, a member of the North Vietnamese Politburo, and Xuan Thuy, head of the North Vietnamese delegation to the Paris peace talks. The meeting, disclosed by the White House, was the 15th between Kissinger and Tho.

Kissinger returned to Washington later Aug. 1 to brief President Nixon. No further details on the Paris meeting were provided by the White House.

The meeting followed a routine session of the Vietnam peace conference in Paris July 27, in which U.S. and Communist negotiators traded charges on damage to North Vietnamese dikes. Xuan Thuy accused the U.S. of "systematic and deliberate" bombing of the dikes, while U.S. Ambassador William J. Porter insisted that "we have not targeted the dikes," adding, "you make no claim that military equipment or installations were not emplaced near dikes or related structures." A Hanoi press spokesman said after the session that "we never put a military installation on a dike."

At the Aug. 3 session of the talks, U.S. and Communist delegates reverted to the sharp recriminations that had characterized previous sessions.

After the meeting, a North Vietnamese spokesman questioned President Nixon's "serenity of mind," asserting there had been no change in "the Nixon Administration's policy of aggression and neocolonialism." Ambassador Porter expressed disappointment in the session, and said he had made a statement to the conference denouncing the Communists' "invective against the President of the United States." However, both sides agreed to another session Aug. 10.

Nonaligned nations criticize U.S. Foreign ministers of more than 60 nonaligned nations, mostly from Asia and Africa, met in Georgetown, Guyana Aug. 8–12 to discuss a wide variety of topics including the Vietnam war. The conference criticized U.S. policy in Indochina, supporting peace proposals made by the Viet Cong in South Vietnam, the Pathet Lao in Laos, and the exile government of Prince Norodom Sihanouk of Cambodia.

The major conflict at the conference, seating delegations representing the Viet Cong and the Cambodian exile government, was resolved after considerable debate Aug. 10. Indonesia, Malaysia and Laos walked out of the conference to protest the decision to seat the two delegations. However, the two new delegations were seated only for the Aug. 10 session. A decision to accept them as permanent members of the nonaligned group was left to a projected conference of nonaligned heads of state and government in 1973.

Kissinger in Paris, Saigon talks. A flurry of speculation about a possible new American peace gesture was generated by a round of talks held by Presidential adviser Henry A. Kissinger with North Vietnamese representatives in Paris Aug. 14 and with South Vietnamese President Nguyen Van Thieu in Saigon Aug. 17–18.

Kissinger conferred privately in Paris with Le Duc Tho of the North Vietnamese Politburo, and Xuan Thuy, chief of Hanoi's delegation to the Vietnam peace talks. It was Kissinger's 16th meeting with Tho since 1969. As in the previous discussions, no details were given out by either side.

Ly Van Sau, a spokesman for the Viet Cong's Provisional Revolutionary Government, asserted in Paris after the Kissinger-Tho talks that President Nixon was "using the so-called private meetings to make American opinion believe that something is happening, while in fact he is increasing the escalation of the war."

Kissinger's trip to Saigon was announced by the White House Aug. 15. Press Secretary Ronald Ziegler said the visit had been planned for several weeks and was not connected with Kissinger's latest meetings with Hanoi's representatives in Paris. His forthcoming meeting with Thieu and U.S. diplomatic and military officials was for the purpose of "a general review of all aspects of the Vietnam problem, including the negotiations in Paris," Ziegler said. He cautioned newsmen that "we are in a sensitive time now; it wouldn't be wise to speculate."

The announcement of Kissinger's plans to visit Saigon coupled with Le Duc Tho's departure for Hanoi Aug. 16 heightened speculation that the two men had reached an agreement and that Kissinger was on his way to inform Thieu of these developments. However, before departing Paris, Tho said his return to Hanoi was "routine."

Kissinger arrived in Saigon Aug. 16 and conferred with Thieu Aug. 17–18. The meeting Aug. 18 was regarded as a surprise, since it had been expected that the two men would only confer once. Present at the Aug. 17 meeting were U.S. Ambassador Ellsworth Bunker, Winston Lord, a Kissinger aide, and Nguyen Phu Duc and Hoang Duc Nha, Thieu's security adviser and press secretary. Prior to that meeting, Kissinger had conferred with Bunker, Gen. Frederick C. Weyand, commander of U.S. forces in Vietnam, and Gen. John W. Vogt Jr., commander of the U.S. Seventh Air Force.

Thieu doubts U.S. policy—In a major policy speech Aug. 1, President Thieu had urged that the U.S. must "keep up relentless bombing" of North Vietnam for another six or seven months, but at the same time questioned whether the

U.S. was firmly commited to a policy of intensified raids.

The speech was made at a graduation ceremony at the National Defense College in Saigon. The South Vietnamese news agency at the time only issued a short paraphrased summary of the address, omitting Thieu's remarks about the U.S. commitment. The New York Times reported the speech in greater detail Aug. 13 based on a transcript made from a tape recording and issued by the government a few days after the president's speech.

In the key portion of his address, Thieu said: "There is only one way to force the Communists to negotiate seriously, and that consists of the total destruction of their economic and war potential. We must strike at them continuously, relentlessly, denying them any moment to catch their breath." On the question of Washington's willingness to do this, Thieu declared: "So it all depends on the determination of our allies. If our allies are determined, peace will be restored in Indochina. If they lack determination, the Communists will revert to their half-guerrilla half-conventional warfare, and the war will go on in Indochina forever."

The South Vietnamese leader said the purpose of the North Vietnamese offensive launched March 30 was to create "a stalemate" in the conflict that would cause President Nixon to lose his bid for re-election. "Whether or not the Communists can achieve their objective, ... will depend on the way the incumbent President deals with the problem," Thieu added.

Paris peace talks. The allied and Communist sides remained deadlocked following two more sessions of the Paris peace talks Aug. 10 and 18.

Mrs. Nguyen Thi Binh, chief delegate of the Viet Cong, attacked President Nguyen Van Thieu's regime at the Aug. 10 session, calling it "an administration of repression and terror" that had been established by the U.S. "to serve as an instrument of 'Vietnamization' of the war." She said the only way to end the war was for the U.S. to stop supporting the Thieu regime.

Nguyen Minh Vy, deputy North Vietnamese negotiator, charged that since April U.S. planes had carried out 177 attacks on North Vietnamese dikes and dams, destroying 58 portions of dikes and seven floodgates.

In a New York Times interview Aug. 11, Mrs. Binh said the key issue in the talks remained the necessity of a U.S. agreement to a political settlement leading to a new government in Saigon to bring the war to an end. Speaking to correspondent Flora Lewis, Mrs. Binh said if "an American President wants to end the war—any President—it's logical that he has to make a political settlement."

Asked what effect the U.S. election campaign might have on the Paris talks and questioned about a unilateral American withdrawal from Vietnam, Mrs. Binh replied: "Why unilateral withdrawal? Why not end with a solution? There would be guarantees for all, for us and the United States." She said her side might question whether the U.S. was "seeking a unilateral exit from the war—in order not to make any commitments about returning or not returning." As for the election campaign, Mrs. Binh said "if it has any effect, it will be on Nixon's side." Nixon was "preoccupied with the campaign and he will have to think about" the importance of the talks in relation to the election, Mrs. Binh said.

At the Aug. 18 session, the North Vietnamese delegation spokesman charged after the meeting that President Nixon was attempting to create an air of optimism while intensifying the war. In a prepared statement at the session, Mrs. Binh said that in January 1969 there had been "a most favorable occassion to put an end to the war if President Nixon had wished it." Nixon instead pursued a solution that would "perpetuate the yoke of American neo-colonialism over South Vietnam," Mrs. Binh said.

Rogers' peace optimism questioned. A prediction by U.S. Secretary of State William P. Rogers Aug. 16 that a settlement would soon be reached in negotiations to end the Indochina war was later qualified by the Nixon Administration and denounced by the Viet Cong.

In an interview with Knight newspapers published Aug. 20, Rogers said "I think that either we will have a negotiated settlement before the [November] elections, which I think is a possibility, or we will have one very soon after President Nixon's re-election." Rogers said he based his optimism on the fact that "the North Vietnamese are having serious military, economic and psychological difficulties." "The role of several of their allies," according to Rogers, "indicated that in the international field most nations feel that the war should end by negotiation. And so I think that will be the inevitable result of these pressures."

Rogers said there were four reasons why he believed Hanoi was anxious for a settlement: The North Vietnamese were convinced their invasion of South Vietnam "has not been successful"; the American bombing and mining of North Vietnam's ports "have been successful"; the North Vietnamese people were beginning to realize their fighting was "a hopeless endeavor"; and "the international community is largely supporting" President Nixon's peace proposals.

The White House qualified Rogers' statement Aug. 21 as "a general assessment based on his personal appraisal of the situation." Deputy Press Secretary Gerald L. Warren said Rogers "was expressing the hope of the Administration for an early settlement" and "was not making a prediction based on any event or any exchange that may or may not have occurred."

State Department spokesman Robert J. McCloskey said he was present at the Rogers interview and got the impression that when Rogers predicted a settlement "shortly" after the elections, "he thought in terms of months, rather than days or weeks."

Ly Van Sau, spokesman for the Viet Cong's delegation to the Vietnam peace talks, said in Paris Aug. 22 that Rogers' prediction of an early settlement of the war was "entirely false." "Every evidence indicates that the American Administration is only seeking to fool public opinion to serve its election campaign needs," Sau said.

Nixon conferred Aug. 31 with Ellsworth Bunker, the U.S. ambassador in Saigon. White House Press Secretary Ronald L. Ziegler later told newsmen that Nixon and Bunker had "assessed the entire situation" in Vietnam. Ziegler disclosed that Bunker, 78, would remain in his ambassadorial post for the remainder of Nixon's current term of office.

Kissinger ends talks with Asians. Presidential adviser Henry A. Kissinger returned to Washington Aug. 19 and reported to President Nixon on his private meetings with North Vietnamese representatives in Paris Aug. 14 and with South Vietnamese President Nguyen Van Thieu in Saigon Aug. 17–18. The White House made no disclosure of the contents of Kissinger's briefing.

(Kissinger also briefed Nixon on his meetings with Japanese officials in Tokyo where he had stopped Aug. 18–19 enroute back to Washington. The talks held Aug. 19 between Kissinger and Premier Kakuei Tanaka centered on U.S.-Japanese trade relations, Tanaka's forthcoming meeting with Nixon, and Japan's friendly diplomatic moves toward China. A joint statement by Kissinger and Tanaka merely said both officials had "exchanged candid views on their respective government's policies.")

Hanoi rejects Saigon bid on POWs. South Vietnam Aug. 22 offered to release 600 disabled North Vietnamese prisoners of war as a "humanitarian" gesture. North Vietnam and the Viet Cong rejected the proposal Aug. 24. Hanoi had spurned a similar bid in 1971.

Saigon's offer was turned down by Hanoi's deputy chief negotiator at the Paris peace talks, Nguyen Minh Vy, and by Mrs. Nguyen Thi Binh, head of the Viet Cong delegation, who denounced the proposal as a "maneuver." She said the U.S. and South Vietnam had "no right to capture patriots. They must free them all immediately."

Prior to another meeting of the Paris talks Aug. 24, Mrs. Binh denounced President Nixon's address to the Republican Convention in Miami the previous day. She said there was no need for the President to travel around the world seeking peace when peace "can be found here in this conference and nowhere else."

The Paris session itself produced no results. It was marked by the absence of the chief negotiators of the U.S. and North Vietnamese delegations. Both sides had announced Aug. 23 that William J. Porter was taking a brief holiday in Europe and that Xuan Thuy was tired and had been told by doctors to rest.

Hanoi to free 3 POWs. The North Vietnamese government announced Sept. 2 that it would release three American prisoners of war, the first it would free since 1969. However it warned the U.S. government not to use the freed POWs to "slander" North Vietnam, an action it said would be against "the interests of the families of other captured U.S. pilots."

The statement, broadcast by Radio Hanoi, said it had "temporarily suspended" the release of the POWs after the three pilots freed in 1969 had been "compelled" by the U.S. government to "put forward distortions about the humane policy" of Hanoi's treatment of the Americans. It said the U.S. had also used the freed pilots "in war activities" against the Vietnamese and other Indochinese peoples.

The three POWs to be freed were identified as Navy Lts. (jg) Markham Ligon Gartley and Norris Alphonzo Charles and Air Force Maj. Edward Knight Elias.

Later Sept. 2, David Dellinger and Cora Weiss, antiwar activists and cochairmen of the Committee of Liaison with the Families of Servicemen Detained in North Vietnam said at a press conference in Paris tha they would fly to Hanoi to escort the prisoners back to the U.S. Dellinger said he expected the release to be made "in a matter of weeks." He warned, however, that the release date could be delayed because of "the danger of floods in North Vietnam" which he linked to unusually heavier rains caused by "U.S. meteorological warfare."

Amplifying on the Hanoi statement, Mrs. Weiss and Dellinger both warned that Hanoi would not release any more prisoners until the end of the war if those freed were used "to slander" North Vietnam or to train other American pilots for raids over Indochina. Dellinger charged that previously released POWs had been "kidnaped" and "brainwashed" by the U.S. military on their return home and compelled to alter initial statements about good treatment by the North Vietnamese. He also charged they had been used to train pilots and plan the abortive 1970 raid on the Sontay prison camp.

Dellinger also disclosed that he had received information that 44 American pilots had been captured by the Hanoi government since the U.S. resumed intensive bombing of the North in April. Mrs. Weiss said she had been informed by North Vietnamese sources that 383 American POWs were held by North Vietnam as of Aug. 23. (The U.S. Defense Department listed 1,123 men as prisoners or missing in action in Indochina.)

Defense Department spokesman Jerry W. Friedheim Sept. 2 said the U.S. reserved the right to decide disposition of the POWs until they returned home, adding "the last thing we want to do is endanger getting somebody else back."

(Antiwar statements had been attributed to Elias and Charles, two of the prisoners to be freed, in broadcasts from Hanoi, according to U.S. government records cited in the Washington Post Sept. 7. In one of the statements broadcast July 11, both men had allegedly urged the "American people to require our government to withdraw all military forces from South Vietnam, cease the bombing of Indochina and cease support of an unwanted Saigon government.")

(Radio Hanoi Sept. 4 broadcast a recorded interview with Air Force Capt. William Glen Byrns, who allegedly called for the election of Democratic candidate Sen. George S. McGovern as president. Byrns reportedly said U.S. POWs opposed President Nixon's reelection "because we don't want to go on sitting here for another four years.")

Communists restate peace terms. Communist conditions for ending the war appeared to be unchanged in major statements made by North Vietnam Sept. 1 and the Viet Cong Sept. 11.

In an address marking North Vietnam's National Day, Premier Pham Van Dong declared Sept. 1 that a three-part "coalition government" to replace the South Vietnamese regime of President Nguyen Van Thieu remained Hanoi's basic condition for a settlement. He repeated previous demands for an end to the U.S.' Vietnamization program, and a halt to all air, naval and ground activity.

Dong's speech was monitored by U.S. government agencies in Saigon, which described it as "uncompromising."

The North Vietnamese radio, which broadcast the premier's speech, also carried a message from Chairman Mao Tsetung of China pledging "all-out support and assistance" to North Vietnam in its "war against United States aggression."

(An editorial in the North Vietnamese Communist party newspaper Nhan Dan broadcast Aug. 17 had seemed to take issue with China and the Soviet Union for permitting closer relations with the U.S. to weaken their support for Hanoi. The statement insisted that North Vietnam would not soften its negotiating position and criticized those "who are departing from the great all-conquering revolutionary thoughts of the time and who are pitifully bogging down on the dark, muddy road of compromise.")

The Viet Cong's Sept. 11 declaration, heralded by them as an "important statement," was described by the U.S. government as containing "absolutely no change" in terms. The Viet Cong broadcast, repeating demands for a three-part coalition regime in Saigon, said in part: "A solution to the internal problems of South Vietnam must proceed from the actual situation—that there exist in South Vietnam two administrations, two armies and other political forces. ... To this end it is necessary to form in South Vietnam a provisional government of national accord with three equal segments to take charge of affairs in the period of transition and to organize truly free and democratic elections."

The Communist proposal for a tripartite government was denounced by the U.S. at the Paris peace talks Sept. 14. Chief delegate William J. Porter said it was "nothing more than an undisguised attempt to put the Viet Cong in power in South Vietnam without elections."

Peace conference sessions had been held Aug. 24, 31 and Sept. 7 with no progress reported. Le Duc Tho, chief adviser to North Vietnam's delegation, returned to Paris Sept. 11.

Hoffa Hanoi trip dropped. James R. Hoffa, former president of the International Brotherhood of Teamsters, reported Sept. 7 that he was canceling, at least for the time being, a private trip to Hanoi to negotiate the release of American prisoners. Shortly thereafter, the State Department reported that Hoffa's passport validation to travel to North Vietnam had been improperly granted and would be immediately revoked.

Hoffa said he had been invited by North Vietnamese trade unions, and that he had planned to fly to Paris Sept. 7 on the first leg of the trip. Certain undisclosed problems had caused him to postpone the trip, which had been damaged, he said, by news disclosures. The proposed mission had been reported that morning by the Detroit News.

After the newspaper story appeared, spokesmen for the State Department and for the U.S. Board of Parole confirmed that the agencies had approved the trip, while White House Press Secretary Ronald Ziegler said the trip was "a strictly private effort."

Later, the State Department disclosed that passport validations for Hoffa and his attorney, William L. Taub, had been issued by "a low level official" without such authority. A spokesman said Secretary of State William P. Rogers had investigated the incident when it came to his attention, and revoked the validations after learning of "irregularities" in issuing the permit and in other, undisclosed procedures before his department became involved.

Ziegler denied Sept. 7 Taub's claim that Presidential adviser Henry A. Kissinger had approved the trip in a July meeting between Taub, Kissinger and a Teamster official, although he admitted the meeting had taken place. Ziegler said Kissinger aides had subsequently told Taub that the Administration opposed the plan. President Nixon had recently criticized antiwar activists who had visited Hanoi or had discussed the prisoner issue with North Vietnamese representatives in Paris.

Attorney General Richard G. Kleindienst said Sept. 8 that his deputy, Ralph Erickson, had rejected an offer Aug. 28 from Taub that Hoffa be allowed to resume union activities if he obtained the release of some prisoners. Hoffa had been barred from such activities when paroled after serving nearly five years for jury tampering and fraud. Part of Hoffa's sentence had been commuted by Nixon in order to make him eligible for parole.

Kissinger meets Tho in Paris. Presidential adviser Henry A. Kissinger held his 17th private meeting with Le Duc Tho, chief adviser to the North Vietnamese peace conference delegation, in Paris Sept. 15. The discussions also were attended by Xuan Thuy, Hanoi's chief delegate to the Paris talks.

Kissinger returned to Washington later Sept. 15 and reported to President Nixon the following day on his talks with the North Vietnamese as well as his meetings with Soviet officials in Moscow Sept. 11–13. At a White House news conference following the briefing, Kissinger indicated that little progress had been made in his negotiations with Tho and Thuy. He noted, however, "that the fact that these talks are going on would indicate a certain seriousness." The presidential adviser warned against setting "arbitrary deadlines" for ending the Indochina conflict. He said the U.S. "would not be surprised" if the Communists launched new offensives and "other high points" in South Vietnam in the near future. Commenting on the Viet Cong's Sept. 11 statement on a proposed tripartite government in Saigon, Kissinger said it "leaves something to be desired." The U.S.' "basic principle," he insisted, was its refusal "as a result of negotiations to impose a particular form of government that guarantees predominance of one side" in Saigon.

3 U.S. POWs freed. North Vietnam freed three American prisoners of war Sept. 17. The men, all captured pilots, were Navy Lts. (j.g.) Markham L. Gartley and Norris A. Charles and Air Force Maj. Edward K. Elias.

The Americans were released in Hanoi in formal ceremonies also attended by Gartley's mother and Charles' wife. The two women had arrived in the North Vietnamese capital Sept. 16 with a group of four U.S. antiwar activists.

Among them were Cora Weiss and David Dellinger, co-chairmen of the Committee of Liaison with the Families of American Servicemen Detained in North Vietnam, who had arranged for the prisoners' release and who were to accompany them back to the U.S.

Freed U.S. POWs return home. Three American prisoners of war released by North Vietnam Sept. 17 returned to the U.S. Sept. 28 after stopovers in Peking, Moscow and Copenhagen.

They were accompanied by members of an antiwar group that had arranged for their release. The trip home was marked by a sharp controversy between U.S. authorities who sought to take custody of the men and fly them back to the U.S. in a military plane, and the representatives of the antiwar group—the Committee of Liaison with Families of American Servicemen Detained in North Vietnam. The manner in which the former captives were released also figured in the U.S. presidential campaign.

The former prisoners who arrived in New York aboard a Scandinavian Airlines jet were Navy Lts. (j.g.) Norris A. Charles of San Diego, Calif. and Markham L. Gartley of Dunedin, Fla., and Maj. Edward K. Elias of Valdosta, Ga.

Soon after landing at Kennedy International Airport, Gartley and his mother engaged in a heated argument with a Defense Department official who demanded that the pilot travel under a military escort to St. Albans Naval Hospital in New York for a medical examination. The official, Dr. Roger E. Shields, chief specialist for prisoner affairs, said Gartley's previous request for at least two days to visit with his family would not be approved. Gartley then consented to go to the hospital, at least overnight. Charles and Elias were flown to naval hospitals in San Diego and Montgomery, Ala.

The U.S. pilots were released on the basis of four conditions announced by Hanoi radio Sept. 22 which were cabled to President Nixon. Nixon made no public statement about the terms. The North Vietnamese warned that failure to comply with the conditions would jeopardize the release of other American servicemen held captive. According to the terms of release, the three freed pilots were to do nothing to further promote the U.S. war effort in Indochina, they were to proceed home with the American peace activists and with their own families in a civilian plane, they were to be given 30-day furloughs if they wished, and they were to receive medical checkups at the hospital of their choice, civilian or military.

The Americans had left Hanoi Sept. 25 aboard a Chinese airliner and arrived in Peking the following day. They were accompanied by six persons, including the wife and mother of Charles and Gartley, and Mrs. Cora Weiss and David Dellinger, co-chairmen of the liaison committee. U.S. officials at Vientiane, Laos had waited in vain for the arrival of the three men in the hope of taking custody of the group. (The pilots had been scheduled to leave Hanoi Sept. 23 but it was believed their departure was delayed to permit them to be taken on a two-day inspection tour of U.S. air raid damage south of Hanoi.) They left Peking Sept. 27 on a Chinese airliner, changed to a Soviet plane at Irrutsky in Siberia and landed in Moscow later Sept. 27.

On arrival in the Soviet capital, they met at the airport with American Charge d'Affaires Adolph Dubs and rejected his offer of overnight accommodations at the U.S. embassy and the use of a U.S. medical evacuation plane for the flight home. Dubs later said the men had refused his offer out of "concern for their fellow servicemen who are suffering the same fate they suffered" in North Vietnamese prison camps.

Although the U.S. Administration had held that Charles, Gartley and Elias must place themselves in the custody of U.S. authorities upon their release from prison, it did not appear to press the matter. Defense Secretary Melvin R. Laird said Sept. 22 "I certainly would recommend that these men turn themselves over as soon as possible to their military commanders." A Defense Department official said Sept. 26 that the three pilots were required to turn themselves over to U.S. authorities upon their release from North Vietnam since they were still military officers on active duty. Otherwise, he warned, "they could be considered AWOL" and face penalties.

Laird Sept. 27 did not rule out possible court-martial action against the three men for allegedly permitting themselves to be used for North Vietnamese propaganda purposes. Speaking in a CBS radio interview in Oklahoma City, Laird added: "That does not mean that court-martial or any action will be taken. But I can't state . . . that the Code of Uniform Military Justice will not be followed."

Meeting with newsmen later Sept. 27, Laird was more emphatic in saying that the three pilots "will face no charges as far as the Defense Department is concerned."

Laird had lauded the relatives of Maj. Elias Sept. 24 for refusing to go to Hanoi to take part in the prisoner release ceremonies Sept. 17. Asked if this was meant as criticism of the two other families who did go to Hanoi, Laird said: "We recommended that they not be a part of violations of the Geneva Convention," which he said stated that "prisoners cannot be used as tools of propaganda."

Saigon ousts Indian ICC unit. South Vietnam Sept. 29 expelled the entire Indian delegation to the International Control Commission from the country. The Indians and the Polish members of the ICC then announced that the commission's headquarters would be shifted from Saigon to Hanoi because of South Vietnam's "discriminatory measures" against the Indian delegates. The ICC had always had facilities in Hanoi, but its headquarters had been in Saigon since the late 1950s.

Heading the last group of Indians to leave Saigon was Brig. P.N. Khanduri, acting chairman of the ICC. He had headed the commission since South Vietnam's refusal Jan. 8 to permit L.N. Ray, an Indian and new chairman-designate, to land in Saigon.

The ICC's Canadian commissioner, R.D. Jackson, charged Sept. 30 that India and Poland were responsible for the organization's "long-standing" failure to supervise the 1954 Geneva agreements on Indochina. Jackson said strained relations between South Vietnam and India could not be blamed for the ICC's "inability to fulfill its mandate."

Democrats Challenge War Policies

Democrats focus on war issue. Sen. George S. McGovern's (S.D.) virtual sweep of the Democratic spring primaries and his subsequent capture of the presidential nomination made the war the central issue of the 1972 election race. McGovern had been one of the earliest opponents of U.S. war policy [See Volume II] and had made stronger demands for U.S. withdrawal than almost any other Democratic leader.

McGovern would go to Hanoi. At a news conference in Los Angeles June 7, McGovern pledged to go to Hanoi or Paris or "anywhere in the world," if necessary, to negotiate an end to the Vietnam war, a safe withdrawal of U.S. forces and the release of American prisoners of war.

"If it's necessary to go to Hanoi to accomplish that, I'll go to Hanoi to do it," he said. "If we can do it in Paris, I'll go to Paris. I'll go anywhere in the world to meet with the leaders of the government of Hanoi to work out arrangements for an immediate end to the killing, the safe withdrawal of our forces and the relase of our prisoners. I don't have any doubt at all that I can accomplish all of that, have the prisoners home, have our troops home and have it done within 90 days."

If this could be achieved by other means, he added, he would not go to Hanoi because "there's no point in going to Hanoi just to put on a grandstand act." But, "if it becomes necessary in my judgment to accelerate the end of this war, I'd be willing to go there or anyplace else that I thought would shorten the war by 24 hours."

McGovern told the newsmen the enemy would never release American POWs "until we agree to the full termination of all American military operations in Southeast Asia." President Nixon, he charged, was "perpetrating a hoax on the American people in leaving the impression that aerial bombardment [of North Vietnam] can bring about the release of our prisoners."

Poll shows pessimism. A Harris poll, reported June 12, found that 88% of a cross-section of 1,385 voters believed that the U.S. would still be involved in the Vietnam war by the November election. Although 79% wanted to see an end to "all U.S. ground, naval and air" involvement, the same sampling opposed, by a 75%–13% margin, a complete withdrawal before American prisoners were released. The sampling also opposed, by 45%–38%, a peace settlement providing "a coalition government which included the Communists."

Agnew labels McGovern a 'fraud.' Vice President Agnew, using some of the harshest language of the 1972 campaign, June 30 called Sen. McGovern "one of the greatest frauds ever to be considered as a presidential candidate by a major American party."

Speaking at a Republican fund-raising dinner in New York, Agnew singled out for particular criticism a McGovern remark that, if elected President, he would go to Hanoi to "beg" if necessary for the release of American prisoners. "America," he said, "wants a President like Richard Nixon who negotiates on his feet—not a demagogue who would crawl to his enemies on his knees."

Agnew added: "I find this an incredible admission by a man who would lead the American people. It expresses a philosophy so callow and shortsighted as to be repugnant to the tradition of a free people."

McGovern had made the statement on the prisoner issue during a meeting June 28 in Columbia, S.C. with South Carolina delegates to the Democratic National Convention. McGovern was asked by one of the delegates about his views on Vietnam and the return of American POWs. Pressing McGovern, the delegate asked: "You want us to do all they demand and then beg them to give back our boys?"

McGovern replied: "I'll accept that. Begging is better than bombing. I would go to Hanoi and beg if I thought that would release the boys one day earlier, but begging won't help if we bomb and aid the Thieu government."

In denouncing that statement, Agnew called McGovern "the darling of the advocates of American retreat and defeat."

He also said that "despite the efforts of his [McGovern's] allies in the liberal media to cover up his defects as a candidate, the American people are coming to know, by George McGovern's own words, that in McGovernism we find the seeds of the downfall of our great Republic."

McGovern wins nomination. Sen. McGovern won the presidential nomination at the Democratic National Convention in Miami Beach, Fla. July 12. His victory on the first ballot was assured after he won a crucial early vote on a credentials challenge that gave him all of California's block of 271 delegate votes.

McGovern confronts protesters—McGovern, overruling the advice of the Secret Service agents assigned to guard

him, spoke for nearly half an hour July 12 in a face-to-face meeting with a group of angry young demonstrators who had refused police commands to leave his campaign headquarters hotel.

The demonstrators, about 300 radical students, young blacks and antiwar activists, had surged into the lobby of the Doral Hotel to demand from McGovern an explanation of a statement he had made July 11 about his position on the war.

McGovern assured the protesters that he was "not shifting my positions on any of the fundamental stands that I've taken in this campaign."

McGovern sought to dispel any idea that a statement released by his staff July 11 at a press conference for wives of prisoners of war (POWs) reflected a change in his Vietnam position.

In that statement, McGovern asserted that he would "retain the military capability in the region—in Thailand and on the seas—to signal and fulfill" his resolve to win the release of Americans POWs.

Protesters at the Doral said they saw that statement as a "sellout" of those who supported McGovern's antiwar views.

(At almost the same time that McGovern was speaking to the protesters at the Doral, some young delegates inside the convention hall were meeting in a "youth caucus" to discuss the McGovern statement on POWs.)

McGovern told the demonstrators that his statement did not spell out a change in his antiwar view. He reasserted as "a flat pledge" his commitment to have every American soldier and prisoner out of Indochina within 90 days of his inauguration as President.

(When the McGovern staff had learned of the controversy the POW statement was stirring, a new statement was issued by McGovern July 12 reaffirming his Vietnam position and underscoring his confidence that any troops in Thailand or naval forces would also be withdrawn within 90 days after he took office.)

The protesters left the hotel after their meeting with McGovern.

McGovern pledges campaign to people—Sen. McGovern pledged in his speech accepting the nomination July 14 that he would "dedicate" his campaign for the presidency to the American people.

Much of McGovern's speech dealt with the issue that pushed him into national prominence—the war in Vietnam.

Without specifically naming them, McGovern blamed the Nixon Administration and those of his three predecessors in the White House for charting "a terrible war behind closed doors."

McGovern said his Administration would open the doors of government at the same time it closed down the war.

"I want those doors opened, and I want that war closed. And I make these pledges above all others—the doors of government will be open, and that brutal war will be closed.

"Truth is a habit of integrity, not a strategy of politics. And if we nurture the habit of candor in this campaign, we will continue to be candid once we are in the White House. Let us say to Americans, as Woodrow Wilson said in his first campaign: "Let me inside [the government] and I will tell you everything that is going on in there."

"And this is a time not for death, but for life.

"In 1968, Americans voted to bring our sons home from Vietnam in peace—and since then, 20,000 have come home in coffins.

"I have no secret plan for peace. I have a public plan.

"As one whose heart has ached for 10 years over the agony of Vietnam, I will halt the senseless bombing of Indochina on Inauguration Day.

"There will be no more Asian children running ablaze from bombed-out schools.

"There will be no more talk of bombing the dikes or the cities of the North.

"Within 90 days of my inauguration, every American soldier and every American prisoner will be out of the jungle and out of their cells and back home in America where they belong.

"And then let us resolve that never again will we shed the precious young blood of this nation to perpetuate an unrepresentative client abroad.

"Let us choose life, not death, this is the time."

But McGovern stressed that the war's end would not mean that America's military posture was weakening. He said, "I give you my sacred pledge that if I become President of the U.S., America will keep its defenses alert and fully sufficient to meet any danger."

That readiness, he said, would not only be for the safety of this nation, but for "those who deserve and need the shield of our strength—our old allies in Europe, and elsewhere, including the people of Israel, who will always have our help to hold their promised land."

Antiwar platform adopted—In a marathon 11-hour session July 11–12 the convention adopted with only two minor changes the liberal draft platform prepared by the 150-member platform committee in Washington two weeks before.

The platform proposed: "An immediate and complete withdrawal of all U.S. forces in Indochina," termination of military aid to the Saigon government, and amnesty for draft evaders after prisoners were returned.

Despite a dramatic wheelchair appearance by Gov. George Wallace to support the conservative minority reports, the convention rejected by a large voice vote margin his stand on Vietnam. It also rejected a controversial minority report to strengthen the platform's stand on Vietnam.

The text of the platform plank on the war in Vietnam was as follows:

Nothing better describes the need for a new American foreign policy than the fact that now, as for the past seven years, it begins with the war in Vietnam.

The task now is still to end the war, not to decide who is to blame for it. The Democratic Party must share the responsibility for this tragic war. But, elected with a secret plan to end this war, Nixon's plan is still secret, and we—and the Vietnamese—have had four more years of fighting and death.

It is true that our involvement on the ground has been reduced. Troops are coming home. But the war has been extended in Laos and Cambodia; the bombing of North Vietnam has been expanded to levels of destruction undreamed of four years ago; North Vietnam has been blockaded; the number of refugees increases each day, and the Secretary of Defense warns us of still further escalation.

All this has accomplished nothing except to prolong the war.

The hollowness of "Vietnamization"—a delusive slogan, seeming to offer cheap victory—has been exposed by the recent offensive. The Saigon Government, despite massive U.S. support, is still not viable. It is militarily ineffective, politically corrupt and economically near collapse. Yet it is for this regime that Americans still die, and American prisoners still rot in Indo-China camps.

The plight of these American prisoners justly arouses the concern of all Americans. We must insist that any resolution of the war include the return of all prisoners held by North Vietnam and other adversary forces and the fullest possible accounting for the missing. With increasing lack of credibility, the Nixon Administration has sought to use the prisoners of war as an excuse for its policies. It has refused to make the simple offer of a definite and final end to U.S. participation in the war, in conjunction with return of all U.S. prisoners.

The majority of the Democratic Senators have called for full U.S. withdrawal by October 1, 1972. We support that position. If the war is not ended before the next Democratic Administration takes office, we pledge, as the first order of business, an immediate and complete withdrawal of all U.S. forces in Indo-China. All U.S. military action in Southeast Asia will cease. After the end of U.S. direct combat participation, military aid to the Saigon Government, and elsewhere in Indo-China, will be terminated.

The U.S. will no longer seek to determine the political future of the nations of Indo-China. The issue is not whether we will depose the present South Vietnamese Government, rather when we will cease insisting that it must be the core of any political settlement. We will do what we can to foster an agreement on an acceptable political solution—but we recognize that there are sharp limits to our ability to influence this process, and to the importance of the outcome to our interest.

Disengagement from this terrible war will not be a "defeat" for America. It will not imply any weakness in America's will or ability to protect its vital interests from attack. On the contrary, disengagement will enable us to heal domestic diversions and to end the distortion of our international priorities which the war has caused.

A Democratic Administration will act to ease the hard transitions which will come with an end to this war. We pledge to offer to the people of Vietnam humanitarian assistance to help them repair the ravages of 30 years of war to the economy and to the people of that devastated land.

To our own people, we pledge a true effort to extend the hand of reconciliation and assistance to those most affected by the war.

To those who have served in this war, we pledge a full G.I. Bill of Rights, with benefits sufficient to pay for an education of the veteran's choice, job training programs and the guarantee of employment. . . . To those who for reasons of conscience refused to serve in this war and were prosecuted or sought refuge abroad, we state our firm intention to declare an amnesty, on an appropriate basis, when the fighting has ceased and our troops and prisoners of war have returned.

Rogers briefs Nixon on tour. Secretary of State William P. Rogers briefed President Nixon at the Western White House in San Clemente July 15 on his recently concluded world tour.

After the meeting, Rogers told newsmen that foreign leaders had indicated to him "without exception" that the U.S. proposals for peace in Vietnam provided "a basis for a negotiated settlement." Commenting on Sen. George McGovern's proposal for a pullout of U.S. forces from Vietnam within 90 days after his inauguration, Rogers asserted that the pledge made negotiating "extremely difficult" because it gave "the enemy exactly what he wants without any negotiations."

Laird questions McGovern on POWs. Defense Secretary Melvin R. Laird assailed McGovern July 17 for his pledge to have every American prisoner of war in North Vietnamese hands released within 90 days of his inauguration as President.

Speaking at a Pentagon news conference, Laird questioned the credibility of that pledge. "He has information," Laird said sarcastically, "which is not available to any other sources within government, is not available to any of our allies or to any of the governments that we have been in contact with, including the Soviet Union and the People's Republic of China."

"So I do not believe that that promise is a legitimate promise or one that is credible," Laird said.

Later in the conference, Laird suggested that a political deal had been made in which McGovern backed away from his proposal to cancel the Air Force's new F-15 fighter in return for an agreement by Sen. Thomas F. Eagleton (D, Mo.) to take the Democratic vice presidential nomination. The F-15 was made by the McDonnell-Douglas Corp. in St. Louis, Eagleton's home town.

On Vietnam, Laird repeated his assertion that U.S. pilots were under instruction not to bomb any of North Vietnam's major dams and dikes controlling most of the flood waters in the northern part of the country. He conceded that one or two "minor" dikes or sluiceways "tied in with" surface-to-air missiles or a major bridge network might have inadvertently been hit.

"But there are no dams or dikes that are authorized as military targets," Laird said.

Polls show Nixon support. According to a Harris Survey reported July 17, Americans who were polled agreed with President Nixon rather than with Sen. McGovern on 15 of 16 key policy issues, including ending U.S. involvement in Vietnam—Nixon 52%, McGovern 33%.

End-war measures gain. A strong statement of Congressional support for a military withdrawal from Indochina was approved by the Senate July 24, but Administration forces succeeded in killing the foreign military aid authorization bill to which the measure was attached. The next day, the House Foreign Affairs Committee attached a similar measure to its own version of the aid bill.

The measure approved by the Senate would have ordered a complete withdrawal of American forces from Vietnam, Laos and Cambodia within four months of passage, enforced by a fund cutoff, provided American prisoners of war were released.

The amendment was offered without the provision on prisoners by Sen. John Sherman Cooper (R, Ky.), to replace language inserted in committee by Sen. Mike Mansfield (D, Mont.), which the Senate had deleted by a 49–44 vote. Sen. Edward Brooke (R, Mass.) proposed the prisoner release stipulation, which was approved by a 62–33 vote. The modified withdrawal measure was approved 50–45, with 39 Democrats and 11 Republicans voting for passage, and 12 Democrats and 33 Republicans in opposition. A final attempt by Sen. John Stennis (D, Miss.) to delete the entire section from the bill was defeated 49–46.

Administration forces, joined by such opponents of military foreign aid as Mansfield and Sen. J. W. Fulbright (D, Ark.), then rallied to defeat the entire bill by a 48–42 vote, hoping to revive the aid provisions at a later date.

Senate antiwar forces revived the issue July 25, as Brooke reintroduced the measure approved the previous day as an amendment to the pending defense procurement authorization bill.

The House Foreign Affairs Committee July 25 voted by 18–17 to attach a withdrawal provision to the House version of the military aid bill. It was the first favorable antiwar vote by a House Committee; the Foreign Affairs Committee had rejected the same measure in June.

The provision would order a complete withdrawal from Indochina by Oct. 1, provided American prisoners were released and a cease-fire was arranged between American and North Vietnamese forces to protect the withdrawal, with no assent by the South Vietnamese government required.

Kennedy, Hanoi exchange on POWs. Sen. Edward M. Kennedy (D, Mass.) disclosed July 25 that he had exchanged letters with North Vietnamese President Ton Duc Thang over the question of U.S. prisoners of war in Indochina.

Kennedy made public a letter to Thang dated May 19 and a reply dated June 16 in which Thang indicated Hanoi might ask the Viet Cong to provide a list of Americans captured in South Vietnam. Such a list had never been released.

In his letter, Kennedy asked Thang to have "competent services" of the North Vietnamese government "facilitate the identification of all American personnel" held in North Vietnam, South Vietnam, Cambodia and Laos.

Thang's reply did not mention Laos or Cambodia, but said, "about the intimation of the names of Americans captured in South Vietnam, we will exchange views with the Provisional Revolutionary Government of the Republic of South Vietnam, which will take an appropriate decision on this subject."

Disclosure of the letters came two days after Kennedy received, through North Vietnamese representatives in Paris, letters to their families from 24 men captured in North Vietnam since November 1970. It was the first time such letters had been transmitted through a U.S. official, rather than through U.S. antiwar groups.

McGovern on Vietnam. Sen George McGovern accused President Nixon July 28 of "running the war and peace talks to try to fit his own election timetable." If the Nixon Administration would "quit its immoral insistence on being tied to Gen. Thieu," he said, "the war could be ended and our prisoners of war would be home immediately."

Talking with reporters July 23, McGovern said he "really can't see anything that we're going to accomplish in ending the war now or in ending it the day before the election that we couldn't have accomplished by ending it four years ago when Mr. Nixon first took over the White House. This is a great tragedy."

McGovern had said July 24 he would not resume the bombing of North Vietnam even if there were difficulties in gaining release of prisoners of war after all U.S. forces had been withdrawn from Indochina. "The bombing is how the prisoners got into prison" in the first place, he said.

Referring to an earlier stand that he would leave a residual force in Thailand if necessary to continue pressure on Hanoi to free prisoners after other forces were withdrawn, McGovern, who had encountered some criticism for the stand from liberal sources, said such a residual force "would be more of a gesture than anything else."

Clark visit stirs controversy. A visit by former Attorney General Ramsey Clark to North Vietnam July 29-Aug. 12 to inspect the effects of U.S. bombing generated widespread controversy on the U.S. political scene. Clark's statements from Hanoi describing the air raid destruction and his visits with U.S. prisoners of war drew critical comment from Administration officials and sharpened the current election campaign debate on the Indochina conflict.

Clark visited North Vietnam with other members of the Stockholm-based International Commission of Inquiry into alleged U.S. war crimes in Indochina. The group was investigating charges of bombing of non-military targets.

Clark and two other members of the group—Prof. Yves Lacoste of France and Dr. Nina Kaskhova of the Soviet Union—were driven Aug. 3 to Lan, a hamlet in coastal Thaibinh Province south of Hanoi, and were shown bomb damage to a sluice gate. (The North Vietnamese claimed U.S. air strikes had damaged 35 sections of dikes in Thaibinh.) They also inspected several miles of dikes in Namcuong, where Hanoi officials reported U.S. planes had dropped bombs July 21. Clark filmed several scenes of civilians carrying earth to repair damaged dikes at Namcuong.

In a recorded interview broadcast by Hanoi radio Aug. 6, Clark described the bomb damage he had seen. He said he had observed large bomb craters on the tops of dikes at Vudong in Thaibinh Province and damage to a hospital and school at Phuvang, which had been struck twice by U.S. planes July 31. Clark said three persons had been killed in the attack on the hospital.

Following a visit to Haiphong Aug. 6, Clark was interviewed on damage to the city. In a recording of the interview, broadcast by Hanoi radio Aug. 9, Clark said that air strikes had caused "massive destruction" of many parts of the port city. He said, "There are many, many people killed. Hundreds or even thousands could have been killed in such terrible bombings and destruction of living areas of Haiphong." Clark deplored the American air campaign, saying, "There is absolutely no excuse for bombing North Vietnam and there never has been."

Clark met the U.S. captives at a prisoner of war camp at an unspecified location in North Vietnam and reported his findings at a Hanoi news conference Aug. 12. A Hanoi broadcast later that day quoted him as saying he had interviewd 10 prisoners for more than two hours and found them to be in good health, getting good medical care and that their living conditions "could not be better."

The former attorney general said that during his stay in North Vietnam he had travelled more than 600 miles and encountered "no efforts that I could detect to influence me or prejudice my judgment."

Clark left North Vietnam Aug. 12. At a stopover in Bangkok, Thailand before returning to the U.S., he declared Aug. 13 that he had seen "more apartments, villages, dikes and sluices destroyed than I ever want to see again."

Returning to the U.S. in San Francisco Aug. 13, Clark said he had been given "adequate assurance" by Hanoi officials that U.S. prisoners of war would be released "when we stop this senseless, murderous bombing and end the war and get out." He told newsmen Aug. 14 that some American prisoners would be released if Sen. George S. McGovern, whom he endorsed, was elected and that all of them would be released within three months after that. Clark said this was based on the views of a North Vietnamese newspaper editor, and talks with Foreign Minister Nguyen Duy Trinh. "I urged them to release some prisoners," he said, "and I say frankly I think they will—a few, I don't know when."

He said he had declined North Vietnamese requests to broadcast over radio Hanoi during the tour, and was unaware of what broadcast use was made of his tape-recorded comments to journalists during the visit. He pointed out that newsman present were taking down his remarks and "they could use this to broadcast on radio Hanoi."

Clark reiterated Aug. 14 his reports of seeing extensive bomb damage. "I saw damage to dikes, sluices and canals of a substantial nature at least six places," he said. "At a couple of places, it was evident that it was a massive assault. At the time I saw it, there were no military targets there," although he conceded that such targets could have been moved before his visit. He said, "We are bombing the hell out of that poor land. We are hitting hospitals. I can't tell you whether it's deliberate. But to the people who are getting hit, it doesn't make much difference, does it?"

As for the prisoners he had visited, Clark said they "were unquestionably humanely treated, well treated."

During an appearance Aug. 15 before a convention committee of the American Bar Association, meeting in San Francisco, Clark clashed with Rita E. Hauser, co-chairman of President Nixon's re-election committee. Mrs. Hauser asked him why he had failed "to plead the cause of our own prisoners" while in Hanoi. Clark assured her he had. He suggested that those who claimed the men were mistreated were doing so for "other motives" and possibly cared "more about the Thieu government than getting the boys home."

Clark testified in Washington Aug. 16 before a special Senate sub-committee on refugees headed by Sen. Edward M. Kennedy (D, Mass.). Reiterating that he had seen extensive bomb damage, he exhibited a grapefruit-sized fragmentation bomb he said was given to him by the mayor of Hanoi. "It has only one purpose and that is to kill people," he said. "I know of no justification in law or morality to justify their use."

(Kennedy and McGovern were among 10 senators introducing a resolution in the Senate Aug. 4 calling for a halt to bombing of the North Vietnamese dike system.)

Republicans assail Clark—The former attorney general was assailed by Republicans and supporters of the Administration for his trip and comments.

Secretary of State William P. Rogers denounced Clark's broadcasts over Hanoi radio as "contemptible" Aug. 11. Rogers said he was shocked and thought "the American people would be shocked to hear his voice on radio Hanoi while the war is in progress, while American lives are being lost, particularly a man who was involved in the very decision that made the whole thing come about."

Former Attorney General John N. Mitchell called Clark's conduct "outrageous" Aug. 12 and said Aug. 15 that Clark had been "duped" by the North Vietnamese and permitted himself to be used for propaganda.

Senate Republican Leader Hugh Scott (Pa.) and Sen. Henry M. Jackson (D, Wash.) joined in the criticism Aug. 15. In a Senate speech, Scott said Clark's remarks on release of the American prisoners "has the effect of saying Hanoi is holding prisoners of war hostage to the election of Sen. McGovern. I regret Mr. Clark allowed himself to be used by Hanoi."

Jackson said Clark saw only what Hanoi wanted him to and he should not "make general statements without saying that he was taking a conducted tour."

McGovern rebuttal—Democratic presidential nominee George McGovern Aug. 12 objected to Rogers' criticism of Clark as "beneath the dignity of his office." It "smacks of the divisive innuendos of the old, old Nixon," McGovern said, by questioning the "patriotism of Nixon's political opposition."

After Mitchell's criticism, McGovern accused Nixon Aug. 13 of "taking the low road" in his campaign for re-election "by remote control." As for Hanoi's broadcast of Clark's criticism of U.S. bombing policies, McGovern said, "What he said, if there was anything wrong with it, it pales into insignificance compared to the fact that President Nixon is ordering American bombers out to slaughter, kill and destroy all across the face of Indochina."

McGovern conceded Aug. 15 it "may have been a tactical error" for Clark to criticize American policy while in Hanoi. He suggested that Clark should have held his criticism until he returned to the U.S.

Senate passes end-war amendment. An intensive lobbying effort by the White

House fell short Aug. 2 as the Senate narrowly adopted an amendment requiring the withdrawal of all U.S. forces from Indochina in four months subject only to the concurrent release of prisoners of war.

The proposal, passed by a 49–47 vote, was introduced by Sen. Edward Brooke (R, Mass.) as an amendment to a $20.5 billion military authorization bill.

Following passage of Brooke's amendment, the Senate approved the overall bill, 92–5.

The White House had failed to persuade two pivotal Republican senators to vote against the end-the-war measure. Throughout the day White House Officials maintained that adoption of the Brooke amendment would mean that Congress was exceeding its constitutional authority. They also contended that the amendment would jeopardize the Paris peace talks.

Although the Administration lobbying effort led to the switch of three votes from conservative Democrats, it failed to win over two moderate Republicans—Sens. Marlow Cook (Ky.) and Ted Stevens (Alaska)—whose votes proved to be crucial.

The Brooke amendment was virtually identical to one submitted by him and passed by the Senate July 24, 50–45, as an attachment to a foreign aid bill. That amendment died when the Senate killed the entire bill.

The new Brooke amendment provided that funds could be used by the President "only for the purpose of withdrawing all U.S. ground, naval, and air forces from Vietnam, Laos and Cambodia and protecting such forces as they are withdrawn," with the withdrawal to be completed within four months after enactment of the legislation, "provided that there is a release within the four-month period of all American prisoners of war held by the government of North Vietnam and all forces allied with such government."

The authorization bill would go to a Senate-House conference committee. In the past, both the Senate and House Armed Services Committees had generally supported the Administration's Vietnam policies.

Rainmaking funds cut—Only once did the Senate vote to delete funds from the bill. The Senate July 28 approved an amendment sponsored by Sen. Gaylord Nelson (D, Wis.) to cut off funds for any use of rainmaking or creation of forest fires as weapons of war.

(Nelson and others had charged that the U.S. had been cloudseeding over Vietnam to induce torrential rains. The Defense Department had denied conducting such operations over Vietnam, but had refused to discuss rainmaking elsewhere in Indochina.

House rejects end-war proposal. The House defeated by a 228–178 vote Aug. 10 an end-the-war amendment for withdrawal of all U.S. forces from Indochina by Oct. 1 subject to release of U.S. prisoners and a cease-fire for safe withdrawal of the U.S. forces.

The amendment was attached by the House Foreign Affairs Committee to a $2.1 billion foreign military assistance bill, which the House passed later by a 221–172 vote. The aid bill had been rejected in July by the Senate.

Defeat of the end-the-war proposal was brought about in large part by a split in the anti-war forces over the pull-out date. Foreign Affairs Committee Chairman Thomas E. Morgan (D, Pa.) supported a bid to change the date to Dec. 31, which some war critics, such as Reps. Benjamin Rosenthal (D, N.Y.) and Bella Abzug (D, N.Y.), opposed. The latter was supported by Republican Leader Gerald R. Ford (Mich.), who said the change would "extend the killing by 90 days." The change was rejected, 304–109, with House Speaker Carl Albert and Democratic Leader Hale Boggs (La.) voting on the losing side.

Then when Rep. Richard Bolling (D, Mo.) proposed that the withdrawal amendment be dropped from the bill, Boggs backed the move on the ground that a vote for an Oct. 1 withdrawal date, in view of the impossibility of clearing the bill by that date, would be a "vain and useless act that could be misinterpreted all over the world." Albert joined him in voting to delete the amendment.

The foreign aid bill would authorize appropriations of $730 million in military grants, $529 million in military credit sales, $769 million in supporting economic assistance and $100 million for refugee relief in Bangla Desh.

The bill also would provide Israel with $350 million in credit sales for military equipment and would authorize the President to withhold aid from a nation harboring airplane hijackers.

The House dropped from the bill, on a 253–140 vote, a provision to require U.S. compliance with the United Nations embargo against importing Rhodesian chrome without a presidential determination it was in the national interest.

Defense spending defended. The Pentagon, in a sweeping defense of its economic policies, struck back at its critics Aug. 10 in a report it said was designed to "debunk the view" that defense spending excessively strained the nation's budget.

The 193-page report, entitled "The Economics of Defense Spending—A Look at the Realities," was compiled by Robert C. Moot, comptroller of the Defense Department.

At a press conference following release of the report, Moot said his work "is an attempt to provide the facts for those who want to look it up and check the accuracy of what they read. It is intended to debunk the review that defense spending is the big problem child" in distribution of government spending. Defense Secretary Melvin R. Laird, who also attended the press conference, said the report was "an attempt to explode a lot of myths that have developed."

Without identifying him by name, Laird again attacked Sen. George McGovern, the Democratic Presidential nominee, for his views on defense spending.

Included in the report was the disclosure that the extra cost of the Vietnam war, resulting from the increased military actions of U.S. forces in response to the North Vietnamese spring offensive, would be $1.1 billion. That was less than Laird had estimated in earlier reports.

According to the report, the estimated "incremental" cost of the war in the current fiscal year was $5.8 billion. That was $1.1 billion above the $4.7 billion figure estimated in January, before the North Vietnamese drove southward. The total cost of the war in the current fiscal year was put at $7.1 billion, also up $1.1 billion from the January estimate.

Dispute flares over '69 peace chance. Democratic vice presidential nominee R. Sargent Shriver charged Aug. 10 that President Nixon had lost an opportunity for a Vietnam peace settlement when he took office in 1969. Shriver said "Nixon had peace handed to him literally in his lap. He blew it."

His remarks were taken to imply that a 1969 decrease in battlefield activity had signaled North Vietnam's willingness to negotiate a settlement to the war.

The Shriver statement brought denials from Administration officials and backing from two negotiators at the Paris peace talks during the Johnson Administration.

(Secretary of State William P. Rogers had reported July 2, 1969 that Communist infiltration and combat activities in South Vietnam had decreased since mid-June of that year. A U.S. spokesman had said July 3, 1969 that "there is no military reason for the pullback."

(U.S. officials had predicted July 23, 1969 that the battlefield lull would continue but said, however, there was no evidence of a political motive behind the Communist forces' reduced military activity. "If this is a political signal from Hanoi," intelligence officials said, "the enemy soldiers and commanders in the field don't know it."

Opening his campaign in his home state of Maryland, Shriver rejected reporters' suggestions that his service as ambassador to France in the Nixon Administration until March 1970 indicated support of Nixon's Vietnam policy. Shriver said he had not resigned when Nixon was elected because "I thought he had an historic opportunity to do what Eisenhower did in Korea—to stop the war." "It would not have been difficult," Shriver said. "When Averell Harriman and Cy[rus] Vance [the U.S. negotiators] were there [in Paris] in the summer of 1968, they felt peace was within their grasp then. Certainly Nixon had peace in his lap."

Shriver said he had resigned when it became clear to him that Nixon "did not want to pursue peace through negotiations alone but believed that it was necessary for the country to have a different way towards peace which he called Vietnamization."

Secretary of State William P. Rogers Aug. 11 called Shriver's remarks "bunk" and "political fantasy." He had checked with officials, including Henry Cabot Lodge, the Paris negotiator in 1969, had read all Shriver's messages to the State Department and "I really don't have any idea what he is talking about."

Lodge issued a statement Aug. 13 saying he "neither was informed of any such peace opportunity nor had any reason to believe one existed."

Harriman and Vance supported Shriver's statements Aug. 12. In a joint statement, they said:

"We support completely Sargent Shriver's view that President Nixon lost an opportunity for a negotiated settlement in Vietnam when he took office. At that time North Vietnam had signaled its willingness to reduce the level of violence by withdrawing almost 90% of its troops —22 of 25 regiments—from the northern two provinces which had been the area of fierce fighting. The United States was then in a far better bargaining position, since it had over 500,000 men in South Vietnam. The new Administration should have set a negotiated peace as its first goal. Instead it took as its first task the forging of a closer bond with President Thieu [of South Vietnam]. This meant nullifying the opportunity for a negotiated solution, since compromise would inevitably eliminate Thieu's power."

The State Department later Aug. 12 issued a statement that "no record of any such so-called signal" could be found. "Mr. Harriman reportedly says it came in October or November 1968," it said. "This raises the question as to why no action was taken on the so-called signal for the next three months, before the present Administration took office. It also raises the question as to what the so-called signal consisted of and who in the new Administration was advised of the so-called signal."

Harriman had told a New York Times reporter Aug. 12 he considered the removal of enemy troops a peace gesture. "This was in October or early November" of 1968, he said. Asked why the Johnson Administration had not re-

sponded to it, he said "we couldn't carry on discussions because President Thieu would not permit his representatives to negotiate." Asked whether the new administration had been informed of the situation, he said "they had all the facts—both at the Pentagon and the State Department."

Dean Rusk, who was secretary of state under President Johnson, did not consider the removal of troops in 1968 a signal for negotiations. "There were some people on our side who attached some significance to the withdrawal of the North Vietnamese forces across the DMZ," he said Aug. 16, but if it was a peace sign the North Vietnamese would have implemented it in some way at the Paris talks and "that didn't happen."

McGovern cites security study—Democratic presidential nominee George McGovern issued a statement Aug. 12 saying Nixon was "the political figure seeking office" and "should properly carry the public debate on international matters instead of hiding behind the Departments of State and Defense."

Laird and Rogers "have obviously been given the assignment of chief frightmongers" for the Republican presidential campaign, he said. "That is always the main workload in a Nixon campaign."

On the ABC "Issues and Answers" broadcast Aug. 13, McGovern espoused Shriver's charge that Nixon "blew" a chance for a negotiated settlement when he took office.

"What the American people have to ask," he said, "is what have we gained by the sacrifice of another 20,000 American lives these past three and one half years, the sacrifice of 50 to 60 billions of dollars? We're in no better position now to negotiate an end to this war than we were three and one half years ago."

McGovern charged that the President's policy of bombing North Vietnam was "the biggest hoax ever perpetrated on the American people" and that the President was "deliberately misleading" the people on the purpose and the results of the strategy. "The truth is," he said, "that we continue to stay on for one primary reason and that's to keep General Thieu in power."

McGovern referred to a national security study assembled by Nixon's adviser,

Henry A. Kissinger, in February 1969. The Administration's own documents, he said, proved President Nixon knew of Hanoi's "signal" for serious negotiation. The study had become public earlier in 1972 and had been inserted into the Congressional Record May 10-11 by Rep. Ronald V. Dellums (D, Calif.). Part of the study included a synopsis of answers to a question posed by Kissinger of why the North Vietnamese had withdrawn troops in late 1968. In addition to military factors, the synopsis cited "political factors centered on enemy efforts to make a political virtue out of a military necessity in a talk-fight strategy to influence the Paris negotiations, and the enemy's emphasis on the establishment of 'Liberation Committees' throughout the South Vietnamese countryside."

The State Department's East Asian Bureau, according to the memo, viewed the troop withdrawals as a political gesture. The bureau said it believed "that Hanoi wanted to make a virtue of necessity but it took care to make certain that its gesture was substantial enough to be clearly recognized."

McGovern aide has Paris talks—Pierre Salinger, a co-chairman of the Citizens for McGovern Committee, disclosed Aug. 16 he had met with North Vietnamese negotiators in Paris July 18 and Aug. 9 and they had informed him "that there was no change in their position with regard to prisoners of war, that the release has to be in the context of an overall peace settlement as outlined at the negotiations."

Salinger said he had told the North Vietnamese that if there was any possibility "to negotiate a peace agreement with President Nixon that they should do so without regard to the American election, that Sen. McGovern's desire for peace was greater than his desire for the issue of the Vietnam war to continue as a central issue in this campaign."

McGovern confirmed Aug. 16 that Salinger had met with the North Vietnamese at his request. "The only purpose of the discussion," he said, "was to determine if any change had occurred which would permit the return of the prisoners prior to the end of hostilities."

The Nixon Administration objected to the Salinger probe Aug. 17. White House Press Secretary Ronald L. Ziegler said McGovern representatives "might say something in contact with the enemy that could jeopardize [President Nixon's] peace efforts."

McGovern responded Aug. 17 that Salinger's "brief, middle-level inquiry about prisoners" could not have interfered with serious negotiations. The larger issue was, he said, whether the Paris negotiations were a serious peace effort. "Mr. Nixon has manipulated Mr. Kissinger" in his dramatic global trips "and he has manipulated American public opinion," McGovern charged, "to appear to be negotiating seriously when actually he has been stalling to prop up Gen. Thieu's government in Saigon."

Kissinger briefings declined. McGovern declined Aug. 15, a White House offer of briefings on Vietnam by presidential aide Henry A. Kissinger. McGovern commented that White House briefings generally "go wide of the mark," and "I've frankly learned more about the realities of Vietnam from following the dispatches of good newspapermen than I have from official briefings in the White House."

He had met Kissinger officially or socially about a dozen times in the past four years, McGovern said, and while the sessions were "interesting" they "haven't shed any new light on the Vietnam problem."

McGovern said he had asked Paul C. Warnke, a former assistant secretary of defense, to receive any information on Vietnam "that the White House thinks would be useful." A Kissinger aide would brief Warnke.

McGovern predicts Thieu exile. Democratic Presidential nominee George McGovern said Aug. 19 that, if elected, he expected President Nguyen Van Thieu and his South Vietnamese "cohorts" to flee into exile.

McGovern predicted that following the collapse of the Saigon regime, the Viet Cong would form a coalition government and seek "accommodation" with Hanoi. Eventually, McGovern said, North and South Vietnam would be reunited.

He added that "arrangements should
be made to try to provide easy exit or
exile for these people that want to leave"
South Vietnam.

McGovern made his remarks in Mil-
waukee. In a break with past election
year traditions, when active campaigning
did not begin until Labor Day, the
Democratic Presidential candidate and
his running mate, R. Sargent Shriver,
were speaking to voters throughout the
country while the Republicans were
holding their convention.

McGovern disputed President Nixon's
claim that a Communist-dominated coalition in power in South Vietnam would
engage in assassination and terror, arguing that the Viet Cong would require a
broad base of popular support to maintain its role in government.

"The bloodbath is really what's going
on now, not the fact that several hundred people might be assassinated in the
event of our withdrawal," McGovern
declared.

He continued, "Our withdrawal is not
going to mean automatic stability in that
part of the world but it does mean that
the political, revolutionary forces that
are moving will work themselves out
without the kind of massive introduction
of modern weapons and killing that
we've brought in."

McGovern contended that the Communists were more politically astute
than the U.S. in dealing with the villagers
and rank and file people in South Vietnam.

"We're the ones that have applied
massive firepower and free-fire zones and
this word, 'pacification,'—and cleared six
million people out of their homes,"
McGovern added.

**GOP convention hits McGovern Vietnam
policy.** The Republican convention
opened in Miami Aug. 21. The party
chairman, Sen. Robert J. Dole (Kan.),
who welcomed the delegates to the convention Aug. 21, set the antiMcGovern
theme sounded by later speakers in con-
trasting the Nixon political philosophy
and "the belief of George McGovern that
what is radical is right and that things
as they are—or ever have been—are always wrong."

Dole, who also appeared on television
Aug. 20, charged that McGovern had

"thrown in with the North Vietnamese
and the Viet Cong." He urged an investigation based on the Logan Act of the
recent contacts with the North Vietnamese by former Attorney General Ramsey Clark and McGovern aide Pierre
Salinger.

Platform backs Nixon peace plan—
The convention approved by voice vote
Aug. 22 a platform endorsing the President's peace offer to withdraw all U.S.
forces from Vietnam four months after
release of all U.S. prisoners of war and
after an internationally supervised cease-
fire had been implemented throughout Indochina. It said the U.S. should not perform an "act of betrayal" by overthrow-
ing the Saigon government. And, in a
reference to a statement by Democratic
presidential nominee George McGovern,
the Republicans said "we most emphatically say the President of the U.S. should
not go begging to Hanoi."

The text of the Republican platform
plank on the war in Vietnam was as follows:

In Vietnam, too, our new policies have been dra-
matically effective.

In the the 1960's, our nation was plunged into
another major war—for the fourth time in this century, the third time in a single generation.

More than a half-million Americans were fighting
in Vietnam in January 1969. Fatalities reached 562
in a single week. There was no plan for bringing
Americans home, no hope for an end of the war.

In four years, we have marched toward peace and
away from war. Our forces in Vietnam have been cut
by 93%. No longer do we have a single ground combat
unit there. Casualties are down by 95%. Our young
draftees are no longer sent there without their consent.

Through it all, we have not abandoned an ally to
aggression, not turned our back on their brave defense against brutal invasion, not consigned them to
the bloodbath that would follow Communist conquest. By helping South Vietnam build a capability to
withstand aggression, we have laid the foundation
for a just peace and a durable peace in Southeast
Asia.

From one sector of the globe to another, a sure
and strong America, in partnership with other nations, has once again resumed her historic mission
—the building of lasting peace.

We will continue to seek a settlement of the Vietnam war which will permit the people of Southeast
Asia to live in peace under political arrangements of
their own choosing. We take specific note of the remaining major obstacle to settlement—Hanoi's demand that the United States overthrow the Saigon
government and impose a Communist-dominated
government on the South Vietnamese. We stand un-
equivocally at the side of the President in his effort
to negotiate honorable terms, and in his refusal to
accept terms which would dishonor this country.

We commend his refusal to perform this act of
betrayal—and we most emphatically say the Presi-

dent of the United States should not go begging to Hanoi. We believe that the President's proposal to withdraw remaining American forces from Vietnam four months after an internationally supervised ceasefire has gone into effect throughout Indochina and all prisoners have been returned is as generous an offer as can be made by anyone—by anyone, that is, who is not bemused with surrender—by anyone who seeks, not a fleeting peace at whatever cost, but a real peace that will be both just and lasting.

We will keep faith with American prisoners of war held by the enemy, and we will keep faith, too, with their families here at home who have demonstrated remarkable courage and fortitude over long periods of uncertainty. We will never agree to leave the fate of our men unclear, dependent upon a cruel enemy's whim. On the contrary—we insist that, before all American forces are withdrawn from Vietnam, American prisoners must be returned and a full accounting made of the missing in action and of those who have died in enemy hands.

We pledge that upon repatriation our returned prisoners will be received in a manner befitting their valor and sacrifice.

We applaud the Administration's program to assure each returned prisoner the finest medical care, personal counseling, social services and career orientation. This around-the-clock personal service will ease their reintegration into American life.

North Vietnam's violation of the Geneva Convention in its treatment of our prisoners of war has called forth condemnation from leaders around the world—but not by our political opposition at home. We denounce the enemy's flagrant breach of international law and common decency. We will continue to demand full implementation of the rights of the prisoners.

If North Vietnam continues obdurately to reject peace by negotiation, we shall nevertheless achieve peace for our country through the successful program of Vietnamization, phasing out our involvement as our ally strengthens his defense against aggression.

Nixon sees 'progress'—In his acceptance speech Aug. 23, President Nixon appealed to the nation to give him a "new majority" of support so his Administration could continue the progress of the past four years and "the progress we have made in building a new structure of peace in the world." As for his own policy, he reminded the convention of his pledge four years ago to seek an honorable end to the Vietnam war. He saw "great progress" toward that goal and said the Administration had "gone the extra mile" in negotiations.

But there were three things "that we have not and that we will not offer," he stressed:

■ "We will never abandon our prisoners of war."

■ "And second, we will not join our enemies in imposing a Communist government on our allies—the 17 million people of South Vietnam."

■ "And we will never stain the honor of the United States of America."

Nixon assured "our friends and allies in Europe, Asia, and Mideast and Latin America" that the U.S. would "continue its great bipartisan tradition" to stand by its friends and never desert them.

In discussing Vietnam, the President referred briefly to the issue of amnesty for those who "chose to desert their country" rather than fight. The real heroes, he said, were those who chose to serve.

Demonstrators fail to delay speeches—Protesters failed in their stated aim to delay the acceptance speeches of President Nixon and Vice President Agnew Aug. 23 by staging a massive sitdown outside the convention. More than 1,129 demonstrators were arrested during the day and evening as splinter groups roamed streets in the convention area trying to block traffic. Some slashed tires and overturned garbage cans.

Members of the Vietnam Veterans Against the War (VVAW), which had been consistently peaceful and well-disciplined throughout the convention demonstrations, tried to restrain the more damage-prone members of the crowd, the Washington Post reported Aug. 23. One demonstrator warned others, "Don't trash, we're after Republicans."

Protesters were prevented from gathering in large groups by extensive police use of CS or "pepper" gas, a crowd-control device, the New York Times reported Aug. 23. Only 38 minor injuries were reported as police adopted the highly mobile, but low profile tactics urged by Miami Beach Police Chief Rocky Pomerance.

Protesters were arrested on misdemeanor charges involving, in most cases, nominal $10 bail fees. Most demonstrators were free on bond by Aug. 24 as 25 judges in 11 courtrooms worked to process those arrested.

The convention session was delayed only seven minutes, but the stinging gas affected delegates trying to enter the hall through the bus barricade which police had used to seal off the convention site.

The Aug. 23 protests brought to a close three days of demonstrations emphasizing opposition to the war and Republican policies.

A debate over protesters' tactics used during the convention had preceded the gathering of more than 3,000 demonstrators in the Flamingo Park campsite in Miami Beach and was not resolved as the convention ended Aug. 23.

The aims of the demonstrators were as varied as the activist groups represented. Protesters had been organized by the Miami Conventions Coalition (MCC), an umbrella group comprised of the Youth International party (Yippies), the Peoples Coalition for Peace and Justice, the Coalition of Gay Organizations and the Miami Women's Coalition.

An MCC spokesman told the Washington Post Aug. 18, "We'd like to see the convention hall surrounded by National Guardsmen for all the world to see on prime TV time. We want to show that Nixon has to be nominated in the atmosphere of an armed camp."

(Paratroopers from the 82nd Airborne, several Marine units and Florida National Guard were on call at the nearby Homestead Air Force Base. The Secret Service, the Federal Bureau of Investigation (FBI) and local police officials at Miami Beach brought the total force to 8,500.)

Veteran activists David T. Dellinger and the Rev. Daniel J. Berrigan announced plans for the protest Aug. 16 in New York. They stressed that demonstrations would be nonviolent and were not aimed at shutting down the convention.

Copies of the protesters' tactical manual were delivered to the FBI and the New York State Committee to Re-elect the President later that day.

"We cannot win in a military confrontation. But we can win in a moral confrontation," Dellinger said.

Dellinger and Berrigan said the Vietnam war issue would be emphasized in the planned protests, including a film taken during former Attorney General Ramsey Clark's visit to North Vietnam to substantiate his claims of deliberate U.S. bombing of the dikes. (The film was not shown.)

They also announced that protesters would form a "gauntlet of shame" Aug. 22 which would be composed of protesters bearing evidence of the Administra-

tion's "war crimes." In addition, a "war crimes tribunal" was held Aug. 21 to hear a former prisoner of war and the sister of a POW denounce Nixon's policies in Indochina.

About 350 demonstrators Aug. 20, marched on the Fontainebleu Hotel, Republican party headquarters, where a $500-a-plate gala honoring Mrs. Nixon was held. Police dispersed the crowd after 45 minutes when several persons trying to enter the hotel were roughed up by demonstrators, who also damaged cars.

The action was organized by the Students for a Democratic Society (SDS), who together with the Zippie faction of the Yippie party, planned protests separate from the nonviolent actions of MCC, according to the Post Aug. 20.

Representatives of the VVAW joined protesters in Miami Beach Aug. 21 for a demonstration in front of the Miami Beach High School, which was occupied by National Guardsmen. Actress Jane Fonda and Black Panther leader Bobby G. Seale addressed the crowd of 1,500 for the rally honoring George Jackson, the black prisoner killed at San Quentin Prison in California. Several arrests were made when demonstrators tried to climb to the roof.

More than 200 were arrested Aug. 22 when demonstrators, led by Zippies, converged on the gates of the convention hall in the afternoon. They were charged with blocking traffic, damaging cars and assaulting delegates. Earlier an SDS-led group of 300 marched down the center of the city ripping flags and bunting and smashing windows in two buildings. No arrests were made.

Another group of 1,200, led by the VVAW, held a peaceful afternoon rally near the Fontainebleu Hotel and were joined by Rep. McCloskey.

That evening, 3,000 demonstrators staged their planned guerrilla theater tactics. They formed a "Street without Joy," as the French had named the Vietnamese Route 1, recreating scenes of the war. An elephant pulled a coffin symbolizing the deaths of Vietnamese and the shootings at Kent State University and Attica Prison. Delegates were assailed with cries of "murderers, murderers," as they tried to enter the hall. Sen. James

L. Buckley (R-Conservative, N.Y.) was chased by protesters.

Daniel Ellsberg, whose Pentagon Papers trial had been suspended, addressed the crowd. Earlier that day, he told a news conference called by McCloskey that Nixon had planned an escalation of the war almost since the beginning of his term in office.

Ellsberg said he had drawn up a list of war options for the President in December 1968 at the request of Henry A. Kissinger, the President's adviser for national security. The seventh alternative, unilateral withdrawal, was immediately rejected, Ellsberg said.

Ellsberg charged that Nixon took three overt steps to indicate to the North Vietnamese his support for South Vietnam during the early part of 1969: Marine ground operations in Laos, termed Dewey Canyon I; B-52 bombing raids in Cambodia; and a reconnaissance operation by Navy frogmen in Haiphong harbor, which was meant to be observed by the North Vietnamese as a signal of the President's intentions. Nixon's aim, Ellsberg said, was the gradual withdrawal of American ground troops and the gradual intensification of other aspects of the war to prevent the collapse of the South Vietnamese government.

Nixon opens campaign. President Nixon opened his campaign Aug. 24 with a slashing attack on McGovern's proposals to cut the defense budget.

Addressing the 54th annual convention of the American Legion in Chicago, Nixon drew cheers by stating his policy to keep the U.S. from having a defense "second" to that of any other nation and by praising the servicemen who served in Vietnam. "What they fought for and what we seek today," he said, "is a true generation of peace, not a short, humiliating truce that will encourage aggression and have the effect of rewarding the foes of freedom."

His Administration had economized on defense spending, he told the legionnaires, and would continue to economize "whenever it is safe to do so." But, he continued, "I have never gambled, and I never will gamble, with the safety of the American people under the false banner of economy."

McGovern's defense proposals, Nixon warned, would undermine the credibility of the nation's defenses and destroy hopes for a mutual troop reduction agreement and lessen the incentive for a further round of arms control negotiations.

McGovern addresses VFW. McGovern addressed the Veterans of Foreign Wars convention Aug. 24 in Minneapolis. The VFW members sat silently while McGovern talked about the swollen defense budget and the demoralizing effects of the Vietnam war on the nation's military tradition.

"If you doubt that judgment, ask the men who are quitting West Point and the other military academies. Ask the enlisted men who are marking time and counting the hours until their service is over," McGovern said.

Shriver calls Nixon No. 1 warmaker. Democratic vice presidential nominee Sargent Shriver called President Nixon Aug. 24 "the No. 1 warmaker of the world at this time." Campaigning in Cincinnati, Shriver said Nixon talked about a full generation of peace "but during the 1,403 days since he was elected America has not enjoyed even one day of peace."

In Houston Aug. 18, addressing the Jewish War Veterans convention, Shriver accused the President of "playing politics" with the relationship between the U.S. and Israel but that under McGovern the Democratic party would "continue its historic commitments" to "our sister democracy in Israel."

In Philadelphia Aug. 18, Shriver told a black audience the Nixon Administration "hides the real problems of Americans behind a smokescreen of neglect, of inaction and double talk."

Shriver also paid campaign visits to New York Aug. 24 and to Georgia and Louisiana Aug. 23.

Defense funds OKd, antiwar measure dropped. In action on defense authorization and appropriation bills Sept. 8–13, Congress whittled away at Administration requests, although most major Pentagon weapons programs were continued.

McGovern answers Agnew attack. In his Detroit talk Sept. 22, McGovern responded to a charge by Agnew in Chattanooga Sept. 21 that McGovern was "parroting the propaganda of North Vietnam" and helping to destroy "the morale of thousands of Americans who are not in possession of the facts" about Communist brutality in Indochina.

McGovern said he saw Agnew on television "crying about my statements on the war" and "I want to say to Mr. Agnew," he continued: "Don't you dare challenge my patriotism or my loyalty to this country."

McGovern repeated his phrase before a campaign crowd of 5,000-6,000 in Rochester, N.Y. later Sept. 22.

McGovern charges politics on POWs. Sen. McGovern charged Sept. 24 that the Nixon Administration was "playing politics" with the three POWs released by Hanoi. McGovern made the charge in impromptu remarks to a street crowd in New York City.

"There is nothing in the Geneva accords that requires that they be turned over to Army officers or go through a long period of indoctrination or briefing or debriefing," he said. McGovern called on Defense Secretary Melvin R. Laird and President Nixon "to let these three come home just as quickly as possible."

In comments on the POW situation earlier Sept. 24, Laird had accused the North Vietnamese of using the POWs' families as propaganda tools "in violation of the Geneva conventions." In a statement issued Sept. 24 after McGovern's remarks, Laird accused McGovern of apparently being willing to "act as an agent for Hanoi" and said "it is a despicable act of a presidential candidate to make himself a spokesman for the enemy."

During a TV appearance in San Francisco Sept. 26 with a POW wife, Mrs. Barbara Mullen of Oakland, McGovern repeated his charge. The Administration was delaying the POWs' travel, he said, because "the President is afraid these prisoners will tell the awful truth about the war—that it is the bombing which keeps them in prison." Mrs. Mullen said the President "seems to resent a mother and a wife going to Hanoi to bring their own loved ones home."

End-war amendment loses. The Senate rejected by a 45-42 vote Sept. 26 a Vietnam war fund cutoff proposal requiring a complete U.S. military withdrawal from Indochina within four months provided that U.S. prisoners of war were released. The proposal was in the form of an amendment by Sen. Edward W. Brooke (R, Mass.) to a $1.8 billion foreign military aid authorization bill, which the Senate passed by a 46-41 vote later Sept. 26. In July, the Senate had approved the Brooke amendment and rejected the aid bill.

More than enough past supporters of the Brooke amendment were absent from the Senate Sept. 26 to cause the defeat. Among the absentees were Sen. George McGovern, the Democratic presidential candidate, and Sen. Hubert H. Humphrey (D, Minn.), who was campaigning with McGovern. But the dwindling support for the antiwar amendment also was viewed in light of the House's consistent refusal to accept such proposals.

The conference committee killed a Senate provision that would have cut off all funds for the Indochina War within four months, subject to release of American prisoners. The House had rejected similar language in an Aug. 12 vote. The conference report, however, included a statement that a provision enacted in the 1971 procurement bill, stating that it was U.S. policy to set an Indochina withdrawal date, was still valid. President Nixon had said the bill was "without binding force or effect."

McGovern: Nixon lies about bombing. Democratic presidential candidate George McGovern accused President Nixon Sept. 30 of lying about the reasons the U.S. remained in the Vietnam war and pursued a bombing policy. In a speech at the Baltimore City Fair, McGovern attributed the continued U.S. involvement in the war to the Nixon Administration's attempt to keep President Nguyen Van Thieu of South Vietnam in power. Nixon "would have you believe that we are staying there and bombing to secure the release of our prisoners," McGovern said. "That is a lie. The truth is that each day this war continues is just one more day that our prisoners remain in their cells. And if we want to release our prisoners, the way to do it is to put an end to this war that put them in jail in the first place."

McGovern repeated his charge later Sept. 30 in meeting in Atlantic City, N.J. with the state AFL-CIO Council. Nixon "will tell you that he has kept us there [in Vietnam] for 3½ years to . . . get the prisoners out," he said. "Now that's a plain deceit, a plain falsehood."

Senate OKs $76 billion for defense. The Senate Oct. 2 passed a $76 billion defense appropriations bill, the largest since World War II. The measure was passed, 70–5, after a handful of amendments which sought to slash billions of dollars from the final bill was rejected.

Among those amendments was a proposal by Sen. William Proxmire (D, Wis.) to cut off funds for further bombing in Indochina. The Proxmire amendment, rejected 55–26, would have deleted about $2 billion from the bill. It was defeated after stormy debate.

As passed the bill included $6.1 billion for the Vietnam war. Overall, the bill provided $3.6 billion less than the Administration had sought.

The bill went to conference with the House, which had passed a slightly different version Sept. 14.

Much of the debate on the bill centered on Proxmire's proposal to end the U.S. bombing over Vietnam, Laos and Cambodia with no conditions attached and without any requirement for prior release of U.S. prisoners of war.

A number of senators who had voted for past "end-the-war" amendments voted against Proxmire's because of the absence of any condition about release of American POWs. Sen. John Stennis (D, Miss.), chairman of the Armed Services Committee and a staunch supporter of the President's Vietnam policy, called Proxmire's amendment "the most dangerous" of all the end-the-war proposals that the Senate had considered. Sen. John L. McClellan (D, Ark.) said "Hanoi wants this amendment."

The Senate, however, adopted by voice vote a much milder end-the-war amendment offered by Sen. Charles McC. Mathias (R, Md.).

The Mathias proposal specified that defense funds could not be used for com-

bat operations in Indochina that were inconsistent with the 1971 amendment declaring it to be "the policy of the U.S." to end all hostilities in Indochina "at the earliest practicable date" and to withdraw all its forces by "a date certain," subject only to release of American POWs.

Shriver denounces Nixon policies. In a Philadelphia speech Oct. 4, Democratic vice presidential nominee R. Sargeant Shriver advocated establishment, after the Vietnam war was ended, of a "State Department which serves as a ministry of peace." He denounced the Nixon Administration's "obsession with power" in foreign policy, which, he said, had led America to become "a patron of oppression." "The American people don't expect their government to declare war on other countries every time there is evil in the world, but Americans have always expected their government to declare us on the side of life and justice."

Nixon sees talks at sensitive stage. President Nixon told reporters at a news conference Oct. 5 in his office that the election "will not in any way influence what we do at the negotiating table." He did not want to discuss the current negotiations in the private channel except to say they were "in a sensitive stage." "If we have the opportunity," he said, "we will continue to talk before this election and we will try to convince them that waiting until after the election is not good strategy."

Nixon said he did not want to repeat the "very, very great mistake" made by "well-intentioned men" in 1968 when the bombing was stopped "without adequate agreements from the other side."

Nixon defended the bombing and mining of North Vietnamese ports as essential "to turn around what was a potentially disastrous situation." "The back of the enemy offensive has been broken," he said, and the mining and bombing would continue "until we get some agreements on the negotiating front."

McGovern presents peace plan. McGovern presented his plan for peace in a televised speech Oct. 10 (taped Oct. 8). Indicting President Nixon for failure to end the war despite 1968 campaign statements, McGovern said the Vietnam issue constituted the "most important" and "fundamental" difference between Nixon and himself.

Nixon regarded the Vietnam war "as our finest hour," McGovern said, "I regard it as the saddest chapter in our ... history." Nixon said in his 1968 campaign he had a plan to end the war, McGovern said, and that "those who have had a chance for four years and could not produce peace should not be given another chance." But "the answer to failure is not more of the same," McGovern contended. Nixon "has had his chance. He could not produce peace in four years. And we have every indication that he cannot produce peace in eight years."

If he were elected president, McGovern said, he would (1) immediately order an end to "all bombing and acts of force in all parts of Indochina," a halt to all "shipments of military supplies that continue the war" and an orderly withdrawal of all U.S. forces from Vietnam, Laos and Cambodia "along with all salvageable" U.S. military equipment, the process to be completed within 90 days.

(2) He would notify the enemy peace negotiators that these steps had been taken and "that we now expect that they will accept their obligation under their own seven-point proposal of 1971—to return all prisoners of war and to account for all missing in action," this process to be completed within 90 days to coincide with the total U.S. withdrawal from the war.

All parties would be notified that the U.S. "will no longer interfere in the internal politics of Vietnam, and that we will allow the Vietnamese people to work out their own settlement," McGovern said, and the U.S. would cooperate "to see that any settlement, including a coalition government, gains international recognition."

(3) He would send the vice president to Hanoi "to speed the arrangements for the return of our prisoners and an accounting of the missing." U.S. diplomats would "contact the opposing parties in Laos and Cambodia in order to secure release of prisoners held in those coun-

tries, and an accounting of missing in action, including American civilian newsmen now missing in Cambodia."

(4) After the return of all U.S. POWs and "a satisfactory accounting for any missing men," U.S. bases in Thailand would be closed and troops and equipment brought home from there and ships stationed adjacent to Indochina reassigned elsewhere.

(5) As the political solution was worked out by the Vietnamese, "we should join with other countries in repairing the wreckage left by this war," McGovern said.

(6) Congress would be asked to expand educational and job programs for Vietnam veterans.

After the war had ended, the POWs were home and the veterans provided for, McGovern said, he favored extending an opportunity to come home to those "who chose jail or exile because they could not in conscience fight in this war." If he were in their position, he said, "I would volunteer for two years of public service on subsistence pay simply to demonstrate that my objection was not to serving the nation but to participating in a war I thought was morally wrong."

In the same spirit, he said, he would oppose "any so-called war crimes trials to fix the blame for the past" on any citizen or group of citizens.

McGovern urged the nation to "seize the chance to lift from our sons and ourselves the terror of this war." Then, he said, "we can restore our sense of purpose and our character as a great nation," there will be "a new birth of confidence and hope," a start could be made toward "the rebuilding of our own land" and "America can begin to be America again."

In his indictment of the Nixon Administration for having broken its promise to end the war, McGovern noted the Administration's troop withdrawal program but said half a million U.S. troops were still "ranged in the Pacific, Thailand and Guam" engaged in the war. Since Nixon took office, he said, 20,000 Americans had been killed in the war, 40% of total U.S. deaths; 550 Americans had been captured or listed as missing; $60 billion had been spent on the war, which was costing $250 million each week; and the Indochinese were "being crushed under the weight of the heaviest bombardment the world has ever known," a bombing, he said, that "does not save their land" but "destroys it."

"Sixty billion of your taxes to kill human beings in Asia instead of protecting and improving human life in America," McGovern said. "Sixty billion in the last four years—not for a cause, but for a mistake—not to serve our ideals, but to save the face of our policymakers."

He contended that, "incredible as it seems, when all is said and done, our purpose in Vietnam now comes down to this—our policymakers want to save face and they want to save the Saigon regime of General [Nguyen Van] Thieu," a regime McGovern considered a "corrupt dictatorship." He represented this as the "fundamental" difference between Nixon and himself.

McGovern saw as another "fundamental" difference his disagreement with Nixon's attempt to end the war by "decisive military action." This was persistence in "the belief that we can find peace only in a wider war," he said, and it "only increased the killing and increased the costs."

McGovern expressed opposition to acceptance of the current situation "because the toll of suffering now includes more Asians and fewer Americans." Surely, he said, "conscience says to each of us that a wrong war is not made right because the color of the bodies has changed. We are all created in the image of God."

In a reference to President Nixon's visits to Peking and Moscow, he asked, "How can we really argue that it is good to accommodate ourselves to a billion Russian and Chinese Communists—but that we must somehow fight to the bitter end against a tiny band of peasant guerrillas in the jungles of little Vietnam?"

McGovern plays vets tape. At the University of Minnesota in Minneapolis Oct. 12, an audience of 15,000 persons listened in silence, some crying, to a recorded voice, self-identified as that of a Vietnam veteran, giving a remorseful eyewitness account of the results of bombing and the use of napalm in Vietnam.

McGovern had been given the tape earlier in the day by a Boston radio interviewer.

Nixon scores 'opinion leaders.' In an extemporaneous talk to a meeting in Washington Oct. 16 of relatives of U.S. prisoners of war and the missing in Southeast Asia, President Nixon attacked "the so-called opinion leaders of this country" for failing to support him in his decision to bomb North Vietnam and mine its ports.

He said the decision had been made when "we were faced with the specter of defeat" in Vietnam and when he was preparing for his Moscow trip. He described it as "the hardest decision" he had made as president and as "a potentially unpopular" one. He described the "opinion leaders" as "supposed to be the leaders of the media, the great editors and publishers and television commentators," university presidents and professors and "our top businessmen."

He said when a president made such a decision "the so-called opinion leaders of this country can be counted upon to stand beside him, regardless of party." In this instance, when he made the bombing and mining decision, "there was precious little support from any of the so-called opinion leaders of this country."

Nixon also told the group he would not abandon the POWs "to the goodwill of the enemy" and that draft evaders and deserters "will pay a price for their choice." When thousands had died and hundreds were prisoners or missing in action "for their choice," he said, "it would be the most immoral thing I could think of to give amnesty to draft dodgers and those who deserted. Your loved ones have and are paying a price for their choice, and those who deserted America will pay a price for their choice."

Nixon lauds Vietnam veterans. In a campaign radio address Oct. 22, President Nixon called upon the nation to honor those who served in Vietnam and promised to continue the Administration's job program for them. (The nation celebrated Veterans Day Oct. 23.)

It was more important than ever to honor the Vietnam servicemen, he said, "at a time when a small minority has tried to glorify the few who have refused to serve." While the problem of drug abuse "has made itself felt in our armed forces," Nixon said, "the vast majority of Vietnam veterans have come out of this war with a clean slate and a record of honor." He said he would not "make a mockery of their service by surrendering to the enemy, or by offering amnesty to draft dodgers and deserters."

Nixon said the Administration's goal of placing a million veterans in jobs by June 30 had been exceeded by 300,000 jobs, and he said "we are now working to provide jobs and training placements for another 1.3 million by next June."

The President said "most of the challenges that we face as a nation are bigger than party politics" and no challenge was greater than "keeping the peace in a dangerous world." He stressed that keeping America strong was vital to the peace effort.

"Some of the voices we hear today calling for a weak America, for an isolationist America," Nixon said, were typical of the "misguided thinking" that "led an unprepared America into two world wars in this century."

Nixon wins landslide victory. In the presidential balloting Nov. 7 President Nixon won reelection by an overwhelming majority in both the popular and electoral college vote. Sen. McGovern carried only one state, Massachusetts, and the District of Columbia. Nixon's victory was widely interpreted as a mandate to continue his policy of gradual and negotiated withdrawal from Indochina.

Candidates react to peace announcement. Less than two weeks before the presidential election, Presidential adviser Henry A. Kissinger told a Washington press conference that he believed "peace is at hand" in all of Indochina. Most observers of the campaign believed the announcement would diminish the impact of Sen. McGovern's vigorous criticism of President Nixon's Indochina policies. [For the details of the announcement .and the reactions of McGovern and Nixon see pp. 177–184, 195–196.]

Combat Developments

Saigon troops open Quangtri drive. An estimated 20,000 South Vietnamese troops launched a major drive June 28 to retake Quangtri Province captured by the North Vietnamese in April–May. The Saigon troops pushed into the province in force across the Mychanh River, their northernmost defense line, and were last reported 10 miles from Quangtri city, regarded as a major objective.

The South Vietnamese push was preceded and accompanied by the war's biggest concentration of firepower, nearly all of it American. Seventeen U.S. cruisers and destroyers offshore and more than 100 B-52 bombers were said to be pounding Communist positions in Quangtri almost continuously. A U.S. communique said a cruiser and destroyer were hit by North Vietnamese shore batteries receiving only "minor exterior damage with no casualties."

A South Vietnamese army report said Saigon troops made contact with North Vietnamese troops several hours after the start of the drive and were meeting "fierce resistance."

The South Vietnamese counteroffensive followed a government sweep into Quangtri on a smaller scale June 18–20. The foray followed an order from President Nguyen Van Thieu June 19 that all territory lost to the North Vietnamese since the start of their offensive be recaptured within three months. The heaviest fighting occurred June 20 when 237 North Vietnamese and 31 government troops were killed, the Saigon command reported. Field reports said 10 North Vietnamese tanks were knocked out by antitank weapons and air strikes.

North Vietnamese troops June 22 carried out a heavy infantry and armored assault against the Mychanh defense line, but the drive, the biggest in a month, was contained with the support of American air strikes. Government forces claimed 100 Communist soldiers were killed in the attack.

In other military developments, South Vietnam's 21st Division was reported June 22 to have been relieved of the task of lifting the siege of Anloc. (Some units of the division had managed to make their way into the town June 9.) The troops which had taken heavy losses in an unsuccessful attempt to break through the North Vietnamese roadblock on Route 13 were replaced by soldiers of the 25th Division from nearby Tayninh Province. The fresh troops also came under heavy Communist assault and remained stalled 10 miles from Anloc.

Abrams leaves post in Vietnam. Gen. Creighton W. Abrams, appointed the new Army chief of staff, left his post as commander of U.S. forces in Vietnam, it was reported June 30. Abrams was reported to have arrived in Bangkok, Thailand to vacation before leaving for Washington.

Abrams was succeeded in Vietnam by Gen. Frederick C. Weyand, who had been appointed June 28. Weyand, 55, was deputy to Abrams, and for 15 months prior to being appointed to that post had served as the military adviser to the U.S. delegation to the Paris peace talks.

U.S. plans new air raids. The U.S. was preparing to intensify air attacks on North Vietnam to cut off what was believed to be the last remaining trickle of supplies being sent through China, Defense Department sources reported June 30. One department official conceded that the new bombing campaign would not completely halt North Vietnamese military operations in South Vietnam, but said the raids would diminish them to "a much reduced level."

According to Pentagon sources, the projected step-up in the air war on the North would not violate the self-imposed 25-mile bomb-free buffer zone south of the China border. The establishment of this zone had been first disclosed by U.S. officials in Saigon June 26. Its formation followed protests by Peking in May and June against U.S. air strikes close to its frontier along the northeast rail lines supplying Hanoi. The American official said North Vietnam, aware of the presence of the buffer zone, was building up transfer facilities in the area for supplies from China. Trains and trucks were coming from China and unloading equipment inside the buffer zone, according to the official.

In another move aimed at circumventing its blockaded harbors, North Vietnam was constructing a fuel pipeline from Hanoi to the Chinese border, U.S. intelligence officials reported June 26. The pipeline was said to have been discovered by aerial photography.

U.S. military sources had disclosed June 21 that for the past 10 days North Vietnam had been unloading supplies from Chinese ships anchored offshore and hauling them inland aboard barges. U.S. Navy planes had destroyed many of the barges and receiving points on shore, the sources said. The unloading operations were said to have been taking place at two coastal islands—off Haiphong and 250 miles to the south near

Vinh. U.S. planes June 20 had bombed two North Vietnamese navy bases near Vinh as part of the action to interdict supplies unloaded from Chinese ships, U.S. military sources reported the following day.

North Vietnam claimed July 5 that it was receiving supplies through 12 "coastal points." It conceded that Haiphong harbor was effectively sealed. North Vietnam also claimed that despite the U.S. bombing of railroad lines war equipment continued to be transported on these lines because they were being repaired within hours of the raids.

The U.S. Defense Department July 5 denied North Vietnam's claims that it was receiving supplies through 12 coastal points. "No supplies are coming in by sea," the department insisted.

Battle for Quangtri city. South Vietnamese troops that had launched a counteroffensive June 28 to recapture Quangtri Province advanced to the edge of Quangtri city July 7. The government attacks were supported by intense American air strikes.

About 1,000 South Vietnamese marines were flown by U.S. helicopters June 29 into an area between the city and the South China Sea to join the main force. This raised the number of government troops in the area to more than 20,000 men. During the day's fighting, Saigon sources reported 225 North Vietnamese were killed and two enemy tanks destroyed. More government troops were airlifted by helicopter into Quangtri Province June 30 as the Saigon force pushed to within three miles of the provincial capital.

After being slowed by heavy Communist shelling and bad weather for two days, government troops resumed their push and July 4 some advance elements penetrated the southeastern limits of Quangtri city, capturing the Mailinh section. Other troops captured the village of Hailang, six miles southeast, bringing to 14 the number of villages seized in the area since the start of the counterdrive. Saigon said 148 Communists were killed. Close American air support during the day's fighting resulted in the accidental bombing of South Vietnamese positions by two U.S. Marine Phantoms five miles southeast of Quangtri city. Ten government soldiers were killed and 30 wounded.

Saigon reported that since the start of the counteroffensive, 1,200 North Vietnamese had been killed, largely by air strikes. Government losses were placed at about 60 killed.

Communists shell Hue—While South Vietnamese soldiers were pressing their drive in Quangtri, North Vietnamese forces launched diversionary shelling attacks July 2 on Hue, 22 miles to the southeast. Ten civilians were killed and 33 wounded when 40–50 shells hit the city July 2. Hue came under a shelling barrage July 3, with the North Vietnamese using long-range 130-mm. guns for the first time against the city. About 30–40 rockets and shells fired from a distance of 17 miles at the Citadel, the walled inner part of the city, killed 12 persons and wounded more than 50, mostly civilians. Two government positions defending Hue also were shelled. They were Phubai, seven miles away, and Fire Base Bastogne.

Three civilians were killed and seven wounded in the shelling of Hue July 4. A series of ground clashes on the approaches to Hue were fought the same day, resulting in the deaths of 49 North Vietnamese, Saigon reported. Fourteen government soldiers were wounded.

U.S. loses 8 jets. The U.S. command July 2 announced the loss of three jets over North Vietnam, with all six crewmen missing. This brought to eight the number of planes reported lost in the North June 21–27.

According to the command's delayed report, one of the aircraft was destroyed by a North Vietnamese MiG-21 June 27 about 60 miles northwest of Hanoi. The other two were reported lost to unknown causes June 24, about 30 miles northwest and 130 miles northwest of Hanoi.

Since the start of the North Vietnamese offensive March 30, the U.S. had lost 50 planes over the North and 99 in South Vietnam and Cambodia, the command said.

North Vietnam claimed the downing of two U.S. planes during a raid July 4 on Hanoi and surrounding Ninhbinh Province. The North Vietnamese news

agency said July 5 that the planes bombed and strafed residential areas in almost all districts of the capital and its outskirts.

Dike controversy continues—A dike at Phuly, 40 miles north of Hanoi, was reported June 30 to have been seriously damaged by three U.S. air raids earlier in June. Agence France-Presse correspondent Jean Thoraval reported that he and a group of foreign and North Vietnamese journalists led by Deputy Water Conservation Minister Phan My had visited the damaged facility that day. The minister said the dike had been bombed during American air strikes June 2, 12 and 21.

The U.S. Defense Department June 30 again denied American air strikes on North Vietnamese dikes. A spokesman said the department "will stand on the statements we have made in the past and that were made yesterday by the President." Nixon had told a news conference June 29 that the order not to hit dikes remained in effect and that reports of such strikes were not true.

State Department officials July 5 did not rule out accidental attacks on dikes in view of the intense American air campaign. In interviews with New York Times correspondent Bernard Gwertzman, department officials said the dikes could be inadvertently hit when North Vietnamese antiaircraft guns were situated at or near the facility or when American fighter-bombers dropped their bombs during aerial combat to gain speed.

Other officials told Gwertzman that there was a strong possibility North Vietnam would be struck by floods later in the summer, but that the country's defective dike system would be responsible rather than American raids. Spokesmen pointed out that many of the dikes had been heavily damaged in the 1971 floods and that many of them, by North Vietnam's own admission, had not been fully repaired.

Captured U.S. pilots identified—The U.S. Defense Department said June 24 it had received a list of 24 Air Force and Navy airmen identified by North Vietnam as having been captured since 1970. Fifteen of the men had been listed previously as prisoners and nine as missing in action, the department said.

The POW list had been given to the U.S. embassy in Paris by Walter Sohier, an attorney representing Sen. Edward M. Kennedy (D, Mass.).

According to the latest summary released June 22, the Pentagon listed 500 Americans captured and 1,109 missing.

Hanoi claims dikes bombed. Hanoi charged July 1 that U.S. planes in June had bombed "20 times at sections of dikes and water conservation projects that had already been repeatedly hit in April and May." The statement by the Water Conservation Ministry further accused the U.S. of using television and laser-controlled bombs "to strike the dike-repair sites . . . to prevent the people in the localities from repairing and strengthening dikes to prevent flash floods and other flooding."

The U.S. Defense Department July 3 repeated previous assertions that "the dike system of North Vietnam has not been targeted." The North Vietnamese were engaged in a "world-wide propaganda campaign . . . in the hope to explain the normal monsoon flooding by blaming it on us," the department said.

The North Vietnamese Foreign Ministry said U.S. planes July 5 damaged a dike in Nghean Province and a sluice gate in Namha Province south of Hanoi.

Agence France-Presse correspondent Jean Thoraval reported that U.S. jets July 11 bombed a dike system outside Namsach, 37 miles southeast of Hanoi. Thoraval said the attack occurred as North Vietnamese officials were leading him and other foreign correspondents on an inspection tour of other air raid damage in the area. Thoraval said he and the other newsmen agreed that the attack was clearly aimed at the dikes on which they were standing and that "the pilots dropped their bombs at random" during the 10-minute raid. He said there were no military targets in the area.

The Defense Department July 12 conceded the air strike on Namsach, but denied that dikes in the area had been assigned as specific targets. The raids were directed at three military targets—a missile site, a dispersed petroleum area and a fuel pipeline, the department said.

Hanoi claims big U.S. jet toll—North Vietnam claimed the downing of a large number of American planes over the North July 6–11. One report said five U.S. Phantom jets were downed July 8 —three near Hanoi and one in Hatay Province to the west. The raid on Hanoi, the statement said, destroyed 183 houses and killed "a score of people."

The U.S. command said the July 8 raid on Hanoi resulted in the destruction of the country's largest military vehicle repair shop. It said three MiG-21s were shot down while attempting to intercept the U.S. attackers. The U.S. conceded in a delayed report July 8 that two Phantoms had been shot down by MiG-21s northeast of Hanoi July 5. The four crewmen were listed as missing.

North Vietnam claimed it downed six U.S. planes July 11 and that "many U.S. pilots" had been captured. The North Vietnamese press agency report said the loss of these aircraft plus "the inclusion of two F-4s belatedly reported as having been knocked down over Quangbinh Province on July 6 and 8, brought to 3,742 the total of U.S. planes lost over North Vietnam."

Quangtri city drive stalled. South Vietnamese troops attempting to recapture Quangtri city were stalled in their drive by fierce North Vietnamese resistance at the edge of the provincial capital July 7–12.

News reports and Saigon government statements had first indicated that the city either had been retaken or at least entered by government troops. An authoritative military source denied all such reports July 7. A government statement July 11 said the purpose of the South Vietnamese counteroffensive was to crush North Vietnamese resistance by encircling Quangtri rather than by a frontal assault that would result in heavy casualties.

Most of the Communist defenders were deployed just outside the city on its southern and eastern edges. Saigon claimed its forces had taken a heavy enemy toll in men and tanks in assaults on these positions. The heaviest fighting occurred July 10–12. Government troops repelled three enemy attacks around Quangtri July 10–11, killing 149 North Vietnamese and destroying eight of their tanks, it was reported. Saigon said its casualties were 14 killed. South Vietnamese troops July 12 claimed to have killed 155 North Vietnamese around Quangtri, while suffering 21 killed and 75 wounded. More than 20 enemy tanks were destroyed in the battle, the Saigon command claimed.

The erroneous reports of government troops having taken Quangtri city were followed by a military order July 8 barring reporters from traveling on Route 1, the only road leading to the town. A military spokesman in Saigon explained July 9 that the decision, by Lt. Gen. Du Quoc Doc, an airborne division commander in the area, resulted from the "special operation situation" and that the news ban was "only temporary —for a few days."

In other military developments, casualties were inflicted on allied troops in two accidental U.S. artillery and air strikes July 8. The artillery, providing defensive fire for an American security patrol near Danang, mistakenly struck the unit, killing two soldiers and wounding eight. In the other incident, six South Vietnamese were killed and six wounded when their positions near Kontum were hit by two American Phantom jets.

Viet Cong set Quangtri rule—Hanoi radio reported July 11 that the Viet Cong had elected in June a 14-member People's Revolutionary Committee to rule Quangtri Province. According to the broadcast, Do San was elected as chairman of the committee and Nguyen Thanh and Mrs. Tran Thi Hong as co-chairmen.

The committee had been elected at a meeting of leaders of districts, towns, collectives and religious organizations, the broadcast said. It said the group "reflects the spirit of great national union and broad national concord and the will of the people in the province to fight the U.S. aggressors and save their country."

The Communists had announced the establishment of a governing apparatus in Quangtri in May following their capture of the province, but gave no details at the time.

Casualties—The Saigon command reported July 7 that 523 government troops and 2,765 North Vietnamese and Viet Cong had been killed June 25–July 1. This compared to totals of 836 and 3,260, respectively, the previous week. U.S. casualites in the June 25–July 1 period were placed at 14 killed, 23 wounded and four "missing, captured or interned."

Saigon troops open Binhdinh drive. South Vietnamese troops opened a counteroffensive in coastal Binhdinh Province July 19 in an attempt to retake the area captured by the North Vietnamese after the launching of their offensive March 30.

In disclosing the drive July 21, a government spokesman said a force of 8,000–10,000 troops were pushing north toward the Communist-held district capital of Hoainhon Bongson. An element of about 500 men had been airlifted to positions less than a mile south of the city. Thus far only light contact with the enemy was reported.

Meanwhile, other government forces were reported making progress in their counteroffensive in Quangtri Province to the north. South Vietnamese soldiers fighting on the edge of Quangtri city since July 7 pushed into the North Vietnamese-occupied provincial capital July 15 and advanced toward the Citadel, a large walled enclave in the center of the town. The government troops moved to within 50 yards of the Citadel in bitter house-to-house combat by July 19. Meanwhile, heavy fighting also continued on the outskirts of the city.

The Saigon command said that government troops had killed 209 Communist soldiers around Quangtri city July 12–13, while losing 47 men themselves. Another 114 North Vietnamese were reported slain in fighting two to four miles northeast of the city July 14. The Saigon command claimed 295 North Vietnamese were killed in fighting in and around Quangtri city July 19. Government losses were listed at 27 killed and 131 wounded.

The U.S. command reported July 15 that B-52 raids on North Vietnamese bunkers around Quangtri city July 11 had killed about 300 of the enemy. The command said South Vietnamese searching one target struck eight miles south of the provincial capital "found 60 destroyed enemy bunkers containing approximately 250 dead and their equipment." Other government troops found six graves containing the bodies of 48 North Vietnamese about two miles northeast of Quangtri city in another area hit by the B-52s, the command said.

U.S. planes and warships July 17 provided the government offensive in Quangtri Province with the heaviest support of the war. Nearly 100 B-52s and more than a dozen cruisers and destroyers bombarded North Vietnamese positions on both sides of the demilitarized zone. Elements of two North Vietnamese divisions moving south to reinforce Quangtri's defenses were attacked by a dozen B-52s near the port city of Donghoi, 45 miles north of the DMZ. More than 80 B-52s dropped bombs on North Vietnamese positions around Quangtri city. One destroyer, the Warrington, was crippled by two explosions of undetermined origin 20 miles off the coast. The ship was towed to the U.S. Naval base at Subic Bay in the Philippines.

In other military developments, North Vietnamese forces continued their shelling of Hue, 32 miles southeast of Quangtri city. In the worst incident, 10 civilians were killed and three wounded July 18. Hue was shelled July 15 and 20 but few casualties were reported.

U.S. jets bomb Hanoi. U.S. planes bombed Hanoi July 22 for the first time in a month. The American command said the following day that 20 F-4 Phantoms flying from Thailand had destroyed two large North Vietnamese army depots in the capital and heavily damaged 11 others.

According to North Vietnam's account of the attack, "waves" of U.S. jets had raided "a number of populous areas in Hanoi city" and "numerous" civilians had been killed and wounded. The Communists said two of the attacking planes were shot down. The U.S. command conceded the loss of two planes, but said one had been lost south of Thanhhoa and the other in the Gulf of Tonkin after a mission northeast of Vinh.

A North Vietnamese communique later July 23 said at least 20 sections of

Hanoi and its suburbs had been heavily hit by U.S. air strikes the night of July 22 and July 23. The government statement said seven U.S. planes were downed by antiaircraft gunners July 22 and one pilot was captured.

The Hanoi area came under U.S. air attack again July 24. Pilots from an aircraft carrier in the Gulf of Tonkin claimed they had heavily damaged the Vandien battery manufacturing plant, four miles from the capital. In other raids July 24, the U.S. command acknowledged the loss of two planes near Haiphong. One was downed by antiaircraft and the other by a MiG-21. The U.S. had claimed an F-4 Phantom pursued and shot down a MiG-21 15 miles from Hanoi July 18.

U.S., U.N. dispute dike raids. U.N. Secretary General Kurt Waldheim said July 24 that he had received evidence that U.S. planes had deliberately bombed dikes in North Vietnam. President Nixon and Secretary of State William P. Rogers denied the charge.

Waldheim said that according to "private and unofficial" information from Hanoi, the dikes had been bombed and that "even in cases where the dikes are not directly bombed, the nearby bombing causes cracking of the earth of the dams and that in this way the result is the same." The secretary general appealed to the U.S. "to stop this kind of bombing, which could lead to enormous human suffering, enormous disaster."

In response to Waldheim's statement, Rogers said he had directed George Bush, head of the U.S. delegation to the U.N., to meet with the secretary general "to point out that the information he has received concerning alleged deliberate bombing to damage the dikes in North Vietnam is false—as the President stated in his June 29 press conference."

Rogers said he had told Bush to inform Waldheim that "these allegations are part of a carefully planned campaign by the North Vietnamese and their supporters to give worldwide circulation of this falsehood." "We cannot consider helpful any public statements giving further currency to these reports," the secretary added.

Bush met with Waldheim later July 24 and conveyed Rogers' views.

The State Department said July 26 that any American air strikes on the dikes were accidental and the resultant damage was minimal. The statement said "there has been no new indication of anything but the most incidental and minor impact on the system of levees as the result of strikes against military installations" in the vicinity of the dikes. The department later said that its evidence was based on photo reconnaissance and other information.

Nixon rejects Waldheim charge—President Nixon July 27 took issue with Secretary General Waldheim's statements on the bombing of the dikes.

Speaking at an impromptu news conference in Washington, the President asserted that Waldheim "just like his predecessor [U Thant]" and other "well-intentioned and naive people" had been "taken in" by North Vietnam's propaganda "to attack the American bombing of civilian installations and risking civilian lives, and yet not raising one word against the deliberate bombing of civilian installations in South Vietnam." Saying he wanted "to get the record straight," Nixon asserted that 45,000 civilian casualties, including 5,000 dead, had resulted from the North Vietnamese offensive in the South since March 30.

The controversy over the dikes, Nixon said, was "a deliberate attempt on the part of the North Vietnamese to create an extraneous issue, to divert attention from one of the most barbaric invasions of history, compounded by a violation of all concepts of international law on the handling of prisoners."

The President insisted that the Administration's policy was not to bomb the dikes, but if any damage to them had occurred, orders had been issued to make certain it did not happen again. Nixon, praising the restraint being used by American military power in Indochina, said if the U.S. wanted to bomb the dikes, "We could take them out in a week."

He added later, "We are not using the great power that could finish off North Vietnam in an afternoon; and we will not."

Nixon also was critical of domestic opposition to his Indochina policy. He singled out the end-the-war amendments in Congress, which he said should be called "prolong the war" amendments. The Congressional votes on them, Nixon said, were telling the North Vietnamese: "Don't negotiate with the present Administration; wait for us and we will give you what you want in South Vietnam." He urged senators and representatives to "consult their consciences" and to take no action which jeopardizes current peace negotiations, whose chance of success, he said, was "better now than it has ever been" because of military setbacks suffered by the Communists.

Blake appeals to Nixon—The secretary general of the World Council of Churches, the Rev. Dr. Eugene Carson Blake, had appealed to President Nixon July 17 to "use your authority as commander in chief of the military forces of the U.S.A. immediately to cease this bombing" of North Vietnam's dikes. In a letter to the President made public July 20, Blake also urged Nixon "to stop the bombing in the region of the dikes in order that the people of North Vietnam can make the urgent necessary repairs to avoid catastrophe of unthinkable proportions."

The White House, refusing direct comment on Blake's allegations, referred to a statement made earlier July 20 by Press Secretary Ronald L. Ziegler on the controversy. Ziegler said the North Vietnamese were engaging in propaganda. "Every year there is some flooding in Vietnam. We have a policy: There is no targeting of dikes and dams in Vietnam. There will be no such policy," Ziegler said.

U.S. charges North Vietnam buildup. The U.S. delegation to the Paris peace talks charged July 25 "a significant buildup" of North Vietnamese troops was in progress in the northern provinces of South Vietnam. The statement said the U.S. had evidence of 12 North Vietnamese divisions in the area, compared with 10 in April.

The delegation said the massing of Hanoi's forces was taking place "at the very time" when President Nixon's cease-fire proposals "are still on the table and have not yet received serious response" from the Communist delegations. The statement urged North Vietnam to reconsider its "own responsibilities for sustaining and intensifying military operations in South Vietnam. Such operations have already resulted in enormous numbers of casualties and devastated towns in South Vietnam, and the prospects of this continuing must dismay international opinion."

Reds capture Fire Base Bastogne. North Vietnamese troops July 26 captured Fire Base Bastogne, a major stronghold defending the southwest approach to Hue, 11 miles away.

A Saigon report July 27 said the battalion of defenders, about 600 men, was forced to abandon the base in the face of intense communist shelling and heavy infantry assaults. This was the second time Fire Base Bastogne had been abandoned since the start of the North Vietnamese offensive March 30. It had been given up by the South Vietnamese from April 28 to May 15.

In the battle for Quangtri city, the South Vietnamese announced July 27 that all 2,500 government airborne troops fighting in and near the provincial capital would be replaced by marines operating east and north of the city. It was believed the airborne force was being shifted to meet the North Vietnamese threat to Route 1, the supply line leading from Hue to Quangtri city, and the threat to Hue itself. North Vietnamese gunners were firing on government convoys on Route 1 with mortars, rockets and machine guns.

The South Vietnamese command reported a lull in the fighting in Quangtri city, where major action in the past few days had centered in the Citadel, the walled enclave in the center of the town. The Saigon command claimed July 25 its forces had captured the Citadel and the entire city. But a command spokesman the following day said North Vietnamese resistance was continuing. The government attackers hoisted their national flag over the Citadel July 26, while Communist forces continued fighting in and around the fortress.

The worst helicopter crash of the Vietnam war occurred July 11 in operations north of Quangtri city, according to a belated report by the Saigon command July 27. At least 50 South Vietnamese soldiers were killed when a U.S. Marine CH-53 helicopter from an aircraft carrier was shot down by enemy fire during an airborne operation. Twenty-nine of the 31 helicopters involved in the operation were hit by enemy fire. In announcing the incident, the Saigon command said July 27 that it was the responsibility of American military authorities to make the disclosure because the casualties occurred in an American aircraft. The U.S. command and Navy argued that it was the responsibility of the South Vietnamese to make the announcement. The U.S. command had reported the shooting down of the CH-53 July 11, but only reported that two of the American crewmen were missing and several were wounded. It made no mention of the South Vietnamese casualties.

In the government's new offensive in coastal Binhdinh Province, South Vietnamese troops captured two major towns abandoned by the North Vietnamese without a fight. The Saigon soldiers seized the district capitals of Hoainhon July 21 and Tamquan July 23. As a result only two districts towns in the province remained in North Vietnamese hands—Hoaian and Anlac.

Casualty reports—The U.S. command announced July 27 that 10 Americans had been killed and nine wounded in action July 16–22. One American was killed in non-combat duty and two were listed as missing, presumably in an air crash. This compared with eight U.S. soldiers killed in action July 9–15. Five others were listed as killed in non-combat action, 14 were missing or captured and 26 were wounded.

South Vietnamese losses in the July 16–22 period were 630 killed and 2,373 wounded, compared with the previous week's toll of 837 killed and 2,367 wounded.

Allied casualties since the start of the North Vietnamese offensive March 30: U.S.—149 killed in action, 117 killed in non-combat duty and 423 wounded; South Vietnam—13,180 killed and 41,431 wounded.

U.S. intelligence report on dike bombing. The Nixon Administration July 28 issued an intelligence report conceding that U.S. bombing had damaged North Vietnam's dike system at 12 points, but asserting that the hits were unintentional and the damage was minor.

The report, assembled principally by the Central Intelligence Agency, was distributed to newsmen by the State Department to support the Administration's contention that Hanoi was falsely charging the U.S. with deliberate and systematic bombing of the dikes.

According to the report, photographs taken July 10–11 showed that all the dike damage occurred within close range of "specific targets of military value." "Of the 12 locations where damage has occurred, 10 are close to identified individual targets such as petroleum storage facilities, and the other two are adjacent to road and river transport lines," the report said.

Because a large number of dikes served as bases for roadways, "the maze they create throughout the delta makes it almost inevitable that air attacks directed against transportation targets cause scattered damage to dikes," the report continued. However, bomb craters identified by photographic reconnaissance at the 12 locations could "be repaired easily with a minimum of labor and equipment," and "repairs to all the dikes could be completed within a week," the report claimed.

State Department officials refused to show newsmen any of the report's photographic evidence, claiming that it would only provoke Hanoi to issue its own photographs in rebuttal, some of which might be "fabricated."

However, officials said the photographs and report had been presented to United Nations Secretary General Kurt Waldheim by U.S. Ambassador George Bush July 24 after Waldheim said he had received evidence that U.S. planes had deliberately bombed North Vietnamese dikes.

Hanoi denial—North Vietnam rejected the Administration claim that damage to the dikes had been minor and unintentional, the London Times reported July 31.

According to Phan My, deputy minister for water conservation, the U.S. had made 173 strikes against the dikes since April, dropping 1,243 "demolition and magnetic bombs" and hitting the dikes in "149 places." My said the speed with which the dikes had to be rebuilt meant a lowering of construction standards, rendering the dikes vulnerable to serious flooding once the heaviest rains set in.

The North Vietnamese news agency reported July 30 that three waves of U.S. bombers had attacked and destroyed a sluice gate 60 miles southeast of Hanoi. The system was used to drain about 120,000 acres of paddy fields.

Waldheim, Bush meet—Relations between U.N. Secretary General Waldheim and the U.S. grew more strained July 28 as Waldheim, responding to criticism from President Nixon, summoned U.S. Ambassador Bush to a private meeting.

The meeting, resulting from Nixon's assertion July 27 that Waldheim had been "taken in" by North Vietnamese "propaganda" about U.S. bombing of the dikes, lasted about an hour. Bush said afterward that his talk with Waldheim had been "frank and full," but added, "I think the best thing I can do on the subject is to shut up."

Clark, study group in Hanoi. Former U.S. Attorney General Ramsey Clark arrived in Hanoi July 29 with other members of an international committee to investigate the effects of U.S. bombing of areas inhabited by civilians and damage to dikes.

According to Yves Lacoste, a geography professor at the Sorbonne in Paris, the group would be in North Vietnam about two weeks, and would map the damage to dikes in an attempt to establish whether air strikes against them were deliberate.

Heavy fighting erupts in Cambodia. A force of about 2,000 South Vietnamese troops July 31 launched a drive near Kompong Trabek in the Parrot's Beak of eastern Cambodia. In first disclosing the operation Aug. 5, the Saigon command announced that its purpose was to thwart a possible North Vietnamese offensive aimed at cutting Route 4, linking Saigon with the Mekong Delta. Meanwhile, the North Vietnamese opened an attack of their own Aug. 6 against Kompong Trabek itself and engaged Cambodian troops in heavy fighting.

In the initial stages of the South Vietnamese drive, a Saigon command spokesman said 34 Communists were killed Aug. 4 in two clashes 12 miles from Kompong Trabek. Another 79 of the enemy that infiltrated into South Vietnam's Mekong Delta were said to have been slain Aug. 5 about eight miles northwest of Cailay. Government losses were placed at five dead. Government troops captured Nhibinh, a village east of Cailay, killing 16 Viet Cong. Twenty South Vietnamese were reported killed.

Cambodian troops were battered by heavy North Vietnamese attacks around Kompong Trabek Aug. 6–8 and were driven from a large section of the city, 50 miles southeast of Pnompenh. The Communist forces, backed by tanks for the first time, also assaulted the outer defenses of Neak Luong and severed Route 1 west of Kompong Trabek. The highway linked Saigon with Pnompenh.

American jets coming to the aid of the Kompong Trabek defenders destroyed 14 Soviet-made North Vietnamese tanks in two days of strafing, the Cambodian command reported Aug. 8. The command said Cambodian troops destroyed five other tanks in Kompong Trabek Aug. 7.

Cambodian President Lon Nol flew to the battlefront at Neak Luong Aug. 8 and talked with Cambodian and South Vietnamese commanders. During the visit North Vietnamese troops operating six miles away severed another Route 1 section by isolating a remnant of a Cambodian brigade near Kompong Soeung.

Kompong Trabek, first seized by the Communists April 24, had been recaptured by Cambodian and South Vietnamese forces July 24. The fall of the city was preceded by heavy allied bombing of the Communist defenders and fierce ground fighting the previous day.

Communists attack near Saigon—South Vietnamese forces suffered heavy losses in Communist attacks 17 miles east of Saigon Aug. 7–8. It was the closest major fighting to the capital since the start of the North Vietnamese offensive March 30. A Saigon communique Aug.

10 described government militiamen losses as "heavy" in the clashes two miles northeast of the district capital of Longthanh. Field reports said nearly 100 men were killed. The militiamen were attacked during a routine sweep of the area. Government rangers Aug. 10 replaced the battered regional force around Longthanh. Route 15, which connected Saigon with the coastal resort of Vungtau, ran through the city.

Other military developments—Fighting continued in and around Quangtri city with the Saigon command admitting Aug. 5 that its forces were making no significant progress in the drive to recapture the provincial capital from North Vietnamese troops. Hanoi's forces remained in control of the walled Citadel and other parts of the town.

A command report Aug. 5 said 100 North Vietnamese had been killed in the area in the 48-hour period ended Aug. 4. South Vietnamese marine positions were heavily shelled on the outskirts of the city Aug. 5–9. An allied retaliatory air and artillery strike Aug. 9 was said to have killed 61 enemy soldiers.

(The U.S. State Department charged Aug. 7 that North Vietnamese forces had deliberately shelled refugees fleeing Quangtri Province April 29–30, killing 1,000–2,000 of the civilians. The attacks occurred on Route 1, just north Quangtri city, the department said. The department also confirmed a report that the Communists had executed civilians in Binhdinh Province.)

In fighting to the southeast, the North Vietnamese continued to pose a threat to Hue. A force of more than 100 Communist troops seized five hamlets near the city Aug. 6, but they were recaptured by government militiamen the following day.

U.S. casualties increase—American combat casualties increased July 30–Aug. 5 to seven killed and 36 wounded because of Communist rocket attacks on U.S. bases at Danang and Binehoa, the U.S. command reported Aug. 10. U.S. forces had suffered 25 casualties the previous week—eight killed and 17 wounded.

The Saigon command said 463 South Vietnamese had been killed July 30–Aug. 5 and 2,115 were wounded. It reported 2,250 Communists slain in that period and placed their total war deaths at 867,718.

Haiphong shipyard bombed. In a new effort to cut off the flow of war supplies to North Vietnamese troops in the south, U.S. Navy pilots Aug. 1 bombed a shipyard in Haiphong that built and repaired shallow-draft boats. The boats were used to shuttle supplies ashore from freighters unable to enter North Vietnam's mined harbors.

The strike was one of 210 against North Vietnam Aug. 1, fewer than recent daily averages of 300 because of poor flying weather. The U.S. command announced Aug. 2 that two U.S. fighter-bombers had been shot down over North Vietnam, with all four crewmen listed as missing.

The North Vietnamese press agency reported Aug. 2 that U.S. bombers had raided a Haiphong residential area Aug. 1, killing or wounding a large number of North Vietnamese and Chinese. The agency said nearly 400 homes belonging to North Vietnamese workers and some Chinese families were demolished. Three of the Chinese dead were identified by name.

The U.S. command had announced July 31 that three U.S. aircraft including a B-52 bomber had crashed during a day of heavy strikes against the north. The B-52 crashed in a thunderstorm in southeastern Thailand, killing five crewmen. Two Air Force F-4 Phantom jets plunged into the sea off the coast of North Vietnam after they ran out of fuel. All four crewmen were reported rescued.

U.S. planes flew more than 310 strikes over North Vietnam July 30, demolishing the center spans of two bridges on the northeast road and rail line linking Hanoi and China, the U.S. command said. Hanoi claimed two F-4 Phantoms were shot down during the raids, and two U.S. airmen were captured on the outskirts of the capital.

The U.S. command reported July 30 that U.S. planes had shot down two MiG-21 interceptors about 35 miles northeast of Hanoi during raids July 29.

China-North Vietnam pipeline. The construction of a second fuel link be-

tween China and North Vietnam was nearing completion, the U.S. Defense Department reported Aug. 4. The pipeline between the Chinese border town of Pingsiang and Kep, 30 miles northeast of Hanoi, was expected to increase North Vietnam's fuel supplies from China to 1,000 tons a day when completed later in August, according to the department. It ran parallel to another pipeline from Pingsiang to Hanoi, which had been completed in July and carried 400 tons of fuel a day.

U.S. jets raid depot near Hanoi. U.S. jets raided the Vandien truck depot near Hanoi Aug. 5. The U.S. command said returning pilots told of setting off two large explosions at the installation four miles south of the capital. The depot had been struck previously July 22.

Hanoi claimed the downing of two American planes over Nghean Province Aug. 2 and 3, but did not disclose the fate of the pilots.

U.S. jets Aug. 8 bombed the Thanhhoa bridge, rendering it unusable, according to the American command.

The North Vietnamese news agency claimed that U.S. planes carried out an "extermination" raid Aug. 8 on Haiduong, 30 miles east of Hanoi. The agency said "a large number of people" were killed and wounded in the bombing of a medical school and a factory.

Fire Base Bastogne reported retaken. The Saigon command reported Aug. 3 that South Vietnamese troops had reoccupied Fire Base Bastogne, a major stronghold defending the southwest approach to Hue. The base, 11 miles from the city, had been captured by North Vietnamese troops July 26.

A South Vietnamese military spokesman said two government platoons reentered the hill base late Aug. 2, finding it empty.

Two U.S. Navy jets had accidentally dropped 500-pound bombs on South Vietnamese positions near the fire base July 28 killing eight government troops and wounding 25, the U.S. command in Saigon announced July 29. It was the fifth mistaken U.S. bombing attack on the northern front since July 4, with a total of 19 South Vietnamese soldiers killed and 76 wounded.

Meanwhile, Communists staged their first rocket attack on the Danang air base near Hue in three weeks and their most severe in more than a year. The U.S. command said 38 122-mm. rockets struck the base early Aug. 3, killing one U.S. airman and wounding 20. A South Vietnamese spokesman added that four South Vietnamese—three civilians and one soldier—were also killed in the action.

In the battle for Quangtri city, 35 miles north of Hue, fierce fighting reportedly continued after South Vietnamese troops, apparently suffering heavy casualties, abandoned their foothold in the walled Citadel July 27. The troops, from an airborne division, were replaced by marines the same day.

On the central coastal front in Binhdinh Province, fresh fighting was reported in the district capital of Hoainhon (Bongson), retaken by the South Vietnamese July 21. The town was heavily shelled July 29, and North Vietnamese were reported to have seized control of the western half.

With Hoainhon contested, the South Vietnamese retained firm control of only Tamquan among the three northern district capitals which they reported recapturing in an 11-day offensive. Hoaian was reported by the Saigon command to have been retaken with "very light resistance" July 28, but government troops moved out of the town after ordering several thousand civilians to move south into government-controlled territory along Highway 1.

Binhdinh executions—According to the New York Times Aug. 4, allied intelligence officials in Saigon claimed Communist political officers had publicly executed hundreds of government officials and imprisoned thousands since occupying the northern half of Binhdinh Province in April.

The allied officials said they had confirmed the deaths of about 250 persons through eyewitness reports and had additional information indicating the number of dead was as high as 500. The main victims were said to be hamlet and village chiefs and their deputies, pacification workers, policemen and militiamen.

More U.S. troops withdrawn—The U.S. command in Saigon announced

July 31 that U.S. troop strength in Vietnam had dropped by another 500 men, to a total of 46,000.

South Vietnam ground action. South Vietnamese forces Aug. 10 were reported to have cleared North Vietnamese troops from the southern part of Quangtri city and destroyed 14 Communist tanks in an air strike six miles southeast of the provincial capital. Despite the government success, 400 North Vietnamese remained entrenched in the walled Citadel and fierce fighting continued in and around the city.

A North Vietnamese attack on the southern fringes of Quangtri city Aug. 15 was beaten back by South Vietnamese troops. Twenty-one Communists were reported killed in the engagement. In an encounter within a mile of the city, 24 North Vietnamese and five government soldiers were killed. Government troops also were said to have discovered the bodies of 38 Communists killed by a South Vietnamese air raid 700 yards from the Citadel. In addition to the heavy ground fighting in and around Quangtri city, South Vietnamese and Communist forces engaged in a heavy exchange of artillery fire. Nearly 700 rounds were fired on government positions outside the city Aug. 15.

Other military developments—A U.S. C-130 transport plane crashed Aug. 12 while taking off from the Soctrang airport in the Mekong Delta. Thirty persons were killed.

North Vietnamese and Viet Cong forces carried out heavy attacks throughout South Vietnam Aug. 11–12. The Saigon command said 38 Communists killed in the 24-hour raids and gave its losses as four killed and 28 wounded. The heaviest enemy assault was directed at Laikhe, headquarters for the South Vietnamese military operations in the Saigon region and a major artillery and helicopter base. A force of 100 attackers was driven away from the base perimeter after a battle of several hours.

Viet Cong infiltrators blew up two ammunition dumps and a bridge in the vicinity of Saigon and Danang Aug. 13. The raiders destroyed one ammunition dump at a government base at Longbinh, 12 miles northwest of the capital. Three infiltrators were captured, the Saigon command said. The second ammunition dump was blown up at Longthanh, 20 miles east of Saigon. A resultant fire was brought under control two hours later. In the Danang area action, Viet Cong sappers blew up a bridge on the outskirts of the city.

The Communists Aug. 14 blew up another government ammunition dump, three miles northwest of Pleiku in the Central Highlands. Several thousand tons of howitzer ammunition were destroyed, the Saigon command reported.

U.S. B-52s dropped 600 tons of bombs Aug. 15 on Communist positions 24–35 miles from Saigon. The raids were said to be aimed at enemy units that had moved toward Saigon from the Anloc area to the north. Despite the shift of troops from Anloc, the Communist siege of the city remained in force.

Last U.S. combat units leave. The last units of American combat troops left South Vietnam Aug. 12. The men, belonging to the 3rd Battalion, 21st Infantry and G Battery, 29th Field Artillery, departed from Danang without ceremony.

The U.S. command had announced Aug. 11 that the last two combat units and a supporting medical attachment totaling 1,043 men were being withdrawn from the field. Their departure from South Vietnam reduced the American force in the country to 43,500, largely service personnel.

U.S. withdrawals pass 500,000 mark. The U.S. command reported Aug. 14 that the withdrawal of 2,220 Americans from Vietnam the previous week increased to more than one half million the number of U.S. servicemen pulled out since President Nixon had begun the cutback in 1969. American troop strength now stood at 42,400, compared with a peak of 543,000 in April 1969.

'Heaviest' B-52 raids hit North. The U.S. Air Force announced Aug. 12 that B-52 bombers in the past 24 hours had carried out "probably their heaviest raids ever" over North Vietnam. The announcement said the bombers had flown 13 missions against supply targets within

63 miles of Donghoi in the southern panhandle.

Meanwhile, lighter U.S. aircraft flew 200 missions against other Communist targets, mostly in the southern part of North Vietnam. One of the strikes reportedly severed a fuel pipeline seven miles west of Donghoi. An American source said the pipeline had been destroyed in a previous raid, but that the Communists keep repairing it.

The U.S. command reported Aug. 14 the downing of two MiG-21 jets by U.S. planes over North Vietnam the previous week. One was shot down Aug. 12 by a Phantom 50 miles northwest of Hanoi and the other Aug. 10, by a Navy F-4 30 miles southwest of Thanhhoa.

U.S. air strikes over the North Aug. 13 were limited to 140 missions because of overcast skies. In the northernmost strike, 30 miles above Hanoi, U.S. pilots claimed the destruction of two-thirds of the Phuly railroad bridge.

North Vietnam claimed that an American raid on Thanhhoa Aug. 14 had killed or injured 100 civilians. The U.S. command Aug. 16 acknowledged that Navy jets Aug. 14 had struck seven targets outside the port city, but denied any raids inside Thanhhoa. A delayed command report said a Navy F-8 jet had crashed Aug. 13 while returning to its carrier in the Gulf of Tonkin. The pilot was listed as missing.

The power plant at Viettri, 30 miles northwest of Hanoi, was heavily damaged by American planes Aug. 15 for the second time in two months, the U.S. command reported the following day. The complex had been previously damaged June 25, but was rebuilt since then. The latest raid on the Viettri plant destroyed the generator hall and damaged the boiler house and storage buildings, according to the command report. In other air action Aug. 15, U.S. pilots reported destroying the Phutho rail bridge, 45 miles northwest of Hanoi. The span was used to bring supplies into Hanoi from Laocai, on the Chinese border to the northwest. Other U.S. planes continued heavy strikes against supply centers and troop concentrations in the southern part of North Vietnam to hamper reinforcements for the Quangtri front in northern South Vietnam.

A Hanoi broadcast Aug. 17 claimed the downing of five U.S. planes during the Aug. 15 raids, two more during midnight strikes and four Aug. 16.

A delayed U.S. command report Aug. 17 said a Phantom jet had been shot down by Communist ground fire in the demilitarized zone Aug. 13.

North hit by heaviest U.S. raids. U.S. fighter-bombers flew more than 370 strikes against targets in North Vietnam Aug. 16 in what was believed to have been the heaviest day of raids of the year.

The U.S. command reported Aug. 18 that the deepest raid was directed against a radar station 13 miles south of Hanoi. The other targets were trucks, barges, bridges, warehouses, radar equipment, air defenses and barracks. Pilots claimed 42 trucks were destroyed.

B-52s also carried out raids over the North Aug. 17, dropping bombs on supply dumps ranging four to 36 miles from Donghoi.

More than 340 American air strikes were flown against North Vietnam Aug. 17, bringing the total of sorties in three days to about 1,000. The U.S. command acknowledged the loss of a Navy Phantom jet in the Haiphong area. It was the 77th U.S. plane lost since the resumption of heavy bombing in April. A total of 85 airmen were listed as missing.

North Vietnam claimed that many civilians had been killed and wounded in raids Aug. 17 on Thaibinh, 50 miles southeast of Hanoi. The report said the bombings demolished a medical school, a high school and a drug factory in the provincial capital. North Vietnam said its antiaircraft fire had downed five U.S. planes Aug. 17, for a three-day total of 14.

Saigon fatalities increase. The Saigon command reported Aug. 17 that South Vietnamese combat fatalities showed a sharp increase Aug. 6–12. A total of 763 men were killed, an increase of 300 from the previous week. Communist deaths in the same period were claimed to be 3,099.

Four Americans were killed in combat Aug. 6–12, bringing the 11-year total to 45,847. The number of wounded totaled 303,322 and 1,651 were listed as missing, captured or interned.

Communists capture Queson. Communist forces Aug. 19 captured the district town of Queson and a nearby defense base in northern Quangnam Province after a major assault that routed the South Vietnamese defenders.

The enemy force launched a heavy ground and shelling attack Aug. 18 against Queson, 25 miles southwest of Danang, and Base Camp Ross, about two miles to the west. The Communists used 130-mm. artillery in the sector for the first time. Government troops, aided by heavy air support, drove the attackers out of Queson early Aug. 19, but after a lull of a few hours, the enemy resumed the assault and forced the government defenders to pull out. The South Vietnamese, regular troops and militiamen, withdrew to Base Camp Baldy, about two miles southeast of Queson.

Although the Saigon command did not provide details on the engagement, the government withdrawal was believed to have been a rout, with the defenders fleeing and abandoning artillery, tanks and other heavy weapons. Hundreds of civilians also were said to have fled the fighting, heading for the coast.

South Vietnamese forces launched heavy counterattacks Aug. 22–23 in an attempt to recapture Queson, but strong North Vietnamese resistance thwarted their efforts. The Saigon command said that fighting Aug. 22 took place up to three miles from the town and that 108 enemy soldiers were killed. Government losses were put at one killed and 28 wounded.

Another district town near Danang, Duy Xuyen, 15 miles to the south, was attacked by the Communists Aug. 23, but they were thrown back with a loss of 56 men killed, according to a Saigon communique. Seven government soldiers were reported killed.

Other military developments—Heavy fighting continued in and around Quangtri city. In two engagements fought about nine miles south of the city Aug. 17, South Vietnamese airborne troops, supported by artillery and air strikes, killed 68 Communists, the Saigon command said. No government casualties were reported. Another 98 North Vietnamese were reported killed in the area Aug. 18.

Danang, a frequent target of Communist rocket and artillery attacks, was struck Aug. 18 by the heaviest shelling of the year. Twenty-seven South Vietnamese civilians and one American airman were killed by 43 rockets fired at the air base and a nearby residential area. The wounded included 21 Americans, 24 South Vietnamese civilians and one soldier. Two U.S. airplanes were destroyed and 10 damaged. Four South Vietnamese planes were slightly damaged.

Communist attacks Aug. 10 closed three major supply highways to Saigon. Government forces launched a drive the following day to reopen the roads, 25–60 miles from the capital, and reported success Aug. 20. The fighting centered on Route 1 east of Saigon, Route 4 to the southwest, and Route 13 to the north. A fourth highway remained severed about 35 miles north of the city. President Nguyen Van Thieu had predicted that the Communists would attempt to isolate Saigon by cutting highways and creating shortages and political unrest in the capital.

The U.S. command reported Aug. 18 that seven accidental bombing attacks by American planes had killed 25 South Vietnamese soldiers and wounded 85 in the past 45 days.

Navy task force shells Haiphong area. A four-ship U.S. task force led by Vice Adm. J. L. Holloway 3rd, commander of the 7th Fleet, conducted a raid on the Haiphong port area after dark Aug. 27, shelling targets within two miles of the Haiphong city limits, the Navy announced Aug. 29. The raid, by a light cruiser, a heavy cruiser and two destroyers, was only the second such reported action in the Vietnam war.

Several targets were hit, including the Catbi fuel storage area and the Doson army barracks complex southeast of Haiphong, the Navy said. Several coastal gun sites were also reportedly hit and "secondary explosions" were reported in many target areas.

The U.S. ships came under heavy attack from North Vietnamese coastal

batteries, but none of the vessels were hit and there were no casualties, the Navy said. Two North Vietnamese patrol torpedo boats pursuing the ships after the raid were sunk, one by fire from a U.S. destroyer and the other by bombs from an A-7 Corsair jet flying support for the mission, the Navy reported.

According to Adm. Holloway, the attack was "a daring raid into strongly defended territory," reminding North Vietnam of "the mobility of the fleet." There was speculation that the raid might signal an increase in pressure on Haiphong, but a 7th Fleet spokesman cautioned against "reading too much into it . . . Maybe it was felt that the best and least risky way to hit these targets was with the guns of cruisers standing several miles away rather than have planes fly over with bombs and risk heavy anti-aircraft and missile fire."

Battle for Queson continues. North and South Vietnamese troops were reported fighting at close quarters Aug. 28 in the northern district capital of Queson, whose headquarters compound had changed hands three times in nine days. North Vietnamese troops had re-entered the compound Aug. 27, dispersing South Vietnamese troops which had recaptured it Aug. 25.

Communist forces opened fire Aug. 28 from bunkers inside the compound. South Vietnamese attacked but failed to dislodge all North Vietnamese troops after several hours of fighting. At last reports, both sides held parts of the heavily damaged strongpoint.

A U.S. adviser reported that South Vietnamese forces remained in control of the rest of the capital and were still counterattacking in other parts of the strategic Queson Valley. However, North Vietnamese troops still held a high hill dominating the main road into Queson, and a Communist batallion was reported holed up in Base Camp Ross, a former South Vietnamese regimental command post two miles away.

Earlier, the commander of the South Vietnamese army's 2nd Division, Brig. Gen. Phan Hoa Hiep, had been relieved of his command after the heavy losses suffered by the division in Queson district, U.S. officials reported Aug. 25. He was replaced by Col. Tran Van Nhut, who had been chief of Binh Long province north of Saigon.

Another officer, Col. Nguyen Van Lu, commander of the 2nd Division's Fifth Regiment, had been arrested, according to officials. Lu's troops had reportedly fled when Communist forces attacked Base Camp Ross, leading not only to a loss of territory but also to the disintegration of a third of the division.

South Vietnamese forces said Aug. 25 the 2nd Division was temporarily ineffective as a combat force, and as many as 2,500 troops—regulars and militia—were still unaccounted for in the wake of the rout at Queson. They were listed as killed, missing or captured, but some troops were still expected to reach safety. An unknown number of civilians were also casualties in the battle for the district.

In a delayed report Aug. 28, the U.S. and South Vietnamese commands announced that a U.S. adviser and three South Vietnamese airmen had been killed Aug. 26 when an observation plane and an A-37 attack jet collided in the air over Queson.

Government forces suffered a setback in the south when Communist troops cut Route 4, Saigon's link to the rice-producing areas of the Mekong Delta, in heavy fighting 50 miles southwest of the capital, it was reported Aug. 26. An ambush Aug. 22 on a batallion of South Vietnamese rangers 36 miles north of Saigon had left 30 dead, 40 missing and more than 60 wounded.

Heavy fighting in Quangtri—On the northern front, heavy fighting was reported in and around Quangtri city Aug. 28. Government spokesmen said 192 Communist troops had been killed in a dozen engagements, while nine South Vietnamese had been killed and 59 wounded. Heavy fighting in and near the ruined provincial capital had also been reported Aug. 26, with South Vietnamese marines reporting nearly 100 Communist troops killed and at least 10 government soldiers dead.

More troops cross DMZ—U.S. intelligence sources reported Aug. 26 that 20,000 fresh North Vietnamese troops

had crossed the Demilitarized Zone and were replacing battered Communist forces in South Vietnam's three northernmost provinces. The move was seen as confirmation of intelligence estimates that North Vietnam was preparing to renew its military offensive against Hue and possibly Danang.

The sources said they were convinced the six North Vietnamese divisions and several independent regiments in the Quangtri, Hue and Danang areas had been hurt badly by heavy U.S. bombing raids and ground action. The discovery in several instances of mass North Vietnamese graves proved the point, they said.

Combat deaths reported—South Vietnamese combat deaths reported by Saigon in the 20 weeks of the North Vietnamese offensive exceeded 10% of the acknowledged toll for more than a decade in the Indochina war, it was reported Aug. 24. The toll for the offensive, begun in late March, was 15,610 dead and 50,909 wounded. Saigon's total toll for the war was 153,423 killed and 398,161 wounded. U.S. sources estimated the actual death toll in the offensive was at least 3,000 higher than the official figures, adding that thousands of civilians had been killed or wounded.

Heavy toll in Cambodia—The Cambodian command reported Aug. 26 that 117 of its troops had been killed, 107 wounded and 216 were missing and feared dead in eight days of fighting along Route 5, where Communist-led forces had seized a 15-mile stretch of road 60 miles north of Pnompenh, threatening the capital's food supplies. The fighting, which had since diminished, took place Aug. 18–26.

U.S. bombs bases near Hanoi. U.S aircraft raiding North Vietnam Aug. 27 struck at an army barracks and military training grounds near Hanoi, destroying 96 buildings and damaging 78. The targets, the Xombay barracks 37 miles northwest of Hanoi and the Xuanmai training complex 17 miles southwest of the capital, were hit in what was described as the heaviest bombing in the Hanoi-Haiphong area in more than four years.

Air Force Phantoms using 2,000-pound laser bombs destroyed two railroad bridges on the northeast railroad line leading to China, the U.S. Air Force said Aug. 28. In attacks on two other bridges, however, bombs were reportedly off target and the rail approaches rather than the spans were cut. Air Force spokesmen said all the bridges had been attacked before, but the North Vietnamese had rebuilt them.

Hanoi Radio asserted Aug. 28 that five U.S. planes had been shot down and some of the pilots captured. The U.S. command did not mention losses.

U.S. Navy jets had bombed five targets in Haiphong including the Haiphong Shipyard West, a small-boat and barge-repair facility, the Navy said Aug. 27. Pilots also reported attacking the Catbi and Kienan MiG air bases on the southern edge of Haiphong, triggering large explosions in caves used to stockpile supplies. Hanoi Radio said seven U.S. jets had been shot down over North Vietnam Aug. 26–27 and some of the pilots captured. There was no immediate U.S. confirmation.

The U.S. command said an F-4 Phantom had been shot down during heavy raids on the Hanoi-Haiphong area Aug. 25. The command said the two crewmen were missing, but Hanoi reported they had been captured. The U.S. also reported that three fighter bombers had been lost over North Vietnam the previous weekend.

U.S. jets flew more than 310 strikes over North Vietnam Aug. 24, reportedly damaging or destroying 10 ammunition storage buildings, 15 bridges and 31 water supply craft.

Raids near China reported—Pentagon officials reported Aug. 24 that U.S. fighter bombers, in an effort to choke off the flow of war supplies to North Vietnam, had attacked railroad bridges within 25 miles of the Chinese border on several occasions during the past four months. U.S. officials had previously disclosed the existence of a 25-mile buffer zone in which U.S. warplanes were normally forbidden to strike.

Pentagon officials said that in two or three instances, planes strayed very close to Chinese air space before being

warned back by U.S. air controllers in large radar planes. In at least one such case, an official said, the Chinese sent aircraft into the area.

The officials stressed that special permission from Washington was necessary before planes could attack in the buffer zone, and asserted no U.S. plane had ever violated the Chinese border. However, Peking had charged on several earlier occasions that U.S. planes had violated Chinese air space.

Disclosure of the recent raids came amid reports that high Air Force and Defense Department officials were in disagreement about the effectiveness of the U.S. bombing campaign against North Vietnam and the mining aimed at cutting off supplies to the Hanoi regime.

A senior Air Force official who declined to be identified told reporters Aug. 23 that North Vietnam still appeared to be getting between 25%–50% of the supplies it received before the bombing and mining campaign. However, Pentagon spokesman Jerry W. Friedheim said Aug. 24 that even the 25% estimate appeared to be too high.

China charges U.S. attacked lifeboat—China said Aug. 24 it had lodged a strong protest with the U.S. over what it described as an attack by U.S. aircraft against a lifeboat of a Chinese merchant ship, resulting in the death of the ship's captain, a deputy political commissar and three seamen. The alleged attack reportedly took place Aug. 22 off Honngu Island, near the North Vietnamese port of Vinh, where the merchant ship Hung Chi No. 151 was reportedly anchored.

The U.S. command acknowledged Aug. 25 that Navy jets had sunk "one 30-foot supply water craft" in the area Aug. 22, but said "we have no evidence to indicate that we attacked a lifeboat." U.S. spokesmen said pilots and operations officers believed the boat was carrying supplies from a Chinese freighter anchored near Honngu Island in an attempt to circumvent U.S. mining of Vinh harbor.

Chinese minesweeper in harbor—The Pentagon reported Aug. 28 that a small Chinese minesweeper had entered Haiphong harbor the week before, passing through the minefield laid by the U.S. at the harbor's entrance. Officials said the craft had not attempted to sweep any mines and was merely riding at anchor in the inner harbor.

U.S. force reduced by 12,000. A 12,000-man reduction in U.S. forces in Vietnam was announced at the Western White House in San Clemente, Calif. Aug. 29 by White House Press Secretary Ronald L. Ziegler. The authorized troop level would decline from 39,000 on Sept. 1 to 27,000 on Dec. 1. The actual number of troops in South Vietnam was 37,000. This did not include approximately 100,000 uniformed Americans participating in the air-sea war in Indochina from Thailand, Guam and on the vessels of the 7th Fleet off Vietnamese coasts.

The announcement was the 10th in a series of withdrawal announcements since June 1969, when the authorized ceiling was 549,500 troops.

At a news conference later Aug. 29, President Nixon said he would "look at the situation again" before Dec. 1 but said no announcement on further withdrawals would be made before the Nov. 7 presidential election "because we are not going to play election politics with this."

Nixon also said that he would not let political considerations influence his bombing strategy. He would not reduce the bombing without "substantial" progress in the peace negotiations and would not end the bombing of North Vietnam during the election campaign without a peace settlement, he said.

While he said these were the criteria for reducing or ending the bombing, Nixon described as "quite ridiculous" reports "that we probably would be bombing in North Vietnam two or three years from now." He expressed confidence that the South Vietnamese would be able to assume "total defense" of their country in the future "if the enemy still refuses to negotiate."

Nixon said he considered the time ripe for a negotiated settlement, partly because the enemy, while capable of launching "a spurt here and there," was incapable of overrunning South Vietnam. But he said there had been no

"breakthrough" in the recent private consultations conducted by Henry A. Kissinger, his national security adviser, with the North Vietnamese.

U.S. bombs big Hanoi air base. U.S. Air Force jets Sept. 2 pounded the Phucyen air base 10 miles north of Hanoi and shot down a MiG interceptor in a dogfight in the area, the Air Force announced Sept. 3. It was the first U.S. attack in four and a half years on the base, one of North Vietnam's largest.

Pilots reported that their 2,000-pound laser-guided bombs and 500-pound general purpose bombs left craters in the base's runway. The bombs reportedly also wrecked the control tower, operations center, a hangar and more than eight support buildings and set fire to underground fuel storage depots. An Air Force spokesman acknowledged the runway could quickly be put back into operation, but asserted damage to the control tower and other buildings would hamper the base's operations.

A Hanoi broadcast said six U.S. planes were shot down over North Vietnam Sept. 2. They were identified as five Phantom jets, reported downed in Vinhphy province northwest of Hanoi, and one A-7 jet shot down in Hatinh province in the Southern Panhandle.

U.S. air strikes Aug. 30 had destroyed a huge ammunition dump and set fire to a fuel depot in the Vinh area, about 140 miles north of the Demilitarized Zone, the U.S. command reported Aug. 31. In a delayed announcement the same day, the command said two F-4 Phantoms and three fliers had been lost the previous weekend, bringing to 94 the number of airmen lost in North Vietnam since the start of the Communist offensive March 30. A total of 84 U.S. jets had been downed in North Vietnam during the period, the command said.

U.S. Navy fighter bombers Sept. 6 ranged along the North Vietnamese coast from Haiphong about 200 miles south to Hatinh, leaving a trail of fires in fuel depots and barracks, the 7th Fleet reported. Radio Hanoi said five U.S. planes were shot down and their pilots captured.

Two Navy F-8s from the carrier Hancock collided in midair over the

Gulf of Tonkin Sept. 5 while one of them was refueling. The refueling tanker was damaged, but the F-8 pilots parachuted to safety.

Communists take Central Highlands base. South Vietnamese troops lost a base camp in the Central Highlands Sept. 4 in the heaviest Communist attack on that front since the April-May Kontum offensive. The camp, at Leminh near the Cambodian border, had come under strong shelling and ground attack Sept. 3.

A Saigon spokesman said Sept. 4 that most troops had pulled out of the base and were moving toward Pleiku, 12 miles east. He said only a company of rangers was based at Leminh, but military sources said a battalion of 600 rangers and their families were based there.

North Vietnamese soldiers Sept. 5 attacked a government militia post at Baucan, 12 miles southwest of Pleiku, but were reportedly repulsed. The South Vietnamese command said 130 Communist troops were killed with the aid of air strikes, but the figure was questionable because only 26 weapons were reported found. Five South Vietnamese militiamen were reported killed.

North Vietnamese troops were also beaten back Sept. 5 at the Ngotrang fire base five miles northwest of Kontum, according to the Saigon command. Nineteen Communist soldiers were killed while 12 government troops were killed and 107 wounded, the command reported.

About 300 North Vietnamese troops assaulted a South Vietnamese ranger position seven miles southwest of Pleiku Sept. 6, but they were reportedly beaten back with the aid of air strikes and artillery barrages. Fifteen North Vietnamese soldiers were reported killed in the action, with government losses put at two killed and three wounded.

In the south, government and Communist troops suffered heavy casualties Sept. 1–2 in fighting near Laikhe, 37 miles north of Saigon. The battle reportedly erupted when a newly organized South Vietnamese pursuit force met a North Vietnamese regiment pulling back from Highway 13 after being hammered by a U.S. B-52 strike. Government forces reported 130 men dead and 70 wounded, with 180 North Vietnamese troops killed.

Near Anloc, 60 miles north of Saigon, South Vietnamese infantrymen supported by U.S. bombers Sept. 6 reportedly seized the southern sector of the Quanloi airfield, which had fallen to the North Vietnamese in April. However, Communist troops were said to be holding the northern sector of the airfield.

Northern front developments—North Vietnamese troops Sept. 6 reportedly overran Hill 211, a government outpost commanding the district town of Tienphuoc, 10 miles south of the Queson valley. Thousands of refugees reportedly fled east during the attack, which was seen by some South Vietnamese officers as a diversionary move to draw government forces away from the Queson valley.

In Quangtri, more than 100 miles north, South Vietnamese marines were said Sept. 7 to continue a slow and costly drive to root out North Vietnamese troops entrenched in a large bunker complex in the city's southern sector.

Little progress was also reported Sept. 6 in the South Vietnamese attempt to recapture Base Camp Ross, which straddled two hills south of Danang. The base had fallen to North Vietnamese troops Aug. 19.

Cambodian food riots. An acute shortage of rice precipitated riots and looting of food stores in Pnompenh Sept. 7–8. The shortage was attributed partly to the Communists' closure of all but one of the key roads leading into the Cambodian capital. Many city residents, however, charged that the low supply of rice was the result of speculation by merchants, most of whom were Chinese.

Cambodian police and troops in Pnompenh clashed Sept. 7 with civilians trying to storm food shops. Troops later in the day raided more than 100 stores and forced the owners to sell rice at new, lower prices announced earlier by the Commerce Ministry. The ministry had said it was requisitioning all low-grade rice in the city and putting it on sale at less than half the current market place.

Troops joined civilians in the rioting and looting in Pnompenh Sept. 8. Gunfire was heard throughout the city and a Chinese merchant was shot to death. Police did not interfere in any of the incidents.

In a radio appeal for calm, Premier Lon Nol announced Sept. 8 that there was a "large quantity" of rice in the northwestern city of Battambang but that it could not be brought to Pnompenh because the Communists had cut Highway 5, about 60 miles north of the capital.

In a response to a Cambodian appeal, the U.S. announced Sept. 9 that it was preparing to fly supplies of rice from Saigon to Pnompenh. The airlift was expected to start in a week.

ROK troops to withdraw. The South Korean Foreign Ministry disclosed Sept. 7 that the country's remaining 37,000 troops in South Vietnam would be withdrawn starting in December. The pullout was expected to be completed by June 1973.

South Korean Foreign Minister Kim Yong Shik said Seoul had consulted with the U.S. and South Vietnam before announcing the decision.

South Korea had pulled out about 10,-000 troops from South Vietnam between December 1971 and April 1972.

Quangtri fighting intensifies. The battle for Quangtri intensified as South Vietnamese troops again stormed the city's walled Citadel Sept. 11 and engaged in heavy combat with the North Vietnamese defenders.

The Saigon command reported that about 100 marines gained a foothold in the eastern edge of the enclave after breaching a wall through a bomb hole. The Communist forces were said to have responded with firing from artillery posted in the hills of western Quangtri Province. Communist artillery attacks on government forces just outside the Citadel since Sept. 10 resulted in the killing of 24 government troops and the wounding of 87, the Saigon command re-

ported Sept. 13. A total of 280 North Vietnamese were claimed by Saigon to have been killed in and around Quangtri city Sept. 9–10.

Continued heavy Communist shelling and stiff ground resistance Sept. 13 slowed the South Vietnamese advance in the Citadel. North Vietnamese fire also was said to be making it hazardous for government marines on the outside to keep open a 250-yard supply line into the enclave. The Saigon command claimed 64 North Vietnamese were killed in clashes 500 yards south of the fortress, while government losses were five dead and 14 wounded.

A camp housing Quangtri Province refugees on the northwestern edge of Danang was attacked by a Viet Cong demolition squad Sept. 9. Reports from the camp said 20 refugees were killed, 94 were wounded and 200 were left homeless by the barrage of mortar shells, rocket-grenades, rifle fire and explosive charges.

In other action near Danang, more than 1,000 North Vietnamese and Viet Cong soldiers Sept. 7 assaulted the district capital of Tienphuoc, 35 miles south of the city. Street fighting raged around the 33,000 civilians reported trapped in the battle zone. The South Vietnamese brought hundreds of troops into the battle for the town, which was defended by about 1,000 regular troops and militiamen, but not all the reinforcements got in. A Saigon command report Sept. 8 said government defenders had abandoned Tienphuoc, but a report the following day denied this. An American adviser said Sept. 9 that the North Vietnamese had only captured the district headquarters in a corner of the town and that government counterattacks were in progress.

In other developments, South Vietnam's two big airports near Saigon—Tansonnhut and Bienhoa—came under Communist attack Sept. 10. The worst assault occurred at Bienhoa, 15 miles east of the capital, where explosions damaged more than 50 South Vietnamese helicopters and planes. Forty American soldiers were slightly wounded and a U.S. gunship was damaged.

U.S. bombs major Hanoi span. U.S. planes Sept. 11 bombed and destroyed the Longbien railroad and highway bridge over the Red River in downtown Hanoi. The Longbien Bridge had been bombed May 10–11, but had been repaired. It was the principal supply link between Hanoi and southern China, North Vietnam's source of military equipment and petroleum products.

The U.S. command said the attacks that day, involving more than 320 strikes, also damaged three other bridges and hit four military barracks within a 42 mile radius of Hanoi. Two of the installations were two and four miles from the capital, respectively. One U.S. plane was shot down by a surface-to-air missile 14 miles southwest of Hanoi. The pilot was listed as missing.

The southern panhandle of North Vietnam was struck by B-52s Sept. 10 and 11, while three U.S. destroyers shelled a supply transfer point in the panhandle 19 miles northwest of Donghoi.

Among other American air strikes on the North:

Navy planes Sept. 6 bombed a supply storage area in Haiphong and a major petroleum depot on the outskirts of the city. Both facilities were left in flames. Two planes were lost and both pilots were missing. Hanoi said Haiphong was bombed for th: second time Sept. 7, but the U.S. command said it had no knowledge of the attack.

U.S. pilots Sept. 7 knocked out sections of fuel lines northeast of Haiphong during a 260-mission attack.

Two U.S. planes were lost and one pilot was missing in raids Sept. 9. The aircraft crashed 15 and 32 miles north of Vinh. This brought to 88 the number of American planes listed by the U.S. command as downed over the North since the start of the Communist offensive in South Vietnam March 30. The command listed 97 airmen missing in that period, while the Defense Department reported 37 of that number had been captured. The total number of American airmen captured before the offensive was placed at 388.

In the Sept. 9 raids American jets destroyed the Vuchua railroad bridge over the Minh River 46 miles northeast of Hanoi. Another rail span six miles to the north was heavily damaged.

The U.S. command Sept. 11 reported the downing of two North Vietnamese MiGs Sept. 9 in the biggest dogfight since the resumption of heavy bombing of the North in April. The action, involving four U.S. jets and seven MiGs, occurred 15 miles north of Hanoi. One American plane was shot down by antiaircraft fire. The two crewmen parachuted into Laos and were rescued.

North Vietnam claimed the downing of three American planes in new raids over Hanoi Sept. 10.

More than 300 American air strikes were carried out Sept. 11 against roads, rail lines, and army barracks from 120 miles north of Hanoi. Two Navy jets were lost near Haiphong, but all four crewmen were rescued.

Hanoi claimed the downing of six more American planes in provinces around Hanoi and Haiphong during raids Sept. 13. In other action that day, the U.S. Seventh Fleet reported that a Navy task force comprised of a missile destroyer and two destroyers had bombarded supply storage areas north of Donghoi.

U.S. bombing called disappointing. North Vietnam was capable of continuing its military operations in South Vietnam "at the present rate" for the next two years despite the American bombing of the North, according to highlights of two separate U.S. intelligence reports published by the New York Times Sept. 12.

The reports were prepared late in August by the Central Intelligence Agency and the Defense Intelligence Agency for the National Security Council. The analysts said that although the intensified air raids on the North since April had succeeded in hitting designated targets, they had failed to slow down appreciably the flow of Communist men and equipment to the battlefields in South Vietnam. One intelligence official was quoted as saying that the North Vietnamese "have not been hit fatally, but they are slowly bleeding to death—even if it takes two more years."

Principal points of the intelligence reports:

■ About 20,000 additional North Vietnamese troops had infiltrated into the South in the past six weeks, raising Hanoi's force there to 100,000 men.

■ The North Vietnamese had an estimated 20,000–30,000 men in the Mekong Delta, compared with 3,000 in 1971. Most of the buildup had occurred since the start of the Communist offensive March 30.

■ A third pipeline had been completed between Hanoi and Pingsiang on the Chinese frontier. The North Vietnamese had constructed additional fuel lines southward from Hanoi to supply their forces in the South, one of them reaching down to the Ashau Valley. The pipelines were virtually invulnerable to air strikes.

■ The pipelines and the North Vietnamese "ant tactics" used in the movement of supplies had enabled Communist forces to keep fighting.

No American combat fatalities. The U.S. command reported Sept. 22 that there were no American combat fatalities Sept. 10–16. This was the first time since March 1965 that a week had passed without a single U.S. death on the battlefield.

During the Sept. 10–16 period five American deaths were attributed to accidental or natural causes. Seven were listed as wounded and four were missing in action or captured.

Total American war losses since January 1961: 45,857 killed in action; 10,274 deaths resulting from non-combat, accidental and natural causes; 303,387 wounded, 153,161 of whom required hospital care; 1,675 missing, captured or interned; and 118 missing, not as a result of hostile action (largely desertions).

Other casualties in the Sept. 10–16 period: South Vietnamese—409 killed, 1,710 wounded and 75 missing; Communists—4,625 killed and 87 captured.

Saigon troops recapture Quangtri. South Vietnamese forces recaptured the Citadel in Quangtri city Sept. 15 and took virtual control of the entire provincial capital for the first time since its seizure by the North Vietnamese May 1. The Communist soldiers remained in control of the rest of Quangtri Province.

The Saigon command claimed that 8,135 North Vietnamese had been killed

since the South Vietnamese had launched their counteroffensive against Quangtri city June 28. Government losses in the drive were placed at 977 killed and 4,370 wounded. The command said 249 North Vietnamese had been slain in the fighting for the Citadel in the last two days, compared with 10 government marines slain and 43 wounded.

The Citadel was devastated as a result of the savage fighting that had raged in and around it for more than two months. Much of the destruction was attributed to North Vietnamese shelling and U.S. air strikes.

The retreating North Vietnamese defenders fled west to the outskirts of Quangtri city, deploying around the Thachhan River, where they continued to put up fierce resistance. Heavy fighting was reported just outside Quangtri through Sept. 19 with the Communists firing projectiles and long-range artillery on government positions in and around the provincial capital.

President Nguyen Van Thieu had set Sept. 19 as the deadline for the recapture of Quangtri and other territory captured by the Communists' offensive. Lauding government troops for their victory in Quangtri city, Thieu said in a broadcast Sept. 16: "I bow before the fighters who have sacrificed their lives for the national cause and I will come to see you."

Communists open Quangngai drive— The North Vietnamese opened a new offensive Sept. 16 in Quangngai Province, 150 miles south of Quangtri city, and were reported making steady progress.

The attackers were concentrating on five of the province's 10 district capitals, capturing one of them, Bato, Sept. 18. Bato was between Moduc and Ducpho, two other district towns that had come under Communist siege. Forty government soldiers were reported Sept. 19 to have been killed in the fighting at Moduc. South Vietnamese reinforcements were moved into Moduc to relieve a militia force there. Other district towns under attack were Binhson and Tunghia, the latter less than five miles south of the provincial capital of Quangngai itself.

U.S. planes hit North. U.S. planes continued heavy bombing of North Vietnam Sept. 13–17. The immediate Hanoi area, however, was placed off limits to the American pilots Sept. 16 for the arrival that day of an American delegation that was to escort home three U.S. prisoners being released by the North Vietnamese. The Hanoi area raid suspension continued through Sept. 19.

One U.S. aircraft was lost during more than 310 air strikes reported throughout North Vietnam Sept. 13. The jet was said to have been downed by antiaircraft artillery 80 miles north of the demilitarized zone, but the pilot bailed out and was rescued. Pilots reported destroying or damaging half a dozen barracks and support buildings of the Haulan complex 40 miles north of Hanoi.

In raids Sept. 14, pilots flying 290 strikes claimed they had damaged or destroyed 11 bridges and 44 warehouses among other targets. In a delayed report, the U.S. command said a Phantom jet had downed a North Vietnamese MiG-21 three miles north of Hanoi Sept. 11 and was later shot down by ground fire. The two American airmen bailed out over the South China Sea and were rescued.

More than 340 strike missions were flown over the North Sept. 15. A fuel depot near the main China-Hanoi pipeline was among the principal targets of raids Sept. 16. Pilots said they destroyed seven 5,000-gallon fuel tanks and damaged 10 tanks 34 miles northeast of Hanoi.

U.S. fighter-bombers carried out more than 330 strikes across North Vietnam Sept. 17. The targets included a bridge on the Hanoi-China rail line.

F-111s re-enter combat. The U.S. controversial F-111 fighter-bombers re-entered combat over North Vietnam for the first time in four-and-a-half years Sept. 28. Following the loss of one of the planes that day, the Defense Department confirmed Oct. 4 that they had been withdrawn from combat missions for a few days for review but were later returned to service.

The department said it was not certain whether the F-111 lost Sept. 28 during separate missions northeast of Hanoi had been shot down or crashed as a result of pilot error or mechanical trouble. North Vietnam reported Sept. 30 that its antiaircraft gunners had shot down the F-111 near Yenbai airfield, 80 miles northwest of Hanoi.

The F-111s had first entered the war March 1968 but were withdrawn several months later after three of the jet planes crashed. The swing-wing jets, capable of carrying twice the bomb load of any other fighter-bomber, were brought back to the U.S. to undergo tests to correct mechanical problems.

The Air Force had announced Sept. 26 that a squadron of 48 F-111s was being sent to Southeast Asia and would be stationed in Thailand.

U.S. jets bomb air bases in North—In one of the heaviest attacks of its kind in the war, U.S. fighter-bombers Sept. 29 struck at four air bases in North Vietnam, reportedly destroying five MiG interceptors and damaging nine, all on the ground. This represented about 10% of North Vietnam's air force.

The airfields were at Phucyen, 10 miles northwest of Hanoi; Yenbai, 80 miles northwest of the capital; Vinh airfield, five miles north of that city; and Quanglang, 45 miles northwest of Vinh.

In other raids flown Sept. 29, Navy jets attacked the port of Hongai, 23 miles northeast of Haiphong, and the pilots reported setting off two secondary explosions. B-52s also flew a number of missions, dropping bombs in the vicinity of Donghoi, near the South Vietnamese border.

Among other U.S. air strikes on the North:

Communist antiaircraft shot down an American plane during raids Sept. 19. It was the 100th U.S. aircraft to be lost since the resumption of the heavy bombing of the North in April. The pilot was rescued after bailing out over the Gulf of Tonkin.

U.S. planes flying more than 280 strikes across the North Sept. 21 ranged between Hanoi and the Chinese border. Three targets were hit for the first time— the Amthuong military area, 67 miles northwest of Hanoi, the Thandan military storage area 34 miles north of the capital, and the Phutho storage area 51

miles northwest of the city. Two more
U.S. jets were downed in the day's raids.

The 150-mile rail line between Hanoi
and China was attacked by Phantom jets
Sept. 23. In addition, U.S. planes destroyed a railroad span 64 miles northwest
of Hanoi and cut the line 10 miles
farther south.

Hanoi claimed American planes
dropped hundreds of bombs on Haiphong
Sept. 23.

The North Vietnamese Foreign Ministry reported Sept. 25 that American
planes had destroyed the Namdan Dam
near Vinh the previous day. The ministry
said the attack was one of several against
populated centers of the North.

The Air Force reported two MiG-21s
were destroyed and another damaged
on the ground in a raid Sept. 27 on
Yenbai airfield. Other targets struck
that day included two army barracks
installations at Honmot, 31 miles northeast of Haiphong, and at Bengoc, 32
miles southwest of Hanoi.

U.S. planes carrying out 320 strike
missions Sept. 30 struck at Phuqui military base northwest of Vinh and reported
destroying 40 buildings and setting off
15 secondary explosions and 10 fires.
Other aircraft hit the Kep air base and
rail yards within 36 miles of Hanoi.

1972 bomb tonnage up—According to
information obtained from the U.S. Defense Department and made public Oct.
3, U.S. planes had dropped more bombs
over Southeast Asia in the first nine
months of 1972 than in all of 1971. The
figures, supplied to the Senate subcommittee on refugees and made available
to the New York Times, showed that
more than 800,000 tons of "air ammunition" had been used over North and
South Vietnam, Cambodia and Laos
from Jan. 1 to Sept. 30. This compared
with 763,160 tons of bombs dropped over
those countries in 1971.

During the period between February
1965 and August 1972, U.S. planes had
dropped 7,550,800 tons of bombs and
other ordnance missiles on Indochina,
according to department figures. This
was about three-and-a-half times the
tonnage of explosives used during World
War II in all the war theaters.

U.S. Navy attacks North—A U.S.
naval task force of five cruisers and

destroyers exchanged heavy fire with
North Vietnamese coastal defenses in
night raids Sept. 26. The task force
shelled fuel and supply depots, bridges
and an army barracks along a 75-mile
stretch from Thanhhoa to Vinh.

Nineteen sailors were killed Oct. 1
in the explosion of a gun turret aboard
the cruiser Newport News. A 20th sailor
died later. The blast occurred as the
warship was shelling North Vietnamese
positions in Quangtri Province, South
Vietnam.

The Navy termed the explosion accidental.

Bombing reports not always forwarded.
A senior military officer told a
Senate panel in secret testimony Sept.
28 that government leaders in Washington did not always receive reports on
civilian damage and casualties caused
by U.S. bombing raids against North
Vietnam.

Maj. Gen. John W. Pauly, deputy
director of operations for the Joint
Chiefs of Staff, made the disclosure to
the Senate subcommittee on refugees.
The panel was seeking to determine the
extent of damage to civilian life and
property from the bombing.

A declassified version of Pauly's testimony was released Oct. 8 by Sen.
Edward M. Kennedy (D, Mass.), chairman of the subcommittee.

According to Pauly, U.S. air commanders in Vietnam conducted field
"critiques" of the bombing but the reports were not "necessarily" sent on to
Washington. Conceding that there undoubtedly had been some "collateral
damage"—the Pentagon term for hits on
civilian targets—Pauly emphasized that
"our policy has been established that
only military targets will be struck, and
that civilian casualties be minimized."

Pauly said "lucrative targets are often
rejected if, as a result of examination, we
found that the collateral damage would
be substantial."

Cambodian military developments.
Fighting between Cambodian and Communist troops increased Sept. 9–Oct. 2,
with government forces falling back in
most sectors and taking heavy losses.

Among the major developments:

North Vietnamese troops captured the district capital of Kompong Trabek Sept. 9. All three government battalions in the town, 47 miles southeast of Pnompenh, moved out and headed in the direction of the capital, leaving Kompong Trabek in Communist hands. A fourth Cambodian battalion that had been defending a nearby position was reported to have "disappeared."

Government troops Sept. 14 retreated from their positions around Pnom Bat following heavy Communist ground and artillery attacks. Pnom Bat was a long-time Communist strong-hold south of the former capital of Oudong, 15 miles northwest of Pnompenh.

A command spokesman said Cambodian planes attacked 300 North Vietnamese sampans in the Mekong River Valley, 26 miles south of Pnompenh, Sept. 18, causing "important losses."

Cambodian troops Sept. 23 fought their way into the market place of Chambak, 25 miles south of Pnompenh and surrounded three other villages below it along Route 2. The command reported Sept. 24 that 16 government soldiers had been killed in three days of fighting around Chambak.

The Cambodian government disclosed Sept. 29 that its forces had abandoned efforts to dislodge North Vietnamese troops from the ancient temples at Angkor, occupied by the Communists since June 1970. The government operations had begun Jan. 29 and were abandoned Sept. 19, the spokesman said.

U.S. B-52s attacked Communist base camps in eastern Cambodia Sept. 27-28. The strikes were aimed at blocking attacks expected in South Vietnam's 3rd Military Region, which included Saigon and 11 provinces around the capital.

Cambodia reported its troops Sept. 30 lifted the siege of Samrong Yong, 20 miles south of Pnompenh. The village had been surrounded by Communist forces for eight days.

A Cambodian commercial plane was struck by two Communist mortar rounds as it landed Oct. 2 at an airport at Kompot. Nine civilians were killed.

*U.S. aide escapes assassination—*U.S. Charge d'Affaires Thomas Enders es-caped death Sept. 27 when a terrorist bomb wrecked the car he was driving to his office in Pnompenh. Enders' car caught fire when an explosive placed in a parked automobile he was passing detonated. The American aide jumped from his vehicle unscathed. But a motorcycle guard riding behind him and a civilian passerby were killed.

Ground fighting ebbs. U.S. military authorities reported Sept. 26 that ground fighting in South Vietnam had decreased to its lowest level since the start of the North Vietnamese offensive March 30. A sudden upsurge of North Vietnamese and Viet Cong attacks, however, were reported by the South Vietnamese command Oct. 2.

Saigon reported that the Communists had carried out about 100 rocket and mortar attacks and sabotage throughout the country, the highest number since July 25, when 103 were reported. Meanwhile, U.S. B-52 bombers struck at Communist positions and staging areas 17-30 miles from Saigon.

Among the military developments in the South prior to the reported lull:

Heavy fighting occurred in Quangngai Province, where the North Vietnamese had launched a new drive Sept. 16. Communist infantry and demolition squads Sept. 20 stormed into a government ranger compound on the northern edge of the district town of Bato. Bato itself had been captured by the attackers Sept. 18. Two other district towns—Moduc and Ducpho—remained under North Vietnamese threat. Moduc was said to be surrounded by about 1,000 Communist troops, while another 200 were said to have infiltrated into the town since Sept. 17.

Communist forces pressed their assaults Sept. 22 close to Quangngai city, the provincial capital, forcing government defenders to abandon two small outposts to the east and west. Four other government positions were said to have fallen near Ducpho, 25 miles south. Sharp fighting raged near Bato, where allied planes made unsuccessful attempts to drop supplies to beleaguered defenders.

Communist troops Sept. 24 poured more than 1,000 shells into government positions near Ducpho and Bato.

South Vietnamese units began a drive Sept. 25 to clear Communist forces from Route 1, the coastal highway running through Quangngai Province. About six miles of the road were said to be cut between the Songve bridge and Moduc, 15 miles south of Quangngai city. Government forces were reported to have made some progress by Sept. 29, pushing the North Vietnamese out of a hamlet and attacking the last enemy force known to be blocking Route 1.

The Saigon government charged Sept. 28 that North Vietnamese troops had killed "hundreds of inhabitants" of the Quangngai villages of Nangan and Ducquang Sept. 22. Saigon claimed that in one of the incidents the Communists herded a group of civilians into a house and blew it up, killing 48 persons.

In fighting elsewhere, the South Vietnamese were said to have reoccupied the Central Highlands ranger camp at Leminh Sept. 20. A ranger battalion airlifted to the base 20 miles west of Pleiku was said to have encountered little enemy resistance. The North Vietnamese had overrun Leminh Sept. 4.

Thousands of government troops launched a sweep of Quangtri and Thuathien Provinces Sept. 19 to prevent the North Vietnamese from reoccupying territory recaptured by the South Vietnamese soldiers in their three-month old counteroffensive in that area. In first reporting the operations Sept. 24, a Saigon command spokesman said 20,-000 troops and 200 armored vehicles were involved. Thus far little enemy resistance was encountered.

U.S. bases in Thailand attacked. Guerrillas attacked two U.S. air bases in Thailand Oct. 1 and 2. It was the third time that American installations had come under assault in the country in 1972.

In the first incident Oct. 1, guerrillas fired 36 mortar shells at the U.S. base at Ubon, 300 miles northeast of Bangkok. Little damage was reported.

The target of the second attack Oct. 2 was at the air base at Udon. Seven demolition men were said to have broken into the base complex and killed a Thai sentry. Three of the guerrillas were killed.

Ubon and Udon were among the eight bases in Thailand used by U.S. planes to bomb North Vietnam.

Saigon area fighting. Fighting in South Vietnam Oct. 6–11 centered largely around Saigon, the closest to the South Vietnamese capital since the start of the Communist offensive March 30. An estimated 2,000 North Vietnamese were involved in the widespread attacks, which were described by the Saigon command as being on a relatively small scale. Some of the clashes occurred only eight miles from the capital. U.S. B-52 planes dropped thousands of tons of bombs in the battle zone in a move aimed at preventing attempted Communist infiltration toward the capital.

The fighting erupted Oct. 6 along Route 13, 20 miles north of Saigon and in lower Binhduong Province between Bencat and Phucuong, with the attackers seizing a number of hamlets.

Government troops Oct. 7 ousted the infiltrators from three hamlets, but the enemy held three others 20 miles north of Saigon.

The Saigon command reported 22 Communists and three government militiamen killed in scattered clashes Oct. 8. Communist infiltrators were ousted from another hamlet, 10 miles north of the capital. Another hamlet, Tanan, was recaptured by government troops Oct. 11.

An American intelligence official disclosed Oct. 11 that a captured Communist directive issued in mid-September gave orders for the attacks around Saigon. The directive, issued by the Communists' Central Office for South Vietnam, said the assaults were to be the final and "most decisive" phase of the major Communist offensive.

In fighting elsewhere in South Vietnam:

North Vietnamese troops killed or wounded 30 government soldiers in an attack on Mytho, the second largest city in the Mekong Delta, Oct. 6.

In northern Quangtin Province, government troops Oct. 7 recaptured the district capital of Tienphuoc, 15 miles south of Danang. The city had been lost to the Communists Sept. 7.

Government troops engaged in heavy fighting with enemy soldiers near Kontum city in the Central Highlands Oct. 6–7. One government position in the area was abandoned under heavy pressure. The government defenders were reported to have killed 343 enemy soldiers, while suffering 35 dead and 66 wounded.

South Vietnamese marines Oct. 8 recaptured the district capital of Trieuphong in Quangtri Province. It had been abandoned by government troops April 30.

Communists attack Pnompenh. A force of about 200 Vietnamese Communists Oct. 7 carried out one of their heaviest raids inside Pnompenh since the start of the war in Cambodia. The government reported that 36 Cambodian soldiers and civilians and 28 of the attackers were killed in six hours of fighting. Four infiltrators were captured. The fighting drove many Cambodians from their homes.

The raiders, attacking with mortars and rockets, blew up a bridge over the Tonle Sap River, less than two miles from the center of the city. Four or five infiltrators entered the French embassy compound with armored personnel carriers they had seized from the Cambodian̄s and machinegunned the buildings.

A number of Cambodian officers were reported arrested in connection with an attack on an army depot during the Communist raid on Pnompenh. The army launched an inquiry into the assault on the capital.

In other action, Communist troops Oct. 9 overran four Cambodian outposts south of Pnompenh on Route 2 near the South Vietnamese border.

Laotian village bombed. Laotian military sources reported that two North Vietnamese planes Oct. 9 bombed the village of Bouamlong, killing six persons. Communist planes were rarely seen operating outside of North Vietnam. It was believed the North Vietnamese aircraft were supporting Pathet Lao operations in the village area more than 125 miles northeast of the capital of Vientiane.

In previous military developments, an upsurge of fighting was reported in September. Government forces were reported Sept. 11 to have driven North Vietnamese soldiers from Khong

Sedone, at the foot of the Boloven Plateau.

U.S.-supported Laotian Meo tribesmen were forced by North Vietnamese fire to withdraw Sept. 5 from positions around the Plaine des Jarres in northern Laos. The tribesmen, fighting an offensive operation in the area for three weeks, suffered heavy losses and were evacuated by U.S. helicopters.

The North Vietnamese launched their own offensive on the western edge of the Plaine des Jarres Sept. 25. Heavy artillery fire was said to have forced the Meo tribal forces to withdraw southward toward Long Tieng, 87 miles north of Vientiane.

French mission bombed in Hanoi. A U.S. air raid on the Hanoi area Oct. 11 heavily damaged buildings of the French diplomatic mission in the North Vietnamese capital. Hanoi radio reported that a member of the French delegation and four North Vietnamese employes were killed. The report said that Pierre Susini, French delegate general, and Albanian Charge d'Affaires Qemal Rahmanaji, who was visiting the mission, were injured. Susini's wounds were described as serious, but he was expected to recover. The U.S. air strike was reported to have caused lesser damage to the Algerian and Indian missions nearby.

The French government delivered a protest to U.S. Ambassador Arthur K. Watson in Paris. President Georges Pompidou called the incident a "deplorable act." American expressions of regret were contained in messages sent by President Nixon to Pompidou and by Secretary of State William P. Rogers to French Foreign Minister Maurice Schumann.

The Algerian and Indian governments protested to the U.S. Oct. 11 and 12.

The U.S. Navy, whose planes were involved in the attack, said the intended target was the Gialam railroad yard and repair shop, three miles northeast of the French mission. Initial reports said the Gialam facilities had been struck and engulfed in flames.

The Defense Department said the damage to the French center might have been caused by a North Vietnamese antiaircraft missile and not by American bombs. Six missiles were fired at the 20 U.S. raiding planes.

A witness to the bombing incident, Canadian correspondent Michael Maclear, said in a dispatch from Hanoi Oct. 11 that he had seen "at least three jets swoop down repeatedly over the heart of the capital." Maclear said he had "witnessed and filmed bodies taken from the rubble of the French residence, which was shorn in half."

U.S. Defense Secretary Melvin R. Laird was asked at a news conference Oct. 11 whether it was wise to attack targets close to Hanoi while presidential adviser Henry A. Kissinger was concluding four days of peace talks with North Vietnamese representatives in Paris. [See p. 175] He replied: "The situation has been that we will continue the use of our air power during this period. The President has stated that on several occasions, as recently as his last press conference [Oct. 5], we will continue to strike military targets in North Vietnam."

The Chicago Daily news reported Oct. 12 that the previous day's raid followed an order from the Joint Chiefs of Staff two weeks before permitting attacks on former off-limit targets. (The attack on Gialam was believed to have been the first since the resumption of full-scale bombing of the North April 6.) The newspaper said the order was amended as a result of the raid on the French mission.

An Associated Press dispatch from Saigon Oct. 12 said U.S. planes had attacked North Vietnam that day, but were staying clear of a newly-established buffer zone around Hanoi that could not be bombed unless cleared first by the Nixon Administration.

Defense Department officials refused to comment on either report, but they recalled that a buffer zone had existed around Hanoi throughout the war and that a similar bomb-free area had been designated along the China border.

Other U.S. air strikes on North—The U.S.' newly-introduced F-111 fighter-bombers carried out attacks Oct. 5 on a North Vietnamese air defense center one mile south of Dienbienphu and on a railroad siding on the northwest line from Hanoi to China.

The F-111s, which had been withdrawn from combat after the downing of one of the planes Sept. 28, were put back into operation following tests conducted Sept. 29–Oct. 3, the U.S. command reported. (The transfer of two squadrons of 48 F-111s from the U.S. to Thailand was completed Oct. 5.)

In other raids on the North, U.S. aircraft flew more than 300 missions on each day through Oct. 9. Among the developments: A North Vietnamese MiG-21 was shot down during U.S. air strikes Oct. 4–5. It was the 60th MiG downed since Jan. 1.

The U.S. command Oct. 9 reported that American jets had destroyed 10 missile sites within five miles of Hanoi during strikes Oct. 5–6.

The U.S. command reported Oct. 9 that two airmen were missing when their Phantom jet was shot down by North Vietnamese surface-to-air-missile fire Oct. 6. This brought to 108 the number of American planes lost over the North since April. Another MiG-21 was shot down by a Phantom Oct. 8, the command reported.

South Vietnam ground action. Heavy fighting raged in South Vietnam Oct. 12–17 in the northern provinces, the Central Highlands and around Saigon.

South Vietnamese troops Oct. 12 recaptured the Quangngai Province district capital of Bato, first seized by the North Vietnamese Sept. 18.

North Vietnamese troops Oct. 13 captured a South Vietnamese ranger camp at Benhet, in the Central Highlands province of Kontum after two days of heavy artillery barrages. Benhet had been defended by more than 500 troops, but only 27 were known to have reached friendly lines. Also unaccounted for were 180 relatives of the Benhet garrison troops.

Communist troops intensified their attacks in the Central Highlands and captured six villages in the Pleiku area Oct. 17. A Saigon command spokesman described the capture of the villages as a "plant-the-flag" campaign with the objective of amassing as much territory as possible that could be used as a bargaining point in anticipation of a cease-fire. The command said the drive was spurred by a Communist command directive, code-named "Resolution X-10." The directive, captured by government troops, ordered Viet Cong political activists to raise their flags in as many South Vietnamese villages as possible, the command said.

More than 100 Communist troops Oct. 17 attacked a refugee village five miles from Quangngai city, killing 11 refugees and six militiamen. Nine of the attackers were slain before the infiltrators withdrew.

In the fighting around Saigon, continued Communist attacks in the area Oct. 16 were said to have disrupted traffic on several of the major roads leading from the city. Route 1, which had been cut 30 miles from Saigon Oct. 13, was reopened to civilian traffic Oct. 16, but clashes continued within sight of the road. Government troops reopened a 12-mile section of Route 12 between Phucuong and Bencat, 13 miles north of the capital. But only military convoys were able to travel the road, which had first been severed Oct. 9. Route 15, linking Saigon with the coastal recreation area of Vungtau, was closed to Americans, with the exception of armed radio-equipped convoys.

Casualties & troop withdrawals—The U.S. command reported Oct. 12 that 21 Americans had been killed in action Oct. 1–7, the highest weekly loss in a year. Twenty of the deaths had occurred aboard the cruiser Newport News Oct. 1 when a shell exploded accidentally. The command said it was decided to list the accidental fatalities as battle casualties because the warship was shelling North Vietnamese positions at the time. Total war fatalities were placed at 45,882 Americans, 170,361 South Vietnamese and 894,214 Viet Cong and North Vietnamese.

The U.S. command announced Oct. 16 that the withdrawal of 600 men from South Vietnam the previous week reduced the American troop strength in the country to 34,600.

U.S. loses 2nd F-111 over North. A second U.S. F-111 fighter plane was downed over North Vietnam Oct. 17. The U.S. command reported Oct. 19 that the swing-wing jet was lost during an F-111 bombing raid of rail lines leading from Hanoi to China, military barracks, fuel depots and assembly plants for surface-to-air missiles. The two crewmen were listed as missing. Hanoi claimed the F-111 was shot down and its two crewmen were killed.

The downing of the F-111 and the reported crash of an F-4 Phantom Oct. 18 brought to 114 the number of American planes lost since resumption of intensified bombing of the North in April. The Phantom crashed north of its base at Ubon, Thailand as it was returning from North Vietnam. The two pilots were rescued.

The U.S. command said the F-111s had been averaging 20–30 strikes a day on the North since their return to combat Oct. 5.

In other air war developments, U.S. planes Oct. 14 carried out the second heaviest bombing attack of the year on the North. (The heaviest raid had occurred Aug. 16., At the same time, B-52s dropped bombs on suspected Communist positions in all four countries of Indochina—Laos, Cambodia and North and South Vietnam. The fighter-bomber strike on the North, involving nearly 400 planes, ranged from the demilitarized zone to the corridor between Hanoi and the Chinese border. Commenting on the intensity of the strikes, a U.S. command spokesman said "We are maintaining our high level of air activity to destroy military targets supporting the invasion of South Vietnam."

In another action, a Communist MiG-21 was shot down in a dogfight with U.S. Phantom jets west of Hanoi Oct. 13.

U.S. concedes French mission raid—A U.S. official in Washington Oct. 15 said there was a "consensus" in the Nixon Administration that the French diplomatic mission in Hanoi had been destroyed by an accidental U.S. bombing attack Oct. 11, and not by a North Vietnamese antiaircraft missile, as had been suggested by Defense Secretary Melvin R. Laird and other Defense Department officials.

In a television interview Oct. 15, Secretary of State William P. Rogers said "It is regrettable that it happened, . . . but faulty bomb drops do occur." The U.S. would try to avoid similar accidents in the future, but "there is going to be no change in the policy" of the bombing of "military targets" in North Vietnam, Rogers said.

U.S. admits French mission raid. The U.S. formally admitted Oct. 20 that American planes had "inadvertently struck" the French diplomatic mission in Hanoi Oct. 11.

A statement released by the Defense Department in Washington said "one possible cause of the accident is the failure of the ordnance [bombs] to release properly." Asserting that "this was an accident, and not a planned strike," the department insisted that the U.S. aircraft at the time "were attacking authorized military targets, including a railroad yard and transshipment point across the Red River approximately three miles" from the French mission in Hanoi.

The French diplomatic mission chief injured in the attack, Pierre Susini, died in a Paris hospital Oct. 19.

North Vietnam charged Oct. 22 that the U.S. air strike on the French diplomatic mission was a "deliberate attack [that] was in no way due to an error or to a mechanical malfunctioning." The statement, based on a government investigation of the incident, said the raid was planned to "intimidate the population of the sector, which had absolutely no military targets and comprised buildings occupying isolated positions that were immediately discernible on a map."

Ground action increases in South. As a cease-fire apparently approached, heavy fighting continued in South Vietnam Oct. 19–25. U.S. B-52s struck at enemy posi-tions during that period, concentrating most of their raids around Saigon.

North Vietnamese troops Oct. 19 reoccupied two hamlets near Saigon, abandoned two days before. One of the villages was Binhhoa, eight miles north of the capital.

In fighting in the Saigon area Oct. 20, government troops reported driving Communist forces from Bungcau after several hours of fighting. At least seven enemy and two South Vietnamese soldiers were reported killed.

The allied airbase at Bienhoa, 15 miles northeast of Saigon, was struck by Communist rockets Oct. 22. The pre-dawn attack wounded 18 Americans and 10 South Vietnamese. One South Vietnamese helicopter was damaged.

Fighting increased sharply throughout South Vietnam Oct. 23 with Communist forces centering their attacks in the Central Highlands around Pleiku. The Saigon command claimed 25 Communists were killed in four battles in the vicinity of the city near Fire Bases 40 and 41 and at base camps at Mythach and Ducco. Government losses were listed as one killed and 25 wounded. The command also claimed the killing of 73 enemy soldiers in Binhdinh Province, three miles east of the district capital of Phumy.

In attacks Oct. 25, Communist forces briefly cut two main highways leading to Saigon. In the most serious shelling incident of the day, a Communist rocket barrage hit the district capital of Tritam, 36 miles northwest of the capital, killing 11 persons, 10 of them civilians, and wounding 37. Four other civilians were killed in the rocket shelling of Hoian, 15 miles southeast of Danang.

Peace Approaches
& Recedes

Kissinger holds more Paris talks. Presidential adviser Henry A. Kissinger held another round of private talks Sept. 26-27 with North Vietnamese representatives in Paris. Kissinger returned to Washington later Sept. 27 amid rumors that the latest meetings had accomplished a breakthrough in the Indochina peace negotiations. This was quickly denied by the Nixon Administration and the Communists Sept. 28. Kissinger gave President Nixon a preliminary report on his talks Sept. 28.

The reported peace agreement had been spurred by the fact that Kissinger's meeting with North Vietnam's Le Duc Tho and Xuan Thuy Sept. 26 had been extended for a second day. This was the first time in their 19 meetings that a session had lasted more than one day.

The most detailed report of an alleged settlement came from White House radio correspondent Clifford Evans, who said the deadlock in the Paris peace talks "is expected to be resolved by the resignation of [South Vietnamese President Nguyen Van] Thieu, who will be replaced by a three-party coalition government" in Saigon.

The North Vietnamese delegation to the Paris peace talks Sept. 28 denied a peace settlement was imminent. A Communist party journal in Hanoi charged the same day that a U.S. "propaganda machine is trying to give the impression" that the U.S. and North Vietnam were "getting closer" in the Paris talks. The publication, Hoc Tap, said the U.S. and North Vietnam were still far apart on the key issue, which is described as "the future administration in South Vietnam." Further sessions of the Paris talks were held Sept. 21 and 28.

Kissinger aide meets with Thieu. Maj. Gen. Alexander M. Haig Jr., deputy to U.S. presidential adviser Henry A. Kissinger, conferred with South Vietnamese President Nguyen Van Thieu in Saigon Oct. 1-4. The White House had said Sept. 29 that Haig would confer with Thieu on Kissinger's latest peace negotiations with North Vietnamese representatives in Paris and would make a "general assessment" of the political and military aspects of the war.

Thieu Sept. 29 had reiterated his opposition to the Communist proposal for replacement of his government with a tripartite regime in Saigon. In a speech at Saigon University, Thieu said: "If the United States accepts to withdraw its troops unconditionally, the Communists will win militarily. If we accept a coalition, we will lose politically."

Secret Paris talks last four days. U.S. presidential adviser Henry A. Kissinger held an unprecedented four days of peace discussions with North Vietnamese representatives in Paris Oct.

175

8–11. He returned to Washington Oct. 12 and briefed President Nixon on his latest private negotiations with Le Duc Tho, North Vietnam's Politburo official, and Xuan Thuy, Hanoi's chief delegate to the regular Paris peace talks. Tho left for Hanoi Oct. 12.

The unusual length of the Kissinger-North Vietnamese meetings, the longest of their 19 sessions, heightened speculation that both sides were near agreement. Neither side would disclose at their conclusion what progress if any had been made.

A new element in the composition of the conferees was the presence of Maj. Gen. Alexander M. Haig Jr., Kissinger's deputy. The White House had given no reason for the attendance of Haig, who had conferred in Saigon with South Vietnamese President Nguyen Van Thieu Oct. 1–4.

Defense Secretary Melvin R. Laird had told a news conference in Washington Oct. 11 that the private U.S.-North Vietnamese talks "are in a very serious, sensitive and significant stage." French Information Minister Jean-Philippe Lecat had said in Paris that day that the talks "have been making rapid progress."

Prior to the new round of talks, published reports Oct. 6 by the Times of London and United Press International (UPI) said a "broad agreement" had been reached in the secret negotiations. This was quickly denied by the U.S. and North Vietnam. The Times dispatch said North Vietnam had agreed to accept a multi-party coalition government. The newspaper said the details of the accord reached with Kissinger would not be completed or at least announced until after the U.S. presidential elections Nov. 7.

The UPI report from Saigon said Gen. Haig had gone to the South Vietnamese capital to apprise President Thieu of a peace plan that would call for his resignation, U.S. withdrawal from South Vietnam, an end to U.S. military activity against North Vietnam and the release of American prisoners.

Hanoi radio asserted Oct. 6 that President Nixon's statement at his news conference Oct. 5 that the private Paris meetings were in a "sensitive stage" was an attempt "to dupe the American voters."

(The regular sessions of the Paris peace talks were held Oct. 5 and 12, but no progress was reported.)

Thieu again opposes coalition—In one of his strongest statements opposing a coalition government with the Communists, President Thieu declared Oct. 12 that the establishment of this kind of a regime "meant death" for his country.

Stressing the need for a military solution, Thieu said, "We have to kill the Communists to the last man before we have peace."

Thieu cited the case of Laos in rejecting the North Vietnam-Viet Cong proposal for a coalition government composed of representatives of Thieu's regime, of the Viet Cong and of third-force elements acceptable to both sides. "A three-part government in Laos led to the loss of the country," Thieu said.

Kissinger meets with Thieu. Presidential adviser Henry A. Kissinger and other U.S. officials held intensive discussions with South Vietnamese President Nguyen Van Thieu in Saigon Oct. 19–20. Kissinger's latest round of peace negotiations heightened reports that the U.S. and North Vietnam were making considerable progress toward an agreement on a cease-fire in Indochina and a political accord that would replace the current government in Saigon.

Kissinger had arrived in Saigon Oct. 18 from Paris, where he had conferred briefly Oct. 17 with Xuan Thuy, North Vietnam's chief delegate to the Paris peace talks. The White House announcement that President Nixon's foreign affairs adviser was ready to take off for the South Vietnamese capital said he was to continue "the regular consultative process" with Thieu. He had last met with Thieu Aug. 17–18.

Kissinger conferred with Thieu twice Oct. 19 and held another session Oct. 20. Among the U.S. officials joining the talks were Gen. Creighton W. Abrams, Army chief of staff, Ambassador Ellsworth Bunker, Deputy Assistant Secretary of State Walter H. Sullivan and two of Kissinger's aides—Winston Lord and James Engle. The State Department said Oct. 19 that Philip Habib, U.S. ambassador to South Korea, had been summoned to Saigon to join Kissinger in the talks.

(Gen. Abrams had arrived in Saigon Oct. 18 after being sworn in as Army chief of staff in Washington Oct. 16. Defense Secretary Melvin R. Laird had said Oct. 16 that he had sent the general to Saigon "to make an on-the-scene evaluation of Vietnamization progress.")

The other South Vietnamese leaders taking part in the discussions were Vice President Tran Van Huong, Premier Tran Thien Khiem and Foreign Minister Tran Van Lam.

The Communists' proposal for a tripartite government was said to be a major topic of the talks. President Thieu's opposition to this plan was reaffirmed Oct. 19 by the government newspaper Tin Song. Referring to the U.S.-South Vietnamese discussions, the publication said South Vietnam "stressed the right of self-determination of the South Vietnamese people and said clearly that it will not accept any two-part, three-part or four-part government. President Thieu will explain the problem to the people and let them decide."

There was considerable political activity within the Saigon government in connection with the accelerated peace negotiations. Pham Dang Lam, South Vietnam's chief delegate to the Paris peace talks, returned to Saigon Oct. 15 for consultations. Thieu's ambassadors to the U.S. and Britain were also recalled. Thieu conferred with the envoys Oct. 16. The president held other consultation sessions Oct. 18–19 with about 50 South Vietnamese legislators and other politicians, both pro-government and opposition. One of those present at the talks quoted Thieu as expressing "hope that the United States would respect South Vietnamese self-determination and not throw away their years of sacrifices in South Vietnam." Thieu was said to have "reaffirmed that there was no pressure on him from the United States government." Thieu was reported to have told the Oct. 18 gathering that the Communists wanted a three-part coalition government not only in Saigon but also at the hamlet and village levels. This demand, Thieu said, was "unacceptable."

Kissinger had reported to President Nixon in Washington Oct. 13 for the second time in two days on his Oct. 8–11 meetings with North Vietnamese representatives in Paris. A White House statement issued after the talks said the U.S. government agreed with a statement made earlier in the day by North Vietnamese negotiator Le Duc Tho that "there still are many difficult things to settle."

Hanoi's delegation to the peace talks, commenting on the secret U.S.–North Vietnamese discussions, said at a news conference in Paris Oct. 18 that the "Nixon Administration's position remains erroneous and intransigent." The delegation spokesman, Nguyen Thanh Le, said Washington "has not changed its neocolonialist aggressive policy on the two fundamental questions—military and political."

Kissinger: Indochina peace is near. Presidential adviser Henry A. Kissinger told a news conference in Washington Oct. 26 that he believed "peace is at hand" in all of Indochina. Reporting for the first time in public on his intensive secret negotiations with the North Vietnamese in the past few weeks, Kissinger said a final agreement on a truce and a political settlement could be worked out in one more conference with the North Vietnamese "lasting no more than three or four days."

Kissinger, who met newsmen in the White House briefing room, said he believed that "an agreement is within sight on the May 8 proposals of the President and some adaptations of our Jan. 25 proposals, which is just to all parties." He confirmed a Hanoi statement broadcast earlier Oct. 26 that the U.S. and North Vietnam had reached a breakthrough in private talks in Paris Oct. 8 and said he had "no complaint with the general description" of the nine-point agreement which the Hanoi broadcast said had been reached with the U.S.

(The Oct. 8–11 Paris talks had been led by Kissinger, Le Duc Tho and Xuan Thuy.)

Progress in the talks had been accelerated at the Oct. 8 session when the North Vietnamese for the first time submitted proposals "which made it possible to negotiate concretely," Kissinger asserted. At that meeting, he said, the Communist side came around to accepting the American position of concentrating "on bringing an end to the military aspects of the war" and then agreeing "on some very general principles within which the South Vietnamese parties could then determine the political evolution of South Vietnam." According to Kissinger, the North Vietnamese made the following concessions Oct. 8: "They dropped their demand for a coalition government which would absorb all existing authority. They dropped their demand for a veto over the personalities and the structure of the existing government. They agreed for the first time to a formula which permitted simultaneous discussion of Laos and Cambodia."

Kissinger reviewed what he said the U.S. understood to be "the main provisions of the agreement" reached with the North Vietnamese. Kissinger's statement, as recorded by the New York Times through the facilities of ABC News:

The principal provisions were and are that a cease-fire would be observed in South Vietnam at a time to be mutually agreed upon.

It would be a cease-fire in place.

But U.S. forces would be withdrawn within 60 days of the signing of the agreement.

There would be a total prohibition on the reinforcement of troops—that is to say that infiltration into South Vietnam from whatever area and from whatever country would be prohibited.

Existing military equipment within South Vietnam could be replaced on a one-to-one basis by weapons of the same characteristic and of similar characteristics and properties under international supervision.

The agreement provides that all captured military personnel and foreign civilians be repatriated within the same time period as the withdrawal—that is to say, there will be a return of all American prisoners —within 60 days after the agreement comes into force.

North Vietnam has made itself responsible for accounting of our prisoners and missing-in-actions throughout Indochina.

There is a separate provision that South Vietnamese civilians detained in South Vietnam—their future should be determined through negotiations among the South Vietnamese parties.

So the return of our prisoners is not conditional on the disposition of Vietnamese prisoners in Vietnamese jails on both sides of the conflict.

With respect to the political provisions, there is an affirmation of general principles guaranteeing the right of self-determination of the South Vietnamese people and that the South Vietnamese people should decide their political future through free and democratic elections under international supervision.

As was pointed out by Radio Hanoi, the existing authorities with respect to both internal and external politics would remain in office. The two parties in Vietnam would negotiate about the timing of elections, the nature of the elections and the offices for which these elections were to be held.

There would be created an institution called the National Council of National Reconciliation and Concord whose general task would be to help promote the maintenance of the cease-fire and to supervise the elections on which the parties might agree.

That council would be formed by appointment and it would operate on the basis of unanimity. We view it as an institutionalization of the election commission that we proposed on Jan. 25 in our plan.

There are provisions that the disposition of Vietnamese armed forces in the South should also be settled through negotiations among the South Vietnamese parties.

There are provisions that the unification of Vietnam also be achieved by negotiation among the parties without military pressure and without foreign interference, without coercion and without annexation.

There is a very long and complex section on international supervision . . .

But, briefly, it provides for joint commission of the participants—either two-party or four-party— for those parts of the agreement that are applicable either to two parties or to four parties. It provides for an international supervisory commission to which disagreements of the commission composed of the parties would be referred, but which also had a right to make independent investigations.

And an international conference to meet within 30 days of the signing of the agreement to develop the guarantees and to establish the relationship of the various parties to each other in greater detail.

And, finally, a section on Cambodia and Laos in which the parties to the agreement agree to respect and recognize the independence and sovereignty of Cambodia and Laos; in which they agree to refrain from using the territory of Cambodia and the territory of Laos to encroach on the sovereignty and security of other countries.

There is an agreement that foreign countries shall withdraw their forces from Laos and Cambodia.

And there is a general section about a future relationship between the United States and the Democratic Republic of Vietnam in which both sides express their conviction that this agreement will usher in a new period of reconciliation between the two countries and in which the United States expresses its view that it will in the post-war period contribute to the reconstruction of Indochina and that both countries will develop their relationship on a basis of mutual respect and noninterference in each other's affairs, and that they move from hostility to normalcy.

Kissinger said "six or seven concrete issues" remained to be ironed out before a final agreement could be drawn up. As an example, he cited possible temptations by South Vietnamese and Viet Cong forces to make "a last effort to seize as much territory as possible" before a truce went into effect. The U.S., he said, wanted to discuss with North Vietnam measures that the proposed international supervisory body could take "to avoid the dangers of the loss of life . . . that may be inherent in this." The U.S. also wanted to take up with North Vietnam the matter of speeding the separate peace talks now in progress in Cambodia and Laos so that a truce would go into effect in those two countries at the same time as in Vietnam, Kissinger said. He also cited certain "linguistic problems" that had arisen between the English and Vietnamese texts of the U.S.-North Vietnamese agreement. He said the U.S. wanted to make certain that its version of the National Council of Reconciliation, the proposed administrative structure in Saigon, was not interpreted by the North Vietnamese as being "anything comparable to a coalition government."

Kissinger acknowledged there was a "misunderstanding" about signature of the agreement by Oct. 31, a deadline set by the Hanoi representatives. Although the U.S. had agreed that it would "make a major effort to end the negotiations by Oct. 31," it had made clear that it could not set a definite date to conclude the talks, Kissinger asserted. He said there also was the question of representation for the South Vietnamese government, which had "every right to participate in the making of their own peace." Although insisting that the U.S. preserved its "own freedom of judgment" in deciding "how long we believe a war should be continued," Washington had no intention of imposing a solution on Saigon, Kissinger said.

Kissinger commented on his meetings in Saigon Oct. 19-23 with President Nguyen Van Thieu and South Vietnamese officials. (In those talks Kissinger reported on the progress of his negotiations with the North Vietnamese in Paris.) Saigon, Kissinger said, had "expressed its views with customary forcefullness. . . . We agreed with some of their views; we didn't agree with all of them and we made clear which we accepted and which we could not . . ." (Before leaving Saigon Oct. 23, Kissinger had made a quick trip to Pnompenh to meet with Cambodian President Lon Nol on the prospects for peace in Indochina. Kissinger had returned to Washington later Oct. 23 and reported the following day to President Nixon and Secretary of State William P. Rogers. A White House statement said that Kissinger had made "some progress" in his talks with Thieu, but cautioned against "excessive" speculation about the prospects of peace in general.)

Kissinger confirmed that the U.S. had curbed the bombing of North Vietnam. He said the U.S. informed Hanoi Oct. 22 that "we would stop military activities north of the 20th Parallel."

Hanoi report on agreement. In a Hanoi broadcast Oct. 26, the North Vietnamese government gave its version of the nine-point Indochina peace agreement it said had been drawn up by its representatives and Henry Kissinger. [See text at left] The accord was outlined in a detailed account of North Vietnam's interpretation of the secret negotiations held in Paris earlier in October.

Hanoi said the negotiations had taken a turning point Oct. 8 when its representatives proposed to Kissinger an "extremely important initiative." The statement said the North Vietnamese "put forward a draft Agreement on Ending the War and Restoring Peace in Vietnam" and proposed that all four interested parties—North and South Vietnam, the Viet Cong's Provisional Revolutionary Government and the U.S.— "immediately agree upon and sign this agreement to rapidly restore peace in Vietnam."

The North Vietnamese draft agreement, as summarized by the Hanoi broadcast:

[North Vietnam] . . . proposed a cessation of the war throughout Vietnam, a cease-fire in South Vietnam, an end to all U.S. military involvement in Vietnam, a total withdrawal from South Vietnam of troops of the United States and those of the foreign countries allied with the United States and with the Republic of Vietnam, and the return of all captured and detained personnel of the parties.

From the enforcement of the cease-fire to the installation of the government formed after free and democratic general elections, the two present administrations in South Vietnam will remain in existence with their respective domestic and external functions.

These two administrations shall immediately hold consultations with a view to the exercise of the South Vietnamese people's right to self-determination, achieving national concord, insuring the democratic liberties of the South Vietnamese people and forming an administration of national concord which shall have the task of promoting the South Vietnamese parties' implementation of the signed agreements and organizing general elections in South Vietnam within three months after the cease-fire comes into effect.

Thus the Vietnam problem will be settled in two stages in accordance with the often-expressed desire of the American side: The first stage will include a cessation of the war in Vietnam, a cease-fire in South Vietnam, a cessation of the United States military involvement in South Vietnam and an agreement on the principles for the exercise of the South Vietnamese people's right to self-determination; in the second stage the two South Vietnamese parties will settle together the internal matters of South Vietnam. The DRVN side proposed that the Democratic Republic of Vietnam and the United States sign this agreement by mid-October, 1972.

The Hanoi broadcast said the U.S. had called the draft "an important and very fundamental document which opened up the way to an early settlement." Kissinger and North Vietnam's Xuan Thuy had "reached agreement on almost all

Hanoi Version of 9-Point Peace Plan

Text of summary of nine-point peace agreement North Vietnam said it had reached with U.S., as reported by Hanoi radio Oct. 26:

1. The United States respects the independence, sovereignty, unity and territorial integrity of Vietnam as recognized by the 1954 Geneva agreements.

2. Twenty-four hours after the signing of the agreement, a cease-fire shall be observed throughout South Vietnam. The United States will stop all its military activities and end the bombing and mining in North Vietnam.

Within 60 days there will be a total withdrawal from South Vietnam of troops and military personnel of the United States and those of the foreign countries allied with the United States and with the Republic of Vietnam. The two South Vietnamese parties shall not accept the introduction of troops, military advisers and military personnel, armaments, munitions, and war material into South Vietnam.

The two South Vietnamese parties shall be permitted to make periodical replacements of armaments, munitions and war materiel that have been worn out or damaged after the cease-fire, on the basis of piece for piece of similar characteristics and properties. The United States will not continue its military involvement or intervene in the internal affairs of South Vietnam.

3. The return of all captured and detained personnel of the parties shall be carried out simultaneously with the U.S. troops' withdrawal.

4. The principles for the exercise of the South Vietnamese people's right to self-determination are as follows:

The South Vietnamese people shall decide themselves the political future of South Vietnam through genuinely free and democratic general elections under international supervision;

The United States is not committed to any political tendency or to any personality in South Vietnam, and it does not seek to impose a pro-American regime in Saigon;

National reconciliation and concord will be achieved, the democratic liberties of the people insured;

An administrative structure called the National Council of National Reconciliation and Concord, of three equal segments, will be set up to promote the implementation of the signed agreements by the Provisional Revolutionary Government of the Republic of South Vietnam, and the government of the Republic of Vietnam and to organize the general elections, the two South Vietnamese parties will consult about the formation of councils at lower level;

The question of Vietnamese armed forces in South Vietnam shall be settled by the two South Vietnamese parties in a spirit of national reconciliation and concord, equality and mutual respect, without foreign interference in accordance with the postwar situation;

Among the questions to be discussed by the two South Vietnamese parties are steps to reduce the military numbers on both sides and to demobilize the troops being reduced;

The two South Vietnamese parties shall sign an agreement on the internal matters of South Vietnam as soon as possible and will do their utmost to accomplish this within three months after the cease-fire comes into effect.

5. The reunification of Vietnam shall be carried out step by step through peaceful means.

6. There will be formed a four-party joint military commission and a joint military commission of the two South Vietnamese parties.

An international commission of control and supervision shall be established. An international guarantee conference on Vietnam will be convened within 30 days of the signing of this agreement.

7. The government of the Democratic Republic of Vietnam, the Provisional Revolutionary Government of the Republic of South Vietnam, the government of the United States of America and the government of the Republic of Vietnam shall strictly respect the Cambodian and Laos peoples' fundamental national rights as recognized by the 1954 Geneva agreements on Indochina and the 1962 Geneva agreements on Laos, i.e., the independence, sovereignty, unity and territorial integrity of these countries. They shall respect the neutrality of Cambodia and Laos. The government of the Democratic Republic of Vietnam, the Provisional Revolutionary Government of the Republic of South Vietnam, the government of the United States of America and the government of the Republic of Vietnam undertake to refrain from using the territory of Cambodia and the territory of Laos to encroach on the sovereignty and security of other countries. Foreign countries shall put an end to all military activities in Laos and Cambodia, totally withdraw from and refrain from reintroducing into these two countries troops, military advisers and military personnel, armaments, munitions and war material.

The internal affairs of Cambodia and Laos shall be settled by the people of each of these countries without foreign interference.

The problems existing between the three Indochinese countries shall be settled by the Indochinese parties on the basis of respect for each other's independence, sovereignty and territorial integrity and noninterference in each other's internal affairs.

8. With the ending of the war, the restoration of peace in Vietnam will create conditions for establishing a new, equal and mutually beneficial relationship between the Democratic Republic of Vietnam and the United States. The United States will contribute to healing the wounds of war and to postwar reconstruction in the Democratic Republic of Vietnam and throughout Indochina.

9. This agreement shall come into force as of its signing. It will be strictly implemented by all the parties concerned.

problems on the basis of the draft agreement" in secret talks held in Paris Oct. 17, it said.

The North Vietnamese statement added: In a message sent to Premier Pham Van Dong Oct. 10, President Nixon had expressed appreciation of North Vietnam's "goodwill" and had "confirmed that the formulation of the agreement could be considered complete," with the exception of "a number of complex points," which Hanoi cleared up to Nixon's satisfaction. The President, in a message Oct. 22, accepted North Vietnam's explanations and that day "the formulation of the agreement was complete."

The North Vietnamese statement detailed the agreement for scaling down and eventually halting U.S. military activities against North Vietnam and a timetable for signature of the agreement. The latter was the point of "misunderstanding" raised by Kissinger at his news conference Oct. 26. [See above] Hanoi accused the U.S. of changing "the agreed schedule" several times, an action which, it warned, "threatens to jeopardize the signing" of the peace accord.

North Vietnam's version of the schedule and of the agreement to halt military action:

The two parties have also agreed on a schedule for the signing of the agreement. On Oct. 9, 1972, at the proposal of the U.S. side, it was agreed that on Oct. 18, 1972, the United States would stop the bombing and mining in North Vietnam; on Oct. 19, 1972, the two parties would initial the text of the agreement in Hanoi; on Oct. 26, 1972, the foreign ministers of the two countries would formally sign the agreement in Paris.

On Oct. 11, 1972, the U.S. side proposed the following change to the schedule: On Oct. 21, 1972, the United States would stop the bombing and mining in North Vietnam; on Oct. 22, 1972, the two parties would initial the text of the agreement in Hanoi; on Oct. 30, 1972, the foreign ministers of the two countries would formally sign the agreement in Paris. The Democratic Republic of Vietnam agreed to the new U.S. schedule.

On Oct. 20, 1972, under the pretext that there still remained a number of unagreed points, the U.S. side again put forth another schedule: On Oct. 23, 1972, the United States would stop the bombing and mining in North Vietnam; on Oct. 24, 1972, the two parties would initial the text of the agreement in Hanoi; on Oct. 31, 1972, the foreign ministers of the two countries would formally sign the agreement in Paris.

Despite the fact that the U.S. side had changed many times what had been agreed upon, the DRVN side, with its goodwill, again agreed to the U.S. proposal while stressing that the U.S. side should not under any pretext change the agreed schedule.

Thus, by Oct. 22, 1972, the DRVN side and the U.S. side had agreed both on the full text of the

Agreement on Ending the War and Restoring Peace in Vietnam and on the schedule to be observed for the formal signing of the agreement on Oct. 31, 1972. Obviously, the two sides had agreed upon an agreement of extremely important significance, which meets the wishes of the peoples in Vietnam, the United States and the world.

But on Oct. 23, 1972, contrary to its pledges, the U.S. side again referred to difficulties in Saigon, demanded that the negotiations be continued for resolving new problems and did not say anything about the implementation of its commitments under the agreed schedule. This behavior of the U.S. side has brought about a very serious situation, which threatens to jeopardize the signing of the Agreement on Ending the War and Restoring Peace in Vietnam.

North Vietnam charged that South Vietnamese opposition to a political solution was a pretext used by the U.S. "to delay implementation" of the American commitment to a settlement. The Nixon Administration was "not negotiating with a serious attitude and goodwill to end the war and restore peace in Vietnam" and was attempting "to drag out the talks so as to deceive public opinion and to cover up its scheme of maintaining the Saigon puppet regime for the purpose of continued war of aggression," Hanoi stated.

Demands that the U.S. sign the nine-point peace agreement Oct. 31 were voiced Oct. 26 by the North Vietnamese and Viet Cong delegations to the Paris peace talks. Xuan Thuy and Viet Cong spokesman Ly Van Sau made the statement following the 164th session of the formal peace talks.

In a statement to the delegates and at a later news conference, Thuy said Hanoi's release of details about secret negotiations with Henry A. Kissinger "serves the cause of peace and in no way affects negotiations." He said Hanoi had released information on the private talks to let the world "know the truth" about North Vietnam's charge that the U.S. was hedging on signing the agreement.

North Vietnamese acceptance of the cease-fire as a first step in the settlement of the war had been strongly indicated by Premier Pham Van Dong in an interview Oct. 16 with Arnaud de Borchgrave, a senior editor of Newsweek. In the interview, made public Oct. 21, Dong said Hanoi would agree to the following proposal, which turned out to be essentially the same peace plan announced by his government and Henry A. Kissinger Oct. 26:

A cease-fire followed by the withdrawal of all American troops from

South Vietnam; South Vietnam and the Viet Cong would then negotiate arrangements for a tripartite government that would prepare for the general elections within six months of the cease-fire; and all prisoners of war, including U.S. pilots downed and captured in North Vietnam, would be freed as soon as the political settlement was agreed to.

Saigon remains critical of accord. In its first official reaction to the Hanoi broadcast on a U.S.-North Vietnamese peace agreement, the South Vietnamese Foreign Ministry released a statement Oct. 27 indicating the government's readiness "to accept a cease-fire" but expressing reservations about a political settlement. While making clear that South Vietnam wanted a cease-fire, the statement emphasized the country "would never accept a political settlement which goes against the interests and aspirations of the 17 million South Vietnamese people." It said Hanoi radio had been vague about what the details of such a settlement would be and that this was "just a North Vietnamese Communist trick to create suspicion between the Republic of Vietnam and our U.S. ally and to create public pressures for an early end to the bombing and blockade."

Foreign Minister Tran Van Lam was quoted by the official Vietnam Press Agency as saying Oct. 26 that "a cease-fire has not been agreed by all the parties involved" and that he did "not believe" such an agreement could come "before the U.S. presidential election." Lam asserted: "The key condition is the complete withdrawal of North Vietnamese troops to North Vietnam." (The peace plan worked out between Henry Kissinger and North Vietnamese officials appeared to allow some 145,000 North Vietnamese troops to remain in South Vietnam in areas they controlled.)

Ambassador Ellsworth Bunker met twice Oct. 26 with President Thieu but both the U.S. embassy and the Presidential Palace refused to give information about what had been discussed.

In an Oct. 24 broadcast, Thieu had voiced violent objections to the peace proposals reportedly discussed by Kissinger and the North Vietnamese.

The New York Times Oct. 23 quoted a South Vietnamese official, who asked not

to be identified, as saying that President Thieu had ordered the establishment Oct. 7 of a 50-member Central Study Committee headed by his close aide, Lieut. Gen. Dang Van Quang, to determine how government ministries should respond in the event of a cease-fire.

Thieu broadcast—President Thieu had declared in a nationwide broadcast Oct. 24 that the reported peace proposals worked out by Washington and Hanoi were unacceptable. He predicted an early cease-fire but said his government could not accept a truce-in-place prior to a political settlement. Saigon would accept a battle halt only if it applied to all of Indochina and only if all North Vietnamese troops were withdrawn from the South, Thieu said.

The South Vietnamese leader said the Communists were seeking a truce out of military weakness. He said a cease-fire in place was a North Vietnamese ploy "to regain their strength." "After a coalition government has been set up and all American troops have been withdrawn, they would use their invigorated military force to rise up and seize power in a last military coup." The Communist effort would succeed, Thieu said, because it was "unlikely that the U.S. could go back to bombing again."

Expressing equal suspicion of a political settlement that would follow a cease-fire, Thieu said "We know that if we coalesce with the Communists they will take advantage of internal disturbances to try to take over the government." He charged that the Communists' use of the term "national concord" to describe their proposed three-part government was "actually only a deceitful trap to dupe public opinion." He was bitter about his role in a future Saigon government. "They speak of accepting Mr. Thieu as leader of a South Vietnamese faction, but they do not speak of him as president, as he is at present," Thieu said.

U.S. curbs bombing of North. The U.S. ordered a temporary halt to the bombing north of the 20th Parallel in North Vietnam, it was reported Oct. 24. Defense Secretary Melvin R. Laird confirmed the existence of the bombing curb Oct. 27 in comments to newsmen in

London. The directive restricting air strikes to the southern panhandle of the country was said to have gone into effect at 5 p.m. Oct. 23 to signal U.S. recognition of the concessions North Vietnam had made in the secret peace negotiations.

The reduction in American air strikes was implied by a U.S. military spokesman in Saigon Oct. 24. In a briefing for newsmen, the official said fewer than half the daily average of strikes on the North had been flown in the previous two days, with the majority of them concentrated south of the 20th Parallel. The spokesman said 140 missions had been flown Oct. 22 and 120 Oct. 23, compared with a usual daily average of about 300. The curbing of the bombing of the North was coupled with an increase in American air strikes in South Vietnam.

An Agence France-Presse report from Hanoi Oct. 25 said there were three bombing "pre-alerts" in Hanoi Oct. 24. The North Vietnamese Foreign Ministry charged Oct. 25 that a number of U.S. air strikes had been carried out the previous day, all south of the 20th Parallel, in which "many civilians" were killed or wounded.

The Associated Press Oct. 25 reported U.S. Navy acknowledgment of the transfer of three aircraft carriers south from the Gulf of Tonkin to positions off the coast of South Vietnam. This left only one carrier off the coast of North Vietnam for the first time since April.

In a delayed report on air action around Hanoi, the U.S. command reported Oct. 23 the downing of three North Vietnamese MiG-21s by U.S. jets Oct. 15. A command spokesman said the report had been held up because of a lack of confirmation.

Nixon, McGovern comments. Both President Nixon and Sen. McGovern made their first public statements on the cease-fire agreement described by Kissinger during campaign appearances Oct. 26.

Speaking at an airport rally in Huntington, W. Va., President Nixon said he was confident that the remaining details for a Vietnam cease-fire and peace settlement "can and will be worked out." Nixon told the audience, "I can say to you in confidence that we shall succeed in achieving our objective, which is peace with honor and not peace with surrender." He added: "There are still difficulties to be worked out. I am confident that they can and will be worked out."

Without commenting on the specifics of a cease-fire arrangement, Nixon also spoke of peace in Vietnam in a second campaign appearance later Oct. 26 in Ashland, Ky. Addressing a crowd of more than 3,500 people, Nixon said that the object of his foreign policy had been "not only to bring an end to the war in Vietnam" but also to build a new kind of "world order." "What we have done," Nixon said, "is to have replaced what was a hopeless situation with now a hopeful situation." Later he reiterated that America must not abandon its position as the world's foremost military power.

McGovern learned of the apparent peace breakthrough as he was preparing to leave Detroit Oct. 26 for a campaign foray into Iowa. McGovern declined to comment specifically on Kissinger's description of the settlement that was being negotiated but pledged his "full support and cooperation" for any moves toward an end to the fighting.

Later Oct. 26 in a speech to 15,000 persons at the University of Iowa in Iowa City, McGovern said that he hoped that Nixon's confidence about an imminent settlement was well founded. He refused to credit the Administration with ending the fighting; those who had opposed the war deserved "much of the credit," he declared.

McGovern implied that the Administration's recent stepped-up peace effort was timed for the November presidential election. "The question that haunts my mind," McGovern said, "is this: Why, Mr. Nixon, did you take another four more years to put an end to this tragic war? What did either we or the rest of the world gain by the killing of another 20,000 young Americans these past four years?"

Speech on defense policies—President Nixon restated his no-compromise stand on the amnesty issue Oct. 29 in another nationwide radio political speech, this one focusing on national defense policies.

In remarks similar to those he made during an Ohio motorcade Oct. 28, Nixon said "rather than talking about amnesty for the few hundred who chose to desert America, let us honor the millions who chose to serve America in Vietnam. He described those who served, were serving or would serve in the armed forces as "the real heroes of our time."

He continued: "As this long and difficult war draws to an end, it is time to draw the line on this issue for once and for all. There will be no amnesty for draft dodgers and deserters after the war. The few hundred who refused to serve or who deserted their country must pay a penalty for their choice."

China, U.S.S.R. urge pact signing. Soviet Premier Alexei N. Kosygin said Oct. 27 that he favored continued negotiations between the U.S. and North Vietnam to clear up the remaining obstacles to a final Indochina peace settlement. Speaking to the envoys of North Vietnam and the Viet Cong in Moscow, Kosygin expressed hope that the renewed discussions would "lead soon to the signature of an agreement ending the war."

The Soviet premier made the statement as the two envoys presented him with the text of North Vietnam's Oct. 26 report of its version of the U.S.–North Vietnamese agreement.

The Soviet ambassador to France, Pyotr A. Abrasimov, discussed the cease-fire agreement with Foreign Minister Maurice Schumann in Paris Oct. 28. The talks also were said to have dealt with Soviet plans to participate in an international aid program for the reconstruction of Vietnam after the war. Abrasimov said his government, the U.S. and "many other countries" would contribute to the program.

The Soviet Union urged the U.S. Oct. 29 not "to delay the agreed solution to the Vietnam problem," which it claimed was being blocked by South Vietnamese President Thieu. An article in the Communist party newspaper Pravda called Thieu the "main obstacle to peace in Vietnam."

"The exaggeration of the role of this ruler-by-American courtesy may, per-haps, mislead some of the inexperienced voters in the United States, but not world public opinion," Pravda said.

China Oct. 30 supported North Vietnam's position that the U.S. must meet the Oct. 31 deadline in signing the peace agreement. The Communist party newspaper Jenmin Jih Pao charged that Washington "must be held responsible for the acts" of the Thieu government's attempts "to obstruct and wreck the agreement." The newspaper dismissed Thieu's demand that a cease-fire must also apply to Laos and Cambodia. The statement said this demand was "sheer effrontery" because only the U.S. and North Vietnam had taken part in the private Paris talks that drew up the peace settlement.

A Chinese government statement Oct. 30 was more critical of the U.S., charging that it had "repeatedly changed its proposition, created offshoot issues and laid new obstacles to put off the signing of the agreement" on the pretext that Saigon was objecting to terms of the peace plan.

Premier Chou En-lai said Nov. 1 that it was his belief that the U.S. "to a certain extent" was encouraging Thieu in his opposition to the peace agreement. He expressed doubt that the settlement would be signed soon. Chou indicated to newsmen that he was speaking on the basis of contacts he had been having with U.S. and North Vietnamese government officials.

In a further comment on the passing of the Oct. 31 deadline without the signing of the agreement, Jenmin Jih Pao asserted Nov. 1 that the U.S. "was wholly responsible for this complication." The newspaper said it was not credible that Thieu and "his clique could block a settlement of the Vietnam question if the U.S. really wants a solution."

Cambodia Oct. 27 expressed concern over Article 7 of the proposed nine-point peace plan, which called on all "foreign countries" to end their military activities in Cambodia. An Information Ministry communique contended this article applied exclusively to North Vietnam, which it charged had "constantly violated" the 1954 and 1962 Geneva accords guaranteeing the sovereignty of Laos and Cambodia.

Souvanna expects Vietnam truce. Laotian Premier Prince Souvanna Phouma told newsmen at U.N. headquarters in New York Oct. 26 that he welcomed recent developments toward a Vietnam cease-fire, although similar arrangements had not yet been worked out for Laos and Cambodia.

Prince Souvanna remarked: "Up to now the only cease-fire that is being arranged is in Vietnam. Laos and Cambodia will come afterward." He said he would know whether there had been "some changes" when he went to Washington Oct. 27 for talks with Secretary of State William P. Rogers on the 1962 peace agreement negotiated for Laos. Souvanna declared that "the Laotian problem is tied to the Vietnam problem.... We hope that a cease-fire in Vietnam will mean the end of the use of Laos as a transit point for North Vietnamese troops." (Speaking Oct. 23 to a group of journalists in Paris, the Laotian premier had predicted a cease-fire "before the end of the month.")

In a related development, Prince Norodom Sihanouk, the deposed Cambodian head of state, said in Peking Oct. 23 he had been told the previous week by a high North Vietnamese official that Hanoi had not changed its basic attitude on the departure of South Vietnamese President Thieu. Sihanouk said he had been informed by Le Duc Tho, chief adviser to the North Vietnamese delegation at the Paris peace talks, that Hanoi had appeared to soften its attitude toward Thieu "in order to achieve peace that permits reconstruction of Vietnam." This "flexibility," Sihanouk reported, concerned "points of detail" but did not change the "fundamental position" that Thieu would have to relinquish his office.

Laotian peace talks—Preliminary peace talks between the government and representatives of the pro-Communist Pathet Lao began Oct. 17 in Vientiane. They were being led by Pheng Phongsavan, for the government, and Gen. Phoun Sipraseuth, for the Pathet Lao.

The two groups met again Oct. 24 for a second round, with Gen. Phoun denouncing the U.S. influence in Laos. He quoted from a report dated Aug. 3, 1971 by a Senate subcommittee headed by Stewart Symington (D, Mo.) which said the Laotian government "depends almost totally on us, perhaps more than any other government in the world."

The Laotian government Oct. 26 outlined a plan for a cease-fire and general elections. The document, read by Pheng, also called for release of political prisoners and the ending of North Vietnamese activities against Laos. There was no response from the Pathet Lao.

Laotian fighting increases. As in South Vietnam, Communist and government forces in Laos stepped up the fighting in an effort to gain the greatest ground advantage in expectation of a cease-fire.

Government troops that began a drive for Saravane in the south Oct. 22 reoccupied the village Oct. 28. Saravane had been in Pathet Lao and North Vietnamese hands almost continuously since May 1970.

Pathet Lao and North Vietnamese soldiers went on the offensive in many parts of Laos Oct. 28, capturing a number of towns and large amounts of territory. Hanoi's troops occupied the virtually undefended town of Kengkok southeast of Savannakhet in the south. Other Communist soldiers were said to have occupied a large farm owned by King Savang Vathana 10 miles north of the royal capital of Luang Prabang.

A government drive to recapture the Plaines des Jarres north of Vientiane received a serious setback Oct. 27 when strong North Vietnamese counterattacks drove them off the plain into surrounding high ground.

Government troops Oct. 31 fought their way back into Kengkok and Khong Sedone, on the Mekong River in southern Laos.

Communist troops Nov. 1 overran the garrison town of Namthorn Buk Kwang, about 90 miles east of Vientiane, killing an estimated 200 government troops. The remaining 300 base defenders joined 1,000 civilians in fleeing the town and going across the border into Thailand.

Laos peace talks continue—Government and Pathet Lao representatives held a third round of peace talks in Vientiane Oct. 31.

Government representative Oune Sananikone accused the Pathet Lao of refusing to admit the presence of North Vietnamese troops in Laos. The Pathet

Lao countered with submission of a 15-page document outlining the recent history of Laos and declaring that the country had been dominated by "American imperialism" since 1954. The document insisted on linking military and political agreements with ending the war in Laos and scorned the government for "behaving like a victor in a war in which our forces win more victories every day." The Pathet Lao restated its refusal to merge with the present coalition government and demanded formation of a completely new regime.

Although both sides remained deadlocked as in their two previous meetings, they agreed to meet Nov. 7 and each week thereafter as necessary.

Communists increase attacks. North Vietnamese and Viet Cong forces stepped up their attacks in South Vietnam Oct. 26–31 in an apparent attempt to capture as much territory as possible before a truce went into effect. South Vietnamese troops received strong support from U.S. planes, which were attacking Communist troop positions, particularly in the Saigon region where the fighting was heaviest.

The Saigon command reported 113 Communist-initiated assaults throughout the country Oct. 26, the largest number in any 24-hour period since the 1968 Tet offensive. U.S. sources dismissed the raids, 81 of them shelling attacks, as of "no military significance." President Thieu was reported to have issued orders to the nation's four military regions to put down any attempt by the Communists to create "a general uprising."

In response to these orders, government troops Oct. 27 launched a drive aimed at ousting Viet Cong agents from villages and hamlets. Meanwhile, Communist forces maintained heavy military pressure Oct. 27, capturing two hamlets on Route 1 20 and 30 miles northwest of Saigon and beating off government counter-attacks. The enemy force also carried out several rocket attacks in the Central Highlands that day, hitting the towns of Pleiku, Kontum and Dalat.

Viet Cong forces Oct. 28 occupied 10 hamlets around Saigon with the attacks concentrated along major highways leading to the capital. The assaults were among 104 Communist-initiated incidents throughout South Vietnam, the Saigon command said.

Communist forces intensified their infiltration tactics near Saigon Oct. 29, cutting Route 1 both east and west of the capital. Government soldiers, however, were able to oust North Vietnamese and Viet Cong troops from nine other hamlets they had seized the previous day. The Communists carried out 138 attacks throughout the country during the day, with other assaults centered around Kontum and in the U Minh Forest in the Mekong Delta. Government troops reported killing 49 enemy soldiers and losing two dead in three clashes four miles southwest of Quangtri city.

Communist forces overran two government base camps in the Central Highlands Oct. 30 and 31. The first camp, at Dakseang in Kontum Province, was destroyed by Communist bombardment, forcing the 300 government defenders to abandon the base. The second strongpoint, the district town of Bato in Quangngai Province, 100 miles to the east, fell to the Communists after a Ranger battalion withdrew to more secure positions nearby. The Communists scored more gains Oct. 31 by capturing the district capital of Queson, 25 miles south of Danang. It was the fifth time Queson had changed hands since the start of the Communist offensive March 30.

U.S. curbs sea attacks. The U.S. was reported Oct. 30 to have halted all naval bombardment north of the 20th Parallel in North Vietnam. Dozens of warships were said to have steamed south of the 20th Parallel. The sowing of new mines was halted. The curb on naval shelling followed a similar order the previous week declaring the area north of the 20th Parallel off-limits to American planes.

U.S. planes, however, continued pressure against enemy targets in North Vietnam's panhandle south of the bomb-free zone. A Phantom was shot down Oct. 27, the 1,045th reported by the U.S. command lost in operations against the North in the war. The two pilots were rescued.

The U.S. command announced that in the 24 hours ending at noon Oct. 31, B-52s had carried out 13 attacks against North Vietnamese ammunition dumps. U.S. fighter-bombers flew more than 130 strikes against other targets in the North Oct. 29–30.

Hanoi radio reported Oct. 31 that a U.S. pilot shot down over North Vietnam Oct. 29 had been killed during an air raid by other American planes over Nghean Province soon after his capture.

Communists cross Cambodian border. Sources in Pnompenh reported Oct. 31 that several thousand North Vietnamese and Viet Cong troops were moving out of Cambodia into South Vietnam, taking up new positions in the Mekong Delta and around Saigon. The move was believed connected with the Communists' determination to expand their control of South Vietnamese territory before a truce went into effect. The new Communist thrust was said to have started several weeks ago, and intensified in the past few days.

The burden of fighting government forces was being left to the Khmer Rouge, the Cambodian rebel guerrillas. In one recent raid, the Khmer Rouge Oct. 28 attacked an area south of Takhmau near Pnompenh. The assault marked an extension of guerrilla activity into the capital's southwestern approaches.

In other action in Cambodia, a government infantry brigade Oct. 26 captured a Communist staging camp 45 miles west of Pnompenh.

U.S., Communist supply buildup. North Vietnam and the U.S. were reported to be accelerating shipment of war material to South Vietnam before supply levels were frozen by a cease-fire.

According to American intelligence sources Oct. 31, an increase in the "heavy movement" of North Vietnamese supplies into the South had begun about Oct. 21. The infiltration routes into South Vietnam from Laos, from across the demilitarized zone and down the coastal routes and from the Parrot's Beak in eastern Cambodia were being used to funnel artillery pieces, tracked vehicles, fuel and foodstuffs.

In a parallel development, the U.S. was said to have significantly stepped up the shipment of war supplies to South Vietnam's armed forces the previous week. Defense Department officials stressed that equipment would involve only material previously scheduled to be sent to the South.

Thieu calls peace plan a 'sellout.' President Nguyen Van Thieu Nov. 1 denounced the draft peace agreement as "a surrender of the South Vietnamese people to the Communists." In a broadcast marking South Vietnam's National Day, Thieu said the proposed U.S.–North Vietnamese settlement was "only a cease-fire to sell out Vietnam." The president said he was not the only one in South Vietnam "who is an obstacle to this agreement to surrender, but there are 17.5 million South Vietnamese who are opposed to such an agreement."

Thieu did not specifically reject a truce or negotiated settlement, but he outlined several objections to the projected solution. He objected to a cease-fire in place which permitted North Vietnam to keep its forces in South Vietnam. Thieu estimated their number at 300,000–400,000, not the 145,000 estimated by U.S. intelligence sources.

The Saigon leader called the North Vietnamese "perfidious as they ask the Americans and allies to withdraw their troops but they do not mention the withdrawal of their own troops." Thieu also criticized Hanoi for referring to three countries in Indochina when "in reality there are four—Cambodia, Laos and North as well as South Vietnam. By saying that, they reserve for themselves the right to be in South Vietnam and keep their troops there."

As for the political aspects of the agreement, Thieu said the North Vietnamese talk "about the self-determination of the people of Vietnam while they are imposing a dictatorial three-part regime in the South from the top down to the local level in the South and wipe out our constitution." He accused Hanoi of "interfering in bilateral negotiations between the government of South Vietnam and the [Viet Cong's] National Liberation Front."

(The South Vietnamese people were unaware of the details of the agreement reached between the U.S. and North Vietnam because Thieu had seized newspapers that had published an account of Henry A. Kissinger's discussion of the plan at a Washington news conference Oct. 26.)

The demand for total withdrawal of North Vietnamese troops from South Vietnam and objections to other facets of the peace plan had been expressed previously by Thieu and other Saigon officials. Among the statements:

Thieu insisted Oct. 27 that his "minimum demand" before approving a halt to the fighting was the total pullout of Hanoi's troops from his country. Speaking at the Presidential Palace to a rally of 500 National Assembly legislators and provincial councilors, Thieu warned that "any cease-fire without our signature will not be valid. So far we have not agreed to anything." Members of the audience had marched to the palace in an organized demonstration of support. Earlier the lower chamber of the assembly, the House of Representatives, had approved by a 125–4 vote a resolution that would reject any truce without a North Vietnamese withdrawal and any political settlement that included a coalition or three-part government.

Foreign Minister Tran Van Lam Oct. 28 characterized the U.S.–North Vietnamese peace agreement as a "surrender" for South Vietnam which was "unacceptable." In an interview with New York Times correspondent Joseph B. Treaster, Lam disagreed with Henry A. Kissinger's remarks Oct. 26 that "peace was at hand" and that only a few minor issues remained to be resolved. The foreign minister listed the issues which he regarded as still unsettled. North Vietnamese troops, he said, must be pulled out of the South and the size of the demilitarized zone was inadequate and must be widened from the current two miles on each side to nine miles to afford South Vietnamese forces greater protection from North Vietnamese shelling. Lam objected to another aspect of the peace plan that barred either side in South Vietnam from receiving military aid in the form of men and new material. He said since this restriction did not ap-

ply to war supplies that could be sent to North Vietnam, his people feared Hanoi "will import tanks and equipment to start the aggression in two or three years."

Lam said his government accepted in principle the establishment of the National Council of Reconciliation and Concord (composed of government, Communist and neutralist representatives) charged with organizing elections and drafting a new constitution. But he said the Communists were not entitled to one-third membership of the South Vietnamese population and that the council's composition must be determined by an election.

Lam Oct. 30 reiterated his demands for North Vietnamese military withdrawal, Hanoi's recognition of the demilitarized zone (which in effect would mean Communist acceptance of two Vietnams) and revamping of the proposed National Council of Reconciliation, which he called "a coalition government in disguise."

South Vietnamese disapproval of the U.S.–North Vietnamese peace accord also emanated from non-government quarters. Au Truong Thanh, a prominent neutralist mentioned as a possible member of the National Council, asserted in Paris Oct. 30 that there was a lack of political guarantees in the draft agreement. Thanh had served as a finance minister in the 1960s but had since become a political exile.

Opposition leader Duong Van Minh Nov. 1 expressed doubts about the feasibility of a cease-fire in place, asking "Who would police all those little spots" of government and Communist troops scattered throughout South Vietnam? Minh, a retired general, proposed instead the withdrawal of opposing forces into "regrouping areas," which he claimed would be easier to supervise. Despite the altered political climate in South Vietnam resulting from the proposed peace plan, Minh said he was no closer to the Thieu regime. He explained: "Two sides are fighting in this country. I am neither for one nor the other."

The Saigon government Oct. 28 had dispatched envoys to 11 Southeast Asian and Pacific nations to explain its position on the proposed peace plan. The

Foreign Ministry said the ambassadors would visit Laos, Cambodia, Thailand, Singapore, Malaysia, Indonesia, New Zealand, Australia, the Philippines, South Korea and Japan.

Communists demand pact signing. A series of statements by North Vietnam and the Viet Cong Oct. 27–Nov. 1 insisted that the U.S. sign the peace agreement reached by Henry A. Kissinger and Le Duc Tho. As Hanoi's announced Oct. 31 deadline for signing passed, the North Vietnamese became increasingly critical of the U.S. and expressed doubts about its sincerity.

North Vietnamese peace delegation spokesman Nguyen Thanh Le disclosed in Paris Oct. 27 that Kissinger and Tho had reached other agreements that had not been mentioned in the U.S. and North Vietnamese texts released Oct. 26. He listed the points as follows:

■ Detailed arrangements on implementation of the cease-fire and assurances against renewal of clashes as the belligerents enter into political negotiations.

■ Assurances against acts of reprisal.

■ Creation of a new international control commission to supervise the cease-fire. (The nations that would reportedly serve on the commission had been identified by other sources as Hungary, Poland, Canada and Indonesia. Poland and Canada were members of the moribund International Control Commission that had been established to implement the 1954 Geneva accord on Indochina.)

■ The functions of the proposed National Council of Reconciliation and Concord had been clearly delineated. The council would serve alongside the existing Saigon and Viet Cong administrations and would prepare elections.

■ The international conference that would work out a political settlement would be convened 30 days after a cease-fire and its participants had been chosen.

Le warned that North Vietnamese negotiators would not meet with Kissinger unless he decided to sign the peace agreement Oct. 31.

The Viet Cong pledged Oct. 28 to "absolutely respect and carry out all provisions" of the U.S.-North Vietnamese agreement. In its first public reaction to the accord, the Viet Cong National Liberation Forces (NLF) radio also promised "no liquidation" campaign against its opponents in South Vietnam and said its representatives were willing to "immediately conduct negotiations with the present Saigon administration to settle" all existing problems.

An NLF broadcast Oct. 30 urged the people of South Vietnam and the Soviet and Chinese governments to pressure the U.S. to sign the draft agreement Oct. 31. The broadcast accused Washington of endangering the peace and threatened to increase Viet Cong military attacks in South Vietnam if an agreement was not signed.

North Vietnamese Foreign Minister Nguyen Duy Trinh charged Oct. 29 that since the conclusion of the Kissinger-Tho talks Oct. 8–11 in which the peace plan had been agreed to, the U.S. had "repeatedly insisted on altering provisions of the draft agreement." Trinh did not specify the requested alterations. The foreign minister warned that further U.S. delaying tactics would put the entire agreement in jeopardy. Trinh did not mention the "Oct. 31 deadline" and spoke instead of an "immediate" decision.

North Vietnam was reported to have expressed willingness Nov. 1 to have Le Duc Tho hold further negotiations with Kissinger. Agence France Presse quoted a Hanoi official as saying "Whether there is another meeting is not important. What is important is that the United States keep its word."

The North Vietnamese government also was said to have rebutted Kissinger's Oct. 26 statements that another meeting with Le Duc Tho was necessary to resolve some minor issues. The North Vietnamese took particular issue with Kissinger's statement that the Saigon government must take part in deciding peace terms most affecting South Vietnam. Hanoi countered this argument by citing what it called previous Washington statements that all negotiating sessions it had been conducting with the North Vietnamese had been carried out with full consultations with President Thieu. The

North Vietnamese were said to have quoted remarks made to this effect by Kissinger Feb. 9 and by President Nixon Feb. 10.

Nixon bars hasty accord. President Nixon declared in a nationwide television broadcast Nov. 2 that the U.S. would not join North Vietnam in signing the agreement on peace in Indochina until all remaining differences were cleared up. He did not specify the unresolved issues.

Nixon insisted that "the central points be clearly settled, so that there will be no misunderstanding which could lead to a breakdown of the settlement and a resumption of the war." He said "We are going to sign the agreement when the agreement is right, not one day before—and when the agreement is right, we are going to sign, without one day's delay."

The President reiterated his determination not "to allow an election deadline or any other kind of deadline to force us into an agreement, which would be only a temporary peace and not a lasting peace."

North Vietnam had insisted that presidential adviser Henry A. Kissinger had agreed in his negotiations with Le Duc Tho in Paris Oct. 8–11 to sign the draft peace accord Oct. 31. Kissinger had said in his report on the agreement Oct. 26 that he had never committed himself to that date.

(The President's statement was made in his first televised paid political broadcast of the campaign, in which he reiterated his stand on other issues.)

Nixon was reported Oct. 31 to have assured Washington's Southeast Asian allies that even after the U.S. withdrew its military forces from Indochina it would continue to provide economic and other aid to Cambodia, Laos and South Vietnam. The U.S. would not disengage from Southeast Asia because it was vital to maintain non-Communist governments in the region, Nixon said. Among those to whom the President had expressed these views was Laotian Premier Souvanna Phouma at a White House meeting Oct. 27. Secretary of State William P. Rogers also met with Souvanna that day and discussed the Indochina situation with Cambodian Foreign Minister Long Boret Nov. 1.

The arrival of the Oct. 31 target date had brought a reaffirmative statement from the White House that "the only deadline we are operating under is one that will bring about the right kind of agreement." The statement reiterated President Nixon's "firm intention" of not permitting "a deadline this weekend, or a deadline of Election Day, to stampede the United States into an agreement that would be less perfect than we would otherwise achieve."

It was reported in Washington Oct. 31 that the U.S. was seeking assurances from North Vietnam to withdraw many of its 35,000 troops from the northern provinces of South Vietnam. This request contrasted with point two of the nine-point draft agreement which implied that North Vietnam would keep its troops in the South pending a final political settlement.

The U.S. and North Vietnam were reported Oct. 30 to have been in constant private communication, seeking to narrow the differences of the nine-point accord since its public disclosure Oct. 26.

Vice President Spiro Agnew Oct. 29 sought to reassure North Vietnam that the accord reached by Kissinger and Tho would be accepted by the U.S. "Substantially, the agreement has been hammered out and there are just a few matters to be made crystal clear between the parties before it can be made final," Agnew said.

Supply buildup in South continues. North Vietnam and the U.S. accelerated their buildup of military supplies in South Vietnam in advance of a possible cease-fire. Under terms of the proposed truce plan, the introduction of new equipment would be barred, although weapons could be replaced on a one-to-one basis.

The U.S. reported Nov. 3 that South Korea, Nationalist China and Iran had agreed to provide South Vietnam with 30 to 40 F-5A jet fighters originally obtained from the U.S. Defense Department spokesman Jerry W. Friedheim said the shipment of the F-5As along with other aircraft from the U.S. was in part "to try to support the negotiating track." Friedheim confirmed that the U.S. was providing the Saigon government with C-130 transport planes from its reserve stocks in South Vietnam. About 32 of the planes reportedly were to be delivered to South Vietnam; several of them landed at Saigon's airport Nov. 2. More than 700 tons of military equipment carried by at least 30 U.S. military and chartered commercial cargo planes arrived in Saigon Nov. 7.

U.S. Administration officials had disclosed Nov. 2 that the other aircraft it had planned to give to South Vietnam included about 72 A-37 jet close-support fighters, one or two squadrons of A-1 propeller-driven close-support fighters (18 in a squadron), and two or more squadrons of UH-1 helicopters (33 'copters in a South Vietnamese squadron). The U.S. already had begun to turn over all of its remaining A-1s in Thailand to the South Vietnamese air force, it was reported from Saigon Nov. 7.

U.S. military analysts said Nov. 3 that North Vietnam was moving heavy reinforcements into South Vietnam, including an armored regiment with about 100 tanks and about 100 armored personnel carriers. The regiment reportedly had crossed the demilitarized zone into northern Quangtri Province. Other Communist equipment reportedly being shipped into the South included SS-7 infrared antiaircraft missiles and 130-mm. heavy artillery.

Hanoi vows continued struggle. Heavy fighting continued throughout South Vietnam this week. North Vietnam declared in a government statement broadcast Nov. 2 that it had "no other choice than to step up the fight on all fronts" in the light of America's failure to sign the draft peace agreement. The Hanoi broadcast pledged the struggle would also continue on the "political and diplomatic" levels "until complete victory."

In ground action in the South, several sharp clashes were fought in the Saigon area Nov. 1 with 142 Communists reported killed in one engagement around Cuchi. Government losses were put at seven killed and 43 wounded. Thirty-nine more North Vietnamese were said to have been killed in an unsuccessful attempt to infiltrate two hamlets 15 miles

east of Saigon. Six government soldiers were reported slain.

North Vietnamese forces led by tanks Nov. 2 captured the government base of Ducco in the Central Highlands 12 miles from the Cambodian border. Elsewhere in the highlands, North Vietnamese troops were said to have penetrated the hamlet of Pleiblang, less than four miles from Pleiku. In fighting near Saigon, the government reported its troops had driven Communist soldiers from four hamlets they had seized in the area and that all major highways in the capital region were open.

The Saigon command said Communist troops had carried out 142 attacks throughout the country in the 24-hour period ended at dawn Nov. 3, the largest number recorded in any one-day period in several years.

South Vietnamese troops Nov. 3 recaptured Queson in the Central Highlands. Government casualties were described as heavy, and the Communists were said to have lost 81 killed and 11 captured. Fighting erupted Nov. 3 around Anloc, 60 miles northeast of Saigon, with the government command claiming 32 North Vietnamese killed in addition to 151 slain in fighting in the same area the previous day.

Viet Cong forces Nov. 4 broke into the hamlet of Xomsuoi, 23 miles north of Saigon, but were driven out by government soldiers later in the day. The biggest ground battle of the day was reported in Kienphuong Province near the Cambodian border in the Mekong Delta, with government soldiers reported killing 35 of the enemy. A total of 194 North Vietnamese were said to have been killed in six battles fought that day.

(In anticipation of the expected ceasefire, the Saigon government had issued an order Oct. 27 for the display of the national flag to back up claims of territorial control. The emblem was required to be flown from buildings and carried by individuals as a means of identification. Failure to do so was punishable by fines. Textile factories turned over their facilities for the mass production of the banners and individuals in their homes contributed to the output.)

Communist ground gunners Nov. 5 shot down three American helicopters within 14 miles of Danang. Two Americans were killed and three wounded, according to a U.S. command announcement Nov. 7. According to the Associated Press report of the announcement, the losses raised to 8,488 the number of U.S. aircraft reported lost during the war. This included 4,851 helicopters.

Fifteen U.S. servicemen and two civilians were killed when a CH-47 helicopter crashed in the Mekong Delta near Mytho Oct. 31. Associated Press reported officers in the field said they believed the 'copter was brought down by a Communist handfired guided missile.

In the air war, U.S. B-52s spearheaded American strikes against Communist targets in both North and South Vietnam Nov. 1–7. The heaviest raids occurred Nov. 4–5 with the big aircraft dropping nearly 2.5 million pounds of bombs over both Vietnams. North Vietnamese troop concentrations were struck in Binhduong Province north of Saigon in the Nov. 4 raids. In the North, a force of B-52s augmented by fighter-bombers concentrated their attacks north of Donghoi. Heavy U.S. strikes also were directed against Communist positions just south of the demilitarized zone in Quangtri Province.

Communist stockpiles were pounded by B-52s Nov. 3 in Laos as well as in North and South Vietnam. Two-thirds of the day's raids were directed against Communist positions in the Central Highlands of South Vietnam and in provinces north and south of Saigon.

The U.S. lost its third F-111 of the war when one of the swing-wing jets failed to return to its Thailand base Nov. 7 after a mission over North Vietnam. A U.S. command spokesman said the plane's two crewman were listed as missing.

Casualty reports—The U.S. command reported Nov. 9 that 17 Americans had been killed in combat Oct. 29–Nov. 4, the highest weekly fatality rate in a month. Fifteen of the deaths had resulted from the crash of a helicopter in the Mekong Delta Oct. 31. Only three Americans had died in combat Oct. 22–28, the command had announced Nov. 2. South Vietnamese losses also had dropped in the period— 504 killed, 72 fewer than the previous week.

Cambodian rebels offered amnesty. Premier Lon Nol offered amnesty to Cambodia's Khmer Rouge rebels in a declaration broadcast Nov. 4. The Khmer Rouge, who had been fighting alongside the North Vietnamese and Viet Cong against the government, totaled about 30,000 men.

The premier offered the Khmer Rouge a choice of either joining the government army "to protect the country against other foreign invasions" or of surrendering their arms to take up a civilian life and be provided with "some land and adequate jobs." Lon Nol said there was no reason why the Khmer Rouge should continue fighting "since their goal has been attained with the ouster of Prince Norodom Sihanouk [as chief of state] and the creation of the republic."

The Cambodian leader also announced the formation of a high-level committee to carry out national reconciliation and reconstruction after a cease-fire in Indochina.

Prince Sihanouk had declared Oct. 29 that a North Vietnamese-U.S. agreement would not stop the fighting in Cambodia. He said that withdrawal of Saigon forces from Cambodia and the halt of American bombing would enable his forces to overthrow the Pnompenh government. Sihanouk made the statement on his return to Peking after three days of talks with North Vietnamese leaders in Hanoi.

Lon Nol complained Nov. 6 that the U.S. had informed him only of the broad terms, not the details, of the proposed peace agreement. He said that even now Washington was not consulting him or keeping him fully informed on the negotiations with Hanoi. The premier indicated that in his Oct. 23 meeting with Henry A. Kissinger in Pnompenh, President Nixon's national security adviser had not shown him a copy of the proposed nine-point agreement he had reached with Le Duc Tho. He implied that his first specific knowledge of the plan came from a Hanoi broadcast Oct. 26.

Cambodian Foreign Minister Long Boret Nov. 8 expressed doubt about North Vietnamese compliance with any agreement calling for Communist troops to withdraw from Cambodia. As a result, Long Boret said Pnompenh would seek two objectives: international guarantees that Cambodia's sovereignty would be respected and international supervision to prevent foreign military intervention. The foreign minister made the statement at UN headquarters where he was visiting the Cambodian delegation.

Truce argued in Paris talks. The proposed cease-fire draft agreement was the subject of heated debate in the regular session of the Paris peace talks Nov. 2.

The bitterness of the meeting was reflected in conflicting statements made to newsmen by delegates of the four sides. North Vietnamese spokesman Nguyen Thanh Le made it clear that no date had been set for a meeting between Henry A. Kissinger and Le Duc Tho to complete the peace agreement. Le asserted that the U.S. "must honor its agreements," that "everything is ready" and that the accord "can be signed in minutes."

Chief U.S. delegate William J. Porter repeated the American view that "the few remaining problems of substance, and these do exist as you know, should not be dismissed as pretexts for delay." He stated that "misunderstandings on serious points, if they exist, must be faced frankly and dealt with."

Le replied to Porter's remarks by calling them "an escalation of difficulties." He said this statement plus increased American supplies to South Vietnam and a step-up in the war constituted a "dishonest maneuver by the U.S."

South Vietnamese spokesman Nguyen Trien Dan said before a cease-fire could take place two "major, substantive" requirements must be met: total North Vietnamese withdrawal from South Vietnam and provisions for national elections before the Viet Cong was conceded any political power.

The Viet Cong chief delegate, Mrs. Nguyen Thi Binh, demanded the resignation of President Nguyen Van Thieu, even though North Vietnam had abandoned this demand in the draft agreement with the U.S.

Hanoi backs more talks with U.S. North Vietnam's chief delegate to the Paris peace talks, Xuan Thuy, Nov. 4 indicated his government's willingness to hold another meeting with the U.S. to work out a final Indochina cease-fire if Washington was "serious." In an interview with New York Times correspondent Flora Lewis, Thuy said: "At present, we are demanding that Americans honor the agreement" reached by Henry A. Kissinger, President Nixon's national security adviser, and Le Duc Tho Oct. 8 and "sign it." Thuy added: "But we do not have a rigid attitude about another meeting. The question is seriousness."

Thuy warned that if after a further meeting "the U.S. agrees and then proposes more changes, it would be very difficult to settle things." The North Vietnamese official quoted a letter sent by President Nixon to Premier Pham Van Dong Oct. 20 in which he said the President had acknowledged that "the agreement can now be considered complete" and agreed to Oct. 31 as the date for signing the accord.

Thuy took issue with Nixon's statement that the agreement required "clarification" and that some points in the Kissinger-Tho accord required clearance with South Vietnamese President Nguyen Van Thieu. Such clearance was unnecessary since there was an explicit statement in the accord that said "the U.S. side acts with the concurrence of the Saigon administration," Thuy said.

Thuy replied to Thieu's demand for withdrawal of North Vietnamese troops from South Vietnam by saying that "the U.S. had agreed to drop the question."

Thuy contradicted Kissinger's Oct. 26 statement that the accord reached Oct. 8 had been made possible because of concessions by Hanoi. Thuy declared that the U.S. had altered its stand on principal points which, if adopted by Washington in 1969, could have brought an agreement then. The North Vietnamese negotiator said that in the Kissinger-Tho talks the U.S. had reversed its position by agreeing to withdraw all its troops, advisers and military personnel from South Vietnam, "to recognize the realities of two administrations and two armies" in South Vietnam, and to recognize "the existence of the Provisional Revolutionary Government as well as of the Republic of Vietnam [Saigon]."

North Vietnam Nov. 3 criticized President Nixon's statement the previous day that "central points" remained to be cleared up before a final settlement could be signed. A Hanoi broadcast asserted that the President's remarks contradicted Kissinger's Oct. 26 assessment "that the problems to be discussed are not basic." In citing the apparent differences in these remarks, the broadcast questioned whether the U.S. had engaged in the talks "in a serious manner."

The North Vietnamese Nov. 4 accused the U.S. of further attempts to undermine the peace agreement by rushing military supplies to South Vietnam in advance of a possible cease-fire. A Hanoi broadcast said the buildup "definitely rejects Nixon's and other U.S. officials' statements that peace in Vietnam is within reach."

The Viet Cong delegation to the Paris peace talks charged Nov. 4 that the peace accord was jeopardized by American plans to set up a civilian advisory corps to replace American troops that would be pulled out of South Vietnam under terms of the agreement. "This permanent corps of military advisers disguised as civilians" would "take command of the Saigon army," the Viet Cong said. U.S. military sources in Saigon had confirmed that plans were being made to substitute civilian advisers for American troops.

The North Vietnamese Communist party newspaper Nhan Dan reported Nov. 8 that the U.S.-North Vietnamese accord provided for the release of all military and political prisoners in South Vietnam. Hanoi's version of this part of the agreement contradicted Kissinger's Oct. 26 statement that the question of the release of these prisoners "should be determined through negotiations among the South Vietnamese parties." The CP journal also charged that the Saigon regime was planning "to secretly dispose of patriots illegally kept in over 1,000 jails in South Vietnam." The newspaper said in the past two weeks Saigon police had arrested nearly 5,000 persons and shot "several hundred others."

Viet Cong-Saigon contacts—A New York Times report from Saigon Nov. 7 said that National Liberation Front officials had made preliminary contacts in recent weeks with anti-government and non-Communist leaders in South Vietnam. The discussions reportedly centered on expected truce preparations and the

political future of the country. The talks followed an invitation by the NLF to all political factions in the country to negotiate a peace agreement. The negotiations had been suggested at a Nov. 1–2 conference of the NLF's presidium. According to an account of the meeting broadcast by the Viet Cong Nov. 5, "the Front and allied forces are ready to get in touch and hold talks with all forces, political, religious organizations and individuals, at home and abroad, even those in the Saigon army and administration, who aspire to peace and national concord, to end the war soon and restore peace on the basis of the agreement." The broadcast urged continuation of the war until the U.S. signed the peace agreement.

U.S. confident of accord—Secretary of State William P. Rogers said Nov. 5 that the U.S. regarded Xuan Thuy's views Nov. 4 on prospects for further negotiations as "the sort of signal" Washington had wanted from Hanoi to indicate another meeting could take place. Rogers disclosed that the U.S. had been "in communication with the other side" through diplomatic channels and expressed confidence that "negotiations in the private channel will resume in the near future." He said it would take "more than days" to reach a final accord, possible several weeks, but that he was certain the Indochina war "is near an end." Rogers said the U.S. was rushing equipment to South Vietnam "to reassure" the South Vietnamese "that they will have the necessary supplies in the event the agreement does not work out" and the war resumes. Rogers also confirmed that the U.S. would maintain warships off Vietnam and planes in Thailand to bolster the governments in the area after a peace agreement.

Rogers clarified Nixon's Nov. 2 statement that a cease-fire settlement would apply to all of Indochina, not just Vietnam. The secretary said since the accord called for the withdrawal of foreign troops and supplies from Cambodia and Laos, "we expect that the cease-fire which will occur in South Vietnam will also occur in Cambodia and Laos within the same framework. Not necessarily simultaneously, but we hope it will be simultaneously."

Nixon confident of settlement. President Nixon, in a pre-election interview Nov. 5 (published after the election), said he was "completely confident we are going to have a settlement" of the Vietnam war. "You can bank on it," he said.

The U.S. expressed further optimism about prospects for a settlement following the 166th meeting of the Paris peace talks Nov. 9. American spokesman David Lamberton said talks with North Vietnam would be held "relatively soon." The Communist and South Vietnamese delegations were not as confident. North Vietnamese spokesman Nguyen Thanh Le said that optimistic declarations by U.S. chief delegate William J. Porter did not match the actions of the Nixon Administration. Nguyen Minh Vy, substituting for chief North Vietnamese delegate Xuan Thuy, said as he left the meeting, "Peace is not yet for tomorrow." South Vietnamese delegate Nguyen Xuan Phong said the major problems, including North Vietnamese withdrawals from South Vietnam, Cambodia and Laos, remained unresolved.

After a settlement, he said, the U.S. would continue to provide economic assistance and "some military assistance" to allies because the Communist nations would provide assistance to North Vietnam. The U.S. also would provide some economic aid to North Vietnam, he said, and "our interest is not only to bring an agreement that ends the war now but to have an influence on the events in the future, and it is much better to have a relationship with the North Vietnamese than not to have it."

In a five-minute nationwide television speech the night of Nov. 6, rebroadcast election day over the Mutual radio network, Nixon flatly stated that "we will soon reach an agreement which will end the war in Vietnam," although there were "some details that we are insisting still be worked out."

Nixon said the delay was necessary to insure "a peace that will last." The President said he believed the "overriding issue" in the campaign was "peace in Vietnam, and the broader issue of peace in the world."

McGovern hits war, morality issues. Democratic presidential candidate George McGovern concluded his campaign Nov. 3–6 with a strong attack on President Nixon's Vietnam settlement posture as a "cruel political deception."

In a paid television address from Chicago Nov. 3, McGovern charged that President Nixon only "pretended" to be near a negotiated settlement of the Vietnam war "to placate the American people." Nixon promised that peace was near, then rejected the settlement negotiated by Henry A. Kissinger, his national security adviser, with the North Vietnamese, McGovern said.

Both Nixon and South Vietnamese Premier Nguyen Van Thieu rejected the agreement accepted by Kissinger, McGovern said, and "we must draw the painful conclusion that the events of recent weeks were not a path to peace but a detour around Election Day."

The Administration's presentation of the agreement as a "major breakthrough" toward peace with some details to be resolved, McGovern said, was in reality a domestic political strategem "to create the illusion of peace" until the election. Instead of "details" being unresolved, "there has been a fatal breakdown on the central issues," McGovern said, "and now this chance for an agreement is gone."

"In a campaign marked by falsehood, sabotage, secret funds, special interest deals and criminal activity," he said, "this is the worst deceit of all."

"What we are seeing in this campaign," he said, "is the manipulation of our hope by men who know how to get power and want to keep it, but do not know what it is for. In politics, there are some things more precious than victory. One of them is truth. But these men will say anything to win."

At a news conference in Chicago Nov. 4, McGovern gave "one more warning" to the American people not to "buy this Nixon line on peace." The "details" holding up the settlement, he said, were "really the substantive issue about which this war has been fought"—the presence of North Vietnamese troops in South Vietnam and the question of a coalition government in the South.

"He has no plan to end the war," McGovern asserted. "He will not let go of General Thieu. . . . He's going to keep our troops there. He's going to keep the bombers flying. He's going to confine our prisoners to their cells in Hanoi for whatever time it takes for him to keep his friend General Thieu in office."

In another TV address from New York Nov. 5, McGovern warned that "an effort has been made to persuade the American people that the war in Vietnam is virtually over. This is untrue. The fact is that the war is now intensifying."

U.S. revises prisoner, missing list. U.S. authorities in Saigon Nov. 11 issued a revised list of U.S. military men who were missing or captured in Indochina. The total figure was placed at 1,809, including 1,266 missing and 543 known captured in North or South Vietnam or in Laos. As of Oct. 28, 473 Americans were reported missing over North Vietnam and 429 confirmed captured. A total of 496 U.S. servicemen were missing in South Vietnam and 208 were confirmed captured. In Laos, 297 Americans were missing and six confirmed captured. The Air Force had the highest number of losses of all American service branches throughout Indochina—671 missing and 271 known captured.

Soviets criticize U.S. on peace delay. The Soviet Union Nov. 12 criticized the U.S. for delaying the signing of the Indochina peace accord while shipping military supplies to Saigon in increasing quantities.

The armed forces newspaper Krasnaya Zvezda warned that "emergency delivery of arms could just put a mine under the still-unsigned agreement on the cease-fire and restoration of peace in Vietnam."

The Communist party newspaper Pravda accused the U.S. Defense Department of "intensively building up the military potential of the Saigon regime, orienting it toward 'guerrilla warfare' after the withdrawal of American troops."

Soviet Communist party leader Leonid I. Brezhnev Nov. 13 urged Washington to remove "the obstacles created by the American side literally on the eve of signing" the peace accord. Brezhnev indicated that Moscow was willing to help achieve a settlement, saying "We strive to facilitate the end of the war."

Chinese Premier Chou En-lai Nov. 10 questioned the Soviet Union's sincerity in wanting peace in Indochina. He said: "The Soviet Union has publicly expressed the wish to see the war in Vietnam come to an end. But it is very difficult to differentiate between their true and false words."

U.S. intensifies raids on North. U.S. planes, including B-52 bombers, carried out heavy raids on North Vietnam below the 20th Parallel Nov. 9–14 in a concerted effort to interdict the shipment of supplies to Communist forces in South Vietnam before a cease-fire. More than 1,290 strikes were flown in the six-day period. Air strikes on the North had averaged about 110 a day immediately after the U.S. had halted raids above the 20th Parallel Oct. 22.

One of the heaviest bombing raids of the war over the North was carried out Nov. 14 with more than 300 tactical strikes by fighter-bombers and B-52s flown in an area from about 20 miles south of Thanhhoa down to the demilitarized zone.

To counter the increased air strikes, U.S. sources reported Nov. 11 that North Vietnam had moved more heavy antiaircraft guns into the southern panhandle. At the same time, the U.S. command reported Nov. 11 the downing of three Navy A-47 bombers by Communist aircraft over the North in the previous 24 hours. Two pilots were reported rescued and one missing.

In American air activity over South Vietnam, the U.S. command reported Nov. 9 that B-52s had set a record for concentrated bombing in a single province in one day. About 70 of the planes had dropped nearly 2,000 tons of bombs on northern Quangtri Province.

Communist troop pullback reported—Several North Vietnamese battalions had withdrawn from the area near the demilitarized zone and from the provinces around Saigon and Communist forces had reduced their attacks throughout South Vietnam, U.S. and South Vietnamese military sources reported Nov. 14. Clashes had tapered off considerably in the South between Nov. 9 and 14.

In fighting Nov. 14 only 71 Communist-initiated attacks were reported, compared with an average of more than 100 a day at the end of October and the first week of November. Hanoi's forces, however, increased the shelling around Quangtri city for the first time in three weeks, firing about 1,000 rounds of artillery, rockets and mortars.

Laotian airport bombed. Communist forces Nov. 13 bombed the airport of the royal Laotian capital of Luang Prabang for the first time in nearly a year. Rockets damaged two T-28 fighter-bombers and three light observation planes, a military spokesman reported.

Government troops had been forced to abandon a position eight miles southeast of Luang Prabang Nov. 12 in the face of heavy enemy shelling.

A force of about 500 North Vietnamese Nov. 12 launched a heavy attack on Thakhek on the Mekong River bordering Thailand, but withdrew after some fighting inside the town. Elsewhere in southern Laos, government soldiers had completed the capture of Dong Hene Nov. 11 after nearly a week of fighting. The town had been controlled by the Communists since 1971.

Several battalions of the U.S.-supported Meo tribal army were forced to withdraw from the southern edge of the Plaine des Jarres Nov. 13 following a heavy North Vietnamese shelling and ground attack. A U.S. military spokesman in Vientiane reported Nov. 15 that the Meos had retreated after suffering "moderate" losses. The North Vietnamese force of 3,500 men had been pressing the attack in the area since Nov. 4.

Government forces recaptured the town of Kengkok from Communist troops Nov. 2. Two burned bodies found in the town were those of American women missionaries, the U.S. embassy in Vientiane reported Nov. 3. They were identified as Evelyn Anderson, 25, Quincy, Mich., and Beatrice Kosin, 35, Fort Washakie, Wyo. Both were members of the Christian Missions in Many Lands, the American branch of the Swiss Brethren. The two women had been taken prisoner by the North Vietnamese and tied to posts in a house that was later burned.

U.S.-led raids reported—The St. Louis Post-Dispatch reported Nov. 6 that U.S. Army Special Forces men had led groups of Cambodians, Laotians and Vietnamese in commando raids into Laos earlier in 1972. Some of the attacks involved the assassinations of leading North Vietnamese military officers in Laos and sabotage operations, the newspaper said. Its accounts were based on interviews with four American officers who acknowledged participating in the operations. The Post-Dispatch had reported Nov. 5 that regular U.S. Army troops had taken part in intelligence-gathering raids in Laos as late as December 1971.

Peace talks remain deadlocked—Laotian peace talks remained deadlocked after two more sessions in Vientiane Nov. 7 and 14.

Pathet Lao spokesman Soth Phetrasy said after the Nov. 14 meeting that progress could be accomplished if the government accepted certain Pathet procedural demands, one of which included the removal of the government flag from the conference room. The day's conference was devoted to a dispute by both sides over the five-point peace plan advanced by the Pathet Lao in 1970.

Laotian Premier Souvanna Phouma had conferred in Vientiane Nov. 10 with Phoumi Vongvichit, ranking member of the Pathet Lao delegation.

U.S. speeds arms buildup. U.S. military officials in Saigon reported Nov. 14 that the American pre-cease-fire arms buildup of South Vietnam's forces would be completed in the next week or two. Saigon had received 31 amphibious vehicles from the U.S. Nov. 13 in the latest shipment of equipment. The air force buildup was completed with the South Vietnamese having received about 30 C-130 transports, 90 A-37 light attack jets, 120 F-5 fighters and A-1 attack planes and scores of helicopters. The U.S. also had airlifted tons of ammunition, spare parts and communication equipment.

(Japanese students and workers Nov. 8 had attempted to prevent 13 trailers carrying 51 M-48 U.S. tanks for South Vietnam from reaching a Yokohama pier. The demonstrators clashed with police over a 30-mile route as they tried to stop the American supply convoy from reaching the docks. Eighty-eight of the protesters were arrested. The cargo ship carrying the tanks left Yokohama for South Vietnam Nov. 10.)

South Vietnamese get Longbinh base—
The U.S. Nov. 11 formally transferred its Longbinh army base to South Vietnam. The 15,000 acre complex, 16 miles north of Saigon, once housed 30,000 American troops and was currently occupied by 28 South Vietnamese army units.

Meanwhile, the American troops withdrawal continued to near the Dec. 1 deadline of bringing the U.S. force in the country down to the target minimum of 27,000 men. A total of 1,100 men had left the country the previous week, reducing the American force to 31,000 men, the U.S. command reported Nov. 13.

South Korea's force of more than 30,-000 men had ended their combat operations and retired to rear bases, ROK headquarters in Saigon reported Nov. 8.

Cambodians recapture district town. Communist forces Nov. 1 captured Trapeang Kraleng 35 miles west of Pnompenh, but Cambodian troops retook the town Nov. 15. In seizing Trapeang Kraleng, the Communists had temporarily cut Route 4, which connected the capital with the country's deep water port of Kompong Som.

Government troops Nov. 16 reoccupied the last remaining stretch of Route 4 about 40 miles southwest of Pnompenh. The road had been closed for two weeks, halting the flow of imported food and U.S. military supplies to the capital.

Cambodian troops were reported Nov. 17 to have reopened another road, Route 5, leading from Pnompenh to Battambang Province in the northwest. The road had been cut in mid-August, resulting in shortages of rice and rioting in Pnompenh.

In other military developments, Cambodian rebel forces Nov. 7 shelled government positions along a 35-mile stretch of Route 2. The heaviest artillery assault was directed against the provincial capital of Takeo, 55 miles south of Pnompenh, killing at least four persons.

U.S. aircraft Nov. 9 bombed Communist positions near Route 4 in an area 14 miles south of Pnompenh.

Cambodian troops Nov. 11 reoccupied the battered town of Oudong, 20 miles northwest of Pnompenh.

Sihanouk opposes truce—Peking radio reported Nov. 11 that the leader of anti-government forces in Cambodia, Khieu Samphan, had rejected any compromise or cease-fire with the Lon Nol government. Khieu, who also was defense minister of Prince Norodom Sihanouk's government in exile, declared, "Our stand is to drive out United States aggressors, annihilate the Pnompenh traitors and liberate the whole country and people."

U.S. Vietnam aide resigns. Willard E. Chambers resigned his post as a senior official of the U.S. pacification program in South Vietnam, it was reported Nov. 15.

Chambers, assistant deputy for CORDS (civil operations and rural development support) in Military Region I in the five northern provinces, quit to protest what he called maladministration of the program. He asserted that "an entrenched bureaucracy made up of the American civil service and the Vietnam civil service" made it difficult for the pacification agency to attain its goals of "a social, economic and military revolution."

U.S.–North Vietnam talks to resume. The U.S. and North Vietnam were prepared to resume further discussions in Paris Nov. 20 to resolve remaining differences that had delayed the signing of the nine-point Indochina settlement negotiated in a draft in October. The White House announced the date for resumption of the talks Nov. 17.

Le Duc Tho, North Vietnam's chief private negotiator, arrived in Paris Nov. 17 to await the arrival of his American counterpart Henry A. Kissinger. Kissinger had conferred with President Nixon Nov. 14 in preparation for his departure to the French capital.

Hanoi's chief delegate to the Paris peace talks, Xuan Thuy, declared at the Nov. 16 session that Tho would not discuss any modification of the draft agreement with Kissinger. He urged the U.S. to sign the accord and denounced the intensified American bombing of North Vietnam.

Mrs. Nguyen Thi Binh, the Viet Cong's chief delegate, insisted on two conditions not included in the draft accord—a halt to American military aid to South Vietnam before a cease-fire and the resignation of South Vietnamese President Nguyen Van Thieu.

South Vietnam's deputy delegate, Nguyen Xuan Phong, expressed opposition to the cease-fire agreement, arguing that "it will not produce a complete and definite cessation of hostilities" unless it applied to Cambodia and Laos.

Kissinger's deputy, Gen. Alexander M. Haig Jr., had met with Thieu in Saigon Nov. 10–11 to discuss "the progress of the peace negotiations and make a general assessment of the situation in Vietnam." Haig reportedly had given Thieu a personal letter from Nixon, urging him to accept the cease-fire plan. Tin Song, the Saigon newspaper which reflected Thieu's views, said Nov. 10 that the president had informed Haig that day that any peace agreement that did not call for North Vietnam's withdrawal from South Vietnam "would be considered as of no validity."

Before returning to Washington, Haig met with Cambodian Premier Lon Nol in Pnompenh Nov. 12 and with South Korean President Chung Hee Park in Seoul Nov. 13 to brief the two Asian leaders on the peace negotiations.

South Vietnamese Foreign Minister Tran Van Lam said Nov. 13 that Haig's visit had brought the U.S. and his government "closer together on a peace settlement." But some problems required "clarification" before Saigon's acceptance, he said. Lam then reiterated Saigon's three principal demands—North Vietnamese troop withdrawal, reestablishment of the demilitarized zone and assurances that the accord would not create a form of coalition government. Haig returned to Washington Nov. 13.

(The U.S. State Department announced Nov. 15 that Canada, Hungary, Indonesia and Poland had agreed in principle to join the proposed international commission that would supervise the Vietnam cease-fire when it came into effect.)

Pentagon honors newsmen. Defense Secretary Melvin R. Laird dedicated a Pentagon memorial Nov. 21 honoring U.S. war correspondents killed while covering World War II and the Korean and Vietnam wars.

Laird designated that section of the Pentagon housing the press room as "Correspondents Corridor." Pentagon officials converted part of that area into an alcove in which the names of 36 newsmen killed in World War II, 8 in Korea and 16 in Vietnam were listed.

Laotians battle for Saravane. The southern Laotian town of Saravane was the focus of sharp fighting from mid-November to early December between government troops and North Vietnamese and Pathet Lao forces.

A force of about 1,000 North Vietnamese soldiers Nov. 14 drove government troops out of Saravane, which had been reoccupied by the Laotians in mid-October. After a week of heavy fighting, government forces were reported Nov. 22 to have moved back into Saravane. Communist forces launched counterattacks on government positions around the town and were reported Dec. 1 to have retaken it. U.S. officials reported Dec. 4 that Laotian government troops struck back and drove the occupying North Vietnamese soldiers to the northern tip of Saravane, killing 30.

In other action in southern Laos, a North Vietnamese-Pathet Lao force was reported Nov. 27 to have surrounded the provincial capital of Thakhek. The government garrison there had come under heavy attack for the previous two weeks.

Peace talks stalled—Further peace talks between government and Pathet Lao representatives in Vientiane Nov. 21 and 28 produced no results.

The negotiations remained deadlocked over the procedural issues of the Laotian flag's presence in the meeting room, to which the Pathet Lao objected, and Pathet Lao insistence that the Vientiane delegation had no right to call itself representatives of a Laotian government.

Pathet Lao chief delegate Soth Phetrasy said after the Nov. 21 session that "We shall never acknowledge the legality of the so-called Vientiane government or its so-called National Assembly."

A government spokesman said Vientiane had made two important concessions to the Pathet Lao at the conference: it had agreed to negotiate with them as equals, not as rebels; and the government no longer insisted that National Assembly members sit in on the talks as observers.

The issue of North Vietnamese troop withdrawals from Laos raised at the Nov. 28 meeting further widened the gulf between the two sides. The Pathet Lao insisted that North Vietnamese troops remain in the country, while the U.S. should cease its bombings of Laos and pull its troops out. The government demanded that Hanoi take its troops out of Laos.

Laotian Premier Souvanna Phouma said Nov. 22 that he had received a U.S. pledge to continue the bombing of Communist targets in his country if a Vietnam war settlement did not apply to his country. The bombing would continue "as long as the North Vietnamese are here," Souvanna said.

Thieu forming new political party. President Nguyen Van Thieu was reported Nov. 17 in the process of completing the formation of a new mass political party to compete with the Communists in the period after a cease-fire.

The new grouping, called the Democracy party, was to have a membership of 100,000 that would include dozens of generals, most of the country's province and district chiefs, and village and hamlet officials. Four or five of South Vietnam's political parties were reportedly planning to join the organization.

Thieu had started forming the Democracy party in 1971, but ordered its formation completed as soon as possible in view of the imminent Indochina peace settlement.

In another action aimed at preparing the country for a cease-fire, the Saigon government Nov. 21 announced a campaign to establish "peoples' anti-Communist political struggle committees."

"When the shooting war is over," a Saigon broadcast said, "another struggle will begin and the South Vietnamese people will have to fight hard, if they still wish to live in freedom and democracy."

The committees were to be made up of thousands of students, junior army officers, military school cadets, and government officials and militiamen. The committees were to be elected by local people and their object would be to "guide them in anti-Communist struggle activities" with the assistance of the Information Ministry and Political Warfare Department of the army, the broadcast said. The statement said 27 "mobile training teams" were to be formed in the Saigon area to help create the committees, conduct meetings and "lend a hand in tracking down and foiling the Communists' acts of sabotage." According to the broadcast, Saigon Mayor Do Kien Nhieu, a general, had ordered establishment of underground "stationary teams" to coordinate and support the mobile training groups.

Hanoi radio was critical Nov. 21 of the pre-cease-fire political activities. The North Vietnamese broadcast asserted that President Thieu "is increasing his restrictive machinery by sending political cadres to the countryside [the Mekong Delta] . . . in order to break up the struggle movement of our people." The broadcast said the government's mobile teams were being sent into the Saigon area "supposedly to propagate Thieu's latest doctrine but actually to spy on all the people."

The South Vietnamese Senate had approved a resolution by a 36-8 vote Nov. 20 supporting Thieu's opposition to the U.S.-North Vietnamese draft peace accord unless it contained the following three conditions: withdrawal of all North Vietnamese troops from South Vietnam, re-establishment of the demilitarized zone and Saigon government approval.

Saigon troops widen Quangtri control. South Vietnamese troops gained more ground in Quangtri Province in sharp fighting against the North Vietnamese Nov. 21–29 despite heavy Communist mortar and artillery attacks. U.S. B-52s provided support to the government offensive throughout the nine-day period, dropping tons of bombs on Communist troop concentrations in the province.

Government troops suffered 17 killed during a 24-hour period ended Nov. 22 after being subjected to 1,500 rounds of North Vietnamese shelling. The Saigon forces were struck by another 1,400 rounds Nov. 25 as they inched their way toward the Qua Viet estuary near Quangtri city. Government paratroops pushed to within a mile of the estuary Nov. 27. Fighting was sharply reduced as bad weather closed in on the battle area Nov. 29.

Elsewhere in South Vietnam, the Saigon command reported Nov. 23 the killing of 300 North Vietnamese in three days of fighting in the Central Highlands, 15–20 miles southwest of Pleiku. Government losses in that period were listed at 15 dead. Further fighting flared in the Pleiku area Nov. 24–25. North Vietnamese assaults on two government positions near the Thangiao camp both days were repulsed, the Saigon command reported.

U.S. loses first B-52 of war. A U.S. B-52 bomber crashed while returning to its base in Thailand Nov. 22 after being struck by a surface-to-air missile during a mission near Vinh, North Vietnam. It was the first public admission by the U.S. command of the loss of a B-52 to enemy ground fire in the Indochina war. (At least 10 of the big bombers, however, had crashed because of reported operational failures.) Six of the plane's crewmen bailed out near Nakhon Phanom, in eastern Thailand, about 400 miles from the base at Utapo. Two were injured.

A second B-52 was damaged in the same missile attack. The mission around Vinh was the largest B-52 strike against North Vietnamese supply positions. The B-52 raids, increasing in intensity since the drop in tactical fighter raids Nov. 17, continued through Nov. 28.

At least 11 other U.S. planes had been lost over North and South Vietnam, Thailand and Laos between Nov. 20 and 28. The U.S. command said 12 airmen were rescued, four were killed and three were missing. One of the lost planes was an F-111, which was downed Nov. 21 just above the demilitarized zone in North Vietnam. It was the fourth F-111 lost since its return to combat at the end of September.

In one of the worst accidental air attacks of the war, six U.S. aircraft mistakenly dropped 500-ton bombs on a populated center 15 miles south of Danang Nov. 28, killing 21 civilians and wounding 30.

No U.S. fatalities. The U.S. command reported Nov. 30 that no American soldiers had been killed or died of non-hostile causes in the Indochina war Nov. 19–25. Three Americans were listed as missing or captured and 11 were wounded during that period. It was the first time since January 1965, the start of major U.S. involvement in the war, that the weekly casualty summary included no American deaths.

U.S. weekly losses in the past three months had averaged almost five combat deaths and a little more than 2 non-combat fatalities.

South Vietnamese casualties in the Nov. 19–25 period were given as 480 killed and 1,821 wounded, compared with 395 killed and 1,373 wounded the previous week. North Vietnamese and Viet Cong losses were estimated at 1,896 killed, an increase of 276 over the Nov. 12–18 period.

1972 war losses listed—According to figures made public by the Saigon government and the U.S. Defense Department Nov. 27, almost 8,000 South Vietnamese and 280 American troops had been killed in January–October. North Vietnamese and Viet Cong battle fatalities in the 10-month period were said to total 117,255, compared with a previous high of 156,954 killed in the same period in 1969. The Saigon authorities said October had been the bloodiest month of 1972 for the Communists with deaths totaling 9,692, up from the previous high of 8,747 killed in October 1969.

Kissinger-Tho talks resume. Henry A. Kissinger of the U.S. and Le Duc Tho of North Vietnam resumed private discussions Nov. 20 to work out a final Indochina peace agreement. The two men conferred again Nov. 21 and further talks were scheduled to resolve the remaining differences over the nine-point accord drafted in October.

The latest Kissinger-Tho negotiations, the 21st in their series of private talks, were held in the Paris suburb of Gif-sur-Yvette. Each session lasted about five hours. For the first time since the start of the private talks, Kissinger was briefing South Vietnamese Ambassador Pham Dang Lam daily. The North Vietnamese said they were consulting with chief Viet Cong delegate Mrs. Nguyen Thi Binh before and after each day's session.

On arriving in Paris Nov. 19, Kissinger had said that President Nixon, with whom he had conferred the previous day, "has sent me here for what he hopes will be the final phase of the negotiations to end the war in Indochina." The President's adviser said his "instructions are to stay for as long as is useful and to conduct discussions in a spirit of conciliation, moderation and goodwill."

In announcing Kissinger's new travel plans, Nov. 17, the White House had said that after the forthcoming sessions in Paris "there will be further consultations with South Vietnam, and perhaps with North Vietnam."

A North Vietnamese communique issued after the Nov. 21 meeting accused the U.S. of having conducted "savage" air attacks against North Vietnam Nov. 1–19, destroying thousands of homes and causing many civilian casualties. The statement said that during that period 4,000 fighter-bombers and 450 B-52s had dropped 22,300 tons of bombs on North Vietnam's southern panhandle.

U.S. completes arms buildup. The U.S. Defense Department announced Nov. 20 that it had virtually completed the buildup of emergency arms shipments to South Vietnam's armed forces and that only "a few things" were on the way.

Department spokesman Jerry W. Friedheim said most of the deliveries had ended and that American military aid would now revert to regular levels. The shipments during the three-week period included about 600 planes and helicopters. This increased South Vietnam's air force to more than 2,000 planes, making it the fourth largest in the world. Other material, sent largely by airlift, included tanks, armored personnel carriers and artillery.

Weather curbs U.S. air strikes. Bad weather curtailed American bombing raids over North Vietnam Nov. 18–20. Only 30–40 strikes were flown during each of those three days, compared with more than 200 a day on the average since early in November. The drop in the number of strikes also was attributed to the diversion of American air support to Saigon troops fighting in the northern part of South Vietnam.

Prior to the forced bombing curbs, U.S. planes Nov. 15 had carried out 270 strikes below North Vietnam's 20th Parallel, raising to 1,560 the number of tactical strikes reported by the American command since Nov. 9. Pilots said they had destroyed or damaged 68 ammunition trucks during the day's raid on a depot near Quangkhe, 65 miles north of the demilitarized zone.

The southern panhandle was struck Nov. 16 by 140 fighter-bomber missions and 24 strikes flown by 24 B-52s. The B-52s reportedly pounded war stockpiles within 10 miles of the 20th Parallel.

In ground action in South Vietnam, the heaviest fighting centered around Quangtri city, with Saigon forces reportedly killing 59 Communist troops in one engagement Nov. 15. An additional 41 troops were apparently killed by air strikes. Government losses were placed at five killed and 41 wounded.

Saigon troops attempting to expand their control of territory north and east of Quangtri city encountered heavy resistance Nov. 17, the Saigon command reported. The South Vietnamese were subjected to 1,200 rounds of artillery, rocket and mortar fire. Government forces around Quangtri came under more enemy fire Nov. 18. B-52s provided strong support to government troops around Quangtri, dropping 1,200 tons of bombs on North Vietnamese positions during a 24-hour period ending Nov. 20.

Scattered ground action was reported around Saigon Nov. 20.

Kissinger-Tho talks recessed. The U.S. and North Vietnam concluded their latest round of private Indochina peace talks near Paris Nov. 25 and agreed to resume the discussions Dec. 4. The 21st in the series of secret meetings between Henry A. Kissinger and Le Duc Tho had started Nov. 20.

Although neither side provided public assessment of the latest meetings, the North Vietnamese Communist party newspaper Nhan Dan Nov. 25 accused the U.S. of "trying a 180-degree turn in demanding reconsideration of the entire problem, trying to start all over from the beginning." The newspaper said that in response to South Vietnam's opposition, the U.S. had presented new proposals at the talks that were less generous than those contained in the nine-point draft accord made public Oct. 26. Nhan Dan specifically demanded "respect for the military clauses" of the original agreement.

A North Vietnamese communique issued after the Nov. 24 meeting accused the U.S. of having carried out "unprecedented" air strikes on North Vietnam, which it said reflected "a lack of desire to settle the Vietnamese problem peacefully." The statement assailed the U.S. for "indefensible pretexts to delay a signature" on the truce agreement.

Kissinger flew back to the U.S. Nov. 25 and held a series of briefing sessions with President Nixon in New York later that day and again in Washington Nov. 27. Kissinger held a separate meeting with Secretary of State William P. Rogers Nov. 27 to discuss details of the proposed four-power international supervisory team that would observe a cease-fire.

White House Press Secretary Ronald L. Ziegler said after Kissinger's meeting with Nixon Nov. 25 that the President was "confident that we will achieve the right kind of settlement." Ziegler cautioned against speculation that the recess in the talks reflected an impasse. He said the suspension of the meetings "gives us time to consult with the South Vietnamese."

International truce team problem— Kissinger had interrupted his talks with Tho Nov. 22 to fly to Brussels and confer with Indonesian President Suharto and Foreign Minister Adam Malik on their country's role in the proposed four-nation international truce supervisory body. The discussion followed Viet Cong and North Vietnamese objections to Indonesia's participation because of its alleged partiality. The CP journal Nhan Dan charged Nov. 21 that Indonesia was supporting "the U.S.-Thieu clique" and that Jakarta's "actions actually reflect sympathy for the aggressors and their henchmen." The U.S. State Department had asserted Nov. 20 that Hanoi had agreed to Indonesian participation in the truce force.

U.S. officials acknowledged Nov. 22 that although Indonesia and the three other nations had agreed in principle to act as cease-fire supervisors—Hungary, Canada and Poland—it seemed improbable that they would provide more than a token force at the time of a cease-fire. All four nations were said to have expressed misgivings about the mission.

Canada's external affairs minister, Mitchell W. Sharp, expressed reservations about his country's involvement on the truce team at a meeting with Secretary of State Rogers in New York Nov. 20. Returning to Ottawa Nov. 21, Sharp said he had told Rogers that Canada's participation depended on the following conditions: the supervisory commission and its method of operations must be acceptable to all four members; there must be some international authority for the commission to report to; there must be a workable formula for observing and reporting on truce compliance; the commission must have complete freedom of movement to investigate the keeping of the peace; and a terminal date must be set for the commission's activities.

Sharp told a news conference Nov. 22 that Canada's only commitment thus far was to permit 20 of its members now serving on the old International Control Commission in Saigon to act as observers for the new commission in the first month of a cease-fire. Canada would consent to send a larger contingent only if all four parties to the dispute—the U.S., North and South Vietnam and the Viet Cong—agreed on details of the supervisory force, Sharp said.

Nixon meets with Thieu's aide—President Nixon met at the White House Nov. 29 and 30 with Nguyen Phu Duc, President Nguyen Van Thieu's foreign policy adviser, to discuss details of the peace negotiations. A U.S. official said after the meetings that the President had urged the Saigon government to take a more positive position on proposals to end the war.

Nixon discussed the Indochina peace settlement plan Nov. 30 with the Joint Chiefs of Staff, who were said to have approved the terms of the proposal.

The White House announced Nov. 30 that there would be no further public announcements on American troop withdrawals from South Vietnam now that the number of men had been reduced to 27,000. Defense Department sources said there might be some additional pullouts in the coming weeks, but that most of these men would stay until a final agreement was reached.

At another session of the semipublic four-party peace talks in Paris Nov. 30, chief U.S. delegate William H. Porter told the Communist delegates that Nixon intended "to permit no avoidable delay" in ending the conflict.

Kissinger, Tho resume talks. Henry A. Kissinger and Le Duc Tho resumed their private Indochina peace talks near Paris Dec. 4 after a nine-day recess. The Dec. 5 meeting between the American and North Vietnamese negotiators was canceled at the U.S.' request, but discussions were held again Dec. 6–8. No official statements were issued as to whether progress was being made in working out a final cease-fire agreement under terms drawn up in a draft accord in October.

A New York Times dispatch from Washington Dec. 5 said Administration officials reported that Kissinger had queried the North Vietnamese about U.S. intelligence accounts that Hanoi planned to conceal much of its army in South Vietnam in Viet Cong units after a cease-fire. The officials declined to say, however, whether the raising of this question had anything to do with the cancellation of the Dec. 5 meeting.

Another session of the four-party formal peace conference was held in Paris Dec. 7. The Communist delegates said the discussions were at an "impasse" and renewed their demand that the U.S. sign the draft accord without alterations. Nguyen Minh Vy, North Vietnam's deputy chief delegate, accused the U.S. of having "threatened to escalate the war."

North Vietnam's Communist party newspaper Nhan Dan had warned Dec. 3 that if Washington attempted to alter the October draft accord, the U.S.' "real intention would be nothing other than to scrap all the commitments already made in order to prolong its war of aggression in Vietnam and Indochina."

U.S. aides prepare for truce. U.S. State Department officials reported Dec. 7 that the agency was preparing to send 100 Foreign Service officials to South Vietnam once a cease-fire went into effect. All the aides had served in Vietnam. Their function would be to observe the truce and to provide Washington with accurate reports on postwar military and political developments in the country. The truce data might also be transmitted to the international supervisory teams that were to observe the cease-fire, the officials said.

The stand-by orders were issued Dec. 6 to 50 Foreign Service officers now serving in embassies abroad and an equal number stationed in Washington. In Vietnam they were to be assigned for a six-month period to the U.S. embassy in Saigon and to consulate-generals that were to be established in Danang, Nhatrang, Bienhoa and Cantho, where the U.S. operated major aid missions.

Saigon airport shelled. Communist forces shelled Saigon's Tansonnhut airport and nearby areas Dec. 6, killing eight South Vietnamese and one American. Two U.S. helicopters were heavily damaged. Allied military spokesmen said the Communists fired 53 rounds of 122-mm rockets, the worst attack on Tansonnhut in four years.

A force of 1,500 government troops struck out for the area where the attack was believed to have originated. Ground fighting was later reported seven miles north of Saigon. U.S. planes also sought out the North Vietnamese attackers, dropping bombs within 10 miles of Tansonnhut airport.

Among other military developments:

South Vietnam lost its seventh general of the war Dec. 1 in a plane crash on the central coast northeast of Saigon. The accident also killed four other Vietnamese and two American employes of the U.S. Agency of International Development. The aircraft was attempting to land in bad weather at Tuyhoa air base. The dead officer was identified as Maj. Gen. Tran Thanh Phong, deputy commander of Military Region II.

The South Vietnamese offensive in Quangtri Province bogged down Dec. 2 because of heavy monsoon weather. Government troops were seeking to extend a front running south from the capital of Quangtri city. U.S. B-52s struck suspected Communist troop concentrations Dec. 1-2 around the government lines and just below the demilitarized zone to the north. The B-52s continued to hit at North Vietnamese troops and staging areas in the province Dec. 4 to prevent Communist reinforcements from reaching the battle zone. Heavy fighting had flared up in Quangtri Province Dec. 3, with Saigon reporting that its troops killed 37 North Vietnamese in a 10-hour battle northeast of Quangtri city. The command claimed 24 other North Vietnamese were killed south of the city where government forces were trying to push enemy troops back into the foothills.

In the Central Highlands, government and North Vietnamese troops fought sharp skirmishes Dec. 3-4 around the government base camp of Ngotrang, six miles northwest of Kontum city. Saigon claimed 62 North Vietnamese and two government soldiers were killed in the two days of fighting. Communist artillery had driven 300 government troops from a defensive position eight miles southwest of Kontum city Dec. 2.

In another highland clash Dec. 5, Saigon claimed that 33 North Vietnamese were killed in Pleiku Province. Government losses were put at six dead.

American air strikes on North Vietnam's southern panhandle continued, with B-52s carrying out most of the raids Dec. 1-6 against supply roads and other targets.

Cambodians lift Trapeang siege. Cambodian reinforcements Dec. 8 lifted a one-day Communist siege of Trapeang Kraleng, the town which government troops had recaptured Nov. 15. The Cambodian soldiers broke through a ring of Communist forces around the garrison 37 miles from Pnompenh, rescuing two trapped battalions.

In other fighting in the area Dec. 8, Communist forces captured a 2½ mile stretch of Route 4 east of Trapeang Kraleng. But three government battalions pushed through Route 4 in the same vicinity Dec. 9, severing the Communists' hold on the vital road linking Pnompenh with the seaport of Kompong Som.

In previous developments, Cambodian targets came under three shelling attacks. Two rockets struck a government building in Pnompenh Dec. 1, causing extensive damage. The area around the city's international airport had been hit by eight North Vietnamese rockets Nov. 29 wounding eight persons. The provincial capital of Kompong Cham, 70 miles northeast of Pnompenh, was shelled by North Vietnamese and Viet Cong gunners Nov. 30. Two civilians were killed.

Combat casualties. The U.S. command reported Dec. 7 that no Americans had been killed in combat Nov. 26–Dec. 2. It was the second week that no battle deaths were reported, but three Americans had died of noncombat causes that week, one was missing or captured and seven were wounded. Total allied casualties for the war as reported by the American and South Vietnamese commands: U.S.—45,-914 killed in action, 10,290 deaths from non-combat causes, 303,914 wounded and 1,706 missing or captured. South Vietnamese—160,711 killed and 427,922 wounded.

Continued troop withdrawals from South Vietnam since October reduced the American force in the country to 25,200, the U.S. command announced Dec. 11. This was 1,800 fewer men than President Nixon's authorization of 27,000.

U.S. planes bomb DMZ area. U.S. B-52s bombed North Vietnamese supply routes and troop concentrations in and near the demilitarized zone Dec. 7–12. U.S. fighter-bombers carried out tactical strike missions on North Vietnam in the same period, attacking further north in the country's panhandle. Hanoi radio claimed two U.S. planes were downed over the North Dec. 9.

B-52s carried out heavy raids in the Saigon area Dec. 11, operating in an arc 23–48 miles northwest and northeast of the capital. It was the heaviest air assault in the region since Oct. 6.

In the ground war, Saigon reported 244 Communist troops were killed in 82 enemy-initiated attacks in 24 hours that ended Dec. 8. Sixteen government soldiers were reported slain.

Government paratroopers reported killing 30 North Vietnamese near Quangtri city Dec. 9. Seven paratroopers were killed.

Communist attacks across South Vietnam diminished sharply Dec. 10 with only 58 enemy assaults reported. In one of the engagements, government forces killed 53 North Vietnamese in repulsing a sharp attack south of Quangtri city. Another 40 Communists were reported killed around the Quangtin Province capital of Tamky. Sixteen government militiamen and their dependents were killed in a Viet Cong attack in the Mekong Delta.

Acting on the tip of a defector Dec. 11, government forces killed 87 of about 500 North Vietnamese troops infiltrating from eastern Cambodia. The Communist force was intercepted 42 miles northwest of Saigon.

In a further report on the Communists' Dec. 6 shelling of Saigon's Tansonnhut air base, the Saigon command said Dec. 8 the attack had been launched by 145 North Vietnamese from a spot seven miles north of Saigon. The command said 54 of the attackers and nine South Vietnamese were killed.

Several thousand North Vietnamese troops were reported by U.S. sources Dec. 13 to have moved through mountain passes from North Vietnam to the Ho Chi Minh Trail in Laos. The Communist units, with 100 tanks, were being struck repeatedly by U.S. aircraft, the sources said. Another source reported that North Vietnam, in an apparent attempt to replenish its losses, had moved almost 100 tanks and about 8,000 fresh troops into Quangtri Province earlier in December.

Soviet-North Vietnam aid pact renewed. The Soviet Union agreed to continue "large-scale deliveries" of military and economic supplies to North Vietnam in 1973 under a new agreement signed in Moscow Dec. 9.

The accord did not mention specific items, but said the Soviet Union would provide large quantities of "goods, equipment and other property of great significance for the development of North Vietnam's economy and will give necessary assistance in the strengthening of its defense capacity."

The economic-military aid talks had started Nov. 28. The pact was signed by Deputy Premiers Vladimir N. Novikov of the Soviet Union and Le Thanh Nghi of North Vietnam.

North Vietnam-China aid pact. An agreement under which China would provide North Vietnam with continued economic and military assistance in 1973 was signed in Peking Nov. 26 by North Vietnamese Deputy Premier Le Thanh Nghi and Chinese Deputy Premier Li Hsien-nien. No details of the pact were made public.

Saigon may free political POWs. South Vietnamese Foreign Minister Tran Van Lam said Dec. 7 that his government "would not refuse to do whatever can be done to free the American prisoners of war," including a Saigon agreement to release political prisoners held by South Vietnam, to bring about an acceptable peace accord. Lam conceded that it would be "very difficult" for Saigon to put its signature to the accord in its present form, but he did not rule out President Nguyen Van Thieu's eventual approval, either indirectly or by signing. The foreign minister disclosed that his government had been trying to persuade the U.S. "to press the Communists, to wring more concessions out of them. I hope Kissinger is going to succeed." Lam reiterated his government's demands that an agreement provide for withdrawal of North Vietnamese troops from South Vietnam and that the proposed National Council of Reconciliation and Concord should be given only "limited powers." He said that in its current form the body was "a government" which was "very dangerous" to South Vietnam.

(In Washington, President Nixon had met for a third consecutive day Dec. 1 with Nguyen Phu Duc, Thieu's aide, to press Saigon to accept the agreement. An Administration official said Duc had conveyed Thieu's fears of a truce that would leave at least some North Vietnamese troops in the South. The meeting was attended by Kissinger, who flew to Paris Dec. 3 for the resumption of his meetings with Le Duc Tho.)

Viet Cong say U.S. raises new issues. The U.S. was accused by the Viet Cong of raising new points in the Kissinger-Tho talks that were "not at all purely technical issues." In an interview published Dec. 8 by Agence France-Presse, Mrs. Nguyen Thi Binh, head of the Viet Cong delegation to the four-party talks, asserted that the U.S. "wants to reopen the questions of principle, such as withdrawal of North Vietnamese troops, restoration of the demilitarized zone and the formula for a three-component National Council of Concord." She warned against introduction of these issues in the talks, saying, "There will either be an agreement now or the war will be prolonged for a long time."

Mrs. Binh warned that American prisoners might not be released unless political prisoners held in South Vietnam also were given their freedom. She insisted that the U.S.-North Vietnamese draft agreement of October provided for release of all prisoners—military and political—and that the problem was one of difference of interpretation. The Communists claimed Saigon held 300,000 political prisoners, but not all of them were said to be Viet Cong.

Hanoi backs Canada as truce observer. The Canadian Foriegn Ministry disclosed Dec. 12 that North Vietnam had endorsed Canada as a member of the proposed four-nation supervisory team that would observe a cease-fire in Vietnam. Hanoi's views were conveyed to David Jackson, the Canadian member of the International Control Commission in Vietnam, during his visit to the North Vietnamese capital the previous week. Jackson had informed the North Vietnamese of the five conditions under which Canada would accept membership in the new truce body.

Thieu proposes truce, POW exchange. President Nguyen Van Thieu Dec. 12 proposed a truce between North and South Vietnam that would start before Christmas and continue at least until Jan. 1 and an exchange of prisoners between North and South Vietnam if Hanoi released all the American captives it held. Thieu's offer was rejected by Viet Cong spokesmen in Paris and by the U.S. Dec. 14.

Speaking to a joint session of the National Assembly, Thieu warned that "two life and death" issues remained unresolved in the Paris negotiation. He then reiterated his opposition to the peace draft's failure to provide for the withdrawal of North Vietnamese troops from his country and to the proposed National Council of Reconciliation and Concord, which the president charged would pave the way for a coalition government that would include Communists.

Thieu suggested that as a beginning, South Vietnam would "release 1,015 disabled North Vietnamese prisoners of war in exchange for the release of all American prisoners held by North Vietnam." A total of 35,000 North Vietnamese and Viet Cong were in prison camps in the South.

Thieu asserted that the "present scheme of the Communists is to use the lives of a few hundred American prisoners, the state of mind of the American people who want a quick withdrawal from Vietnam, as a pressure on us, to force us to surrender." The president added: "With the Americans, it is total withdrawal from Vietnam. With the Republic of Vietnam, it is the end of the present regime."

(South Vietnamese Foreign Minister Tran Van Lam's statement Dec. 7 that Saigon would free political as well as military prisoners if it would help bring peace was clarified by the Foreign Ministry Dec. 8. The ministry said although Lam had stated that Saigon could agree to let out "all the prisoners," he meant only military captives, and not political detainees, whose release had been demanded by the Communists.)

In announcing American rejection of the Thieu plan, White House Press Secretary Ronald L. Ziegler said Dec. 14, "We have a proposal now being negotiated on a cease-fire, and we support no other position on a cease-fire." Ziegler's statement was designed to dispell an Associated Press report that a statement made that day by the American delegation at the four-party peace talks represented backing for the Thieu proposal. U.S. representative Heyward Isham had urged North Vietnam to consider Saigon's latest suggestion and not reject it out of hand. Ziegler asserted that the AP had taken Isham's statement "out of context," that Isham's remarks could not be interpreted as supporting the Thieu plan.

The 170th session of the Paris talks was marked by routine statements in which each side blamed the other for the negotiating deadlock.

Peace talks recessed with no agreement. The latest round of private U.S.-North Vietnamese cease-fire talks, opened near Paris Dec. 4, concluded Dec. 13 with no agreement reached on the major issues dividing the two sides. The U.S. negotiator, Henry A. Kissinger, flew back to Washington Dec. 13 and reported to President Nixon the following day. His counterpart, Le Duc Tho, left for Hanoi Dec. 15. Before leaving Paris, Kissinger said he would "exchange messages" with Tho "as to whether a further meeting is necessary."

The principal stumbling block to a settlement was said to center on South Vietnam's demand, rejected by Hanoi, that North Vietnam either withdraw all its troops from South Vietnam or at least acknowledge their presence in the country as "illegal" by recognizing the Saigon government's sovereignty over all the territory of South Vietnam.

The talks between Kissinger and Tho and their staffs had been recessed for one day Dec. 10 to permit Gen. Alexander M. Haig, Jr., Kissinger's deputy, to return to Washington to consult with President Nixon. Haig left Paris Dec. 9 and conferred with the President Dec. 10, but he did not return to the Paris discussions.

During the Dec. 10 recess, experts of both sides for the first time held a joint conference to work on technical problems envisaged under the proposed agreement. The secret negotiations resumed Dec. 11 and continued through Dec. 13. Two separate meetings of deputy negotiators and technical experts were held outside Paris Dec. 12.

The American deputy negotiators were Deputy Assistant Secretary of State William H. Sullivan and William J. Porter, chief of the U.S. delegation at the four-party Paris peace talks. (Porter had participated in the private Kissinger-Tho talks for the first time Dec. 11.) Their North Vietnamese counterparts were Xuan Thuy, head of his country's delegation to the four-party sessions, and Deputy Foreign Minister Nguyen Co Thach. The U.S. technical experts included Kissinger's aides on the National Security Council—John D. Negroponte, Peter Rodman, Winston Lord, and David A. Engle.

Following the departure of Kissinger and Tho from Paris, the U.S. and North Vietnamese technical experts remained to continue bargaining sessions on details of the draft cease-fire text and related protocols.

Intensive Bombing Resumes

Kissinger blames Hanoi for deadlock. Henry A. Kissinger told a news conference in Washington Dec. 16 that his secret peace talks in Paris with Le Duc Tho had failed to reach what President Nixon regarded as "a just and fair agreement" because Hanoi had reneged on earlier accords negotiated by the two sides.

Kissinger's statement was contained in a review of his version of the negotiations that had resumed Nov. 20 after the Oct. 26 announcement of a draft accord. He gave no indication when the talks, broken off Dec. 13, would resume, but warned that the U.S. would not be "blackmailed, "stampeded" or "charmed" into an agreement "until its conditions are right." Although he and Tho had pledged not to publicly discuss their meetings, President Nixon had decided to divulge their contents "because we could not engage in a charade with the American people," Kissinger said.

Nixon's adviser said the negotiations were now at "a curious point" where on the one hand "we have an agreement that is 99% completed," but on the other hand the remaining 1% required a major decision by North Vietnam.

Kissinger implied that there were at least two major stumbling blocks to an agreement—the proposed four-nation supervisory team that was to observe a truce and the question of South Vietnam's sovereignty. He said the U.S. envisioned an observer force of "several thousand people . . . to monitor the many provisions of the agreement." North Vietnam, he said, insisted that the number of truce inspectors be limited to "no more than 250, of which nearly half should be located at headquarters" and that their movement and means of communication be severely restricted.

On the question of South Vietnam's sovereignty, Kissinger said the U.S. sought to include in an agreement a statement that would make clear that "the two parts of Vietnam would live in peace with each other." He contended that North Vietnam had accepted this "fundamental point" in negotiations two weeks ago but rejected the idea in subsequent talks. Kissinger did not give any details of the U.S.-North Vietnamese agreement on South Vietnam's sovereignty, but other Administration sources said he was referring to Hanoi's acceptance of the re-establishment of the demilitarized zone, that would in effect mean Vietnam was two countries. North Vietnam had repeatedly stated publicly that it would never accept Saigon's sovereignty over all of South Vietnam, one of the principal conditions of President Nguyen Van Thieu's acceptance of any peace agreement.

On resumption of the talks Dec. 4 after a nine-day recess, Kissinger said the North Vietnamese had switched their position on every major point agreed to Nov. 20. By Dec. 9 the differences were worked out and both sides were so close to an agreement that Nixon had summoned Gen. Alexander M. Haig, Jr. back to Washington Dec. 10 to prepare to go to Saigon with the proposed pact, Kissinger said. But at a meeting of technical experts Dec. 11, the North Vietnamese brought in "17 new changes in the guise of linguistic changes," he said. And when one problem was cleared up, Hanoi negotiators would raise another proposal. Kissinger said he would "not go into details or merits of these changes," but said Nixon decided at that point Dec. 13 to suspend the talks.

Kissinger acknowledged that there were "disagreements" between Saigon and Washington on the approach to peace. Cautioning Saigon against attempting to block any possible future U.S.-North Vietnamese accord, Kissinger said, "We want to leave no doubt about the fact that if an agreement is reached that meets the stated conditions of the President . . . that no other party will have a veto over our action."

(Kissinger had briefed Nixon Dec. 15 for the second consecutive day on his recently-concluded talks with Tho. He also held separate briefings with Defense Secretary Melvin R. Laird, Vice President Agnew, Central Intelligence Director Richard Helms and Adm. Thomas H. Moorer, chairman of the Joint Chiefs of Staff.)

U.S. held responsible for impasse— The Viet Cong and North Vietnam blamed the U.S. for the breakdown in the private Paris negotiations in statements Dec. 16 and 19.

While Kissinger was holding his news conference in Washington, the Viet Cong delegation to the regular Paris peace talks released a statement Dec. 16 assailing the "double-crossing attitude" of the U.S. and accusing it of "schemes to revise the contents" of the Oct. 26 draft accord. The Viet Cong asserted that the U.S. had blocked a final agreement by raising the questions of North Vietnamese troop withdrawal from South Vietnam and restoration of the

demilitarized zone. The DMZ proposal, the statement said, was aimed at turning "the provisional military demarcation line into a territorial boundary, perpetuate the partition of Vietnam and turn South Vietnam into a separate country under United States neocolonialist domination."

Xuan Thuy, North Vietnam's chief delegate to the Paris talks, replied directly to Kissinger's news conference remarks by declaring Dec. 19 that the U.S. was to blame for the impasse. He claimed that Kissinger had returned to Paris Nov. 20 to resume the secret talks with Le Duc Tho and brought with him 126 changes in the October draft accord. "Except for a very small number that were details or technicalities," the changes affected points of "fundamental importance," Thuy said.

A White House statement Dec. 19 denied Thuy's charge that the U.S. had sought 126 changes in the draft agreement.

Haig Mission to Indochina. Gen. Alexander M. Haig Jr., Kissinger's deputy, visited South Vietnam, Cambodia, Laos and Thailand Dec. 19-20 to brief their leaders on the current impasse at the Paris peace negotiations. Haig's mission had been described by the White House Dec. 17 as "a followup" to Kissinger's news conference Dec. 16 in which he had said the peace talks had thus far failed to reach agreement.

Haig arrived in Saigon Dec. 19 and conferred with President Nguyen Van Thieu. Later in the day he flew to Pnompenh, where he met with Cambodian Premier Lon Nol. The American aide returned to Saigon and held another meeting with Thieu the following day. Haig flew to Vientiane later Dec. 20 and met with Laotian Premier Souvanna Phouma and went on to Bangkok to meet with Thailand Premier Thanom Kittikachorn.

South Vietnam had not yet officially reacted to the new American bombing campaign against North Vietnam, but the semi-official newspaper Tin Song, which reflected Thieu's views, praised the U.S.' "tough new measures" Dec. 19.

Tho briefs Russians, Chinese. After leaving Paris for Hanoi Dec. 15, North Vietnamese negotiator Le Duc Tho stopped off in Moscow and Peking to brief the Soviet and Chinese leaders on the peace talk impasse.

Tho arrived in Moscow Dec. 15 and conferred Dec. 16 with two high Soviet Communist party officials—Andrei P. Kirilenko and Konstantin F. Katushev, both national party secretaries. A statement issued after the talks said the Soviet "side voiced unswerving and resolute support for the goodwill and the constructive approach demonstrated" by North Vietnam and the Viet Cong at the Paris talks.

Tho met with Premier Chou En-lai in Peking Dec. 17–18 and received firm support from the Chinese leader. The Dec. 17 meeting also had been attended by Truong Chinh, a member of the North Vietnamese Politburo. The Hsinhua news agency quoted Chou as telling the two men, "The Vietnam question should be settled at an early date on the basis of respect for the Vietnamese people's basic national rights."

Hanoi, Haiphong bombed. North Vietnam was subjected to the heaviest bombing of the Indochina war as hundreds of American planes resumed massive strikes on the northern part of the country Dec. 18. The mining of North Vietnam's harbors also was resumed.

The raids were launched in the wake of a breakdown in the private peace negotiations in Paris between the U.S. and North Vietnam. A White House statement Dec. 18 warned that the bombings "will continue until such a time as a settlement is arrived at."

Saying that the latest action was aimed at meeting the threat of another North Vietnamese offensive, Press Secretary Ronald L. Ziegler said President Nixon "will continue to order any action he deems necessary by air or by sea to prevent any buildup he sees in the South." Ziegler added: "We are not going to allow the peace talks to be used as a cover for another offensive. Neither side can gain from prolonging the war and neither side can gain from prolonging the peace."

The raids marked the first time since Oct. 23 that targets were struck above the 20th Parallel, which had been declared a bomb-free zone in recognition of North Vietnamese peace concessions at the time. In the latest attacks, Hanoi and Haiphong were bombed for the first time since early in October and U.S. warships joined in shelling North Vietnamese ports and coastal installations.

The intensity of the raids continued through Dec. 21 with the U.S. command acknowledging the loss of eight B-52s and four F-111 fighter-bombers in the four-day period. The command spokesmen said 43 airmen had been captured or killed and that North Vietnamese coastal guns Dec. 20 had damaged the U.S. guided missile destroyer Goldsborough off Thanhhoa, killing two sailors and wounding three.

North Vietnam claimed 12 B-52s and at least 14 fighter-bombers were downed. The six-member crew of one downed B-52 was captured Dec. 18 and displayed before a news conference in Hanoi the following day, according to the North Vietnamese.

Hanoi radio reported Dec. 20 that 215 persons had been killed and 325 wounded in the air strikes on the capital Dec. 18 and 19. The attacks on Haiphong Dec. 18 claimed the lives of 45 persons and wounded 131, the broadcast said. "Thousands of homes were demolished and many economic, cultural and social establishments were razed or badly damaged," Hanoi radio added.

A Hanoi dispatch by the Soviet news agency Tass Dec. 20 said the American raids on the city that night and Dec. 19 had caused "heavy civilian casualties" and destroyed thousands of homes. Among the targets struck were the Hanoi Technical Institute and a hospital, the agency said. Tass said bombs kept falling on Haiphong's "densely populated blocks, main streets and suburbs." In the raid on Haiphong Dec. 20, a Polish freighter was sunk and three seamen were killed. The Polish press agency reported that Warsaw had officially protested the attack on the freighter, the 5,720-ton Jozef Conrad. to the U.S.

The U.S. Defense Department said Dec. 20 that "very significant damage" had been inflicted on North Vietnam in the past two days. The department provided the general categories of the bombed targets for the first time since the raids above the 20th Parallel were resumed. Those points were being hit, a statement said, because they "support the continued North Vietnamese infiltration against South Vietnam." Department spokesman Jerry W. Friedheim said "these military targets include such categories as rail yards, ship yards, command and control facilities, power plants, railway bridges, railroad rolling stock, truck parks, MiG bases, air defense radars and gun and missile sites." He ruled out the customary Christmas bombing lull, saying "We are early in this engagement."

The North Vietnamese Foreign Ministry Dec. 19 denounced the resumption of the bombing as a "new war escalation of American imperialism" that was "premeditated and aims at achieving its plot of intensifying its war of aggression and negotiating from a position of force." The ministry asserted: "This insane action by the United States will never be able to remedy its desperate situation in South Vietnam."

To protest the American bombings, North Vietnam Dec. 20 called off the technical talks it had been holding with U.S. representatives and walked out of the regular four-party peace conference Dec. 21. The technical talks on details of a cease-fire had been held in the wake of the conclusion of the last round of secret talks between Henry A. Kissinger and Le Duc Tho Dec. 13. The last two such meetings had been held Dec. 18 and 20.

International reaction—President Nixon's decision to resume heavy bombing north of the 20th Parallel evoked strong criticism Dec. 19 and 20 from foreign governments, including the Soviet Union and China.

The official Soviet news agency Tass remarked Dec. 18 that Nixon's move appeared to cast doubts on his wish to achieve an early end to the war. "This particular decision of Washington flagrantly disagrees with numerous protestations made by U.S. leaders about their wish to seek mutually acceptable solutions for the remaining unresolved problems," Tass said. It described the "new escalation" as an effort "to bring pressure to bear" on the

North Vietnamese and Viet Cong to "accept the American terms" for a settlement.

Tass noted that "massive bombing and strafing raids" had produced "victims among the civilian populations" in the Hanoi and Haiphong areas. "The Soviet people are indignant in their condemnation of the new piratic acts" and "demand immediate stoppage of the actions and speedy signing of an agreement on ending the war," the agency said.

"Tass has been authorized to declare," the statement continued, "that the governing circles of the Soviet Union are giving the most serious consideration to the situation."

(In Paris Dec. 19, Pyotr A. Abrasimov, Soviet ambassador to France, said that in view of the renewed bombing "one can ask if the American leaders did not deceive" Soviet officials during President Nixon's visit to Moscow in May. The latest developments, he said, was "not a proof of force but of the weakness of U.S. policy and diplomacy, which will not succeed in forcing the Vietnamese people to their knees and make them accept a settlement convenient to Saigon and Washington.")

A message made public Dec. 20 from the Soviet leadership to the Viet Cong on its 12th anniversary condemned "efforts by the American side to create various obstacles in the path of a just political settlement in Vietnam."

Chinese Acting President Tung Pi-wu and Premier Chou En-lai sent a note Dec. 19 congratulating the Viet Cong for having "waged protracted and indomitable struggles against the U.S. aggressors and their running dogs and won splendid victories." The Chinese leaders promised support "so long as the U.S. does not stop its war of aggression."

A statement by the Chinese Foreign Ministry Dec. 20, appearing in the Communist party newspaper Jenmin Jih Pao, called the bombing "a new barbarous crime," which "has threatened to wreck a peace agreement which is close at hand." It described the Paris talks as having been adjourned when they "were about to enter their final stage."

U.N. General Assembly President Stanislaw Trepczynski said Dec. 19 that the "new escalation" of the war "jeopardizes the future of detente and carries the grave risk of increased tensions in international life." Secretary General Kurt Waldheim was reported to have expressed concern to George Bush, U.S. ambassador.

Pope Paul VI told his weekly audience Dec. 20 he felt "painful emotion over the sudden renewal of harsh and heavy military operations in blessed Vietnam, which has become a cause of daily grief." The bombing came at a time when the world "thought the beginning of a peaceful solution to this long conflict was at hand."

The French newspaper Le Monde Dec. 20 compared the renewed aerial attacks to the bombing of Guernica during the Spanish Civil War and added: "Perpetually seeking victory, Mr. Nixon is thus brought to strike out harder and harder and everywhere, since his adversaries are everywhere."

A leading British newspaper, the Manchester Guardian, commented Dec. 20: "It is the action of a man blinded by fury or incapable of seeing the consequences of what he is doing."

Finnish Foreign Minister Ahti Karjalainen said Dec. 20 it was "especially difficult to understand on what arguments the vast bombardment of the North Vietnamese territory has been based." Danish spokesman denounced the bombing and said the rebuilding of Vietnam had "suffered a tragic setback." Krister Wickman, Swedish foreign minister, attacked Nixon's "blind and brutal" move. The liberal Swedish newspaper Expressen wrote: "Once again mania fills the air. The outrage against Nixon's order for attack is deepening. Our disappointment is boundless."

In the only reported statement approving the bombing, Cambodian Information Minister Kem Reth said Dec. 20 that "the decision was correctly taken" and would cause the North Vietnamese to "pursue a peace settlement that will be a just one."

Domestic reaction—"Disappointment" was the immediate reaction of many members of Congress to the breakdown in secret Vietnam peace talks in Paris.

Sen. George McGovern (D, S.D.) termed Nixon's action "regrettable" in "misleading many people into believing that the war was virtually over." He said Dec. 17 that "we must look again to the possibility of Congressional action to terminate any further American military involvement in Indochina."

Senate Majority Leader Mike Mansfield (D, Mont.) Dec. 17 expressed a feeling of "great depression" at the news and also suggested there would be renewed Congressional action to end the war. "I anticipate that the Senate, which has been very responsible in keeping silent during the negotiations, will give priority consideration to the matter," Mansfield said.

Mansfield charged Dec. 19 that renewed bombing raids on North Vietnam constituted a "stone age tactic" and warned, "The American people and Congress are entitled to a full explanation of the disastrous turn of events."

Republican reaction was restrained. Sen. Hugh Scott (Pa.), Republican minority leader, predicted Dec. 17 that Congress would be "tolerant" of the bargaining breakdown, in part because Presidential Adviser Henry Kissinger had been "very candid in explaining the difficulties."

But Scott admitted Dec. 20 after bombing of the North had been resumed that "it will be difficult to get any Vietnam legislation" through Congress if peace had not been achieved by Inauguration Day.

Sen. William B. Saxbe (R, Ohio) criticized the Administration Dec. 17 for "misreading North Vietnamese attitudes. "What amazes me is that it took so long to find out," Saxbe said.

Saxbe said his constituents "couldn't care less about the war." He said he had attended a businessmen's luncheon Dec. 17 and "not one word was mentioned about Vietnam although it was the major story in the morning newspapers."

Sen. Jacob K. Javits (R, N.Y.) declared Dec. 19 that the "North Vietnamese have never been bombed into a settlement," but his Republican-Conservative party counterpart in the state, Sen. James L. Buckley, commenting on the breakdown in talks, said Dec. 17: "It continued to be clear that force is the only language which Hanoi understands."

Kissinger lunched Dec. 19 with Sen. J. William Fulbright (D, Ark.), a persistent war critic and chairman of the Foreign Relations Committee. There were no reports of their discussions.

Rep. Benjamin S. Rosenthal (D, N.Y.), and 17 other House Democrats telegraphed the President Dec. 19, telling him, "Your election and re-election were due in large part to your commitment to end the war. . . . If you cannot or will not get us out, then Congress will have to exercise its obligation to do so."

Dow-Jones falls—News of failure at the negotiating table and of resumed bombing caused the Dow-Jones industrial average to fall 13.99 points Dec. 18, its biggest decline in 16 months, to 1,013.25. By Dec. 21, the index was at 1,000 after reaching a record high of 1,036.27 Dec. 11.

Previous air strikes. Prior to resumption of air strikes above the 20th Parallel, U.S. planes had continued to hit heavily at North Vietnam's southern panhandle. The heaviest raid of the war to date was conducted during a 24-hour period that ended at noon Dec. 15. B-52s carried out a record 16-mission attack, concentrating on supply bases around the port of Donghoi.

In South Vietnam ground action, Communist forces shelled the Bienhoa air base, 15 miles north of Saigon, Dec. 15 and 16. Six civilians were slain in the first day's attack and two more Dec. 16. South Vietnam said North Vietnamese troops were massing in the Bienhoa area. The Communist units were said to have moved into an area six miles northeast of the U.S.-South Vietnamese installation.

Heavy fighting was reported near Quangtri city Dec. 16–18, as government troops continued attempts to expand their control of territory in the area. U.S. B-52s provided heavy air support, striking at North Vietnamese troop positions and supply lines in the province. Saigon said that in three clashes Dec. 16, 151 North Vietnamese and six government troops

were killed. The enemy losses were described as the heaviest since the government's recapture of Quangtri city in September. Further clashes were fought around Quangtri city Dec. 20, with the Saigon command claiming 154 North Vietnamese battle fatalities. South Vietnamese losses were placed at eight killed. Many of the North Vietnamese casualties resulted from U.S. fighter-bomber strikes.

A government ammunition dump was blown up Dec. 14 six miles east of Saigon. More than 1,000 tons of bombs and ammunition were reported to have been destroyed at the Laicat depot.

The first U.S. combat fatality in three weeks was reported by the American command Dec. 14. It said one soldier was slain in the Dec. 3–9 period. He was killed in the Communist shelling of Tansonnhut air base Dec. 6.

Thais approve U.S. command shift. Thailand announced Dec. 16 that it had given the U.S. approval to move its military headquarters from Saigon to Thailand in the event a cease-fire went into effect in Vietnam.

Field Marshal Thanom Kittikachorn, the Thai leader, confirmed that plans called for shifting American headquarters to Nakorn Phanom air base, 380 miles northeast of Bangkok and 60 miles from the North Vietnamese border. Nakorn Phanom had formerly served as a major base for close air support of government and U.S.-sponsored troops in Laos. Thanom said he had discussed the projected move with Leonard Unger, U.S. ambassador to Thailand.

Australian troops leave. Australia's military involvement in the Vietnam war ended Dec. 18, when the country's last contingent left Saigon. The force consisted of about 60 military advisers. Australia had ended its combat role in November 1971.

Laotians exchange peace plans. The Pathet Lao offered an immediate cease-fire in Laos and proposed the formation of a new coalition government at the weekly peace negotiating session with

Laotian government representatives in Vientiane Dec. 12. Government representatives made a counter-proposal at the Dec. 19 meeting, but it was rejected by the Pathet Lao.

Among the principal points of the Pathet Lao plan: U.S. and other foreign troops would withdraw from Laos within 90 days of a truce and all their bases in the country would be dismantled; all military operations, repression, arrests and reprisals would be barred "in the zone provisionally controlled" by the Laotian government (no mention was made of similar curbs in areas under Pathet Lao control); neither the Pathet Lao nor the government would be permitted to introduce into their respective zones any foreign troops, advisers, new weapons or war material, but worn out equipment could be replaced on a one-to-one basis with the agreement of both sides; both zones would permit free elections and freedom of speech and assembly; the truce would be supervised by a mixed commission of the two sides, assisted by the existing International Control Commission.

As for the political aspects of the Pathet Lao plan, the present Vientiane government and its National Assembly would be dissolved, but the country, four-fifths of which the Pathet Lao claimed to control, would continue to be administered as at present until a new government and assembly was chosen. A Political Council of Coalition and a new provisional government of national union would be formed prior to the holding of nationwide elections and within 30 days of the signing of the agreement. The council would be comprised of four equal delegations of the Pathet Lao, the Vientiane government, the neutralists, who supported the Pathet Lao, and representatives named by King Savang Vatthana. The new three-part regime would be equally divided among the Pathet Lao, the neutralists and the Vientiane government. The council would control the city of Vientiane, which would become a neutral zone.

Government negotiator Nouphat Counramany rejected formation of the council on the ground it was unconstitutional. He suggested the Pathet Lao could widen their representation in the present government under the current constitution, which he said empowered the king to appoint extra members to the National Assembly. Nouphat added that Vientiane also opposed any governmental changes that recognized a division of Laos into two zones.

Vientiane's peace proposal at the Dec. 19 session was similar to the Pathet Lao plan in that it stressed the neutralization of Laos and the need to form a new coalition government. But Pathet Lao spokesman Soth Phetrasy said after the meeting that "on first examination it is merely a recapitulation of Vientiane's earlier proposals, which we have denounced as unacceptable." The contents of the Vientiane plan were not immediately reported in the Western press.

Government retakes Muong Phalane— Pro-government irregular forces Dec. 12 recaptured the southern Laotian town of Muong Phalane, which had been in North Vietnamese hands since early in 1970.

The town's capture followed a month-long government offensive eastward from Dong Hene, which had been captured by Laotian forces in November. Muong Phalane was on the western approach to North Vietnam's Ho Chi Minh Trail network adjoining South Vietnam. Large caches of Communist arms and ammunition were taken in and around Muong Phalane, including a Soviet-made T-34 tank.

The heaviest fighting in southern Laos continued in and around Saravane, where losses were reported heavy on both sides. Government troops repelled North Vietnamese attacks on the city Dec. 8 and 17.

Communist forces mounted heavy attacks on government strongpoints on the Plaine des Jarres, overruning two defensive positions Dec. 8 and 9. The enemy offensive was aimed at putting pressure on the main government base of Long Tieng to the west.

Haig reports to Nixon on mission. Gen. Alexander M. Haig, Jr., Kissinger's deputy, returned to the U.S. from Indochina Dec. 22 and briefed President Nixon on his Dec. 19–20 meetings with the leaders of South Vietnam, Cambodia, Laos and Thailand. Kissinger attended the talks, held at Key Biscayne, Fla.

The White House later confirmed that Haig had carried a letter from Nixon to President Nguyen Van Thieu and brought back a reply from the Saigon leader. Contents of the messages were not disclosed, but it was reported that Nixon had told Thieu not to advance any more peace proposals on his own, as he had Dec. 12, and to make concessions toward a peace settlement.

A South Vietnamese official Dec. 21 confirmed receipt of the Nixon letter, but denied reports that the President had given Thieu an "ultimatum" to either accept a peace settlement or face the loss of American military and economic aid.

U.S. to bomb until talks resume. A White House statement Dec. 22 said President Nixon was determined to continue his present course of bombing North Vietnam until Hanoi decided to resume negotiations "in a spirit of goodwill and in a constructive attitude." "If they do that," the statement added, "we can have a very rapid settlement of the situation."

Nixon Administration officials had insisted Dec. 20 that North Vietnam was solely to blame for the breakdown of negotiations. Government aides were said to be of the opinion that North Vietnam's leadership had made a "fundamental" decision during the Kissinger-Tho recess between Nov. 25 and Dec. 4 not to sign an agreement. The officials denied reports that the question of South Vietnam's "sovereignty" blocked an agreement.

South Vietnam Dec. 23 repeated its demand for withdrawal of all North Vietnamese troops from the South as its price for accepting a peace accord. Foreign Minister Tran Van Lam reiterated this view in testimony at a closed-door meeting of the National Assembly's Foreign Affairs Committee. He said Saigon's demands for re-establishment of the demilitarized zone and its objections to the proposed National Council of Reconciliation were minor points that could be easily settled.

Hanoi conditions for talks. North Vietnam's chief peace negotiator, Xuan Thuy, said in an interview broadcast Dec. 24 that Hanoi would not resume peace negotiations with the U.S. until it halted air strikes north of the 20th Parallel.

Interviewed in Paris the previous day for the ABC Program "Issues and Answers," Thuy said "the negotiations cannot be carried out under the bombing." He reiterated Hanoi's charge that Washington was to blame for the breakdown in the secret peace talks between Henry A. Kissinger and Le Duc Tho and he accused the U.S. of using the intensified bombings "to compel the Vietnamese people to accept United States terms." During the negotiations between the two men, the U.S. had "insisted upon modifications of the principles of the content, of the substance of the agreement" reached in October, Thuy said. He charged that Kissinger raised "all the demands of the Saigon administration."

The resumption of the American bombing north of the 20th Parallel, Thuy contended, constituted a breach of pledges by President Nixon and Kissinger that the attacks would not be renewed "while negotiations are under way, and until the negotiations are concluded." The U.S. also had promised that "the bombing south of the 20th Parallel would be significantly reduced," Thuy said.

North Vietnam reiterated its conditions for renewal of the peace talks Dec. 26. Nguyen Thanh Le, spokesman for Hanoi's delegation to the Paris peace talks, said that if the U.S. was serious about ending the conflict by negotiation "it must cease immediately the acts of escalation of the war against the Democratic Republic of Vietnam, abandon threats through the use of force and, in the first place, return to the situation existing before Dec. 18," the day the U.S. had resumed the bombings north of the 20th Parallel.

North Vietnamese Defense Minister Gen. Vo Nguyen Giap had declared in a speech made public Dec. 22 that "Hanoi, Haiphong and other cities may be bombed and erased, but the Vietnamese people will never bend."

Bombing raids continue. The Bach Mai Hospital, in the center of Hanoi, was struck Dec. 22 and was virtually destroyed. The North Vietnamese Health Ministry reported Dec. 23 that 25 doctors, pharmacists and nurses had been killed in the attack. The ministry said the hospital previously had been bombed Dec. 19 and in June. U.S. Defense Department spokesman Jerry Friedheim Dec. 28 called the report of the hospital bombing "propaganda," and repeated his denial that the U.S. was bombing civilian targets.

A North Vietnamese broadcast Dec. 21 (Dec. 22, Hanoi time) claimed that U.S. planes had bombed and damaged a prisoner of war camp in the capital Dec. 20 and 21 and that an unspecified number of American airmen held there had been wounded. A Defense Department spokesman said if the Hanoi statement was correct, then North Vietnam was admitting that it was violating the Geneva Convention by keeping prisoners "in areas particularly exposed to the dangers of war." Department spokesman Friedheim said Dec. 21 U.S. aircraft "are not intended to attack any areas that we think the U.S. POWs are being detained in." Hanoi radio charged Dec. 23 that Friedheim was lying when he said the U.S. was not targeting areas in which prisoners were held.

An Agence France-Presse report Dec. 21 said the Cuban embassy in Hanoi had been bombed and heavily damaged. The Soviet news agency Tass said the Egyptian embassy in the city had been damaged. The Indian Embassy was bombed Dec. 21 and New Delhi protested to Washington. The embassies of East Germany, Bulgaria and Albania also were reported damaged.

Hanoi radio reported that a Soviet ship had been damaged by an American raid on Haiphong Dec. 21. Peking radio said a Chinese freighter had been bombed in the same port Dec. 20. The Polish press agency in Warsaw reported Dec. 27 that a fourth seaman had died as a result of injuries suffered in the American sinking of a Polish ship in Haiphong Dec. 20.

An Agence France-Presse report from Hanoi Dec. 26 said the raids on the capital that day were the heaviest of the war. The city was said to have been struck for more than 40 minutes and at least five B-52s were reported shot down

by antiaircraft fire. Hanoi radio claimed another three B-52s were downed in other parts of North Vietnam Dec. 26.

A U.S. military command blackout on reports of raid damage, imposed Dec. 18, was lifted Dec. 27 with a 10-page report on North Vietnamese targets struck during the nine-day period. The news blackout was reimposed Dec. 28 after the command reported the loss of two more B-52s. In its Dec. 27 report the command said that since Dec. 18, 55 North Vietnamese targets had been pounded by 147 B-52 missions and 1,000 tactical air strikes. Half the targets were in the Hanoi-Haiphong area and included airfields, rail yards, power plants, supply depots and communications centers. The report made no mention of such civilian targets as the Bach Mai Hospital and the Gia Lam International Airport in Hanoi, which had been heavily damaged Dec. 21.

The massive air attacks on North Vietnam and American raids elsewhere in Indochina had halted for 36 hours during a Christmas truce Dec. 24–26. The bombing halt overlapped a 24-hour Christmas truce set by the Viet Cong and the Saigon government for the ground fighting in South Vietnam. The South Vietnam command reported that 58 cease-fire violations between Dec. 24 and 25 had killed 40 government soldiers and wounded 47 and killed five civilians and wounded 10. Communists losses in that period were 60 killed, the Saigon command said.

Communist gunners Dec. 25 shelled the Danang air base and surrounding civilian areas. Two Vietnamese civilians were killed and five American helicopters were damaged or destroyed. A South Vietnamese training post near Danang came under Communist shelling Dec. 28. The attack killed three persons and wounded 13 others.

A South Vietnamese fighter-bomber Dec. 27 accidentally bombed a village 20 miles northeast of Saigon, killing nine civilians and wounding 10. Six homes were reported destroyed.

Congressional reaction to raids. Congressional reaction to the bombing took on a bipartisan tone as Republican and

Democratic members became increasingly critical of President Nixon's actions.

The harshest attack was delivered by Sen. William B. Saxbe (R, O.), who declared in a Cleveland Plain Dealer interview published Dec. 29, "I have followed President Nixon through his convolutions and specious arguments but he appears to have left his senses on this issue. I can't go along with him on this one."

Among other statements Dec. 29: Sen. Charles McC. Mathias Jr. (R, Md.) said even if the raids were to succeed, the cost would be too high in lives and the U.S. would suffer a blow to its "moral leadership in the world."

Sen. Clifford P. Case (R, N.J.) declared if the air assaults continued "Congress, when it meets next Wednesday, will have an obligation to bring about a complete termination of American involvement."

Sen. John V. Tunney (D, Calif.) called on the Nixon Administration to provide a public explanation of the bombing.

House Speaker Carl Albert (D, Okla.) received a written request from 22 Democratic representatives for a vote at the Jan. 2 Democratic Caucus in favor of an immediate termination of the bombing and "prompt signing of a peace agreement," it was reported Dec. 29. Albert had said Dec. 27 that Congress should first receive a full report from the Administration. "I don't think we should pull the rug out from under him if there is hope of success," Albert said.

President Nixon's decision to curb the bombing of North Vietnam brought expressions of relief from his Congressional critics Dec. 30.

U.S. prelates assail bombings—The American bombing of North Vietnam was assailed as "an unspeakable assault upon this season's message of peace" by an interfaith group of 44 U.S. religious leaders in a letter made public Dec. 22. The group accused the Nixon Administration of "aborting the possibility and betraying the duty of peace." It called for a national "religious convocation for peace" in Washington Jan. 3 and 4, 1973.

Leaders of 10 religious organizations in Chicago appealed Dec. 22 to the Rev. Billy Graham "to implore President Nixon to stop the bombing of North Vietnam in the name of the Christmas Christ."

Peace demonstrations on a small-scale were held in various cities throughout the U.S. Dec. 19–22. Protest rallies were conducted in various parts of New York Dec. 21.

Anti-war leaflets were passed out by demonstrators outside Westover Air Force Base, Mass. Dec. 22. There were small demonstrations in Boston Dec. 19 and 21, and in Madison, Wis. Dec. 20.

International protests continue. The resumption of American air strikes on North Vietnam continued to evoke widespread foreign protests. Among the major developments:

Soviet Communist party leader Leonid I. Brezhnev declared Dec. 21 that his government "angrily and resolutely condemns these acts of aggression" against North Vietnam. Addressing a meeting honoring the 50th anniversary of the formation of the Soviet Union, Brezhnev warned that any Soviet-American detente "will depend on the course of events in the immediate future and, in particular, on what kind of turn is taken on the issue of ending the war in Vietnam."

Addressing a similar gathering in Moscow Dec. 22, Cuban Premier Fidel Castro accused President Nixon of "thoughtless bloodshed, barbarous destruction and diplomatic perfidy."

Pope Paul VI said Dec. 22 the "unforeseen worsening of events has intensified bitterness and anxiety in world opinion." Addressing the Sacred College of Cardinals in Rome, the Pope said the reasons for the breakdown in the U.S.-North Vietnamese peace talks were not "sufficiently apparent."

Australian Prime Minister Gough Whitlam was reported Dec. 22 to have sent a "strongly worded" protest message to President Nixon over the renewed bombing.

Demonstrations against the bombing were held Dec. 22–23 in London, Rome, Copenhagen, Zurich and Amsterdam. Bangla Desh students Dec. 23 ransacked the U.S. Information Service building in Dacca. Another USIS building was set fire by students Dec. 26 in Rajashahi, 90 miles north of Dacca. About 200 Japanese demonstrated Dec. 23 in front of the U.S. embassy in Tokyo.

U.N. Secretary General Kurt Waldheim expressed concern Dec. 23 over the resumption of bombing and called for a renewal of efforts to end the war.

Yugoslavia Dec. 25 condemned the U.S. air strikes, denouncing "the massacre of the civil population and the systematic destruction of cities."

In a Christmas Day message, Stefan Cardinal Wyszynski, Roman Catholic primate of Poland, called on American Catholics Dec. 25 to halt "the bloodshed of the innocent children and brothers in Vietnam."

Yugoslavs smeared red paint on the American consulate in Zagreb Dec. 26 and staged a protest outside the building Dec. 27.

Chinese Premier Chou En-lai said Dec. 28 that U.S.-Chinese relations were imperiled by the raids. Chou told Washington Post correspondent Marilyn Berger in Peking that the rift could be healed if the U.S. stopped the bombing.

Roy Jenkins, a leader of the British Labor party, called the bombings Dec. 28 "one of the most cold-blooded actions in recent history." Jenkins' statement was contained in a letter sent to Prime Minister Heath, whom he urged to speak out against the raids.

The Seamen's Union of Australia Dec. 28 announced a boycott against all American shipping in Australian ports. Two more Australian maritime unions joined the boycott action Dec. 29.

The governments of Italy, the Netherlands and Sweden had officially condemned the intensified American air war, it was reported Dec. 29. Deep concern over the air war was expressed by political leaders in Norway, Denmark, Belgium, Finland and West Germany.

U.S. rebuffs Sweden on protest—In response to a statement by Swedish Premier Olof Palme Dec. 23 comparing the bombing of North Vietnam to Nazi atrocities of World War II, the U.S. told Sweden not to send a new ambassador to Washington, it was disclosed Dec. 29. The protest was delivered orally Dec. 23 by Acting Secretary of State U. Alexis Johnson to the current Swedish Ambassador Hubert de Besche, who was scheduled to leave Washington in January 1973.

Johnson also notified de Besche that the U.S. charge d'affaires in Sweden, John C. Guthrie, would not return to Stockholm "at this time."

De Besche allegedly told Johnson that initial news reports had distorted Palme's statement. According to a Swedish text released Dec. 24, Palme had called the bombing "a form of torture" and an "outrage" similar to those "often connected with names—Guernica, Oradour, Babi Yar, Katyn, Lidice, Sharpeville, Treblinka." Several of those names were linked with Nazi atrocities.

The leaders of all Sweden's political parties issued an unprecedented declaration Dec. 28 urging Nixon to halt the bombing and sign a peace treaty with Hanoi. The leaders called for two million signatures of the declaration.

Bombings disrupt 4-party talks. The American raids on North Vietnam disrupted the four-party peace talks in Paris and the discussions between U.S. and North Vietnamese technical experts, which were an offshoot of the Kissinger-Tho meetings.

The North Vietnamese and Viet Cong delegations had suggested another regular meeting of the four-sided discussions be held Dec. 28 before they walked out of the Dec. 21 session in protest against the raids. The meeting never took place.

A meeting Dec. 23 in which U.S. and North Vietnamese delegates were discussing the technical aspects of the peace negotiations was adjourned suddenly when the Hanoi representatives walked out of the talks after accusing the U.S. of "savage attacks" on North Vietnam.

Another technical meeting scheduled for Dec. 27 was called off at the last moment when the North Vietnamese informed the Americans they would not attend until "the situation existing before Dec. 18, 1972 has been restored."

Moscow meeting on bombings. Soviet and North Vietnamese leaders held two separate meetings in Moscow Dec. 29 to discuss possible action to counter the intensified American bombing of North Vietnam. Premier Aleksei N. Kosygin met with North Vietnamese Ambassador Vo Thuc Dong. This conference was followed by talk between two other Soviet officials—Politburo member Mikhail Suslov and Dimitri F. Ustinov, a Communist party secretary—and Truong Chin, of North Vietnam's National Assembly.

Chinese support for the Vietnamese Communists was expressed by a mass rally held Dec. 29 in Peking's Great Hall of the People. Addressing an audience of 10,000, Viet Cong Foreign Minister Nguyen Thi Binh charged that the U.S. was attempting to split the Vietnamese people from China and other Communist countries.

Mrs. Binh had arrived in Peking from Moscow Dec. 27.

Nixon curbs raids on North. The massive American bombing north of North Vietnam's 20th Parallel, in progress since Dec. 18, were halted Dec. 30 on the orders of President Nixon. The raids on North Vietnam's southern panhandle, the area below the 20th Parallel, however, were to continue. The White House statement on the bombing curb was coupled with an announcement that Henry A. Kissinger and Le Duc Tho of North Vietnam would resume their secret peace discussions in Paris on Jan. 8, 1973. Lower-echelon technical talks were to be renewed in Paris Jan. 2.

A separate 36-hour New Year's truce declared by the U.S. was to start Jan. 1, 1973 and temporarily halt American air attacks on North and South Vietnam. A 24-hour cease-fire accepted by Saigon and the Viet Cong to halt ground action in South Vietnam went into effect at 6 p.m. Dec. 31.

The reasons behind the halt in the American air offensive and the resumption of private peace talks were disputed by Washington and Hanoi.

Gerald L. Warren, a deputy White House press secretary, told newsmen Dec. 30 that "as soon as it was clear that the serious negotiations could be resumed at both the technical level and between the principals, the President ordered that all bombing be discontinued above the 20th Parallel."

North Vietnam denied that it had been pressured by the bombing to return to the negotiations. A statement issued by Hanoi's delegation to the regular Paris peace talks Dec. 30 said, "The resumption of the bombings, while negotiations were proceeding, did not succeed in subjugating the Vietnamese

people." The statement indicated that "heavy" American air losses and world condemnation of the raids were responsible for the bombing halt.

During the 12-day bombing period the U.S. command acknowledged that 15 B-52s and 11 fighter-bombers had been shot down. The official toll of American airmen missing between Dec. 18 and 30 stood at 93, with 31 men reported captured by the North Vietnamese.

Hanoi radio claimed Dec. 29 that its antiaircraft fire and missiles had brought down 76 planes, including 33 B-52s since Dec. 18. Nguyen Thanh Le, spokesman for the North Vietnamese delegation to the Paris peace talks, had said Dec. 28 that "The number of pilots killed or captured has also reached a record," but he did not give any figures.

In the first official report on North Vietnamese casualties from the bombings, the head of a Hanoi hospital reported Dec. 29 that about 2,000 civilians had been killed and more than 10,000 wounded since Dec. 18.

The North Vietnamese press agency had reported Dec. 25 that 40,000 tons of bombs had fallen on the country between Dec. 18 and 24, which it said was equal to two of the atomic bombs dropped on Hiroshima in World War II.

Total U.S. air losses—According to Defense Department figures made public Dec. 30, the U.S. had lost more than 8,500 planes and helicopters worth an estimated $10.5 billion in the Indochina war since 1961. About 2,000 airmen had been killed in air action over North and South Vietnam, Cambodia and Laos, and 1,236 were missing and 525 were captured by the North Vietnamese and Viet Cong, the report said.

Cambodian military developments. Communist forces attacked two Cambodian army positions 12 miles southwest of Pnompenh Dec. 14. Government planes bombed suspected Vietnamese Communist troop concentrations 12–16 miles from the capital Dec. 17 and 18. The government command reported Dec. 20 that fighting had broken out again 12 miles south of the capital.

Elsewhere in Cambodia, heavy fighting raged around Kompong Thom, 77 miles north of the capital, besieged since Dec. 7. North Vietnamese forces launched an all-out assault Dec. 20, forcing government troops to abandon at least two defensive positions just outside the town. The attackers tightened their grip around the city and by Dec. 24 the government reported fighting less than two miles away. A Cambodian garrison commander said Dec. 25 that in four days of fighting, government forces had lost 17 killed, 36 wounded and 265 missing.

Cambodian soldiers joined South Vietnamese troops Dec. 21 in a joint operation aimed at clearing a Communist-occupied area 55 miles south of Pnompenh. The area bordered the westernmost section of the Mekong Delta in South Vietnam.

Cambodian army scandal. Although Cambodia had an army of 200,000 men, the government acknowledged Dec. 27 that because of corruption by military commanders and other "irregularities" it had "at times" paid salaries to as many as 100,000 soldiers who did not exist. It was estimated that the false payrolls submitted by unit commanders had resulted in a loss of $2 million a month, virtually all of which came from U.S. aid, about $300 million in 1972.

Communists seize Laos bridgehead. North Vietnamese troops Dec. 23 captured a Laotian government position at a bridge spanning the Se Bang River, 24 miles north of Seno in southern Laos and 15 miles from the Thai border. The Se Bang bridge was part of Route 13, which extended along the western border of Laos from one end to the other. The key strongpoint was captured by a battalion of North Vietnamese troops.

The 11th weekly peace-negotiating meeting of Pathet Lao and Laotian government representatives was held in Vientiane Dec. 26 with both sides reiterating their former positions and agreeing that the main issues were unresolved.

Australia ends arms aid. Australia announced Dec. 27 that it was halting military assistance to South Vietnam and abandoning its program for training Cambodian troops.

Defense Minister Lance H. Barnard said that of the $31.8 million in assistance Australia had allocated for Saigon in 1971, about $2.5 million had gone to the military.

24,200 GIs remain. The U.S. command reported Dec. 25 that 700 American troops had been withdrawn from South Vietnam the previous week, reducing the total American force in the country to 24,200.

South Vietnam ground action. Communist ground attacks in South Vietnam intensified following expiration of the 24-hour New Year's cease-fire Jan. 1.

Communist troops Jan. 2 carried out a major assault against a government militia unit along Route 1, about 40 miles northeast of Saigon. Initial reports said at least two militiamen were killed.

Viet Cong forces were reported to have doubled their attacks Jan. 3 to the highest number in nearly a month, initiating 81 such incidents. The most serious involved mining of a bridge on Route 4 about five miles from Cantho, linking Saigon with the Mekong Delta.

The allied air base at Bienhoa, 15 miles northwest of Saigon, was shelled by Communist forces Jan. 4. The 16-rocket attack killed three civilians and wounded 10. The incident was one of 116 initiated by the enemy in a 24-hour period.

U.S. resumes raids on North Vietnam. U.S. planes resumed raids on North Vietnam's southern panhandle Jan. 2 after a 36-hour New Year's truce. The attacks continued at an intensified rate through Jan. 6. The suspension of air strikes above the country's 20th Parallel, which had started Dec. 30, 1972, remained in effect. The New Year's bombing pause was not officially confirmed until its termination was announced by the U.S. command Jan. 2.

American air strikes on Communist targets in South Vietnam were renewed at dusk Jan. 1. The 36-hour air truce did not apply to Cambodia and Laos, and U.S. jet attacks on enemy bases and supply routes in those countries had continued.

The Saigon military command reported Jan. 2 that during a 24-hour truce in South Vietnam that had ended at 6 p.m.

Jan. 1 Communist forces had committed 49 violations, resulting in the death of eight government soldiers and three civilians and 44 Communists. The number of South Vietnamese wounded had totaled 79, including 10 civilians, the command reported. The only major fighting during the truce occurred around Quangtri city.

A U.S. Defense Department spokesman confirmed Jan. 4 that the Bach Mai Hospital and the Gia Lam civilian airport, both in Hanoi, had been damaged during American raids in December. But Jerry W. Friedheim said that contrary to "Hanoi's propaganda claims of massive destruction at these sites," the damage was "accidental" and its extent and cause were "uncertain." He said he was not sure whether the damage had been caused by bombs, by downed American or North Vietnamese aircraft or by falling North Vietnamese antiaircraft missiles. Friedheim added: "We regret any such accidental damage from whatever source, but we reiterate that our strikes have been targeted only at military targets."

Friedheim disclosed that in addition to the 15 B-52s shot down over North Vietnam during December, he believed another six had been damaged and that some presumably were put out of action permanently.

In a delayed report, the U.S. command Jan. 4 announced the loss of an A-6 fighter-bomber over North Vietnam Dec. 28 with two of its crewmen missing. This brought to 28 the number of planes acknowledged by the U.S. command to have been lost since Dec. 18 and to 97 the number of airmen killed, captured or missing.

According to the command's weekly casualty summary issued Jan. 4, 109 Americans had been killed, captured or were missing during the two-week period ending at midnight Dec. 31. The command acknowledged that virtually all the casualties were the result of the air and naval campaign against North Vietnam.

The U.S. command reported another B-52 had been shot down over North Vietnam Jan. 4, the 16th since Dec. 18. The bomber had been fired at over the southern panhandle and the six crewmen bailed out safely, the command said.

Hanoi radio claimed Jan. 4 that 1,318 persons had been killed and 1,261 wounded in Hanoi alone during the U.S. raids Dec. 18–30. The broadcast, quoting a report by a special government investigating committee, said that in 10 days of bombing starting Dec. 18 American planes had made more than 1,000 sorties against the capital, among them 500 B-52 attacks. The broadcast charged that the workers' quarter of An Duong had been wiped out by 600 B-52 bombs dropped Dec. 21. The report said the Bach Mai Hospital in Hanoi was destroyed and 28 persons were killed.

The U.S. was reported Jan. 4 to have decided not to make public a comprehensive account of the bomb damage inflicted on North Vietnam for fear of harming the peace talks that were scheduled to be resumed in Paris. A partial summary of the Dec. 18–25 raids had been issued Dec. 27 and a follow-up report on the attacks through Dec. 29 was to have been given out no later than Jan. 3.

North Vietnam charged that U.S. planes had raided targets north of the 20th Parallel Jan. 5 in violation of the U.S.' suspension pledge. The Foreign Ministry said bombs were dropped on Dong Lai district of Hoabinh Province, about 50 miles southwest of Hanoi between the 20th and 21st Parallels. The U.S. Defense Department denied the report Jan. 5.

A private delegation of four Americans who had returned from a two-week visit to North Vietnam reported Jan. 1 that the American raids had caused widespread destruction in Hanoi. The group, which had met with American prisoners of war, had arrived in the North Vietnamese capital Dec. 16 for a one-week stay, but the American bombing forced a one-week delay in their departure. They returned to New York Dec. 31. The members of the group were folk singer Joan Baez, Telford Taylor, professor of law at Columbia University, Michael Allen, associate dean of the Yale University Divinity School, and Barry Romo, national coordinator of Vietnam Veterans Against the War. A statement issued by the group said part of an American prisoner camp they had visited in Hanoi had been "wiped out" by the bombs.

Antiwar efforts as Congress convenes. The 93rd Congress convened Jan. 3 amid decisions by the Democratic party, in control of both houses, to approve antiwar resolutions.

The House Democratic Caucus, meeting Jan. 2, adopted by a 154–75 vote a policy declaration "that no further funds be authorized, appropriated or expended for U.S. military combat operations in or over Indochina and that such operations be terminated immediately subject only to arrangements necessary to insure the safe withdrawal of American troops and the return of American prisoners of war." The resolution, sponsored by Rep. Lucien N. Nedzi (Mich.), condemned the "recent unprecedented and reprehensible bombing of North Vietnam" ordered by President Nixon and further objected that "extensive" military combat operations had been undertaken "without notification of, consultation with or explanation to the Congress."

The Senate Democrats, meeting Jan. 4, adopted a similar policy statement by a 36–12 vote. Sponsored by Sen. Edward M. Kennedy (Mass.), the statement called for an end to funding of American military operations in Indochina and said all such operations should be stopped immediately subject only to arrangements for release of prisoners and an accounting of the missing in action.

There were other Democratic initiatives on the war. Sen. George McGovern (S.D.), the defeated Democratic presidential candidate, introduced a bill Jan. 4 to cut off funds for U.S. operations in Indochina within 60 days. He denounced the December bombing of North Vietnam as "the cruelest and most insane act of a long and foolish war."

Sen. Edward W. Brooke (R, Mass.) told the Senate Jan. 4 "Congress has no more compelling obligation than to bring and maintain peace" in Indochina. He introduced a bill similar to McGovern's. It was co-sponsored by Sen. Alan Cranston (D, Calif.).

Sen. J. W. Fulbright (D, Ark.) said after an informal meeting of his Senate Foreign Relations Committee Jan. 2 that its membership was determined "that the legislative powers of the Congress should be brought to bear" if peace were not negotiated by Jan. 20, the date of Nixon's second inauguration.

Republicans back Nixon—Senate Republicans passed a resolution Jan. 3 declaring full support for "the efforts of the President to end the tragic conflict in Indochina now through a negotiated settlement." The vote was 16–10. The resolution was sponsored by Sen. Charles H. Percy (Ill.).

A similar resolution backing the Administration's negotiation effort to end the war was adopted by the House Republican Conference Jan. 6 by a 135–7 vote. An effort by Paul N. McCloskey Jr. (Calif.) to amend the resolution to call for an end to bombing of "inhabited areas" was rejected 91–43.

A White House statement from Press Secretary Ronald L. Ziegler Jan. 3 cautioned the Democrats in Congress against any steps that could jeopardize the peace negotiations being undertaken in Paris.

In rebutting Democratic antiwar critics on the floor Jan. 4, Senate Republican Leader Hugh Scott (Pa.) suggested the senators "temper our language" and "remember there is something more important than headlines and that is national security."

Nixon meets Congressional leaders. President Nixon told a group of Republican and Democratic Congressional leaders at a White House meeting Jan. 5 that although he was aware that many of them opposed his Vietnam policy, he was determined to achieve "a proper kind of settlement." One congressman quoted Nixon as having told the gathering that "We should know fairly quickly next week whether the North Vietnamese, as they claimed, are ready to negotiate seriously the three major issues of the October agreement."

The three issues were identified as the return of U.S. war prisoners, a cease-fire in Vietnam and an agreement to permit all parties in South Vietnam to determine their future.

Nixon Administration officials had said Jan. 3 that the U.S. was resuming the peace talks with North Vietnam without assurances that a settlement would be reached. The view was conveyed in conversations with members of Congress, legislative staff members and newsmen. The aides confirmed that the American air strikes north of North Vietnam's 20th Parallel had been suspended solely in exchange for a North Vietnamese pledge that the forthcoming negotiations would be "serious."

White House Press Secretary Ronald L. Ziegler warned that the antiwar mood in Congress could threaten the negotiations. He said "Members of Congress should ask themselves if they want to take the responsibility of raising doubts in the minds of the enemy about the United States position and thereby prolong the negotiations."

Klein attacks war critics. White House Communications director Herbert G. Klein attacked Congressional war critics Jan. 7 as "irresponsible" and said President Nixon "had a very clear mandate" from the presidential election "to proceed the way he has on Vietnam." Saying "some of the more irresponsible members" of Congress "have been critical in a way which could slow down" the U.S. peace effort, Klein called for "less rhetoric and more support in the Congress."

Replying to a question whether the U.S. might resume bombing such as in the B-52 raids of the Hanoi-Haiphong area in December 1972, Klein said, "I would not rule out any tactic that is necessary to protect American lives or to carry out the military objectives which are essential."

Klein made the remarks during an appearance on NBC's "Meet the Press" with John D. Ehrlichman, Nixon's chief domestic adviser.

Ehrlichman, responding to a question why the President had not consulted with Congressional leaders before making the bombing raid decision, said it was "simply not appropriate for a president to do things by committee" in that situation. It was "a question whether that would add anything to the success of the negotiations," which was "what we have to look at, . . . the ultimate outcome of this," he added.

Canadian House deplores U.S. raids. In an unprecedented action, the Canadian House of Commons Jan. 5 unanimously adopted a resolution deploring the U.S. raids on North Vietnam and calling on Washington to refrain from further

bombing on the Hanoi-Haiphong area. The resolution, drawn up by the government of Prime Minister Pierre Elliott Trudeau, was introduced by External Affairs Minister Mitchell W. Sharp. Sharp said in a speech that although Canadians were distressed by violence perpetrated by all sides in the Vietnam conflict, they were "shaken by the large-scale bombing in the Hanoi-Haiphong area. We found it very difficult to understand the reason for that bombing, . . . We deplore that action."

Among other international repercussions to the bombing:

A joint statement Jan. 4 by 40 nonaligned members of the United Nations charged that the U.S. bombing of North Vietnam was "indiscriminate and savage" and called for its immediate halt.

British Labor party leader Harold Wilson was reported Jan. 3 to have canceled a lecture tour of the U.S. because of his objections to the American bombing.

West German Chancellor Willy Brandt's silence on the American bombing was criticized Jan. 2 by the Young Socialists, the junior arm of his governing Democratic Socialist party. The statement accused Brandt of "hush-up tactics."

The Danish government Jan. 2 proposed a $750,000 humanitarian gift to North Vietnam. Premier Anker Jorgensen said the assistance was proposed by his Cabinet because of the great need created by the raids on the Hanoi-Haiphong area.

The U.S. protested to Australia Jan. 3 and 4 over the decision by Australian unions to boycott American ships. Thirty Australian labor unions Jan. 4 countered the protests with a warning that they would intensify their actions against U.S. firms in Australia unless President Nixon reached a peace agreement soon with North Vietnam. Their statement was handed to the U.S. consulate general in Sydney. The American protests were conveyed Jan. 3 by Secretary of State William P. Rogers to Australian Charge d'Affaires Roy Fernandez and Jan. 4 by U.S. Ambassador Walter L. Rice in Canberra.

An anti-American protest in Dacca, Bangla Desh Jan. 1 resulted in the death of two persons and the wounding of six others. Police reportedly opened fire after a demonstrator threw a Molotov cocktail into the U.S. Information Service building and set it afire.

Laird says Vietnamization completed. Defense Secretary Melvin R. Laird told Congress Jan. 8 that "from a military standpoint, the Vietnamization program has been completed" and that "the Vietnamese people today, in my view, are fully capable of providing for their own in-country security."

"Should negotiations fail," Laird added, "Vietnamization makes possible the complete termination of American involvement in the war, contingent always on the safe return of American prisoners-of-war and an accounting for those missing in action throughout Indochina."

Laird gave these assessments before the House Armed Services Committee in his final report after four years as defense secretary. His term would end with the second inauguration of President Nixon, who had chosen Elliot L. Richardson, secretary of health, education and welfare, as his successor.

Laird said Vietnamization had been "the most impressive logistics story the past four years." He said more than $1 billion worth of U.S.-built facilities had been turned over to the South Vietnamese armed forces during the U.S. troop withdrawal and more than $5.3 billion worth of new military equipment had been delivered to Saigon in just over three years. He also said more than $400 million in "usuable property" had been disposed of in Vietnam during the process.

The U.S. would continue to maintain a military "presence" in Vietnam, he said, but he stressed that this was not being done "because of a lack of capability on the part of the South Vietnamese" but primarily because of the Administration's pledge to remain until the POWs were released.

Laird declined to discuss the Paris peace talks or the December, 1972 B-52 bombing raids in the Hanoi-Haiphong area except to say the raids were ordered "when we determined negotiations were not going forward." The raids, he said, were a return to Nixon's policy announced May 8, 1972 of bombing and mining North Vietnam harbors until it agreed to negotiate an internationally

supervised cease-fire, release of POWs and an accounting of the missing.

(Outgoing Central Intelligence Director Richard Helms briefed the Senate Armed Services Committee at a closed session Jan. 8. Sen. William B. Saxbe [R, Ohio] disclosed afterwards the "prime thing" he had talked about was the North Vietnamese "ability to wage war," which was "not much diminished.")

Australians end U.S. ship boycott. The Australian Maritime Union voted Jan. 9 to call off the boycott of U.S. ships, imposed Dec. 28–29, 1972 to protest the intensive U.S. bombing of North Vietnam. A union official said the move had been taken at the request of the Australian Trade Union.

The U.S. International Longshoremen's Association (ILA), which had taken retaliatory action against Australian ships Jan. 3, called off its boycott Jan. 10. The ILA ban had affected Australian ships in eight Eastern and Southern ports of the U.S.

Australian Prime Minister Gough Whitlam warned Jan. 9 that any resumption of massive American raids on North Vietnam would again evoke critical and public reaction from him. Whitlam, however, disassociated himself from the sharp attacks recently directed against President Nixon over the bombing by three of his Cabinet ministers. Whitlam told his ministers that any more criticism of the U.S.' Indochina policy would be made by him in his additional capacity as foreign minister. One of the officials, Regional and Urban Development Minister Thomas Uren, had accused Nixon at an antiwar rally in Sydney Jan. 7 of "false pretentions," "double dealing" and "a mentality of thuggery" in his Vietnam policy.

Other international reaction: The executive committee of the World Council of Churches Jan. 9 called on all U.S. churches to "do everything in their power" to protest the American raids north of the 20th Parallel. The plea was issued at the end of an 11-day conference in Bangkok, Thailand.

Netherlands Premier Barend Bisheuvel received a letter Jan. 8 from 120 prominent Dutch scholars, artists and newspapermen requesting that the Dutch

Washington be recalled if continued the war in Indochina.

group of U.S. religious leaders, on a tour of Europe, stopped off in London Jan. 7 and appealed to British churches and politicians to press the U.S. for peace in Indochina.

In a related development, Iceland announced Jan. 8 that it would recognize North Vietnam, but would continue to recognize the Saigon regime as the legitimate government of South Vietnam.

The North Vietnamese Communist party newspaper Nhan Dan Jan. 10 thanked Sweden, Norway, Denmark, Finland and Iceland for their criticism of the U.S. bombing of North Vietnam in December 1972. The CP journal called the statements made by the Scandinavian leaders "a brilliant example of international solidarity."

King Gustav VI Adolf of Sweden called for an immediate peace in Vietnam Jan. 11 and said the U.S. must not resume its "merciless bombing" of Hanoi and Haiphong.

Indian Prime Minister Indira Gandhi Jan. 11 expressed "horror" at the "savage bombing" of North Vietnam.

The America House library in Frankfurt, West Germany was broken into by vandals and set afire Jan. 10. The U.S. consulate in Lyons, France was invaded by antiwar demonstrators, who pulled down the American flag and raised a swastika flag.

In his first public response to the American bombing, West German Chancellor Willy Brandt Jan. 15 joined his Social Democratic party (SDP) in warning the U.S. that its relations with Western European states would deteriorate if the Vietnam war did not end quickly. Later, upon hearing that the U.S. had halted the bombing, the SDP called the action an "important step" on the way to peace.

The U.S. consulate in Amsterdam was occupied Jan. 15 by 34 Dutch antiwar demonstrators.

The World Council of Churches had announced in Geneva Jan. 11 that it was sending North Vietnam $300,000 worth of medical supplies.

Lower-echelon peace talks resume. Technical experts of the U.S. and North Vietnam conferred in the Paris suburb of Gif-sur-Yvette Jan. 2–5 in preparation for the resumption of the private peace talks scheduled to be resumed between Henry A. Kissinger and Le Duc Tho Jan. 8. The lower-echelon meetings presumably were dealing with the technical aspects of a cease-fire.

The U.S. and North Vietnamese delegations were headed by Deputy Assistant Secretary of State William H. Sullivan and Deputy Foreign Minister Nguyen Co Thach.

French Foreign Minister Maurice Schumann, who had been in contact with both sides, said after the Jan. 2 meeting, the first since Dec. 23, 1972, that the U.S. and North Vietnam "have not drawn closer together." Schumann had acknowledged earlier in the day that France had played "an essential role" in getting the U.S. and North Vietnam to resume negotiations. This had been indicated earlier by French President Georges Pompidou who had disclosed Jan. 1 that he had exchanged letters with President Nixon "in addition to the usual contacts with both sides."

The regular four-party peace conference in Paris, in recess since Dec. 21, resumed Jan. 4. A spokesman for the North Vietnamese delegation said after the meeting that the principal impediment to a settlement remained U.S. policy which "is an invariable one that has been practiced for decades—to perpetuate the division of Vietnam." "Vietnam is one, the Vietnamese nation is one," the spokesman said.

The South Vietnamese delegation leader, Pham Dang Lam, countered the Hanoi position by stating that there would be lasting peace "only if North Vietnam and South Vietnam respect each other's territorial integrity and sovereignty."

Chief U.S. delegate William J. Porter said during the meeting that negotiations and subsequent relations would require "continuing work, patience and a large measure of understanding."

On arriving in Paris Jan. 6 in preparation for his talks with Kissinger, Le Duc Tho said it was up to the U.S. to reach a settlement. Referring to the nine-point draft agreement reached in October 1972, Tho said, "Now the decisive moment has come either to settle the Vietnam problem quickly and sign the agreed accord or to continue the war. The American Administration has to make a definite choice; the responsibility rests entirely on the United States."

Tho denounced the American air strikes on North Vietnam in December as "the most inhuman and barbarous ever seen in the history of the war." He asserted their purpose was "to make the Vietnamese people bow and accept the conditions posed by the United States in the negotiations." Although the raids had killed thousands of innocent civilians, Tho said, the U.S. had "obtained no result."

Kissinger-Tho talks resume. Henry A. Kissinger of the U.S. and Le Duc Tho of North Vietnam resumed their secret Indochina peace talks near Paris Jan. 8. Further sessions were held through Jan. 12, but no substantive reports came from either side. The last round of talks between the two negotiators had collapsed Dec. 13, 1972 and was followed by massive U.S. air strikes on North Vietnam.

On arriving in Paris Jan. 7, Kissinger had said "President Nixon has sent me back to make one more major effort to conclude the negotiations." He said the U.S. expected "the talks this time will be serious and worthy of the yearnings of the people all over the world for an early end to the war."

North Vietnam expressed pessimism about the future negotiations. The Communist party newspaper Nhan Dan was quoted as saying Jan. 7 "There are no signs showing any intention by the American government to abandon its demands nor any will to sign the [October 1972] accord on the cessation of the war and the establishment of peace in Vietnam." Following the Jan. 9 session, Nhan Dan said "There is no indication that the negotiations may achieve results."

U.S. and North Vietnamese technical experts continued to hold separate meetings near Paris Jan. 8–10 on secondary aspects of a cease-fire, and joined the Jan. 11 meeting of Kissinger and Tho.

The delegates to the four-sided formal peace talks held another session in Paris Jan. 11 and concentrated on the basic issue of whether there was to be one or two Vietnams. Heyward Isham, acting chief of the U.S. delegation, called for "a sober de-escalation of rhetoric." (Isham was replacing William J. Porter, who had returned to Washington Jan. 10 to assume a new post in the Nixon Administration)

Pentagon secrecy protested. The Amerian Civil Liberties Union Jan. 8 protested a Pentagon order barring all Defense Department civilian and military employes from commenting on the resumption of the Vietnam peace talks and suspension of the bombing of North Vietnam above the 20th Parallel.

The order, made public by the Pentagon Jan. 9, was issued Dec. 30, 1972, the day the bombing was curtailed, under the signature of Pentagon spokesman Jerry W. Friedheim.

Defense Secretary Melvin R. Laird implemented the order at a Pentagon ceremony Jan. 5 by declaring that, "during the next week to 10 days, no information will be put out of this building at any time that would possibly jeopardize the success of these negotiations."

Moorer says raids effective. Adm. Thomas H. Moorer, chairman of the U.S. Joint Chiefs of Staff, said Jan. 9 that the Hanoi-Haiphong bombing raids against "military targets" had been "very effective" in reducing North Vietnam's "warmaking potential." Moorer made the remarks after briefing the House Military Appropriations Committee and the Armed Services Committee at closed sessions. Moorer reportedly reaffirmed the military reason for the raids as being to blunt an enemy buildup being conducted during peace negotiations. He also reportedly denied bomb hits against U.S. prison camps, including one known as the Hanoi Hilton, although the possibility of shrapnel damage was left open.

After the Armed Services Committee hearing, Chairman F. Edward Hebert (D, La.) defended the bombing. "We brought them to the conference table in the beginning by bombing and we brought them back to the conference table by bombing."

One of the congressmen at the Armed Services Committee hearing, Rep. Michael J. Harrington (D, Mass.), reported that Moorer had told them he had not been consulted by the White House specifically on Oct. 23, 1972 when bombing north of the 20th Parallel was halted, or on Dec. 18, 1972, when it was temporarily resumed. Harrington said Moorer told them contingency plans had been in readiness and President Nixon put them into effect without specific prior consultation on the decision with the military.

(At a confirmation hearing by the Senate Armed Services Committee Jan. 11, William P. Clements Jr., designated deputy defense secretary, refuted this. He said "Moorer was consulted" on the December bombing and had suggested it as "a contingency plan.")

Richardson questioned on bombings. Elliot Richardson, President Nixon's nominee to be the new defense secretary, appeared Jan. 9 before the Senate Armed Services Committee for the first day of questioning in his confirmation hearings.

Richardson refused to give his personal view of the U.S. bombing campaign in December 1972 against North Vietnam or to answer a query about the next Administration step in Vietnam if the peace negotiations failed to produce a settlement.

Richardson pleaded unfamiliarity with defense policy in declining to discuss details of that policy. He declined to discuss the bombing in order not to jeopardize the sensitive peace talks.

During his second appearance before the armed services panel Jan. 10, Richardson did offer a comment on the bombing. While he was not cognizant of all the factors that led to the President's "agonizing decision" to resume the heavy bombing, he said, he could understand how it might have been made in an effort to end the war. Asked if that meant he favored the bombing, Richardson said, "I think it would be more accurate to say I support it."

The committee approved Richardson's nomination Jan. 16.

A member of the Armed Services Committee, Sen. Harold E. Hughes (D, Iowa), suggested at the Jan. 10 hearing the possibility of delaying confirmation of Cabinet nominees "so we can stop the war." While he was not opposed to Richardson's confirmation, he said, "the goal is to stop the mechanism of the Senate, including bills and nominations, so we can stop the war."

Clements questioned on atomic weapons—When William P. Clements Jr., nominated to be deputy defense secretary, appeared before the committee Jan. 11, he refused to rule out the possible use of nuclear weapons against North Vietnam. Asked by Hughes if he would "recommend use of nuclear warheads in North Vietnam if no agreement is reached" on ending the war, he replied that "I would have to study the answer to that" and "I wouldn't say I either would not or would."

"You won't eliminate in your own mind," Hughes pursued, "the use of nuclear warheads in Vietnam?" "No sir," Clements answered. "I would not eliminate it . . . and that is not to say I would be in favor of it either."

"If the President recommended it," Hughes continued, "you would support it?" "I'd either support the President," Clements replied, ". . . and if I didn't, I'd be on my way back to Dallas."

Later Hughes asked Clements if the peace talks failed and the war resumed if he would be willing to condone use of nuclear weapons in the war. "As I understand the situation today," Clements said, "with my limited knowledge, the answer would be no."

Clements' refusal to disavow use of nuclear weapons in Vietnam evoked domestic and foreign protests, and statements reaffirming the Administration's rejection of use of nuclear weapons in the Vietnam war were issued Jan. 12 by the White House and the Defense and State Departments.

White House Press Secretary Ronald L. Ziegler said "the President has made clear that nuclear weapons were not one of the contingent elements he would use in relation to Vietnam. He has said that repeatedly."

The Pentagon also released a memorandum quoting Clements as saying he was "in complete agreement" with the policy expressed by Secretary of State William P. Rogers April 17, 1972 that "we are not going to reintroduce American ground combat troops to South Vietnam and we are not going to use nuclear weapons in South Vietnam or North Vietnam."

The committee approved Clements' nomination Jan. 16.

South Vietnam ground, air action. Viet Cong and North Vietnamese troops carried out attacks throughout South Vietnam Jan. 5–7 that were twice the average number of the previous two months. Allied military sources described the assaults as the Communists' "winterspring campaign."

A Saigon command spokesman said there were 116 separate Communist assaults Jan. 4, 97 Jan. 5 and 106 Jan. 6. The number of enemy raids in the 24-hour period ending at dawn Jan. 8 totaled 77, the first time in five days that the daily average dropped below 100. The heaviest fighting centered around Quangtri city and in the vicinity of Kontum city and Pleiku in the Central Highlands.

Communist shells struck the Longbinh army post, 12 miles northeast of Saigon, Jan. 9 and destroyed 135,000 gallons of fuel oil.

U.S. planes continued to strike at Communist targets in South Vietnam Jan. 5–9. Fourteen B-52 missions and 229 fighter-bomber strikes were flown Jan. 5. B-52 raids were directed at Communist positions in the Central Highlands Jan. 8–9. The U.S. command reported the loss of a helicopter just below the demilitarized zone Jan. 10. All seven crewmen were missing.

Five U.S. planes Jan. 8 accidentally dropped 35 bombs on the allied air base at Danang. Nine Americans and one Vietnamese on the base were wounded. A fuel tank was hit and burned with a loss of 875,000 gallons of fuel.

Communists renew Laos attacks. Communist forces in Laos were reported Jan. 2 to have launched a strong drive north of Vientiane during the New Year's holiday weekend, overrunning a number of government positions and inflicting heavy casualties. A government statement Jan. 9 said "we have intelligence from captured documents that they [the Communists] are about to open a general offensive."

Pathet Lao and North Vietnamese troops scored a number of successes Dec. 30, 1972. They captured the government strongpoint of Sala Phou Khoun, on Route 13 about 100 miles north of the capital. Communist forces ambushed a government convoy to the south and many of the Laotians were presumed killed or captured. Government troops were reported to have recaptured the Se Bang River bridgehead, following its seizure by the Communists Dec. 23. The Communists were said to have blown up the span before government forces could retake it.

Government troops abandoned the southern town of Saravane Jan. 9 in the face of a heavy Communist ground attack and artillery barrage.

Heavy fighting was raging along Route 13 north from Vientiane to the royal capital of Luang Prabang. Following the Communist capture of Sala Phou Khoun, government troops reportedly demolished some sections of the highway to slow down the Communist advance.

The upsurge of fighting in Laos was creating a new movement of civilian refugees. More than 1,000 persons had fled the town of Vang Vieng as a result of Communist shelling Jan. 4. Other refugees were said to have moved south to Phonhong, 40 miles north of Vientiane, and to the Laotian capital itself.

Peace talks deadlock continues— Laotian peace talks remained deadlocked following two more sessions Jan. 2 and 9 between government and Pathet Lao representatives in Vientiane.

The Jan. 2 meeting was taken up with Pathet Lao denunciation of reportedly government-inspired newspaper accounts that heroin had been found in the baggage of a Pathet Lao delegation member boarding a plane for Hanoi. Gen. Phoune Sipreseuth, leader of the delegation, asserted that the delegate in question had left for Hanoi on a different day and that his baggage was not searched and he was not carrying heroin.

Key members of the Pathet Lao and government delegations were absent from the Jan. 9 meeting.

Cambodian military action. Cambodian troops engaged in sharp fighting with local and Vietnamese Communist soldiers in the vicinity of Pnompenh. Jan. 2–8.

Two government positions 24 miles southwest of the capital were overrun Jan. 2 by Cambodian Khmer Rouge rebel forces. A combined rebel-Viet Cong drive against a government strongpoint 10 miles from the Pnompenh airport was beaten back. In one of the Communist assaults, against Prey Totung, 20 Cambodians were killed and 40 were wounded, the Cambodian command reported.

Pnompenh's Pochentong airport and military base were struck by Communist rockets Jan. 4. More than 30 persons were killed and wounded.

A Communist commando force Jan. 4 infiltrated the provincial capital of Tram Khnar, 25 miles south of Pnompenh. Government troops reoccupied the town Jan. 6, but heavy fighting continued around Tram Khnar through Jan. 8. A 2,-000-man Cambodian force, supported by waves of air strikes, renewed a drive Jan. 8 to push a combined force of Khmer Rouge and Viet Cong troops from the outskirts of the battered town. Government defenders inside Tram Khnar had come under harrassing fire through the night.

Communist troops Jan. 8 overran Prek Prasap, 15 miles northwest of Pnompenh, but were ousted from the town the following day by a government counterattack.

U.S. to keep Thailand bases. Premier Thanom Kittikachorn announced Jan. 10 that his government had granted a U.S. request to keep American troops and planes in Thailand after a Vietnam ceasefire. It had been agreed previously that the U.S. would keep its 49,000 troops and seven bases in Thailand only for the duration of the Vietnam war.

U.S. losses & troop withdrawals—The U.S. command reported Jan. 11 that three Americans had been killed in action Dec. 31–Jan. 6. The toll was two fewer than the previous week and raised total American combat deaths in the Indochina war to 45,931.

South Vietnamese losses Dec. 31–Jan. 6 were the highest in six weeks, with 385 killed and 1,449 wounded, compared with 293 killed and 1,056 wounded the previous week.

The Saigon command estimated that 923 North Vietnamese and Viet Cong had been killed Dec. 31–Jan. 6, a drop of 365 from the previous week.

The U.S. command reported Jan. 15 that 200 American troops had left Vietnam the previous week, reducing the total U.S. force in the country to 23,800.

U.S. raids hit panhandle. U.S. B-52s and fighter-bombers struck the areas below North Vietnam's 20th Parallel Jan. 7–11 in the continuing campaign to prevent Communist war supplies from reaching battle zones in South Vietnam, Laos and Cambodia. Targets struck during the five-day period included trucks, antiaircraft sites, military warehouses and supply routes.

The heaviest raid on the southern panhandle since the halt in the strikes above the 20th Parallel Dec. 30, 1972 occurred Jan. 10. A total of 15 B-52 missions and 140 fighter-bomber strikes was reported carried out. Hanoi radio claimed North Vietnamese gunners shot down two B-52s Jan. 10 and a fighter-bomber Jan. 8. The U.S. command denied the loss of any B-52s but conceded the loss of a fighter-bomber Jan. 10.

Despite the ban on raids above the 20th Parallel, the U.S. Defense Department Jan. 9 confirmed a report that American planes were being permitted to operate in the bomb-free zone to pursue North Vietnamese jets that attempted to attack U.S. planes on missions in the southern panhandle. One such incident was reported to have occurred Jan. 6 when a U.S. F-4 Phantom pursued and shot down a North Vietnamese MiG-21. U.S. officials disclosed that two types of American reconnaissance craft continued to operate above the 20th Parallel—unmanned photo drones and SR-71 spy planes, which fly about 80,000 feet, above the range of North Vietnamese air defenses.

The U.S. command reported a Navy fighter-bomber Jan. 12 downed a North Vietnamese MiG-17 "a few miles north" of the 20th Parallel, the northern limits set by President Nixon for air operations. It was the 184th MiG downed by American planes in the war, according to official U.S. statistics.

The U.S. command reported that a B-52 was damaged by an enemy missile Jan. 13, but the bomber returned safely to its base at Danang in South Vietnam.

The command confirmed the downing of a fighter-bomber by North Vietnamese gunners near Thanhhoa Jan. 14, but said the two pilots were rescued.

Hanoi radio claimed Jan. 16 that North Vietnamese antiaircraft artillery had shot down two B-52s over Nghean Province Jan. 14. The North Vietnamese press agency said this brought to six the number of B-52s shot down over the province since Jan. 4.

The North Vietnamese Foreign Ministry had charged Jan. 13 that B-52s were "carpet-bombing" populated areas in four provinces below the 20th Parallel. The ministry said reconnaissance missions being flown above the line "were in preparation for new acts of war" against the Hanoi-Haiphong area.

Hanoi takes action against damage— North Vietnam had declared a national emergency as a result of the heavy damage inflicted on its heartland by U.S. bombing raids in December. Hanoi radio reported Jan. 6 that Premier Pham Van Dong had ordered an emergency relief program "to stabilize production activities and the people's living conditions in areas hit by bombs."

A Hanoi broadcast Jan. 7 said government officials had visited military units and devastated regions in Hanoi Jan. 5. One of the installations inspected was the Yen Phu power plant, one of the five power plants in the Hanoi-Haiphong area reported by the U.S. command to have been heavily damaged in the raids.

An Agence France-Presse (AFP) report from Hanoi Jan. 7 said more bodies were found that day in the city's rubble. In one section alone 1,445 dead were said to have been counted.

An AFP report from Haiphong Jan. 6 said the U.S. raids had virtually destroyed the port city's industrial zone. Haiphong officials were said to have told journalists Jan. 5 that U.S. planes had flown 366 sorties against the port area Dec. 18-30, and that 15,000 tons of bombs dropped during that period had killed 305 civilians, wounded 882 and destroyed 5,800 homes.

North Vietnam announced Jan. 8 that hundreds of antiaircraft units had been formed in the Hanoi-Haiphong area in anticipation of a possible resumption of American air raids north of the 20th Parallel. The units were to be manned by home guards and militia.

Raids cost $500 million—The 12-day bombing campaign against North Vietnam Dec. 18-30, 1972 added about $500 million to the cost of the Vietnam war, according to Pentagon sources Jan. 5. Estimated total Vietnam war costs, including the 12-day bombing campaign, were said to have increased by $1 billion–$2 billion above previous estimates.

U.S. jet raids in South. Despite the halt in American air action over North Vietnam, U.S. planes continued to carry out heavy air strikes Jan. 10-17 in South Vietnam, in support of government forces engaged in scattered clashes. Ground fighting during the week was generally light.

B-52 bombers struck traditional Communist staging areas northwest of Saigon Jan. 12. The U.S. command said 14 three-plane formations pounded targets between the former Michelin and Lai Khe rubber plantations, 40 miles from the capital. The raids followed reports of North Vietnamese attempts to move heavy artillery across the Cambodian border into South Vietnam.

In the second mistaken air attack in the Danang area in a week, a U.S. plane Jan. 14 dropped a bomb on a populated region, killing one civilian and wounding 12.

The U.S. command reported that American raids during a 24-hour period Jan. 17-18 were the heaviest in more than a month. The command said fighter-bombers had carried out 311 strikes and B-52s about 90. The B-52 attacks ranged from Quangtri Province to the Mekong Delta. For the second time in a week the planes struck at a suspected North Vietnamese buildup in the Michelin-Lai Khe rubber plantation areas.

Thieu asked invasion of North. In an interview made public Jan. 13, President Thieu had suggested that if current peace talks failed, the U.S. and South Vietnam should intensify the conflict "in all possible ways," including an invasion of North Vietnam.

Thieu expressed this view in a lengthy interview Dec. 30, 1972 with Italian journalist Oriana Fallaci, the day the U.S. had halted bombing raids north of North Vietnam's 20th Parallel.

Thieu reiterated his objections to the efforts of Henry A. Kissinger to negotiate a settlement with North Vietnam. He asserted that "if I had signed what Kissinger wanted, within six months there would be bloodshed." Thieu said Kissinger and President Nixon "were too impatient to get a peace, too impatient to negotiate and sign. When you negotiate with the Communists, you shouldn't fix a deadline ... otherwise they exploit you."

Thieu was also critical of U.S. military policy, saying "For years they bomb, they stop bombing, they bomb again, they reduce, they escalate, they reduce over the 20th Parallel, under the 20th Parallel. What's that. A war?" "Had we bombed North Vietnam continuously, had we landed in North Vietnam, the war could be over by now," Thieu said.

Ceasefire Ends U.S. Military Role

Nixon announces truce pact. In a television and radio report to the American people Jan. 23, President Nixon announced that his special adviser, Henry A. Kissinger, and Le Duc Tho of North Vietman had initialed an agreement in Paris that day "to end the war and bring peace with honor in Vietnam and Southeast Asia."

The President then read the statement, that also was being issued simultaneously in Hanoi, announcing the action taken by the two negotiators and the full-fledged signing ceremony that was to be held Jan. 27 in Paris.

Nixon provided only a sketchy account of the agreement, whose details were subsequently made public Jan. 24. He said the accord met "all the conditions I laid down" Jan. 25 and May 8, 1972 and had "the full support" of South Vietnamese President Nguyen Van Thieu.

The President reiterated support for South Vietnam, saying that the U.S. "will continue to recognize" the Saigon regime "as the sole legitimate government of South Vietnam" and would "continue to aid South Vietnam within the terms of the agreement." He promised strict U.S. adherence to terms of the accord and appealed to the other interested parties to extend similar cooperation. Nixon urged "the other major powers" involved indirectly in the conflict to exert "mutual

restraint" to assure that "the agreement is carried out and peace is maintained."

Explaining his public silence during the private Kissinger-Tho discussions the past several weeks, Nixon said if he had spoken out then, he "would not only have violated our understanding with North Vietnam," but also "would have seriously harmed and possibly destroyed the chances for peace."

Nixon said he was proud of the Americans who had served in Vietnam, and especially of those "who gave their lives." He cited "some of the bravest people I have met"—the families of American prisoners of war and the missing in action.

Nixon lauded his predecessor, former President Lyndon B. Johnson, who had died Jan. 22. Noting that Johnson during his administration had "endured the vilification of those who sought to portray him as a man of war," Nixon said "no one would have welcomed this peace more than he."

Thieu cautious about peace—President Nguyen Van Thieu simultaneously joined President Nixon in announcing the Paris agreement. In a radio broadcast Jan. 24 (Saigon time), the South Vietnamese leader said he regarded the accord only as a battlefield truce and not as a guarantee of "a stable, long, lasting peace."

Discussing future political prospects, Thieu said if his government and the National Liberation Front (Viet Cong) agree on an election, "it remains to be seen whether the Front will accept the result of the election."

"The political struggle phase," he said, "although not as bloody, will be as tough and dangerous as the military struggle phase."

The main point of Thieu's address was that the Paris agreement confirmed his government's victory over · the Communists, that after 18 years of war they were forced to stop the conflict and acknowledge the existence of two Vietnams—South and North—and the sovereignty of South Vietnam.

The Communists, he said, had failed "in their demands for neutralism, ... and to overthrow the legal institutions of Vietnam." They also had failed in their efforts to force the Saigon regime to recognize the Viet Cong's Provisional Revolutionary Government, Thieu said. He took note of the fact, however, that his government would negotiate with the Viet Cong "in regard to the participation of members of the National Liberation Front" in the government of South Vietnam.

Kissinger gives details of pact. At a news conference in Washington Jan. 24, Henry A. Kissinger, President Nixon's national security adviser, released the text of the Vietnamese cease-fire agreement that he and Le Duc Tho of North Vietnam had initialed in Paris Jan. 23. The accord had been drawn up in the final round of the two negotiators' secret protracted discussions concluded in the French capital Jan. 8–13.

The settlement included these principal provisions:

■ A cease-fire throughout North and South Vietnam effective Jan. 28 (Jan. 27 at 7 p.m. EST).

■ Complete withdrawal of all U.S. troops and military advisers and dismantling of American bases in South Vietnam within 60 days of the signing of the agreement.

■ The return of all U.S. and other prisoners of war and civilians throughout Indochina and the release of captured North Vietnamese and Viet Cong troops within 60 days. The first POWs were to be freed within 15 days, and the rest in equal installments at intervals of about 15 days. The matter of the release of imprisoned

Vietnamese civilians was to be negotiated by the Vietnamese themselves over a period of three months.

■ North Vietnamese troops were to remain in place in South Vietnam but they could not be replaced. Additional arms could be introduced into South Vietnam, but only to replace existing weapons.

■ Foreign troops were to be withdrawn from Cambodia and Laos, with no deadline set. Bases were barred in those two countries and the movement of troops and supplies through Laos and Cambodia was banned.

■ The demilitarized zone (DMZ) separating North and South Vietnam at the 17th Parallel was to remain as a provisional dividing line, with the eventual reunification of the country to be settled "through peaceful means."

■ The formation of a 1,160-man International Commission of Control and Supervision (ICCS) to supervise the release of prisoners, troop withdrawals, elections and other aspects of the agreement. The force was to be comprised of Canada, Hungary, Indonesia and Poland.

The commission was to be based throughout South Vietnam, including at border crossings. Preliminary probes of truce violations were to be handled first by a Joint Military Commission with forces from the U.S., South Vietnam, the Viet Cong's National Liberation Front and North Vietnam which would report its findings to the ICCS. The U.S. and North Vietnam would withdraw from the joint military commission within 60 days.

■ An international political conference on Indochina would be called within 30 days to "acknowledge the signed agreements." Its participants would include China and the Soviet Union.

■ The South Vietnamese government of President Nguyen Van Thieu would remain in office pending elections. The U.S. and North Vietnam were to respect "the South Vietnamese people's right to self-determination." A National Council of National Reconciliation and Concord would supervise the South Vietnamese elections. Its members would be representatives of the Saigon government, Communists and neutralists. All sides would respect the DMZ, there was to be no military movement across the strip and

Nixon's Jan. 23 Address to Nation on Vietnam War

Good evening. I have asked for this radio and television time tonight for the purpose of announcing that we today have concluded an agreement to end the war and bring peace with honor in Vietnam and Southeast Asia.

The following statement is being issued at this moment in Washington and Hanoi:

"At 12:30 Paris time today, Jan. 23, 1973, the agreement on ending the war and restoring peace in Vietnam was initialed by Dr. Henry Kissinger on behalf of the United States and Special Adviser Le Duc Tho on behalf of the Democratic Republic of Vietnam.

"The agreement will be formally signed by the parties participating in the Paris Conference on Vietnam on Jan. 27, 1973, at the International Conference Center in Paris. The cease-fire will take effect at 2400 Greenwich Mean Time Jan. 27, 1973. The United States and the Democratic Republic of Vietnam express the hope that this agreement will insure stable peace in Vietnam and contribute to the preservation of lasting peace in Indochina and Southeast Asia."

That concludes the formal statement.

Throughout the years of negotiations, we have insisted on peace with honor.

In my addresses to the nation from this room on Jan. 25 and May 8, [1972] I set forth the goals that we considered essential for peace with honor. In the settlement that has now been agreed to, all the conditions that I laid down then have been met—a ceasefire internationally supervised will begin at 7 p.m. this Saturday, Jan. 27, Washington time. Within 60 days from this Saturday all Americans held prisoners of war throughout Indochina will be released.

There will be the fullest possible accounting for all of those who are missing in action.

During the same 60-day period all American forces will be withdrawn from South Vietnam.

The people of South Vietnam have been guaranteed the right to determine their own future without outside interference.

By joint agreement, the full text of the agreement and the protocols to carry it out will be issued tomorrow.

Throughout these negotiations we have been in the closest consultation with President Thieu and other representatives of the Republic of Vietnam.

This settlement meets the goals and has the full support of President Thieu and the government of the Republic of Vietnam as well as that of our other allies who are affected.

The United States will continue to recognize the government of the Republic of Vietnam as the sole legitimate government of South Vietnam. We shall continue to aid South Vietnam within the terms of the agreement, and we shall support efforts for the people of South Vietnam to settle their problems peacefully among themselves.

We must recognize that ending the war is only the first step toward building the peace.

All parties must now see to it that this is a peace that lasts and also a peace that heals, and a peace that not only ends the war in Southeast Asia but contributes to the prospects of peace in the whole world. This will mean that the terms of the agreement must be scrupulously adhered to. We shall do everything the agreement requires of us, and we shall expect the other parties to do everything it requires of them. We shall also expect other interested nations to help insure that the agreement is carried out and peace is maintained.

As this long and very difficult war ends I would like to address a few special words to each of those who have been parties in the conflict.

First, to the people and government of South Vietnam. By your courage, by your sacrifice, you have won the precious right to determine your own future and you have developed the strength to defend that right. We look forward to working with you in the future, friends in peace as we have been allies in war.

To the leaders of North Vietnam: as we have ended the war through negotiations, let us now build a peace of reconciliation. For our part, we are prepared to make a major effort to help achieve that goal. But just as reciprocity was needed to end the war, so too will it be needed to build and strengthen the peace.

To the other major powers that have been involved, even indirectly, now is the time for mutual restraint so that the peace we have achieved can last.

And finally, to all of you who are listening, the American people, your steadfastness in supporting our insistence on peace with honor has made peace with honor possible.

I know that you would not have wanted that peace jeopardized. With our secret negotiations at the sensitive stage they were in during this recent period, for me to have discussed publicly our efforts to secure peace would not only have violated our understanding with North Vietnam, it would have seriously harmed and possibly destroyed the chances for peace.

Therefore I know that you now can understand why during these past several weeks I have not made any public statements about those efforts. The important thing was not to talk about peace but to get peace and to get the right kind of peace. This we have done.

Now that we have achieved an honorable agreement, let us be proud that America did not settle for a peace that would have betrayed our allies, that would have abandoned our prisoners of war or that would have ended the war for us but would have continued the war for the 50 million people of Indochina.

Let us be proud of the two and a half million young Americans who served in Vietnam, who served with honor and distinction in one of the most selfless enterprises in the history of nations.

And let us be proud of those who sacrificed, who gave their lives, so that the people of South Vietnam might live in freedom, and so that the world might live in peace.

In particular, I would like to say a word to some of the bravest people I have ever met—the wives, children, the families of our prisoners of war and the missing in action.

When others called on us to settle on any terms, you had the courage to stand for the right kind of peace, so that those who died and those who suffered would not have died and suffered in vain and so that where this generation knew war, the next generation would know peace. Nothing means more to me at this moment than the fact that your long vigil is coming to an end.

Just yesterday, a great American who once occupied this office died. In his life, President Johnson endured the vilification of those who sought to portray him as a man of war, but there was nothing he cared about more deeply than achieving a lasting peace in the world.

I remember the last time I talked with him. It was just the day after New Year's. He spoke then of his

inging peace, with making it the right
and I was grateful that he once again
pport for my efforts to gain such a
ould have welcomed this peace more

And I know he would join me in asking for those
who died and for those who live, let us consecrate this
moment by resolving together to make the peace we
have achieved a peace that will last.
Thank you, and good evening.

the use of force to reunify the two Vietnams was prohibited.

Kissinger said he expected the truce to take effect in Laos "within a short period of time" and that a "de facto" cease-fire would eventually take place in Cambodia.

The actual text of the military and political accord was called "Agreement on Ending the War and Restoring Peace in Vietnam." It was accompanied by four protocols, outlining the procedures for putting the cease-fire into effect. They dealt with (1) the return of military and civilian captives, (2) U.S. obligation to remove the mines planted in North Vietnamese waters since May 8, 1972, (3) the carrying out of the truce and the joint U.S.-Vietnamese military commission, and (4) the four-nation International Commission of Control and Supervision.

The signing of the documents in Paris Jan. 27 involved a complex procedure, in which the signatures of the four ministers were affixed to three documents. The Agreement on Ending the War was signed by Secretary of State William P. Rogers of the U.S. and Foreign Minister Tran Van Lam of South Vietnam on one page, and by Foreign Minister Nguyen Duy Trinh of North Vietnam and Nguyen Thi Binh, foreign minister of the Provisional Revolutionary Government (PRG), on another page. This was described by Kissinger as "a document involving the four parties," the preamble of which vaguely referred to them as "the parties participating in the Paris conference on Vietnam" and the "two South Vietnamese parties." Its deliberate vagueness was designed to circumvent the problem that Saigon and the Viet Cong "have not yet been prepared to recognize each other," Kissinger had said.

Later in the day Rogers and Trinh signed two documents, labeled "2-Party Versions," that were substantially similar to the four-party document signed earlier, except that they mentioned the names of all four parties, including the PRG.

Following the release of the documents at his news conference, Kissinger said the Nixon Administration had "substantially achieved" the negotiating goals it had es-

tablished for "an honorable agreement." In reviewing the course of his negotiations with Le Duc Tho in December 1972, Kissinger noted that the talks had broken down and that the U.S. had carried out the massive bombing of North Vietnam Dec. 18–29 "to make clear that the United States could not stand for an indefinite delay in the negotiations." He declined, however, to attribute the success of the resumed discussions with Tho solely to the bombing raids. ". . . the North Vietnamese are the most difficult people to negotiate with that I have ever encountered when they do not want to settle, they are also the most effective that I have to deal with when they finally decide to settle," Kissinger said. He added:

"We have gone through peaks and valleys in these negotiations of extraordinary intensity."

The documents released by Kissinger were said to be essentially the same as the nine-point draft agreement made public in October. Kissinger had said at the time that while the U.S. was seeking modifications, it did not intend to reject the accord altogether.

At his news conference he listed a number of changes the U.S. had sought and achieved. He said the U.S. wanted the international control commission to be in place at the time of the cease-fire to avoid last-minute attempts by the Communists to seize territory. The current agreement provided for the observers to meet within 24 hours of the truce, with some forces in place within 48 hours, and the rest within 15–30 days. The size of the force, however, represented a compromise. The U.S. had sought 5,000 men, North Vietnam insisted on only 250 and it was finally agreed that the force should total 1,160 men.

Kissinger said another point the U.S. had succeeded in obtaining was a cease-fire in Laos and Cambodia at about the same time as the one in Vietnam.

Kissinger noted:

"The provisions of the agreement with respect to Laos and Cambodia reaffirm as an obligation to all the parties of the provisions of the 1954 agreement on Cambodia and of the 1962 agreement on Laos, which affirms the neutrality and right to self-determination of those two countries. And they are therefore consistent with our basic position with respect also to South Vietnam.

"The provisions of the agreement specifically prohibit the use of Laos and Cambodia for military and any other operations against any of the signatories of the Paris agreement or against any other country. In other words, there is a flat prohibition against the use of base areas in Laos and Cambodia. There is a flat prohibition against the use of Laos and Cambodia for infiltration into Vietnam or for that matter into any other country.

"Finally, there is a requirement that all foreign troops be withdrawn from Laos and Cambodia and it is clearly understood that North Vietnamese troops are considered foreign with respect to Laos and Cambodia.

"Now as to the conflict within these countries, which could not be formally settled in an agreement which is not signed by the parties of that conflict. Let me make this plain without elaborating.

"It is our firm expectation that within a short period of time there will be a formal cease-fire in Laos, which in turn will lead to a withdrawal of all foreign forces from Laos and, of course, to the end of the use of Laos as a corridor of infiltration.

"The situation in Cambodia, as those of you who have studied it will know, is somewhat more complex because there are several parties headquartered in different countries and therefore we can say about Cambodia that it is our expectation that a de facto cease-fire will come into being over a period of time relevant to the execution of this agreement."

Kissinger said the U.S. had also obtained a clarification of the linguistic problem as it related to the functions of the National Council of National Conciliation and Concord and to the question of making it clear that the two Vietnams should live in peace with each other. Kissinger insisted that "We did not increase our demands after Oct. 26 and we substantially achieved the clarifications which we sought."

On the matter of North Vietnam's estimated 145,000 troops in the South, Kissinger said that although the agreement provided for their remaining in place, the U.S. expected a gradual reduction in the force since the pact stipulated they could not be replaced.

Kissinger concluded that "whether this agreement brings a lasting peace or not depends not only on its provisions but also on the spirit in which it is implemented." He expressed hope that "in a short time the animosities and the hatred and suffering of this period will be seen as aspects of the past. Of course the hatred will not rapidly disappear, and of course people who have fought for 25 years will not easily give up their objectives. But also people who have suffered for 25 years may at last come to know that they can achieve their real satisfaction by other and less brutal means."

(The U.S.' Indochina allies had given their approval of the Vietnam peace pact in meetings with Gen. Alexander M. Haig, Jr., Kissinger's aide, during his visit to their capitals Jan. 16–20. Haig returned to Washington Jan. 21 and briefed President Nixon and Kissinger on his mission. Before leaving Indochina, Haig had held another round of meetings with President Nguyen Van Thieu in Saigon Jan. 20. Nixon's emissary had returned to the South Vietnamese capital from Bangkok where he had held two days of meetings with Thai officials. After his conference with Thieu, Haig flew to Seoul and met briefly with South Korean President Chung Hee Park.)

Tho claims 'great victory.' At a news conference in Paris Jan. 24, chief North Vietnam negotiator Le Duc Tho hailed the agreement he had initialed with Henry A. Kissinger the previous day as a "great victory for the Vietnamese people." He said the accord was "basically the same" as the draft that had been reached in October 1972, before the negotiations with the U.S. had collapsed.

Tho said the "victory crowned a valiant combat conducted in unity by the army and the people of Vietnam." He lauded "the combat solidarity of the three Indochinese people," "the Socialist countries, the oppressed and all the peace-loving

Map shows approximate areas held by Allied and Communist forces in South Vietnam, Laos and Cambodia at cease-fire Jan. 28. While Communists control large regions, population concentrations are mostly in Allied-dominated areas.   Map by Wide World Photo

peoples of the world, including the American people who displayed their solidarity and gave devoted support to the just struggle of our people."

Tho took issue with Kissinger that their talks had broken down in December. He said: "At the time the negotiations were in the progress of developing, and I had returned home to report to my government. The first waves of bombing took place a few hours after my arrival in Hanoi." Tho denounced the bombings, saying they "in no way helped the negotiations. On the contrary, they contributed to delay."

Turning to some of the specific aspects of the accord, Tho indicated that he and Kissinger had solved the thorny question of the National Council of National Reconciliation and Concord by simply ignoring it. He said Hanoi favored calling the council a "structure of power," while Kissinger opposed this phrase and suggested instead that it be designated "an administrative structure." Hanoi also objected, and as a result both phrases were dropped along with detailed provisions of the composition of the body, Tho said.

Tho said from Hanoi's point of view the accords contained 13 cardinal points, which formed "a juridical base of great import." 'He listed one of them as American recognition of the "independence, sovereignty, unity and territorial integrity" of Vietnam, the same wording contained in the 1954 Geneva accords, which the U.S. had refused to sign. Tho hailed the recognition of what he called the "actual situation" in Vietnam, the existence of "two armies, two zones of control and other political forces." This phrase did not apear in any of the documents released that day. It was believed that Tho's phrase was one of the key "interpretations" that Kissinger had said had been read into the formal records of the talks.

Among the other cardinal points cited by Tho were the cease-fire and the removal of U.S. mines from North Vietnamese waters, withdrawal of all U.S. forces from Vietnam, the release of prisoners, the restrictions on troops and arms, the prohibition of reprisals, the guarantee of democratic liberties, "never before applied in South Vietnam," the establishment of the Council of Reconcilia-

tion on a basis of "mutual respect," the redesignation of the DMZ that stressed its "provisional" nature, and American recognition of its responsibility to furnish rehabilitation aid to North Vietnam.

World reaction to cease-fire. The initialing of the Vietnamese cease-fire agreement Jan. 24 evoked international expressions of relief coupled with the hope that the truce would lead to a permanent peace. Many nations pledged aid to rehabilitate the war-devastated nations.

A Soviet Foreign Ministry statement called the pact "a serious realistic step toward a peaceful settlement in Vietnam" and "a success for the Vietnamese people and the forces of peace and freedom."

The Chinese Foreign Ministry said the agreement was "not only in conformity with the interests of the Vietnamese people and the American people but will also be conducive to the relaxation of tension in the Far East and Asia."

French Foreign Minister Maurice Schumann said after a Cabinet meeting that his government welcomed the cease-fire accord and reaffirmed "its determination to contribute to the reconstruction and development" of the countries damaged by the conflict. Similar promises of assistance were made by Belgium, West Germany, Sweden, Denmark and the Netherlands.

The British Foreign Office said "the opportunity is now there to convert it [the truce agreement] to an enduring peace throughout Indochina."

South Korean President Chung Hee Park said his country's 37,000 troops would be withdrawn "immediately" from South Vietnam. He said he hoped "the cease-fire will lead to a lasting peace in Vietnam."

Thailand Premier Thanom Kittikachorn praised the agreement and said there must be "effective measures to insure that all parties abide" by it.

Indian Prime Minister Indira Gandhi called on all nations to "turn their attention to the task of collaborating and cooperating in the reconstruction of the war-ravaged nation" of Vietnam.

Australian Prime Minister Gough Whitlam said "conclusion of a cease-fire agreement is a hopeful first step toward eventual reconciliation between the contending forces in Vietnam."

U.N. Secretary General Kurt Waldheim said he was gratified by the truce agreement and announced that the U.N. "stands ready to play any role which may be required of it."

The cease-fire agreement for Vietnam spurred hopes in the Middle East that similar international efforts could also resolve the dispute in that region. Israeli Foreign Minister Abba Eban issued a statement to that effect, directing his words particularly to Egypt.

Jordanian Premier Ahmed al-Lawzi said the peace in Vietnam "will open the door to a solution of the Palestinian question."

Congress backs agreement. The announcement of a cease-fire agreement was greeted with praise by most Congressmen, although some said they would continue to press for limitations of the presidential war-making power.

President Nixon received a standing ovation from 25 Congressional leaders at a Jan. 24 White House briefing. According to Senate Minority Leader Hugh Scott (Pa.), "there wasn't a dry eye in the house" when Nixon completed his presentation. Sen. J. William Fulbright (D, Ark.), a leading critic of the American role in the war, said he had personally congratulated the President.

Another antiwar leader, Sen. Frank Church (D, Idaho) said he would introduce legislation to bar "re-entry" of U.S. combat forces in Vietnam, including air forces, even if the cease-fire broke down, which he said was "probable, if not predictable." But Senate Majority Leader Mike Mansfield (Mont.) said the accord "negated" the need for further Vietnam debate in Congress. Instead, Mansfield said, he would work for a bill that had been sponsored by 58 senators to limit the President's power to wage undeclared war. The bill would specifically exclude Vietnam from its scope, in response to Administration fears that North Vietnam would otherwise be encouraged to violate the cease-fire. Rep. Robert Leggett (D, Calif.) said he would introduce a similar bill in the House.

Nixon's decision to offer rehabilitation aid to North Vietnam provoked some dissent. Rep. Wayne Hays (D, Ohio) said Congress would have to move "over my dead body" to vote the funds, but House Appropriations Committee Chairman George H. Mahon (Tex.) said the assistance "must be accepted as a fact of life."

One of the few negative reactions came from Sen. Harold E. Hughes (D, Iowa), who said he was sorry that Nixon's Jan. 23 television address avoided "healing words" to encourage "reconciliation here at home." But Sen. Barry Goldwater (R, Ariz.) praised Nixon for facing up to "unprecedented criticism at home" on his conduct of the war.

Stocks decline—Despite the President's peace announcement, the Dow Jones industrial average registered its worst loss in 17 months Jan. 24 as the index fell 14.07 pts. to close at 1,004.59 on the New York Stock Exchange.

Analysts said the market had already absorbed the bullish effect of a peace settlement after progress in Paris negotiations toward the end of 1972. They attributed the new decline to purely economic factors, including fears of renewed inflation and higher interest rates as a result of President Nixon's easing of economic controls.

U.S. raids on North prior to halt The U.S. command reported Jan. 16 that in the final hours before the bombing halt in all of North Vietnam went into effect at 11 p.m. Jan. 15, American planes had destroyed three bridges near Vinh and started large oil fires near Quangkhe in the southern panhandle. A total of 87 fighter-bomber strikes and four missions by three-plane formations of B-52s were involved in the final 15 hours of operations Jan. 15.

Meeting soon to complete text of pact. President Nixon ordered a halt to all U.S. offensive military action against North Vietnam Jan. 15, including air strikes, shelling and mining operations. A White House statement said Nixon had taken the action "because of the progress made" in the recent Vietnam peace negotiations between Henry A. Kissinger and Le Duc Tho.

A joint U.S.-North Vietnamese statement Jan. 18 said Kissinger and Tho would meet again Jan. 23 "for the purpose of completing the text of an agreement." The statement was issued simultaneously by the White House (at Key Biscayne, Fla.) and the North Vietnamese delegation in Paris.

Asked by newsmen for clarification, Press Secretary Ronald L. Ziegler said Kissinger would be returning to Paris "to complete the text of an agreement that has the objective of stopping the fighting, ending the war and restoring peace."

The U.S. issued the statement after a series of telephone conversations between Nixon, Kissinger in Washington, and Kissinger's aide Gen. Alexander M. Haig Jr., who had been meeting with President Nguyen Van Thieu in Saigon.

The cessation of hostilities against North Vietnam was not extended to South Vietnam, where U.S. planes continued heavy strikes against Communist targets and South Vietnamese forces were engaged in scattered ground clashes with Viet Cong and North Vietnamese troops.

In the Jan. 15 announcement on the halt to American military action against the North, Ziegler had said the move was unilateral. He explained: "The North Vietnamese knew and we were aware that once progress in the negotiations was being made, that the United States was prepared to take unilateral steps, make a unilateral gesture such as we have announced today in relation to the entire situation."

Ziegler said that although no new mining operations would be conducted against North Vietnamese ports, "the mines that are there will remain in place" and "is a subject of negotiations and is being dealt with in the negotiations."

Hanoi radio Jan. 16 acknowledged the halt in all U.S. attacks on North Vietnam, but warned "This had been done before, and afterwards U.S. imperialists had resumed even more fierce and barbarous bombing and shelling."

The latest round of Kissinger-Tho talks that had apparently brought both sides closer to agreement had been conducted Jan. 8–13. (Both men had conferred for a total of 27 hours during the six days.) Before departing from Paris later Jan. 13 to report to President Nixon, Kissinger said his meetings with Tho had been "very extensive, very useful negotiations."

In its first public comment since resumption of the Kissinger-Tho talks in October 1972, the North Vietnamese representatives issued a short statement saying the latest meetings "have made progress."

Kissinger flew to the Florida White House and met with Nixon Jan. 14–15 to give him a detailed report on his meetings with Tho. Gen. Haig had attended the Jan. 14 discussions and was later dispatched by Nixon to Indochina to apprise President Thieu and other leaders of the status of the peace negotiations.

Haig met with Thieu and other high-ranking South Vietnamese officials Jan. 16–18 and reportedly presented copies of a draft of a new peace agreement. Haig was accompanied in the talks by U.S. Ambassador Ellsworth Bunker. After leaving Saigon, Haig made scheduled stops Jan. 18 in Vientiane, Pnompenh and Bangkok, where he briefed the leaders of Laos, Cambodia and Thailand on the peace talks. The general conferred Jan. 19 with Thai Premier Thanom Kittikachorn.

Formal peace talks suspended—The formal four-sided Vietnam peace conference in Paris was suspended Jan. 18 after its 174th weekly meeting. Although no official reason was given for the decision, the comments of the delegates implied they were waiting to see whether the secret Kissinger-Tho discussions would reach a final agreement by Jan. 25, the normal meeting day of the semi-public conference.

World reaction to bombing halt—International reaction Jan. 16 to the cessation of U.S. offensive action against North Vietnam was generally favorable.

Swedish Foreign Minister Krister Wickman said his government was "very happy about the halt of the bombing." Similar expressions were voiced by a spokesman for Japanese Premier Kakuei Tanaka, West Germany's ruling Social Democratic party and Norwegian Foreign Minister Dagfinn Vaarvik.

The East European Communist press welcomed the bombing halt, but questioned whether it meant the end of the conflict. The Czechoslovak CP journal Rude Pravo said "This is not the first time that bombing in Vietnam halted only to be resumed with even greater brutality." The Polish newspaper Zycie Warszawy said "President Nixon's decision does not mean the end of the war, but it certainly means that the chances for a final settlement have clearly increased."

Conservative senators warn Saigon. Statements cautioning Saigon not to be an obstacle to a peace agreement were delivered Jan. 18 by U.S. Sens. Barry Goldwater (R, Ariz.) and John C. Stennis (D, Miss.), chairman of the Senate Armed Services Committee, two of Saigon's strongest supporters in the Senate.

Stennis, in a Senate speech, and Goldwater, in a statement "directed to" South Vietnamese President Nguyen Van Thieu, made the same point, that objection to minor points in a peace agreement would diminish support for Thieu in the U.S. and jeopardize future aid to South Vietnam.

Another Saigon viewpoint on a peace settlement was publicly expressed Jan. 17 by Foreign Minister Tran Van Lam, who declared that his government would refuse to sign an agreement that mentioned the Viet Cong's Provisional Revolutionary government. Lam's statement was consistent with Saigon's position that it would never accept the Viet Cong as an equal. South Vietnam, he said, would welcome the Viet Cong, but still regarded it as "an opposition group which has neither army nor territory." Any peace accord must be signed on the same basis as the four-party peace talks that were being held in Paris, the minister said. He explained it as "the principle of two sides: our side, the Republic of Vietnam and the United States and the other side, North Vietnam and the people of the National Liberation Front."

Viet Cong seek political support. The Viet Cong's Provisional Revolutionary Government (PRG) issued a call for political support to confront the Saigon regime in the post-war period, according to a communique published Jan. 18 by the North Vietnamese Communist party newspaper Nhan Dan.

The PRG statement had been drawn up after a meeting Jan. 8–10 in South Vietnam. It said "The most important thing

is to broaden the national front, rallying to it patriotic, democratic and pacifist forces of various tendencies." The PRG leaders urged all South Vietnamese who were opposed to the U.S. and the Thieu regime to rally to its side and "intensify the movement of offensive and uprisings on all battlefields in coordination with the diplomatic offensive."

Laird urges arms curtailment. In his last press conference Jan. 19, outgoing Secretary of Defense Melvin R. Laird urged the major powers to negotiate curbs on arms deliveries to Vietnam.

Laird added that the $5 billion in weapons supplied to South Vietnam would be sufficient for defense against any threat now posed by North Vietnam, although this would quickly change if large shipments of arms to Hanoi upset the balance of power. "It depends really upon China and the Soviet Union," he continued, "and I do not believe it is their intention to do that."

Military action prior to truce. South Vietnamese and Communist forces engaged in heavy combat Jan. 18–26 as both sides attempted to gain as much territory as possible before a cease-fire went into effect. U.S. planes continued to provide strong support to government troops in the South with fighter-bombers and B-52s carrying out nearly 3,000 strikes Jan. 17–25.

Among the major developments:

U.S planes Jan. 18 bombed Communist targets with 32 B-52 missions flown largely in northern Quangtri Province. The U.S. command acknowledged Jan. 19 that American planes Jan. 17 had carried out their third accidental attack against friendly targets in 10 days. In the latest incident, one South Vietnamese soldier was killed and four were wounded when three Phantom jets mistakenly dropped three 500-pound bombs near a government unit operating in the Hiepduc Valley below Danang.

Hanoi claimed Jan. 19 that a U.S. reconnaissance plane had been shot down Jan. 17 over North Vietnam just above the demilitarized zone in Quangbinh Province.

South Vietnamese troops began a series of offensive thrusts Jan. 18 with the heaviest operation centered in the Queson Valley just below the DMZ. The attacks were said to have been personally ordered Jan. 17 by President Nguyen Van Thieu at a meeting with the commanders of the country's four military regions. The Saigon command reported Jan. 21 that more than 300 Communists had been killed in the Queson fighting.

In a delayed report, the Saigon command disclosed Jan. 23 that heavy fighting had erupted in the Saigon area Jan. 13, with field reports indicating government troops had taken a severe beating. The battle occurred in the former Michelin rubber plantation, 40 miles northwest of the capital. Field accounts said at least 80 government troops had been killed, 245 wounded and 40 missing before contact was broken off Jan. 20. The Saigon command had acknowledged Jan. 21 that 45 of its men were killed and 120 wounded in the Michelin clashes, but claimed the North Vietnamese had suffered more than 300 killed.

An upsurge of Communist attacks was initiated throughout South Vietnam in the 24-hour period ending at 8 a.m. Jan. 24. The command said there were 95 incidents, two-thirds of them shelling attacks, compared with 52 reported in the previous 24 hours.

U.S. planes Jan. 23 conducted their heaviest raids in five months over South Vietnam. Fighter-bombers carried out 374 strikes and B-52s flew 27 missions. The command also reported that American planes Jan. 23 had bombed the Ho Chi Minh Trail in Laos and targets in Cambodia.

A U.S. Marine was killed in the Communist shelling Jan. 26 of the Bienhoa air base near Saigon. Nine U.S. servicemen and 12 civilian advisers and six South Vietnamese were wounded. The dead American was the first U.S. fatality since the intialing of the Vietnam truce agreement Jan. 23. The assault on Bienhoa followed 112 Communist attacks on government positions and civilian centers in the 24-hour period which ended at 6 a.m. Jan. 25. The Saigon command reported that 242 Communists and 58 South Vietnamese soldiers had been killed in that period.

Pnompenh supply route reopened. A mixed force of North Vietnamese and Cambodian rebels Jan. 12 seized a number of Mekong River outposts near Pnompenh, threatening a vital supply route between the Cambodian capital and the South Vietnamese border. The Communists captured nine government positions along a 12-mile stretch of the Mekong just south of Neak Luong, 32 miles southeast of Pnompenh.

Government forces launched a counter-attack and recaptured the last of the river bank positions by Jan. 16. Seventeen cargo ships that had been held up in the South Vietnamese port of Vung Tau during the fighting made their way into Pnompenh Jan. 18.

In other developments, Cambodian troops were reported Jan. 23 to have lifted the siege of Romeas, a railway center 46 miles northwest of Pnompenh. The town had been surrounded by the Communists since Jan. 5.

Protests mar Nixon inaugural. President Richard M. Nixon was inaugurated for his second four-year term Jan. 20. While the President did not specifically mention Indochina in his inaugural speech, he asserted twice that "America's longest and most difficult war" was coming to an end.

The day was also marked by dissent in Washington. Three antiwar demonstrations were staged in the capital at the time, one drawing a crowd variously estimated at from 25,000 to 100,000 persons. The protesters were kept from the immediate area of the proceedings by security forces augmented by National Guardsmen and federal troops. The largest protest gathering massed at the foot of the Washington Monument after a march from the Lincoln Memorial along Constitution Avenue. The march was joined by Vietnam Veterans Against the War marching from Arlington National Cemetery. This effort was sponsored by the National Peace Action Coalition and the People's Coalition for Peace and Justice, both umbrella groups. Sen. Philip A. Hart (D, Mich.) and Rep. Bella S. Abzug (D, N.Y.) were among the speakers at this rally.

A second rally was held on the steps of the Capitol by Students for a Democratic

Society and the Progressive Labor party joined by members of the Youth International party.

Shouts from a third antiwar rally at Union Station Plaza could be heard at the inauguration site.

No major incidents were reported during the demonstrations, although at one point objects apparently were thrown at the President's car as it returned to the White House for the parade. Security men walking escort were seen to bat down a few objects thrown, apparently fruit and pebbles.

Demonstrations against the Vietnam war also were staged abroad on inauguration day in Paris, Berlin, Stockholm, Tokyo and New Delhi. One of the largest was held in Dortmund, West Germany, attended by an estimated 10,000 persons.

War powers bill introduced. A bill to limit the President's authority to involve the U.S. in undeclared wars was introduced in the Senate Jan. 18 by Sen. Jacob K. Javits (R, N.Y.) in co-sponsorship with 57 other senators, including the majority and minority leaders, Sens. Mike Mansfield (D, Mont.) and Hugh Scott (R, Pa.).

The bill, identical to one passed by the Senate in 1972 but expiring in conference with the House, condoned use of military force by the President in an emergency without advance notification to Congress but provided that such hostilities could not be carried on for more than 30 days without specific approval by Congress. The bill applied only to future conflicts.

"It is a bill to end the practice of presidential war and thus to prevent future Vietnams," Javits told the Senate. The Nixon Administration opposed the legislation in 1972, but Scott said Jan. 18 he hoped to persuade the Administration not to oppose it this year.

Hanoi Gives U.S. prisoner lists. At the signing of the Vietnam truce agreement in Paris Jan. 27, North Vietnam handed U.S. representatives lists of American servicemen and civilians captured in North and South Vietnam. The U.S. in exchange turned over a list of about 26,-000 Communist prisoners held by South Vietnam.

One North Vietnamese list contained the names of 555 U.S. military prisoners held in North and South Vietnam and 55 who had died in captivity. The other showed 27 American civilians held prisoner by the Viet Cong in South Vietnam and the names of seven who had died. Among those civilians cited as being alive were State Department officers Philip M. Manhard, 52, taken prisoner in Hue in 1968, and Douglas K. Ramsey, captured Jan. 17, 1966 in Haung Hia.

North Vietnamese officials in Paris Feb. 1 handed the U.S. a list of American prisoners held by the Pathet Lao in Laos. They included seven Air Force officers and two civilians. The list also carried the name of a Canadian civilian. U.S. officials were disappointed with the information. While the Defense Department had reported only six servicemen captured in Laos, it had placed the number of missing there as 311. Henry A. Kissinger said later Feb. 1 that "we have queried Hanoi about the discrepancy" between the number of missing and those listed as prisoners.

The State Department had listed six American civilians as captured or missing in Laos.

Defense Department spokesman Jerry W. Friedheim said Jan. 29 that "56 men that we have previously carried on our list of prisoners of war" were not on the lists furnished by the Communists. He pointed out that the total of all American military prisoners and missing had been revised to 1,935 men—including the 555 awaiting release from camps in North and South Vietnam, the 55 prisoners who died, the 56 still unaccounted for and 1,269 carried as missing.

Fighting continues despite truce. Although a cease-fire officially went into effect in South Vietnam Jan. 28, the fighting between Saigon government and Communist troops continued throughout the country. The pace of combat through Feb. 1, however, was described by American officials as on a downward trend and "inconsequential." One U.S. official said Jan. 31 "the fighting is definitely stopping."

The Saigon command claimed the Communists had committed 1,034 violations of the cease-fire between 8 a.m. Jan. 28 and 6 a.m. Feb. 1. The command said 2,434 Communists had been killed and 113 captured in that period. It placed its own losses at 434 killed and 1,633 wounded. In addition, 15 civilians were killed and 90 were wounded since the start of the truce, the command said.

The Viet Cong command Jan. 30 accused South Vietnamese troops of violating the cease-fire repeatedly, while insisting that its own forces were "scrupulously" observing the terms of the Paris truce agreement. Since the international truce machinery had not yet begun to function, it was not possible to verify the claims of truce breaches of either side.

Among the major military actions:

The Saigon command said a Communist attempt the night of Jan. 28 to cut Route 14 north of Pleiku was beaten back with 200 enemy soldiers killed. Government losses were placed at five killed in the six-hour battle. Another 32 Communists were slain as government troops repelled an attack on a hamlet south of Danang, the command said.

Two American planes were downed Jan. 28 by Communist ground fire in northeastern Quangtri Province. The four crewmen of a Navy F-4 Phantom and an observation plane were listed as missing. (Two F-4s crashed into the Gulf of Tonkin Jan. 31 after colliding. Two of the four crewmen were rescued.)

The Saigon command reported Jan. 30 that three main highways had been cut by enemy forces since the truce went into effect. Route 1 was severed at two points east of Saigon and in one place at Tayninh Province west of the capital. Route 14 was reported cut between Pleiku and Kontum, and Route 13 was said to be cut south of Chonthanh. A subsequent command report Jan. 31 said the Tayninh road had been reopened the previous day, as well as Route 20 between Dalat and Saigon, and Route 15, southeast of Bienhoa, about 15 miles northeast of the capital.

South Vietnamese planes Jan. 28–30 bombed North Vietnamese tanks in the Queson Valley. Six of the tanks were reported destroyed Jan. 29. The government planes flew the bombing missions despite the Paris accord which stipulated that they fly only unarmed training missions.

U.S. pledges combat aid to Saigon—An unidentified South Vietnamese official reported Jan. 27 that President Nixon had assured President Nguyen Van Thieu and warned North Vietnam that "if the cease-fire is violated in a blatant way, the United States will intervene again immediately." He described blatant violations as "large-scale fighting" or "important infiltration of North Vietnamese troops into the South."

A letter sent by Thieu to Nixon Jan. 27 expressed his "heartfelt gratitude for the great sacrifices the United States has made throughout so many years to help us defend our freedom and our right of self-determination." Commenting on the truce agreement signed in Paris that day, Thieu said that while the accord "can be only a first important step" toward permanent peace, "it is nevertheless encouraging that after many long years of fighting, the killings and destruction are to stop at last."

Thieu sent a similar letter to South Korean President Chung Hee Park.

Fighting prior to cease-fire—The Saigon command reported Jan. 29 that the 26 hours before the cease-fire went into effect were among the most violent of the entire war. The command said the Communists had initiated 451 attacks in that period. U.S. planes also were active, carrying out 494 tactical strikes and 29 B-52 missions. A U.S. military spokesman said the number of strikes was the largest since May 2, 1972, when 618 tactical strikes were flown in one day.

In other developments before the truce went into effect, an American frigate was shelled Jan. 26 by Communist guns off Quangtri Province. There were no injuries to the crew, but some minor damage to the warship was reported.

The heaviest ground fighting Jan. 26 was north of Quangtri city. South Vietnamese marines attempting to advance in recent days to the Cuaviet River north of the town were struck by 448 rounds of Communist rocket, mortars and heavy artillery fire. Casualties were reported to be light. Fighting also raged that day to the south of Quangtri city, with Saigon claiming 131 Communist soldiers killed. Government losses were put at three killed and 21 wounded.

Communist forces carried out 160 attacks in the 24-hour period ended at 6 a.m. Jan. 27, the Saigon command reported. One of the assaults was directed Jan. 27 at Tayninh city, west of Saigon. The fighting first broke out in a temple of the Cao Dai sect and then spread to the rest of the city. South Vietnamese intelligence officials had predicted that the Communists might attack Tayninh just before a truce in an attempt to establish their capital for South Vietnam there.

U.S. continues to bomb Laos. Despite the cease-fire in Vietnam, the U.S. continued air operations in Laos, while Laotian government and Pathet Lao and North Vietnamese forces remained locked in heavy combat.

A U.S. State Department statement Jan. 29 said, "We are continuing air operations in Laos in support of the Royal Laotian government. We are doing that in response to some Communist movements in Laos." The department declined to say what Communist activity the raids were being directed against. Another department statement Jan. 30 said the U.S. was continuing the bombing of Communist forces in Laos for the third day since the signing of the Viet truce accord.

U.S. Senate Majority Leader Mike Mansfield (D, Mont.) disclosed Jan. 29 that he had sent Secretary of State William P. Rogers a telegram asking why Laos was being bombed after a Vietnam truce accord was signed. Mansfield said he had warned Rogers that the raids "create a very dangerous situation and will not be in the spirit of the accords as described" by President Nixon and his chief Vietnam negotiator, Henry A. Kissinger.

In the ground action in Laos, heavy fighting continued in the region between Savannakhet, on the Mekong River, and North Vietnam's Ho Chi Minh Trail to the east. Communist movement along the supply route did not appear to have diminished despite the Paris agreement, it was reported.

Laotian Premier Souvanna Phouma had charged Jan. 26 that the Communists had launched a general offensive in Laos

to seize as much territory as possible prior to a truce. Souvanna said he had been assured by the U.S. that he would receive full American air support to counter the new enemy thrusts and the raids would be resumed if the Communists violated any Laos truce that might go into effect.

In fighting earlier in the month, Laotian troops Jan. 12 knocked out two North Vietnamese tanks and captured a third in fighting around Muong Kassy in southern Laos. The airport at the royal capital of Luang Prabang was shelled by 30 Communist rockets. A light observation plane was damaged.

Cambodia announces truce. Cambodian Premier Lon Nol Jan. 27 announced his government's approval of the Vietnam cease-fire agreement signed in Paris that day and Jan. 28 ordered a test truce in Cambodia, effective at 7 a.m. Jan. 29. Sporadic fighting continued at a low level, however, after the truce went into effect. At least two government soldiers were killed and 12 wounded in scattered clashes around Pnompenh.

In announcing his approval of the Paris agreement, Lon Nol Jan. 27 called on North Vietnam to respect the accord "by ceasing its acts of aggression against Cambodia." He said the pact specifically stipulated respect for the rights of the Cambodian people as guaranteed by the 1954 Geneva agreements. North Vietnam, as a party to the Geneva accord, "must order its troops and their Viet Cong auxiliaries to withdraw from Cambodia territory and cease all acts of destruction, sabotage and subversion," the premier said.

Under the cease-fire ordered by Lon Nol Jan. 28, government troops were to suspend offensive military operations to enable the North Vietnamese and Viet Cong to leave Cambodia in the shortest possible time. The government said "we will retain the right to defend ourselves if attacked." Speaking to a special convocation of the two houses of the National Assembly, Lon Nol appealed to all Cambodian rebel factions fighting his government to join the regime "against the expansionist and imperialist aims of our enemy." He also urged the four parties that signed the

Paris agreement, the U.N. and "all countries that cherish peace and justice" to aid Cambodia in assuring strict adherence to the Paris accord.

Prince Norodom Sihanouk, exiled Cambodian head of state, declared Jan. 27 that the Cambodian guerrilla forces supporting his Peking-based Government of National Union would not lay down their arms despite the cease-fire in Vietnam. Speaking at a news conference in the Chinese capital, Sihanouk said "we will continue fighting until we wipe out Lon Nol and his clique." "We do not see any possibility of stopping the war in Cambodia unless Nixon abandons Lon Nol or until the traitorous regime in Pnompenh is wiped out," the prince said.

Sihanouk was denounced Jan. 29 by an official of the National Union regime, who had defected from his post Jan. 18. Ker Chhieng, Sihanouk's former director of protocol, told a news conference in Pnompenh that Sihanouk was a puppet, who "has sold his country to North Vietnam and China."

(Pakistan had recognized Sihanouk's government Jan. 25. An official statement said Pakistan questioned the legality of the Lon Nol regime.)

Joint truce commissions meet. The two joint military commissions that were to monitor the Vietnam cease-fire held their first combined meeting in Saigon Jan. 31 following several days of a procedural dispute involving one of the commissions. Already behind schedule in carrying out their functions, it was not certain when either of the groups might actually begin its truce observation work in the field. According to the Paris agreement, each commission was to begin operating no later than the morning of Jan. 29 and was to have seven regional inspection teams in place in South Vietnam by Jan. 30.

The Saigon meeting was attended by the deputy delegates of the Joint Military Commission (JMC), representing the U.S., North and South Vietnam and the Viet Cong, and the International Commission of Control and Supervision (ICCS), comprised of military officers of Canada, Hungary, Indonesia and Poland.

The procedural dispute erupted Jan. 28 when an advance 13-member Viet Cong delegation to the JMC, arriving in Saigon

from Hanoi aboard a South Vietnamese air force plane, refused to fill out South Vietnamese landing cards. The officials stayed on the plane overnight and were permitted to disembark Jan. 29 without signing the forms. A government statement said its actions did not constitute a waiver of the rules, but was taken to permit the JMC to start its work, and that the commission should take up the matter of Saigon immigration laws. The Communists reportedly had refused to sign the documents because they felt it would be tantamount to recognizing the sovereignty of the Saigon government. However, another group of 19 North Vietnamese and Viet Cong delegates that had arrived in Saigon from Hanoi an hour earlier Jan. 28 were not asked to fill out the landing cards and were permitted to get off the plane and go to their quarters.

A group of 90 North Vietnamese and Viet Cong representatives arrived in Saigon aboard two U.S. Air Force planes Jan. 29, and they, too, refused to fill out the immigration forms. They were finally permitted to disembark Jan. 30 without signing the documents.

The North Vietnamese Foreign Ministry charged Jan. 31 that the U.S. and South Vietnam had "blatantly violated" the Paris agreement by attempting "every way to cause troubles" for the two Communist delegations to the military commission.

The JMC's first meeting of deputy representatives Jan. 29 bogged down over Viet Cong refusal to present their credentials or to submit a list of their 290 members. (The meeting had been scheduled for Jan. 28, but was postponed because the Viet Cong were not present.) The JMC held further meetings Jan. 30 and Feb. 1, with discussions centered on administrative arrangements for a later meeting of the chief delegates.

The ICCS had held its first meeting Jan. 29 to discuss procedure. The heads of each delegation were Michel Gauvin of Canada, Ferenc Esztergalyos of Hungary, Lt. Col. Samsudin of Indonesia, and Bogdan Wasilewski of Poland.

Brezhnev hails accord. At a dinner given in Moscow Jan. 30 for Le Duc Tho, the chief North Vietnamese negotiator, So-

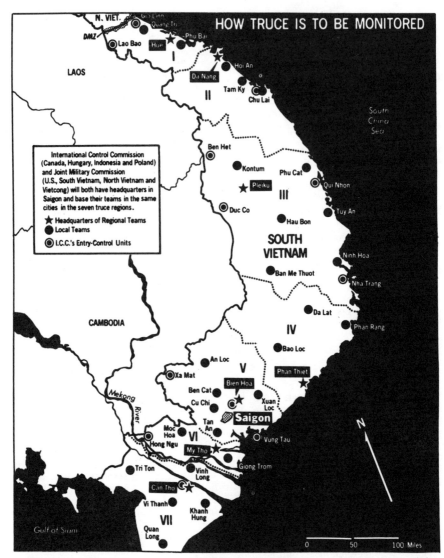

HOW TRUCE IS TO BE MONITORED

International Control Commission
(Canada, Hungary, Indonesia and Poland)
and Joint Military Commission
(U.S., South Vietnam, North Vietnam and
Vietcong) will both have headquarters in
Saigon and base their teams in the same
cities in the seven truce regions.

★ Headquarters of Regional Teams
● Local Teams
◉ I.C.C.'s Entry-Control Units

SOUTH
VIETNAM

Map showing cities where ICC and Joint Military Commission representatives will be
based, drawn from data supplied by the White House.

viet Communist Party General Secretary
Leonid I. Brezhnev described the Vietnam
cease-fire agreement as "a victory of
realism and sanity in international
affairs."

He said the "decisive step for complete
restoration of peace in Vietnam has been
made." North Vietnam would now be able
"to concentrate its efforts on Socialist
construction." For South Vietnam there
were new prospects "for upholding true
independence and for conducting the
policy of national concord and unification." Brezhnev added: "More favorable conditions are created for ending
the bloodshed in Laos and Cambodia."

Because "the most dangerous seat of war in the world is being liquidated," there were "possibilities for easing tensions, for consolidating security and world peace," Brezhnev continued. It "can be expected that the political settlement in Vietnam will have a positive effect on the relations among the states that were involved in one way or another in the events in Indochina. Moreover, this shows that it is possible to find a peaceful and just solution of other conflicts, to liquidate the seats of war danger that exist so far, above all in the Middle East."

Brezhnev said North Vietnam and the Viet Cong had "solemnly declared they will strictly observe" all provisions of the agreement. "The peoples expect that other parties to the agreement will honor and completely observe the commitments assumed," he noted. (The New York Times Jan. 31 reported a commentary by Izvestia, the Soviet government newspaper, accusing South Vietnam of preparing to break the peace agreement. The paper declared: "Even before the ink on these documents has dried, President Thieu in Saigon has come out with a speech full of malicious attacks on the patriotic forces of South Vietnam. The Saigon administration has already undertaken its first attempts to violate the documents signed in Paris.")

In reply to Brezhnev's remarks, North Vietnamese Foreign Minister Nguyen Duy Trinh said the main task ahead was "stronger unity in the struggle for strict and full compliance with the Paris agreements." He asked the Soviet Union to "continue to give us support and assistance" in the "completion of the national democratic revolution in South Vietnam and the peaceful reunification of the fatherland."

Soviets laud Communist forces—In a congratulatory message sent to the Viet Cong leadership Jan. 27, the Soviet Union had pledged to provide it with continued support. It said the withdrawal of American forces under the truce agreement would provide "favorable conditions for a final and just settlement of the Vietnam problem" through reunification of North and South Vietnam.

The Soviet Union disclosed Jan. 28 that it had rushed arms to North Vietnam at the height of the American bombing raids

over the North in December 1972. The Communist party newspaper Pravda said the U.S.S.R. had shipped "the latest weapons—antiaircraft missiles, guns and fighter planes—" to help the North Vietnamese counter the U.S. air assaults.

Nixon press conference. President Nixon announced Jan. 31 that Henry A. Kissinger, his national security adviser, would travel to Hanoi for meetings Feb. 10–13 to discuss implemention of the Vietnam cease-fire agreement and arrangements for postwar economic aid, which the President described as "incentives for peace."

Nixon said he would also meet "this spring" with South Vietnamese President Nguyen Van Thieu for similar talks at the Western White House in San Clemente, Calif.

(The White House announced Feb. 3 that Kissinger would consult in Peking Feb. 15–19 with Chinese leaders, "to further the normalization of relations.")

The announcement came at an impromptu, 30-minute news conference at the White House. The briefing was Nixon's first since Oct. 5, 1972.

The President said he would send to Congress a "reconstruction plan for all of Indochina." No dollar figure for the aid program was released, but, according to the Washington Post Feb. 1, Administration estimates made in 1972 for planned reconstruction totaled 7.5 billion for Southeast Asia, spread over five years, with North Vietnam receiving about $2.5 billion. (No provision for any rebuilding program had been included in the President's budget submitted to Congress.)

Discussing other aspects of the Vietnam peace, Nixon reiterated his opposition to amnesty for draft evaders and derserters. "Amnesty mean forgiveness. We cannot provide forgiveness for them. Those who served paid their price. Those who deserted must pay their price, and the price is not a junket in the Peace Corps, or something like that, as some have suggested. The price is a criminal penalty for disobeying the laws of the United States."

At the same time, he lashed out at war foes, "the so-called better people, in the media and the intellectual circles," who criticized his efforts to win a "peace with honor." Referring to the reporters present, Nixon said, "I know it gags some of you to write that phrase, but it is true and most Americans realize it is true."

The President also tied the issue of the release of Vietnam war prisoners to the release of two U.S. pilots. Maj. Philip E. Smith and Lt. Cmdr. Robert J. Flynn, held in China since 1965 and 1967.

The President said he anticipated no immediate release for another China captive, John T. Downey, who, for the first time, was officially acknowledged to be a Central Intelligence Agency operative.

In domestic matters, the President expressed no preference for candidates seeking the 1976 Republican presidential nomination, although he repeated that he held "very high respect" for former Treasury Secretary John B. Connally Jr.

"I have stated my belief that he could handle any job that I can think of in this country, or in the world for that matter," Nixon said.

Agnew starts Indochina mission. U.S. Vice President Spiro T. Agnew met with President Nguyen Van Thieu in Saigon Jan. 30–31 to discuss postwar relations between the U.S. and South Vietnam.

In a brief written statement issued on his arrival, Agnew said the U.S. would work with "the people and the government of South Vietnam as partners in peace as we have been allies in war." He said the U.S. recognized the Saigon government as "the sole legitimate government of South Vietnam" and did not recognize the right of any foreign troops to remain in South Vietnam.

On departing for Pnompenh Feb. 1, the U.S. embassy in Saigon distributed a statement by Agnew in which he said his two days of talks with Thieu dealt with the "prospects of postwar relations between our two countries." Agnew said he was "impressed by the confidence in which the South Vietnamese government is approaching the challenges it faces." He said he assured Thieu and his advisers "of the strong and abiding interest of the United States in the security and well-being of South Vietnam."

Agnew held a five-hour meeting with Cambodan Premier Lon Nol in Pnompenh Feb. 1 and assured him of continued U.S. support. Agnew backed Cambodia's demands for the withdrawal of Communist troops from its country, saying that peace in Indochina would not be complete "as long as a formal cease-fire has not been established here and as long as all foreign forces have not been withdrawn from Cambodia."

German Indochina aid approved. The West German Cabinet approved an Indochina aid program totaling DM130 million Jan. 31. Of the total, DM30 million was earmarked for emergency relief aid and DM100 million was allotted for a long-term recovery program. The aid would be apportioned among North and South Vietnam, Laos and Cambodia.

Minister for Economic Cooperation Erhard Eppler told a news conference Jan. 31 that the aid would be granted only if the cease-fire terms were followed. He said "if peace is not concluded in the foreseeable future, the question of whether reconstruction aid can still be given will have to be reconsidered."

Final U.S. death toll. The U.S. command reported Feb. 1 that four Americans had been killed in South Vietnam during the week that ended with the start of the cease-fire Jan. 28. This was expected to be the command's final report on American casualties, since the U.S. combat role had come to an end.

The four deaths brought to 45,941 the number of Americans killed in combat in Indochina since Jan. 1, 1961. The number of wounded requiring hospitalization was placed at 150,303. Another 150,332 were wounded but did not require hospital treatment, the command said. The command listed 1,811 men as missing, captured or interned during combat.

The Defense Department Jan. 28 identified Lt. Col. William B. Nolde, 43, as the last American to die in the Vietnam war. Nolde was killed the night of Jan. 27 by an artillery shell at Anloc, 11 hours before the truce went into effect.

Nixon nominated for peace prize. The Norwegian Nobel Committee Feb. 1 accepted the nomination of President Nixon for the 1972 Nobel Peace Prize on the basis of his accomplishments in foreign affairs.

Miss Elizabeth MacDonald Manning, publisher of Finance magazine, initiated the action with the aid of five Republican House and Senate lawmakers.

Prayer breakfast. In an address to the 21st National Prayer Breakfast in Washington Feb. 1, President Nixon cautioned that the recently signed Vietnam ceasefire pact would "mean peace only to the extent that leaders on both sides have the will to keep the agreement." He added, "We will keep the agreement. We expect others to keep the agreement."

"Let there be peace on earth and let it begin with each and every one of us in his own heart," the President said.

Sen. Mark Hatfield (R, Ore.), a persistent war foe, also addressed the 3,000 government and military leaders and representatives of the diplomatic corps.

Hatfield declared that the Vietnam war had been a "sin that has scarred the national soul. . . . If we as leaders appeal to the god of an American civil religion, our faith is in a small and exclusive deity, a loyal spiritual adviser to American power and prestige, a defender of only the American nation, the object of a national folk religion devoid of moral content."

Kissinger explains Hanoi mission. Henry A. Kissinger said Feb. 1 that his Feb. 10–13 visit to Hanoi would be "an exploratory mission to determine" how the U.S. and North Vietnam "can move from hostility towards normalization." "The basic purpose," he said, "is to establish a new relationship similar perhaps to my first trip to Peking."

President Nixon had announced the proposed trip at his press conference Jan. 31.

Kissinger made his remarks in a CBS television interview with correspondent Marvin Kalb. He covered other aspects of the Indochina problem, including prospects for a lasting peace, the American decision to bomb North Vietnam in December 1972 and the role of China and the Soviet Union in preserving peace in Indochina.

Asked what American policy would be if South Vietnam requested a renewal of the bombing, Kissinger said "it would be extremely unwise for a responsible American official at this stage ... to give a checklist about what the United States will or will not do in every circumstance that is likely to arise." Kissinger expressed confidence that the South Vietnamese could handle "most of the [truce] violations that one can now foresee."

Kissinger stressed that "the biggest task now is to move a generation that has known nothing but war towards an attitude of peace—and that is an intangible quality." Asserting that good-will alone was not enough to achieve a lasting peace, Nixon's national security adviser said "A lot depends on the actions of the Soviet Union and the People's Republic of China, and on the sort of relationship we'll be able to establish with North Vietnam." He said "we would like the Chinese and the Russians to behave responsibly in preserving the peace in Indochina" by holding down their arms shipments to Vietnam.

Kissinger denied speculation that his visit to Hanoi "is for determining aid" for North Vietnam. He explained: Assistance was one of "the possible middleterm outcomes. The real problem in relation to North Vietnam is that here is a country that has been almost constantly at war throughout its existence. Now we would like to explore the possibility of whether after the experiences of the last decade, having established a pattern of coexistence with Moscow and Peking, it seems to us not inconceivable that if we can coexist with Peking we can coexist with Hanoi."

Kissinger gave the first detailed explanation of Nixon's decision in December 1972 to bomb Hanoi and Haiphong when the Paris peace negotiations collapsed. He said Nixon had decided to resume the bombing after "we came to the conclusion that the negotiations as they were then being conducted were not serious, that ... the North Vietnamese at that point had come to the conclusion that protracting the negotiations was more in their interest than concluding them." He noted that "the more difficult Hanoi was, the more rigid Saigon grew, and we could see a prospect, therefore, where we would be caught between the two contending Vietnamese parties with no element introduced that would change their opinion." Fearing that his talks with North Vietnamese negotiator Le Duc Tho would gradually degenerate into propaganda, Kissinger said, "therefore it was decided to try to bring home really to both Vietnamese parties that the continuation of the war had its price."

Kissinger said the U.S. decided to employ the B-52 to bomb North Vietnam because the rainy season required the use of an all-weather plane. He said "major efforts were made to avoid residential areas" in the bombing of Hanoi and Haiphong, and that the casualty figures of about one thousand released by the North Vietnamese "tend to support that this was the case."

Kissinger briefs Congress—In two closed door sessions Jan. 26 to brief members of the House and Senate on the terms of the cease-fire, Presidential adviser Henry Kissinger promised lawmakers that the White House would seek consultations with Congress before committing the U.S. to a postwar reconstruction plan.

Kissinger, who received a standing ovation from those present, reportedly told Congress that there were no secret agreements attached to the cease-fire. He also voiced optimism that the cease-fire would be upheld and said he anticipated that President Thieu could make political gains in the postwar period, according to the New York Times Jan. 26.

Kissinger did not appear before regular Congressional committee hearings because the White House refused to waive its right of executive privilege.

In related developments:

Sen. Frank Church (D, Ida.) and Sen. Clifford P. Case (R, N.J.) introduced a bill Jan. 26 which would prohibit, without Congressional approval, the involvement of U.S. military forces in Vietnam, Laos and Cambodia after the last U.S. war prisoners were released.

The State Department announced Jan. 26 that the cease-fire accord signed Jan. 27 in Paris was an executive agreement and would not, therefore, require Senate approval.

The White House issued a proclamation Jan. 26 calling on the public to observe a "national moment of prayer and thanksgiving" at 7 p.m. (EST) Jan. 27 when the cease-fire took effect.

Hanoi demands eventual reunification. North Vietnamese Premier Pham Van Dong declared Feb. 2 that although his government had signed the Paris truce agreement, North and South Vietnam must eventually be reunified.

Dong was sharply critical of President Nixon's Jan. 23 statement in which he had said the U.S. recognized the Saigon regime of President Nguyen Van Thieu "as the sole legitimate government of South Vietnam." "To say that is to violate the agreement," the premier said. He added: "In the South there is another government, the [Viet Cong's] Provisional Revolutionary Government. The PRG is a signatory of the agreement. How can you erase that?"

As for merging the two Vietnams, Dong said: "No one can live with a body cut in half. We cannot live with our country cut in half. We must have reunification."

Dong asserted that "it was a calumny" to "say we want to impose a Communist government on South Vietnam." "We have signed a peace agreement," he said, and "we have no other course than to abide by it."

Dong made his remarks in an interview given to U.S. representatives of the Women's International League of Peace and Freedom who were visiting North Vietnam. The interview was written by Louise Hickman Lione of the Philadelphia Inquirer and was published Feb. 7.

U.S. seeks Laos truce. The U.S. was reported Feb. 2 to have urged the government of Laos to conclude a quick truce with the rebel Pathet Lao. The appeal was made as the fighting in Laos intensified and the U.S. continued to provide heavy air support to the embattled government forces.

The U.S. Pacific forces command in Honolulu reported Feb. 7 that American planes bombed Laos that day for the 11th straight day since the start of the Vietnam cease-fire Jan. 28. The command said the jets continued to concentrate on Communist positions and supply lines in northern Laos. As many as 120 aircraft were said to be involved in each day's mission.

In ground action, Pathet Lao and North Vietnamese forces were reported Feb. 6 to have made widespread gains. Three government positions near the Burmese border north of Houei Sai were captured by the Pathet Lao. The key supply base at nearby Nam Yeu was reported by the government Feb. 5 to have fallen. Communist forces launched a drive to recapture the important road junction at Sala Phou Khoun, southeast of the royal capital of Luang Prabang. The government stronghold of Long Tieng came under heavy shelling from North Vietnamese guns positioned in the Plaine des Jarres.

In southern Laos, North Vietnamese troops pushed government soldiers westward all the way to Muong Phalane, while other Communist troops began a major drive to take Thakhek on the Mekong River, opposite the U.S. air base at Nakhon Phanom in Thailand. Paksong in southernmost Laos was the scene of heavy fighting, with government forces under increasing Communist pressure. The city had been shelled and attacked by Communist troops Feb. 5, but government soldiers started a counterattack.

Laotians start secret peace talks— Government and Pathet Lao representatives started secret talks in Vientiane Jan. 31 in a new effort to reach a peace agreement. The discussions had been proposed by the Pathet Lao at the regular public session of the negotiations Jan. 30. The two sides agreed to continue the formal talks, held each week, along with the private sessions. Another regular peace session was held Feb. 6. One of the Pathet Lao negotiators condemned the American raids on Laos. He told the meeting that B-52s had "intensified their bombardment of the Plaine des Jarres and Xieng Khouang zones in a perfidious and barbarous manner. The combat aircraft of the U.S. Air Force flying from bases in Thailand and the 7th Fleet have used their full power to bomb, destroy, burn and devastate Laotian territory."

Premier Souvanna Phouma held private discussions Feb. 5 and 6 with Phoumi Vongvichit, chief Pathet Lao negotiator. Souvanna declined to say what the talks

were about, but he expressed confidence Feb. 6 that a truce would be concluded in Laos by Feb. 15 at the latest.

Agnew vows U.S. aid to Cambodia. Continuing his tour of Asia, U.S. Vice President Spiro T. Agnew visited Pnompenh Feb. 1 and conferred with Premier Lon Nol and other Cambodian leaders. In a statement issued at the conclusion of his five-hour visit, Agnew said he had reaffirmed American "respect for Khmer independence, unity, sovereignty, neutrality and territorial integrity." The statement added: "I also conveyed our intention to provide continued support for Cambodia. Peace will be incomplete in Indochina until a formal cease-fire is achieved here, and all foreign forces are withdrawn from Cambodia."

Agnew flew to Bangkok later Feb. 1 and in talks with Thailand's leaders Feb. 2 pledged more military and economic aid. The vice president conferred with Premier Thanom Kittikachorn and also met with King Phumiphol Aduldet.

Agnew met with U.S. officials and Laotian Premier Souvanna Phouma in Vientiane, Laos Feb. 3 and then returned to Bangkok. He left the Thai capital Feb. 4 and arrived that day in Singapore. In talks with Prime Minister Lee Kuan Yew Feb. 5, Agnew was said to have assured the Singapore leader that the U.S. would retain its military bases in Thailand to prevent possible Communist expansion to the south.

Agnew went on to Jakarta where he conferred Feb. 6 and 7 with Indonesian President Suharto and Foreign Minister Adam Malik. The vice president arrived in Kuala Lumpur Feb. 7 on next to the last leg of his Asian tour and met the following day with Malaysian Prime Minister Abdul Razak to discuss the U.S. role in Southeast Asia.

Communist rebels attack in Cambodia. Communist-led Khmer Rouge rebel troops continued their offensive operations in Cambodia Feb. 2–7 despite the cease-fire announced by the Pnompenh government and reported truce contacts with the regime of Premier Lon Nol. At the same time, government officials reported Feb. 2 that some North Vietnamese troops appeared to be leaving combat zones and heading toward border regions. A spokesman said most of the fighting was being waged by the Khmer Rouge insurgents and that clashes involving Vietnamese Communists could have resulted from diversionary actions aimed at covering up their pullout.

The government command reported that Communist troops Feb. 2 closed Route 4 connecting Pnompenh with the port of Kompong Som. The attacks occurred 36 miles south of the capital and cut off the city's main supply route. Heavy fighting continued in the area Feb. 4, with the guerrillas attacking government positions on both sides of Route 4. The command also reported heavy clashes on Route 2 around Prey Sandek, 57 miles south of Pnompenh. Six government soldiers were killed, the command said.

Five government posts were attacked along the South Vietnamese frontier, the government command said Feb. 7. Seven government troops and eight Communist guerrillas were reported killed during the night in one of the clashes on the Mekong River, 35 miles southeast of Pnompenh.

Cambodian Information Minister Keam Reath had announced Jan. 31 that government troops and Khmer Rouge leaders had made "promising" truce contacts since Premier Lon Nol ordered a halt in offensive military operations. Keam expressed confidence that Cambodia would soon have peace "because we have no reason to remain in conflict when the war in Vietnam is reaching its end."

Prince Norodom Sihanouk, exiled Cambodian leader, said Jan. 31 that his anti-government forces in Cambodia would "not launch offensive actions" under a new policy being evolved by the resistance forces. But he told newsmen in Hanoi, where he had begun a visit Jan. 30, that a final policy had not yet been worked out by the resistance leaders in Cambodia, who were headed by Khieu Samphan, deputy premier and defense minister of Sihanouk's Peking-based Government of National Union.

Sihanouk's support of a military standdown in Cambodia followed his refusal Jan. 27 to abide by any cease-fire in the country. He said he had asked resistance leaders in Cambodia for permission to enter their territory "as soon as possible."

"If they refuse to let me return to Cambodia within two months at the latest, I will offer to them my resignation from my present position," Sihanouk said.

U.S. on arms to Cambodia, Laos. Continued American arms shipments to Cambodia and Laos would not be in violation of the Vietnam truce agreement, the U.S. State Department said Feb. 5.

The department statement was issued in response to a Feb. 2 New York Times report that the State and Defense Departments were in disagreement over whether the accord with North Vietnam barred such supplies to Cambodia and Laos. Defense Department spokesman John King said Feb. 5 that Article 20 of the Vietnam accord permitted arms to be sent to those two countries for self-defense. He said that "in negotiating Article 20 of the Vietnam agreement there was no intention to change" the 1954 and 1962 Geneva accords, which permitted shipment of military equipment for self-defense.

The Times reported that some Defense Department officials had questioned whether continued American arms shipments to Cambodia and Laos were permissible under terms of the Vietnam pact.

Truce commissions take to field. International truce supervisory teams left Saigon Feb. 5 to take up positions in the South Vietnamese countryside from which they would monitor the cease-fire. Representatives of the International Commission of Control and Supervision (ICCS) and the Four-Party Joint Military Commission (JMC) were in place by Feb. 6 at the seven regional headquarters at Hue, Danang, Pleiku, Phanthiet, Bienhoa, Mytho and Cantho. The ICCS teams were made up of five to nine soldiers from each of the commission's four members—Canada, Hungary, Indonesia and Poland.

The North Vietnamese and Viet Cong teams of the JMC were being severely restricted by the South Vietnamese government. The Communists were stationed at highly guarded South Vietnamese military installations, where they were unable to make contacts with civilians.

An artillery duel Feb. 6 blocked a 12-man ICCS team from reaching Quangtri city. The group had set out from Hue but stopped at Hailang, six miles from Quangtri city, under orders not to move into hazardous situations.

The truce commissions took to the field following high-level meetings held earlier in Saigon. The chief delegates of the JMC held their first conference Feb. 2. In a separate meeting Feb. 2, the ICCS decided to send observers that day to inspect the regional headquarters facilities in Hue, Danang and Pleiku without waiting until all the teams were in place.

(The JMC chief delegates were Maj. Gen. Gilbert H. Woodward of the U.S., Lt. Gen. Tra Van Tra of the Viet Cong, Maj. Gen. Le Quang Hoa of North Vietnam and Lt. Gen. Ngo Dzu of South Vietnam.)

The heads of the ICCS and JMC held their first joint meeting Feb. 4. Michel Gauvin of Canada later described the talks as "one of the most constructive steps" accomplished by the two bodies in a week.

At a separate meeting of the ICCS Feb. 5, Gauvin was named chairman of the commission. He had been serving as its temporary chairman since Jan. 28 and was to continue in that post for one month, to Feb. 28. The chairmanship was to rotate monthly among the four participants of the commission.

The two peace-keeping commissions held another joint meeting in Saigon Feb. 7. A spokesman for the Canadian delegation to the ICCS said the commission members had agreed to use English as a working language.

Saigon releases prisoners. The New York Times reported Feb. 5 that the South Vietnamese government had released thousands of Communist military prisoners and civilian captives in recent days without turning them over to North Vietnam or the Viet Cong as required by the Paris truce agreements. The Viet Cong denounced the action. The U.S. and South Vietnam defended it.

The Times report said about 20,000 Communist military captives and about an equal number of civilian political prisoners were affected by the release order. Each captive was given the equivalent of $2.50 when set free, the report said.

The Paris accord on the captives stipulated that "all captured Vietnamese personnel whether regular or irregular shall be returned to that South Vietnamese party under whose command they served."

The Viet Cong delegation in Paris Feb. 6 denounced the Saigon government's action as "a flagrant violation" of the truce agreements and "a perfidious maneuver." A spokesman said the unscheduled release of the prisoners "puts the goodwill of the Saigon government in doubt."

U.S. State Department officials in Washington Feb. 6 said the Communist prisoners had been processed and released before the cease-fire began.

A South Vietnamese government spokesman Feb. 7 denied the release of the Communist prisoners was a violation of the Paris agreements. Pham Duong Hien said President Nguyen Van Thieu had taken the decision to give the POWs their freedom Jan. 25, two days before the Paris agreement was signed, and their release therefore did not constitute a breach of the peace terms. Hien said a total of 10,600 Viet Cong war prisoners and 380 civilian political prisoners had been freed as part of the traditional amnesty for Tet, the Lunar New Year. Hien said the prisoners had applied in writing to enter the government's "chieu hoi" or "open arms" program, which permitted Viet Cong defectors to return to their native villages after a period of indoctrination.

On another matter, Hien announced "new regulations" and "new ground rules" for foreign newsmen in Saigon. He said correspondents who engaged in "un-Vietnamese activity" by giving out "misleading" or "distorted" reports about South Vietnam, would be expelled from the country. Hien apologized for the obstacles encountered by foreign newsmen attempting to cover the activities of the peace-keeping mission at Saigon's Tansonnhut air base. Several newsmen had been detained for three or four hours during the first few days of the truce because they entered the base without authority.

U.S. starts mine-clearing operations. The U.S. began preparatory work to clear

North Vietnamese waters of American mines planted in 1972, the Defense Department announced Feb. 6. Four U.S. Navy minesweepers were clearing an anchorage 40 miles southeast of Haiphong harbor as an initial step toward destroying hundreds of mines that had blocked the North Vietnamese port for nine months. These operations were being conducted as a safety precaution for a larger fleet of American vessels that would clear mines from North Vietnamese ports and waterways under terms of the Paris truce agreement. The job was expected to take several months.

Arrangements for clearing the mines had been worked out in talks held in Haiphong Feb. 5 between North Vietnamese officials and an American delegation headed by Rear Adm. Brian McCauley.

Saigon, Viet Cong in political talks. Viet Cong and Saigon government representatives met in Paris Feb. 5 and 7 and reported progress on arranging for the start of political negotiations on the future of South Vietnam as called for in the Paris agreements. The meetings were being held in the Hotel Majestic, where the cease-fire pact had been signed Jan. 27.

The initial talks dealt with preliminary procedures. Pham Dang Lam, the chief South Vietnamese negotiator in Paris, had said after the Feb. 5 session that both sides had agreed that substantive talks should be held at a high level in Saigon.

The two sides were represented by deputy delegation leaders—Nguyen Phuong Thiep for the Saigon government and Dinh Ba Thi for the Viet Cong's Provisional Revolutionary Government.

South Vietnam had taken the initiative in starting the political discussions with the Viet Cong, according to an announcement made by President Nguyen Van Thieu Feb. 3. In a radio and television address welcoming Tet, Thieu said he believed the Viet Cong would seek to delay talks with the Saigon government because "they want to get more land and more people for a general election in the future." Thieu, however, insisted that "we should force the Communists to negotiate in order to have a political solution as soon as possible."

Truce violations continue. Sporadic clashes in violation of the South Vietnam cease-fire continued in various parts of the country Feb. 2–7. The fighting between government and Communist troops, however, was described largely as minor, with the number of truce breaches showing a steady decline.

The worst outbreak of combat occurred Feb. 6 around Pleiku, where Saigon claimed 233 Communists and five government soldiers were killed. The fighting erupted after government positions came under attack near Fire Base 41, between Pleiku and Kontum city, 18 miles south of Pleiku.

A Saigon spokesman reported that the Communists had committed 121 truce violations during the 24-hours ending at dawn Feb. 7.

The ground fighting Feb. 3 had come to a virtual standstill. A South Vietnamese spokesman said "there is no major ongoing action now." The Communists had violated the truce 38 times between 6 a.m. and noon Feb. 3. According to figures released by Saigon, 175 Communist troops and 22 government soldiers were killed in fighting in the 24-hour period ending at 6 a.m. Feb. 3, the smallest number of combat deaths for one day since the cease-fire went into effect Jan. 28.

U.S. policy in Indochina criticized. Indian Prime Minister Indira Gandhi Feb. 6 criticized U.S. policy in Indochina and expressed doubts that the Vietnam cease-fire agreement would bring peace.

Speaking in New Delhi at the One-Asia Assembly, sponsored by the Press Foundation of Asia, Mrs. Gandhi asked: "Would this sort of war or the savage bombing which has taken place in Vietnam have been tolerated for so long had the people been European?" Asserting that "the very manner of ending the Vietnam war may create tensions," Mrs. Gandhi said "the cease-fire should not lull us into comfort that there will be peace all the way. To many nations, peace itself has often been war by other means."

The U.S. State Department Feb. 7 expressed shock at Mrs. Gandhi's statement, noting that it was "quite inconsistent with the messages we have received from the government of India expressing gratification for the peace which has been achieved in Vietnam." Mrs. Gandhi's remarks, the department said, "contradicted the recent indications from New Delhi suggesting a desire to improve relations between our two countries."

The department disclosed for the first time a letter Mrs. Gandhi had sent President Nixon in November 1972. The message, referring to the Vietnam negotiations, said: "We now have the best opportunity for building a new structure of lasting peace. The vision itself is inspiring."

In a further reaction to the Indian leader's critical appraisal of American policy in Indochina, the State Department said Feb. 7 that it was holding up the departure to New Delhi of the newly-appointed U.S. ambassador to India, Daniel P. Moynihan. He had been scheduled to leave Washington Feb. 11 to assume his new post, but the department now said there were "no firm departure plans."

Moynihan, whose appointment was approved by the Senate Feb. 8, had told the Senate Foreign Relations Committee Feb. 5 that Nixon and Mrs. Gandhi had exchanged notes recently and that U.S.-Indian relations seemed to be improving.

Ottawa recognizes North Vietnam. The government announced Feb. 7 it had extended formal recognition to North Vietnam, giving it "equal diplomatic status" with Saigon.

Mitchell W. Sharp, secretary of state for external affairs, said Canada's "act of recognition" had taken the form of a letter from Prime Minister Pierre Elliott Trudeau to Premier Pham Van Dong and was intended to promote "friendly relations" during the postwar period in Vietnam.

Sharp noted, however, that the move did not amount to "full diplomatic relations" and that neither government had immediate plans to exchange envoys.

Nixon briefed on Agnew mission. Vice President Spiro T. Agnew Feb. 10 briefed President Nixon on his tour of eight Southeast Asian nations that had started Jan. 28. Agnew had returned to the U.S. Feb. 9.

Nixon had said before the briefing at the Western White House at San Clemente, Calif. that no official statement would be issued on Agnew's trip until after the National Security Council had evaluated his report and until after Henry A. Kissinger had returned from his current trip to Hanoi and Peking.

Before returning to the U.S., Agnew had visited Manila Feb. 9 to confer with President Ferdinand E. Marcos and other Philippine leaders.

Rebels press drive in Cambodia. Rebel Khmer Rouge troops made widespread gains in their continued offensive against government positions in Cambodia Feb. 8–12.

The U.S. Defense Department said American planes attacked guerrilla forces in Cambodia Feb. 8 and again Feb. 11 at the request of the Pnompenh government. This was the first time the U.S. announced air strikes in Cambodia since Premier Lon Nol had declared a unilateral truce Jan. 29.

Guerrilla forces Feb. 10 captured the Mekong River port city of Banam, three miles north of the Neak Luong naval base. Neak Luong itself, 32 miles southeast of Pnompenh, was struck by Khmer Rouge artillery. Farther north, government troops abandoned four positions on Route 1, 15 miles southeast of the capital, and more than 120 Cambodian defenders were reported captured. Rebel troops also severed the road connecting the capital and the Mekong River ferry crossing at Phumi Prek Khsay, 32 miles east.

GIs who balked discharged. Two much-decorated Vietnam soldiers were discharged from the armed services because of their opposition to the Indochina war.

Capt. Michael J. Heck, 30, a B-52 pilot who refused to fly a Dec. 27, 1972 bombing mission over North Vietnam, was discharged from the Air Force, it was announced Feb. 8. Heck flew 175 missions in Vietnam and was decorated with the Distinguished Flying Cross and the Air Medal with 22 clusters.

Heck's lawyer, Marvin M. Karpatkin of the American Civil Liberties Union, said the discharge was for "other than honorable reasons." Heck applied for an honorable discharge and was rejected, since the Air Force was considering court-martial on the charge of refusing to obey a legal order. Heck said he acted because "the goals do not justify the mass destruction and killing."

Sgt. Ernest R. Pounder, 28, a Green Beret paratrooper and winner of 24 medals for bravery in Vietnam, was discharged from the Army Jan. 20 as a conscientious objector. Pounder, a 12-year veteran, had previously returned his medals to the Pentagon. He said he went to Vietnam in 1964 "100% in favor" of the war, but he said he quickly soured, disillusioned by the "death and destruction" and the corruption of South Vietnamese military officials.

U.S. shifting base to Thailand. The U.S. Defense Department announced Feb. 12 that it was establishing a new Southeast Asian headquarters at a base at Nakhon Phanom, Thailand. After March 28 the base was to be used to control teams searching for missing U.S. servicemen and to direct any future air activity.

The Vietnam cease-fire agreement required the U.S. command and the 7th Air Force to withdraw from their Saigon headquarters by the end of March. Air Force Gen. John W. Voigt Jr. was to head the new Thailand base, with a staff of 1,-000 men, including 800 assigned to air operations.

Truce violations charged. The Viet Cong and North Vietnam Feb. 12 accused South Vietnam and the U.S. of repeatedly violating the cease-fire since it had gone into effect Jan. 28.

Asserting that its side "will not go on tolerating" the truce breaches, Viet Cong delegation spokesman Ly Van Sau said in Paris that the U.S. had refused to dismantle all its military bases in South Vietnam and that Saigon's troops were attacking Communist-controlled zones. Saigon's actions threatened to "lead to the complete sabotage of the Paris cease-fire and peace accord," Sau charged.

The North Vietnamese Foreign Ministry claimed that Saigon, "tolerated and shielded by the United States," had violated the Paris agreement more than 2,000 times in 15 days.

South Vietnam's delegation spokesman in Paris, Nguyen Trieu Dan, denied Sau's accusations and countercharged that the Communists had committed 2,671 violations of the cease-fire between Jan. 28 and Feb. 12.

A South Vietnamese spokesman had reported Feb. 10 that 870 government soldiers and 5,218 North Vietnamese and Viet Cong troops had been killed since Jan. 28. The Saigon command said the Communists had violated the truce 215 times in the 30-hour period ended at noon Feb. 10.

Although the two truce observation commissions had taken up positions in the field, they had not yet inspected a single incident.

Chairman Michel Gauvin of the International Commission of Control and Supervision (ICCS) conceded in Saigon Feb. 9 that an effective truce was not being implemented because of the inability of the Saigon government and the Viet Cong to agree on clear lines separating the territories they held. Gauvin said establishment of lines of demarcation between the opposing forces was the responsibility of the Four-Party Joint Military Commission, which he said "is not operating to a sufficient degree." The demarcation problem reportedly was supposed to have been settled in negotiations preceding the signing of the Paris agreement Jan. 27. The matter, however, was turned over to the JMC after the political representatives of the U.S., North and South Vietnam and the Viet Cong had apparently failed to come up with a solution.

South Vietnamese President Nguyen Van Thieu declared Feb. 8 that "there's no cease-fire at all" and that "the war continues." He said it was difficult to enact a truce "as long as the Communists continue to violate the cease-fire." The president expressed satisfaction with the Jan. 27 Paris agreement, but said he was "not satisfied with the attitude of the Communists."

Mistreatment charged—Lt. Col. Bui Tin, a spokesman for the JMC's North Vietnamese delegation, said Feb. 9 that members of its team that day had been "attacked by a group of hooligans" when they arrived for a truce assignment in the

Central Highlands town of Banmethuot. He said eight North Vietnamese had been injured and that South Vietnamese had robbed the group. The incident was confirmed by sources in Saigon.

Lt. Col. Le Quang Hoa, head of the North Vietnamese delegation, protested to the U.S. and South Vietnam at a meeting of the JMC Feb. 10. Tin said no more North Vietnamese members of the JMC would be sent to inspection sites until security and living conditions were guaranteed.

Mistreatment of the Communist JMC delegates was charged Feb. 10 by the Viet Cong at another meeting in Paris between Viet Cong and Saigon government representatives. Delegate Dinh Ba Thi, without elaborating, said "We demand that the Saigon administration cease all acts that hamper the application of the Paris agreement and its protocols." The third meeting had been held by both sides Feb. 8 to prepare for substantive political talks in Saigon.

Saigon delegate ousted—Gen. Ngo Dzu was reported Feb. 11 to have been ousted as head of the South Vietnamese delegation to the JMC and replaced by Lt. Gen. Du Quoc Dong, a former com-.nander of a paratroop division.

A government spokesman said Dzu had been removed Feb. 10 because of his "physical condition." Saigon sources said Premier Tran Thien Khiem had ordered Dzu's ouster because he was dissatisfied with his performance. Dzu had been relieved of his Central Highlands post May 10, 1972 because his troops had performed poorly in combat.

War prisoner release begins. The release of U.S., North and South Vietnamese and Viet Cong prisoners of war began Feb. 12 and 13. The first phase of the repatriation was being carried out under terms of the Jan. 27 Paris cease-fire agreement, which provided for the return of all captives within 60 days of the signing of the pact.

A group of 116 American prisoners were freed by North Vietnam Feb. 12, another 27 Americans were released by the Viet Cong in South Vietnam, the South Vietnamese repatriated 250 North Vietnamese and Viet Cong and the Communists returned 140 Saigon troops. In the Feb. 13 exchange, 450 Viet Cong and 571 South Vietnamese soldiers were removed from war prisoner camps.

The Americans released in Hanoi were flown from the North Vietnamese capital to Clark Air Force Base in the Philippines in U.S. C-141 medical evacuation planes on the first leg of their eventual trip home. Three planes carrying 116 prisoners arrived at the base Feb. 12 and four more evacuation aircraft landed Feb. 13 with 19 military men and seven civilians. After preliminary medical checkups, the base's hospital commander pronounced the general health of the men as "reasonably good."

Ninety-seven of the Americans had been imprisoned six or more years. Of those, 36 were captured in 1966, 60 in 1965 and one—Lt. Cmdr. Everett Alvarez Jr.—was the first captured in 1964. Only 19 had been captured after 1966.

President Nixon Feb. 12 spoke by telephone to one of the released prisoners as he arrived at Clark Air Base. The four-minute conversation Nixon held with Air Force Col. Robinson Risner was described by the President, through his press secretary, as "one of the most moving" he had ever had in the White House.

The release by the Viet Cong of the 27 American prisoners—19 servicemen and eight civilians—had been delayed for half a day because of a dispute between American and Viet Cong officers over whether the men could be freed before Saigon turned over the 2,000 Communist prisoners it had announced Feb. 11 it would be exchanged for 1,020 government soldiers. The 27 Americans were finally set free in Communist-controlled Locninh, about 72 miles north of Saigon, and were flown to Clark Air Force Base later Feb. 12 after a brief stopover at Saigon's Tansonnhut air base. The majority of the Communist prisoners at the South Vietnamese camp at Bienhoa, 20 miles north of Saigon, had refused to leave unless they were reassured that they would be taking part in a bona fide release and would not be subjected to new dangers.

An additional 100 sick and disabled North Vietnamese were to have been freed by South Vietnam in Quangtri Province Feb. 12, but North Vietnamese officers were said to have refused to accept them because they were "not ready."

Rogers on POW return. Commenting on the returning POWs brought tears to the eyes of Secretary of State William P. Rogers Feb. 15. If watching the returning POWs "doesn't make America proud, then I don't know what will," he said. "I think it is time that all of us took a little pride in our country."

He stressed the Administration's desire "to get on with the business of peace and reconstruction here" and the importance for the nation "to attempt to get together and to have a period of reconciliation."

In cases "where people resisted [the draft] and fled or deserted," Rogers said, "that means that someone else had to take their place; someone else had to serve for them; someone else may have been killed because they refused to serve."

Agnew scores deserters—Vice President Spiro T. Agnew told a Republican Lincoln Day audience in Los Angeles Feb. 12 the nation "must be particularly hard and tough in our treatment of deserters" who evaded Vietnam service.

U.S. to channel aid to North Vietnam. An agreement to create a Joint Economic Commission to provide North Vietnam with postwar American reconstruction assistance was announced jointly by the U.S. and North Vietnam Feb. 14. The announcement was contained in a joint communique based on talks held in Hanoi Feb. 10–13 by Henry A. Kissinger, President Nixon's national security adviser, and Premier Pham Van Dong and other North Vietnamese officials.

The joint commission would be composed of an equal number of representatives from each side, and "will be charged with the task of developing economic relations" between the two countries. It was expected to become operative in about a month.

The communique said Kissinger and the Hanoi representatives had "examined concrete steps which can be taken to normalize the relations" between the two countries. The conferees listed these "general principles" which they said "should govern their mutual relations":

"All provisions of the Paris agreement on Vietnam and its protocols should be fully and scrupulously implemented.

"The Democratic Republic of Vietnam and the United States should strive for a new relationship based on respect for each other's independence and sovereignty, noninterference in each other's internal affairs, equality and mutual benefit.

"The normalization of the relations between the Democratic Republic of Vietnam and the United States will help to insure stable peace in Vietnam and contribute to the cause of peace in Indochina and Southeast Asia."

The communique said both sides had "reviewed the implementation of the Paris agreement" and discussed "various imperative measures" to accelerate its implementation, "welcomed the discussions" between the Saigon government and the Viet Cong, and "exchanged views on the convening of the international conference on Vietnam" to start Feb. 26.

Kissinger and the North Vietnamese officials expressed the hope that his "visit will mark the beginning of new bilateral relations" between Washington and Hanoi.

White House Press Secretary Ronald L. Ziegler said the "imperative measures" mentioned by the communique to speed up the carrying out of the Paris accord included agreement to determine the fate of the 1,300 Americans listed as missing in action.

In addition to Premier Dong, Kissinger had conferred with Le Duc Tho, Hanoi's chief peace negotiator, Foreign Minister Nguyen Duy Trinh and Vice Foreign Minister Nguyen Co Thach. He had been accompanied to Hanoi by Herbert Klein, the Nixon Administration's communications director, Deputy Assistant Secretary of State William H. Sullivan, and National Security Council Staff members Richard Kennedy, Winston Lord, Peter Rodman and David Engel.

Before arriving in Hanoi, Kissinger had visited Thailand and Laos for talks on expanding the Vietnam cease-fire to include Laos and Cambodia. The Presidential aide met with Thai Premier Thanom Kittikachorn in Bangkok Feb. 8 and with Laotian Premier Souvanna Phouma in Vientiane Feb. 9.

Ending his Hanoi meetings Feb. 13, Kissinger flew to Hong Kong for a rest and left for Peking Feb. 15 for five days of talks with Chinese leaders.

Rogers testifies on Vietnam aid—U.S. Secretary of State William P. Rogers testified before the House Foreign Affairs Committee Feb. 8 on the Vietnam situation. It was his first public appearance before a Congressional group in nine months.

Committee chairman Thomas E. Morgan (D, Pa.) said many members were being pressed by constituents to oppose rehabilitation aid for North Vietnam. He asked Rogers whether the Administration had plans for "a real costly effort for the American taxpayer." Rogers responded that no firm plans had been made nor commitment given for a rehabilitation effort. "We did say we would be helpful," he said, and the Administration considered such an effort "an investment in peace."

Other committee members also questioned Rogers on the aid issue. Rep. Donald M. Fraser (D, Minn.) brought up the question of aid to North Vietnam in context with the Administration's refusal to exchange ambassadors with Sweden because its premier, Olof Palme, had criticized American bombing of North Vietnam. Rogers said he thought it "would be best for Sweden" if its premier refrained "from gratuitous statements that are not helpful at all.... I think his statements have been outrageous ... [and he] should resist the temptation to say so much." "We believe," Rogers continued, "that if a lot of people were quieter, the peace would have come quicker."

Fraser asked if the Administration similarly would refrain from sending an ambassador to India because of recent criticism from Prime Minister Indira Gandhi. "It's a possibility," Rogers said.

Rep. Benjamin S. Rosenthal (D, N.Y.) asked Rogers how aid to North or South Vietnam could be voted "after the President has cut off 100 domestic programs." Rogers replied he was "not requesting your vote" that day.

(Sen. J. W. Fulbright [D, Ark.] introduced an amendment to the foreign aid bill Feb. 8 to cut off foreign aid funds unless the funds impounded for domestic programs were released.)

In summarizing Vietnam developments since negotiation of the cease-fire, Rogers said there were "many remaining problems to be worked out, but so far developments certainly support our expectations that the agreement will work, that the South Vietnamese people have a reasonable chance to sort out their own political destiny and that peace with honor is being achieved."

End to Vietnam fighting urged. The heads of the Four-Party Joint Military Commission (JMC) appealed Feb. 17 to the commands of Saigon and Communist forces to "promptly issue" orders to cease further combat in South Vietnam as there appeared to be no letup in the fighting since the truce went into effect Jan. 28. The Saigon command complied with the appeal and directed its troops Feb. 18 to halt all military action. The Communist command was said to have issued a similar order to its soldiers.

The JMC declared in its statement that "the fighting had not yet stopped, the cease-fire has not yet been consolidated in South Vietnam in accordance with the agreement and protocol concerning the cease-fire." The commission called on the Viet Cong, North Vietnamese and Saigon troops "to strictly respect the cease-fire, settle all questions by peaceful negotiations in the spirit of national reconciliation and concord with a view to averting conflicts and preserving a lasting peace."

The commission also urged the commands to order their forces to stop "armed patrols into areas controlled by opposing armed forces," to stop all plane flights, except training missions, to end "all combat operations on the ground, on rivers, on the sea and in the air," and to cease "all hostile acts, terrorism or reprisals" and "all acts endangering" lives and property.

Maj. Gen. Gilbert H. Woodward, chief U.S. delegate to the JMC, had urged the Viet Cong commission members Feb. 14 to speed deployment of their observer teams. Woodward issued his appeal in a letter to the chief Viet Cong delegate, Lt. Gen. Tran Van Tra. The plea was made on the day with the highest reported number of Communist truce breaches since Feb. 2. The Saigon command said the Communists had committed 188 violations in the 24-hour period ended at dawn Feb. 14, killing 44 government troops and wounding 314.

The seven regional truce teams and 26 local teams were to have been in place by Feb. 12 under terms of the Paris accord. The Viet Cong had deployed only parts of four regional teams and no local teams at all. The U.S. had all its regional teams and all but two of its local teams in position. Saigon had deployed all its regional and local teams. The North Vietnam had sent out all its regional teams but disposition of its local teams was not clear.

Despite the JMC's appeal for a halt to the fighting, the clashes continued unabated Feb. 18, diminished Feb. 19 and increased sharply Feb. 20. According to the Saigon command: The Communists committed 194 truce violations in the 24 hours that ended at 6 a.m. Feb. 19. Communist violations dropped to 134 during the 24-hour period that ended at 6 a.m. Feb. 20. An upsurge in Communist attacks resulted in 200 truce violations in the 24 hours that ended at 6 a.m. Feb. 21. Communist truce violations since the Jan. 28 truce totaled 4,000 incidents, resulting in the killing of 7,470 Communist and 1,280 Saigon troops, according to the South Vietnamese command. The Communists claimed South Vietnamese forces had violated the truce more than 2,000 times since Jan. 28.

North Vietnamese Premier Pham Van Dong charged Feb. 20 that South Vietnam was "sabotaging the Paris agreements with United States support and approval." Saigon, Dong asserted, "not only does not want to carry out all its provisions but is deliberately trying to torpedo their execution."

U.S. helicopter downed—In a related development, a U.S. helicopter flying a supply mission for the JMC was shot down by ground fire Feb. 16 three miles south of Anloc, near the Cambodian border. Five U.S. crewmen were injured. Gen. Woodward called on the International Commission of Control and Supervision (ICCS) Feb. 18 to investigate the incident. Woodward said a preliminary investigation by "United States experts"

indicated that the Viet Cong were responsible for the shooting down of the helicopter. The U.S. chief delegate said he was asking the ICCS to initiate the probe because Viet Cong Gen. Tra had refused his request to investigate the attack.

U.S. members of the JMC complained Feb. 22 that although the North Vietnamese and Viet Cong delegates had attended an inquiry at the helicopter crash site Feb. 20, they displayed little interest in pursuing the probe.

Gen Woodward filed a formal complaint with the JMC Feb. 22 about the Communists' refusal to investigate another alleged truce violation. According to Woodward, a JMC team was to have flown Feb. 20 to the central coastal town of Thach By, the scene of the principal fighting in South Vietnam. The Viet Cong had requested the inquiry Feb. 19. The investigators reached only as far as Danang, the JMC's nearest regional headquarters, and were unable to proceed further because of the Communists' delaying tactics, Woodward said.

Saigon forms new political front. The South Vietnamese government Feb. 17 announced the formation of a new political front "to prepare the peace and to prepare the political struggle against [the Viet Cong's] National Liberation Front."

The new organization, called the People's Front to Safeguard Peace and to Realize the People's Right to Self-Determination, was under the chairmanship of President Nguyen Van Thieu. It was formed at a meeting of members of the national legislature, chairmen of provincial and municipal councils and political, religious and professional leaders. Two principal leaders of the non-Communist opposition—Maj. Gen. Duong Van Minh and former Vice President Nguyen Cao Ky—did not attend. Government spokesman Pham Duong Hien said Thieu had no current plans to ask the two men join the front.

Thieu had indicated at the meeting that the People's Front would be active in the national elections provided for by the Paris peace agreement and in the selection of Saigon representatives to serve on the proposed National Council of National Reconciliation and Concord.

The political talks leading to the formation of the front had started Feb. 8.

More U.S. prisoners freed. North Vietnam released 20 more American prisoners of war Feb. 18. The men were flown to Clark Air Force Base in the Philippines before their scheduled return to the U.S. North Vietnam freed the Americans ahead of schedule as a goodwill gesture, following the recent visit to Hanoi by President Nixon's national security adviser Henry A. Kissinger.

The airlift from the Philippines to the U.S. of the first group of 143 U.S. prisoners released by North Vietnam and the Viet Cong Feb. 12–13 started Feb. 14 and was completed Feb. 17. Air Force evacuation planes landed the men at Travis Air Force Base and Alameda Naval Air Station in California.

Saigon frees POWs—South Vietnam released 175 disabled North Vietnamese prisoners Feb. 14. They were repatriated in northern Quangtri Province after crossing the Thach Han River in 10 boats. One hundred of the men had been held at the Phubai airport, 35 miles south of the release point, since Feb. 12, when they first had been scheduled to be set free. North Vietnamese officers in Quangtri Province had said at the time they were not prepared to accept the released men. A Viet Cong spokesman in Saigon, however, had said the delay was caused by a South Vietnamese artillery barrage on the area of release Feb. 11.

South Vietnam Feb. 15 released 1,604 Communist captives, including 904 women. The women, who had been serving with the Viet Cong in a combat and noncombat capacity, were taken from a camp at Cantho in the Mekong Delta and flown to Locninh, a Communist-controlled district capital 77 miles north of Saigon, and turned over to the Viet Cong. All the women had been captured in action.

Another 982 Communist prisoners were released by Saigon Feb. 19. The former captives were ferried across the Thach Han River to the Communist side. South Vietnam set free 200 POWs Feb. 20. This brought to 6,500 the number of Communists repatriated. Saigon said 830 government soldiers had been released from Communist prison camps.

U.S. captives supported war aims—One of the released American captives said Feb. 15 that to his knowledge most of his fellow prisoners had supported the U.S.' war aims. Speaking to a news conference at Clark Air Base, Col. Robinson Risner said "as far as I know, every man that has been in prison in North Vietnam supports and has supported our President and his policies." Risner was one of many captives to whom anti-U.S. statements had been attributed by the North Vietnamese.

The first two released American prisoners to land in the U.S. Feb. 13 were Cmdr. Brian D. Woods and Maj. Glendon W. Perkins. They had been flown back early in order to be at the bedsides of their critically ill mothers. On landing at Travis Air Force Base, the two men expressed sentiments that were generally repeated by other freed captives who followed. Woods said: "This homecoming is not only for myself and Glendon Perkins, but for all the POWs. We are grateful and overwhelmed. We are proud to be Americans. We are proud to have served our country and our commander in chief."

Cambodia plans united front. The Cambodian government announced Feb. 20 that negotiations were in progress to form a united front, composed of the government and its non-Communist opposition, to establish future contacts with the warring Communist movement. The U.S. reportedly had urged the government of President Lon Nol to undertake the move to pave the way for peace talks with the Communists.

Information Minister Keam Reth said the ruling Social-Republican party had proposed creation of a council of national reconciliation and the opposition Republican party had agreed to join. Talks were under way to get the Democrats, the other major opposition party, to enter the coalition. Keam Reth said the council would be an extragovernmental organization with advisory powers only.

The leader of the Democrats, Brig. Gen. In Tam, had been appointed by Lon Nol Feb. 7 as a special presidential adviser with the rank equivalent to premier to make contacts with the Communists. In Tam resigned Feb. 24, saying he was leaving the post because he had not been given the executive powers sufficient to carry out his duties.

Fighting continues in South Vietnam. Despite appeals by the International Commission of Control and Supervision (ICCS) for a halt to the fighting in South Vietnam, U.S. and South Vietnamese officers in Saigon were reported as saying Feb. 21 that government troops in the central provinces had not been ordered to halt operations. Small-scale ground attacks and shelling incidents by both sides were also continuing in other parts of the country since the truce formally went into effect Jan. 28.

The Saigon command was reported as saying Feb. 18 that it was complying with a Joint Military Commission (JMC) appeal of the previous day to stop the fighting. But allied officers said there had been no general directives to government soldiers in the central provinces, particularly in Binhdinh, to observe the cease-fire. The same applied to the Communists. Government intelligence agents Feb. 19 were said to have intercepted a Viet Cong military radio message directing their forces to continue operations and to prepare for long-term combat.

Chairman Michel Gauvin of the ICCS Feb. 19 again complained about the unabated fighting. He accused the U.S., North and South Vietnam and the Viet Cong of "having failed up to now to abide" by the Paris truce agreement and deplored their "evident inability" to stop the combat. Gauvin said the JMC bore the burden of ending the fighting. The ICCS, he said, was not going to send its observers "to go out in cross-fire and get killed." Gauvin explained that his group "is not a peace-keeping force. It is principally an observer group for reporting on the implementation or non-implementation of the Paris agreement by the four parties who signed and are under obligation to respect that agreement."

Gauvin's criticisms were contained in a letter he had sent to the JMC Feb. 16, whose text he made public. In it he reminded the JMC that it was "responsible for this deplorable situation," that "the cease-fire is being violated."

Gauvin said despite the JMC's failure to become "fully operative," the ICCS was increasing the effectiveness of its own

mission by preparing to deploy from its seven regional headquarters supervisory teams to the 26 towns around South Vietnam from which actual inspections would take place. He said the ICCS also would send teams to designated points of entry for military supplies to the demilitarized zone and to military bases to "observe the withdrawal of U.S. forces and those of other foreign nations" allied to Saigon.

In related developments, the Saigon command reported that the Communists had committed 222 truce violations in the 24-hour period ending at noon Feb. 19. This represented a 15% increase over the daily average the previous week.

A U.S. helicopter carrying a Canadian and Indonesian member of the ICCS was struck by small-arms fire Feb. 28, 12 miles south of Danang. The American pilot was wounded. The ICCS said the shooting was one of four similar incidents involving ICCS aircraft that day. As a result the ICCS grounded all helicopter flights in South Vietnam for an indefinite period.

The Viet Cong claimed Feb. 28 that four of its JMC members were killed in a South Vietnamese ambush Feb. 25.

The U.S. command had reported Feb. 23 that the American wounded in the shooting down of a helicopter at Anloc Feb. 16 died in an Okinawa hospital. [See p. 134C2] He was identified as Spec. 5 James L. Scroggins. He was the second American fatality since the truce went into effect Jan. 28. The first GI killed was a pilot whose helicopter was fired on Jan. 30.

Communist gunners Feb. 24 fired three shells at separate intervals into Tri Ton in the Mekong Delta, killing 12 South Vietnamese and wounding 10. One shell burst in a school yard next to a conference room of the JMC.

Nixon justifies Vietnam decisions. President Nixon addressed the South Carolina General Assembly in Columbia Feb. 20 on the Vietnam war settlement. The legislature had been the first of several state legislatures to endorse the settlement.

In his 25-minute address, Nixon said peace with honor was attained in Vietnam, that the U.S. goal to prevent "imposition by force of a Communist government" on South Vietnam had been achieved, that "we can be proud that we stuck it out until we did reach that goal" and that as a result the U.S. could "exercise more effective leadership in the cause of world peace."

"The chances for us to build a peace that will last are better than they have been at any time since the end of World War II," he said.

The President emphasized that the U.S. must remain strong militarily and that it must not go to the negotiating table "the second strongest nation in the world." Referring to the war, he said: "Had we taken another course—had we, for example, followed the advice of some of the well-intentioned people who said, 'Peace at any price. Get our prisoners of war back in exchange for withdrawing'— had we taken that course, then respect for America not only among our allies but particularly among those who might be our potential adversaries would have been eroded, perhaps fatally."

Nixon asserted that the men who died or served in Vietnam had not done so in vain and "the way to honor them—is for us to work together to build a lasting peace in the world."

The President had touched upon the same theme in other recent statements. Stressing to newsmen at the White House Feb. 15 the importance of having ended the war "the right way—peace with honor," Nixon said he was "strongly" convinced "that in the perspective of history that many of our allies, particularly, will look back and realize that had we taken the easy way out, which we could have done years ago, certainly when I came into office in 1969, our failure there would have eroded and possibly destroyed their confidence in the United States and, of course, enormously encouraged those who might have aggressive intentions toward us."

In Jacksonville, Fla. Feb. 16, Nixon noted that the first words of many of the returning American prisoners of war were "God bless America." "When anyone can say that after 6½ years in prison, it has all been worthwhile," he commented.

Brezhnev lauds Vietnam pact. Soviet Communist party General Secretary Leonid I. Brezhnev praised the Vietnam peace agreement in a letter to President Nixon, White House officials disclosed Feb. 21.

Brezhnev said the accord opened up "new possibilities" for improving U.S.-Soviet relations and generally improved the world situation. "We are confident that the end of bloodshed in Vietnam has a tremendous significance and will be warmly welcomed not only by the Vietnamese and the American people but also by all people of good will," the Soviet leader said.

Nixon host to backers in Congress. President Nixon held a White House party Feb. 22 for about 200 members of the Senate and House who had supported him on the Vietnam war issue. He told them that without their help "we couldn't have had a peace with honor" and the POWs "wouldn't have been able to come home full of pride and assurance in their country's willingness to see it through."

Kissinger comments on postwar aid. At a press briefing Feb. 22 in Washington, Henry Kissinger, in response to questions from newsmen, said the government was asking for support for the aid program to be launched by the joint economic commission with North Vietnam, announced Feb. 14, "not on economic grounds and not even on humanitarian grounds primarily, but on the grounds of attempting to build peace in Indochina and therefore to contribute to peace in the world."

He said the "basic purpose" of his trip to Hanoi had been to "establish contact with the leadership of the Democratic Republic of Vietnam in order to see whether it would be possible to establish with it in Indochina something like the relationship that we have managed to establish with the People's Republic of China in Asia in general."

The U.S., he said, intended to "work on a settlement in Cambodia with energy," although the situation there was "complicated by the fact that there are three or four different groups, rather than one homogeneous opposition group, to the government that we recognize."

Meeting of U.S. draft evaders banned.
Police Feb. 17 banned a conference of
U.S. draft evaders and military deserters
scheduled to meet in Paris Feb. 20–21.
The police said the planned meeting was
potentially "disruptive to public order" in
view of the fact that the international
conference on Vietnam was scheduled to
open less than a week later.

Accord ends 20 years of war. The
government of Premier Souvanna
Phouma and the Communist Pathet Lao
signed an agreement in Vientiane Feb. 21
aimed at ending the 20-year war in Laos.
A truce in place went into effect at noon
Feb. 22

With the signing of the accord, U.S.
officials made immediate contact with the
Pathet Lao to seek the release of
American prisoners believed held by the
Communist forces.

The peace agreement was reached
earlier Feb. 21 and was signed later in the
day by Pheng Phongsavan, chief negotiator for the Vientiane government, and
Phoumi Vongvichit, a Pathet Lao leader.

The principal terms of the pact provided for an immediate halt to military
activities by all forces in Laos, including
those of North Vietnam and the U.S. All
foreign troops were to be withdrawn from
Laos within 60 days after the establishment of a new National Provisional
Coalition Government and a National
Political Coalition Council. The
government was to be formed within 30
days of the signing of the accord. The
temporary regime and the council were to
be composed of representatives of the
Vientiane government and the Pathet Lao
in equal numbers. The government also
was to include "two intellectuals who
advocated peace, independence, neutrality and democracy, who will be agreed
upon by both sides." The new prime
minister was not to be "a member of the
representatives in the government." The
new government was empowered "to implement all agreements reached and the
political program agreed upon by both
sides." The Coalition Council's function
was "to consult and express views" to the
coalition government and to assist it in implementing the agreements.

The two sides were to retain the territories in Laos under their control, pending
the establishment of a national assembly

and the installation of a permanent
coalition government.

The International Control Commission
(Canada, Poland and India), established
under the 1962 Laos accords, would
oversee compliance of the truce until a
mixed commission of Vientiane and
Pathet Lao representatives worked out a
new supervisory system.

The text of the agreement made no
mention of North Vietnam by name, but
did specifically call on the U.S. and Thailand to respect the "peace, independence
and neutrality" of Laos.

Another clause of the pact said
Vientiane and the royal capital of Luang
Prabang would be "neutralized." This
presumably meant that the Pathet Lao
would be guaranteed complete safety and
protection in the two cities, which were in
government-held territory.

Two U.S. officials of the American embassy in Vientiane discussed the prisoner
issue earlier Feb. 21 with Pathet Lao
officials at their headquarters in the city.
The two were John G. Dean, deputy chief
of mission, and Consul S. Richard Rand.
At a news conference following the
signing of the agreement, Pathet Lao
leader Phoumi Vongvichit made no
mention of the two Americans' visit.
Phoumi said, however, that U.S. Ambassador G. McMurtrie Godley had
"congratulated us on the accord and said
the United States would do all it could to
help realize the terms of the accord."

On the question of the captives, Phoumi
said: "Do not call them prisoners of war. I
call them people who were captured and
held during the war." He promised
release of the prisoners.

The Vientiane agreement followed
intensified private talks held in the
Laotian capital Feb. 12–16 between
government and Pathet Lao officials.

Laotian clashes prior to truce—Major
military developments in Laos prior to announcement of the truce pact included
intensified ground fighting and a step-up
in the American air war Feb. 8–20. Except for U.S. air activity, details of other
fighting were scanty following announcement by a U.S. spokesman in
Vientiane Feb. 9 of a halt to military
briefings. The spokesman said the request
for the news blackout had been made by
the Laotian government "in view of the

current sensitive stage of peace negotiations" between the Laotian government and the Pathet Lao.

A U.S. Defense Department announcement Feb. 15 said American air strikes against North Vietnamese and Pathet Lao troop and supply movements had increased from an average of about 280 a day the previous week to about 380 during the current week. The intensified raids by B-52s and fighter-bombers was attributed by the department to

"increased enemy activity and further requests for assistance by the Royal Lao government."

The U.S. Pacific forces command in Honolulu announced Feb. 9 the downing of an American EC-47 electronic intelligence plane over southern Laos Feb. 5, presumably by Communist ground fire. The Defense Department said Feb. 17 that one of the eight crewmen was killed and that the others were missing. The EC-47 was supporting U.S. air strikes when it was downed.

Text of Laotian Cease-fire Agreement Signed Feb. 21

In response to the supreme desire of His Majesty the King and the earnest aspirations of the people of all nationalities throughout the country, who want to end the war as soon as possible and restore and safeguard lasting peace, in order to achieve national concord and unification and build Laos as a country of peace, independence, neutrality, democracy, unity and prosperity, and to diligently contribute to improving peace in Indochina and Southeast Asia on the basis of the 1962 Geneva agreement on Laos and the present reality in Laos, the Vientiane Government side and the Patriotic Forces side have agreed on the following provisions:

CHAPTER I

General Principles

Article 1
A. The desires of the Lao people to safeguard and exercise their cherished fundamental national rights—the independence, sovereignty, unity and territorial integrity of Laos—are inviolable.

B. The 9 July 1962 communiqué on the neutrality of Laos and the 1962 Geneva agreement on Laos are the correct basis of the policy for peace, independence and neutrality of the Kingdom of Laos. The parties concerned in Laos, the United States, Thailand and other foreign countries must strictly respect and implement this agreement. The internal affairs of Laos must be conducted by the Lao people only, without external interference.

C. To achieve the supreme objective of restoring peace, enhancing independence, implementing national concord and restoring national unification, and due to the present reality in Laos, which has two zones under the control of two sides, the internal problems of Laos must be solved in the spirit of national concord and on the basis of equality and mutual respect, with neither side trying to swallow or oppress the other side.

D. To safeguard national independence and sovereignty, implement national concord and restore national unification, the people's various rights and freedoms must be absolutely respected—for example, privacy, ideology, speech, press, writing, assembly, establishing political organizations and associations, candidacy and elections, traveling, living where one wants and establishing business enterprises and ownership. All acts, regulations and organizations that violate these rights and freedoms must be abolished.

CHAPTER II

Provisions on Military Affairs

Article 2
Beginning at 1200 (0500 G.M.T.—F.B.I.S.) on 22 February 1973, a cease-fire in place will be observed simultaneously throughout the territory of Laos. This includes:

A. Foreign countries must completely and permanently cease the bombing against the territory of Laos, all acts of intervention and aggression in Laos, and all military involvement in Laos.

B. All armed forces of foreign countries must completely and permanently cease all military movements in Laos.

C. The armed forces of all sides must completely cease all military movements encroaching upon one another both on the ground and in the air.

Article 3
As soon as the cease-fire goes into effect:

A. It is definitely forbidden to commit small encroachment attacks or threats by army or air forces against the territory temporarily controlled by the other side.

B. It is definitely forbidden to commit any military acts that antagonize the other side, including the movement of bandits [word indistinct] and armed air reconnaissance. In case a particular side wants to transport food supplies across the territory under the control of the other side, the committee for implementation of the agreement must discuss and lay down a clear-cut procedure for this.

C. It is definitely forbidden to carry out mop-up, intimidation and suppression drives against the lives and property of the people or to discriminate against those who participated with the opposite side during the war. The people who were forced to evacuate from their native land during the war must be assisted to freely return to their domiciles to earn their living in accordance with their desires.

D. It is forbidden to bring into Laos military personnel of any type, regular forces or irregular forces, and all kinds of weapons and war means of foreign countries, as mentioned in the 1954 and 1962 Geneva agreements. In case it is necessary to replace damaged or out-of-order weapons and war means, the two sides will discuss this and come to an agreement among themselves.

Article 4
Within 60 days at the latest after the establishment of the National Provisional Coalition Government and

the National Political Coalition Council, the withdrawal of all military personnel and regular and irregular forces from Laos and the dissolution of all military and paramilitary organizations of foreign countries must be completed. The special forces organized, armed, trained and commanded by foreign countries must be disbanded, and their bases, military positions and strongholds must be completely dismantled.

Article 5
The two Lao sides will repatriate all persons, regardless of nationality, who were captured or detained because they collaborated with one side or the other in the war. The repatriation will be carried out in accordance with the principles agreed upon by the two sides and be completed within 60 days at the latest after the establishment of the National Political Coalition Council. Following the completion of the repatriation of captured personnel, each side will have the responsibility to provide the other side with information on those reported missing during the war in Laos.

CHAPTER III

Provisions on Political Affairs
Article 6
General free and democratic elections are to be carried out to establish the national assembly and permanent national coalition government, which are to be the genuine representatives of the people of all nationalities in Laos. The principles and procedures of the general elections will be discussed and agreed upon by the two sides. Pending the general elections, the two sides must set up a National Provisions Coalition Government and a National Political Coalition Council within 30 days at the latest after the signing of this agreement, to implement all the agreements signed and to administer national tasks.

Article 7
The new National Provisional Coalition Government is to be composed of representatives of the Vientiane Government side and the Patriotic Forces side, in equal proportions, and two intellectuals who advocate peace, independence, neutrality and democracy, who will be agreed upon by both sides. The prime minister must be a person who is not a member of the representatives in the government. The National Provisional Coalition Government is to be set up in accordance with special procedures by royal decree of His Majesty the King. It will perform its duties in accordance with principles unanimously agreed upon by both sides. It will have the responsibility to implement all agreements reached and the political program agreed upon by the two sides—for example, in implementing and maintaining the cease-fire, permanently safeguarding peace, completely implementing popular rights and freedoms, implementing the policy for peaceful foreign relations and for independence and neutrality, for coordinating all economic development plans, expanding culture and accepting and distributing all aid materials from all countries aiding Laos.

Article 8
The National Political Coalition Council is to be an organization of national concord and to be composed of representatives of the Vientiane Government side and of the Patriotic Forces side in equal proportions, as well as intellectuals who advocate peace, independence, neutrality and democracy, whose number will be determined by the two sides. It will perform its duties in accordance with principles unanimously

agreed upon by both sides. It has the responsibility to consult with and express views to the National Provisional Coalition Government on major problems relating to domestic and foreign policies, to support and assist the National Provisional Coalition Government as well as the two sides in implementing the agreements signed, to bring about the realization of national concord, to scrutinize and endorse the electoral coalition government in holding general elections to establish the national assembly and the permanent national coalition government. The procedures in detail on the establishment of the National Political Coalition Council will be discussed and agreed upon by the two sides and will be sent to the National Provisional Coalition Government to be forwarded to His Majesty the King for his decree of appointment. The abolition of the National Political Coalition Council must go through the same procedures as its establishment, as mentioned above.

Article 9
The two sides agree to neutralize the royal capital of Luang Prabang and the city of Vientiane and to take all measures to guarantee the security of the National Provisions Coalition Government and the National Political Coalition Council so they can carry out their tasks effectively, and to prevent all acts of sabotage or threats from any force from within or without.

Article 10
A. Pending the establishment of the national assembly and the permanent national coalition government, in the spirit of Article 6 in Chapter II of the joint Zurich communiqué of 22 June 1961, the two sides will maintain the territories under their temporary control, and will endeavor to implement the political program of the National Provisional Coalition Government, as agreed upon by both sides.
B. The two sides will promote the establishment of normal relations between the two zones, and create favorable conditions for the people to move about, make their living and carry out economic and cultural exchanges with a view to consolidating national concord and bringing about national unification at an early date.
C. The two sides acknowledge the declaration of the United States government that it will contribute to healing the wounds of the war and the postwar reconstruction in Indochina. The national coalition government will hold discussions with the United States Government in connection with such a contribution regarding Laos.

CHAPTER IV

The Coalition Commission for Implementation of the Agreement and the International Commission for Supervision and Control
Article 11
The implementation of this agreement is the responsibility of the two sides concerned in Laos. The two sides will immediately establish a commission for implementation of the agreement, comprising representatives of both sides in equal proportions. This commission will begin functioning immediately after the cease-fire goes into effect. It will perform its tasks in accordance with the principles unanimously agreed upon by both sides.

Article 12
The International Commission for Control and Supervision, which was established in accordance with the 1962 Geneva agreement on Laos, is composed of

the representatives of India, Poland and Canada, and is chaired by India. It will continue to perform its duty in accordance with its rights and principles of work as provided for in the subagreement of the Geneva agreement mentioned below.

CHAPTER V

Other Provisions

Article 13

The Vientiane Government side and the Patriotic Forces side pledge to implement this agreement and to continue discussions in order to effect all the provisions already agreed upon and to settle the other pending problems concerning them, in the spirit of equality and mutual respect with a view to ending the war, to restore and safeguard lasting peace, achieve national concord, create national unity in order to proceed to build a peaceful independent, neutral, democratic, united and prosperous Laos.

Article 14

This agreement is effective from the date of its signing.

Done in Vientiane 21 February 1973, in the Lao language in five copies. One copy will be submitted to His Majesty the King. Each side will retain one copy. The remaining two copies will be kept in the files of the National Provisional Coalition Government and the National Political Coalition Council.

On behalf of the Patriotic Forces side:

Phagna Phoumi Vongvichit

Plenipotentiary special representative of the Patriotic Forces.

On behalf of the Vientiane Government side:

Phagna Pheng Phongsavan

Plenipotentiary representative of the Vientiane Government.

Laos truce implementation talks start. Laotian government and Pathet Lao representatives opened talks in Vientiane Feb. 26 to work out details of the cease-fire agreement signed Feb. 21. The conference started amid a gradual decrease in fighting after an upsurge of combat that was marked by resumption of U.S. air strikes.

Both sides agreed on meeting sites for the political and military sections of the joint commission authorized to oversee the cease-fire and negotiate a new coalition government. Formation of the mixed commission had been completed Feb. 23.

Nine U.S. B-52s struck at targets around the Bolovens Plateau town of Pak Song Feb. 22, after its capture that day by Communist forces.

Premier Souvanna Phouma requested the air strikes after charging that the Communists had launched a general offensive throughout Laos Feb. 22 the date the truce was to have gone into effect. At a meeting with Pathet Lao chief negotiator Phoumi Vongvichit earlier Feb. 22, Souvanna had warned that the raids would be renewed unless the Pathet Lao and the North Vietnamese ended their "general offensive."

Souvanna told a news conference Feb. 23 that the Communists had committed 29 truce violations in less than 24 hours after the cease-fire was to go into effect. He said North Vietnamese troops were responsible for more than 90% of the violations. The premier said "I deeply regret that the accord signed two days ago has not been respected by the other side despite the good faith we have displayed."

Pathet Lao spokesman Soth Phetrasy said in Vientiane Feb. 24 that he doubted his side was violating the truce. He said the "trouble was being caused by rightists and by Thai mercenary troops." "The right-wing Vientiane generals held a meeting a few days ago at which they decided the [truce] agreement was only political and would not apply to the military," Soth Phetrasy said.

In addition to Pak Song, heavy clashes were being fought 25 miles north of Vientiane for control of a road leading to the Nam Ngum Dam. Communists also were attacking near the southern town of Khong Sedone, forcing government troops to abandon a position there Feb. 25. Further north two North Vietnamese battalions overran Xieng Khouang at the edge of the Plaine des Jarres.

Diplomatic sources in Vientiane said three B-52 sorties had been carried out Feb. 23 near Pakse, in southern Laos.

The Laotian command reported a sharp decrease in fighting Feb. 24, saying that Communist truce violations dropped to 20 during the past 24 hours. Pathet Lao officials, however, contended that government bombardment of their areas was continuing "as usual." The government said Feb. 27 the relative battle lull was continuing with only 20 Communist violations during the 24 hours ended at 10 a.m. Feb. 26. This brought to 106 the total number of truce breaches since Feb. 22.

Accord formally signed. A North Vietnamese threat to suspend the scheduled release of more American prisoners of war until the U.S. and South Vietnam "correctly implemented" the truce agreement disrupted the 13-party international conference on Vietnam soon after it convened in Paris Feb. 26. North Vietnam subsequently agreed to free the POWs, allowing the conference to proceed. The parley was concluded March 1 with the initialing by the attending foreign ministers of an agreement providing for reconvening the conference if the truce broke down. The accord was formally signed March 2.

Meanwhile, the Communists agreed to release additional American POWs March 4. North Vietnam March 1 submitted a list of 106 Americans and two Thais to be freed. The Viet Cong March 2 turned over the names of 34 captives to be repatriated.

The international conference was convened to guarantee the truce agreement signed in Paris Jan. 27. The approval of that agreement and its protocols was contained in the first part of the latest accord. The second point said the Jan. 27 agreement fulfilled the hopes and fundamental rights of the Vietnamese people to independence, sovereignty, unity and territorial integrity and the rights of the South Vietnamese to self-determination.

The conferees also acknowledged the commitments undertaken by the four parties to the cease-fire accord—the U.S., North and South Vietnam and the Viet Cong—and to respect the national rights of the Vietnamese people.

Among other points of the agreement:

■ The U.S., North and South Vietnam and the Viet Cong could jointly or individually inform other conference participants about application of the truce, and could also receive reports from the International Commission of Control and Supervision (ICCS) and submit them jointly or individually to the other conference participants. U.N. Secretary General Kurt Waldheim could also receive these reports on the truce, but "only for information."

■ In the event of breaches of the cease-fire, the four signers of the truce could jointly or separately consult with other participants on what action to take. The conference could be reconvened jointly by the U.S. and North Vietnam, or by six of the 12 participants to the agreement.

■ The independence, sovereignty, unity, territorial integrity and neutrality of Cambodia and Laos were also acknowledged.

Secretary of State William P. Rogers signed the agreement for the U.S. The others who signed were foreign ministers of Britain, France, the Soviet Union, China, North and South Vietnam, the Viet Cong's Provisional Revolutionary Government and of the four members of the ICCS countries—Canada, Poland, Hungary and Indonesia. Although U.N. Secretary General Waldheim attended the conference, he did not sign the document at the insistence of the Communists that he be considered only a witness.

Canadian External Affairs Minister Mitchell W. Sharp expressed disappointment with parts of the text on truce supervision after initialing it March 1. Sharp had proposed at the opening of the conference Feb. 26 the establishment of an independent outside authority to receive reports from the international control teams on truce violations. He said this was necessary because the ICCS had not been able "to meet its obligations" to supervise the cease-fire. In his March 1 statement, Sharp warned that if the new truce arrangement did not work Canada would "pull out."

Background to prisoner dispute—The dispute over further release of U.S. prisoners of war was precipitated with a North Vietnamese declaration Feb. 27 that the captives would not be returned "until the United States stops concentrating their efforts on getting back the prisoners while failing to correctly implement the Paris agreement." Col. Bui Tin, a spokesman for the North Vietnamese delegation to the Four-Party Joint Military Commission (JMC), said South Vietnamese forces had violated the truce 20,000 times since Jan. 28. He repeated the Communist demand that the next group of prisoners to be released by South Vietnam include political detainees.

Tin also complained that the North Vietnamese and Viet Cong delegations to the JMC had been "subjected to provocation, isolation, and, in some cases, violence" since the body's formation. He cited the latest incident Feb. 25 in which anti-Communist demonstrators threw rocks at barracks housing North Vietnam's JMC observers in Hue and Danang. Five North Vietnamese officers in Hue were slightly injured. Gen. Le Quang Hoa, chief North Vietnamese delegate to the JMC, charged that the mobs were "a gang of hooligans hired by the Saigon administration."

The South Vietnamese had charged Feb. 25 that the Communists had violated the cease-fire by installing three surface-to-air missile sites near Khesanh, just below the demilitarized zone, after the truce was signed. Saigon asked the ICCS to investigate.

Col. Tin denied the Saigon charge later Feb. 25 and said the missiles had been in place before the truce.

In a retaliatory action against North Vietnam, the U.S. Feb. 28 abruptly terminated minesweeping operations which had begun Feb. 27 in North Vietnam's Haiphong harbor and halted the withdrawal of U.S. troops from South Vietnam.

The international conference's U.S. delegation charged Feb. 27 that it had "continuing evidence that there are gross violations of the Communist side that include infiltration of several thousand North Vietnamese forces into South Vietnam since Jan. 28." Rejecting the accusation, the North Vietnamese delegation replied that they were "aimed at simply camouflaging and justifying" the violations of the truce accord committed by the U.S. and South Vietnam.

Two JMC subcommittee meetings to discuss the prisoner exchanges were boycotted by North Vietnam Feb. 27. The North Vietnamese and Viet Cong attended further subcommittee meetings Feb. 28, at which they apparently decided to end the suspension of prisoner release.

The U.S. Feb. 27 assailed North Vietnam's decision to halt the release of more American prisoners. White House Press Secretary Ronald L. Ziegler asserted that the U.S. would not accept "the linking of release of American prisoners to any other aspect of the [Jan. 27 truce] agreement other than the rate of [troop] withdrawal." Ziegler also noted that "there was no relationship between the release of the United States prisoners of war and civilian prisoners held in the South. This point is clearly spelled out in the agreement and clearly spelled out in the protocol."

President Nixon Feb. 27 ordered Secretary Rogers in Paris "to demand clarification" from the North Vietnamese delegation "on a most urgent basis." Rogers met with North Vietnamese Foreign Minister Nguyen Duy Trinh Feb. 28 and received assurances that discussions would start in Saigon immediately for the freeing of the additional American prisoners.

Hanoi ties established. Australia established diplomatic relations with North Vietnam Feb. 26. The agreement was signed in Paris by Alan Renouf, ambassador to France, and Vo Van Sung, North Vietnam's delegate general in France. Talks had begun in Paris Feb. 14.

Prime Minister Gough Whitlam said in Canberra that day that ambassadors of the two countries would be exchanged later in 1973. He said Australia would continue to be represented in South Vietnam by an ambassador.

The agreement had been preceded by the arrival in Melbourne Feb. 2 of a three-man North Vietnamese trade union delegation. The visit, arranged by Australian unions, had sparked protests and hostile demonstrations. Whitlam had met with two members of the delegation in Canberra Feb. 7. They had discussed Australian representation in Hanoi.

The Senate Foreign Relations Committee had voted along party lines Feb. 26 to approve a bill cutting off foreign aid spending after April 30 unless the Administration agreed to release $4.5 billion in impounded funds for domestic programs. The bill also called for a ban against aid to North Vietnam without specific Congressional approval.

Fighting rages near Pnompenh. Communist forces continued to press their attacks in Cambodia Feb. 20–27, concentrating their push just south of Pnompenh.

Meanwhile, government troops continued to receive heavy U.S. air support that included the resumption of B-52 attacks. The U.S. Pacific command in Honolulu said the strikes were being carried out at the request of the Cambodian government. It was reported Feb. 27 that some American planes were using the Pnompenh airport for refueling for the first time. These were largely observation and forward air control aircraft with insufficient range to return to their bases in Thailand without a refueling stop.

The government command reported three of its soldiers were killed in one of several Communist attacks Feb. 20 on or near two main highways 14 miles from the center of the capital. Another 27 Cambodian troops were said to have been killed in other engagements that day. Communist troops were reported Feb. 23 to have advanced to within three miles of the Pnompenh suburbs. One enemy unit occupied a road outside the industrial suburb of Takhmau to the south, while another unit captured Siem Reap, nine miles from the city limits on Route 2. All main roads and secondary highways in the area were reported cut.

Communist forces stepped up their attacks Feb. 24 and threatened to capture the provincial capital of Tram Khnar, 22 miles southwest of Pnompenh. Widespread desertions to the Communist side from the 1,800-man government garrison in Tram Khnar were reported.

Government forces launched an offensive, reopening Highway 3 between Pnompenh and Tram Khnar, the Cambodian command reported Feb. 27. The command also reported the recapture by government troops of Phumi Banam on the east bank of the Mekong River, 32 miles southeast of the capital. The town had been under guerrilla control for nearly a month.

In an earlier action, Communist guerrilla forces Feb. 16 sank a U.S. barge on the Mekong River carrying napalm bombs to Pnompenh. The Communist shelling attack took place 32 miles southeast of the capital.

U.S. hails international pact. The March 2 international agreement endorsing the Vietnam truce pact was lauded by U.S. Secretary of State William P. Rogers as having "met all our principal goals."

Rogers made the statement at a news conference after the ceremonies in which he and 11 other foreign ministers signed the document at the conclusion of the five-day conference in Paris. [See p. 273 for text of agreement] Rogers said he also was pleased that China and the Soviet Union, North Vietnam's principal arms suppliers, had pledged by their signing to "refrain from any action" conflicting with the truce pact. The document was formally described as the "act" of the Vietnam conference.

Rogers said U.N. Secretary General Kurt Waldheim would be making a "wrong decision" in permitting the Viet Cong's Provisional Revolutionary Government to establish a liaison office at U.N. headquarters in New York. Waldheim had said March 1 that he had discussed such a possibility in Paris Feb. 28 with PRG Foreign Minister Nguyen Thi Binh. Binh had said the PRG favored opening a liaison office at the U.N.

Immediately after signing the agreement, Chinese Foreign Minister Chi Peng-fei accused South Vietnam of committing truce violations. But he promised that Peking would "strictly abide by the provisions of the act" and expressed hope that others would do the same.

As for the document itself, Article 9 was said to have been the most contentious in drawing up. Over Saigon's objections, the Communist representatives had succeeded in having the Viet Cong listed as the Provisional Revolutionary Government of the Republic of South Vietnam. But the U.S. was able to include a qualifying statement which said "Signature of this act does not constitute recognition of any party in any case in which it has not previously been accorded."

In return for the clause that acknowledged the sovereignty of Cambodia and Laos, the U.S. dropped efforts to have the signers pledge rehabilitation aid for the area.

Accompanying Rogers at the signing ceremonies were a U.S. Congressional

Text of Paris Declaration on Vietnam Signed March 2

Act of the International Conference on Vietnam

the Government of Canada;

the Government of the People's Republic of China;

the Government of the United States of America;

the Government of the French Republic;

the Provisional Revolutionary Government of the Republic of South Vietnam;

the Government of the Hungarian People's Republic;

the Government of the Republic of Indonesia;

the Government of the Polish People's Republic;

the Government of the Democratic Republic of Vietnam;

the Government of the United Kingdom of Great Britain and Northern Ireland;

the Government of the Republic of Vietnam, and

the Government of the Union of Soviet Socialist Republics; in the presence of the Secretary General of the United Nations:

With a view to acknowledging the signed agreements guaranteeing the ending of the war, the maintenance of peace in Vietnam, the respect of the Vietnamese people's fundamental national rights, and the South Vietnamese people's right to self-determination, and contributing to and guaranteeing peace in Indochina;

Have agreed on the following provisions, and undertake to respect and implement them:

Article 1

The parties to this act solemnly acknowledge, express their approval of and support the Paris agreement on ending the war and restoring peace in Vietnam signed in Paris on Jan. 27, 1973, and the four protocols to the agreement signed on the same date (hereinafter referred to respectively as the agreement and the protocols).

Article 2

The agreement responds to the aspirations and fundamental national rights of the Vietnamese people, i.e., the independence, sovereignty, unity and territorial integrity of Vietnam, to the right of the South Vietnamese people to self-determination, and to the earnest desire for peace shared by all countries in the world. The agreement constitutes a major contribution to peace, self-determination, national independence and the improvement of relations among countries. The agreement and the protocols should be strictly respected and scrupulously implemented.

Article 3

The parties to this act solemnly acknowledge the commitments by the parties to the agreement and the protocols to strictly respect and scrupulously implement the agreement and the protocols.

Article 4

The parties to this act solemnly recognize and strictly respect the fundamental national rights of the Vietnamese people, i.e., the independence, sovereignty, unity and territorial integrity of Vietnam, as well as the right of the South Vietnamese people to self-determination. The parties to this act shall strictly respect the agreement and the protocols by refraining from any action at variance with their provisions.

Article 5

For the sake of a durable peace in Vietnam, the parties to this act call on all countries to strictly respect the fundamental national rights of the Vietnamese people, i.e., the independence, sovereignty, unity and territorial integrity of Vietnam and the right of the South Vietnamese people to self-determination and to strictly respect the agreement and the protocols by refraining from any action at variance with their provisions.

Article 6

(A) The four parties to the agreement or the two South Vietnamese parties may, either individually or through joint action, inform the other parties to this act about the implementation of the agreement and the protocols. Since the reports and views submitted by the International Commission of Control and Supervision concerning the control and supervision of the implementation of those provisions of the agreement and the protocols which are within the tasks of the commission will be sent to either the four parties signatory to the agreement or to the two South Vietnamese parties, those parties shall be responsible, either individually or through joint action, for forwarding them promptly to the other parties in this act.

(B) The four parties to the agreement or the two South Vietnamese parties shall also, either individually or through joint action, forward this information and these reports and views to the other participant in the international conference on Vietnam for his information.

Article 7

(A) In the event of a violation of the agreement or the protocols which threatens the peace, the independence, sovereignty, unity or territorial integrity of Vietnam, or the right of the South Vietnamese people to self-determination, the parties signatory to the agreement and the protocols shall, either individually or jointly, consult with the other parties to this act with a view to determining necessary remedial measures.

(B) The international conference on Vietnam shall be reconvened upon a joint request by the Government of the United States of America and the Government of the Democratic Republic of Vietnam on behalf of the parties signatory to the agreement or upon a request by six or more of the parties to this act.

Article 8

With a view to contributing to and guaranteeing peace in Indochina, the parties to this act acknowledge the commitment of the parties to the agreement to respect the independence, sovereignty, unity, territorial integrity, and neutrality of Cambodia and Laos as stipulated in the agreement, agree also to respect them and to refrain from any action at variance with them, and call on other countries to do the same.

Article 9

This act shall enter into force upon signature by plenipotentiary representatives of all 12 parties and shall be strictly implemented by all the parties. Signature of this act does not constitute recognition of any party in any case in which it has not previously been accorded.

Done in 12 copies in Paris this 2d day of March, 1973, in English, French, Russian, Vietnamese and Chinese. All texts are equally authentic.

for the Government of the United States of America, the Secretary of State,

WILLIAM P. ROGERS

for the Government of the French Republic, the Minister for Foreign Affairs,
MAURICE SCHUMANN
for the Provisional Revolutionary Government of the Republic of South Vietnam, the Minister for Foreign Affairs,
NGUYEN THI BINH
for the Government of the Hungarian People's Republic, Minister of Foreign Affairs;
JANOS PETER
for the Government of the Republic of Indonesia, the Minister for Foreign Affairs.
ADAM MALIK
for the Government of the Polish People's Republic, the Minister for Foreign Affairs.
STEFAN OLSZOWSKI
for the Government of the Democratic Republic of Vietnam, the Minister for Foreign Affairs,

NGUYEN DUY TRINH
for the Government of the United Kingdom of Great Britain and Northern Ireland, the Secretary of State for Foreign and Commonwealth Affairs,
ALEC DOUGLAS-HOME
for the Government of the Republic of Vietnam, the Minister for Foreign Affairs,
TRAN VAN LAM
for the Government of the Union of Soviet Socialist Republics, the Minister for Foreign Affairs,
ANDREI A. GROMYKO
for the Government of Canada, the Secretary of State for External Affairs,
MITCHELL SHARP
for the Government of the People's Republic of China, the Minister for Foreign Affairs,
CHI PENG-FEI

delegation consisting of Senate Majority Leader Mike Mansfield (D, Mont.), Senate Minority Leader Hugh Scott (R, Pa.) and House Republican Leader Gerald Ford (Mich.).

Nixon's news conference. Indochina was the major topic at an impromptu, 32-minute news conference called by President Nixon March 2.

It was important to note, he told the reporters, "that the number of violations [of the cease-fire agreement], the intensity of the fighting, has been reduced." While it was "not zero yet" and he doubted if it would "become zero in any time in the foreseeable future," Nixon said "the main point is it is going down and we expect adherence to the agreement from both sides." Nixon pointed out "a guerrilla war having been fought for 25 years, off and on, is not going to be ended by one agreement, not in one month, not in two months."

The President said the key to the Laotian cease-fire agreement was the "unequivocal provision" for the withdrawal of all foreign forces from Laos. "We expect that to be adhered to and when that is adhered to, we believe the chances for peace in Laos will be very considerable."

The prospects in Cambodia were not as "positive as those in Laos," Nixon said, but if the North Vietnamese forces were withdrawn from the country the chances for a viable cease-fire there "will be very substantial."

In response to a question, the President said the provision of aid to North Vietnam was not a condition of the cease-fire

agreement. He supported the theory of providing aid to North Vietnam on the ground it would be in the interest of peace. He said he believed Congress would make a similar decision when it considered the matter.

Such assistance, he said, would not require a reduction of domestic programs but would be taken out of the existing budget levels for national security purposes, i.e., "the whole area of defense and foreign assistance."

The President called "completely wrong" the suggestion that the recent U.S. POW return had been brought about by "some action" or "some assurance" by the U.S. to get better compliance with the cease-fire. The agreement "clearly provides," he said, "that in return for withdrawal, the POWs will be returned" and the U.S. expected the agreement "to be complied with."

The President restated his opposition to amnesty for Vietnam draft evaders. "These men have broken the law," he said, and "we are not going" to provide amnesty for them "and I do not intend to change my position."

Communists withdraw some truce units. The Communists March 2 withdrew 156 of their Joint Military Commission observers from the Hue and Danang regional headquarters following complaints about the lack of security. The observers—152 North Vietnamese and four Viet Cong—were flown back to Saigon.

Col. Bui Tin, a spokesman for the North Vietnamese delegation, said the teams had been pulled out because "the People's Liberation Army [the Viet Cong] felt it has been dishonored and our army and people in North Vietnam are strongly resentful." Tin referred to the recent attacks by South Vietnamese demonstrators against Communist JMC observers. The Communists had also complained repeatedly about the poor food and quarters provided by the Saigon government for their JMC men. Tin said the Communist truce groups would return to Hue and Danang "as soon as their working conditions can be insured."

In related developments, the U.S.' JMC delegation March 3 urged the commission to issue another joint appeal for a halt to fighting in South Vietnam. A draft appeal handed by Maj. Gen. Gilbert H. Woodward, the chief U.S. delegate, to the North Vietnamese and Viet Cong delegation leaders, said: "While the level of hostilities in South Vietnam has steadily declined since the proclamation of the cease-fire and the issuance of a joint appeal of the JMC on Feb. 17, the purpose of renewing the joint appeal is to call for a full implementation of the cease-fire."

Six of Canada's 12 Red Cross workers left South Vietnam March 3 after blaming the North Vietnamese and the Viet Cong for preventing them from inspecting prisoner of war camps. The Canadians had spent three weeks in Saigon without being permitted to carry out their assignment.

The Indonesian government warned March 5 that it would withdraw its team from the International Commission of Control and Supervision if continued truce violations prevented the ICCS from conducting its mission.

A South Vietnamese spokesman March 6 revised its list of casualties for the fighting since the truce went into effect Jan. 28. A spokesman said "updated reports from the field" placed the Communist death toll at 12,192, rather than 8,-884 as reported March 4. Government combat deaths were listed at 2,156 rather than 1,616 reported in the previous count.

Prisoner release resumes. North Vietnam resumed the release of war prisoners March 4, freeing 106 Americans and two Thais. The men were flown to Clark Air Force Base in the Philippines. Another 34 prisoners, including 27 American soldiers

and three civilians, were set free by the Viet Cong in Hanoi March 5. They were also flown to the Philippine base.

Eighty of the freed Americans arrived in the U.S. March 7, returning to military bases across the country for reunions with their families. The remaining 56 were brought back to the U.S. March 8.

Among the 34 POWs freed by the Viet Cong were two West German medical missionaries and two Filipino employes of the Voice of America. Their release brought to 306 the number of captives turned over by the North Vietnamese and the Viet Cong since the signing of the Jan. 27 truce agreement.

With the release of the American prisoners, the U.S. March 4 resumed the withdrawal of its forces from South Vietnam and renewed preparations for the clearing of mines from Haiphong harbor. Both actions had been suspended by the U.S. to show displeasure over North Vietnam's delay in the repatriation of the U.S. captives.

(The U.S. force in South Vietnam was down to 10,787 men, fewer than half of the 23,500 that were there when the truce agreement was signed, American military officials reported March. 4.)

POW's comments restrained—Most of the returning U.S. prisoners of war refrained from immediate comment upon their ordeal. Pride in their country, its leadership, gratitude and belief in the cause of the war effort were recurring themes.

"God bless the President and God bless you, Mr. and Mrs. America, you did not forget us," Navy Lt. Cmdr. Everett Alvarez said upon arriving at Travis Air Force Base, Calif. Feb. 16. Captured in August 1964 during the U.S. retaliatory air strikes after the Gulf of Tonkin incident, Alvarez was the first American flier shot down in the Vietnam war.

The reluctance to disclose details of their ordeal stemmed from caution against jeopardizing the release of the POWs still in custody. It reflected a discipline within the returning contingents, composed mostly of mature, highly-trained officers, to unify their reaction during the homecoming. This in turn reflected an apparent adherence during captivity to the Code of Conduct proclaimed by President Eisenhower after the Korean War to govern conduct of U.S. prisoners of war. The code called for the senior man in a prison camp to take command and provide an ethic for the POW to "keep faith with my fellow prisoners." The command officer was in evidence aboard the returning planeloads of POWs. One of the freed POWs, Lt. Col. Richard Keirn told newsmen in Tampa, Fla. March 2 the senior officers among them had decided what the returning men would and would not say, based on what would be "better for the service, better for the government:" Government officials, he said, had nothing to do with the comments. There had been such speculation because of the uniformity of the POWs' comments.

Several did speak out against the antiwar protesters. Navy Capt. Harry T. Jenkins Jr. said in San Diego Feb. 23 he was "a little disgruntled" at the "small minority" of protesters and particularly those who visited Hanoi during the war. "I think they shamed our nation in the eyes of the enemy," he said. Asked about the issue of amnesty, Jenkins said, "I don't know a single man who fought in this war who would accept amnesty and I don't know why anyone who didn't fight should be offered amnesty."

As for the the war effort itself, Jenkins said, "We started out to assure the self-determination of the Vietnamese people and I think we have. I really don't believe we wasted our efforts."

Air Force Col. Robinson Risner, POW for 7½ years at a camp in Hanoi, said in Oklahoma City Feb. 26 he felt the war dissenters "kept us in prison an extra year or two, not just the people demonstrating but the people who were downing or bad-mouthing our government and our policies." He said he and his fellow prisoners had felt only anger and dismay at the dissenters and draft-dodgers and were willing to remain POWs years longer if necessary to gain peace with honor. He said their captors had kept the imprisoned pilots informed on "anything that was against our government, our policy or our way of life."

One of many captive POWs to whom statements condemning U.S. war policies had been attributed by the North Vietnamese, Risner said the source of the statements should be taken into consideration as they were "made from the prison in North Vietnam."

Another freed POW, Douglas Ramsey, a U.S. Foreign Service officer, acknowledged to newsmen March 1 he had made antiwar statements to his captors. Asked if the statements were made under duress, he replied: "I was told that all statements were voluntary and then reminded that I had received good treatment, including medicines and vitamins." He asked the newsmen to judge whether this constituted duress. He did not consciously disclose intelligence-related information in such statements, he said, and they were intended to relay word of his survival.

Ramsey, 38, captured Jan. 17, 1966 delivering rice to refugees from a village near Saigon, made the most extensive comment of any POW about his ordeal. Among his comments, at a State Department press conference March 1:

He had spent six of his seven years of capture in solitary confinement. "I spent several years in cages which were too small for me to pace in," although "I was never in one in which I couldn't run in place." Physical exercise, for which he had "a compulsive neurosis," and mental mathematics—he "finally worked up to where I could multiply four digits by four digits"—were key factors in his survival.

Ramsey had contracted beri-beri and malaria, the latter reaching crisis stage on Christmas Eve 1966, when he was in a coma for 60 hours and went into convulsions. A prison camp doctor arrived within 60 seconds, Ramsey said, "and if he'd been another two minutes I would not be here."

He had had occasional meals of dog and monkey meat and "enjoyed" it. Another factor in his survival was an ability "to overcome constant nausea." He cited the example of an undernourished and sick fellow prisoner who could not bring himself to eat his regurgitated food and grew weaker.

As for the prison camp commanders, "I ran into dogs and real jewels. Some people I would invite today into my home for a drink; others I'd invite behind a woodshed and only one of us would return."

Saigon, Communists end POW dispute—South Vietnam and the Viet Cong agreed March 7 to end a dispute over the second phase of prisoner exchanges. The impasse, involving a dispute over the number of Communist captives to be freed, had led to a two-day Communist boycott of hearings of the Four-Party Joint Military Commission (JMC) to support demands for the release of more prisoners.

The trade of the captives began March 8 as five U.S. C-130 transports carried 500 Communist prisoners from South Vietnamese camps on Phu Quoc island, off the southern tip of the country, to the Communist-controlled sector in northern Quangtri Province.

In the latest exchange, Saigon agreed to turn over 6,300 Communist prisoners, while the Viet Cong were to free 1,200 South Vietnamese. (Almost 7,000 Communists had been exchanged for 1,000 government soldiers in the first round of prisoner releases in February.) Government representatives at the JMC's March 7 meeting had met the Communists' demands by announcing Saigon would free 3,300 more men than it had originally planned. A South Vietnamese spokesman, Lt. Col. Le Trung Hien, said the Communists also had compromised by dropping their insistence that all civilians detained by both sides be released before the exchange of military prisoners.

The Communist boycott of the JMC hearings had been announced March 5 by Col. Bui Tin, North Vietnam's JMC delegation spokesman. Speaking in an interview in Saigon, Tin said his side would return to the meetings only if Saigon freed more prisoners. He did not specify the number of captives the Communists wanted released. Tin contended that his position had been supported by Maj. Gen. Gilbert H. Woodward, chief U.S. delegate to the JMC. He quoted Woodward as having said at the JMC's March 5 meeting that "during the first and second phase of prisoner exchanges each side should release a number of prisoners no less than 50% of the total prisoners they held."

The underlying cause of the Saigon-Communist disagreement stemmed from the differing number of prisoners each side claimed it held. The Communists said they had 4,000 South Vietnamese captives, while Saigon insisted 30,000 government forces were in Communist captivity. Saigon said it held 28,000 Communist prisoners.

Fearing the Saigon-Communist dispute might delay the further release of American prisoners, the White House again insisted March 5 that the repatriation of all U.S. captives was linked to no other provision than withdrawal of U.S. forces from South Vietnam.

U.S. journalists expelled. South Vietnam March 7 ordered the expulsion from the country of a U.S. journalist on charges of "un-Vietnamese activities." The action was taken under a strict new press law instituted Feb. 7. The government said the visa for Donald A. Davis, acting bureau chief of United Press International in Saigon, expired March 8 and would not be renewed because UPI had filed dispatches that were "pure fabrications" and "entirely inaccurate." Davis had to leave South Vietnam in seven days.

Government spokesman Pham Duong Hien said that UPI Feb. 26 had falsely reported that a Saigon hotel visited by Communist delegates to the Joint Military Commission was subject to the same rules as a military compound. Hien also asserted that UPI had reported on atrocities "based on Communist sources" while ignoring Saigon government reaction to these stories.

Saigon said punitive action was being considered against other foreign journalists in the country and that some who might be planning to return to South Vietnam would be barred. In the latter category were two correspondents from the National Broadcasting Co. and one from Agence France-Presse.

NBC correspondent Ronald Nessen had been ejected from South Vietnam in late February in a dispute with the government over the right of newsmen to visit the North Vietnamese and Viet Cong delegates to the Joint Military Commission at Saigon's Tansonnhut air base. The government informed Nessen of the ouster order Feb. 27, charging that he had "distorted" and falsely attributed the remarks of a military spokesman.

The Saigon government March 5 lifted its ban against newsmen visiting the Communist JMC delegates at Tansonnhut. However, only 16 newsmen, chosen by the Foreign Correspondents Association, would be permitted to go the compound once a week. A government spokesman said there would be no blanket permission for any correspondent to visit Tansonnhut because "many people in the press corps have served as messengers for the Communists."

Laos truce accord talks at impasse. Laotian government and Pathet Lao representatives made no progress in talks held in Vientiane March 5, 6 and 8 to work out details of the political and military aspects of the cease-fire accord signed Feb. 21.

Premier Souvanna Phouma expressed concern about the stalemate in a letter March 8 to Prince Souphanouvong, the Pathet Lao leader. Souvanna noted that half of the 30-day period stipulated for formation of a new provisional coalition government and creation of a mixed military commission to observe the truce had passed without progress.

The dispute over the mixed commission centered on a government demand that three teams of observers be stationed in Vientiane and 46 in the countryside, in both government-controlled sectors and Pathet Lao-held areas. The Pathet Lao insisted at the March 8 meeting that the observer groups come into being only as part of a general settlement embodied in the cease-fire protocols.

Pathet Lao spokesman Soth Phetrasy had charged at a Vientiane news conference March 6 that the U.S. and the Laotian government were attempting to "sabotage" the accord. He said the government thus far had not issued specific truce instructions to its troops. Soth Phetrasy claimed that in the first week after the cease-fire went into effect Feb. 22 government troops had committed 68 violations and American planes 162.

The Vientiane Defense Ministry reported the Pathet Lao had carried out two violations during a 24-hour period ending at 10 a.m. March 6, for a total of 173 since Feb. 22.

Laotian National Assembly President Phoui Sananikone March 6 questioned the constitutionality of the truce accord. He said the Assembly should have been consulted before its signing and that the proposed national consultative council would be given legislative powers invested in the National Assembly.

Right-wing and some neutralist members of Souvanna's Cabinet also had denounced the accord, centering their criticism on Interior Minister Pheng Phongsavan, the premier's chief negotiator in the conferences that led to the agreement. These critics had speculated that Pheng had reached agreement on Communist terms in order to replace Souvanna as premier with Communist support.

Souvanna March 2 issued a statement defending Pheng's role in the negotiations by saying that the premier accepted full responsibility for the talks and the agreement. Souvanna's statement said Pheng "had been the object of violent criticism and even threats" since the signing of the agreement Feb. 21.

U.S. officials were reported March 8 to have called on the Laotian government to halt at least one military operation which they regarded as a violation of the truce. The area in question was near Thakhek on the Mekong River border between Laos and Thailand in central Laos. When the truce had gone into effect Feb. 22, government forces had pushed back Communist forces surrounding the town. Since then however, Vientiane soldiers had been driving deeper into traditional Communist-held positions in the area, it was reported.

Cambodian forces under attack. Cambodian government forces came under constant Communist rebel attacks in the vicinity of Pnompenh March 2–13. U.S. planes struck repeatedly at Communist positions during that period at the request of the Cambodian government, the U.S. Pacific command in Honolulu reported.

Communist attacks March 2 along Route 2, 13 miles south of Pnompenh, forced hundreds of Cambodian troops to flee north to the suburb of Takhmau. At least 60 government soldiers were reported wounded and hundreds were missing. Fighting along Route 2 continued through March 5.

Supply convoys heading up the Mekong River toward Pnompenh were attacked twice by Communist forces March 6.

Stepped-up Communist attacks March 12 forced the government abandonment of Samrong Yong and Chambak, 20 miles south of the capital. More than 100 wounded government soldiers were said to have been abandoned by retreating forces. The government troops had given up two other positions on Route 2 March 10–11 despite their offensive aimed at opening the vital roadway to the border with South Vietnam.

Government forces at Prasat Neang Khmau, just south of Chambak, came under heavy Communist attack March 13.

Lon Nol urges Communist withdrawal— President Lon Nol March 6 called for discussions with North Vietnam and the Viet Cong on removing their forces from Cambodia and exchanging prisoners. In a national radio address following a Cabinet meeting, Lon Nol said he had issued instructions to facilitate the withdrawal of the Vietnamese Communist troops. "As for those Cambodian soldiers and civilians who are collaborating with the enemy we welcome them with open arms if they agree to return into the national community," the president said.

China releases U.S. fliers. John T. Downey, a CIA agent shot down over China in 1952, arrived in New Britain, Conn. March 12 after he had been released by Chinese authorities that day.

Three days later, two U.S. airmen imprisoned in China after being shot down during missions in the Indochina war were released. They were Lt. Cmdr. Robert J. Flynn, 35, of Colorado Springs, Colo., shot down Aug. 21, 1967 aboard an A-6 in southern China and Maj. Philip E. Smith, 38, of Roodhouse, Ill., shot down Sept. 20, 1965 over Hainan Island near the Gulf of Tonkin when his F-104 veered off course. Flynn and Smith crossed the border into Hong Kong and were flown to Clark Air Force Base.

Downey had been flown via Clark Air Force Base in the Philippines and Elmendorf Air Force Base in Alaska in order to be with his mother, who was suffering from a stroke in a New Britain hospital. His impending release had been announced March 9 by Ronald L. Ziegler, White House press secretary, who said Premier Chou En-lai had agreed to free Downey earlier than planned after being informed by the U.S. of his mother's illness. Ziegler said also China would release Flynn and Smith March 15.

At a March 13 news conference in New Britain, Downey said he looked on his 20-year imprisonment as "to a large extent wasted," adding: "I don't see that it benefited anybody."

Downey noted that during his first eight or nine months in jail he was questioned closely by his captors and that he "revealed about every bit of information I had."

Asked about the Chinese people, he said he felt "sympathy for them in some respects" and they were "more behind their government than I dreamed would be possible."

North Vietnamese infiltration charged. The U.S. March 13 expressed concern over reports of large-scale movements of North Vietnamese troops and supplies, some of them allegedly infiltrating into South Vietnam in possible violation of the Paris truce agreement. (At a news conference March 15, President Nixon warned that North Vietnam "should not lightly disregard such expressions of concern.")

The White House statement said the U.S. was "using every means of communication we have" to inform Hanoi of Washington's interest in the reports of continued movement of men and material. State Department spokesman Charles W. Bray 3rd said the U.S. was watching the North Vietnamese activity "very closely and with some concern in the context of Articles 7 and 20 of the Paris agreement." Article 7 barred introduction of foreign troops or weapons into South Vietnam, except for replacement purposes. Article 20 prohibited introduction of foreign troops into Cambodia and Laos.

According to U.S. intelligence reports disclosed March 12 by the Defense Department, since Jan. 1 North Vietnam had infiltrated down the Ho Chi Minh Trail in Laos toward the South more than 310 tanks, 150 artillery pieces, 150 antiaircraft guns and some 30,000 troops. Several thousand of those troops were believed to have actually moved into South Vietnam through the demilitarized zone since the truce went into effect Jan. 28.

Nixon warns Hanoi on infiltration— U.S. concern over the reported infiltration of North Vietnamese troops into South Vietnam was sharply emphasized by President Nixon March 15. He hinted at possible retaliation.

Speaking at a news conference, Nixon said: ". . . we have informed the North Vietnamese of our concern about this infiltration and what we believe it to be, a violation of the cease-fire, and the peace agreement. Our concern has also been expressed to other interested parties [reportedly China and the Soviet Union] and I would only suggest that based on my actions over the past four years, that the North Vietnamese should not lightly disregard such expressions of concern, when they are made, with regard to a violation."

Because of the guerrilla nature of the war, truce violations were to be expected, the President said. But the infiltration of North Vietnamese forces into South Vietnam "with equipment exceeding the amounts that were agreed upon" in the Jan. 27 truce accord was a "more important point," he asserted.

In response to a question, Nixon said the U.S. also was raising its complaints with the International Commission of Control and Supervision, although that body was having "some problems" in supervising the truce. "We will continue through the ICCS, and any other body that we can effectively appeal to, to attempt to get action there," the President said.

Khesanh missile dispute—In another incident involving an alleged truce violation, U.S. Secretary of State William P. Rogers disclosed March 11 that a protest by Michel Gauvin, head of Canada's delegation to the International Commission of Control and Supervision (ICCS), was instrumental in North Vietnamese withdrawal of missiles installed at a former U.S. Marine Corps. airstrip at Khesanh near the demilitarized zone.

Maj. Gen. Gilbert H. Woodward, head of the U.S. delegation to the Joint Military Commission (JMC), had warned the Hanoi delegation in February that if the missiles were not removed, the U.S. "reserves the right with its allies to take such actions as it deems appropriate."

South Vietnam and the U.S. had filed a protest with the ICCS Feb. 26 after producing U.S. air reconnaissance photographs of the missile installations, which they claimed had been built after the Jan. 28 truce. U.S. intelligence reports also said the North Vietnamese had hastily rebuilt the Khesanh airstrip and were using it for courier flights into South Vietnam in violation of the truce.

At a news conference in Saigon March 10, Gauvin had accused two ICCS members—Hungary and Poland—of three times rejecting a Canadian request to investigate the Khesanh missiles. Gauvin asserted that although the Paris accord made it mandatory for the commission to probe a complaint by "any party," the two delegations had "refused to agree to an investigation on the ground that no evidence existed to justify an investigation." Gauvin warned that the dispute over the missiles "could even lead to action by one side or another resulting in a resumption of general hostilities."

In response to Gauvin's criticism, the Hungarian delegation said March 10 "our standpoint has not changed. There was no proof" of North Vietnamese missiles at Khesanh.

Gauvin also accused the Poles and Hungarians of preventing publication of an ICCS report on the fighting at the central port of Sa Huynh, 315 miles northeast of Saigon. The North Vietnamese and Viet Cong had asked for an investigation into South Vietnamese attacks on the town when they claimed it was under their control. Saigon's forces recaptured Sa Huynh by the time an ICCS team arrived on the scene. According to commission sources, a report saying the town was under Saigon's control was prepared but shelved when the Hungarians and Poles refused to endorse it.

President Nguyen Van Thieu had visited Sa Huynh March 9 to show that government troops were in firm possession. Sa Huynh became a major target of Communist forces the day the truce went into effect.

At a meeting of the JMC March 9, the Communist delegations rejected an appeal by South Vietnam that commanders of both sides discuss halting the sporadic fighting. A Saigon command report March 13 said the Communists were committing 125–150 truce violations daily, and that 12,590 Communists and 2,597 government troops had been killed since Jan. 28. In fighting the previous week, government forces killed almost 1,000 Communists, compared with 4,000 reported killed in the first week of the truce, the command said.

Hungarian ICCS member defects. A Hungarian army sergeant serving with the International Commission of Control and Supervision defected to Australia March 14. The Australian Foreign Affairs Department said Sgt. Gyorgy Wallner, 22, had applied to the Australian embassy in Saigon March 10 for permission to emigrate to Australia and his request was granted. Wallner had disappeared that day from the Hungarian military compound at Saigon's Tansonnhut air base, an embassy spokesman said.

Communists free 140 U.S. POWs. The Communists released 140 more U.S. prisoners of war in Hanoi March 14 and 16. All were flown to Clark Air Force Base in the Philippines. This left 147 U.S. captives in North and South Vietnam and Laos to be released by March 28, the deadline for freeing prisoners under terms of the Jan. 27 cease-fire agreement.

The first group of POWs were released by North Vietnam and included 107 pilots, held since 1967 or 1968, and a U.S. civilian. Among the pilots was Lt. Cmdr. John S. McCain 3rd, 36, son of Adm. John S. McCain Jr., recently retired commander of U.S. forces in the Pacific.

The freed American civilian was identified as Bobby Joe Keesee, 39, of Amarillo, Tex., who reportedly had comandeered a Thai plane in September 1970 and forced the pilot to fly him to North Vietnam, where he was imprisoned as a war captive.

Thirty-two Americans were set free by the Viet Cong March 16. They included 27 servicemen and five civilians.

The U.S. had suspended the withdrawal of troops from South Vietnam March 11 to await the further release of American prisoners. The pullout was resumed March 14 after the 108 POWs were turned over by North Vietnam. As of March 14 the American force in South Vietnam had been reduced to 6,900 men. South Korea's force dwindled to less than 4,000 as a main group of its headquarters in Saigon returned to Seoul March 14.

More Communist prisoners freed—South Vietnam March 13 released 1,200 Communist prisoners at Lochninh near the Cambodian border. The exchange was momentarily interrupted when two of the prisoners reportedly tried to stay behind by breaking ranks and running for the cease-fire teams. One was caught by his fellow prisoners and taken back and beaten. A North Vietnamese spokesman said only one prisoner was involved and that he had been "subjected to propaganda and beatings" by a South Vietnamese officer March 12.

The release of the 1,200 men ended the second phase of Vietnamese prisoner exchanges. Thus far 5,796 captives had been turned over to the Communists and 1,004 had been returned to Saigon.

A group of 250 South Vietnamese POWs were to have been freed by the Viet Cong March 11, but the Communists March 10 called off their release after charging that government forces had attacked one of the two turnover points and occupied it. Saigon spokesmen denied their forces had been fighting in the vicinity of the exchange sites, at Tam Ky and Duc Pho on the central coast.

The alleged South Vietnamese attack was protested by Lt. Gen. Tran Van Tra, chief of the Viet Cong delegation to the Joint Military Commission, in notes sent to the U.S. and South Vietnamese delegations.

U.S. to search for MIAs—Plans to establish a Joint Casualty Resolution Center in Nakhon Phanom, Thailand to search for Americans still missing or unaccounted for in Southeast Asia were announced by the U.S. Pacific command in Honolulu March 9. The command said JCRC air and ground teams would scour the region for air crash sites or grave locations.

Communist infiltration continues. The U.S. reported the continued infiltration of North Vietnamese troops and equipment into South Vietnam, but later accounts told of a considerable decrease in these movements. The Communists denied the infiltration charges and leveled a counterclaim of American introduction of military equipment into South Vietnam in violation of the truce agreement.

A Washington dispatch March 16 cited American analysts as saying that most of the 300 North Vietnamese tanks and hundreds of artillery pieces that had been moving down the Ho Chi Minh Trail in Laos from the North were either in South Vietnam or arrayed along its border. The Communist troops had received orders for a possible offensive in the South in the summer or fall following the total withdrawal of U.S. troops March 28, according to the report. Until that time, Viet Cong and North Vietnamese troops were said to be under orders to limit their activities to mortar and terror attacks.

Although conceding that the Communist buildup in the South was greater than it had been before their 1972 offensive, their combat units were below fighting strength, U.S. intelligence officials in Saigon said March 17. Nevertheless, the officials expressed fear that the presence of the huge amount of war materiel could lead to an increase in the fighting.

U.S. and South Vietnamese officials in Saigon said March 15 and 16 that the Communists were massing large amounts of troops and equipment in Tay Ninh Province, just north of Saigon. They said the Communists had also brought advance equipment into the area never seen before. The weaponry was said to include Soviet-made 130-mm. artillery with a range of nearly 17 miles, SA-7 heat-seeking missiles and AT-3 guided missiles.

A South Vietnamese division commander in the area, Brig. Gen. Le Van Tu, estimated March 15 that as many as 100 Soviet-made T-54 tanks had arrived at Tay Ninh in the past month.

The U.S. March 19 reiterated the charge of Communist infiltration from the North. Defense Department spokesman Jerry W. Friedheim said: "There is continued movement on the trail, but I am not in a position to quantify it with statistics and figures. We judge some of the equipment is in South Vietnam."

U.S. officials in Washington said March 20 that American intelligence believed that in the past two to three weeks the North Vietnamese had considerably reduced the shipment of men and equipment from the North into Laos for eventual entry into South Vietnam. Administration officials, however, said they could not determine the significance of this alleged slowdown.

Communists deny infiltration charges— The chief of the Viet Cong delegation to the Joint Military Commission charged in Saigon March 16 that the U.S. was violating the cease-fire agreement by shipping uninspected war materiel into South Vietnam. Lt. Gen. Tran Van Tra, in a letter to Maj. Gen. Gilbert H. Woodward, head of the U.S. delegation, attributed the reports of the alleged illegal shipments "to many foreign sources." Tra said the Japanese Socialist party reported that U.S. munitions had been shipped from Japan to Da Nang March 9 and 10 and the U.S. would transport 9,000 tons more between those two points March 17 and 18.

A U.S. command statement later March 16 denied Tra's charges, saying that since the start of the truce Jan. 28 the U.S. had been bringing supplies into South Vietnam only "on a one-for-one replacement basis in accordance" with the terms of the cease-fire accord.

President Nixon's warning March 15 of possible retaliation for North Vietnam's alleged infiltration activities was denounced by the North Vietnamese and Viet Cong March 16 and 17. Xuan Thuy, head of Hanoi's delegation to the Paris peace talks, said in Paris March 16 that "history shows that threats do not lead very far." He insisted that his side was respecting all terms of the agreement.

Elaborating on his remarks of the previous day, Gen. Tra stated March 17 that the U.S. accusation that 30,000 North Vietnamese troops and 300 tanks had infiltrated into South Vietnam "has no grounds whatsoever." Referring to his previously cited story of American supplies from Japan, Tra said "it is crystal clear which party is illegally introducing weapons into South Vietnam." Tra accused South Vietnamese forces of having violated the cease-fire 46,188 times between Jan. 28 and March 10. Saigon accused the Communists of 7,400 breaches of the truce.

A North Vietnamese official in Hanoi March 17 denounced Nixon's accusation as "slander." Asserting that "the people in the liberated areas need food and medicine and other nonmilitary supplies," Col. Ha Van Lau, an adviser to the Hanoi Paris peace delegation, said "we have the right to provide them with this as is made clear in the Paris agreements." Lau in turn accused the U.S. of possible violations of the agreement. He said the U.S. was procrastinating in clearing the mines from North Vietnamese ports and rivers. Lau claimed the U.S. had planted more than 8,000 mines, while "according to their statements, they have deactivated only one or two." Lau also complained about the American troop pullout, asserting that the Joint Military Commission "still has no satisfactory means to check whether all the troops from the U.S. command really have been withdrawn." The departing American troops were leaving their weapons with South Vietnamese forces, Lau said.

Canadian foreign minister visits. Canadian External Affairs Minister Mitchell W. Sharp visited South and North Vietnam and Laos March 15–18 to decide whether his country should continue to serve on the International Commission of Control and Supervision. Canada had repeatedly complained about the ineffectiveness of the ICCS and had threatened to pull out.

Returning to Ottawa March 19, Sharp said his trip confirmed previous reports that the ICCS "is not working well." In a report to the House of Commons March 20 Sharp said the commission had not been permitted to investigate "thousands" of truce violations in Vietnam. He said the information he gathered on his visit "tends to confirm" the infiltration of thousands of North Vietnamese troops into South Vietnam since the Jan. 28 cease-fire.

Sharp conferred in Saigon March 15 with South Vietnamese Foreign Minister Tran Van Lam and March 16 with President Nguyen Van Thieu. Thieu urged Canada not to resign from the commission. Sharp quoted the South Vietnamese leader as having told him that the ICCS "may not be working effectively but it will be much less effective if Canada left."

Sharp met with Laotian Premier Souvanna Phouma in Vientiane March 17 and with North Vietnamese Premier Pham Van Dong in Hanoi March 18.

Cambodian palace bombed. A pilot flying a stolen Cambodian air force plane March 17 bombed the presidential palace in Pnompenh in an apparent attempt to kill President Lon Nol, who was holding a Cabinet meeting at the time. The plane, a T-28 light bomber, missed a direct hit on the building and dropped two bombs instead on an army barracks on the palace grounds, killing 43 persons and wounding more than 50.

Lon Nol declared a state of emergency and siege and suspended civil liberties. More than 100 persons were detained as suspects, including opposition party members, journalists and about 20 members of the royal family. The pilot of the plane was identified by the government as So Potra, a son-in-law of Prince Norodom Sihanouk, exiled former chief of state. So Potra landed the plane safely March 18 in the Communist-controlled zone of Cambodia, the Chinese Hsinhua news agency reported March 20.

Lon Nol's emergency measures also suspended publication of all newspapers and periodicals, except government journals, ordered the return to work of 20,000 Cambodian teachers on strike for a month for more money, imposed an overnight curfew and barred all Cambodians and foreign residents from leaving the country, except diplomats and tourists. In a radio broadcast of his emergency declaration, Lon Nol said "This was a clear attempt on my life."

Information Minister Keam Reath said March 17 there was a link between the palace raid and a hand grenade attack earlier in the day on a Pnompenh University rally in which 10,000 teachers and students were protesting inflation. Two persons were killed and several wounded. Both incidents were "part of the subversive plan which the government cannot reveal at this time," Keam Reath said.

U.S., Hanoi open aid talks. The U.S. and North Vietnam held private preliminary talks in Paris March 15 and 19 on how their newly-formed Joint Economic Commission would funnel postwar American aid to North Vietnam. The three-man U.S. delegation was led by Maurice J. Williams, deputy director of the Agency for International Development. Finance Minister Dang Viet Chau headed the North Vietnamese delegation.

South Vietnamese open political talks.
Representatives of the Saigon government and the Viet Cong's Provisional Revolutionary Government (PRG) opened full-scale talks in Paris March 19 on the political future of South Vietnam. The discussions were mandated by the Jan. 27 Paris truce agreement.

Each side submitted a three-point agenda for the negotiations. Each list contained one point excluded from the other and in different order. The Saigon delegation, led by Nguyen Trieu Dan, proposed discussion of general elections in South Vietnam, formation of the proposed National Council of National Reconciliation and Concord and reduction and demobilization of armed forces. A delegation spokesman later explained that the last point referred to withdrawal of North Vietnamese troops from South Vietnam, which he called "the fundamental question."

The agenda submitted by the PRG delegation, headed by Nguyen Van Hieu, provided for negotiations on guarantees of democratic liberties and "realization of national concord," formation of the National Council and general elections.

Agreement to hold the talks had been reached in Paris Feb. 23 by PRG Foreign Minister Nguyen Thi Binh and South Vietnamese Foreign Minister Tran Van Lam following preliminary discussions that had begun earlier in February. The date for the formal conference had been set at the conclusion of the last preparatory meeting March 8.

Saigon troops open major attack. South Vietnamese forces launched a major assault March 20 to break a Viet Cong siege of a small government outpost at Rach Bap, 22 miles north of Saigon. The Saigon command announced March 21 that its force of more than 2,000 men had broken into the outpost that day without encountering Communist resistance. A second government outpost was also under Communist siege at Tong Le Chan, 63 miles north of the capital. Communist forces had surrounded the two bases March 11.

Government troops started the drive on Rach Bap after the Joint Military Commission and the International Commission of Control and Supervision had failed to act on Saigon's complaints. The JMC was asked March 18 to investigate, but was unable to send out observer teams after the body's North Vietnamese and Viet Cong members denied any Communist violations of the cease-fire. Saigon then took its case to the ICCS, which agreed March 19 to carry out an inquiry. However, the departure of the commission teams was called off when the Hungarian and Polish members refused to leave, presumably because they were unable to obtain Viet Cong assurances that the teams could enter the area safely.

The ICCS met March 21 in another unsuccessful effort to investigate the Viet Cong attacks on the two South Vietnamese outposts. After the session, Canadian delegate Michel Gauvin said the required unanimous agreement was not forthcoming despite Canada's demand for "immediate action." "We are not getting anywhere in getting satisfactory answers to our questions about why the investigation is not proceeding," Gauvin said.

In a related development, an ICCS team flew to the Mekong Delta March 15 to investigate what was described as the worst terror attack of the truce. A Buddhist pagoda in Tra Cu was struck by explosions which killed at least 20 persons and wounded more than 80 during a predawn service. The Saigon command said Communists had hurled grenades into the building.

The Saigon delegation to the JMC charged March 15 that the Communists had committed 146 more truce violations in the 24 hours ended at 6 a.m. that day, raising their total truce breaches since Jan. 28 to 7,154. A total of 13,757 North Vietnamese and Viet Cong, 2,668 government soldiers and 319 civilians had been killed since Jan. 28, according to government estimates.

Sweden seeks improved ties. Foreign Minister Krister Wickman, in a foreign policy statement to the Riksdag (parliament) March 21, said his government wanted to restore normal diplomatic relations with the U.S. A U.S. State Department spokesman responded in Washington the same day, "We have a frosty 'no comment.'"

Diplomatic relations between the two nations had been frozen since the end of 1972, when Premier Olof Palme compared the U.S. bombing of North Vietnam to Nazi atrocities. President Nixon was reported to have been personally incensed by the statement.

Wickman's statement echoed the stand expressed by Palme in a London Times interview published March 8. Palme urged the normalization of relations with the U.S. The premier had added, however, that Sweden would not compromise its convictions.

Communists delay release of POWs. A dispute between the U.S. and Communists over American prisoners in Laos delayed the release of the last group of 138 U.S. captives held by the Viet Cong and North Vietnam. The Communists had announced March 21 that the Americans would be freed March 24 and 25. The Viet Cong delegation to the Joint Military Commission (JMC) said March 22 that it was suspending release of the remaining U.S. prisoners in its custody until the dispute was resolved.

The controversy was touched off with the delivery March 22 of a letter to the Viet Cong by Brig. Gen. John A. Wickman Jr., deputy chief of the U.S. delegation to the JMC. He said the continued withdrawal of U.S. troops from South Vietnam, which were suspended while the list of prisoners from the Communists was being awaited, would not be resumed until the U.S. had been "provided with a complete list of all U.S. POWs including those held by the Pathet Lao [in Laos], as well as the date, time and place of release, and after the first group of POWs has been physically transferred to United States custody." (It was reported that the Pathet Lao held 10 Americans—seven military men and three civilians.)

Wickman recalled that the North Vietnamese had assured the U.S. March 21 that "it would arrange with the Pathet Lao for the release of U.S. POWs held in Laos, although it did not indicate the date, place or circumstances of release."

Wickman also said that 1,034 American servicemen would remain in South Vietnam after the U.S. military withdrawal was officially completed March 28, the deadline for troop pullout as stipulated by the Paris agreement. They would include 50 men to be attached to a new defense office in the U.S. embassy in Saigon, 150 to serve as security for the embassy, and the 825 JMC team members, whose departure date was not specified.

A U.S. source contended that the release of the U.S. prisoners in Laos had been part of an understanding reached in Paris by Henry A. Kissinger of the U.S. and Le Duc Tho of North Vietnam when they negotiated the Vietnam peace agreement in January. Kissinger had said at a Jan. 24 news conference that "American prisoners held in Laos and North Vietnam will be returned to us in Hanoi."

A Viet Cong spokesman rejected the alleged Kissinger-Tho understanding on prisoners held by the Pathet Lao, asserting that the American demand for the release of prisoners outside Vietnam constituted "new conditions" that were unacceptable. As a result, he said, the Viet Cong's Provisional Revolutionary Government "reserves the right to suspend handing over the list of American prisoners" in preparation for their scheduled release March 24–25 until those "new conditions" were clarified.

Gen. Tran Van Tra, head of the Viet Cong delegation to the JMC, accused the U.S. March 22 of "an about-face" and "a most serious violation of the Paris agreement and its protocols." He said his delegation "energetically protests all the illogical demands" by the U.S. delegation.

Saigon-Communist POW exchange—South Vietnam announced March 22 the release of 1,200 more Communist prisoners in exchange for 585 government soldiers turned over by the Communists. Meanwhile, the South Vietnamese accused the Communists of freeing only a small fraction of government soldiers it actually held. According to Saigon, the Communists had scheduled the release of only 3,250 of 31,818 government troops held captive. South Vietnam said it had repatriated more than 19,000 Communist prisoners so far.

U.S. charges missiles at Khesanh. The U.S. charged March 23 that North Vietnam had installed missiles at Khesanh just below the demilitarized zone in violation of the cease-fire. The allegation was made at a meeting of the Joint Military Commission. It was the second time in a month that the Communists had been accused of installing missiles near the DMZ. The first missiles set up in the area were subsequently withdrawn by the North Vietnamese in February.

The Viet Cong March 24 denied the charges of a truce violation, saying the missiles at Khesanh had been installed before the Jan. 28 cease-fire. A Viet Cong spokesman said the accusation was made to cover up the illegal arms shipments into Danang by the U.S.

In other military developments, a Communist rocket fired March 23 into a resettlement camp in Chau Doc Province, 95 miles southwest of Saigon, killed 24 refugees and wounded 40.

U.S. raids continue in Cambodia. U.S. planes, including B-52s, bombed Communist rebel targets in Cambodia March 27 for the 21st consecutive day. The raids were centered about 12 miles south of Pnompenh, where Cambodian rebels continued to make gains against government defenders.

The army announced that rebel forces March 27 captured Trapeang Thnot, only 10 miles from the capital, following abandonment of the village by two government battalions the previous night.

Government and Communist troops had clashed March 26 five miles west of Pnompenh, near the capital's airport.

Communist forces March 26 severed Route 4, which linked Pnompenh with the port of Kompong Som. As a result, only one of Cambodia's national highways remained open—Route 4, connecting the capital with the rice-growing regions of the northwest. One of the other highways cut previously was Route 1 leading from Pnompenh to Saigon, the government reported March 21.

Bombing criticized in Congress—There was growing U.S. Congressional criticism of the continuing bombing raids in Cambodia. Three Republican senators joined Democrats in criticizing President Nixon's continued authorization of bombing raids in Cambodia. The three—Sen. Jacob Javits (N.Y.), Sen. Charles Mathias (Md.) and Sen. Mark Hatfield (Ore.)—in March 29 speeches on the Senate floor questioned Nixon's constitutional and legal authority to order the bombings, since the Vietnam war had ended.

Javits said the issue was not the desirability of the bombings, "but who is to determine that fact for the U.S." He said the decision had to be jointly made by Congress and the President.

Mathias charged that Nixon had no "legal warrant or constitutional authority." Hatfield said if the bombing continued, "we will be on our way to making the Constitution the last casualty of the war."

Democrats Mike Mansfield (Mont.), Senate majority leader, and Sen. J. William Fulbright (Ark.), chairman of the Senate Foreign Relations Committee, also criticized Administration policy. Mansfield said March 28 the President had no authority to bomb Cambodia when all American forces had been withdrawn from South Vietnam. Fulbright had issued a statement March 27 demanding the Administration issue a public explanation for the purpose and authority for continued actions in Cambodia.

Fulbright received a partial answer to his demands when Secretary of Defense Elliot Richardson testified before his Foreign Relations Committee March 28. Richardson said the raids were being conducted in response to requests from the Cambodian government.

Speaking to newsmen before testifying, Richardson said the U.S. was continuing to support "our ally" against Communist isolation of Pnompenh. Richardson failed to note, the New York Times said March 28, that Cambodian President Lon Nol, following a policy laid down by Prince Norodom Sihanouk, who was deposed as Cambodian head of state in 1970, had explicitly withdrawn Cambodia from the aegis of the 1954 South East Asian Treaty Organization (SEATO). Richardson himself, as acting secretary of state, had written the Senate Foreign Relations Committee May 30, 1970 that "the SEATO treaty has no application to the current situation in Cambodia."

Negotiations rejected—The government was reported March 24 to have rejected a proposal by Prince Norodom Sihanouk's government in exile to hold peace negotiations. The offer, contained in a letter sent by Sihanouk's Interior

Minister Hou Youn to Premier Hang Thun Hak, was rejected because it conditioned the discussions on the exclusion of President Lon Nol.

In a statement issued in Shanghai, China March 24, Sihanouk asserted that the U.S. had rebuffed offers he had made in January and February that American representatives meet with him to discuss the fighting in Cambodia. Sihanouk said the U.S. "must be held responsible for the starting of the war in Cambodia and for the existence of the present Khmer political problem."

Arrests continue—The Cambodian government was continuing to conduct mass arrests in the wake of the air attack on the presidential palace in Pnompenh March 17, it was reported March 22. Although Information Minister Keam Reath said only 20 persons were imprisoned and 100 were under house arrest, other official sources said about 400 were being held.

Among those reportedly under house detention was Lt. Gen. Sisowath Sirik Matak, former deputy premier, a longtime associate of President Lon Nol and critic of his regime. After government troops and armor had surrounded Sirik's home in Pnompenh March 21, Keam Reath announced March 22 that the action was taken to protect him and denied reports that he was under arrest. "Measures to protect him include not allowing anyone to enter his home or allowing him to get out," Keam said.

Sirik said in a government-approved interview at his home March 22 that there was "only a light margin of difference between the protection they are giving me and house arrest." He said the Lon Nol regime "must not survive and will not last. It is not supported by the people." Sirik criticized the government for failing to reach an agreement with the Communist rebels to end the fighting.

The Cambodian National Assembly March 21 had ratified the emergency rule imposed after the palace bombing. The decree empowered police to search and arrest and prohibited meetings of more than five persons.

Canada to stay in ICCS. External Affairs Minister Mitchell W. Sharp announced March 27 that Canada would remain a member of the International Commission of Control and Supervision (ICCS) for at least 90 days more. In a report to the House of Commons, he warned, however, that "unless there is a substantial improvement in the situation or some signs of imminent political agreement" in South Vietnam, Canada would "cease to participate" in the ICCS by June 30. Ottawa's 60-day commitment to serve on the truce observer body expired March 28.

Complaining about the commission's inability to cope with the constant violations of the truce, Sharp said "We will not take part in a charade nor will we tacitly condone inaction when we believe action is required." He said Canada had decided that the Communist and Saigon sides "need a little more time to demonstrate the feasibility" of ending the conflict.

A Washington Post report published March 26 quoted Canadian government sources as saying that the U.S. State Department had "misled" Canada to believe that the signing of the Vietnam truce agreement "hinged almost exclusively on Canadian acceptance of a peace-keeping role in Vietnam." Deputy Assistant Secretary of State William H. Sullivan was said to have apprised Ottawa of these conditions soon after Presidential adviser Henry A. Kissinger had said Oct. 25, 1972 that "peace was at hand." Sharp had discussed Canada's commitment to a Vietnam peace role with Secretary of State William P. Rogers in November 1972.

The State Department denied March 26 that it had provided Canada with misleading information to get it to join the ICCS. A department statement said "quite to the contrary, . . . communications between the two governments were quite open and straightforward."

Dzu released. Truong Dinh Dzu, a peace candidate in South Vietnam's 1967 presidential elections, was released from a Saigon jail March 26. He had been imprisoned since 1968 on charges of advocating neutrality and negotiations with the Viet Cong.

Dzu's five-year term had been commuted to four years in 1971 and he was eligible for release May 1, 1972. But Dzu's wife claimed that the day her husband was to be freed he was detained at the national police center and then returned to the

Saigon prison, where he had been held for "temporary detention" since. The decision to release Dzu came after his wife had sent letters of appeal earlier in March to President Thieu and legislative leaders.

Democracy party inaugurated. President Nguyen Van Thieu formally inaugurated his Democracy party at its first national convention in Saigon March 28.

The new organization, with a membership estimated at half a million, was one of only three parties to meet the requirements of a new government regulation restricting the number of parties. It went into effect March 27. The other two were the Socialist Democratic party and the Roman Catholic Freedom party. Seventeen other parties, including all Buddhist and leftist groups, were officially dissolved under the new law.

Thieu was elected Democracy party chairman at the Saigon convention. He told the 1,000 delegates that the party's principal goal was to compete with the Communists in the national elections called for by the Paris truce agreement and to "point out to the people the Communist danger."

Paris truce agreement terms met. The withdrawal of all American troops from South Vietnam and release of the last of the U.S. war prisoners held by the Communists were completed March 29. Both actions fulfilled the terms of the Paris truce agreement that called for the pullout of all U.S. forces and the freeing of all captives within 60 days of the signing of the pact.

The POW release ended one day later than the 60-day schedule because of a delay that developed over U.S. insistence that nine Americans and one Canadian held by the Pathet Lao in Laos also be freed. The U.S.-Communist disagreement over this issue had erupted March 21, halting the further release of the prisoners and the pullout of the American forces. The Vietnamese Communists had insisted that the prisoners held in Laos were not covered by the Paris agreement and that it was up to the Pathet Lao to decide when to release them. The Pathet Lao then announced March 26 their willingness to free the 10 POWs, and a meeting of the Four-Party Joint Military Commission

(JMC) in Saigon March 27 formalized the agreement, ending the impasse.

President Nixon March 26 expressed gratification with the resolution of the deadlock and ordered resumption of the troop withdrawal. The President March 25 had repeated a previous order for the remaining American forces to stay in South Vietnam until all U.S. POWs were released.

At a meeting of the JMC March 24, the North Vietnamese and Viet Cong delegates had introduced two new demands that threatened to intensify the impasse. They insisted that the U.S. withdraw all its 825 JMC personnel and the Marine security guard at the U.S. embassy in Saigon by March 29. The U.S. rejected the demands.

In the final prisoner release carried out by the North Vietnamese in Hanoi, 32 were freed March 27, another 49, including the 10 from Laos, were returned March 28 and the final 67 were liberated March 29. All were flown to Clark Air Force Base in the Philippines before returning to the U.S.

The Communists had freed a total of 595 prisoners. Of these, 587 were Americans, including 24 civilians. The others were two each from West Germany, Thailand, Canada and the Philippines. According to the Defense Department, 1,328 Americans were missing in action or unaccounted for. The department also listed 1,100 men killed in action whose bodies had not been recovered.

Formal ceremonies were held at Saigon's Tansonnhut airport March 29 marking the final departure of the last of the more than 5,000 of American troops from Vietnam and the deactivation of the U.S. Military Assistance Command, Vietnam. Addressing the U.S. troops, Gen. Frederick C. Weyand, U.S. commander in South Vietnam, declared the U.S. had completed its mission "to prevent an all-out attempt by an aggressor to impose its will through raw military force." He said "the rights of the people of the Republic of Vietnam to shape their own destiny and to provide their self-defense have been upheld."

In a second speech addressed later to the South Vietnamese in their own language just before he boarded a plane to leave the country, Weyand said: "Our mission has been accomplished. I depart with a strong feeling of pride in what we have achieved, and in what our achievement represents."

The troops to leave Vietnam departed for the U.S. or to bases in Japan, Thailand and Guam. A total of 2,501 troops were flown from Saigon and Danang March 29.

With the formal end of the American military mission, 8,500 U.S. civilians were to remain in South Vietnam, most of them technicians helping Saigon's armed forces. The civilians, employees of the State Department, were to serve under Maj. Gen. John E. Murray, the highest-ranking American military man remaining in the country as the senior defense attache.

U.S. POWs tell of torture—Former American prisoners of war who already had returned to the U.S. related March 29 they had been subjected to physical and mental torture by their North Vietnamese captors. The men told of their experiences in news conferences across the country after the last of the American captives had left North Vietnam that day. Heretofore, they had refused to discuss their lives in the prison camps for fear of endangering POWs who had not yet been released. The men said they had been beaten, tied, shackled and starved until they gave their captors information on U.S. war plans or signed antiwar confessions.

Among the statements:

Col. Robinson Risner, speaking at Andrews Air Base in Maryland, said he had been tied so tightly, that in hunching over, his shoulders popped out of their sockets and his toes were pushed against his mouth. At other times, he said, an iron bar was tied to his ankles, where it gradually bit into his flesh. Risner described the treatment as "severe torture, degradation, deprivation, humiliation." Although neither he nor any other prisoner had actually seen a fellow captive die in prison, Risner said he was certain that some men had "died at the hands of the North Vietnamese."

Lt. Cmdr. Everett Alvarez, shot down over North Vietnam in 1964, said he had not been tortured until mid-1966, when he was made to sit on a stool for four or five days, without sleep or food.

Capt. Wendell Rivers t[...] ference at Bethesda Naval [...] had spent nine days in isol[...] only bread and water. He c[...] ever, that while the priso[...] badly, they usually ate alm[...] their guards, and sometimes even better.

Air Force S. Sgt. Arthur Cormier of Bayshore, N.Y. said his captors "a couple of times" had tied him with ropes "to cut the circulation of the arms."

Air Force Capt, David E. Baker said in Huntington, N.Y. that he had been shot in the leg while trying to escape after being captured in June 1972 and later was denied treatment because he would not speak out against the war.

Cmdr. Richard A. Stratton said in San Francisco that he believed the North Vietnamese should be tried for "war crimes" for their treatment of the POWs. Stratton explained his bowing to his captors at a Hanoi news conference, a picture of which had been widely circulated. He said he had been forced to attend the conference and had decided to act drugged to discredit his appearance.

One of the few prisoners to express open opposition to American war policy in Indochina gave his views in an interview in Sacramento, Calif. March 7. Maj. Hubert K. Flesher, a pilot shot down in December 1966, said the U.S. had no right to intervene in the war and that President Nixon could have settled the conflict on the same terms in 1969. He said the prisoners in North Vietnam were divided into two factions, the "superpatriots who felt we should be in there killing them by the thousands," and those who "felt the bombing and that sort of thing was not doing any good."

Nixon speaks on Vietnam. President Nixon, in a nationwide address March 29, hailed the completion of the U.S. military withdrawal from Vietnam. He stressed the necessity to keep America strong economically, militarily and spiritually. In speaking of Vietnam, he warned Hanoi to comply with the truce agreement or suffer "the consequences."

Despite the end of "America's longest war" and other "progress toward peace" in U.S. relationships with the Soviet Union and China, the President emphasized that the U.S. must not reduce its military strength by cuts in his defense budget. "What is at stake is whether the United States shall become the second strongest nation in the world" when "the chance for building a new structure of peace in the world would be irreparably damaged and free nations everywhere would be living in mortal danger."

Nixon opened his address by noting that "the day we have all worked and prayed for has finally come"—for the first time in 12 years no American military forces were in Vietnam, all of the American prisoners of war were on the way home, the South Vietnamese people had "the right to choose their own government without outside interference" and, because of the Vietnamization program, they had "the strength to defend that right."

There were still "some problem areas," he conceded: "The provision of the [truce] agreement requiring an accounting for all missing in action in Indochina; the provision with regard to Laos; the provision prohibiting infiltration from North Vietnam into South Vietnam have not been complied with."

"We have and will continue to comply with the agreement," he continued, and "we shall insist that North Vietnam comply with the agreement and the leaders of North Vietnam should have no doubt as to the consequences if they fail to comply with the agreement."

The President paid tribute to the "two and a half million Americans who served honorably" in the war. "Never have men served with greater devotion abroad with less apparent support at home," he said. "Let us provide these men with the veterans' benefits and the job opportunities they have earned, and let us honor them with the respect they deserve."

"And I say again tonight," he added, "let us not dishonor those who served their country by granting amnesty to those who deserted America."

"The great majority of Americans" had "stood firm for peace with honor" despite "an unprecedented barrage of criticism from a small but vocal minority," he said. Recalling some of the difficult decisions he

had faced with the war, the Cambodia attack in 1970 and the mining of Haiphong and air strikes in 1972, he said "perhaps the hardest decision I have made as President" was in December, 1972, "when our hopes for peace were so high, and when the North Vietnamese stone-walled us at the conference table" and I "found it necessary to order more air strikes on military targets in North Vietnam in order to break the deadlock."

The "voices" of opposition" were loudly raised on each instance, he recalled, but "the overwhelming majority stood firm against those who advocated peace at any price—even if the price would have been defeat and humiliation for the United States."

The President ended his speech with an appeal to "put aside those honest differences about war which had divided us and dedicate ourselves to meet the great challenges of peace which can unite us." Other nations in history had fallen "by the wayside," he said, "because their people became weak, soft and self-indulgent and lost the character and the spirit which had led to their greatness."

Battle Losses in Vietnam

With the American military role in Vietnam officially terminating March 29, the following statistics on troops and war casualties were compiled by the U.S. and South Vietnamese commands, covering the period Jan. 1, 1961–March 29, 1973:

Maximum American troop level: 543,000 in April 1969.

U.S. losses: combat deaths 45,948; wounded 303,640; deaths from non-combat causes 10,298.

South Vietnamese losses: deaths 184,546; wounded 495,931.

Viet Cong and North Vietnamese combat deaths: 937,562.

Civilians killed: 415,000 (based on U.S. Senate Subcommittee on Refugees estimates covering 1965–1972).

Civilians wounded: 935,000 (Senate subcommittee estimates).

U.S. expenditures since start of buildup in 1965: $109.5 billion.

Political Developments in South Vietnam

Thieu decrees new curbs. A decree issued by President Nguyen Van Thieu provided the Saigon government with control over all clubs and associations in the country, it was reported Jan. 6.

The new law gave the interior minister the authority to approve the formation of religious, charitable, cultural, educational, social, scientific, artistic, entertainment and friendship associations. Founders of these groups would be required to convene a general assembly within six months after their permits were issued and to provide the government with minutes of the meeting and a list of elected officers.

In other South Vietnamese political developments:

The House of Representatives Jan. 8 approved by a 69–50 vote a bill sponsored by Thieu that would consolidate the country's political parties.

An opposition leader, Deputy Le Dinh Duyen, denounced the measure as a violation of the "citizens' political rights."

In conformity with the party-consolidation measure, a group of Roman Catholic politicians were reported Jan. 5 to have merged their three groupings to form a single pro-government organization called the Tu Do (Freedom) party. The merged party was comprised of one group headed by Senate Chairman Nguyen Van Huyen, the Greater Unity Force and the Social Humanistic party.

Saigon bars Gen. Thi. Lt. Gen. Nguyen Chanh Thi, a former South Vietnamese commander, was refused entry into South Vietnam Feb. 23 after an exile of nearly six years.

Thi, who had been living in the U.S. since his ouster from the country in 1966, landed in Saigon in an American jet airliner, but police refused to let him debark, reportedly on the personal order of President Nguyen Van Thieu. Thi flew back to the U.S. on the same plane.

Thi had been relieved of his command of Military Region I in 1966 and was forced to leave South Vietnam after being convicted with others of being involved in anti-government demonstrations carried out by Buddhists.

Former deputy sentenced. Former opposition Deputy Ngo Cong Duc, a political opponent of President Thieu, was convicted and sentenced in absentia to three years imprisonment Feb. 9 on charges of leaving South Vietnam illegally. The Saigon court also ordered confiscation of his properties. Duc, who was believed to have gone to Europe, was among 400 candidates disqualified for the Aug. 29, 1971 National Assembly elections.

Another leading critic of the Saigon government and the war, Mrs. Ngo Ba Thanh, went on trial before a Saigon

291

military court March 22 on charges of engaging in activities harmful to the state. The trial, however, was postponed indefinitely after a doctor testified that Mrs. Thanh was ill and in critical condition. She had been arrested Sept. 18, 1971 after participating in an anti-government demonstration led by Ngo Cong Duc.

Saigon newspapers seized. Eleven of Saigon's 40 Vietnamese language newspapers were seized by police March 11. The journals had published articles regarded as "harmful to national security," it was reported March 12 by the official press agency Vietnam Press.

A government-ordered increase of 125% in the price of newsprint had resulted in a halt in publication of nearly half of Saigon's newspapers, official sources reported March 17. Opposition leaders accused President Thieu of using the cost boost to silence the antigovernment press.

Defense aides ousted. Five top aides of the South Vietnamese defense minister were ousted by President Nguyen Van Thieu March 22 following a scandal involving possible misuse of a soldiers' retirement fund. The minister, Lt. Gen. Nguyen Van Vy, offered to resign after learning his aides had been dismissed.

No specific charges had been filed against the five officials, pending an investigation. They were administrators of the Mutual Aid and Savings Fund for Soldiers and had been subjected to recent press criticism for their handling of the job. Soldiers had complained that they had not benefitted from the fund, although some money had been distributed to orphans, widows and the severely disabled.

Thieu declares martial law. As part of his plan to counter the major spring Communist offensive, President Thieu May 10 declared martial law throughout South Vietnam. [For details, see pp. 91–92]

Senate rejects Thieu decree bid. By a 27–21 vote June 2, the South Vietnamese Senate rejected President Nguyen Van Thieu's request for legislative authority to rule by decree for six months because of the Communist offensive.

The action followed approval of the measure by the lower House of Representatives by an 81–49 vote May 14. The bill was sent back to the House, which could override the Senate rejection by a two-thirds vote.

In a related development, all of South Vietnam's colleges and universities were closed May 17 in accordance with Thieu's May 11 emergency mobilization decree. About 60,000 students affected faced conscription into the regular armed forces or a period of training in the People's Self Defense Force. The schools, whose normal academic year was only cut by several weeks, were expected to reopen in October.

Thieu to rule by decree. A rump session of South Vietnam's Senate June 27 approved by a 26–0 vote a bill granting President Nguyen Van Thieu authority to rule by decree on matters of defense and economics for six months. The 26 senators represented less than a quorum of the 57-member chamber. Thieu signed the bill later June 27.

The vote was held after Saigon's 10 p.m. curfew when no opposition senators were present. The 26 opponents of the bill had walked out in protest against the invocation by government supporters of a rule permitting five members to start a session. Until then debate had been delayed by the absence of five of the 57 members. The anti-decree faction argued that the calling of a Senate meeting by five members required the approval of the Senate chairman.

The decree measure had been passed twice by the lower House of Representatives and once before by the Senate and slightly rewritten.

Saigon eases draft. South Vietnamese President Nguyen Van Thieu July 8 rescinded a May 11 edict that would have raised the maximum draft age from 39 to 43 and lowered the minimum from 18 to 17.

Thieu also ordered the cancellation of the existing "parallel" rates for the exchange of the piaster. This had enabled South Vietnamese students studying abroad to purchase U.S. dollars at 118 piasters to the dollar compared with the prevailing rate of 425:

Thieu's action was followed by a national bank announcement July 10 of a unified rate of 425 piasters to the dollar. A lower rate of 290 remained in effect for importers purchasing goods under U.S. import projects.

Martial-law decree signed—A martial-law decree signed into law by Thieu July 15 provided jail terms for strikers, curfew violators, employers who fired workers during the state of war and for persons who circulated news or pictures "detrimental to the national security." The edict also permitted police to shoot to kill motorists, looters, arsonists or saboteurs who attempted to flee.

Thieu curbs press. President Nguyen Van Thieu announced a decree Aug. 5 restricting South Vietnam's newspapers. The country's newsmen and diplomatic observers regarded the move as an attempt to stifle criticism of the Saigon regime.

Under the decree every daily newspaper was required to deposit about $47,000 with the government treasury within 30 days. The money would be a guarantee to cover possible fines and court charges resulting from violations of the already strict press rules. The decree also provided for government shutdown of any newspaper, pending a court decision, if its daily issue was confiscated the second time for publishing "articles detrimental to the national security and public order."

Information Minister Truong Buu Dien expressed hope that the national press "will be more progressive as well as more responsive to the needs of national security and public order." He said the government's aim was "to promote the merging of small newspapers into big ones."

Two opposition Saigon dailies ceased publication rather than pay the required deposit, the Information Ministry announced Aug. 8. The editor of one of the newspapers, Ly Qui Chung, said he was closing "until the decree is abolished."

The government had disclosed July 1 that 42 newsmen had been convicted since June 22 on unspecified charges. The penalties included heavy fines and prison terms up to one month, the announcement said.

Defense minister ousted. South Vietnam's defense minister, Lt. Gen. Nguyen Van Vy, was ousted from his post in connection with a financial scandal involving the possible misuse of a soldiers' retirement fund, Saigon radio reported Aug. 6.

Under a decree signed by President Thieu, Vy was retired and barred from traveling abroad until completion of a government investigation of the case. Seven colonels and three civilians were also dismissed from the Defense Ministry and were refused permission to leave South Vietnam.

The defense portfolio was turned over to Premier Tran Thien Khiem, who also served as interior minister.

Saigon torture of opponents reported. Widespread torture of political prisoners rounded up in South Vietnam as suspected Communist sympathizers since the start of the Communist offensive March 30 was reported by the New York Times Aug. 12. The article, written by Sydney H. Schanberg, brought a denial Aug. 14 from the South Vietnamese Interior Ministry, which said "there is no such torture of prisoners."

The report was based on smuggled interviews and documents purportedly written by the inmates, and in some cases by sympathetic guards. According to the Times, most foreign diplomats believed that more than 10,000 persons had been imprisoned. An American source placed the figure at 15,000, with about 5,000 freed later. The arrests were believed to be continuing.

Many of the prisoners were being taken to the Con Son jail. They were said to have been transported there in planes of Air America, the airline operated for the U.S. Central Intelligence Agency. Schanberg said he sought to discuss the matter with two top American advisers to the South Vietnamese on police and prison matters—Michael G. McCann and Theodore D. Brown—but an interview was denied.

South Vietnamese Sen. Nguyen Huy Chieu charged Aug. 15 that 920 innocent persons, "mostly women and children," had been taken to Con Son and held as suspected Communists without trial. Chieu, who had visited Con Son Aug. 10 with several other senators, said they might be released later in the week. He said they were among 1,250 persons rounded up in Quangtri Province and in the Hue area shortly after the start of the North Vietnamese drive. He said the 330 others already had been freed.

Hamlet elections abolished. The South Vietnamese government issued a decree Aug. 22 abolishing popular democratic elections in the country's 10,775 hamlets. The decree, signed by Premier Tran Thien Khiem and made public Sept. 6, superseded a 1966 law establishing the election of hamlet and village officers. The new statute ordered the 44 province chiefs, military men appointed by President Nguyen Van Thieu, to reorganize local governments and appoint all hamlet officials.

Khiem's decree was coupled with the issuance to the province chiefs of "general guidelines for the explanation and implementation" of the directive abolishing hamlet elections. It said, "In sum, the administration in villages and hamlets is advanced but not quite adequate, and it doesn't satisfy the needs of the nation in the present phase of the struggle against the Communists."

The province chiefs were told "to screen the ranks of village and hamlet officials including hamlet chiefs" and to dismiss those found "unqualified, negative or who had bad behavior."

Khiem's decree went beyond recent instructions issued by Thieu to the province chiefs that they could replace elected village and hamlet officials at their discretion. U.S. officials said the reason for Khiem's harsh measures was the discovery during the Communists' offensive that many of the hamlet chiefs were Communists, who had provided assistance to the enemy forces.

The U.S. State Department said Sept. 7 that the Nixon Administration had been neither consulted nor informed by the Saigon government of its decision to abolish hamlet elections. It expressed hope that "when the situation stabilizes itself these measures could be relaxed."

Saigon newspapers seized. The South Vietnamese government Aug. 27 announced the seizure of three Saigon newspapers for violating the new press code, which curbed the criticism of the regime or the armed forces. Three more Saigon dailies were confiscated Aug. 30 and the government announced that a court had sentenced 60 other alleged press violators. The sentences were mainly fines, but one publisher also received a one-month jail term.

A Saigon court Sept. 6 fined 48 more newspaper and magazine publishers for violations of the press law. The fines ranged up to about $700.

Thus far only a few of South Vietnam's newspapers had met the Sept. 1 deadline for depositing the required $47,000 with the government treasury in order to continue publishing. As a result, the deadline was extended to Sept. 15.

About one third of Saigon's 43 newspapers had stopped publishing for one day Aug. 22 to protest the press law. Most of the city's politically-oriented dailies were involved.

The publisher of a pro-government newspaper, Phan My Truc, was shot and killed by an unidentified assassin in a Saigon restaurant Aug. 26. The assailant escaped. Truc had urged other newspapers to cooperate with the government's stringent press curbs.

Anti-McGovern broadcasts curbed— High-ranking South Vietnamese officials were reported Sept. 11 to have ordered the government-controlled television and radio networks to stop their sharp attacks on Sen. George McGovern, the U.S. Democratic presidential candidate. The action followed a U.S. embassy protest to Saigon.

Since McGovern's nomination in July, editorials read over TV and radio had been critical of the senator's opposition to the Saigon regime, calling him a "mad dog" and an "enemy of the South Vietnamese people."

A U.S. embassy spokesman said "we deplore the very strong and personal attacks on Sen. McGovern."

Death penalty extended. President Thieu signed a decree ordering the death penalty for persons convicted of hijacking, armed robbery and rape, the official government press agency announced Sept. 4. Thieu also decreed the death penalty for persons who forced women into prostitution and five years' imprisonment for persons involved in organized gambling.

He signed the new laws under the special powers granted him to deal with the national emergency stemming from the North Vietnamese offensive.

Opposition press folds. Fourteen of Saigon's 41 newspapers ceased publication Sept. 15 when they failed to meet the government deadline for posting $47,000 bonds as guarantees against possible fines for violating the country's press code. Most of the newspapers were either opposed to the government or politically neutral; none were pro-government. Also shut down were 15 of 18 periodicals that had not paid the bonds.

Two opposition newspapers paid their deposits and continued publishing. They were Dai Dan Toc and Dien Tien. Dai Dan Toc was published by opposition Deputies Ho Ngoc Nhuan and Vo Long Trieu. Dien Tin described itself as the journal of Gen. Duong Van Minh, the country's major opposition political figure.

Another press decree issued Sept. 15 barred servicemen from working as journalists when off duty. It charged that servicemen employed by domestic or foreign news organizations had "sometime disseminated arguments harmful to the nation."

Senate scores Thieu decree. The South Vietnamese Senate Sept. 23 approved a resolution asserting that President Nguyen Van Thieu had no legal authority to rule by decree. A group of 21 of the body's 57 senators adopted the resolution, which was not legally binding.

An opponent of Thieu, Sen. Nguyen Van Huyen, was re-elected chairman of the Senate Oct. 6 by a 30–25 vote. Huyen's support came largely from Roman Catholic and Buddhist senators.

Saigon newspapers penalized. Two opposition Saigon newspapers were pe-

nalized after being found guilty of violating government press laws. ·

The Sept. 20 issue of Dai Dan Toc was confiscated after publishing an Agence France-Presse report dealing with the tonnage of bombs dropped by U.S. planes over Quangtri Province during the last five months. The government did not give any reason for the seizure, but an editorial appearing in the newspaper Sept. 21 said it had been "confiscated because of a news report extolling the wholehearted air support the United States gave in the battles in the province of Quangtri and for the reoccupation of Quangtri's old Citadel during the last five months."

The newspaper's editor and publisher, Vo Long Trieu, said Sept. 22 that he believed Dai Dan Toc had been seized under the press law which forbade "the sowing of confusion among the masses."

A military tribunal in Saigon Sept. 22 convicted the editor of the newspaper Dien Tin of charges of "confusing public opinion and harming security." The court sentenced Vo Thi Suong to one year in prison and fined him $2,500. The newspaper itself was fined $2,300. The publication's business manager, Mrs. Vo Ngoc Suong, also received a one-year prison term. The publisher, Sen. Hong Son Dong, was ruled exempt from a jail sentence because of his parliamentary immunity.

The newspaper was cited for having published an article Aug. 16 dealing with the U.S. Pentagon papers and the 1971 Cornell University report on American bombing in Indochina. The article was deemed "harmful to the national security."

Thieu forming new political party. President Nguyen Van Thieu was reported Nov. 17 in the process of completing the formation of a new mass political party, to be called the Democratic party, to compete with the Communists in the period after a cease-fire. [For details, see p. 200]

Thieu signed the statute on the last day before the expiration of the special decree powers granted him in June. The new regulations required that every party must within three months set up branches in at least a quarter of the villages of half of South Vietnam's 44 provinces and in every city. Each branch must enroll as members at least 5% of the registered voters in each area. A party would be required to win at least 20% of the vote in any national election or be "automatically dissolved."

Deputy Tran Van Tuyen, leader of the opposition Vietnam Quoc Dan Dang party, charged that the bill would "drive the people underground and into the Communist side. Only Thieu's Democracy party can meet the criteria."

War Protests, Trials & Amnesty

Bar group asks probe. The New York City Bar Association, in a Jan. 12, 1972 letter to President Nixon, the vice president and speaker of the House, asked that a commission be appointed to probe "evidence that serious breaches of the laws of war have been committed by all parties" in Vietnam.

The panel would investigate "the compatibility of certain policies of the United States with the laws of war and the adequacy of governmental processes for assuring compliance with such laws." These policies would include the use of "free-fire zones," enforced population relocation, treatment of refugees, and the use of environmentally damaging weapons.

Religious assembly asks pullout. Religious leaders from 46 Protestant, Catholic and Jewish denominations meeting Jan. 16 in Kansas City, Mo. to discuss Vietnam, asked the Administration "to withdraw its armed forces immediately and totally and refuse to supply the Indochinese governments with military, economic or political aid, which has simply postponed the political solution" by the Vietnamese themselves.

The message, approved by the 650 delegates to the meeting, charged that President Nixon had deceived the public into thinking his troop withdrawal policy was winding down the war, while in fact it "forces Asian people to be our proxy army, dying in our places for our supposed interests."

Seven bishops were among the 200 Roman Catholics present. The Most Rev. Thomas J. Gumbleton, auxiliary bishop of Detroit, said Catholics were changing their interpretation of patriotism, since "now they're seeing that the Catholic must analyze the actions of his government in light of his faith."

The conference adopted an amendment asking the Soviet Union and China to stop military assistance to North Vietnam, so "all the peoples of Indochina may indeed determine their own future without outside military support and interference."

Kent defendant sentenced. Jerry Rupe, one of three defendants found guilty of charges connected with the May 1970 disorders at Kent State University, was sentenced to six months in jail Jan. 21 by Common Pleas Court Judge Edwin W. Jones in Ravenna, Ohio. His sentence would run concurrently with an unrelated 10–20 year drug sentence imposed in 1971.

Stanford professor dismissed. Howard Bruce Franklin, a Stanford University tenured professor of English suspended since March 1971, was fired by the university board of directors Jan. 22 for his role in February 1971 campus violence protesting U.S. actions in Laos.

The faculty Advisory Board had ruled Jan. 5 after six weeks of hearings that Franklin's speeches at the time "included a general call to employ immediately a wide range of actions including violent and illegal behavior," and that he had incited the occupation of a campus facility and urged refusal of a police dispersal order. Following the faculty decision, Franklin said he hoped for "revolutionary counter-violence."

A fire laid to arsonists damaged university offices Jan. 17. The same day a bomb was discovered in a power station near the Palo Alto campus.

War protest at White House. A substitute member of the Ray Conniff singers chorus line, Carol Feraci, 30, startled President Nixon and his White House dinner guests Jan. 28 when she suddenly unfurled a cloth sign reading "Stop the Killing." Stepping forward she spoke directly to the President, who was sitting several feet away, denounced the war and praised ". . . the Berrigans and Daniel Ellsberg." She left the room after shouts of "throw her out" from other guests. The dinner was held for Mr. and Mrs. DeWitt Wallace, co-founders of the Reader's Digest, to present them with Medal of Freedom Awards.

Draft raiders sentenced. U.S. District Court Judge Alexander J. Napoli Feb. 7 sentenced four protesters in Chicago who had been convicted of pouring blood over Evanston, Ill. Selective Service files in April 1971. The four, who were convicted Dec. 1, 1971, were Thomas P. Clark, 22, John W. Baranski, 23, Eileen Kreutz, 24, and Mary E. Lubbers, 23. They were sentenced to one-year prison terms.

Laird bars amnesty now. Defense Secretary Melvin R. Laird told a student group Feb. 3 that he did not think there should be amnesty for draft evaders so long as other American boys were drafted to fight in Vietnam or U.S. soldiers were held as prisoners of war.

Laird's statement repeated what had come to be the Administration's position on amnesty. President Nixon had indicated that stance in a television interview Jan. 2.

In response to a question from a member of the student group, Laird said the U.S. had always "tried to temper justice with mercy," but that this was "not the time" to consider the question of granting amnesty to the young men who fled the country rather than face military service in Vietnam.

In another development, Laird went before the House Armed Services Committee Jan. 25 to ask for $254 million in extra appropriations for the Defense Department for fiscal 1972.

About half of those funds would be used to control electromagnetic pulses, which would presumably be one result of a hostile nuclear attack against the U.S. According to Laird, those pulses could paralyze the emergency command system that would control the nation's response to the attack.

11,000 draft orders canceled. The Selective Service System announced Feb. 8 that it had instructed local draft boards to cancel the induction orders for the more than 11,000 men who had been scheduled to report in the first three months of 1972.

The cancellation orders were sent out because all draft calls had been suspended until April.

Local boards were instructed to place those men and about 115,000 others who had low lottery numbers and were eligible for the draft but were not inducted in 1971 into a second priority category. Their new status virtually assured them that they would not be drafted.

Jurors picked for Harrisburg trial. The trial of the Rev. Philip F. Berrigan and six colleagues in the Catholic antiwar movement moved a step closer Feb. 8 as nine women and three men were selected in Harrisburg, Pa. for the jury that would rule on charges of conspiring to kidnap Presidential adviser Henry Kissinger, bomb Washington, D.C. heating tunnels, and raid draft offices in several states.

U.S. District Court Judge R. Dixon Herman Jan. 17 ordered a separate trial for the eighth defendant, John

Theodore Glick, who had asked permission to be his own lawyer. (Glick was free on bail pending appeal after serving 11 months of an 18-month sentence for an earlier federal office raid.)

The jurors included one black, one Catholic, and a member of a pacifist religious sect. Although three jurors expressed some opposition to the Vietnam war, only one held that position strongly. During 12 days of jury selection, when over 80 prospective jurors were questioned, little familiarity with the anti-war movement seemed evident among the veniremen from the strongly Republican, white Protestant section of Pennsylvania.

The defendants had unsuccessfully requested a change of venue Jan. 10 to the southern district of New York. The overt acts mentioned in the indictment occurred in nine different judicial districts, in any of which the trial could have been called. After final jury selection, defendant Eqbal Ahmad said "we knew it was a political and social milieu extremely hostile to us," but hoped the 12 finally selected would be fair.

The defendants had lost another pretrial move Jan. 7, when the U.S. Court of Appeals for the 3rd Circuit in Philadelphia refused without comment to order Judge Herman to conduct an immediate hearing concerning the government's alleged use of electronic surveillance to gather evidence.

During jury selection, a variety of protest activities was conducted in Harrisburg, including nightly meetings in local Protestant churches. One such meeting Feb. 2 was addressed by National Council of Churches President Dr. Cynthia Clark Wedel, National Federation of Priests' Councils President Rev. Frank Bonnike, and New York Board of Rabbis President Dr. Harold I. Saperstein.

Besides Berrigan and Ahmad, the defendants were Sister Elizabeth McAlister, Rev. Neil R. McLaughlin, Rev. Joseph Wenderoth, Anthony Scoblick, a separated priest, and Scoblick's wife Mary Cain Scoblick, a former nun. All were Catholics except Ahmad, a Pakistani national studying in the U.S.

Related developments—The Rev. Daniel J. Berrigan, brother of Philip Berrigan, was paroled Jan. 26 for the duration of his three-year sentence for destroying draft records at Catonsville, Md. in 1968. The U.S. Parole Board ordered his release effective Feb. 24, after he pleaded ill health and affirmed his "respect for the law of the land" and his "firm determination henceforth to obey the law." Until his parole expires Aug. 2, 1973, Berrigan was to remain in New York City at Woodstock College, a seminary of his Jesuit order. Rep. William R. Anderson (D, Tenn.) appeared in his behalf before the board.

Two members of the Swedish parliament nominated the Berrigan brothers for the Nobel Peace Prize Jan. 26.

Anti-war rally scores U.S. An anti-war rally in Versailles, France Feb. 11–13 denounced American policy in Indochina and pledged support for the Vietnamese Communists' plans for ending the conflict.

A resolution adopted at the conclusion of the World Assembly for Peace and Independence of the Peoples of Indochina called for backing of "progressive and anti-war forces in the United States" and urged governments "to grant asylum to deserters and to support their right to repatriation." The resolution added: "All together the peoples of the world will efficiently help impose on the United States government the restoration of peace, independence and freedom in Vietnam, Laos and Cambodia."

Plans for a six-week campaign of peace demonstrations in the U.S. starting April 1 were disclosed Feb. 13 by the American delegation to the meeting.

The conference was attended by about 800 delegates, including 147 from the U.S., representing 75 countries.

Wisconsin bomb suspect held. Canadian authorities in Toronto Feb. 16 arrested Karleton L. Armstrong, charged in the August 1970 bombing at the University of Wisconsin at Madison, in which a graduate student was killed.

Extradition proceedings were scheduled for Armstrong, one of four charged for the bombing and with an attempted Jan. 1, 1970 bombing of a Baraboo, Wis. ordnance works. Armstrong had been individually charged Sept. 1, 1971 with three additional bombings in 1969 and 1970.

Berrigan trial begins. The trial of the Rev. Philip Berrigan and six other activists of the Catholic Left on charges of plotting to kidnap Presidential adviser Henry Kissinger, bomb Washington heating tunnels and raid draft board offices began in Harrisburg, Pa. Feb. 21.

The opening weeks of the trial centered on the testimony of chief prosecution witness Boyd F. Douglas Jr., whom the defense attempted to portray as an agent provocateur enlisted by the government to discredit the antiwar movement.

Douglas had been serving a five-year term in the Lewisburg, Pa. federal prison for passing bad checks and resisting arrest when in May 1970 he met Berrigan, who had been jailed for destroying draft records in Catonsville, Md. in 1968. In direct testimony and cross examination Feb. 28–March 15, Douglas said he smuggled letters between Berrigan and other defendants, in particular Sister Elizabeth McAlister, which discussed the alleged plot, and that he participated in meetings and telephone calls with the defendants and other activists at which the plot was mentioned.

Douglas said he conveyed the letters (copies of which he later turned over to the Federal Bureau of Investigation [FBI]) from the prison, which had granted him the privilege to attend nearby Bucknell University, between May and August 1970, when Berrigan was transferred from the prison. He maintained contact with some of the defendants until January 1971.

Douglas testified Feb. 28 that Berrigan told him he had at one time inspected Washington heating tunnels, with their eventual destruction in mind. Another defendant, the Rev. Joseph Wenderoth, allegedly told Douglas in June 1970 that dynamite was available to blow up the tunnels, and later said that Washington's Birthday 1971 had been chosen as a target date.

Anthony and Mary Cain Scoblick, two other defendants, were implicated in March 2 Douglas testimony, as having discussed with him the use of explosives for the project, which he said

he would assist. Eqbal Ahmad, a Pakistani national who tried unsuccessfully Feb. 17 to have his trial transferred to another district because of "prejudice against non-Caucasian aliens," was implicated by a reference to "Eq" in a McAlister letter to Berrigan suggesting a political kidnap, and by two telephone calls, which Douglas said March 15 he had received from "Eq" or "Eqbal" August 20, 1970, exploring the idea of a kidnap.

In his opening statement Feb. 21, defense attorney and former Attorney General Ramsey Clark admitted that some of the defendants had been involved in draft raids, but denied any conspiracy, or that the antiwar activists were capable of violence. He said the trial was intended to intimidate the peace movement and to "justify a leak" by FBI Director J. Edgar Hoover, who first made the charges public, before an indictment was handed down, during Senate testimony requesting increased appropriations.

Douglas admitted March 8 he had received over $9,000 from the FBI in rewards and expenses while informing on the defendants and others, and acknowledged he had unsuccessfully asked the FBI for a further tax-free $50,000. Earlier testimony by prison officials revealed that Douglas had concealed his smuggling activities until a routine search turned up one of the letters. Douglas admitted March 7 that the FBI indicated to him that he would not be prosecuted for the smuggling, which carried a heavy penalty, when he was requested to become an informer.

A major aim of the defense was to picture Douglas as an instigator who initiated contact with Berrigan, who passed on advice about explosives to the defendants, and who raised the subject of the plot in letters and conversations with them after they had themselves ceased to discuss it.

Douglas admitted arranging meetings, inviting individuals to join the movement, and posing as a demolitions expert. Two Bucknell students testified that Douglas had introduced them to the defendants, and advised one of them to engage in draft board raids.

Hearings on amnesty. The Senate Judiciary Committee's Administrative Practice and Procedure Subcommittee held hearings Feb. 28–March 1 on a major issue evolving from the war in Indochina—disposition of draft dodgers or deserters from the armed forces.

At the center of the subcommittee's hearings was the question of whether those who evaded the draft or deserted should be granted amnesty.

The hearings had been called by Sen. Edward M. Kennedy (D, Mass.), subcommittee chairman. Kennedy's subcommittee had no authority to consider legislation on amnesty, but it could study the administrative possibilities involved in such a move.

(According to unofficial government figures, 50,000 men had broken the law by evading the draft or deserting the armed forces since 1964. The actual number of draft evaders was thought to be much higher for there were perhaps thousands of young men throughout the U.S. who had never registered for the draft thereby escaping the government's attention.)

The hearings day-by-day:

Feb. 28—Selective Service Director Curtis W. Tarr testified that it would be unfair and dangerous to grant amnesty to Vietnam war evaders and deserters. Tarr said of such an amnesty: "The nation would accept a precedent for permitting the evasion of Selective Service law that might some day be an unwelcome tradition." He added that amnesty would be unfair to those who had entered the service when drafted.

Feb. 29—Henry Steele Commager, historian and Amherst College educator, said he supported "sweeping amnesty" for all deserters and draft evaders to "wipe the slate clean and start over."

March 1—John H. Geiger, national commander of the American Legion, said his group steadfastly opposed any amnesty for draft evaders and deserters. Geiger urged full prosecution for those men.

Maj. Gen. Leo E. Benade, deputy assistant secretary of defense for military personnel policy, said amnesty for deserters "would have a serious, detrimental impact on our armed forces."

Kennedy entered into the record a letter from Assistant Attorney General Robert C. Mardian who wrote that proposals to grant amnesty to draft evaders while the country was at war were "without precedent."

Said Kennedy, who himself favored unconditional amnesty: "How much of a penalty are we going to ask these people to pay? Most of the political leaders of this country are asking for amnesty from their past positions on war, and they're going to the American public to try to get it."

FBI charged in Camden raid. Robert W. Hardy, the informer who aided the Federal Bureau of Investigation (FBI) in the August 1971 Camden, N.J. draft office raids, said in an affidavit filed March 15 in U.S. district court in Camden that he had been used by the bureau as a "provocateur," without whom the raid could never have taken place.

Hardy's affidavit was filed in support of a pretrial motion to dismiss charges against 20 defendants for breaking and entering federal property and stealing and destroying federal records, and against eight others charged with conspiring and abetting the crimes.

Hardy's affidavit said the plot had been abandoned before he first reported it to the FBI, which paid him about $60 a day plus expenses thereafter to keep the agency posted, to help plan the raid, to provide tools, instructions and supplies, including groceries and the van and gasoline used in the raid. He said he "provided 90% of the tools necessary for the action. They couldn't afford them, so I paid and the FBI reimbursed me. It included hammers, ropes, drills, bits, etc. They couldn't use some of the tools without hurting themselves, so I taught them." He also provided the defendants with diagrams of the draft office and the entire building.

In explaining why he was filing the affidavit, Hardy said the FBI had first told him arrests would take place before the building was actually entered, limiting the charges to conspiracy and ruling out jail terms. He was later told by the FBI that "the higher-ups, someone at the Little White House in California, they said, which I took to mean someone high in the FBI or Justice Department, then in California, wanted it to actually happen."

Defense attorney David Kairys said in his motion that his clients had been "as a matter of law, entrapped" by the government. He called the incident "a case of manufacturing crimes to support repressive policies and the political futures of persons in power," and cited as a similar case the role of FBI informer Boyd Douglas in the Harrisburg 7 conspiracy trial.

In a reply reported April 18 the government argued that the "defense of entrapment is available only to a person who is otherwise innocent, i.e., one who had no predisposition to commit the crime," and that the predisposition should be determined in a jury trial.

Leslie Bacon indicted. Antiwar activist Leslie Bacon was indicted March 24 in Seattle on charges of perjuring herself while testifying in May 1971 as a material witness before a grand jury investigating a bomb blast at the Capitol building in Washington, D. C.

Miss Bacon, who had been indicted in 1971 for allegedly conspiring to bomb a New York City bank, was ordered to appear in Seattle May 5, with a trial to follow within 60 days, according to U.S. Attorney Stan Pitkin. The indictment contended that Bacon had been "at the U.S. Capitol building and the U.S. House of Representatives office building", on or about Feb. 28, 1971, which she had specifically denied.

No other criminal charges had been brought in the Capitol bombing.

Church to sell military stock. The 200,000-member pacifist Church of the Brethren voted to sell all its stock in corporations that produced weapons or defense products, it was reported March 26. It was believed to be the first such action by a major American denomination.

York, Pa. bomb plant sabotaged. The American Machine & Foundry Co. announced March 27 that 300 bomb casings had been found damaged and splashed with red paint at its York, Pa. plant. The Washington Post reported

April 1 it had received a statement claiming responsibility from the Commission to Demilitarize Industry and the Citizens' Commission to Investigate the FBI, which had earlier claimed credit for the unsolved 1971 theft of documents from the FBI office in Media, Pa.

Mistrial in Harrisburg 7 case. The federal jury deliberating charges against the Rev. Philip F. Berrigan and six fellow antiwar activists, April 5 reported itself unable to reach a verdict on the charges of conspiracy to kidnap Presidential adviser Henry Kissinger, blow up Washington, D. C. heating tunnels and raid draft board offices.

But the jury, sitting in Harrisburg, Pa., found Berrigan and Sister Elizabeth McAlister guilty on four and three counts respectively of smuggling contraband letters at the Lewisburg, Pa. federal prison.

The jury had deliberated 59 hours. During that period it had three times requested clarification from U.S. District Court Judge R. Dixon Herman of his instructions on the conspiracy law. The defense charged that his answers, as well as his summation to the jury March 30 were prejudicial to their clients.

According to juror Mrs. Vera Thompson, only two jurors at the close of deliberations voted for a guilty verdict on Count One, the general conspiracy charge.

Defense attorney Ramsey Clark said April 5 that he would argue at a scheduled hearing in Harrisburg May 2 that the smuggling charges be dropped as "discriminatory prosecution." He said his research indicated this was the first time anyone was prosecuted for letter smuggling, which he contended was a commonly tolerated practice. The contraband law, defense attorneys charged, applied to weapons and drugs, and was routinely enforced by administrative actions within the prison involved.

After the 64 prosecution witnesses completed 24 days of testimony March 23, the defense rested its case the following day without calling a witness. At a meeting March 23 the defendants had decided on that course by a 4–3 vote. The majority, including the Rev. Joseph Wenderoth, the Rev. Neil R. McLaugh-

lin, and Mary Cain and Anthony Scoblick, concluded that an active defense
would be crippled if Judge Herman denied, as he did March 24, a motion to
hold a hearing before the jury on
whether the government had engaged in
discriminatory prosecution, and another
motion asking immunity for witnesses
to describe non-violent, although illegal
acts by the Catholic Left. Berrigan, Miss
McAlister and Dr. Eqbal Ahmad had
dissented.

Judge Herman had ordered Ahmad
cleared of two of three charges March
27. The government's charge that he had
smuggled contraband into Lewisburg
and that he suggested through the mails
that Kissinger be kidnaped had been
based solely on a reference to "Eq" in
one of the smuggled letters from Miss
McAlister to Berrigan, and on testimony
by government informer Boyd Douglas
Jr., who claimed he identified Ahmad's
voice as that of a person with whom he
discussed the kidnaping by telephone in
1970.

Chief prosecutor William S. Lynch
refused to say April 5 whether any of the
conspiracy charges would be dropped.

Some 10,000 supporters of the defendants attended a rally at the state Capitol in Harrisburg April 1, addressed by
some of the defendants and by Rep.
Bella Abzug (D, N.Y.), Daniel Ellsberg,
under indictment in the Pentagon Papers case, and Rev. Ralph D. Abernathy,
president of the Southern Christian
Leadership Conference. A telephone
conversation between Berrigan and Mrs.
Nguyen Thi Binh, foreign minister of
the South Vietnam Provisional Revolutionary Government stationed in Paris,
was broadcast to the rally.

On March 29, 166 protesters had been
arrested after surrounding the federal
building in Harrisburg.

Federal court to hear war plea. A
three-judge federal panel was named
in Philadelphia April 6 to hear a suit
asking them to enjoin Defense Secretary Melvin Laird from spending further funds on the Vietnam war.

U.S. District Court Judge Joseph
S. Lord 3rd had refused to dismiss
the suit, which charged Presidents
Johnson and Nixon with unconstitu-

tionally waging war without a Congressional declaration of war. Judge Lord
said March 28 that "alleged economic
injury caused by the prosecution of the
war" and the hundreds of thousands
of American casualties conferred standing on any citizen to sue.

(The Supreme Court had refused in
1971 to rule on the war's legality, and
the First Circuit Court of Appeals had
ruled the war was being pursued with
Congressional support.)

Chicago 7 contempt retrial ordered. The
7th U.S. Circuit Court of Appeals May
11 ordered retrials on contempt of court
charges for the Chicago 7 defendants,
their two lawyers and Bobby Seale,
whose case had been separated from the
main trial.

The 10 had been sentenced to prison
terms ranging from two months to four
years by U.S. District Court Judge Julius
Hoffman for alleged disrespect and disorderly behavior during the 1969–70 riot
and conspiracy trial.

The circuit court was also deliberating
on an appeal by five of the defendants of
their convictions for incitement to riot,
but did not indicate when it would issue a
ruling. Conspiracy and riot charges
against Seale had been dropped.

The three-judge panel cited a 1971
Supreme Court ruling that a judge might
impose contempt sentences only at the
time of the contempt, but if action were
deferred to the end of the trial (as was
the case with the Chicago 7) the sen-
tencing must be left to another judge.
The panel ruled in addition that no contempt sentences longer than six months
could be imposed without a jury trial.

Ten district court judges sitting in the
Northern Illinois district who had
sought to intervene in the contempt appeal were barred from presiding at the
new trial. Judge Hoffman himself had
announced his resignation in December
1971.

The panel left most of the charges
pending, but struck down half the charges
against attorneys William Kunstler and
Leonard Weinglass. The judges said "attorneys have the right to be persistent,
vociferous, contentious and imposing,
even to the point of being obnoxious,
while acting on a client's behalf." They

also ruled that defendants could refuse to rise when a judge entered or left the chamber. Four of 12 contempt counts against Seale were reversed.

The other defendants were Abbie Hoffman, Rennie Davis, David Dellinger, Tom Hayden, Jerry Rubin, John Froines and Lee Weiner.

Seale to enter mayor race—Bobby Seale, chairman of the Black Panther Party, announced May 14 he would run for mayor of Oakland in the 1973 election, on a platform of rent ceilings and community control of police.

Buffalo draft raiders probated. Five defendants were sentenced to one year's probation in U.S. district court in Buffalo May 18 after their conviction April 27 for conspiracy and intent to commit third-degree burglary in connection with a 1971 draft office raid.

Judge John T. Curtin praised the defendants' "love of country," and said that "if others had the same sense of morality, the war would have been over a long time ago."

Those sentenced were Mr. and Mrs. Charles L. Darst, Jeremiah Horrigan, Ann Marie Masters and James Martin.

Ground attacks, bombing spark protests. Increased fighting in South Vietnam and President Nixon's May 8th decision to mine North Vietnamese ports resulted in widespread antiwar protests in the U.S. during April and May. [For the details of these protests see pages 60, 61, 64, 67–68, 89–91, 98–99.]

Charges against nuns dropped. A New York City criminal court judge ordered charges dropped June 23 against 7 nuns and a teacher who had been arrested after lying down in the aisles of St. Patrick's Cathedral in New York April 30. Roman Catholic authorities had declined to prosecute.

In other war protest developments, 115 protesters were arrested June 27 while blocking the entrance to the Senate chambers in the Capitol Building in Washington, and 52 others were arrested June 11 for trespassing after blocking a railroad spur leading to the Naval Ammunition Depot in Earle, N.J.

Labor peace group formed. Members of 35 labor unions from 31 states met in St. Louis June 24–25 at the founding meeting of Labor for Peace. Although some of the 986 delegates advocated calling a one-day national strike against the Vietnam war, the conference confined itself to plans for a permanent national headquarters, a monthly newspaper, and educational and lobbying efforts.

Among those attending the conference were Harry Bridges, president of the West Coast International Longshoremen's Union, Emil Mazey, secretary-treasurer of the United Auto Workers and Harold Gibbons, a vice president of the International Brotherhood of Teamsters. It was the first national antiwar labor meeting since 1968.

Vietnamese student killed. A young South Vietnamese student was shot and killed by an armed passenger July 2 after he tried to divert a Pan American Airways flight to Hanoi.

The would-be hijacker, identified as Nguyen Thai Binh, was shot to death when the plane landed at the Tansonnhut Airport in Saigon. When he took over the plane, Binh said his hijacking attempt was an "act of revenge" for American bombing of North Vietnam.

The plane Binh had sought to commandeer had left San Francisco at midnight June 30 and was bound for Saigon after stops at Honolulu, Guam and Manila. Binh sought to force the plane off its course by showing a stewardess a knife and a package he said contained a bomb. When alerted of the youth's threat to blow up the plane if he was not flown to Hanoi, the pilot told the hijacker that he would have to refuel in Saigon.

Upon landing, the pilot grabbed the hijacker and a passenger shot the youth five times in the chest.

Jane Fonda rebuked for broadcasts. The State Department July 14 rebuked actress Jane Fonda over reports that she had made anti-war broadcasts in Hanoi. A department spokesman said "it was always distressing to find American citizens ... lending their voice in any way to a government" such as North Vietnam.

The North Vietnamese press agency said July 14 that in a broadcast the previous day Miss Fonda, appealing to American pilots, had said· "I implore you, I beg you to consider what you are doing." Relating her visit to damaged dikes in the Namsach district July 13, Miss Fonda said "In the area where I went in it was easy to see that there are no military targets, there is no important highway, there is no communication network."

Six antiwar vets indicted. Six members of the Vietnam Veterans Against the War (VVAW) were indicted in Tallahassee, Fla. July 14 on charges of conspiring to disrupt the Republican National Convention in Miami Beach in August with bombings and shootings.

The six were John W. Kniffen of Austin, Tex., William J. Patterson of El Paso, Tex., Peter P. Mahoney of New York, Alton C. Foss of Hialeah, Fla., Donald P. Perdue of Gainesville, Fla. and Scott Camil of Gainesville, who was also indicted for manufacture and possession of a firebomb and with instructing others in the use of explosives. Perdue and Mahoney were still at large July 16.

The conspiracy charges were based on provisions in the 1968 civil rights bill against crossing state lines to stir disorder, used to convict the Chicago Seven after the 1968 Democratic National Convention. According to the indictment, at least four meetings were held April 1–June 24 to plan the disorders, and a variety of weapons were assembled.

VVAW leaders charged July 15 that the indictments were based on false evidence given by William Lemmer, a former VVAW official who they said had been an informer for the Federal Bureau of Investigation and provocateur. The group claimed to have tape recordings in which Lemmer admitted the charges.

The Fifth U.S. Circuit Court of Appeals ordered the release July 18 of four VVAW members—not among the six indicted—who had been jailed in Tallahassee July 13 by U.S. District Court Judge David L. Middlebrooks for refusing to testify before the grand jury that handed down the indictments. The government had subpoenaed 23 VVAW members July 7, prompting the Demo-

cratic convention to adopt by voice vote July 13 a resolution charging the Administration with trying to "intimidate and discredit" VVAW in a "political" case.

Hoffman, Plamondon charges dropped. In two separate cases, the Justice Department dropped charges July 28 against Yippie leader Abbie Hoffman in Washington and against Lawrence Plamondon and two other White Panther Party leaders in Detroit, rather than disclose transcripts of unauthorized national security wiretaps.

Hoffman had been charged with crossing state lines to participate in a riot, in connection with the 1971 Mayday demonstrations. Plamondon had been charged in a 1968 bombing case that led to the Supreme Court's wiretap decision.

Leslie Bacon cleared in bombing. The Justice Department announced Aug. 4 that it had secured the dismissal of a perjury indictment against Leslie Bacon, an antiwar activist, in connection with the March 1971 bombing of the U.S. Capitol in Washington.

The charge against Miss Bacon, 21, was dropped by District Court Judge Walter T. McGovern in Seattle at the department's request.

A department spokesman said the dismissal was sought "because the decision was made not to answer defendant's motions of disclosure of electronic surveillance" regarding the case.

The perjury charge against Miss Bacon had alleged that she had given false testimony to a grand jury in Seattle when she was questioned about the Capitol bombing.

Left unchanged, however, were federal charges against Miss Bacon in connection with an alleged plot to bomb a New York bank in May 1970.

Antiwar suit dismissed. A three-judge federal panel voted 2–1 Aug. 7 to dismiss a suit asking for a ban on further funds for the Vietnam War.

The majority opinion, written by U.S. Appeals Court Judge Arlin M. Adams, said "Congress possesses whatever power is necessary" to end the war, and to redress any imbalance of power between the executive and legislative branches. The court said federal courts should "move with extreme caution in the sensitive area of foreign policy," or risk "inflicting a grievous wound on our democratic system."

U.S. District Court Judge Joseph S. Lord 3rd dissented in the case, which had been brought by the National Emergency Civil Liberties Committee. U.S. District Court Judge Daniel H. Huyett 3rd voted with the majority.

Protests held at GOP convention. Antiwar protesters Aug. 23 sought to delay acceptance speeches by President Nixon and Vice President Spiro Agnew before the Republican National Convention in Miami Beach, Fla. More than 1,129 demonstrators were arrested during a massive sitdown outside the convention hall. [For details, see pages 137–139.]

Vietnam Vets trial set. Six members of Vietnam Veterans Against the War pleaded innocent Aug. 24 in Gainesville, Fla. to charges of planning to disrupt by violence proceedings at the Miami Beach Republican National Convention in August.

U.S. District Court Judge David L. Middlebrooks set an Oct. 10 trial date for the six, who would remain free under $25,000 bail each.

The U.S. 5th Circuit Court of Appeals in New Orleans dismissed contempt of court charges against four members of the antiwar group Sept. 26, ruling that the government had not adequately denied charges that it had used illegal wiretaps at the group's Gainesville headquarters and at defense attorneys' Tallahassee, Fla. homes. The four had been freed on their own recognizance Sept. 7 by Middlebrooks, after Supreme Court Justice William O. Douglas ordered their release. They had been held in contempt for refusing to testify before the grand jury that handed down the six indictments, after being granted immunity.

Douglas acted Sept. 5, after Justice Lewis F. Powell refused to accept the defense plea. Douglas gave as reasons the possibility that illegal wiretapping had been used to obtain evidence leading to the subpoena of the four veterans, and that the grand jury might have abused its powers in questioning the men after indictments had already been handed down. The four had been freed once before, only to be jailed again Aug. 9 after a contempt hearing, that had been ordered by the 5th U.S. Circuit Court of Appeals, was held.

Berrigan, McAlister sentenced. The Rev. Philip F. Berrigan was sentenced Sept. 5 in U.S. district court in Harrisburg, Pa. to four concurrent two-year terms, and Sister Elizabeth McAlister to a one-year-and-a-day term for smuggling letters at Lewisburg, Pa. federal penitentiary. Immediately after the sentences were read, U.S. attorneys moved to drop all conspiracy charges against the two and their fellow defendants in the "Harrisburg Seven" case, which had ended in a mistrial on the major charges in April.

Judge R. Dixon Herman ruled that Berrigan's sentence would be served concurrently with the three years remaining of a six-year term for destroying draft board records in Baltimore in 1967 and in Catonsville, Md. in 1968. Berrigan could be released immediately if his parole application, which had been held up by the trial, was accepted. Sister McAlister would also be eligible for immediate parole, since her sentence exceeded one year. The smuggling charges had carried maximum possible sentences of 10 years each.

Defense lawyers said they would appeal the smuggling sentences before the Third U.S. Circuit Court of Appeals. Judge Herman had rejected, in a 41-page opinion released Aug. 28, their plea that the conviction be set aside as "discriminatory prosecution." The defense contended that no prosecution had ever been brought in similar letter-smuggling cases. The Federal Bureau of Prisons had dropped restrictions on the flow of mail in its penitentiaries before the Harrisburg trial had gone to the jury.

In denying the motion for acquittal Aug. 28, Judge Herman said the defense had failed to prove discrimination, and he rejected another defense charge, that illegal wiretaps had "tainted" the government's case, since the transcripts of the tapes, handed over to the defense, contained only "innocuous" and "insignificant" conversations.

Mayday damages granted. U.S. District Court Judge Gerhard A. Gesell ordered the District of Columbia to pay $4,500 civil damages Oct. 3 to each of two persons arrested during the Mayday demonstrations in 1971.

Peter Roberts and Dennis Lieberman, Labor Department employes, had been among 13,000 arrested and detained the week of May 2. Only 200 convictions had been obtained so far.

The plaintiffs said they had been arrested May 3 while on their way to work and after showing police their Labor Department identifications. Disorderly conduct charges against the two had later been dismissed.

Gesell rejected the District's contention that the emergency situation confronting the police should be taken into account. He said constitutional protections "must be zealously safeguarded and the appropriate time to safeguard them particularly is in times of stress and strain." He ordered the District to pay each of the plaintiffs $500 in punitive damages, $3,000 in compensatory damages and $1,000 in legal costs.

U.S. drops Seale charges. The Justice Department said Sept. 27 it would drop contempt charges against Black Panther leader Bobby Seale imposed by U.S. District Court Judge Julius Hoffman during the "Chicago 7" trial in 1969.

The 7th U.S. Circuit Court of Appeals in Chicago had ordered the charges dropped unless the department turned over to Seale's attorney a transcript of electronically overheard conversations that had been introduced in Hoffman's chambers during the trial. The department had admitted that the conversations, overheard while Seale was in jail, were relevant to the contempt charges.

The conversations had been intercepted by a "national security" wiretap installed without court approval, a practice recently ruled unconstitutional by the Supreme Court. U.S. Attorney James R. Thompson told the appeals court that disclosure of the transcripts "would be inimical to our national security interests."

In a related development, Edwin A. Robson, chief U.S. judge for the Northern Illinois district, accepted a government request July 10 that the retrials of the Chicago 7 defendants and two of their attorneys on contempt charges be heard by a judge outside the district.

Bacon charge dropped. The Justice Department said in New York Nov. 1 it was dropping a bomb conspiracy charge against Leslie Bacon, rather than reveal the contents of surveillance material.

Miss Bacon, an antiwar activist, had been charged in connection with a 1970 plot to bomb a New York branch of First National City Bank. An earlier perjury charge, relating to testimony about a 1971 bomb blast in the Capitol in Washington, had also been dropped for similar reasons.

Ban on Capitol protests lifted. Without hearing arguments, the court unanimously affirmed Nov. 6 a lower court ruling that held as unconstitutional an 1882 law banning all unauthorized demonstrations on the U.S. Capitol grounds.

The law had often been used by District of Columbia prosecutors as the basis for federal "unlawful entry" charges against antiwar and other protesters demonstrating on the Capitol grounds.

The decision upheld a May ruling by a three-judge federal court in Washington that the law was an improper restriction on the public's First Amendment rights of free speech and free assembly. At the same time, the federal court issued an injunction against Capitol police from enforcing the law.

The case grew out of attempt by a now-defunct peace group, the Jeanette Rankin Brigade, to stage a protest against the Vietnam war in January 1968 on the Capitol grounds.

Antiwar vets plead innocent. Seven members of the Vietnam Veterans against the War (VVAW) and a nonmember sympathizer pleaded innocent in U.S. district court in Gainesville, Fla. Nov. 6 to a total of five counts relating to their alleged conspiracy to disrupt the Republican National Convention in Miami Beach in August.

Two additional counts and two additional names had been added to the indictment by a federal grand jury, and announced by the Justice Department Oct. 18. The new defendants were VVAW member Stanley K. Michelson and John King Briggs, both of Gainesville. Briggs was brought under the original conspiracy charge, and Michelson was charged with misprision, or concealing an unlawful act, and with being an accessory after the fact.

U.S. District Court Judge David L. Middlebrooks set bail at $10,000 for each of the defendants, a reduction from $25,-000 for the six original defendants, but refused a defense plea to free the accused on their own recognizance.

In pleading innocent, the VVAW members said they had been guilty of "war crimes against the people of Indochina."

Protest charges dropped. Only one person had been found guilty in connection with mass protest activities during the Republican convention in Miami Beach in August, when court records were closed in Dade County Metropolitan Court, under a Florida law requiring all misdemeanor cases to be brought to court within 90 days. Hundreds had been arrested.

All but 115 cases had been dropped by Judge C. P. Rubiera two weeks before because the arresting warrants had not been properly witnessed. Rubiera ruled Nov. 21 that Barbara Slack, one of only two persons to appear in court out of 47 scheduled for trial that day, was guilty of disorderly conduct. No sentence was imposed.

Chicago case overturned. The U.S. Court of Appeals for the 7th Circuit Nov. 21 overturned the convictions of five defendants in the "Chicago 7" trial because of improper rulings and conduct by District Court Judge Julius J. Hoffman during the 1969 trail.

But the appeals court refused, by a 2-1 vote, to find unconstitutional the interstate riot act under which the five had been tried.

The judges found that there was enough evidence to legally justify another trial, but said the Justice Department would then have to disclose electronically overheard conversations made under national security wiretaps, since found unconstitutional by the Supreme Court.

The five defendants, all antiwar leaders charged with crossing state lines with the intent to incite a riot at the 1968 Democratic National Convention in Chicago, were David T. Dellinger, Rennard C. Davis, Thomas E. Hayden, Jerry C. Rubin and Abbie Hoffman.

The opinion, supported by Judges Wilbur Pell, Thomas Fairchild and Walter J. Cummings Jr., rebuked Judge Hoffman in unusually emphatic terms for his "deprecatory and often antagonistic attitude toward the defense," from "the very beginning of the trial," both "in the presence and absence of the jury." Judge Hoffman's statements, tinged with "sarcasm," and a series of incidents and rulings "must have telegraphed to the jury the judge's contempt for the defense."

The trial judge's attitude alone would have justified reversal of the conviction, the court wrote. In addition, the court said Hoffman had not adequately questioned potential jurors about their attitudes toward the defendants and about the effect of pre-trial publicity, had improperly sent notes to the jury during deliberation without telling the defense, had rejected defense evidence relating to the defendants' intentions and had excluded expert witnesses who would have testified on police tactics.

The court said the prosecution, led by U.S. Attorney Thomas A. Foran, had frequently made remarks before the jury "not called for by their duties," which "fell below the standards applicable to a representative of the United States."

Two other defendants, Lee Weiner and John R. Froines, had been acquitted, and charges were dropped against the eighth, Bobby G. Seale. Of eight Chicago policemen indicted for civil rights violations during the disorders, seven had been acquitted and charges against the other were dropped after a mistrial.

In his minority dissent, Judge Pell, an appointee of President Nixon, argued that the interstate riot law was too vague and too broad. He wrote "suppression of the free interchange of ideas and beliefs would be pyrrhic sacrifice of a precious freedom for an illusory safety." But the majority found the law's restraints to be closely enough linked to the risk of physical violence to justify the potential infringement of free speech.

Berrigan paroled. The Board of Parole announced Nov. 29 that the Rev. Philip F. Berrigan would be freed on parole Dec. 20 from the Federal Correctional Institution at Danbury, Conn., after serving 38 months for various antiwar activities.

Berrigan, 49, had been serving three concurrent terms, one of six years for damaging draft board records in Baltimore in 1967, one of three and one half years for damaging records in Catonsville, Md. in 1968, and one of two years for smuggling letters in and out of the Federal Penitentiary at Lewisburg, Pa.

The board. which had denied parole July 28 and had refused a request for a special hearing in October, gave no reason for its latest action.

Berrigan and Sister Elizabeth McAlister, convicted with him on the smuggling charge, were still appealing that verdict.

Vets judge withdraws. U.S. District Court Judge David L. Middlebrooks withdrew Dec. 17 from the case of seven antiwar veterans and a supporter accused of planning to disrupt the Republican National Convention in Miami Beach. The defense had requested him to step down Sept. 18 because of alleged personal bias.

5 held in sabotage. Five antiwar activists were arrested near York, Pa. Dec. 18 after attempting to pour concrete on Penn Central Railroad tracks near an American Machine and Foundry Corp. bomb casing factory.

Police said the five were members of the East Coast Conspiracy to Save Lives, a group which the late Federal Bureau of Investigation director J. Edgar Hoover had said in 1970 was led by the Revs. Daniel and Philip Berrigan. The five, all New Jersey residents, were Eugene William Daniel Galvin Jr., Thomas E. Korkames, Rollin D. Kirk, Patricia Kirk, and Monica McKig, all in their 20s.

Prosecutor vs. Chicago 7 retrial. U.S. Attorney James R. Thompson said in Chicago Dec. 18 he had written Attorney General Richard G. Kleindienst advising him not to appeal an appeals court ruling that overturned the 1970 riot convictions against five Chicago 7 defendants, and recommending against a retrial, which the court had not barred.

Thompson said the "numerous grounds cited for reversing the original conviction" made it unlikely that the Supreme Court would back the prosecution in an appeal.

U.S. District Court Judge Edward T. Gignoux had ruled Nov. 17 that contempt charges against Bobby Seale arising from the 1969 Chicago 7 trial be dropped, and that contempt charges against the other defendants and two of their lawyers be limited to a maximum of 177 days, to avoid the necessity of a jury trial.

Both rulings came on government motions, and the defendants' attorney said he would still request a jury trial. Judge Gignoux had been brought into the case from Portland, Me.

Protests held at inaugural. Antiwar protestors attempted to disrupt the inauguration of President Nixon and Vice President Spiro T. Agnew in Washington Jan. 20, 1973. The demonstrations did not seriously disrupt the ceremony or the inaugural parade. For details, see pp. 243–244

Pentagon Papers Case & Other Developments

Pentagon Papers Case

Senate decision on Gravel case. The Senate adopted by a 55–27 vote March 23, 1972 a resolution authorizing the Senate to file a friend of the court brief in the Supreme Court case involving Sen. Mike Gravel (D, Alaska) and his release of part of the Pentagon papers before they were officially declassified.

As originally presented, the resolution authorized payment of Gravel's legal fees in the case, but this was altered, in the face of Republican opposition, to payment only of the cost of printing Gravel's legal brief for the court.

At issue in the court case was whether Congressional immunity could be extended to cover Congressional aides.

1965–68 documents disclosed. More secret material from the Pentagon Papers, a government study of U.S. involvement in Vietnam, was made public by syndicated columnist Jack Anderson June 26. Material from 43 of 47 volumes of the papers had been disclosed in 1971.

The newly-released material was in volumes covering Johnson Administration efforts in 1965–68 to get peace talks started.

In releasing the top secret material, Anderson said President Nixon had made public "even more sensitive negotiations." Much of the material had already been made public by other means, such as in President Lyndon B. Johnson's memoirs. Some items had appeared in Anderson's columns the previous three weeks.

This had led to government complaints at the "Pentagon Papers" trial of Daniel Ellsberg and Anthony J. Russo Jr. in Los Angeles of "a high likelihood" that the defense had leaked the latest four volumes to Anderson, an activity denied by Anderson and the defendants.

One of the findings of the Pentagon analysis disclosed June 26 was that "it has always been clear that insofar as Hanoi is interested in negotiations, it is only as another way of achieving its objectives."

Some other disclosures June 26:

■ Soviet Premier Aleksei N. Kosygin had "startled" the British during an official visit to London in February 1967 by being willing to act as a mediator with the North Vietnamese. Kosygin reportedly later told the U.S. ambassador his intervention in London, which came to nought, had provoked "fury" in Peking.

■ Norwegian efforts as an intermediary were highly regarded by the Pentagon analysts but not "treated with great importance in Washington."

311

■ Henry A. Kissinger, an assistant to President Nixon for national security affairs, had attempted in 1967 (when he was a Harvard professor) to arrange a direct peace-talk discussion between North Vietnamese leader Ho Chi Minh and Ho's friend, Raymond Aubrac, and another Frenchman, Herbert Marcovich. The Frenchmen conferred in Hanoi with Premier Pham Van Dong, who told them, according to the account, his people had been fighting for independence for 4,000 years and had defeated the Mongols three times and the U.S. Army, "strong as it is, is not as terrifying as Genghis Khan."

The way to peace, Dong told Washington, was for the U.S. to withdraw and allow formation of a neutral regime in Saigon.

The Pentagon analysts found the unwillingness of either side to compromise on political control of South Vietnam to be a basic cause of inability to reach a peace settlement. The enemy cherished its long-term objective of a united Vietnam under a Communist form of government, the U.S. the objective of a divided Vietnam and a non-Communist South.

The study found Hanoi's diplomacy relatively consistent in private and in public efforts, with the theme of extending to the U.S. a face-saving way to pull out and deferring its long-term goal of a Communist-run South by creation of an outwardly neutral regime. The study said U.S. public negotiations pointed diplomatically toward private evolvement of a face-saving way for Hanoi to end its war in the South in exchange for an end to the U.S. bombing and ground combat.

The Communist attitude that U.S. military power would not win out in the end, as Dong pointed out, was a basic difference between the two sides emphasized in the study. The U.S. thought its military "pressures could accomplish our goals," as the Pentagon analysts put it, "the Communists did not."

Ellsberg trial delayed. The Supreme Court Aug. 5 refused a government request to convene a special summer session to consider overturning Justice William O. Douglas's stay of the trial of

Daniel Ellsberg and Anthony J. Russo Jr. in the Pentagon papers case.

The Justice Department had asked the court to vacate Douglas' order so that the trial of the defendants, charged with leaking the secret war study to the press, could resume in Los Angeles. A legal controversy over a government wiretap had led to a halt in the proceedings July 26.

With Douglas's stay in force, it was unlikely that the trial would resume before October.

Chief Justice Warren E. Burger announced the court's decision in a one-paragraph statement from Washington. Referring to the Justice Department's request for a summer session, Burger said that "after consultation with all members of the court except Justice Douglas, who granted the stay, the motion to call a special term of the court is denied."

Burger's comment that he had polled all the justices except Douglas indicated that Justice William H. Rehnquist apparently did not disqualify himself from considering the case. Lawyers for Ellsberg and Russo had asked Rehnquist to excuse himself because of his alleged connection with phases of the Pentagon papers case when he was an assistant attorney general in the Justice Department.

Douglas stay halts trial—Douglas stayed the opening of the trial July 29, 48 hours before opening arguments were to be heard. Douglas said he was granting the stay to allow attorneys for Ellsberg and Russo to appeal to the Supreme Court their contention that the government be required to divulge details of a wiretapped conversation involving a defense lawyer or consultant.

Douglas gave defense attorneys until Aug. 28 to file a petition for review of the wiretap question by the full court. If the court agreed to hear the appeal when it convened Oct. 2, the opening of the trial could be delayed until 1973.

At issue in the wiretap controversy was whether the defendants had a right to see transcripts of a telephone conversation involving a member of the Ellsberg-Russo defense team that was monitored by the government as part of a "foreign intelligence" investigation unrelated to the Pentagon papers case.

The government had refused to make available to defense attorneys the details of that wiretap on the ground that it was not related to the Ellsberg-Russo trial.

The 9th U.S. Circuit Court of Appeals in San Francisco upheld the government's position July 27.

According to the New York Times, Douglas' stay marked the first time a Supreme Court justice had ever blocked a trial after the jury was sworn in.

Douglas conceded that he was "exceedingly reluctant" to stay a trial in which the jury had already been selected and seated. (The jury of eight women and four men had been sworn in July 21.)

But he said he was granting the stay out of concern that the defendants' constitutional rights might have been violated by "the powerful electronic ear of the government."

Ellsberg appeal rejected. The Supreme Court cleared the way Nov. 13 for the government to resume its prosecution of Daniel Ellsberg and Anthony J. Russo Jr., who were accused of making public the Pentagon Papers.

With two justices dissenting, the court refused to hear the defendants' appeal that the presiding trial judge should have allowed them to see the transcript of a defense lawyer's conversation that had been monitored by a government wiretap.

The decision in effect dissolved a stay issued by Justice William O. Douglas July 29 that stopped the trial in Los Angeles 48 hours before opening arguments were to be heard.

Douglas and Justice William J. Brennan Jr. dissented Nov. 13, saying that the court should hear the Ellsberg-Russo appeal. That the court refused to hear the appeal now, however, did not mean that it would not reconsider it if the defendants were convicted, raising the point in a subsequent appeal.

In arguing against the appeal, the Justice Department maintained that the court would encourage "piecemeal" appeals if it held up the case for months while considering the wiretap issue.

In a related development, the court had refused Nov. 10 to stay the jailing of a Harvard University professor for his refusal to answer questions about the Pentagon Papers case.

Samuel L. Popkin, a political scientist, had been sentenced to 18 months in jail for contempt after he declined to answer seven questions before a U.S. grand jury in Boston in March. Popkin was a friend of Ellsberg.

The 1st Circuit Court of Appeals upheld Popkin's right to refuse replies to four of the seven questions. Those four had to do with his opinions of who might have had copies of the 47-volume war study. But the appeals court ruled that the three others were germane and should have been answered. Only Douglas dissented in the court's 8–1 decision.

Popkin freed in contempt case. Prof. Samuel L. Popkin, the Harvard scholar who was jailed for refusing to answer certain questions about the Pentagon papers, was released from a Dedham, Mass. jail Nov. 28 in a surprise move by the government.

Popkin gained his freedom when the Justice Department unexpectedly dismissed the Boston grand jury before which he had refused to answer the questions. He was jailed for contempt Nov. 21 and had been expected to remain there until Jan. 12 when the jury was to end its investigation into the Pentagon papers case.

The U.S. attorney's office in Boston said the jury was dismissed to avoid any conflict with the government's case against Daniel Ellsberg and Anthony J. Russo Jr. on criminal charges involving the once-secret war study. [See below]

According to published reports, the decision to dismiss the jury and in effect free Popkin was made within the Justice Department's Internal Security Division. During the week that Popkin was imprisoned, Harvard officials, including President Derek C. Bok, sought to have Popkin released.

Popkin's release did not necessarily mean that the government was no longer interested in the information he withheld from the grand jury. If the government wanted to continue its investigation into the distribution of the Pentagon papers, it could impanel a new grand jury to ask Popkin the same questions he refused to answer before. They dealt with identification of government officials and others who had talked confidentially with him during his research on Vietnam.

Ellsberg mistrial sought—Defense attorneys in the Pentagon papers case, soon to begin in Los Angeles, asked a federal judge Nov. 25 to dismiss the charges against Daniel Ellsberg and Anthony J. Russo Jr. on the ground that remarks made by Vice President Spiro T. Agnew prejudiced the defendants' case. Agnew, during a nationally televised interview Oct. 29, used the word "steal" to describe both the Watergate bugging incident and publication of the secret Vietnam War study.

Mistrial declared in Ellsberg case. The judge in the Pentagon Papers trial in Los Angeles declared a mistrial Dec. 8 because of an unparalleled lapse between the time a jury was seated and the actual opening of the trial.

Attorneys for Daniel Ellsberg and Anthony J. Russo Jr., principal defendants in the case, had sought a mistrial on different grounds.

Federal District Court Judge William M. Byrne Jr. announced his decision and dismissed the jury after Ellsberg and Russo had waived their double jeopardy protection.

At issue was the Pentagon's once-secret, 47-volume study of the Vietnam war and its origins and who released it to the press. Ellsberg was charged with 12 counts of espionage, conspiracy and theft. Russo was charged with three counts.

Shortly after Byrne announced his decision, defense attorneys said they would challenge the new jury selection on several grounds. One reason cited by defense attorneys was their charge that the chief federal judge of the district had prejudiced the case with remarks he had made about the case.

2nd Pentagon Papers trial begins. The second Pentagon Papers trial began Jan. 18, 1973 in Los Angeles. The first had been declared a mistrial by Federal District Court Judge William M. Byrne Jr., Dec. 8, 1972 after a four-month lapse between the time the jury was seated and the trial opened.

Defendants were Daniel Ellsberg and Anthony J. Russo Jr., former employes of the Rand Corp., a concern that did extensive consultant work for the Defense Department, and from which the Pentagon Papers were taken. There were 15 counts in the indictments against Ellsberg and Russo that covered the period March 1, 1969 to Sept. 30, 1970, at least nine months before the Pentagon Papers were revealed to the public by the New York Times June 13, 1971. The counts included: conspiring to obtain classified government documents and to show them to unauthorized persons (one count); stealing, concealing, and receiving stolen government property (six counts); and espionage (eight counts).

The trial took a major turn Jan. 27, when chief prosecutor David R. Nissen turned over to the defense, secret analyses made by the Defense Department on the impact of the release of the Pentagon Papers. Judge Byrne ordered Nissen to hand over the studies after reviewing them and concluding that they might contain evidence of an exculpatory nature.

During arguments over the introduction of the new evidence, the jury was excluded from the courtroom by the judge.

Existence of the studies had been confirmed Jan. 18 in testimony by Frank A. Bartimo, assistant general counsel for the Defense Department. Nissen had denied knowledge of such analyses, although Judge Byrne, at the request of the defense, had ordered the U.S. attorney to produce them in April 1972.

Disclosure of the analyses (called "damage reports" by the Defense Department) began Jan. 31 with the testimony of Lt. Col. Edward A. Miller (ret.), who authored one study on nine volumes of the Pentagon Papers. Miller said he had been asked to determine if disclosure of the material in the nine volumes was harmful to the national security. He testified that in his review of 800 documents, "only about 140 or 150 of these items had been correctly classified" top secret. Miller's testimony related to six of the eight espionage charges against Ellsberg and Russo. In order to prove them, the government had to establish that injury was done to national security.

Miller added that a few days after completing his "damage report," he saw a memorandum written by his direct superior Charles W. Hinkle, director of security review for the Defense Department, ordering his study removed from the files, although not destroyed. Miller said it was his understanding that the directive originated with J. Fred Buzhardt, general counsel to the Defense Department.

Hinkle, when questioned about the memorandum, testified Feb. 1 that he did not "recollect" writing it nor did he "recollect" ever hearing of such a memo.

Buzhardt had said in testimony Jan. 30 he never knew Miller had done analyses of the Pentagon Papers.

Another "damage report" prepared by William Gerhart of the National Security Agency, turned over to the defense Jan. 30, stated flatly that the volume dealing with Franco-American relations during the 1950s did not damage national interest, as the information was already in the public domain.

Walter Cutler of the State Department, who studied the impact of one of the four volumes dealing with diplomacy, adjudged it as not relating to the "national interest." This material was also given to the defense Jan. 30.

Earlier testimony before the jury—In earlier testimony before the jury, two Army generals said the data contained in the Pentagon Papers was an aid to the enemy. Lt. Gen. William G. DuPuy testified Jan. 18 that Hanoi would have found it "interesting and useful" to have had access to a 1968 report on the effects of the 1968 Tet offensive, written by Gen. Earle G. Wheeler, then chairman of the Joint Chiefs of Staff. Eight pages of this report—co-authored by DuPuy—were among the documents that the government said Ellsberg and Russo duplicated. DuPuy said the North Vietnamese would find the report useful, "particularly if they intend to do it (mount an offensive in the South) again. . . . and they did it in 1972."

However, upon being questioned by defense, DuPuy admitted that he had helped Gen. William C. Westmoreland with a report that contained the same statistics as the sensitive Wheeler report. The Westmoreland report was sold by the Government Printing Office for $6 shortly after President Nixon's inauguration in 1969.

Brig. Gen. Paul F. Gorman, in similar testimony Jan. 24, said the revelations contained in the Pentagon Papers "could have damaged the national defense." He cited specifically a volume titled "The Overthrow of Ngo Dinh Diem," which detailed the part that U.S. Ambassador Henry Cabot Lodge played in the overthrow of Diem. According to the volume, Lodge told the plotters that the U.S. would not interfere and would offer the aid of the Central Intelligence Agency for tactical planning.

Ellsberg-Russo charges reduced. The judge in the Pentagon Papers trial Feb. 26 ordered two of the 15 counts against defendants Daniel Ellsberg and Anthony J. Russo Jr. dropped. Federal District Judge William M. Byrne struck the counts because of insufficient evidence.

One count against Ellsberg was for espionage in connection with a Rand Corp. study of the 1954 Geneva Accords. Byrne Feb. 7 had banned presentation of any evidence by the prosecution on this count as punishment for withholding other evidence from the trial.

The count dismissed against Russo alleged he obtained nine volumes of the Pentagon Papers from Ellsberg "knowing and having reason to believe at the time . . that said documents would be . . . disposed of contrary" to the espionage act.

Another major development in the trial was disclosure that Samuel A. Adams, a former analyst for the Central Intelligence Agency (CIA), possessed information that might discredit important prosecution testimony. Adams, employed by the CIA from 1965 to 1972 as an analyst of enemy troop strength in Vietnam, said he read accounts of the testimony of Lt. Gen. William DePuy (reported previously as DuPuy), who testified that disclosure of material from a 1968 Joint Chiefs of Staff memo could have been helpful to the enemy.

Statistics in the memo (called "the Vietnamese Communist order of battle) were among those studied by Adams in his capacity as a CIA analyst. In an affidavit given to the defense Feb. 17, Adams said the "statistics were derived from numbers which had been deliberately fabricated in late 1967" by American military officers in Vietnam.

The prosecution completed its case Feb. 26. During the latter stages, it attempted to establish that Ellsberg had no special relationship to the documents and therefore no right to remove them from the offices of the Rand Corp., and that he allowed unauthorized persons to see top-secret documents.

Richard H. Moorstein, a Rand consultant, testified Feb. 16 that Ellsberg had no special arrangement in 1969 and 1970 guaranteeing him unrestricted and confidential access to the Pentagon Papers. He said he always assumed the documents were to be treated in the same way as other classified documents.

Moorstein denied the defense contention that he knew three retiring Pentagon officials had made a special arrangement with the Rand Corp concerning the papers, and that he participated in that arrangement, obtaining confidential access only a few months after Ellsberg.

The three Pentagon officials were Paul C. Warnke, then assistant secretary of defense for international affairs, and two of his top aides, Leslie Gelb and Morton H. Halperin.

In Feb. 15 testimony, the Rand Corp. chief of security, Richard H. Best, conceded that the Pentagon Papers had not been entered into the corporation's top secret control system until 16 months after they had been acquired.

The prosecution said the papers were protected by the "industrial security" manual which was attached to all contracts between Rand and the government. Although no such contract ever involved the Pentagon Papers, the prosecution contended other contracts with Rand were broad enough to include the Pentagon Papers.

The defense contended throughout the Rand testimony that the Pentagon Papers were at Rand merely for storage and that Ellsberg had control over access to them.

In other testimony, a friend of Russo, Lynda Sinay Resnick, conceded Feb. 21 that she helped the defendants copy the documents in her Los Angeles advertising office. She said, however, she had not read the contents of the documents on orders from Ellsberg, who told her she did not have top secret clearance.

Pentagon Papers defense begins case. The defense in the Pentagon Papers trial began its case Feb. 27, promising to show that the controversial documents had no relationship to the national security and that they were "needed by the country" in order to evaluate the war in Vietnam.

Seeking to discredit the espionage charges against Daniel Ellsberg and Anthony J. Russo Jr., defense lawyers called expert witnesses to testify that the Pentagon Papers and the 1968 Joint Chiefs of Staff memorandum on the 1968 Tet offensive in South Vietnam did not constitute useful intelligence for foreign analysts.

The most prominent witness was Ford Foundation President McGeorge Bundy, a special assistant for national security affairs under Presidents Kennedy and Johnson. Bundy, considered a chief architect of American policy in Vietnam, testified March 9 that the three of the 19 documents he was concerned with did not damage the U.S. nor did they aid Hanoi. Bundy referred to the documents as "the first cut of history" and said they could best be understood that way, "not as an intelligence account."

Bundy said the Joint Chiefs of Staff memo was meant only as argument to impress upon President Johnson the need to increase U.S. troop strength in Vietnam. Besides, the memo became public two weeks after it was written, when the New York Times disclosed its thrust, he said. Later, he added, a more comprehensive version of the memo written by Gen. William C. Westmoreland was issued by the Government Printing Office—six months before Ellsberg and Russo allegedly committed their offenses.

The other two volumes that concerned his testimony simply lost their importance when there was a change of administrations in 1969, Bundy said.

Also testifying was Central Intelligence Agency (CIA) analyst Samuel A. Adams, who said in testimony March 6 that the Army had deliberately fabricated enemy troop strength figures in the Joint Chiefs of Staff memorandum. Adams called the falsifications "a result of political pressures within the military to display the enemy as weaker than he actually was." He said the military gave enemy troop figures during the 1968 Tet offensive as 240,000 when they should have been 400,000.

On the third day of his testimony March 8, the issue of suppression of exculpatory evidence that Adams possessed was raised before the jury for the first time. The jurors had previously been sent from the courtroom by Judge William M. Byrne when the question was raised. Under questioning from both the defense and Byrne, Adams said he had been "lied to" in a definite attempt "to prevent me from testifying in this court."

Among the other defense witnesses called were:

Rear Adm. Gene LaRocque (ret.) former Pentagon analyst, and current director of the Center for Defense Information, a private organization that collected and disseminated defense information to the public, Feb. 28 called the Joint Chiefs of Staff memo "absolutely unintelligible." He said March 2, "nothing the U.S. did in Vietnam had any relation to the national defense. . . . to defend the U.S. you have to have a credible foe."

Rep. Paul N. McCloskey (D, Calif.) was also called to testify March 2, but most of his testimony was blocked by the judge who ruled against a "justification defense," whereby a defendant would prove the evil he was doing was less than the evil he was preventing.

City University of New York history professor Arthur M. Schlesinger, an adviser to President Kennedy, testified March 12 that the Pentagon Papers were better suited to foreign historians than foreign intelligence analysts.

Byrne dismisses charges. Judge Byrne May 11 dismissed government charges of espionage, theft and conspiracy against Ellsberg and Russo, citing government misconduct during the case as the reason for his action. The government had admitted breaking into the office of Ellsberg's former psychiatrist, discussing with Byrne the directorship of the FBI during the trial and tapping Ellsberg's phone and then losing the records of the tap.

War Atrocity Reports

Higher Mylai death toll reported. Seymour Hersh, the free-lance journalist who won a Pulitzer Prize for his account of the Mylai massacre, said in a magazine article Jan. 18, 1972 that Army investigators had found that 347 South Vietnamese men, women and children were killed by U.S. soldiers in that hamlet in 1968.

It had been widely believed that less than 200 civilians were slain at Mylai. That figure had been used because of the 109 murders initially charged to 1st Lt. William L. Calley Jr., a platoon commander of the rifle company that swept through Mylai.

Hersh, in the first installment of a two-part article to appear in The New Yorker magazine, accused the Army of covering up factual material about another alleged incident in which he said 90 civilians were slain on the same day as the Mylai attack in a hamlet known as Mykhe 4. Military maps placed Mykhe 4 two miles northwest of Mylai.

Hersh identified the source of his information as the transcript of the Army's 1969–70 inquiry into the massacre at Mylai. That report had not yet been made public by the Defense Department.

Hersh said a secret investigation conducted by the Army's Criminal Investigation Division at the request of the Army inquiry board concluded that 347 civilians died at Mylai, a total he said, that was "twice as large as had been publicly acknowledged."

Hersh says Army destroyed papers. In the second of a two-part article in The New Yorker, Seymour Hersh, who first reported the Mylai massacre, charged Jan. 25 that members of the Army's American Division destroyed documents about the Mylai incident to protect officers involved in the attack.

Soldiers of the American Division's 11th Infantry Brigade were the ones who swept through Mylai on March 16, 1968.

Hersh based the new charge on an examination of the Peers inquiry, a report by an Army panel under Lt. Gen. William R. Peers that studied whether the Army covered up the Mylai incident. The Peers report had not yet been made public by the Defense Department.

Hersh contended the Peers panel finished its inquiry "without being able to discover how the Mylai 4 files had disappeared" from the American's record in South Vietnam.

Jerry W. Friedheim, Pentagon press spokesman, had said Jan. 19 the Pentagon would withhold comment on Hersh's charges. "Our legal officers feel public comment at this time is inappropriate because the Calley case is still pending review."

Friedheim was referring to the case of Lt. William L. Calley Jr., the only U.S. soldier to be convicted in the Mylai incident.

U.S. sued for Mylai report. Rep. Les Aspin (D, Wis.) filed a suit in federal district court in Washington April 3 to force the Pentagon to release the unpublished report of the Army's Peers Commission on the mass slayings of civilians at Mylai.

The Army inquiry, headed by Lt. Gen. William R. Peers, had taken up the question of whether the Army had covered up the Mylai incident.

Aspin, a member of the House Armed Services Committee, asked the court to order that the Peers' report be made public under the Freedom of Information Act. Named as defendants were Defense Secretary Melvin Laird and Secretary of the Army Robert F. Froehlke.

Aspin charged that the "defendants are improperly withholding the material contrary to statute, contrary to the intent and policy of the Freedom of Information Act."

Panel indicts American Command. The Army panel which investigated the Mylai 4 massacre concluded in its official report that the entire command structure of the American Division, whose soldiers were responsible for the murder of South Vietnamese civilians at the Mylai village complex, was guilty of misconduct in connection with the March 16, 1968 incident.

At the same time, the Army panel said it had found that a second massacre involving the killing of as many as 90 civilians by U.S. riflemen "did in fact" take place two miles south of Mylai on the same day. [See below]

The Army investigating team which prepared the report was headed by Lt. Gen. William R. Peers, after whom the panel's official analysis was named. The Peers Report, which covered 260 pages, had not yet been made public by the Army and was still considered classified material. But the basic findings of the report were made public in news dispatches by Seymour Hersh in the New York Times June 3–4. According to Hersh, a complete copy of the document had been made available to the Times. Accompanying Hersh's June 3 dispatch, the newspaper published almost a full-page of excerpts from one chapter of the Peers Report.

The report's most serious finding was that the American Division's two top generals had committed 43 specific acts of misconduct or omission in connection with the initial field investigations of the Mylai incident.

Maj. Gen. Samuel W. Koster, then commander of the American Division, was cited for 27 acts of misconduct or omission. His chief deputy, Brig. Gen. George H. Young Jr., was accused of 16 acts of similar wrongdoing.

The official inquiry report said there was no direct evidence that the two knew in full the details at Mylai. But it said "they probably thought they were withholding information concerning a much less serious incident than the one which had actually occurred."

But the Peers panel, which concluded its report after a four-and-a-half-month study of Mylai, went farther than accusations of Koster and Young. The report was sharply critical of all aspects of the division's command and company network as of March 1968. The report stated:

"At every command level within the American Division, actions were taken, both wittingly and unwittingly, which effectively suppressed information concerning the war crimes committed at Son[g]my Village."

"At the company level there was a failure to report the war crimes which had been committed. This, combined with instructions to members of one unit not to discuss the events of 16 March, contributed significantly to the suppression of information."

The report also concluded that many high-ranking officers learned of the extent of the massacre at Mylai within days or weeks but did nothing.

"Reports of alleged war crimes, noncombatant casualties, and serious incidents concerning the Son[g]-my operation of 16 March were received at the head-quarters of the Americal Division but were not reported to higher headquarters despite the existence of directives requiring such action.

"Reports of alleged war crimes relating to the Son-[g]my operation of 16 March reached Vietnamese Government officials, but those officials did not take effective action to ascertain the true facts.

"Efforts of the ARVN-GVN [South Vietnamese Army and government] officials discreetly to inform the U.S. commanders of the magnitude of the war crimes committed on 16 March, 1968 met with no affirmative response."

In other parts of the report, the Peers panel made these other basic findings:

■ Koster had failed "to insure that a thorough investigation would be conducted" and had accepted at face value patently fraudulent reports from subordinates.

■ Both Koster and Young had failed to inform other Americal command officers of the complaints and allegations about Mylai. That omission, the panel said, "effectively suppressed" information about the killings.

■ Lower-ranking Americal officers "probably conspired" to make false reports about the activities at Mylai 4 and participated in investigations that were "little more than a pretense."

■ A platoon of U.S. infantrymen under the command of Lt. William L. Calley Jr., the only defendant convicted in connection with the Mylai case, killed between 90 and 130 noncombatants at the village. A second American platoon was said to have killed another 100. One hundred or more were also believed to have been killed as a result of actions by the company's third platoon and helicopter gunships.

At the close of its inquiry, the Peers panel made three specific recommendations to Army Chief of Staff Gen. William C. Westmoreland and Stanley R. Resor, then secretary of the Army.

The recommendations were: (1) that the officers accused of wrongdoing be required to undergo investigations pursuant to possible courts martial; (2) that combat troops be more carefully advised about the international rules of war; and (3) that the U.S. consider revising the procedures for reporting war crimes through the chain of command in which an officer in that command structure "participated in or sanctioned a war crime."

2nd massacre described—In his second article June 4, Hersh said the Peers panel concluded that as many as 90 South Vietnamese civilians were gunned down by U.S. soldiers in a village two miles south of Mylai on the same morning of the Mylai massacre—March 16, 1968.

According to the Peers report, the soldiers involved in the second massacre were attached to the Bravo Company in Task Force Barker. A sister Task Force Barker unit, Charlie Company, had been responsible for the Mylai killings.

The Peers report identified the site of the second massacre as the Mykhe 4 hamlet near the South China Sea. Bravo Company infantrymen, the panel said, stormed into the hamlet March 16, 1968 and began shooting indiscriminately at civilians.

"It appears ... that the number of noncombatants killed by [the company] on 16 March 1968 may have been as high as 90," the report said. "The company reported a total of 38 VCKIA [Viet Cong killed in action] on 16 March, but it is likely that few if any were Viet Cong."

The Peers panel had publicly announced some of its findings in March 1970, but there was no mention of the Mykhe 4 incident. At that time, Gen. Peers told newsmen that he had "no knowledge" of any incidents similar to the massacre at Mylai. (NBC-TV news had reported Feb. 18, 1970 that the Peers panel had uncovered another incident nearby in which about 100 civilians were reported slain by U.S. troops.)

The Peers report said most of the Bravo Company soldiers who took part in the assault on Mykhe 4 "have either refused to testify about the event or disclaimed any recollection of their observations."

The panel added: "For this reason, it has not been possible to establish the facts with any degree of certainty." But the Peers panel said that "both testimony and circumstantial evidence strongly suggest that a large number of noncombatants were killed during the search of the hamlet."

Up to the present time, only one member of Bravo Company had been publicly charged or prosecuted in connection with the slayings at Mykhe 4. That soldier was then Capt. Thomas K. Willingham, the platoon leader of Bravo Company. Willingham had been accused of the unpremeditated murder of 20 civilians and with suppressing information about the Mylai killings. In June 1970, the Army dropped both the murder and coverup charges against Willingham because, according to an official statement, "based on available evidence, no further action should be taken in the prosecution of these charges."

Vietnam pacification assailed. A correspondent who reported on the war in Vietnam for four years charged in an article that U.S. soldiers had deliberately killed thousands of Vietnamese civilians under the guise of "pacification."

Writing in the June 19 issue of Newsweek magazine, Kevin Buckley said: "It can, I believe, be documented that thousands of Vietnamese civilians have been killed deliberately by U.S. forces."

At one point in his report, Buckley said that in 1968 748 weapons were captured in an operation code-named "speedy Express," a pacification effort in the Mekong Delta province of Kien Hoa. In that same operation, Buckley said, the Americans listed 10,899 "enemy" killed. He concluded that "a staggering number of noncombatant civilians—perhaps as many as 5,000 according to one official—were killed by U.S. firepower to "pacify" Kien Hoa.

Buckley said Vietnamese civilians repeatedly told him that those "enemy" fatalities were in many instances unarmed farmers working in their rice fields.

Buckley said the death toll during the Kien Hoa operation "made the Mylai massacre look trifling by comparison."

U.S. admits forest burnings. The U.S. had made three attempts to start fire storms in forests in South Vietnam in 1965–67 to deprive Communist military forces of cover, but abandoned the effort because the moist tropical rain forests would not burn, it was reported July 21

by the New York Times and Science magazine. The Defense Department July 21 acknowledged the attempts to set the fires, but denied they had been secret or were intended to produce devastating fire storms.

According to Science, the targets were first defoliated and then bombed with incendiary devices. The forests were in the Boiloi woods near Tayninh, in the Chupong Mountains, halfway between Pleiku and Kontum, and in the Iron Triangle region northwest of Saigon. The magazine said the project had been carried out by the Defense Department's Advanced Research Projects Agency in collaboration with experts from the U.S. Forest Service. The Times said fire-prevention experts of the Agriculture Department's forest service in Montana and California also were involved.

Diplomat tied to Mylai denied promotion. The Senate Foreign Relations Committee was reported Aug. 3 to have blocked, at least temporarily, the promotion of a career U.S. diplomat accused of suppressing news of the Mylai massacre. Pending an investigation, the committee removed James May's name from a State Department promotion list.

May was now an administrative officer in the U.S. embassy at Mogadishu, Somalia. At the time of the Mylai killings, he was provincial senior adviser to the governor of Quangnai Province, which encompassed the hamlet of Mylai.

Disclosure of the committee action was made by Rep. Samuel S. Stratton (D, N.Y.), who urged the panel in private testimony not to approve May's promotion until the full facts of the case were known.

Stratton had served on a House Armed Services Committee panel which had investigated the Mylai incident and its aftermath.

As a result of that investigation, the House panel had published a report charging May and others with having "suppressed" widespread stories of the incident.

May's name had been sent to the Senate committee June 20 along with the names of 229 others up for promotion.

Army's Mylai case nears end. The Army moved a step closer Sept. 2 to disposing of the Mylai case, disciplining three more men in connection with the March 1968 killings. In the latest actions, the Army formally reprimanded a colonel and a captain and ordered a sergeant dismissed from the service.

With those steps, the Army completed its administrative measures against those involved in the incident. The only loose ends in the case were a review of the murder conviction of Lt. William L. Calley Jr., the only soldier to be convicted of a criminal charge in the incident, and a suit filed by the sergeant whose dismissal was announced Sept. 2.

The sergeant, Kenneth L. Hodges, had filed a suit in federal district court in Georgia protesting his ouster.

The other two men disciplined Sept. 2 were Col. Nelson A. Parson and Capt. Dennis H. Johnson. All three were disciplined on orders by Secretary of the Army Robert F. Froehlke.

Parson, who had been chief of staff of the Americal Division—whose soldiers were responsible for the killings at Mylai—was stripped of his Legion of Merit decoration and given a letter of censure.

Johnson, an Americal Division intelligence officer, was given a letter of reprimand, virtually ending any chance for promotion.

Hodges, whose murder charges stemming from Mylai were dismissed by the Army, had served in Calley's company.

South Korean massacre charged—Two South Vietnamese legislators called for a government investigation into the alleged slaying of 29 civilians by South Korean troops July 31, it was reported Sept. 9.

The request was submitted to Premier Tran Thien Khiem's office by Deputies Nguyen Cong Hoan and Pham Xuan Huy. They charged that the South Korean troops had killed the civilians during an operation in Phuyen Province and buried the bodies in three graves.

A South Korean military spokesman said ROK and South Vietnamese military officials had probed the alleged incident and found it to be "not true." Saigon siad it had no information on the allegation.

More slayings near Mylai alleged. The Daily Oklahoman, an Oklahoma City newspaper, disclosed Sept. 27 that the Army was investigating allegations that another of its infantry units committed war crimes in May 1967 in the same area as the 1968 massacre at Mylai.

The Army confirmed the existence of such an inquiry the same day.

According to the newspaper, former members of the company involved were reported to have said that the number of executed civilians and prisoners ranged from 80 to "the hundreds." Army investigators were also said to be looking into charges that villages and crops were burned and dead bodies mutilated.

The newspaper identified the unit as Company C, 2nd Battalion, 35th Infantry, 3rd Brigade of the 25th Infantry Division. According to the Oklahoman, more than 100 witnesses, some former members of Company C, had been questioned.

The Oklahoman said Company C took part in a search and destroy operation between May 18 and May 23, 1967, when the alleged atrocities were said to have taken place.

An Army public affairs officer, Lt. Col. Leonard F. B. Reed, said Sept. 27 that an internal Army investigation into allegations against Capt. James W. Lanning in connection with the alleged 1967 crimes was completed in August and forwarded to Lanning's commanding officer at Ft. Bragg, N.C. Lanning was commander of Company C at the time of the alleged incidents.

Kotouc ties ouster to Mylai. Capt. Eugene M. Kotouc, who was exonerated in 1971 on charges stemming from the Mylai massacre, charged Oct. 10 that the Army was trying to dismiss him as part of a program to discharge all those connected with the incident.

Kotouc had been the intelligence officer of the task force that swept through Mylai in March 1968, killing Vietnamese men, women and children. He was charged with murder and maiming in connection with the raid but was acquitted by a court-martial panel.

According to an Associated Press report, the Army had said it was seeking Kotouc's dismissal because of his below-par performance.

Calley verdict upheld. The Army Court of Review Feb. 16, 1973 upheld the conviction and sentence of 1st Lt. William L. Calley Jr. for his part in the 1968 Mylai massacre. Calley had been found guilty March 29, 1971, of the premeditated murder of "not less than 22 Vietnamese" and of assault with intent to murder a Vietnamese child. He was sentenced to life in prison, which was later reduced to 20 years at hard labor.

In upholding the sentence, which also included dismissal from the Army and forfeiture of all pay and allowances, the court said the prison term "is not too severe a consequence of his choosing to commit mass murder." The court rejected Calley's contention that he was simply following orders and did not mean to commit murder. It found "despite the absence of any combat in the area [Mylai], Lieutenant Calley caused villagers to be herded together and killed."

Also rejected were appeals made on technical grounds: that Calley was not subject to military jurisdiction; that the court martial was improperly constituted, unlawfully controlled by military superiors and influenced by pretrial publicity; and that his case was prejudiced by the refusal of a House armed services subcommittee to release testimony it had received in executive session.

Calley could appeal his case to both the civilian constituted Court of Military Appeals and the Supreme Court. The White House had said April 29, 1971 it would not review the case until Calley had completed the appellate process or until he accepted the decision handed down by one of the appeals courts.

Unauthorized Bombing Reports

U.S. air chief removed. The commander of the U.S. 7th Air Force in Vietnam, Gen. John D. Lavelle, 55, was dismissed from his post "because of irregularities in the conduct of his responsibilities," the Defense Department in Washington disclosed May 16, 1972. Lavelle had been recalled to the U.S. in March and retired April 7 with a

disability pension. He was replaced as 7th Air Force commander by Gen. John Vogt.

Lavelle was said to have been involved in a controversy with Gen. John D. Ryan, Air Force chief of staff, over the tactics of his pilots. At the time, a Defense Department spokesman citing conflicting reports in the case, had said: "Some said that his pilots flew too low and took too many risks. Others said that they flew too high and did not take enough."

Defense Secretary Melvin R. Laird had confirmed earlier in May that Lavelle "had been relieved of his command responsibility because the chief of staff of the Air Force had lost confidence" in his leadership.

Dismissal of Air Force chief probed. Gen. John D. Lavelle, former commander of U.S. Air Force units in Vietnam, acknowledged June 12 that he had been relieved of his post in March and later demoted after ordering repeated and unauthorized bombing strikes of military targets in North Vietnam.

Testifying before an investigating subcommittee of the House Armed Services Committee, Lavelle said that "in certain instances I made interpretations that were probably beyond the literal intention of the rules."

Lavelle said he had ordered his planes to make "in the neighborhood" of 20 unauthorized raids on military targets in North Vietnam and had reported them to command headquarters as "protective-reaction" missions.

(In Air Force parlance, protective-reaction described either offensive or defensive actions taken by U.S. pilots when they were fired upon or pinpointed by enemy radar controlling surface-to-air missiles.)

Lavelle said he had taken full responsibility for the false bombing reports. "I'm the commander and the buck stops here," Lavelle told the subcommittee.

Lavelle had been ordered to return to the U.S. and retire in March. In May, the White House nominated him for retirement at the three-star rank of lieutenant general, making him the only four-star general in modern U.S. military history to be demoted upon retirement.

Lavelle and the officer who relieved him of his command, Air Force Chief of Staff Gen. John D. Ryan, spent more than four hours testifying before the subcommittee June 12.

Almost all of the final two hours of testimony took place behind closed doors. According to one report, part of that secret session sought to establish what was known about the unauthorized raids at the highest American command in Saigon, the Military Assistance Command, Vietnam, headed by Gen. Creighton W. Abrams.

Whether Abrams himself knew about the raids was also discussed at the open-door morning session.

Lavelle said: "I think Gen. Abrams knew what I was doing. But I'm positive that Gen. Abrams had no idea what the reporting requirements were. He never worried about or sat down and debated on rules of engagement before we did it."

The raids, Lavelle said, took place between November 1971 and March 1972. He said the targets pinpointed for the strikes included "airfields, radar sites, missile sites, missiles on transporters, equipment with the missiles and heavy guns." He added that the strikes were "very successful."

Lavelle said that most of the targets were in an area 11–15 miles north of the demilitarized zone between North and South Vietnam. He said he issued the unauthorized bombing orders after failing to get permission from officers higher up in the command to attack the sites.

In his testimony, Ryan disclosed that a letter from an Air Force sergeant had led to Lavelle's dismissal. Ryan said the letter showed that "some missions had not been flown in accordance with the rules of engagement and there were irregularities in the operational reports."

Ryan told the subcommittee that an official Air Force investigation had concluded that at least 28 unauthorized missions involving 147 aircraft had been sent out on Lavelle's orders.

When Lavelle returned to Washington, he was offered the opportunity to remain in the Air Force as a two-star general. When he demurred, he was retired. In April, an official Air Force announcement said Lavelle had retired "for personal and health reasons."

Ryan said no disciplinary action had been taken against either the pilots involved in the raids or their officers for the falsification of the records.

Reports said to be falsified—The unidentified sergeant whose letter led to Lavelle's dismissal charged in the same letter that one American photo-reconnaissance team had been ordered to falsify classified documents about air strikes over North Vietnam.

In the letter, released in full June 13, the sergeant said "we have been reporting that our planes have received hostile reactions whether they have or not." He added: "We have also been falsifying targets struck and bomb damage assessments."

The letter was released by Sen. Harold E. Hughes (D, Iowa), who said the sergeant was from his state.

The sergeant wrote that "authorization for this falsification of classified documents comes from secure telephone communications from the Deputy of Operations, 7th Air Force." (Air Force officials identified that officer as Maj. Gen. Alton D. Slay, who was still on duty with the 7th Air Force in Vietnam.)

In his letter, the sergeant described himself as an intelligence specialist for a reconnaissance wing stationed at the Udorn Air Force base in Thailand. He told Hughes that "I do not know where the original authorization comes from—and this is my major concern," He added: "I am writing this letter to inform you of what is happening and to find out if this falsification of documents is legal and proper."

Officer files Lavelle charges. An Air Force lieutenant swore out court martial charges against Gen. John D. Lavelle in Washington June 21, and said he would ask Defense Secretary Melvin Laird to investigate "the propriety of the conduct" of Lavelle's superiors during the general's unauthorized raids against North Vietnam.

1st. Lt. Delbert R. Terrill Jr. said he had acted because no fellow or superior officer had done so, and "any oath of allegiance requires that I at least speak out." He said military discipline could not be maintained if "commanders are relieved and retired while others for like offenses are court-martialed and given dishonorable discharges."

Terrill charged that Lavelle willfully disobeyed a lawful order and falsified official documents, and he demanded that Air Force Secretary Robert C. Seamans Jr. initiate a formal probe. The Uniform Code of Military Justice required that all charges be followed by at least an informal inquiry. If found guilty, Lavelle could face criminal penalties of up to six years in jail and immediate discharge from the Air Force.

Terrill asked Laird to set up a court of inquiry to examine how Lavelle's alleged misconduct was handled by Gen. John D. Ryan, Air Force chief of staff, Gen. Creighton Abrams, then head of U.S. forces in Vietnam, Adm. John S. McCain, Pacific commander, and Adm. Thomas H. Moorer, chairman of the Joint Chiefs of Staff.

Terrill, who had been a member of the Concerned Officers Movement, submitted his resignation from the Air Force effective in August because of unfavorable reaction among fellow officers, but said he would have preferred to remain in the service.

Sens. Harold Hughes (D, Iowa) and Stuart Symington (D, Mo.) of the Armed Services Committee asked June 21 that the committee conduct a complete investigation of the incident before approving Lavelle's pending retirement. Hughes said "the violations in question are far too serious and far-reaching in their implications to be adequately handled by disciplining one violator when a number were involved."

U.S. tightens air war control—The U.S. command in Saigon announced June 26 that it had imposed stricter controls over the air war in Indochina. A command spokesman, however, denied that the action had any connection with the case of Gen. John D. Lavelle, who had been dismissed for ordering unauthorized raids on North Vietnam.

According to the U.S. spokesman, the new policy reflected a shift from the American ground combat role to the air war. The reorganizational move involved incorporation of the operations and intelligence components of the 7th Air Force at the Tansonnhut air base outside Saigon into the Saigon headquarters of the U.S. Military Assistance Command, Vietnam (MACV). The 7th Air Force was to continue to operate as a separate entity.

Senate panel probes Lavelle case. The Senate Armed Services Committee opened a full-scale investigation Sept. 11 to determine if others shared the responsibility with Lt. Gen. John D. Lavelle for a series of unauthorized air sorties against North Vietnam in late 1971 and early 1972.

Lavelle was relieved as commander of the 7th Air Force in March and later demoted for sending his planes out on those raids without authorization. The raids violated the Air Force's rules of engagement in effect at the time.

The most important question facing the committee was whether any of Lavelle's superior officers knew about the unauthorized bombing. When the first round of the hearings were concluded Sept. 18, the committee was no closer to unraveling the case.

The case became further complicated when Lavelle testified that he had kept some of his superior officers—among them Gen. Creighton W. Abrams—informed of what he was doing.

Abrams, who was awaiting Senate approval as Army chief of staff, was commander of U.S. forces in Vietnam at the time of the unauthorized raids. (Consideration of Abrams' nomination was delayed by the committee pending the outcome of the hearings.)

The question of others involved in the raids arose even before the hearings began.

Sgt. Lonnie D. Franks, the Air Force sergeant who first reported the bombing, said Sept. 6 that more than 200 men were involved in falsely reporting the raids. In an interview with Seymour Hersh of the New York Times, Franks said pilots and officers at the Udorn Air Base in Thailand faked classified after-action reports to cover up the unauthorized missions before routinely sending the reports on to higher headquarters.

The Air Force had maintained that Lavelle "alone was responsible" for the raids, which took place between November 1971 and March 1972.

Franks said "everybody knew we were falsifying these reports. Everybody was doing it. I kept on saying 'Why' and they said, 'That's the way we do it.'"

Franks later repeated his contention in testimony before the committee. [See below]

The hearings day by day:

Sept. 11—Lavelle, who was the lead-off witness, testified behind closed doors that he had "committed no wrong" in connection with the raids. His testimony conflicted with his testimony in June before a House panel in which he acknowledged responsibility for the unauthorized air strikes.

But in his Senate testimony, Lavelle changed that view. Committee Chairman John C. Stennis (D, Miss.) said that under Lavelle's "interpretation of what his authorization was, he considered that he was authorized" to order the raids. Stennis said of Lavelle: "In his view he had committed no wrongs, either as to the mission or those reports."

• The reports were the after-action summaries, which Lavelle allegedly ordered his subordinates to falsify.

Sept. 12—Lavelle reportedly testified that he had received permission from Abrams and Adm. Thomas H. Moorer, chairman of the Joint Chiefs of Staff, for a number of the bombing raids for which he was later relieved of his command. Lavelle said the strikes involved attacks on North Vietnamese air fields in November 1971—five months before President Nixon ordered the resumption of bombing over North Vietnam.

At one point during his four hours of testimony, Lavelle reportedly said he received permission for the air field attacks at a meeting in Saigon with Abrams and Moorer.

Sept. 13—Abrams denied Lavelle's allegations during his appearance before the committee in a closed-door session. Abrams reportedly told the panel that he did not know that Lavelle's raids were unauthorized nor did he know

that false after-action reports were covering up the nature of the missions.

Following Abrams' appearance, Stennis told newsmen that "a conflict" between the testimony of Abrams and Lavelle had developed "over the strikes that were made, the extent to which they were planned and whether they came within the rules."

Stennis refused to specify over which points the conflict had arose.

But Sen. Peter H. Dominick (R, Colo.) quoted Abrams as having said that he had never been told that the raids were unauthorized. Dominick said Abrams testified "that, of course, he knew of the raids but did not know they were being conducted outside the rules of engagement."

Sept. 14—Franks, who also testified in a closed-door session, reportedly said that more than 200 pilots and officers of the 7th Air Force at the Udorn Air Base were involved in falsifying the air reports following the controversial raids.

After Frank's testimony, Sen. Harold E. Hughes (D, Iowa) said "the evidence has proven beyond a doubt that there was knowledge from top to bottom" in the 7th Air Force about the fake reports. Hughes, who had first urged the committee to launch its investigation, said Franks' testimony demonstrated that there was "an entire breakdown in the command structure of the 7th Air Force."

Sept. 15—The committee made public a censored transcript of Lavelle's testimony in which he said he was criticized by superior officers not for a violation of Air Force rules but because his planes missed their targets. The transcript also showed that Lavelle had said he had received authority from Abrams and Moorer for at least a few of the raids.

Sept. 18—Gen. John D. Ryan, the Air Force chief of staff, defended his decision to punish Lavelle for the unauthorized raids. Ryan had removed Lavelle in March from his post as commander of the 7th Air Force and later demoted him because of the raids.

At the same time, Ryan told the panel that unauthorized bombing against North Vietnam could happen again without the highest-ranking officers knowing about it. He said he "couldn't guarantee" that such incidents "wouldn't happen again."

Navy role in Lavelle raids probed. The Senate Armed Services Committee Sept. 29 ended its three-week inquiry into the unauthorized bombing of North Vietnam by the Air Force after first looking into allegations that the Navy had also violated the rules of engagement set down by Washington.

In the first weeks of the probe, the committee had sought to determine if others had shared the responsibility with Lt. Gen. John D. Lavelle for a series of unauthorized raids against North Vietnam in late 1971 and early 1972.

The investigation was widened Sept. 27 to include the Navy by Sen. John C. Stennis (D, Miss.), the committee chairman. Stennis said he had "received direct allegations of violations of the rules by the Navy" in a letter from a former Navy pilot who saw duty in Southeast Asia from October 1971 to July 1972. The ex-pilot was identified as William Gregg Groepper, whose four-year tour of duty expired in September.

Groepper and Lt. Charles William Moore Jr., a shipmate of Groepper's aboard the aircraft carrier Constellation, appeared before the committee Sept. 28, giving conflicting testimony on whether the Navy had violated the rules of the air war.

Groepper said the pilots aboard the Constellation had been ordered to bomb targets in North Vietnam regardless of whether they were fired upon first. Such action would have violated the rules of engagement in effect at the time.

According to committee members, Groepper said he and the other Constellation pilots were given closed-circuit television briefings before they were sent out on escort duty to protect reconnaissance planes in case of enemy attack.

Groepper was reported to have told the committee that on at least three occasions the pilots were instructed to drop their bombs even if they did not draw fire from the ground.

Moore, while acknowledging the television briefings, said the pilots were told not to drop their bombs over North Vietnam if they were not fired upon.

Moore told the senators he had conferred with Pentagon officials regarding his testimony before he went before the committee.

Adm. Thomas H. Moorer, chairman of the Joint Chiefs of Staff, appeared before the committee Sept. 29 to assert that the Navy had not violated the rules of engagement in the air war against North Vietnam.

Also disputing Groepper's testimony were Adm. John S. McCain, former commander in chief in the Pacific, and Cmdr. John A. Willer, Groepper's squadron commander.

Following his testimony, Moorer, speaking to newsmen, said that the rules of the air war were "strictly obeyed" by the Navy. He said that the decision to send along additional carrier-based fighter-bombers with the reconnaissance planes was prompted by increased ground-to-air fire against the scout planes by North Vietnamese gunners.

The testimony of Moorer, McCain and Willer marked the end of the committee's investigation into the Lavelle case. After the final witness was heard, Stennis and most of the other committee members seemed to agree that there had been no violation of civilian authority by either the Air Force or the Navy. Stennis told newsmen that "the facts do not show any drastic challenge or drastic violation of civilian authority."

Other developments—Defense Secretary Melvin Laird said Sept. 24 that the Air Force had "under current review" possible court-martial charges against Lavelle in connection with the unauthorized raids. But Defense Department officials later said that Laird had simply stated the present legal situation as a result of formal charges of "criminal misconduct" filed against him by a junior Air Force officer.

Testimony released Sept. 25 by the Senate Armed Services Committee from the earlier round of hearings disclosed that Gen. John D. Ryan, the Air Force chief of staff, had singled out Lavelle as the sole instigator of the unauthorized air strikes. Ryan also testified that removal of Lavelle from command of the 7th Air Force was adequate punishment.

Ryan added that he did not think a court-martial would be appropriate and said he thought no one else should be punished.

Additional testimony released Sept. 26 showed that Ryan was at odds with Laird over the latter's decision to withhold from key members of Congress the reason behind Lavelle's removal. Public disclosure of the action against Lavelle for the unauthorized raids was not made until June.

Senate confirms Abrams. After weeks of delay, the Senate Oct. 12 approved, 84-2, the nomination of Gen. Creighton W. Abrams as Army chief of staff. Consideration of Abrams' nomination had been sidetracked while Senate hearings were under way into unauthorized bombing raids against North Vietnam.

Abrams had testified during those hearings that he did not know a series of bombing strikes ordered by Lt. Gen. John D. Lavelle were unauthorized. Lavelle, who was stripped of his command for the raids, had charged otherwise.

Abrams, 58, was commander in chief of all U.S. forces in Vietnam during the time of the Lavelle raids.

The confirmation vote followed six hours of debate Oct. 11. Only Sens. William Proxmire (D, Wis.) and Frank Church (D, Idaho) opposed the nomination.

Before the confirmation vote, Sen. Harold Hughes (D, Iowa), speaking at a news conference, threatened to delay future Senate action on the promotion of senior military offices unless the Pentagon improved its command and control procedures. Hughes warned that "unless there is some action, there will be pressure from the Congress for more hearings into the unauthorized bombings.

He also called on the Air Force and Navy to conduct a court of inquiry into the air war "with the authority to recommend a court martial, if the evidence warrants it."

In an earlier development, the Senate Armed Services Committee voted Oct. 6 to strip Lavelle of another star recommended for him by the Air Force.

By a 12-2 vote, the committee proposed that Lavelle be retired at the permanent rank of a two-star major general and not that of a lieutenant general, three-star rank. As commander of the 7th Air Force Lavelle had been a four-star general. He was reduced in rank for the unauthorized bombings.

The committee's vote was largely symbolic, since Lavelle would continue to receive a full general's retirement pay of $27,000 a year, all but $2,900 of which was tax free. Retirement pay for officers was figured according to rank during their last active service.

Joint chiefs, Navy tied to raids— Although the Armed Services Committee ended its investigation into the Lavelle affair with the general conclusion that the responsibility for the unauthorized raids lay solely with Lavelle, new developments Oct. 5-9 cast doubt on that judgment.

Lavelle himself prompted much of the new speculation. In a private letter dated Sept. 26, but not made public until Oct. 5, Lavelle wrote to the committee that others were involved in the raids. He said representatives of his 7th Air Force were told in a December 1971 meeting that the Joint Chiefs of Staff "would not question" enemy targets hit during protective-reaction missions. Excerpts of Lavelle's letter were published by the New York Times Oct. 5.

Lavelle said his officers were told that "in the event of adverse publicity" from the raids, "we could expect full backing" from the joint chiefs.

(Adm. Thomas H. Moorer, chairman of the joint chiefs, Gen. John D. Ryan, Air Force chief of staff, and Gen. Abrams had already denied earlier allegations that they had known of and at least expressed tacit approval of the unauthorized missions.)

Conceding that he had not been specifically instructed to plan bombing strikes in the guise of protective-reaction missions, Lavelle maintained that he began doing so because of what he took to be private encouragement from his superiors.

In another part of his letter, Lavelle again tied higher authorities to the unauthorized raids. "It seemed clear to me," he wrote, "that higher authorities had recommended, encouraged and commended an extremely liberal policy, well beyond the literal language of the rules of engagement."

In another development, five Navy pilots corroborated Oct. 9 much of the testimony of another pilot in their squadron who said they had made bombing strikes which violated the air war rules against North Vietnam.

The five pilots said their squadron had made at least three planned raids against a North Vietnamese airfield beginning Dec. 13, 1971, all of which they said were carried out under the guise of "protective reaction."

The pilots gave their accounts of the raids in separate telephone interviews with Seymour Hersh of the Times. They were essentially the same details as those given to the committee Sept. 28 by William G. Groepper, a former Navy lieutenant who flew in the same squadron.

The five said the three planned raids were directed against the Quanglang airfield, 180 miles north of the demilitarized zone. As a forward base for North Vietnamese MiG fighters, the airfield was a frequent target for sorties by U.S. pilots.

All five pilots said that on at least one raid against Quanglang, the reconnaissance plane, which was ostensibly deployed to take pictures of the airfield, actually flew behind the bombers and took photographs after the strike.

One of the pilots, James D. Hyberg, said the reconnaissance plane "was more or less a secondary thing. They just run it through to make it look good. Our intention was to get rid of the bombs whether or not we were fired upon."

Command procedures revised. Faced with growing Congressional concern over the unauthorized bombing of North Vietnam, Defense Secretary Melvin Laird Oct. 19 described new steps he said were aimed at "further strengthening" civilian control over the military.

Laird's announcement followed threats of Senate action unless the Pentagon improved its command and control procedures. There were also direct Senate inquiries to Laird to explain how he intended to prevent future unauthorized bombing raids.

In speaking to newsmen, however, Laird insisted that the bombing ordered by Maj. Gen. John D. Lavelle without authorization did not represent a breakdown in civilian control of the military. But Laird said the new steps should prevent a recurrence of unauthorized strikes and false post-mission reporting about the circumstances of the strikes.

Among the new steps was creation of a new group of inspectors general in unified command headquarters to conduct regular checks of procedures to insure that orders from Washington were scrupulously carried out. The new panel was to report to Laird through the Joint Chiefs of Staff.

In another change, the Army, Navy, Air Force and Marine inspectors general would now report not only to their respective military chiefs but to their civilian service secretaries as well.

Under the new setup, the defense secretary also had authority to direct the work of the newly established Defense Investigative Service, an agency which centralized the investigative units of each of the armed services. In the past, the Investigative Service worked under the orders of the chiefs of the individual services.

Another step would direct a second deputy secretary of defense—a post just approved by Congress—to concentrate on maintaining operational control of forces in the field.

Lavelle charges dropped—The Air Force Oct. 24 dismissed charges filed by 1st Lt. Delbert R. Terrill Jr. against Maj. Gen. John D. Lavelle, whose planes conducted unauthorized bombing missions against North Vietnam.

The Air Force said it had made a "thorough investigation of all facts and material" and dropped the charges because the "interests of discipline" had already been served.

Air Force Secretary Robert Seamans Jr. noted that Lavelle had been relieved of his command and that the action "has served the interests of discipline by its punitive impact and by placing commanders on notice that the Air Force does not and will not condone the manner in which General Lavelle discharged his duties."

New Lavelle charges dismissed. The Air Force Nov. 21 dismissed new court-martial charges against Maj. Gen. John D. Lavelle and 23 other officers accused of carrying out unauthorized bombing raids against North Vietnam. The Air Force said "no new information was presented which would warrant further action."

The charges had been filed Nov. 3 by Sgt. Lonnie Franks, the officer who first reported the unauthorized bombing strikes. Franks had filed the charges after the Air Force ruled out further disciplinary action against Lavelle.

House committee backs Lavelle. The House Armed Services Investigating Subcommittee report released Dec. 18 said the U.S. bombing strikes over North Vietnam authorized in 1971 and 1972 by Gen. John D. Lavelle "were not only proper but essential," although the committee refrained from deciding whether the raids had been legal.

Other Military Scandals

Ex-general and aide convicted. Former Brig. Gen. Earl F. Cole and his secretary, Catherine Jean Baker, were each convicted Jan. 16 of seven counts of making false statements to the Army.

The government prosecution charged Cole had authorized trips by Mrs. Baker from Vietnam to the U.S. for the purpose of visiting friends and relatives rather than tracing missing soldiers in hospitals and missing supply shipments as she and Cole had stated. Other charges said that Cole and Baker collaborated to collect overtime when she was actually on leave.

The one charge not connected with trips said Mrs. Baker had falsely filed claims for rent allowances when she lived in government-furnished quarters.

Each count carried a maximum sentence of five years in jail and a $10,000 fine.

USO probe expanding. The government's month-old investigation into reports of alleged fraud in the worldwide operations of the United Service Organizations (USO) was given new leads April 18–19 as the USO president and a congressman gave unofficial accounts of wrongdoing by USO personnel in South Vietnam.

Retired Gen. Francis L. Sampson, president of the USO, said April 18 that "preliminary findings" of an internal investigation indicated that four or five former USO employes had been involved in alleged financial irregularities. The USO probe, under way since March, was independent of the government's investigation conducted by the Defense Department.

According to Sampson, the "alleged irregularities have to do principally with certain individuals allegedly using certain USO clubs in Vietnam as a conduit for converting black market money into U.S. dollars."

But Sampson denied that U.S. soldiers had been defrauded by USO personnel. He asserted that no funds had been "misappropriated or used improperly" and that "no serviceman was in any way damaged, defrauded or denied the services he could expect from USO by the alleged activities."

Alleged black market activites by USO personnel also came under Congressional scrutiny April 19 when Rep. Les Aspin (D, Wis.) made public the text of purported interviews with two former USO employes giving details of alleged fraud and financial wrongdoing.

Aspin read the text of interviews into the Congressional Record. He refused to identify the informants other than as "two women formerly employed by USO."

Among them were charges involving the alleged diversion of cigarettes to the black market, the theft and black market sales of USO equipment and reports that alleged black market activity was common knowledge among USO personnel.

USO acknowledges corruption. The United Service Organizations (USO) said June 15 that an internal investigation had turned up evidence substantiating charges of corruption by USO personnel in South Vietnam.

But USO officials said the inquiry failed to show that the corruption was as widespread as indicated in a report by the U.S. military command in Saigon in March. In that report, USO personnel were accused of dealing in narcotics and other dangerous drugs.

According to USO officials, the organization's report failed to prove that charge. It did find, however, evidence of currency manipulations, black-market activities, mail order fraud and other corrupt activities.

Copies of the USO's report were sent to the Justice Department, Internal Revenue Service and appropriate Congressional committees for possible legal action.

U.S. rain-making charged. U.S. Sen. Claiborne Pell (D, R.I.) said June 25 that he believed U.S. armed forces had used rain-making technology for military purposes in Indochina, causing torrential downpours that had killed several thousand persons. The New York Times confirmed July 3 that the U.S. had been secretly using this cloud-seeding method since 1963 over North and South Vietnam and Laos.

Pell, in an interview published in the Providence Journal, said "I strongly believe clouds have been seeded in Southeast Asia for military reasons. There is little doubt in my mind, but I cannot go any further than that."

Pell, a member of the Senate Foreign Relations Committee, had introduced a draft of a treaty barring weather and climate-modification activities as weapons of war. He said the Defense Department was non-committal when questioned about these alleged activities.

The Times report, written by Seymour M. Hersh, said the purpose of the rain-making, according to civilian and military officials interviewed, was to neutralize the radar used for the operation of North Vietnamese surface-to-air missiles, to provide rain and cloud cover for South Vietnamese commando operations in North Vietnam, to frustrate North Vietnamese ground attacks in South Vietnam and to divert North Vietnamese men and material from military operations to clear muddied roads and lines of communications.

The Times report quoted a former Central Intelligence Agency agent as saying that the cloud-seeding operation was first used in South Vietnam in August 1963 to dispel anti-government

Buddhist demonstrators. A similar cloud-seeding was carried out by CIA aircraft in Saigon at least once during the summer of 1964, the agent said.

Hersh said the CIA had spread its rain-making activities over the Ho Chi Minh Trail in Laos in the middle 1960s, and quoted a Nixon Administration official as saying that the practice was extended to North Vietnam in late 1968 or early 1969 to impede antiaircraft missiles' ability to hit U.S. jets then bombing the southern panhandle of the country. More than half the cloud-seeding operations in 1969–70 took place in South Vietnam, another government official was reported as saying.

Starting in 1967 there was some opposition in the State Department to the use of artificial rainfall for military purposes on the ground that it could endanger the environment, the report said. But advocates of the method apparently had prevailed.

Ex-general indicted. Former Brig. Gen. Earl F. Cole, a key figure in the 1971 Senate probe of Army service clubs, was indicted with his former secretary Oct. 12 in Alexandria, Va. on charges of defrauding the government of $7,500.

Cole and Catherine Jean Baker were each charged with one count of conspiring to defraud the government by making false statements and claims and 15 counts alleging the actual making of false statements and claims. Each count carried a maximum penalty of five years in prison and a $10,000 fine.

The charges against Cole and Miss Baker did not, however, specifically relate to the service club case. The indictment charged them with wrongdoing involving illegal statements over transfers, overtime pay and business expenses.

Racial Problems

46 hurt in carrier brawl. Forty-six black and white crewmen were injured Oct. 12–13 in racial brawls involving more than 100 men aboard the aircraft carrier Kitty Hawk off North Vietnam. Some 5,000 men were aboard the ship at the time of the fighting.

The Navy said Oct. 17 that the clash began as a fight between black and white crewmen in the ship's mess deck and then spread to other parts of the Kitty Hawk. A Navy spokesman said three men seriously injured in the fighting had been evacuated to a base hospital in the Philippines.

The Navy announced Oct. 22 that 25 black crewmen aboard the ship had been charged with assault and rioting. The men were to face courts-martial on the Kitty Hawk.

White acquitted in Kitty Hawk riot. The only white sailor to go on trial for the Oct. 12–13, 1972 riots aboard the aircraft carrier Kitty Hawk was acquitted Feb. 12, 1973 of the charge of assault.

Fifteen black crewman had been tried in connection with the riot. Nine were convicted.

Navy purges undesirables—The Navy confirmed Feb. 2 that it had discharged nearly 3,000 enlisted men whom it considered a "burden to the command." Adm. Elmo R. Zumwalt Jr., chief of naval operations, had issued the order Dec. 26, 1972. The directive provided for voluntary-for-mutual-benefit-discharges for sailors with at least one year of service "whose records reflect marginal performance or substandard conduct." Of the number discharged, about 14% were black.

At the same time the Navy said it was tightening its standards of recruitment, with a new emphasis on education and character qualifications. According to the New York Times Feb. 2, one of every four enlistees was at level 4 of the Armed Forced Qualifications Tests during 1972, indicating a sixth grade reading level. The 1971 figure was 14%. One of every six 1972 recruits had a police record.

The Navy said the discharges would be mostly under honorable conditions, with no stigma attached. The Times said, however, that the discharges would carry code numbers, which knowledgable employers could understand to mean "undesirable" or "unsuitable" for reenlistment."

A Navy spokesman said: "There are too many recruits—not only blacks but members of other minorities and under-privileged whites as well—who cannot cope with the technical training in the skills needed to operate our sophisticated weapons and navigational systems. As a result they are forced into menial jobs, in the laundries, in mess galleys and in deck crews. Their work performance is poor and their opportunities for advancement are very limited. This frequently produces festering resentment which may erupt violently. The blame is not the Navy's, it goes deeper into the American social system."

Drug Use by Servicemen

Heroin trend reversed. The Defense Department's chief medical officer said Jan. 8, 1972 that the Army had reversed what had been a rising rate of heroin use among servicemen.

Dr. Richard S. Wilbur, assistant secretary of defense for health, said the number of servicemen who were hard-core drug addicts had fallen from a peak of 600 in June and July of 1971 to slightly more than 200 in October. Wilbur said the downward trend was continuing.

Wilbur also said that 2.5% of the GIs from Vietnam who returned to the U.S. in December were using drugs, compared with 4.2% of those tested in August shortly after the tests had begun.

Wilbur attributed the downward trend to the military's mandatory drug tests, the success of the rehabilitation programs for drug users and the education program alerting soldiers about the dangers of hard drugs.

Most drug use in Vietnam. The Pentagon made available Jan. 16 the results of its latest tests for drug use by servicemen which indicated that the drug problem was largely confined to Vietnam and soldiers stationed there.

Some of the test results had been published previously, but the Jan. 16 figures further detailed the extent of drug use for each branch of the armed forces in each major geographic area.

The urinalysis tests turned up men on hard drugs, such as heroin, amphetamines and barbiturates. The Pentagon had begun the tests in Vietnam in June 1971 and later extended them to include U.S. servicemen at bases all over the world.

The new figures showed that worldwide .2% of Marines tested were on drugs, .3% in the Navy and .5% of the Air Force. The urinalyses showed that 2.8% of those Army men tested were drug users.

The geographic breakdown showed that 4.1% of the soldiers in Vietnam were on drugs. In other Pacific area countries, 1.6% of those tested were found to be on drugs, .9% in Europe and 1.3% in other areas overseas.

For the U.S., the urinalysis tests were given to men entering and leaving the Army. Of 64,000 soldiers tested just after entering the Army, 1.4% were detected to be drug users. The tests showed that 2.1% of the 63,000 others who were leaving the Army were drug users.

Appendix

VIETNAM AGREEMENT AND PROTOCOLS

Texts of the Vietnam cease-fire agreement initialed in Paris Jan. 23 by Henry A. Kissinger of the U.S. and Le Duc Tho of the Democratic Republic of Vietnam (North Vietnam), and of the four accompanying protocols detailing means of carrying it out. The agreement and three of the protocols were drafted in two versions. The "four-party" versions were signed the morning of Jan. 27. Because the Republic of Vietnam (South Vietnam) was unwilling to imply recognition of the Viet Cong's Provisional Revolutionary Government, "two-party" versions mentioning that government were signed only by the U.S. and North Vietnam the afternoon of Jan. 27.

The Cease-Fire Agreement

Agreement on Ending the War and Restoring Peace in Vietnam

The parties participating in the Paris conference on Vietnam,

With a view to ending the war and restoring peace in Vietnam on the basis of respect for the Vietnamese people's fundamental national rights and the South Vietnamese people's right to self-determination, and to contributing to the consolidation of peace in Asia and the world,

Have agreed on the following provisions and undertake to respect and to implement them:

CHAPTER I

The Vietnamese People's Fundamental National Rights

Article 1

The United States and all other countries respect the independence, sovereignty, unity and territorial integrity of Vietnam as recognized by the 1954 Geneva Agreements on Vietnam.

CHAPTER II

Cessation of Hostilities, Withdrawal of Troops

Article 2

A cease-fire shall be observed throughout South Vietnam as of 2400 hours G.M.T., on Jan. 27, 1973.

At the same hour, the United States will stop all its military activities against the territory of the Democratic Republic of Vietnam by ground, air and naval forces, wherever they may be based, and end the mining of the territorial waters, ports, harbors and waterways of the Democratic Republic of Vietnam. The United States will remove, permanently deactivate or destroy all the mines in the territorial waters, ports, harbors and waterways of North Vietnam as soon as this agreement goes into effect.

The complete cessation of hostilities mentioned in this article shall be durable and without limit of time.

Article 3

The parties undertake to maintain the cease-fire and to insure a lasting and stable peace.

As soon as the cease-fire goes into effect:

(a) The United States forces and those of the other foreign countries allied with the United States and the Republic of Vietnam shall remain in place pending the implementation of the plan of troop withdrawal. The

Four-Party Joint Military Commission described in Article 16 shall determine the modalities.

(b) The armed forces of the two South Vietnamese parties shall remain in place. The Two-Party Joint Military Commission described in Article 17 shall determine the areas controlled by each party and the modalities of stationing.

(c) The regular forces of all services and arms and the irregular forces of the parties in South Vietnam shall stop all offensive activities against each other and shall strictly abide by the following stipulations:

■ All acts of force on the ground, in the air and on the sea shall be prohibited.

■ All hostile acts, terrorism and reprisals by both sides will be banned.

Article 4

The United States will not continue its military involvement or intervene in the internal affairs of South Vietnam.

Article 5

Within 60 days of the signing of this agreement, there will be a total withdrawal from South Vietnam of troops, military personnel, including technical military personnel and military personnel associated with the pacification program, armaments, munitions and war material of the United States and those of the other foreign countries mentioned in Article 3 (a). Advisers from the above-mentioned countries to all paramilitary organizations and the police force will also be withdrawn within the same period of time.

Article 6

The dismantlement of all military bases in South Vietnam of the United States and of the other foreign countries mentioned in Article 3 (a) shall be completed within 60 days of the signing of this agreement.

Article 7

From the enforcement of the cease fire to the formation of the government provided for in Articles 9 (b) and 14 of this agreement, the two South Vietnamese parties shall not accept the introduction of troops, military advisers and military personnel, including technical military personnel, armaments, munitions and war material into South Vietnam.

The two South Vietnamese parties shall be permitted to make periodic replacement of armaments, munitions and war material which have been destroyed, damaged, worn out or used up after the cease-fire, on the basis of piece-for-piece, of the same characteristics and properties, under the supervision of the Joint Military Commission of Control and Supervision.

CHAPTER III

The Return of Captured Military Personnel and Foreign Civilians, and Captured and Detained Vietnamese Civilian Personnel

Article 8

(a) The return of captured military personnel and foreign civilians of the parties shall be carried out simultaneously with and completed not later than the same day as the troop withdrawal mentioned in Article 5. The parties shall exchange complete lists of the above-mentioned captured military personnel and foreign civilians on the day of the signing of this agreement.

(b) The parties shall help each other to get information about those military personnel and foreign civilians of the parties missing in action, to determine the location and take care of the graves of the dead so as to facilitate the exhumation and repatriation of the remains, and to take any such other measures as may be required to get information about those still considered missing in action.

(c) The question of the return of Vietnamese civilian personnel captured and detained in South Vietnam will be resolved by the two south Vietnamese parties on the basis of the principles of Article 21 (b) of the Agreement on the Cessation of Hostilities in Vietnam of July 20, 1954. The two South Vietnamese parties will do so in a spirit of national reconciliation and concord, with a view to ending hatred and enmity, in order to ease suffering and to reunite families. The two South Vietnamese parties will do their utmost to resolve this question within 90 days after the cease-fire comes into effect.

CHAPTER IV

The Exercise of the South Vietnamese People's Right to Self-Determination

Article 9

The Government of the United States of America and the Government of the Democratic Republic of Vietnam undertake to respect the following principles for the exercise of the South Vietnamese people's right to self-determination:

(a) The South Vietnamese people's right to self-determination is sacred, inalienable and shall be respected by all countries.

(b) The South Vietnamese people shall decide themselves the political future of South Vietnam through genuinely free and democratic general elections under international supervision.

(c) Foreign countries shall not impose any political tendency or personality on the South Vietnamese people.

Article 10

The two South Vietnamese parties undertake to respect the cease-fire and maintain peace in South Vietnam, settle all matters of contention through negotiations and avoid all armed conflict.

Article 11

Immediately after the cease-fire, the two South Vietnamese parties will:

■ Achieve national reconciliation and concord, end hatred and enmity, prohibit all acts of reprisal and discrimination against individuals or organizations that have collaborated with one side or the other.

■ Insure the democratic liberties of the people: personal freedom, freedom of speech, freedom of the press, freedom of meeting, freedom of organization, freedom of political activities, freedom of belief, freedom of movement, freedom of residence, freedom of work, right to property ownership and right to free enterprise.

Article 12

(a) Immediately after the cease-fire, the two South Vietnamese parties shall hold consultations in a spirit of national reconciliation and concord, mutual respect and mutual nonelimination to set up a National Council of National Reconciliation and Concord of three equal segments. The council shall operate on the principle of unanimity. After the National Council of National Reconciliation and Concord has assumed its functions, the two South Vietnamese parties will consult about the formation of councils at lower levels. The two South Vietnamese parties shall sign an agreement on the internal matters of South Vietnam as soon as possible and do their utmost to accomplish this within 90 days after the cease-fire comes into effect, in keeping with the South Vietnamese people's aspirations for peace, independence and democracy.

(b) The National Council of National Reconciliation and Concord shall have the task of promoting the two South Vietnamese parties' implementation of this agreement, achievement of national reconciliation and concord and insurance of democratic liberties. The National Council of National Reconciliation and Concord will organize the free and democratic general elections provided for in Article 9 (b) and decide the procedures and modalities of these general elections. The institutions for which the general elections are to be held will be agreed upon through consultations between the two South Vietnamese parties. The National Council of National Reconciliaton and Concord will also decide the procedures and modalities of such local elections as the two South Vietnamese parties agree upon.

Article 13
The question of Vietnamese armed forces in South Vietnam shall be settled by the two South Vietnamese parties in a spirit of national reconciliation and concord, equality and mutual respect, without interference, in accordance with the postwar situation. Among the questions to be discussed by the two South Vietnamese parties are steps to reduce their military effectives and to demobilize the troops being reduced. The two South Vietnamese parties will accomplish this as soon as possible.

Article 14
South Vietnam will pursue a foreign policy of peace and independence. It will be prepared to establish relations with all countries irrespective of their political and social systems on the basis of mutual respect for independence and sovereignty and accept economic and technical aid from any country with no political conditions attached. The acceptance of military aid by South Vietnam in the future shall come under the authority of the government set up after the general elections in South Vietnam provided for in Article 9 (b).

CHAPTER V
The 'Reunification of Vietnam and the Relationship Between North and South Vietnam
Article 15
The reunification of Vietnam shall be carried out step by step through peaceful means on the basis of discussions and agreements between North and South Vietnam, without coercion or annexation by either party, and without foreign interference. The time for reunification will be agreed upon by North and South Vietnam.

Pending reunification:

(a) The military demarcation line between the two zones at the 17th Parallel is only provisional and not a political or territorial boundary, as provided for in paragraph 6 of the Final Declaration of the 1954 Geneva Conference.

(b) North and South Vietnam shall respect the demilitarized zone on either side of the provisional military demarcation line.

(c) North and South Vietnam shall promptly start negotiations with a view to re-establish normal relations in various fields. Among the questions to be negotiated are the modalities of civilian movement across the provisional military demarcation line.

(d) North and South Vietnam shall not join any military alliance or military bloc and shall not allow foreign powers to maintain military bases, troops, military advisers and military personnel on their respective territories, as stipulated in the 1954 Geneva Agreements on Vietnam.

CHAPTER VI
The Joint Military Commissions, The International Commission of Control and Supervision, The International Conference.
Article 16
(a) The parties participating in the Paris conference on Vietnam shall immediately designate representatives to form a Four-Party Joint Military Commission with the task of insuring joint action by the parties in implementing the following provisions of this agreement:

■ The first paragraph of Article 2, regarding the enforcement of the cease-fire throughout South Vietnam.

■ Article 3 (a), regarding the cease-fire by U.S. forces and those of the other foreign countries referred to in that article.

■ Article 3 (c), regarding the cease-fire between all parties in South Vietnam.

■ Article 5, regarding the withdrawal from South Vietnam of U.S. troops and those of the other foreign countries mentioned in Article 3 (a).

■ Article 6, regarding the dismantlement of military bases in South Vietnam of the United States and those of the other foreign countries mentioned in Article 3 (a).

■ Article 8 (a), regarding the return of captured military personnel and foreign civilians of the parties.

■ Article 8 (b), regarding the mutual assistance of the parties in getting information about those military personnel and foreign civilians of the parties missing in action.

(b) The Four-Party Joint Military Commission shall operate in accordance with the principle of consultations and unanimity. Disagreements shall be referred to the International Commission of Control and Supervision.

(c) The Four-Party Military Commission shall begin operating immediately after the signing of this agreement and end its activities in 60 days, after the completion of the withdrawal of U.S. troops and those of the other foreign countries mentioned in Article 3 (a) and the completion of the return of captured military personnel and foreign civilians of the parties.

(d) The four parties shall agree immediately on the organization, the working procedure, means of activity and expenditures of the Four-Party Joint Military Commission.

Article 17
(a) The two South Vietnamese parties shall immediately designate representatives to form a Two-Party Joint Military Commission with the task of insuring joint action by the two South Vietnamese parties in implementing the following provisions of this agreement:

■ The first paragraph of Article 2, regarding the enforcement of the cease-fire throughout South Vietnam, when the Four-Party Joint Military Commission has ended its activities.

■ Article 3 (b), regarding the cease-fire between the two South Vietnamese parties.

■ Article 3 (c) regarding the cease-fire between all parties in South Vietnam, when the Four-Party Joint Military Commission has ended its activities.

■ Article 7, regarding the prohibition of the introduction of troops into South Vietnam and all other provisions of this article.

■ Article 8 (c), regarding the question of the return of Vietnamese civilian personnel captured and detained in South Vietnam;

■ Article 13, regarding the reduction of the military effectives of the two South Vietnamese parties and the demobilization of the troops being reduced.

(b) Disagreements shall be referred to the International Commission of Control and Supervision.

(c) After the signing of this agreement, the Two-Party Joint Military Commission shall agree immediately on the measures and organization aimed at enforcing the cease-fire and preserving peace in South Vietnam.

Article 18

(a) After the signing of this Agreement, an International Commission of Control and Supervision shall be established immediately.

(b) Until the international conference provided for in Article 19 makes definitive arrangements, the International Commission of Control and Supervision will report to the four parties on matters concerning the control and supervision of the implementation of the following provisions of this agreement:

■ The first paragraph of Article 2, regarding the enforcement of the cease-fire throughout South Vietnam.

■ Article 3 (a), regarding the cease-fire by U.S. forces and those of the other foreign countries referred to in that article.

■ Article 3 (c), regarding the cease-fire between all the parties in South Vietnam.

■ Article 5, regarding the withdrawal from South Vietnam of U.S. troops and those of the other foreign countries mentioned in Article 3 (a).

■ Article 6, regarding the dismantlement of military bases in South Vietnam of the United States and those of the other foreign countries mentioned in Article 3 (a).

■ Article 8 (a), regarding the return of captured military personnel and foreign civilians of the parties.

The International Commission of Control and Supervision shall form control teams for carrying out its tasks. The four parties shall agree immediately on the location and operation of these teams. The parties will facilitate their operation.

(c) Until the international conference makes definitive arrangements, the International commission of Control and Supervision will report to the two South Vietnamese parties on matters concerning the control and supervision of the implementation of the following provisions of this agreement:

■ The first paragraph of Article 2, regarding the enforcement of the cease-fire throughout South Vietnam, when the Four-Party Joint Military commission has ended its activities.

■ Article 3 (b), regarding the cease-fire between the two South Vietnamese parties.

■ Article 3 (c), regarding the cease-fire between all parties in South Vietnam, when the Four-Party Joint Military Commission has ended its activities.

■ Article 7, regarding the prohibition of the introduction of troops into South Vietnam and all other provisions of this article.

■ Article 8 (c), regarding the question of the return of Vietnamese civilian personnel captured and detained in South Vietnam.

■ Article 9 (b), regarding the free and democratic general elections in South Vietnam.

■ Article 13, regarding the reduction of the military effectives of the two South Vietnamese parties and the demobilization of the troops being reduced.

The International Commission of Control and Supervision shall form control teams for carrying out

its tasks. The two South Vietnamese parties shall agree immediately on the location and operation of these teams. The two South Vietnamese parties will facilitate their operation.

(d) The International Commission of Control and Supervision shall be composed of representatives of four countries: Canada, Hungary, Indonesia and Poland. The chairmanship of this commission will rotate among the members for specific periods to be determined by the commission.

(e) The International Commission of Control and Supervision shall carry out its tasks in accordance with the principle of respect for the sovereignty of South Vietnam.

(f) The International Commission of Control and Supervision shall operate in accordance with the principle of consultations and unanimity.

(g) the International Commission of Control and Supervision shall begin operating when a cease-fire comes into force in Vietnam. As regards the provisions in Article 18 (b) concerning the four parties, the International Commission of Control and Supervision shall end its activities when the commission's tasks of control and supervision regarding these provisions have been fulfilled. As regards the provisions in Article 18 (c) concerning the two South Vietnamese parties, the International Commission of Control and Supervision shall end its activities on the request of the government formed after the general elections in South Vietnam provided for in Article 9 (b).

(h) The four parties shall agree immediately on the organization, means of activity and expenditures of the International Commission of Control and Supervision. The relationship between the international commission and the international conference will be agreed upon by the International Commission and the International Conference.

Article 19

The parties agree on the convening of an international conference within 30 days of the signing of this agreement to acknowledge the signed agreements; to guarantee the ending of the war, the maintenance of peace in Vietnam, the respect of the Vietnamese people's fundamental national rights and the South Vietnamese people's right to self-determination; and to contribute to and guarantee peace in Indochina.

The United States and the Democratic Republic of Vietnam, on behalf of the parties participating in the Paris conference on Vietnam, will propose to the following parties that they participate in this international conference: the People's Republic of China, the Republic of France, the Union of Soviet Socialist Republics, the United Kingdom, the four countries of the International Commission of Control and Supervision, and the Secretary General of the United Nations, together with the parties participating in the Paris conference on Vietnam.

CHAPTER VII

Regarding Cambodia and Laos
Article 20

(a) The parties participating in the Paris conference on Vietnam shall strictly respect the 1954 Geneva Agreements on Cambodia and the 1962 Geneva Agreements on Laos, which recognized the Cambodian and the Lao peoples' fundamental national rights, i.e., the independence, sovereignty, unity and territorial integrity of these countries. The parties shall respect the neutrality of Cambodia and Laos.

The parties participating in the Paris conference on Vietnam undertake to refrain from using the territory of Cambodia and the territory of Laos to encroach on the sovereignty and security of one another and of other countries.

(b) Foreign countries shall put an end to all military activities in Cambodia and Laos, totally withdraw from and refrain from reintroducing into these two countries troops, military advisers and military personnel, armaments, munitions and war material.

(c) The internal affairs of Cambodia and Laos shall be settled by the people of each of these countries without foreign interference.

(d) The problems existing between the Indochinese countries shall be settled by the Indochinese parties on the basis of respect for each other's independence, sovereignty and territorial integrity, and noninterference in each other's internal affairs.

CHAPTER VIII

The Relationship Between the United States and the Democratic Republic of Vietnam

Article 21

The United States anticipates that this agreement will usher in an era of reconciliation with the Democratic Republic of Vietnam as with all the peoples of Indochina. In pursuance of its traditional policy, the United States will contribute to healing the wounds of war and to postwar reconstruction of the Democratic Republic of Vietnam and throughout Indochina.

Article 22

The ending of the war, the restoration of peace in Vietnam and the strict implementation of this agreement will create conditions for establishing a new, equal and mutually beneficial relationship between the United States and the Democratic Republic of Vietnam on the basis of respect for each other's independence and sovereignty and noninterference in each other's internal affairs. At the same time this will insure stable peace in Vietnam and contribute to the preservation of lasting peace in Indochina and Southeast Asia.

CHAPTER IX

Other Provisions

Article 23

This agreement shall enter into force upon signature by plenipotentiary representatives of the parties participating in the Paris Conference on Vietnam. All the parties concerned shall strictly implement this agreement and its protocols.

Done in Paris this 27th day of January, 1973, in Vietnamese and English. The Vietnamese and English texts are official and equally authentic.

For the Government of the
United States of America
William P. Rogers
Secretary of State
For the Government of the
Republic of Vietnam
Tran Van Lam
Minister for Foreign Affairs

For the Government of the
Democratic Republic of Vietnam
Nguyen Duy Trinh
Minister for Foreign Affairs

For the Provisional Revolutionary
Government of the Republic of
South Vietnam
Nguyen Thi Binh
Minister for Foreign Affairs

2-Party Version

Agreement on Ending the War and Restoring Peace in Vietnam

The Government of the United States of America, with the concurrence of the Government of the Republic of Vietnam,

The Government of the Democratic Republic of Vietnam, with the concurrence of the Provisional Revolutionary Government of the Republic of South Vietnam,

With a view to ending the war and restoring peace in Vietnam on the basis of respect for the Vietnamese people's fundamental national rights and the South Vietnamese people's right to self-determination, and to contributing to the consolidation of peace in Asia and the world,

Have agreed on the following provisions and undertake to respect and to implement them:

[Test of agreement Chapters I-VIII same as above]

CHAPTER IX

Other Provisions

The Paris agreement on Ending the War and Restoring Peace in Vietnam shall enter into force upon signature of this document by the Secretary of State of the Government of the United States of America and the Minister for Foreign Affairs of the Government of the Democratic Republic of Vietnam, and upon signature of a document in the same terms by the Secretary of State of the Government of the United States of America, the Minister for Foreign Affairs of the Government of the Republic of Vietnam, the Minister for Foreign Affairs of the Government of the Democratic Republic of Vietnam and the Minister for Foreign Affairs of the Provisional Revolutionary Government of the Republic of South Vietnam. The agreement and the protocols to it shall be strictly implemented by all the parties concerned.

Done in Paris this 27th day of January, 1973, in Vietnamese and English. The Vietnamese and English texts are official and equally authentic.

For the Government of the
United States of America
William P. Rogers
Secretary of State

For the Government of the
Democratic Republic of Vietnam
Nguyen Duy Trinh
Minister for Foreign Affairs

Protocol on the Cease-Fire

Protocol to the Agreement on Ending the War and Restoring Peace in Vietnam; Concerning the Cease-Fire in South Vietnam and the Joint Military Commissions

The parties participating in the Paris conference on Vietnam.

In implementation of the first paragraph of Article 2, Article 3, Article 5, Article 6, Article 16 and Article 17 of the Agreement on Ending the War and Restoring Peace in Vietnam signed on this date which provides for the cease-fire in South Vietnam and the establishment of a Four-Party Joint Military Commission and a Two-Party Joint Military Commission,

Have agreed as follows:

Cease-Fire in South Vietnam

Article 1

The high commands of the parties in South Vietnam shall issue prompt and timely orders to all regular and irregular armed forces and the armed police under their command to completely end hostilities throughout South Vietnam, at the exact time stipulated in Article 2 of the Agreement and insure that these armed forces and armed police comply with these orders and respect the cease-fire.

Article 2

(a) As soon as the cease-fire comes into force and until regulations are issued by the Joint Military Commissions, all ground, river, sea and air combat forces of the parties in South Vietnam shall remain in place; that is, in order to insure a stable cease-fire, there shall be no major redeployments or movements that would extend each party's area of control or would result in contact between opposing armed forces and clashes which might take place.

(b) All regular and irregular armed forces and the armed police of the parties in South Vietnam shall observe the prohibition of the following acts:

(1) Armed patrol into areas controlled by opposing armed forces and flights by bomber and fighter aircraft of all types, except for unarmed flights for proficiency training and maintenance;

(2) Armed attacks against any person, either military or civilian, by any means whatsoever, including the use of small arms, mortars, artillery, bombing and strafing by airplanes and any other type of weapon or explosive device;

(3) All combat operations on the ground, on rivers, on the sea and in the air;

(4) All hostile acts, terrorism or reprisals; and

(5) All acts endangering lives or public or private property.

Article 3

(a) The above-mentioned prohibitions shall not hamper or restrict:

(1) Civilian supply, freedom of movement, freedom to work and freedom of the people to engage in trade, and civilian communication and transportation between and among all areas in South Vietnam.

(2) The use by each party in areas under its control of military support elements, such as engineer and transportation units, in repair and construction of public facilities and the transportation and supplying of the population.

(3) Normal military proficiency conducted by the parties in the areas under their respective control with due regard for public safety.

(b) The Joint Military Commissions shall immediately agree on corridors, routes and other regulations governing the movement of military transport aircraft, military transport vehicles and military transport vessels of all types of one party going through areas under the control of other parties.

Article 4

In order to avert conflict and insure normal conditions for those armed forces which are in direct contact, and pending regulation by the Joint Military Commissions, the commanders of the opposing armed forces at those places of direct contact shall meet as soon as the cease-fire comes into force with a view to reaching an agreement on temporary measures to avert conflict and to insure supply and medical care for these armed forces.

Article 5

(a) Within 15 days after the cease-fire comes into effect, each party shall do its utmost to complete the removal or deactivation of all demolition objects, minefields, traps, obstacles or other dangerous ob-jects placed previously, so as not to hamper the population's movement and work, in the first place on waterways, roads and railroads in South Vietnam. Those mines which cannot be removed or deactivated within that time shall be clearly marked and must be removed or deactivated as soon as possible.

(b) Emplacement of mines is prohibited, except as a defensive measure around the edges of military installations in places where they do not hamper the population's movement on waterways, roads and railroads. Mines and other obstacles already in place at the edges of military installations may remain in place if they are in place where they do not hamper the population's movement and work, and movement on waterways, roads and railroads.

Article 6

Civilian police and civilian security personnel of the parties in South Vietnam, who are responsible for the maintenance of law and order, shall strictly respect the prohibitions set forth in Article 2 of this protocol. As required by their responsibilities, normally they shall be authorized to carry pistols, but when required by unusual circumstances, they shall be allowed to carry other small individual arms.

Article 7

(a) The entry into South Vietnam of replacement armaments, munitions and war material permitted under Article 7 of the agreement shall take place under the supervision and control of the Two-Party Joint Military Commission and of the International Commission of Control and Supervision and through such points of entry only as are designated by the two South Vietnamese parties. The two South Vietnamese parties shall agree on these points of entry within 15 days after the entry into force of the cease-fire. The two South Vietnamese parties may select as many as six points of entry which are not included in the list of places where teams of the International Commission of Control and Supervision are to be based contained in Article 4 (d) of the protocol concerning the international commission. At the same time, the two South Vietnamese parties may also select points of entry from the list of places set forth in Article 4 (d) of that protocol.

(b) Each of the designated points of entry shall be available only for that South Vietnamese party which is in control of that point. The two South Vietnamese parties shall have an equal number of points of entry.

Article 8

(a) In implementation of Article 5 of the agreement, the United States and the other foreign countries referred to in Article 5 of the agreement shall take with them all their armaments, munitions and war material. Transfers of such items which would leave them in South Vietnam shall not be made subsequent to the entry into force of the agreement except for transfers of communications, transport and other non-combat material to the Four-Party Joint Military Commission or the International Commission of Control and Supervision.

(b) Within five days after the entry into force of the cease-fire, the United States shall inform the Four-Party Joint Military Commission and the International Commission of Control and Supervision of the general plans for timing of complete troop withdrawals which shall take place in four phases of 15 days each. It is anticipated that the numbers of troops withdrawn in each phase are not likely to be widely different, although it is not feasible to insure equal numbers. The approximate numbers to be withdrawn in each phase shall be given to the Four-Party Joint Military Commission and the International Commission of Control and Supervision sufficiently in advance of actual withdrawals so that they can properly carry out their tasks in relation thereto.

Article 9

(a) In implementation of Article 6 of the agreement, the United States and the other foreign countries referred to in that article shall dismantle and remove from South Vietnam or destroy all military bases in South Vietnam of the United States and of the other foreign countries referred to in that article, including weapons, mines and other military equipment at these bases, for the purpose of making them unusable for military purposes.

(b) The United States shall supply the Four-Party Joint Military Commission and the International Commission of Control and Supervision with necessary information on plans for base dismantlement so that those commissions can properly carry out their tasks in relation thereto.

The Joint Military Commissions

Article 10

(a) The implementation of the agreement is the responsibility of the parties signatory to the agreement.

The Four-Party Joint Military Commission has the task of insuring joint action by the parties implementing the agreement by serving as a channel of communication among the parties, by drawing up plans and fixing the modalities to carry out, coordinate, follow and inspect the implementation of the provisions mentioned in Article 16 of the agreement, and by negotiating and settling all matters concerning the implementation of those provisions.

(b) The concrete tasks of the Four-Party Joint Military Commission are:

(1) To coordinate, follow and inspect the implementation of the above-mentioned provisions of the agreement by the four parties.

(2) To deter and detect violations, to deal with cases of violation, and to settle conflicts and matters of contention between the parties relating to the above-mentioned provisions.

(3) To dispatch without delay one or more joint teams, as required by specific cases, to any part of South Vietnam, to investigate alleged violations of the agreement and to assist the parties in finding measures to prevent recurrence of similar cases.

(4) To engage in observation at the places where this is necessary in the exercise of its functions.

(5) To perform such additional tasks as it may, by unanimous decision, determine.

Article 11

(a) There shall be a Central Joint Military Commission located in Saigon. Each party shall designate immediately a military delegation of 59 persons to represent it on the central commission. The senior officer designated by each party shall be a general officer, or equivalent.

(b) There shall be seven Regional Joint Military Commissions located in the regions shown on the annexed map and based at the following places:

REGIONS	PLACES
I	Hue
II	Danang
III	Pleiku
IV	Phanthiet
V	Bienhoa
VI	Mytho
VII	Cantho

Each party shall designate a military delegation of 16 persons to represent it on each regional commission. The senior officer designated by each party

shall be an officer from the rank of lieutenant colonel to colonel, or equivalent.

(c) There shall be a joint military team operating in each of the areas shown on the annexed map and based at each of the following places in South Vietnam:

Region I	Region III	Region IV
Quangtri	Kontum	Dalat
Phubai	Haubon	Baoloc
Region II	Phucat	Phanrang
Hoian	Tuyan	
Tamky	Ninhhoa	
Chulai	Banmethuot	
Region V	Region VI	Region VII
Anloc	Mochoa	Triton
Xuanloc	Giongtrom	Vinhlong
Bencat		Vithanh
Cuchi		Khanhhung
Tanan		Quanlong

Each party shall provide four qualified persons for each joint military team. The senior person designated by each party shall be an officer from the rank of major to lieutenant colonel, or equivalent.

(d) The Regional Joint Military Commissions shall assist the Central Joint Military Commission in performing its tasks and shall supervise the operations of the military teams. The region of Saigon-Giadinh is placed under the responsibility of the central commission, which shall designate joint military teams to operate in this region.

(e) Each party shall be authorized to provide support and guard personnel for its delegations to the Central Joint Military Commission and Regional Joint Military Commissions, and for its members of the joint military teams. The total number of support and guard personnel for each party shall not exceed 550.

(f) The Central Joint Military Commission may establish such joint subcommissions, joint staffs and joint military teams as circumstances may require. The central commission shall determine the numbers of personnel required for any additional subcommissions, staff or teams it establishes, provided that each party shall designate one-fourth of the number of personnel required and that the total number of personnel for the Four-Party Joint Military Commission, to include its staffs, teams and support personnel, shall not exceed 3,300.

(g) The delegations of the two South Vietnamese parties may, by agreement, establish provisional subcommissions and joint military teams to carry out the tasks specifically assigned to them by Article 17 in the agreement. With respect to Article 7 of the agreement, the two South Vietnamese parties' delegations to the Four-Party Joint Military Commission shall establish joint military teams at the points of entry into South Vietnam used for replacement of armaments, munitions and war material which are designated in accordance with Article 7 of this protocol. From the time the cease-fire comes into force to the time when the Two-Party Joint Military Commission becomes operational, the two South Vietnamese parties' delegations to the Four-Party Joint Military Commission shall form a provisional subcommission and provisional joint military teams to carry out its tasks concerning captured and detained Vietnamese civilian personnel. Where necessary for the above purposes, the two parties may agree to assign personnel additional to those assigned to the two South Vietnamese delegations to the Four-Party Joint Military Commission.

Article 12

(a) In accordance with Article 17 of the agreement, which stipulates that the two South Vietnamese parties shall immediately designate their respective representatives to form the Two-Party Joint Military Commission, 24 hours after the cease-fire comes into force, the two designated South Vietnamese parties' delegations to the Two-Party Joint Military Commission shall meet in Saigon so as to reach an agreement as soon as possible on organization and operation of the Two-Party Joint Commission, as well as the measures and organization aimed at enforcing the cease-fire and preserving peace in South Vietnam.

(b) From the time the cease-fire comes into force to the time when the Two-Party Joint Military Commission becomes operational, the two South Vietnamese parties' delegations to the Four-Party Joint Military Commission at all levels shall simultaneously assume the tasks of the Two-Party Joint Military Commission at all levels, in addition to their functions as delegations to the Four-Party Joint Military Commission.

(c) If, at the time the Four-Party Joint Military Commission ceases its operation in accordance with Article 16 of the agreement, agreement has not been reached on organization of the Two-Party Joint Military Commission, the delegations of the two South Vietnamese parties serving with the Four-Party Joint Military Commission at all levels shall continue temporarily to work together as a provisional two-party joint military commission and to assume the tasks of the Two-Party Joint Military Commission at all levels until the Two-Party Joint Military Commission becomes operational.

Article 13

In application of the principle of unanimity, the Joint Military Commissions shall have no chairmen, and meetings shall be convened at the request of any representative. The Joint Military Commissions shall adopt working procedures appropriate for the effective discharge of their functions and responsibilities.

Article 14

The Joint Military Commissions and the International Commission of Control and Supervision shall closely cooperate with and assist each other in carrying out their respective functions. Each Joint Military Commission shall inform the international commission about the implementation of those provisions of the agreement for which that Joint Military Commission has responsibility and which are within the competence of the international commission. Each Joint Military Commission may request the international commission to carry out specific observation activities.

Article 15

The Central Four-Party Joint Military Commission shall begin operating 24 hours after the cease-fire comes into force. The Regional Four-Party Joint Military Commissions shall begin operating 48 hours after the cease-fire comes into force. The joint military teams based at the places listed in Article 11 (c) of this protocol shall begin operating no later than 15 days after the cease-fire comes into force. The delegations of the two South Vietnamese parties shall simultaneously begin to assume the tasks of the Two-Party Joint Military Commission as provided in Article 12 of this protocol.

Article 16

(a) The parties shall provide full protection and all necessary assistance and cooperation to the Joint Military Commissions at all levels, in the discharge of their tasks.

(b) The Joint Military Commissions and their personnel, while carrying out their tasks, shall enjoy privileges and immunities equivalent to those accorded diplomatic missions and diplomatic agents.

(c) The personnel of the Joint Military Commissions may carry pistols and wear special insignia decided upon by each Central Joint Military Commission. The personnel of each party while guarding commission installations or equipment may be authorized to carry other individual small arms, as determined by each Central Joint Military Commission.

Article 17

(a) The delegation of each party to the Four-Party Joint Military Commission and the Two-Party Joint Military Commission shall have its own offices, communication, logistics and transportation means, including aircraft when necessary.

(b) Each party, in its areas of control, shall provide appropriate office and accommodation facilities to the Four-Party Joint Military Commission and the Two-Party Joint Military Commission at all levels.

(c) The parties shall endeavor to provide to the Four-Party Joint Military Commission and the Two-Party Joint Military Commission, by means of loan, lease or gift, the common means of operation, including equipment for communication, supply and transport, including aircraft when necessary. The Joint Military Commissions may purchase from any source necessary facilities, equipment and services which are not supplied by the parties. The Joint Military Commissions shall possess and use these facilities and this equipment.

(d) The facilities and the equipment for common use mentioned above shall be returned to the parties when the Joint Military Commissions have ended their activities.

Article 18

The common expenses of the Four-Party Joint Military Commission shall be borne equally by the four parties, and the common expenses of the Two-Party Joint Military Commission in South Vietnam shall be borne equally by these two parties.

Article 19

This protocol shall enter into force upon signature by plenipotentiary representatives of all the parties participating in the Paris conference on Vietnam. It shall be strictly implemented by all the parties concerned.

Done in Paris this 27th day of January, 1973, in Vietnamese and English. The Vietnamese and English texts are official and equally authentic.

For the Government of the
United States of America
William P. Rogers
Secretary of State

For the Government of the
Republic of Vietnam
Tran Van Lam
Minister for Foreign Affairs

For the Government of the
Democratic Republic of
Vietnam
Nguyen Duy Trinh
Minister for Foreign Affairs

For the Provisional
Revolutionary Government of
the Republic of South Vietnam
Nguyen Thi Binh
Minister for Foreign Affairs

2-Party Version

Protocol to the Agreement on Ending the War and Restoring Peace in Vietnam Concerning the Cease-Fire in South Vietnam and the Joint Military Commissions

The Government of the United States of America, with the concurrence of the Government of the Republic of Vietnam,

The Government of the Democratic Republic of Vietnam, with the concurrence of the Provisional Revolutionary Government of the Republic of South Vietnam,

In implementation of the first paragraph of Article 2, Article 3, Article 5, Article 6, Article 16 and Article 17 of the Agreement on Ending the War and Restoring Peace in Vietnam signed on this date which provide for the cease-fire in South Vietnam and the establishment of a Four-Party Joint Military Commission and a Two-Party Joint Military Commission,

Have agreed as follows:

[Text of protocol Articles 1–18
same as above]

Article 19

The protocol to the Paris Agreement on Ending the War and Restoring Peace in Vietnam Concerning the Cease-fire in South Vietnam and the Joint Military Commissions shall enter into force upon signature of this document by the Secretary of State of the Government of the United States of America and the Minister for Foreign Affairs of the Government of the Democratic Republic of Vietnam, and upon signature of a document in the same terms by the Secretary of State of the Government of the United States of America, the Minister for Foreign Affairs of the Government of the Republic of Vietnam, the Minister for Foreign Affairs of the Provisional Revolutionary Government of the Republic of South Vietnam. The protocol shall be strictly implemented by all the parties concerned.

Done in Paris this 27th day of January, 1973, in Vietnamese and English. The Vietnamese and English texts are official and equally authentic.

For the Government of the
United States of America
William P. Rogers
Secretary of State

For the Government of the
Democratic Republic of Vietnam
Nguyen Duy Trinh
Minister for Foreign Affairs

Protocol on Control Commission

Protocol to the Agreement on Ending the War and Restoring Peace in Vietnam; Concerning the International Commission of Control and Supervision

The parties participating in the Paris conference on Vietnam,

In implementation of Article 18 of the Agreement on Ending the War and Restoring Peace in Vietnam signed on this date providing for the formation of the International Commission of Control and Supervision,

Have agreed as follows:

Article 1

The implementation of the agreement is the responsibility of the parties signatory to the agreement.

The functions of the international commission are to control and supervise the implementation of the provisions mentioned in Article 18 of the agreement. In carrying out these functions, the international commission shall:

(a) Follow the implementation of the above-mentioned provisions of the agreement through communication with the parties and on-the-spot observation at the places where this is required.

(b) Investigate violations of the provisions which fall under the control and supervision of the commission.

(c) When necessary, cooperate with the Joint Military Commissions in deterring and detecting violations of the above-mentioned provisions.

Article 2

The international commission shall investigate violations of the provisions described in Article 18 of the agreement on the request of the Four-Party Joint Military Commission, or of the Two-Party Joint Military Commission or of any party, or, with respect to Article 9 (b) of the agreement on general elections, of the National Council of National Reconciliation and Concord, or in any case where the international commission has other adequate grounds for considering that there has been a violation of those provisions. It is understood that, in carrying out this task, the international commission shall function with the concerned parties' assistance and cooperation as required.

Article 3

(a) When the international commission finds that there is a serious violation in the implementation of the agreement or a threat to peace against which the commission can find no appropriate measure, the commission shall report this to the four parties to the agreement so that they can hold consultations to find a solution.

(b) In accordance with Article 18 (f) of the agreement, the international commission's reports shall be made with the unanimous agreement of the representatives of all the four members. In case no unanimity is reached, the commission shall forward the different views to the four parties in accordance with Article 18 (b) of the agreement, or to the two South Vietnamese parties in accordance with Article 18 (c) of the agreement, but these shall not be considered as reports of the commission.

Article 4

(a) The headquarters of the international commission shall be at Saigon.

(b) There shall be seven regional teams located in the regions shown on the annexed map and based at the following places:

REGIONS	PLACES
I	Hue
II	Danang
III	Pleiku
IV	Phanthiet
V	Bienhoa
VI	Mytho
VII	Cantho

The international commission shall designate three teams for the region of Saigon-Giadinh.

(c) There shall be 26 teams operating in the areas shown on the annexed map and based at the following places in South Vietnam:

Region I	Baoloc
Quangtri	Phanrang
Phubai	*Region V*
Region II	Anloc
Hoian	Xuanloc
Tamky	Bencat
Chulai	Cuchi
Region III	Tanan
Kontum	*Region VI*
Haubon	Mochoa
Phucat	Giongtrom
Tuyan	*Region VI*
Tinhhoa	Triton
Banmethuot	Vinhlong
Region IV	Vithanh
Dalat	Khanhhung
	Quanlong

(d) There shall be 12 teams located as shown on the annexed map and based at the following places:
Giolinh (to cover the area south of the provisional military demarcation line)

Laobao	Vungtau
Benhet	Xamat
Ducco	Bienhoa Airfield
Chulai	Hongngu
Quinhon	Cantho
Nhatrang	

(e) There shall be seven teams, six of which shall be available for assignment to the points of entry which are not listed in paragraph (d) above and which the two South Vietnamese parties choose as points for legitimate entry to South Vietnam for replacement of armaments, munitions and war material permitted by Article 7 of the agreement. Any team or teams not needed for the abovementioned assignment shall be available for other tasks, in keeping with the commission's responsibility for control and supervision.

(f) There shall be seven teams to control and supervise the return of captured and detained personnel of the parties.

Article 5
(a) To carry out its task concerning the return of the captured military personnel and foreign civilians of the parties as stipulated by Article 8 (a) of the agreement, the international commission shall, during the time of such return, send one control and supervision team to each place in Vietnam where the captured persons are being returned, and to the last detention places from which these persons will be taken to the places of return.

(b) To carry out its tasks concerning the return of the Vietnamese civilian personnel captured and detained in South Vietnam mentioned in Article 8 (c) of the agreement, the international commission shall, during the time of such return, send one control and supervision team to each place in South Vietnam where the above-mentioned captured and detained persons are being returned, and to the last detention places from which these persons shall be taken to the places of return.

Article 6
To carry out its tasks regarding Article 9 (b) of the agreement on the free and democratic general elections in South Vietnam, the international commission shall organize additional teams, when necessary. The international commission shall discuss this question in advance with the National Council of National Reconciliation and Concord. If additional teams are necessary for this purpose, they shall be formed 30 days before the general elections.

Article 7
The international commission shall continually keep under review its size, and shall reduce the number of its teams, its representatives or other personnel, or both, when those teams, representatives or personnel have accomplished the tasks assigned to them and are not required for other tasks. At the same time, the expenditures of the international commission shall be reduced correspondingly.

Article 8
Each member of the international commission shall make available at all times the following numbers of qualified personnel:
(a) One senior representative and 26 others for the headquarters staff.
(b) Five for each of the seven regional teams.
(c) Two for each of the other international control teams, except for the teams at Giolinh and Vungtau, each of which shall have three.
(d) One hundred sixteen for the purpose of providing support to the commission headquarters and its teams.

Article 9
(a) The international commission, and each of its teams, shall act as a single body comprising representatives of all four members.
(b) Each member has the responsibility to insure the presence of its representatives at all levels of the international commission. In case a representative is absent, the member concerned shall immediately designate a replacement.

Article 10
(a) The parties shall afford full cooperation, assistance and protection to the international commission.
(b) The parties shall at all times maintain regular and continuous liaison with the international commission. During the existence of the Four-Party Joint Military Commission, the delegations of the parties to that commission shall also perform liaison functions with the international commission. After the Four-Party Joint Military Commission has ended its activities, liaison shall be maintained through the Two-Party Joint Military Commission, liaison missions or other adequate means.
(c) The international commission and the Joint Military Commissions shall closely cooperate with and assist each other in carrying out their respective functions.
(d) Wherever a team is stationed or operating, the concerned party shall designate a liaison officer to the team to cooperate with and assist it in carrying out without hindrance its task of control and supervision. When a team is carrying out an investigation, a liaison officer from each concerned party shall have the opportunity to accompany it, provided the investigation is not thereby delayed.
(e) Each party shall give the international commission reasonable advance notice of all proposed actions concerning those provisions of the agreement that are to be controlled and supervised by the international commission.
(f) The international commission, including its teams, is allowed such movement for observation as is reasonably required for the proper exercise of its functions as stipulated in the agreement. In carrying out these functions, the international commission,

including its teams, shall enjoy all necessary assistance and cooperation from the parties concerned.

Article 11

In supervising the holding of the free and democratic general elections described in Articles 9 (b) and 12 (b) of the agreement in accordance with modalities to be agreed upon between the National Council of National Reconciliation and Concord and the international commission, the latter shall receive full cooperation and assistance from the national council.

Article 12

The international commission and its personnel who have the nationality of a member state shall, while carrying out their tasks, enjoy privileges and immunities equivalent to those accorded diplomatic missions and diplomatic agents.

Article 13

The international commission may use the means of communication and transport necessary to perform its functions. Each South Vietnamese party shall make available for rent to the international commission appropriate office and accommodation facilities. The international commission may receive from the parties, on mutually agreeable terms, the necessary means of communication and transport and may purchase from any source necessary equipment and services not obtained from the parties. The international commission shall possess these means.

Article 14

The expenses for the activities of the international commission shall be borne by the parties and the members of the international commission in accordance with the provisions of this article:

(a) Each member country of the international commission shall pay the salaries and allowances of its personnel.

(b) All other expenses incurred by the international commission shall be met from a fund to which each of the four parties shall contribute twenty-three per cent (23%) and to which each member of the international commission shall contribute two per cent (2%).

(c) Within 30 days of the date of entry into force of this protocol, each of the four parties shall provide the international commission with an initial sum equivalent to four million five hundred thousand (4,500,000) French francs in convertible currency, which sum shall be credited against the amounts due from that party under the first budget.

(d) The international commission shall prepare its own budgets. After the international commission approves a budget, it shall transmit it to all parties signatory to the agreement for their approval. Only after the budgets have been approved by the four parties to the agreement shall they be obliged to make their contributions. However, in case the parties to the agreement do not agree on a new budget, the international commission shall temporarily base its expenditures on the previous budget, except for the extraordinary, one-time expenditures for installation or for the acquisition of equipment, and the parties shall continue to make their contributions on that basis until a new budget is approved.

Article 15

(a) The headquarters shall be operational and in place within 24 hours after the cease-fire.

(b) The regional teams shall be operational and in place, and three teams for supervision and control of the return of the captured and detained personnel shall be operational and ready for dispatch within 48 hours after the cease-fire.

(c) Other teams shall be operational and in place within 15 to 30 days after the cease-fire.

Article 16

Meetings shall be convened at the call of the chairman. The international commission shall adopt other working procedures appropriate for the effective discharge of its functions and consistent with respect for the sovereignty of South Vietnam.

Article 17

The members of the international commission may accept the obligations of this protocol by sending notes of acceptance to the four parties signatory to the agreement. Should a member of the international commission decide to withdraw from the international commission, it may do so by giving three months' notice by means of notes to the four parties to the agreement, in which case those four parties shall consult among themselves for the purpose of agreeing upon a replacement member.

Article 18

This protocol shall enter into force upon signature by plenipotentiary representatives of all the parties participating in the Paris conference on Vietnam. It shall be strictly implemented by all the parties concerned.

Done in Paris this 27th day of January, 1973, in Vietnamese and English. The Vietnamese and English texts are officially and equally authentic.

For the Government of the
United States of America
William P. Rogers
Secretary of State

For the Government of the
Republic of Vietnam
Tran Van Lam
Minister for Foreign Affairs

For the Government of the
Democratic Republic of Vietnam
Nguyen Duy Trinh
Minister for Foreign Affairs

For the Provisional
Revolutionary Government of
the Republic of South Vietnam
Nguyen Thi Binh
Minister for Foreign Affairs

2-Party Version

Protocol to the Agreement on Ending the War and Restoring Peace in Vietnam Concerning the International Commission of Control and Supervision

The Government of the United States of America, with the concurrence of the Government of the Republic of Vietnam,

The Government of the Democratic Republic of Vietnam, with the concurrence of the Provisional Revolutionary Government of the Republic of South Vietnam,

In implementation of Article 18 of the Agreement on Ending the War and Restoring Peace in Vietnam signed on this date providing for the formation of the International Commission of Control and Supervision,

Have agreed as follows:

[Text of protocol Articles 1-17 same as above]

Article 18

The Protocol to the Paris Agreement on Ending the War and Restoring Peace in Vietnam concerning the International Commission of Control and Supervision shall enter into force upon signature of this document by the Secretary of State of the Government of the United States of America and the Minister for Foreign Affairs of the Government of the Democratic Republic of Vietnam, and upon signature of a document in the same terms by the Secretary of State of the Government of the United States of America, the Minister for Foreign Affairs of the Government of the Republic of Vietnam, the Minister for Foreign Affairs of the Government of the Democratic Republic of Vietnam and the Minister for Foreign Affairs of the Provisional Revolutionary Government of the Republic of South Vietnam. The protocol shall be strictly implemented by all the parties concerned.

Done in Paris this 27th day of January, 1973, in Vietnamese and English. The Vietnamese and English texts are official and equally authentic.

For the Government of the
United States of America
William P. Rogers
Secretary of State

For the Government of the
Democratic Republic of Vietnam
Nguyen Duy Trinh
Minister for Foreign Affairs

Protocol on the Prisoners

Protocol to the Agreement on Ending the War and Restoring Peace in Vietnam; Concerning the Return of Captured Military Personnel and Foreign Civilians and Captured and Detained Vietnamese Civilian Personnel

The parties participating in the Paris conference on Vietnam.

In implementation of Article 8 of the Agreement on Ending the War and Restoring Peace in Vietnam signed on this date providing for the return of captured military personnel and foreign civilians, and captured and detained Vietnamese civilian personnel.

Have agreed as follows:

The Return of Captured Military Personnel and Foreign Civilians

Article 1

The parties signatory to the agreement shall return the captured military personnel of the parties mentioned in Article 8 (a) of the agreement as follows:

■ All captured military personnel of the United States and those of the other foreign countries mentioned in Article 3 (a) of the agreement shall be returned to United States authorities.

■ All captured Vietnamese military personnel, whether belonging to regular or irregular armed forces, shall be returned to the two South Vietnamese parties; they shall be returned to that South Vietnamese party under whose command they served.

Article 2

All captured civilians who are nationals of the United States or of any other foreign countries mentioned in Article 3 (a) of the agreement shall be re-

turned to United States authorities. All other captured foreign civilians shall be returned to the authorities of their country of nationality by any one of the parties willing and able to do so.

Article 3

The parties shall today exchange complete lists of captured persons mentioned in Articles 1 and 2 of this protocol.

Article 4

(a) The return of all captured persons mentioned in Articles 1 and 2 of this protocol shall be completed within 60 days of the signing of the agreement at a rate no slower than the rate of withdrawal from South Vietnam of United States forces and those of the other foreign countries mentioned in Article 5 of the agreement.

(b) Persons who are seriously ill, wounded or maimed, old persons and women shall be returned first. The remainder shall be returned either by returning all from one detention place after another or in order of their dates of capture, beginning with those who have been held the longest.

Article 5

The return and reception of the persons mentioned in Articles 1 and 2 of this protocol shall be carried out at places convenient to the concerned parties. Places of return shall be agreed upon by the Four-Party Joint Military Commission. The parties shall insure the safety of personnel engaged in the return and reception of those persons.

Article 6

Each party shall return all captured persons mentioned in Articles 1 and 2 of this protocol without delay and shall facilitate their return and reception. The detaining parties shall not deny or delay their return for any reason, including the fact that captured persons may, on any grounds, have been prosecuted or sentenced.

The Return of Captured and Detained Vietnamese Civilian Personnel

Article 7

(a) The question of the return of Vietnamese civilian personnel captured and detained in South Vietnam will be resolved by the two South Vietnamese parties on the basis of the principles of Article 21 (b) of the agreement on the Cessation of Hostilities in Vietnam of July 20, 1954, which reads as follows:

"The term 'civilian internees' is understood to mean all persons who, having in any way contributed to the political and armed struggle between the two parties, have been arrested for that reason and have been kept in detention by either party during the period of hostilities."

(b) The two South Vietnamese parties will do so in a spirit of national reconciliation and concord with a view to ending hatred and enmity in order to ease suffering and to reunite families. The two South Vietnamese parties will do their utmost to resolve this question within 90 days after the cease-fire comes into effect.

(c) Within 15 days after the cease-fire comes into effect, the two South Vietnamese parties shall exchange lists of the Vietnamese civilian personnel captured and detained by each party and lists of the places at which they are held.

Treatment of Captured Persons During Detention

Article 8

(a) All captured military personnel of the parties and captured foreign civilians of the parties shall be treated humanely at all times, and in accordance with international practice.

They shall be protected against all violence to life and person, in particular against murder in any form, mutilation, torture and cruel treatment, and outrages upon personal dignity. These persons shall not be forced to join the armed forces of the detaining party.

They shall be given adequate food, clothing, shelter and the medical attention required for their state of health. They shall be allowed to exchange postcards and letters with their families and receive parcels.

(b) All Vietnamese civilian personnel captured and detained in South Vietnam shall be treated humanely at all times, and in accordance with international practice.

They shall be protected against all violence to life and person, in particular against murder in any form, mutilation, torture and cruel treatment and outrages against personal dignity. The detaining parties shall not deny or delay their return for any reason including the fact that captured persons may, on any grounds, have been prosecuted or sentenced. These persons shall not be forced to join the armed forces of the detaining party.

They shall be given adequate food, clothing, shelter and the medical attention required for their state of health. They shall be allowed to exchange postcards and letters with their families and receive parcels.

Article 9
(a) To contribute to improving the living conditions of the captured military personnel of the parties and foreign civilians of the parties, the parties shall, within 15 days after the cease-fire comes into effect, agree upon the designation of two or more national Red Cross societies to visit all places where captured military personnel and foreign civilians are held.

(b) To contribute to improving the living conditions of the captured and detained Vietnamese civilian personnel, the two South Vietnamese parties shall, within 15 days after the cease-fire comes into effect, agree upon the designation of two or more national Red Cross societies to visit all places where the captured and detained Vietnamese civilian personnel are held.

With Regard to Dead and Missing Persons
Article 10
(a) The Four-Party Joint Military Commission shall insure joint action by the parties in implementing Article 8 (b) of the agreement. When the Four-Party Joint Military Commission has ended its activities, a Four-Party Joint Military Team shall be maintained to carry on this task.

(b) With regard to Vietnamese civilian personnel dead or missing in South Vietnam, the two South Vietnamese parties shall help each other to obtain information about missing persons, determine the location and take care of the graves of the dead, in a spirit of national reconciliation and concord, in keeping with the people's aspirations.

Other Provisions
Article 11
(a) the Four-Party and Two-Party Joint Military Commissions will have the responsibility of determining immediately the modalities of implementing the provisions of this protocol consistent with their respective responsibilities under Articles 16 (a) and 17 (a) of the agreement. In case the Joint Military Commission, when carrying out their tasks, cannot reach agreement on a matter pertaining to the return of captured personnel they shall refer to the international commission for its assistance.

(b) The Four-Party Joint Military Commission shall form, in addition to the teams established by the protocol concerning the cease-fire in South Vietnam and the Joint Military Commissions, a subcommission on captured persons and, as required, joint military teams on captured persons to assist the commission in its tasks.

(c) From the time the cease-fire comes into force to the time when the Two-Party Joint Military Commission becomes operational, the two South Vietnamese parties' delegations to the Four-Party Joint Military Commission shall form a provisional subcommission and provisional joint military teams to carry out its tasks concerning captured and detained Vietnamese civilian personnel.

(d) The Four-Party Joint Military Commission shall send joint military teams to observe the return of the persons mentioned in Articles 1 and 2 of this protocol at each place in Vietnam where such persons are being returned, and at the last detention places from which these persons will be taken to the places of return. The Two-Party Joint Military Commission shall send joint military teams to observe the return of Vietnamese civilian personnel captured and detained at each place in South Vietnam where such persons are being captured, and at the last detention places from which these persons will be taken to the places of return.

In implementation of Articles 18 (b) and 18 (c) of the agreement, the International Commission of Control and Supervision shall have the responsibility to control and supervise the observance of Articles 1 through 7 of this protocol through observation of the return of captured military personnel, foreign civilians and captured and detained Vietnamese civilian personnel at each place in Vietnam where these persons are being returned, and at the last detention places from which these persons will be taken to the places of retun, the examination of lists and the investigation of violations of the provisions of the above-mentioned articles.

Article 13
Within five days after signature of this protocal, each party shall publish the text of the protocol and communicate it to all the captured persons covered by the protocol and being detained by that party.

Article 14
This protocol shall come into force upon signature by plenipotentiary representatives of all the parties participating in the Paris conference on Vietnam. It shall be strictly implemented by all the parties concerned.

Done in Paris this 27th day of January, 1973, in Vietnamese and English. The Vietnamese and English texts are official and equally authentic.

For the Government of the
United States of America
William P. Rogers
Secretary of State

For the Government of the
Republic of Vietnam
Tran Van Lam
Minister for Foreign Affairs

For the Government of the
Democratic Republic of Vietnam
Nguyen Duy Trinh
Minister for Foreign Affairs

For the Provisional
Revolutionary Government of
the Republic of South Vietnam

Nguyen Thi Binh
Minister for Foreign Affairs

2-Party Version

Protocol to the Agreement on Ending the War and Restoring Peace in Vietnam; Concerning the Return of Captured Military Personnel and Foreign Civilians and Captured and Detained Vietnamese Civilian Personnel

The Government of the United States of America, with the concurrence of the Government of the Republic of Vietnam,

The Government of the Democratic Republic of Vietnam, with the concurrence of the Provisional Revolutionary Government of the Republic of South Vietnam,

In implementation of Article 8 of the Agreement on Ending the War and Restoring Peace in Vietnam signed on this date providing for the return of captured military personnel and foreign civilians, and captured and detained Vietnamese civilian personnel,

Have agreed as follows:

[Text of protocol Articles 1–13 same as above]

Article 14

The protocol to the Paris Agreement on Ending the War and Restoring Peace in Vietnam concerning the Return of Captured Military Personnel and Foreign Civilians and Captured and Detained Vietnamese Civilian Personnel shall enter into force upon signature of this document by the Secretary of State of the Government of the United States of America and the Minister for Foreign Affairs of the Government of the Democratic Republic of Vietnam, and upon signature of a document in the same terms by the Secretary of State of the Government of the United States of America, the Minister for Foreign Affairs of the Government of the Republic of Vietnam, the Minister for Foreign Affairs of the Government of the Democratic Republic of Vietnam and the Minister for Foreign Affairs of the Provisional Revolutionary Government of the Republic of South Vietnam. The protocol shall be strictly implemented by all the parties concerned.

Done in Paris this 27th day of January, 1973, in Vietnamese and English The Vietnamese and English texts are official and equally authentic.

For the Government of the
United States of America
William P. Rogers
Secretary of State

For the Government of the
Democratic Republic of Vietnam
Nguyen Duy Trinh
Minister for Foreign Affairs

Protocol on Clearing Sea Mines

Protocol to the Agreement on Ending the War and Restoring Peace in Vietnam; Concerning the Removal, Permanent Deactivation or Destruction of Mines in the Territorial Waters, Ports, Harbors and Waterways of the Democratic Republic of Vietnam

The Government of the United States of America,
The Government of the Democratic Republic of Vietnam,

In implementation of the second paragraph of Article 2 of the Agreement on Ending the War and Restoring Peace in Vietnam signed on this date,

Have agreed as follows:

Article 1

The United States shall clear all mines it has placed in the territorial waters, ports, harbors and waterways of the Democratic Republic of Vietnam. This mine-clearing operation shall be accomplished by rendering the mines harmless through removal, permanent deactivation or destruction.

Article 2

With a view to insuring lasting safety for the movement of people and watercraft and the protection of important installations, mines shall, on the request of the Democratic Republic of Vietnam, be removed or destroyed in the indicated area; and whenever their removal or destruction is impossible, mines shall be permanently deactivated and their emplacement clearly marked.

Article 3

The mine-clearing operation shall begin at twenty-four hundred (2400) hours G.M.T. on Jan. 27, 1973. The representatives of the two parties shall consult immediately on relevant factors and agree upon the earliest possible target date for the completion of the work.

Article 4

The mine-clearing operation shall be conducted in accordance with priorities and timing agreed upon by the two parties. For this purpose, representatives of the two parties shall meet at an early date to reach agreement on a program and a plan of implementation. To this end:

(a) The United States shall provide its plan for mine-clearing operations, including maps of the minefields and information concerning the types, numbers and properties of the mines.

(b) The Democratic Republic of Vietnam shall provide all available maps and hydrographic charts and indicate the mined places and all other potential hazards to the mine-clearing operations that the Democratic Republic of Vietnam is aware of.

(c) The two parties shall agree on the timing of implementation of each segment of the plan and provide timely notice to the public at least 48 hours in advance of the beginning of mine-clearing operations for that segment.

Article 5

The United States shall be responsible for the mine clearance on island waterways of the Democratic Republic of Vietnam. The Democratic Republic of Vietnam shall, to the full extent of its capabilities, actively participate in the mine clearance with the means of surveying, removal and destruction, and technical advice supplied by the United States.

Article 6

With a view to insuring the safe movement of people and watercraft on waterways and at sea, the United States shall in the mine-clearing process supply timely information about the progress of mine clearing in each area, and about the remaining mines to be destroyed. The United States shall issue a communique when the operations have been concluded.

Article 7

In conducting mine-clearing operations, the U.S. personnel engaged in these operations shall respect the sovereignty of the Democratic Republic of Vietnam and shall engage in no activities inconsistent with the Agreement on Ending the War and Restoring Peace in Vietnam and this protocol. The U.S. personnel engaged in the mine-clearing operations shall be immune from the jurisdiction of the Democratic Republic of Vietnam for the duration of the mine-clearing operations.

The Democratic Republic of Vietnam shall insure the safety of the U.S. personnel for the duration of their mine-clearing activities on the territory of the Democratic Republic of Vietnam, and shall provide this personnel with all possible assistance and the means needed in the Democratic Republic of Vietnam that have been agreed upon by the two parties.

Article 8

This protocol to the Paris Agreement on Ending the War and Restoring Peace in Vietnam shall enter into force upon signature by the Secretary of State of the Government of the United States of America and the Minister for Foreign Affairs of the Government of the Democratic Republic of Vietnam. It shall be strictly implemented by the two parties.

Done in Paris this 27th day of January, 1973, in Vietnamese and English. The Vietnamese and English texts are official and equally authentic.

For the Government of the
United States of America
William P. Rogers
Secretary of State

For the Government of the
Democratic Republic of Vietnam
Nguyen Duy Trinh
Minister for Foreign Affairs

Index

Note: This index follows the Western usage in regard to most Vietnamese names. A Vietnamese individual, therefore, would be listed not under his family name but under the last section of his full name. *E.g.,* Mrs. Nguyen Thi Binh would be indexed thus: BINH, Mrs. Nguyen Thi (not NGUYEN Thi Binh, Mrs.). Exceptions are usually the cases of monks or others (*e.g.,* Ho Chi Minh) who use adopted names; such persons are generally listed under the first sections of their names (HO Chi Minh, not MINH, Ho Chi).

PEOPLE'S Front to Safeguard Peace and to Realize the People's Right to Self-Determination—262
PERCY, Sen. Charles H. (R., Ill.)—59, 223
PERDUE, Donald P.—305
PERKINS, Maj. Glendon W.—263
PETER, Janos—274
PETERSON, Peter G.—85
PEVEK (Soviet vessel)—101
PHAN Trong Tue, Brig.—97
PHENG Phongsavan—266, 269
PHONG, Nguyen Xuan—195, 199
PHONG, Maj. Gen. Tran Thanh—205
PHOUI Sananikone—278
PHOU Ke, Laos: Airbase—31
PHOU Khoun, Laos—23, 26
PHOUMI Vongvichit—197, 253, 266, 269
PHOUN Sipraseuth, Gen—185, 229
PHUBAI, South Vietnam—147
PHUCYEN, North Vietnam: Airbase—162, 167
PHULOI, South Vietnam: U.S. airbases—31
PHUMIPHOL Aduldet, King—253
PHUQUI, North Vietnam: Government post—168
PHUYEN Province, South Vietnam—321
PITKIN, Stan—302
PLAIN of Reeds, South Vietnam—106
PLAINE de Jarres, Laos—26, 31–2, 171, 185, 215, 253
PLAMONDON, Lawrence—305
PLEIBLANG, South Vietnam—191
PLEIKU Province, South Vietnam—35, 172, 174, 186, 201, 205, 229, 256
PNOM Bat, Cambodia—169
PNOMPENH, Cambodia—35–6, 72, 163, 171, 205, 230, 243, 283
PODGORNY, Nikolai V.—114
POLAND—6, 82, 211, 217, 234, 242
POMERANCE, Rocky—137
POMPIDOU, Georges—171, 226
POPKIN, Prof. Samuel L.—313–4
PORTER, William J.—10, 13, 16, 19–20, 54–5, 73, 113–4, 116–7, 121, 208, 227. Peace agreement—193, 204
POST-Dispatch (St. Louis newspaper)—197
POUNDER, Sgt. Ernest R.—258
POWELL, Justice Lewis F.—306
PRAPHAS Charusathien, Gen—34
PRASAT Neong Khmau, Cambodia—279
PRAVDA (Soviet newspaper)—184, 196, 249
PREK Prasap, Cambodia—230
PRESBYTERIANS—99
PREY Totung, Cambodia—230
PREYVENG, Cambodia—36, 64
PRINCETON University—90
PRISONER of Wars (POWS): Antiwar groups—123. China—279. Inspections—19. Laos—266. Lists—10, 129, 147–8, 270, 196, 244. North Vietnam—30. Peace agreement—334, 346. POWS families—89–90, 140. Release & aftermath—123–4, 167, 255, 259–60, 263, 266, 269–70, 275–7, 281, 288–9; negotiations 3–5, 120–3, 234, 270–1, 277, 285; POWS statements—123, 275–6,

289. South Vietnam—63, 255; political prisoners—206-7. Search for MIAs—281. U.S.—21; pilots (missing or captured)—147, 155, 158, 161–2, 165, 172, 211, 220, 222. War advocates—263
PROGRESSIVE Labor Party—244
PROTESTANTS—297
PROVIDENCE Journal (newspaper)—330
PROXMIRE, Sen. William (D., Wis.)—141, 327
PULITZER Prize—317
PUSAN Port, South Vietnam—32

Q

QUANG, Lt. Gen. Dang Van—182
QUANGBINH Province, North Vietnam—29, 33, 47, 148
QUANGLANG, North Vietnam: Air base—167, 328
QUANGKHE Port, North Vietnam—82
QUANGNAM Province, South Vietnam: Base Camp Baldy—158
QUANGNGAI Province, South Vietnam—24, 35, 92, 166, 170, 172–3, 186. Government post—166
QUANGTIN Province, South Vietnam—170-1
QUANGTRI Province, South Vietnam—23, 29, 46–8, 51–2, 69–70, 75, 92, 94, 99–100, 145–6, 148–9, 156, 158–60, 163–4, 166, 170, 192, 196, 199, 202, 205–6, 242
QUANGTRI Provincial Capital Provisional People's Revolutionary Committee (Viet Cong regime in South Vietnam)—70–1
QUANLOI, South Vietnam: Airfield—47
QUESON Valley, South Vietnam—31–2, 158, 186, 191, 243, 245. Base Camp Ross—159–60, 163
QUINHON, South Vietnam—23. U.S. base—31
QUOC Dan Dang Party (South Vietnam)—296

R

RACH Bap, South Vietnam: Government post—284
RAHMANAJI, Qumal—171
RAMSEY, Douglas K.—244, 276
RAND, S. Richard—266
RAND Corp.—315–6
RATHER, Dan—3–4
RAY, L. N.—6, 124
RAYFORD, Pfc. King D.—107
RAZAK, Abdul—253
REAGAN, Gov. Ronald (R., Calif.)—90
RED River, North Vietnam—97, 107, 110
REED, Lt. Col. Leonard F.—321
REED College (Portland, Ore.)—68
REHNQUIST, Justice William H.—312
RENOUF, Alan—271
REPUBLICAN National Convention:—136-8, 305-9
REPUBLICAN Party—8, 59–60, 223